CAMBRIDGE STUDIES IN AMERICAN LITERATURE AND CULTURE

American Catholic Arts and Fictions

In *American Catholic Arts and Fictions*, Paul Giles describes how secular transformations of religious ideas have helped to shape the style and substance of works by American writers, film-makers, and artists from a Catholic background, such as Orestes Brownson, Theodore Dreiser, Mary McCarthy, Robert Mapplethorpe, Alfred Hitchcock, and Robert Altman. The book also explores how Catholicism was represented and mythologized by other American writers. By highlighting the recurring themes and preoccupations of American Catholic fictions, Giles challenges many of the accepted ideas about the centrality of romanticism to the American literary canon. He reconstructs the different social, historical, and philosophical contexts from which aesthetics in the "Catholic" tradition has emerged, and he shows how these stand in an oblique relationship to the assumptions of the American Enlightenment.

CAMBRIDGE STUDIES IN AMERICAN LITERATURE AND CULTURE

Editor
Eric Sundquist, University of California, Los Angeles

Advisory Board
Nina Baym, University of Illinois, Champaign-Urbana
Sacvan Bercovitch, Harvard University
Albert Gelpi, Stanford University
Myra Jehlen, University of Pennsylvania
Carolyn Porter, University of California, Berkeley
Robert Stepto, Yale University
Tony Tanner, King's College, Cambridge University

Continued on pages following the Index

American Catholic Arts and Fictions

Culture, Ideology, Aesthetics

PAUL GILES
Portland State University

CAMBRIDGE
UNIVERSITY PRESS

Published by the Press Syndicate of the University of Cambridge
The Pitt Building, Trumpington Street, Cambridge CB2 1RP
40 West 20th Street, New York, NY 10011–4211, USA
10 Stamford Road, Oakleigh, Victoria 3166, Australia

First published 1992

Printed in the United States of America

Library of Congress Cataloging-in-Publication Data
Giles, Paul.
American Catholic Arts and Fictions: culture, ideology, aesthetics
/ Paul Giles.
p.   cm. – (Cambridge studies in American literature and
culture)
Includes index.
ISBN 0-521-41777-5
1. American literature – Catholic authors – History and criticism.
2. Christian literature, American – History and criticism.
3. Catholics – United States – Intellectual life.   4. Authors,
American – Religious life.   5. Catholic Church in literature.
6. Christianity and literature.   7. Catholics in literature.
I. Title.   II. Series.
PS153.C3G55   1992
810.9'9222 – dc20   91–36223
                                                              CIP

A catalog record for this book is available from the British Library

ISBN 0-521-41777-5 hardback

Contents

v

Preface

This book, like those other fictional texts I discuss here, is the product of specific times and places. The early reading was done in Oxford and London during the first half of the 1980s; the actual writing begun in Stafford, England, in January 1987; the final version completed in Portland, Oregon, in February 1991. My move to the United States occurred between the first drafts of chapters on Scott Fitzgerald and Allen Tate. Though the prefatory phrase about indispensable support has become something of a cliché, it has never been truer than in my indebtedness to Portland State University, which bailed me out of the unpropitious academic landscape of Britain in the late 1980s and furnished me with the circumstances in which I could complete this book. Peter Carafiol, who back in 1987 first disturbed my BBC television snooker with a phone call from six thousand miles away, now claims my stylistic circumlocutions derive all too clearly from the Old World rather than the New. If, therefore, the reader should experience any disjunction between American grammatical conventions and an English idiom, this transatlantic relocation in medias res may be part of the reason.

The passage of writing this book also encompassed the death of a number of authors discussed within its pages: Mary McCarthy, Donald Barthelme, Walker Percy. In each case, natural regret at their demise was tempered with a wry satisfaction at knowing they would not now be able to produce a later work that might undermine my carefully crafted arguments. In this respect, I have not been so fortunate in the case of some of the younger writers, and I realize that an even greater air of provisionality than usual necessarily hovers over any attempt critically to analyze contemporary authors. Conversely, I also regret certain omissions, such as Martin Scorsese's excellent film *Goodfellas* (1990), which appeared just too late for me properly to consider here, or the novels of Don DeLillo, or those of Frederick

Barthelme. I console myself with Valéry's perception that a text is never finished, only abandoned: "It is always an accident that terminates it, that is, gives it to the public." Still, my hope is that the ideas and styles outlined here will be clear enough for readers to be able to recognize them in various other works of American "Catholic" fiction, past, passing, and to come.

It is a pleasure to acknowledge again the valuable guidance provided by my friends at the Cambridge University Press: Andrew Brown in Cambridge, England, who first expressed interest in this work; Julie Greenblatt in New York, who put up with my frequent changes of mind about the title; Janis Bolster, who coordinated the production process; Patricia Woodruff, whose copyediting skills shifted all my British scepticisms into American skepticisms. Since this was one of the last books he oversaw as series editor of the Cambridge Studies in American Literature and Culture, it may be appropriate to note a special debt of gratitude to Al Gelpi, whose generous encouragement all along has been more than any anxious author could hope for. I should like to acknowledge also the help of Peter Conn, who made many perspicacious suggestions about the manuscript, and of Robert S. Levine, who commented more specifically upon the Brownson chapter. Evelyn J. Hinz assisted me with stylistic details of the Fitzgerald section when that was first published in a shorter form in *Mosaic,* 22, No. 4 (Fall 1989), 1–12. An earlier version of the Ford and Altman chapter appeared in *Unspeakable Images: Ethnicity and the American Cinema,* edited by Lester Friedman (University of Illinois Press, 1991); Les's astute editorial remarks on that occasion were especially valuable because they helped me develop a critical style for incorporating film into my larger projects. I do not, of course, mean to implicate any of the above in the idiosyncrasies of this particular end product.

In addition, I should like to thank the Robert Mapplethorpe Estate for allowing me to reproduce within the text four of Mapplethorpe's works, as well as the Galerie Bruno Bischofberger in Zurich and the Estate and Foundation of Andy Warhol for permitting us to have Warhol's *Black-and-White Retrospective* on the jacket. Tim Hunt, who used to lean heavily upon my translations of the Anglo-Saxon poets in our undergraduate days, handsomely repaid that service by helping me obtain these permissions. Film stills were provided by Jerry Ohlinger's Movie Material Store, New York, while important assistance with the index and proofs was given by my research assistant, Mark Lloyd, whose work was funded by a grant from Portland State University's Research and Publications Committee. I should mention also my wife, Nadine, who married me between the final drafts of Martin

Scorsese and Katherine Anne Porter, and who bore with me during our first year of marriage as I became more and more heavily pregnant with book. Through this cerebral offspring, we would both like to be remembered by our friends and relatives back in the old country, whom we in turn keep always in mind.

Portland, Oregon
February 1992

The man who believes that his truth on religious
matters is so absolutely the truth, that say it when,
and where, and to whom he will, he cannot but do
good with it, is in our day almost always a man
whose truth is half blunder, and wholly useless.

Matthew Arnold, *Literature and Dogma*, 1873

The task of these principles was to derive the
necessity of a philosophy of man, that is, of
anthropology, from the philosophy of the absolute,
that is, theology, and to establish the critique of
human philosophy through the critique of divine
philosophy.

Ludwig Feuerbach, Preface to *Principles of the
Philosophy of the Future*, 1843

One does not begin with the part in order to reach
the whole: one begins by infinitizing the totality in
order to reach, only later, the finite meaning of each
part.

Julia Kristeva, "The Novel as Polylogue," 1974

The *whole* of anything is never told; you can only take
what groups together.

Henry James, *Notebooks*, 1881

1

Methodological Introduction: Tracing the Transformation of Religion

The purpose of this book is to examine the continuing significance of religion, and specifically Roman Catholicism, as an ideological force within modern American literature, film, and photography. My aim is not to consider Catholicism as a theological entity – except incidentally, insofar as that impinges upon my main theme – but as a residual cultural determinant and one aspect of the social context within which various American artists of this century have been working. Because Catholicism so clearly defines itself within a metaphysical context, we should not make the mistake of ignoring the fact that it functions within particular social contexts as well, contexts that consist of more than simple historical facts about immigration from Europe, or the war between the United States and Mexico, or whatever. The point is that this social and historical framework of Catholicism cannot be apprehended in isolation from the mythology of the supposedly "metaphysical" sphere, because the power of this mythology actually affects action and reaction within the secular world.

The way in which religious ideas can help to determine patterns of thought is clear enough to contemporary students of ancient civilization. It is of no consequence that we no longer believe in the literal "truth" of these old religious mythologies: few classical scholars today believe the pagan deities ever enjoyed a literal existence, throned resplendently on Mount Olympus, but equally few scholars would deny the historical significance and pertinence of religious ideas to ancient Greek tragedy or politics. Much recent literary criticism has sought to recover a cultural matrix for any given writer – assessing James Joyce and W. B. Yeats in the light of Irish political history, for instance, rather than viewing them in the old romantic way as isolated geniuses – and this book is working toward something similar, except that it offers religion rather than politics as the milieu within which modern American authors can be seen to be operating. Sometimes this ideology of Catholicism is explicit, as in the

I

poems of Allen Tate and Robert Lowell, the novels of Walker Percy and
J. F. Powers, the films of Alfred Hitchcock and Martin Scorsese. At
other times this ideology is concealed and implicit, though still a determining factor, as in the poetry of John Berryman and Frank O'Hara,
the novels of Mary McCarthy and Jack Kerouac, the films of John Ford
and Robert Altman.

By drawing a parallel with the study of religious conceptions in Greek
tragedy, it is not my intention to propose the starkest kind of structuralist
approach whereby American works of fiction are seen simply as anthropological rituals sanctifying an archaic central myth. I use the term
"fictions" to hold in suspension any putative equation between this cultural Catholicism and a "transcendental signified" or ultimate truth. But
I believe the purely naturalistic accounts of religion as false consciousness
outlined in various forms by Marx, Freud, Durkheim, and others can
also be misleading, insofar as they tend often to underestimate the lingering force of religious ideas, the (often insidious) ways in which religion
can affect textual production in some circuitous or unconscious fashion
long after the forces of rationality have deconstructed and rejected such
an idiom as anachronistic. Before discussing these various theories of
religion further, it is worth making clear at the outset that this book is
not designed to be a Marxist satire on ignorant irrationality any more
than it follows the example of Jesuit intellectuals like Walter J. Ong by
heralding the presence of a triumphal Catholic spirit within the lapsed
modern world.

We run immediately, of course, into problems of definition. In her 1971
Ewing lectures, *Religion and Literature,* the critic Helen Gardner declared
her intention to concentrate on writing with a manifest and overtly
religious content. The term "religious sensibility," said Gardner, is "so
wide as to be meaningless" and "does not provide a sufficiently firm
delimitation of the subject-matter of the poems assembled for comparison."[1] Here Gardner was taking issue with T. S. Eliot's 1935 essay
"Religion and Literature," where Eliot had suggested a much broader
approach to the problem. Eliot dismissed minor "devotional" poets as
being of limited interest and he aspired instead toward a redefinition of
the relationship between religion and "major" literature. "I am not concerned here with religious literature," concluded Eliot, "but with the
application of our religion to the criticism of any literature." Eliot asserted
that François Villon and Charles Baudelaire, "with all their imperfections
and delinquencies," are greater Christian poets than Henry Vaughan or
George Herbert because the works of Villon and Baudelaire introduce

1 Helen Gardner, *Religion and Literature* (London: Faber, 1971), pp. 133–4.

more complex issues and interrogate the uneasy juxtaposition of spiritual and material inclinations within the context of a fragmented modernist environment.[2]

Eliot's approach undoubtedly carries more risks, but it is ultimately more satisfactory than Gardner's. Whereas Gardner saw religion as functioning within a highly limited and demarcated area, Eliot viewed the concept of religion as more widely pervasive, part of the consciousness of some writers who had rejected its more explicit premises. Indeed, in his 1939 treatise, *The Idea of a Christian Society,* Eliot expanded on this notion of religion as an unconscious habit to posit the idea of a "community of Christians" whose allegiance to that system of religious belief would depend upon routine and instinctive patterns of behavior rather than any conscious act of will. Although their political positions could hardly be more distinct, Eliot's nostalgia for a spontaneous, unreflective allegiance to Christendom has something in common with that of more recent social theorists like the French Marxist Louis Althusser, who insisted upon the material nature of ideology, the ways in which ideology is not merely a specific category or false chimera, but instead functions as a latent force which radically affects human perceptions and operations within a social environment. Rather than seeing power as residing in the more overt manifestations of political control – the church, the family, the law, and so on – Althusser declared that the more profound implications of ideological control were to be found in a person's unconscious activities, his or her mode of implicit thought and behavior within everyday life. For Althusser, more could be inferred about the sinister ubiquity of ideology from shopping expeditions than from government elections: "Ideology never says, 'I am ideological,'" asserted Althusser, instead it "hails or interpellates concrete individuals as concrete subjects," ordaining their ways of life by its overarching, all-encompassing, but intangible structure.[3] Through this process of interpellation, said Althusser, the human subject is necessarily constituted as a "subject" of the larger ideological matrix. Althusser played with this double meaning of "subject" so as to imply the symbiotic quality of such cultural operations, the way a relatively autonomous human subject is at the same time interpellated within (under the "subjection" of) a dominant ideology.

The Marxist Althusser was of course antipathetic toward these dominant social categories while Eliot was friendly toward the Christian religion, but both men postulated an intimate and labyrinthine relation-

---

2 T. S. Eliot, "Religion and Literature," in *Selected Essays,* 3rd ed. (London: Faber, 1951), pp. 389, 391.

3 Louis Althusser, "Ideology and Ideological State Apparatuses (Notes towards an Investigation)," in *Lenin and Philosophy and Other Essays,* trans. Ben Brewster (London: New Left Books, 1971), pp. 162–4.

ship between the individual human person and the cultural system he or she was necessarily part of. It is, though, significant that Althusser was himself an ideological product of Catholic France: indeed, Althusser stated that he saw the church as a "duplicate mirror-structure of ideology," the paradigm whose form was being imitated by the modern secular state. As Althusser pointed out, the crucifix was a ubiquitous image in eighteenth-century France, even for those who did not meditate consciously upon its meaning.[4] Significant also is the fact that the English historian E. P. Thompson, in his savage attack on Althusser in *The Poverty of Theory,* ridiculed Althusser's notions of the interpellation of individuals within corporate systems as an idealistic "theology" which takes no account of "humanism" or "empiricism." Thompson's view was that Althusser was too easily inclined to incorporate human beings within facile "systems and subsystems," viewing them as "*träger* or vectors of ulterior structural determinations" rather than as actual people engaged in the process of making their own history.[5] Like Helen Gardner, the humanistic Thompson preferred to stress the free will and rational consciousness of individual people; like T. S. Eliot, the structuralist Althusser preferred to stress unconscious allegiance to a predetermined group.

The relative merits of these two positions are no concern of ours here. This kind of argument has been going on for many centuries and is in many ways a reconstruction of that eternal argument between Aquinas and Luther, Catholicism and Nonconformism, the organization and the individual. When he was appointed to a chair of history at Oxford in 1984, Norman Stone was asked which topics he would choose if he could give only three lectures in his field, and Stone's second choice was: "the history of religion – the fantastic tenacity of religious attitudes, the way in which what purport, nowadays, to be straightforward political or social or even technological responses often go back to the Reformation and the Counter-Reformation."[6] Still, to recognize the historical specificity of Althusser's discourse, the way it is located within a particular social context, is not to annul its significance. Instead it renders that discourse provisional, valid within its own cultural terms, but not adequate as an ultimate solution to the problem of history or ideology. In the same way, to relocate "Catholic" discourses within specific cultural frameworks will be one of the aims of this book: deprived of their idealist and universalist inclinations, Catholic fictions will nevertheless be

---

4 Althusser, "Ideology," p. 168.
5 E. P. Thompson, *The Poverty of Theory and Other Essays* (London: Merlin, 1978), pp. 267, 194–6.
6 Miriam Gross, "A New Turning for Mr. Stone," *Times* (London), 6 Oct. 1984, p. 8.

granted a particular and historical existence as one form of discourse as valid, within its own terms, as any other. To deconstruct the signs of the cross is not to destroy them, but to hold in doubt the pertinence of their claim to a conclusive "reality" of the signified. While not claiming Catholic ideas are "true" in either a theological or a sociological sense, we can nevertheless analyze the internal consistency of Catholic culture and its power to shape thought in the world.

The ways in which religion continues to be a powerful ideological force are often especially evident to minority groups within any given society. In France, it is no coincidence that two of the great postwar protesters against mythology and icon were raised as part of the small Protestant minority of that country. The films of Jean-Luc Godard, born in Paris into a French-Swiss Protestant family, insist upon the arbitrary and artificially constructed nature of visual signs: the relevance of Godard's maxim "Ce n'est pas une image juste, c'est juste une image" (it's not a just image, it's just an image) should be seen as not confined merely to the cinema world, for it is also an implicit comment upon the wider realms of "official" French culture, toward whose institutionalized tableaux the film director takes an iconoclastic attitude. Godard himself lived in Switzerland as a youth and, according to John Kriedl, his films retain a "Genevan" style of "austere protest," a "puritanic" idiom that is "at once envious of the moral license and theatrical excesses of its loosely Catholic neighbor, France, and distrustful of it."[7] The other famous Protestant demystifier was Roland Barthes, who again took an ironic stance toward dominant French mythologies and who in his last work, Camera Lucida, directly associated his own attitude toward photography with a specific religious heritage: "Although growing up in a religion-without-images where the Mother is not worshipped (Protestantism) but doubtless formed culturally by Catholic art, when I confronted the Winter Garden Photograph [of my mother] I gave myself up to the Image, to the Image-Repertoire."[8] Being caught between two religious cultures, Barthes is able to gain some critical perspective upon the idiosyncrasies he perceives within each of them. American Catholic writers and artists find themselves, of course, in a similar minority position within the United States.

Despite all this, it is still not easy to discuss religion within a contemporary cultural context. Few readers would fail to recognize how the rituals of Catholicism influence not only the works of "believers" like

7 Colin MacCabe, Godard: Images, Sounds, Politics (London: British Film Institute-Macmillan, 1980), p. 111; John Kriedl, Jean-Luc Godard (Boston: Twayne, 1980), p. 25.
8 Roland Barthes, Camera Lucida: Reflections on Photography, trans. Richard Howard (New York: Hill and Wang, 1981), p. 75.

François Mauriac or Graham Greene but also those of declared nonbe-
lievers, as they do the poems of Baudelaire, the plays of Genet, the novels
of James Joyce, the films of Luis Buñuel. But these traces of Catholicism
are often thought of as a regressive and relatively uninteresting phenomenon by comparison with the more avant-garde elements in these texts:
Joyce's linguistic experiments, Buñuel's black satire, and so on. George
A. Panichan has written of how the attempt to speak about literature
within a framework of religion has customarily been unwelcome within
the modern academic world because it is to reveal a "metaphysical...
predisposition that, in a strictly intellectual sense, was completely unacceptable." The idea here is that academic study of literature and culture
is, per se, a rationalistic enterprise, with no room for the mumbo jumbo
of spiritual belief. It was in this rationalist light that F. R. Leavis, in *The
Common Pursuit,* declared literary criticism and Christian ideologies
should henceforth be seen as mutually incompatible. William Empson,
in *Milton's God,* similarly abhorred the attempts of amateur theologians
like C. S. Lewis to circumscribe Milton's artistic genius by rebuking the
epic poet when he erred on a point of Christian dogma. The dichotomy
here is between rationalism on the one hand and religious sensibility on
the other, a dichotomy Panichan in fact perpetuates by his final invective
against "the deconstructionist invaders" and his proposition instead of
the need for some "transfiguring visionary power... the moral and spiritual acceptation that must ultimately govern a 'theory of literature.'"[9]

However, such a dichotomy is, I believe, unwelcome and in the end
false. If Norman Stone is correct in his assertion that contemporary
political arguments can be traced back to religious traditions implicit
within societies for hundreds of years, then it follows that a recognition
of the ways in which this residual religious force operates is crucial for
an understanding of the complexity of modern literature and indeed the
modern world. It is not my intention to denigrate Panichan's "transfiguring visionary power"; indeed, it is not my intention to denigrate any
particular ideological position. But the most significant aspect of religion
in terms of contemporary cultural studies lies in its continuing influence,
often unconscious, upon the secular and material world. This unsatisfactory binary opposition between intellectual skepticism on the one hand
and nonintellectual belief on the other fails to comprehend the motives
and actions of vast numbers of people, including writers and artists, who
are not "believers" in any orthodox theological sense. The fact that
analysis of any religious sensibility must involve a study of nonbelief as
well as of belief has too often been overlooked; as Clifford Geertz put

9 George A. Panichan, "Literature and Religion: A Revelatory Critical Confluence," *Studies
in the Literary Imagination,* 18, no. 1 (1985), 3, 9–10.

it: "If the anthropological study of religious commitment is underdeveloped, the anthropological study of religious non-commitment is non-existent." Geertz's 1966 essay, "Religion as a Cultural System," is in fact one of the clearest theoretical statements of how religious thought, recast within demystified forms, becomes an active agent within the secular world:

> It seems to me that it is best to begin any approach to this issue with frank recognition that religious belief involves not a Baconian induction from everyday experience – for then we should all be agnostics – but rather a prior acceptance of authority which transforms that experience. ... Religious concepts spread beyond their specifically metaphysical contexts to provide a framework of general ideas in terms of which a wide range of experience – intellectual, emotional, moral – can be given meaningful forms. ... In the doctrine of original sin is embedded also a recommended attitude toward life, a recurring mood, and a persisting set of motivations.[10]

Geertz's theory of symbolic action is presented here as a model for systems of cultural anthropology rather than literature as such; nevertheless, his critique of excessively narrow and empirically minded definitions of religious influence is just as relevant for literary analysis. Geertz's article also highlights the controversial and relatively unexplored nature of this conceptual area, and it is worth briefly examining theories of the transformation of religion over the last two centuries to suggest why this continues to be such awkward terrain for contemporary academic discourse to negotiate.

One of the earliest and most subtle proponents of transformation theory was Ludwig Feuerbach. In *The Essence of Christianity* (1841) and other works, Feuerbach proposed to dissolve theology into anthropology, to remove God and enthrone man in his place. Feuerbach believed that man externalizes and projects his best qualities, attempting to dignify them by giving them the name of divinity. However, the modern era, said Feuerbach, ought to recognize that these "divine" qualities in fact emanate from within human beings: man should restore his sense of inner value, power, and autonomy by canceling the fiction of heaven. Feuerbach vehemently opposed both the idealism of Hegel, which proposed to reconcile contradictions within some grand architectonic synthesis, and also the aesthetic and moral idealism of Kant, which, said Feuerbach, indicated the extent to which Kant's mentality was "still bound by

---

10 Clifford Geertz, "Religion as a Cultural System," in *Anthropological Approaches to the Study of Religion,* ed. Michael Banton (New York: Praeger, 1966), pp. 43, 25, 40.

theism."[11] Feuerbach preferred to locate truth with the concrete and the particular, those down-to-earth phenomena which could be empirically verified by science and by ordinary human processes of perception. He preached a gospel of human limitation rather than human transcendence, although he liked the idea of preserving a "religious" sensibility, provided it was clearly acknowledged how this was a strictly human affair where "god" had descended into man so that man himself was now the divinity.

There are several problems with Feuerbach's philosophy from the perspective of my particular argument. In the first place, Feuerbach cherishes a millennial notion that the residue of metaphysical displacement can finally be overcome, that all traces of the transcendent can one day be removed, that alienation can apocalyptically be alleviated as humanity itself assumes the role of godhead. This kind of romanticism reveals an impossible nostalgia for Eden: the idea of totally overcoming alienation, of removing all elements of spiritual aspiration and yearning, is a form of pastoral utopia. In the second place, the "anthropology" with which Feuerbach proposes to supplant "theology" is in fact a specifically Protestant anthropology. The opening of *Principles of the Philosophy of the Future* (1843) finds Feuerbach openly asserting that the Catholic conceptualization of divinity within the figure of God himself has now given way to a Protestant concern with Christ, the God of man. Protestantism, says Feuerbach, "is essentially Christology, that is, religious anthropology," and he clearly sees himself as advancing this project one logical stage further by his proposed demystification of Christ and relocation of all Christ's divine aspects within a human incarnation.[12] Feuerbach liked to think of himself as a second Luther, and, like Luther, Feuerbach recommends the prioritizing of an individual's "inner light" over every pernicious attempt to systematize and objectify the spirit. The systems and generalizations Luther was escaping were those of the papacy, of course, whereas Feuerbach primarily was fleeing the universalist impulses of Hegel and Kant, but the underlying premises in each case are very similar: an impulse of resistance, a refusal of the individual to succumb or be "interpellated," as Althusser would say, into any kind of cultural network. As we have already seen in the controversy between Althusser and E. P. Thompson, this kind of nonconformity itself betokens a Protestant cultural mentality; Catholic anthropology, by contrast, works toward patterns of analogy and universalism, conformity and ritual. In some ways, the methodology of this book could be seen as based upon a more "Catholic" version of Feuerbach's transformation theories: like

11 Ludwig Feuerbach, *Principles of the Philosophy of the Future*, trans. Manfred H. Vogel (Indianapolis: Bobbs-Merrill, 1966), p. 29.
12 Feuerbach, *Principles*, p. 5.

Feuerbach, it dissolves theology into anthropology, but it considers that cultural anthropology within a less Germanic, less millennial, and more "Catholic" light.

Yet if Feuerbach's ideas are not universally valid, they are still more apposite than a lot of those that came after him in the nineteenth century. Abhorred, of course, by conventional Christian thinkers, Feuerbach also found himself dismissed by positivists and materialists who found his idea of lingering religious sensibilities to be an idealistic irrelevance. Karl Marx as a young man had great respect for Feuerbach's iconoclasm, but Marx clearly saw his task as to redefine Feuerbach's paradoxical ambivalence within a tougher and more radically materialist idiom. Thus in their 1844 essay, *On Religion,* Marx and Friedrich Engels famously declared religion to be "the opium of the people," a sanctification of this earthly "vale of woe" and a chimera designed to prevent oppressed classes from seeking justice in this world by offering them the promise of greater rewards in the next. Insisting that "religion is only the illusory sun which revolves around man as long as he does not revolve around himself," Marx and Engels thought the essential business of a criticism of religion should be rational disillusionment, with discussions of theology becoming superseded by discussions of politics. Engels, for instance, admonished those German historians who failed to recognize that the religious disputes and heresies of medieval times were all simply class conflicts in disguise. Like Feuerbach, Marx and Engels viewed the psychological experiences of religion as a "saintly form of human self-alienation," a culturally induced pathology which prevents man from realizing that it is in fact he himself who invents religion; but for Marx and Engels, the crucial problem was that this obsession with affairs metaphysical impeded mankind's full participation in the historical process. It was in his 1845 *Theses on Feuerbach* that Marx concluded philosophers like Feuerbach "have only *interpreted* the world . . . the point, however, is to *change* it."[13]

The context for Marx's writing was the scientific intellectual atmosphere of the mid-nineteenth century, and this environment produced various other attempts to subsume religion and mythology under a rationalist umbrella. George Eliot, for instance, wrote her novels in the shadow of the "Higher Criticism" of German biblical scholars like Feuerbach and David Friedrich Strauss, who placed a new emphasis upon the allegorical and fictional status of the Bible. Although this skeptical, de-

13 Karl Marx and Friedrich Engels, "On Religion," in *Sociological Perspectives: Selected Readings,* ed. Kenneth Thompson and Jeremy Tunstall (Harmondsworth: Penguin-Open University, 1971), pp. 439–40; Karl Marx and Friedrich Engels, *Opposition of the Materialist and Idealist Outlooks* (London: Lawrence and Wishart, 1973), p. 95.

mythologizing project caused much dismay among the more literal-minded clergymen of the time, George Eliot's sophisticated mind experienced no difficulty in working within the framework of Christian mythology without at all believing in Christian doctrines. In her 1859 novel, *Adam Bede,* for example, as Valentine Cunningham has said: "George Eliot as it were demythologizes the traditional formulas of repentance and conversion as Feuerbach had reinterpreted, humanistically, the Christian symbols and theology. Hetty repents superficially to God, but most movingly to Adam: the human connection is the most prominent."[14] George Eliot herself translated Feuerbach's *Essence of Christianity* and also, in 1846, Strauss's iconoclastic *Life of Jesus,* which similarly rejected Christ's supernatural aspirations and dealt with him simply on a human level.

This rationalizing and scientific outlook took a different direction toward the end of the nineteenth century, as Sir James Frazer and other anthropologists set about the task of demonstrating the essential equivalence of myth, ritual, and religion across primitive and supposedly "civilized" communities. These anthropologists disseminated a new awareness of how myth should be seen not just as an archaic form confined to jungles and rain forests but as a vital organizing principle of Western societies. Their work was taken up around the turn of the century by a number of intellectuals who became interested in how the conceptual implications of religion and ritual could be deemed to carry significant weight within the material world even if their metaphysical premises were ignored or invalidated. Whereas Engels saw religion as simply a delusion, and whereas, according to John Addington Symonds, prosaic nineteenth-century historians generally regarded religious myths as "a thickly-tufted jungle of inexplicable stories" and proceeded to discount them, there was by contrast between 1890 and 1930 an increasing emphasis upon the psychological rather than scientific accuracy of symbol and myth.[15]

Stating that "the truth to be looked for in myths is psychological, not historical, aesthetic rather than positive," Symonds's 1893 *Studies of the Greek Poets* proceeds to pour scorn on Professor Max Müller's disregard of mythology as "the bane of the ancient world" and "a disease of language." The philologist Müller shared the general belief of nineteenth-century historians that mythology was simply a series of unverifiable propositions; but Symonds's critique of this pedantic and "unimaginative habit of mind" is consonant with the outlook of Joyce, Ezra Pound,

14 Valentine Cunningham, *Everywhere Spoken Against: Dissent in the Victorian Novel* (Oxford: Oxford Univ. Press, 1975), p. 169.
15 John Addington Symonds, *Studies of the Greek Poets,* 3rd ed. (1893; rpt. London: Black, 1920), p. 31.

T. S. Eliot, D. H. Lawrence, and many other modernist writers of fiction who were to deploy the icons of ancient Greek or Old Norse not for their literal significances but for their mythopoeic qualities, the ways in which such archaic symbolism could offer a medium for the imaginative expression of intangible truths. For Pound and Joyce, as for Marx, all myth and religion was finally an anthropomorphic conception. But whereas Marx castigated such anthropomorphism as human self-deception, Pound and Joyce believed this anthropomorphism, though necessarily fictive and man-made, could still be useful as a means of lending some kind of shape and order to the anarchy and "futility" (as Eliot called it) of the lapsed modern world.[16] Joyce, who read Strauss's *Life of Jesus* in 1905, clearly follows the modernist line of exploiting the cultural power of religious myths without literally believing in them. Stephen Dedalus's sermon on art in *A Portrait of the Artist as a Young Man,* with its emphasis on aesthetic radiance, harmony, and wholeness, is a demystified reworking of the theological conceptions of Thomas Aquinas, who had said the same thing about divine presence; and the religious sensibility in *Ulysses* is evident from the very first page of the novel, when Buck Mulligan mimics the Eucharist service by holding up his shaving mirror – rather than the Communion host – and declaiming "Intribo ad altare Dei" (I will go unto the altar of God). Despite remaining a fervent atheist throughout his mature life, Joyce used to sneak into the back of Catholic churches during services on the pretext that he was admiring the liturgical form of the mass, and his works are proof, if ever it existed, of the potency with which Catholic fictions can operate within an overtly skeptical and secular context.

The single most famous transformation theory also dates from the turn of the century: Max Weber's 1904–5 treatise, *The Protestant Ethic and the Spirit of Capitalism.* Here Weber associated the rise of capitalism in the seventeenth century with the characteristics of asceticism, self-discipline, and systematic self-control, which the new ideas of Calvinism enjoined upon its followers in the wake of the Reformation. Weber explicitly refused to make any moral judgments on the issues under consideration: "The question of the relative value of the cultures which are compared here will not receive a single word." Nor did Weber claim that the Reformation had originated capitalism, merely that it had helped capitalism on its way:

> We have no intention whatever of maintaining such a foolish and doc-
> trinaire thesis as that the spirit of capitalism. . . . could only have arisen
> as a result of certain effects of the Reformation, or even that capitalism

16 Ibid., pp. 35–6. Eliot used the word "futility" in his 1923 essay on Joyce, "*Ulysses:*
  Order and Myth," rpt. in *Selected Prose of T. S. Eliot,* ed. Frank Kermode (New York:
  Harcourt Brace Jovanovich, 1975), p. 177.

> as an economic system is a creation of the Reformation. . . . On the
> contrary, we only wish to ascertain whether and to what extent religious
> forces have taken part in the qualitative formation and the quantitative
> expansion of that spirit over the world.[17]

Weber's disclaimer has not prevented him from being criticized by more
empirically minded historians on the grounds that he oversimplified complex issues through neglecting time sequences and telescoping various
data. Some social scientists have also been unhappy with Weber's tendency toward "idealization": the whole idea of a disembodied "spirit"
of capitalism is anathema to many radical sociologists who insist the
economic base must precede any abstract idea. Although Weber himself
claimed that "it is, of course, not my aim to substitute for a one-sided
materialistic an equally one-sided spiritualistic causal interpretation of
culture and of history," nevertheless for some modes of more traditional
Marxist thought any nonmaterial idea is necessarily an illusory phenomenon which must emerge from a state of false consciousness.[18]

Luciano Pellicani, in fact, has asserted that Weber's attempt to prove
the autonomy of ideas and the power of ethical values within history
was a direct response to what Pellicani called the "obsessive" economic
materialism of Marxism. The result of this implied argument with Marx,
according to Pellicani, was to make Weber's thesis too polemical and
overgeneralized. Pellicani pointed out that "capitalists" can easily be
found in the Middle Ages, that Calvin and other Puritan leaders publicly
attacked the acquisitive instinct, and that Calvinism among the Scots
actually helped to slow down Scotland's rate of economic development
by comparison with that of England. In a rejoinder to Pellicani, Guy
Oakes replied that the early medieval capitalists were simply adventurers
and the "spirit" of capitalism became institutionalized only much later
on. According to Oakes, Weber openly acknowledges that these Puritans
ostensibly reviled mammon but he also analyzes that "paradoxical quality
of history" whereby the Calvinists' achievement of wealth was one of
the unintended consequences of their religious sensibility.[19]

The debate about Weber's thesis is a long and complex one, but one
of the most unconvincing attacks on it is the notion that this is merely
a "bourgeois" response to the intellectual challenge of Marx. For while
Weber happened to be writing about the development of the bourgeoisie,
that is not his central theme: his central theme is the transformation of

---

17 Max Weber, *The Protestant Ethic and the Spirit of Capitalism*, trans. Talcott Parsons (New
York: Scribner's, 1958), p. 91.

18 Ibid., p. 183.

19 Luciano Pellicani, "Weber and the Myth of Capitalism," *Telos*, no. 75 (1988), pp. 57–
85; Guy Oakes, "Farewell to *The Protestant Ethic*?" *Telos*, no. 78 (1988–9), pp. 81–94.

theology into social anthropology. If his subject had been other religious groups, the bourgeoisie would not have figured so prominently; indeed, a consideration of the transformation of Catholic theology into Catholic anthropology and aesthetics within the United States will involve investigation of the fortunes of more working-class and immigrant groups. Merely to equate religion with "bourgeois" false consciousness is far too simplistic. Because Christianity continues to exert a powerful social and psychological charge even if its theological premises are ignored, any critic who seeks to dismiss religion as irrelevant to contemporary material concerns runs the risk of making an erroneous analysis of the forces currently governing society. This was not, of course, a mistake Marx himself made: Marx was very interested in the all-pervasive ideologies of religion and knew that any attempt to root out the "opium of the people" would be a long-term and very difficult project. To take just one example, Hasia R. Diner has written of how Irish immigrant workers in the United States in the nineteenth century found their inclinations toward feminist independence usurped not so much by external social pressures as by the psychology of their own Irish-Catholic heritage: "In the final analysis," noted Diner, "ethnicity and cultural values proved to be more significant than gender. Despite the strides Irish women had made towards acculturation, their commitment to their Irish heritage remained intact."[20] Here the traditional Catholic model of male dominance continued to reign supreme. It is one of the puzzles for rationalist historians, and one of the frustrations for rationalist philosophers, why "reason" continues to exert such a slim and tenuous hold upon the general consciousness of mankind, and the perseverance of old religious attitudes is one explanation for this.

More obviously in tune with the positivism of the sociologists was Emile Durkheim, whose *Elementary Forms of the Religious Life* appeared in 1912. For Durkheim, the various forms of "mystery" surrounding religion were "wholly superficial" and he claimed "it is enough merely to set aside the veil with which mythological imagination has covered them for them to appear such as they really are." In recommending that religion should become the object of scientific enquiry, Durkheim regretted how "the obscure intuitions of sensation and sentiment" associated with religion too often hindered the processes of rational enlightenment, although he went on to assure his readers that these barriers of prejudice would without doubt eventually give way. However, Durkheim did believe that religion was a deep-rooted social practice, and he feared that a society's "collective sentiment" and "collective

20 Hasia R. Diner, *Erin's Daughters in America: Irish Immigrant Women in the Nineteenth Century* (Baltimore: Johns Hopkins Univ. Press, 1983), p. 153.

ideas" (which were intimately tied to particular systems of divine belief) would be in danger of disintegrating if religion itself were to suffer a loss of prestige. Hence Durkheim's notions of alienation and "anomie," the prospect of individuals adrift on a sea of social isolation as a direct consequence of increasing agnosticism. One possible solution to this problem, thought Durkheim, was to transform religious ritual into secularized formats so as to preserve society's collective spirit, just as "the French Revolution established a whole cycle of holidays to keep the principles with which it was inspired in a state of perpetual youth."[21]

This idea of religion as a self-consciously fictive antidote to contemporary social dissolution was taken up by the Marxist critic Fredric Jameson in his 1981 book, *The Political Unconscious*, where Jameson quoted Rousseau on how festivals signify those moments when a society celebrates its own unity. Jameson went on to envisage the possibility of transforming the residual power of this collective religious impulse into a collective political force. His desire was to rework the lingering (and symbolic) power of religious ideas for different social purposes:

> To stress the purely *symbolic* character of such unification . . . is to place this theory in a perspective in which religious practices and cultural production – the nostalgia for the collective and the Utopian – are harnessed to ideological ends. . . . The problem of the ideological function of religion must be raised more urgently than at any other nexus of the Marxian theory of modes of production, and in a far more concrete and historical way than in Durkheim's ahistorical theory of religion.[22]

Like George Eliot, James Joyce, and Max Weber, Jameson considered the significance of religion to lie in its potential for transforming itself from spiritual into material forms so as to exert continuing influence within the modern secular and political world.

However, the evident difficulty both with Durkheim's dystopian theory and with its utopian counterpart in Jameson is the problem of oversimplification. In his concentration on religion's function as social ritual, Durkheim neglects the less obvious psychological ramifications of religion and the ways religion can affect the behavior of people who have no interest whatsoever in symbolic affirmations of community life. Durkheim's dystopia is, in a way, merely an inversion of G. K. Chesterton's sentimental view of medieval "Merry England," where peasants were supposed to dance gleefully round the maypole, their social good cheer

---

21 Emile Durkheim, "The Elementary Forms of the Religious Life," in *Sociological Perspectives*, pp. 442–5.
22 Fredric Jameson, *The Political Unconscious: Narrative as a Socially Symbolic Act* (Ithaca: Cornell Univ. Press, 1981), pp. 292–5.

mirroring their confidence in Christianity. But in the novels of Mary McCarthy or John O'Hara, for instance, religion operates in a much less obtrusive and apocalyptic fashion than this. The characters in O'Hara's novels accept religion casually, as part of a social heritage, as a (sometimes latent) psychological determinant, and (occasionally) as a theological system of belief. Yet, if they are not believers, they do not become irredeemably alienated, as the Durkheim model would suggest; nor are they necessarily inspired to transform religious icons into emblems of political collectivism, as Jameson would hope. O'Hara is perhaps an extreme example of this, in that the characters in his novels, with their beady eye for social distinctions and classes, tend to take a very down-to-earth attitude toward religious appurtenances; it is true enough that there are several examples, particularly in the literature of modernism, of idealistic Catholicism becoming metamorphosed into idealistic Marxism, as for instance with the character of Jim Nolan in Steinbeck's 1935 novel, *In Dubious Battle*. But my point is that Durkheim's utopian–dystopian paradigm is not the only possible model. Especially in the postmodernist era, as we shall see later – in the poetry of Frank O'Hara, the films of Robert Altman – cultures of Catholicism usually operate in a much more relaxed and playfully ironic fashion than foreseen in Durkheim's angst-ridden modernist idiom.

It may be also that "Catholic" writers and artists, as individuals, have generally tended to be less anxious than Reformists about the status of their own religious beliefs. Whereas in the sixteenth century Erasmus and Montaigne cheerfully combined a Catholic sensibility with theological skepticism, Luther by contrast insisted that "a Christian ought . . . to be certain of what he affirms, or else he is not a Christian." Luther told Erasmus that the latter's skeptical attitudes implied no belief at all in God, but was rather a way of mocking him: "The Holy Ghost is not a Sceptic," thundered Luther.[23] Again, what we see here is a cultural confrontation going back hundreds of years. Protestantism foregrounds the importance of free choice, individual conscience, and individual belief, while Catholicism places more emphasis upon a (religious or artistic) tradition which necessarily incorporates and objectifies the individual, with his or her own particular attitude toward that tradition being of secondary importance. This is to describe a complex historical affair in the most general terms, of course, and we shall see more detailed modifications of these patterns later; still, as James Turner has noted, while Protestantism chooses to emphasize conscious belief, Catholicism stresses altogether vaguer conceptions of "the Faith." Thomas Paine remarked

---

23 See Richard H. Popkin, *The History of Scepticism from Erasmus to Spinoza* (Berkeley: Univ. of California Press, 1979), pp. 6–7.

on this phenomenon back in the eighteenth century, when he complained that Catholics were too prone to fall back into a position of mere *assensus,* passive obedience, rather than striving to cultivate an active virtue.[24] Yet the lingering perseverance of this cultural notion of assensus helps to explain why many Catholic writers have not been especially tormented about issues concerning the private experience of God but have been more willing, especially in the postmodernist period, to take or leave religion as one possible fiction among others.

Recent proponents of the transformation of theology, however, have tended to be of a more idealistic bent. Harvey Cox's famous 1965 book, *The Secular City,* welcomed the fact that modern, flexible "technopolitan" humanity was at last sloughing off the old neuroses and fetishes of organized religion. By turning its attention away from archaic visions of the next world, thought Cox, secular man could concentrate instead upon the pressing problems of the earthly city. Cox distinguished his notion of "secularization" – "an authentic consequence of biblical faith" – from mere secularism, or atheistic materialism: secularization did not necessarily involve abandoning God, simply abandoning the old notion of God as a father figure.[25] Nevertheless, Cox's vision of a demystified world guided by the impetus of rationality and (more distantly) the Holy Spirit now seems no less a product of its era than many of the other utopian pronouncements in popular culture of that time. Andrew M. Greeley's *Unsecular Man* (1972) was conceived largely as a direct response to *The Secular City:* Greeley, a Catholic sociologist, strenuously maintained that the persistence of religious belief was an "observable, verifiable, empirical fact" and he inveighed against "those divinity school professors who believe that contemporary man no longer needs or wants the sacred."[26] Both Greeley's unsecular man and Cox's secular utopianism, however, ignore the crucial problem of what happens in the gray, uncertain areas in between the secular and the unsecular; it is this paradoxical interrelation between belief and disbelief that is so unsettling and so disruptive of fixed academic concepts. If it were a question of individuals or society being simply either "secular" or "unsecular," then the whole issue would become much more straightforward. It is the psy-

24 James Turner, *Without God, Without Creed: The Origins of Unbelief in America* (Baltimore: Johns Hopkins Univ. Press, 1985), p. 278. For Paine and *assensus,* see Jay Fliegelman, *Prodigals and Pilgrims: The American Revolution against Patriarchal Authority, 1750–1800* (Cambridge: Cambridge Univ. Press, 1982), p. 186.
25 Harvey Cox, *The Secular City: Secularization and Urbanization in Theological Perspective* (New York: Macmillan, 1965), p. 18.
26 Andrew M. Greeley, *Unsecular Man: The Persistence of Religion* (New York: Schocken, 1972), pp. 7, 153.

chological and cultural ambiguities at work here that polemical writers like Cox and Greeley tend to ignore.

Cox himself, in fact, later retracted the philosophy behind *The Secular City,* saying that while he used to believe mankind "might someday outgrow its religious phase and live maturely in the calm, cool light of reason," he no longer seriously believed this would happen, "nor do I hope it will."[27] In his 1974 book, *The Seduction of the Spirit,* Cox argued more moderately that the "religious" impulse is a constant in human life, an idealistic essence which outlives any particular social forms, and that when the established churches have declined, this impulse will manifest itself in other ways. Bryan Wilson, a sociologist who has written extensively about the role of religion within a secular society, has often taken a similar stance. In a series of 1974 lectures later published under the title *Contemporary Transformations of Religion,* Wilson asserted, in an echo of Durkheim, that "secularization is intimately related to the decline of community, to increased social mobility, and to the impersonality of role-relationships. . . . Contemporary society is less legitimated than any previously existing social system and part of that lack of legitimation stems from the collapse of a shared conception of transcendent order." Declaring himself in favor of old custom and "social control," Wilson nevertheless revealed a certain amount of sympathy for newly established religious cults and sects – Californian mysticism, Scientology, Latin American Pentecostal worship – all of which Wilson saw as a wholly understandable reaction against the increasingly banal ecumenical nature of socially established churches and the equally mundane "rational principles that govern the modern world."[28]

The difficulty here seems to be that Wilson places altogether too great a faith in the efficacy of these "rational principles." While he may himself feel only lukewarm toward this rationalism, Wilson nevertheless accepts the effects of Durkheim's positivism and Weber's notions of *Zweckrational* and *Entzanberung* – those rationalizing and demystifying categories Weber claimed were superseding the archaic religious world – as a fait accompli in social terms. Believing that "men act less in response to religious motivation: they assess the world in empirical and rational terms," Wilson sought to come out from the other side of this particular tunnel, as it were, and to reclaim some of the lost religious sensibility within society.[29] Yet to apprehend the modern world as a purely secular entity is

27 Quoted in Garry Wills, *Bare Ruined Choirs: Doubt, Prophecy, and Radical Religion* (Garden City, N.Y.: Doubleday, 1972), p. 96.
28 Bryan Wilson, *Contemporary Transformations of Religion* (London: Oxford Univ. Press, 1976), pp. 99, 90.
29 Bryan Wilson, *Religion in Secular Society: A Sociological Comment* (London: Watts, 1966), p. x.

to ignore the wells of primitive beliefs through which social theories of various kinds are refracted. Many secular modes are, to some extent at least, rationalizations of irrational or supernatural beliefs. Wilson's 1966 book, *Religion in Secular Society*, included one particularly unfortunate example of the kind of rationalizing process he claimed was prevalent in the modern world: "The marked loss of religious fervour in Northern Ireland in the decades since the end of the Second World War," he said, "and their diminished consequence in political terms, illustrates the declining relevance of religion for politics."[30] It would be unfair to pick on this one unhappy prophecy were it not for the fact that it brings into focus the more general point about how covert religious codes often continue to underlie overtly political ideas. To take another example from recent British history, Jonathan Raban has analyzed how Margaret Thatcher's economic ideas – emphasizing "individual responsibility," free choice, and "the divinely created sovereignty of individual conscience" – were "informed throughout by her theological upbringing in the Methodist Church."[31] While one would not seek to explain politicians simply in terms of implicit religious motivation, Raban made a good case for seeing this subliminal or transformed Calvinism as one important component of Thatcher's political outlook. The insidious aspect of this rhetoric is not, of course, the propagation of Calvinist views in themselves. The danger lies in suppression (or ignorance) of where the cultural origins of this rhetoric lie and the pretence, instead, that this particular and limited religious ideology might constitute a universal truth.

The political significance of the critical demystification of religion was also urged in a 1986 essay by Jonathan Culler. Here Culler noted that the traditional religious tolerance and right of privacy in America, together with the separation of church and state, have made it difficult to "mock, criticize, or even discuss other people's religious beliefs." Nevertheless, he concluded that religion contains any number of unexamined assumptions that might be used to justify racism, sexism, violence, and the like, and so in his opinion religious beliefs should be fully open to the processes of rational interrogation: "The political and intellectual health of our nation requires, I submit, that the religious justifications of political positions and thus religious discourse be as much a subject of debate and critique as other ideological formations and discourses."[32] However, one caveat that should be inserted here is that Culler's own preferred ideology of "radical skepticism" is, in its way, no less of a

30 Ibid., p. 60.
31 Jonathan Raban, *God, Man and Mrs. Thatcher* (London: Chatto and Windus, 1989), pp. 14, 32, 3.
32 Jonathan Culler, "Comparative Literature and the Pieties," *Profession, 86* ([New York]: Modern Language Association of America, 1986), p. 31.

partial position than the rational utopias of Marx and Durkheim, and no less chimerical. Pure skepticism can never be attained, any more than pure reason or pure innocence can. In this sense, the dogmatically atheistic critic – the Harold Bloom or the William Empson who takes religious belief in a writer to be a sign of weakness – is simply an inverted mirror image of the old-style Christian critic, the C. S. Lewis or the Northrop Frye. Traces of religious sensibility cannot simply be abolished by programs in deconstruction, though deconstruction may admittedly help the rational mind to preserve a more paradoxical awareness of the discrepancy between its own lucidity and every form of religious conditioning or assertion of metaphysical truth.

Paradox, in fact, is the area within which some of the most challenging contemporary theorists of religion locate their discourse. For the explicitly Christian thinker Paul Ricoeur, critiques from the atheistic school are welcome because they enable us finally to dispose of the old-fashioned "moral God" predicated upon "an ethics of prohibition and condemnation." By abandoning this superannuated deity who was equated with the psychological superego and with social conventions, the philosopher of religion – who, said Ricoeur, "stands midway between atheism and faith" – will be empowered to move toward the more intangible essence of spiritual belief. Georges Bataille's *Theory of Religion* similarly postulated a world where religion, situated "at the boundary of that which escapes cohesion," engages in transgression against all rational social codes.[33] For Bataille, mankind is forever stranded between his desire for what is holy and sacred and his awareness of a human condition that is animalistic and profane, and this contradiction can be resolved only in extreme circumstances such as violent intimacy, sacrifice, or death. So both Ricoeur and Bataille, in their different ways, confront a rupture between human reason and "divine" irrationality. This is the kind of dualism and irony more characteristic of French cultural traditions, an outlook substantially different from the self-sufficient radical skepticism of Jonathan Culler, which emerges from a more typically American Enlightenment perspective. For the French philosophers, religion connotes a shifting, amorphous force that bifurcates the human ego and subverts human aspirations to independent autonomy.

We discover in Ricoeur and Bataille, then, the kind of paradox in which modern consciousness is split between rational disbelief and irrational belief. Rather than society being comfortably divided into two

33 Paul Ricoeur, "Religion, Atheism, and Faith," in Alasdair MacIntyre and Paul Ricoeur, *The Religious Significance of Atheism* (New York: Columbia Univ. Press, 1969), pp. 68, 70; Georges Bataille, *Theory of Religion,* trans. Robert Hurley (New York: Zone, 1989), p. 10.

opposed camps of atheists and believers, this opposition becomes a contradiction within each individual person. This is a paradox taken up in
a more secular sense by late-twentieth-century theorists of religion who
have pursued such notions of a "divided self" into the realms of psychoanalysis. In his 1967 book, *The Sacred Canopy*, Peter Berger aligned
religion with masochism, the "key characteristic" in both cases being
"the intoxication of surrender to an other." Drawing upon Sartre's analysis, in *Being and Nothingness*, of the masochistic enterprise as a predestined failure and as one example of man's "bad faith" or refusal to take
existential responsibility for his own actions, Berger raised the question
of whether religion should not be seen as a purely pathological phenomenon: "Masochism, by its radical self-denial, provides the means by
which the individual's suffering and even death can be radically transcended. . . . Not being able to stand aloneness, man denies his separate-
ness, and not being able to stand meaninglessness, he finds a paradoxical
meaning in self-annihilation."[34]

Another psychological version of religious transformation is to be
found in Thomas Luckmann's 1963 account, *The Invisible Religion*. Luckmann maintained that everything human is also innately religious, religion being defined as the capacity of the human organism for
"transcendence" of its "biological nature" through the construction of
wider systems of meaning. Setting himself in opposition to "visible" and
"objective" manifestations of "religiosity," Luckmann sought to aggrandize to the status of religious acts anything capable of providing a
"subjectively meaningful system of 'ultimate' significances," including
"such 'ultimately' significant hobbies as wife-swapping."[35]

These various analyses of religious transformation are worth keeping
in mind, and they introduce ideas we will encounter again later: Kerouac's
notion of the "beat" or beatific as a rupture of the real is not too far
from Bataille's concept of religious transgression, for example. All such
theories, however, seem finally inadequate as a universal explanation of
the phenomenon of religious culture. Ricoeur and Bataille idealize the
category of religion without taking account of material and cultural differences between different forms of divine worship. Luckmann's theory
is vague: wife-swapping may indeed be cherished as though it were a
divine object, but this parallel must remain at a level of mere fancy,
because (pace John Updike) there is no direct causal or historical link
between religion and extramarital sex. Berger's analysis of religious ma-

---

34 Peter L. Berger, *The Sacred Canopy: Elements of a Sociological Theory of Religion* (Garden
    City, N.Y.: Doubleday, 1967), pp. 55–6.
35 Thomas Luckmann, *The Invisible Religion: The Problem of Religion in Modern Society*
    (1963; rpt. London: Collier–Macmillan, 1967), pp. 49, 101, 106.

sochism might shed light on Scott Fitzgerald's "cheap Irish love of defeat," as Hemingway called it, and also on the heroines of Mary Gordon, but it hardly seems appropriate for the villains of Mario Puzo or for the lawyers of George V. Higgins.[36] Harvey Cox's idea of innate religious impulses becoming frustrated by secular society and so emerging in new and indirect ways may be relevant to Frank O'Hara, but it is rather less helpful when considering the work of William Kennedy, for whom Catholicism operates on an unabashed material and metaphorical rather than transcendent level. Thus the focus here will be upon how different writers and artists refract their religious heritage in different ways: pluralism is all. The aim is not to deny the putative validity of "spiritual" impulses, as the nineteenth-century positivists would have done, but to examine how affairs of the spirit are also necessarily grounded in material culture. Like Max Weber, I am not of course attempting to gainsay the existence of other, perhaps more important and immediate pressures within an artist's culture. I am merely seeking to point out how various patterns of "Catholic" ideology and aesthetics can illuminate one specific aspect of an author's work.

What I am moving toward, then, is an explication of some of those structures of thought that have become hidden or latent within modern American writing. The aim is an elaboration of the "positive unconscious" of knowledge, as Michel Foucault described it in *The Order of Things,* an attempt "to know, with a positive knowledge, that which is given to or eludes [the subject's] consciousness," an illumination of those dark areas within texts that have been suppressed by modern rationalist philosophies.[37] In Mary McCarthy's writing, for instance, we will be able to unravel unconscious traces of Catholic ideologies that have been ignored or dismissed as insignificant by purely formalist critical standards. There will, of course, be no attempt finally to "explain" McCarthy's work in terms of these ideas, any more than one can "explain" Margaret Thatcher in terms of Methodism. The more modest ambition will be to demonstrate how these patterns of cultural Catholicism recur across texts in a variety of media – poetry, photography, and films, as well as novels – and so to reveal how a secularized form of religious consciousness has become implanted within twentieth-century American art. This is not to resurrect the specter of "myth" in any idealist or essentialist or rigidly structuralist way: it is not the purpose here to

36 Hemingway quoted in André Le Vot, *F. Scott Fitzgerald,* trans. William Byron (Harmondsworth: Penguin, 1985), p. 300.
37 Michel Foucault, *The Order of Things: An Archaeology of the Human Sciences* (London: Tavistock, 1970), p. xi; p. 378.

suggest that these cultural patterns are timeless or archetypal, but rather that they are observable historical realities, changing their shape across time.

Literature is an appropriate area for this kind of investigation, because within fiction deep layers of social and psychological consciousness manifest themselves, often in circuitous ways, but also in ways that permit the reader the possibility of recognizing how these preconceptions are built into the text. By raising these obscure and irrational aspects of any given text to a level of reason and reflection, the reader is able to transform the work of art into a self-reflexive entity meditating upon its own conditions of production and self-consciously displaying the ways it has originated from a specific cultural context. To quote from Wolfgang Iser's *The Act of Reading:*

> We recognize in a novel, for instance, so many of the conventions that regulate our society and culture. But by reorganizing them horizontally, the fictional text brings them before us in unexpected combinations, so that they begin to be stripped of their validity. As a result, these conventions are taken out of their social contexts, deprived of their regulatory function, and so become objects of scrutiny in themselves. . . . The repertoire of the novel both reflects and reveals the rules that govern its own communication.[38]

By examining these silent, unconscious religious determinants, the reader can move toward deconstructing and demystifying the power of mythology. As Foucault said, silence reinforces power, whereas an acknowledgment of the way power operates within a framework of discourse renders power fragile and liable to be thwarted.

These silent spaces are the areas ventured into by good writers and artists. This is why it is important to preserve a sense of aesthetic value when considering such large cultural questions. The good writer does not follow rigidly any prescribed pattern of thought, religious or otherwise, but instead reveals a cultural heritage in "unexpected combinations," to take up Iser's phrase, thereby defying the conceptual reifications of theologians and philosophers and demonstrating how individual sensibilities manifest themselves amid the particular quirks and idiosyncrasies of human experience. Nobody could imagine Milton was a typical seventeenth-century English Puritan, and yet Milton's works can tell us more about the complexities of the seventeenth-century Puritan temperament than any run-of-the-mill Leveller pamphlet because Milton's work is not just an expression of what he himself "thought" but is replete with the density, ambiguities, and silences of the great artist. The more

38 Wolfgang Iser, *The Act of Reading: A Theory of Aesthetic Response* (London: Routledge and Kegan Paul, 1978), pp. 61, 84.

an author is willing to expose his writing to the unconscious and impersonal forces acting upon it, the more interesting that writing is likely
to be. This is not, of course, to relapse into the old romantic myth of
the creative genius isolated from social and cultural concerns. It is, on
the contrary, to insist that the greater the writer, the more he or she will
have to tell us (often in an implicit way) about the world in which he
or she is living.

This is why Kerouac or Mary McCarthy or indeed Flannery O'Connor
can reveal more about the Catholic experience in the United States than
many wearisome issues of the *Catholic Digest*. Texts that not only emerge
from within the framework of Catholic orthodoxy but also choose simply
to reproduce that framework as a fait accompli tend to lack subtlety.
The Jesuit critic Harold C. Gardiner in his "Christian Appraisal" of *Fifty
Years of the American Novel,* for instance, represents this didactic approach
at its least attractive. Gardiner, disparaging "the unmuscular and weak-
willed exercise of merely narrating 'what had happened,'" urged instead
the ranking of authors according to their "realization of man as fundamentally a religious being," and he presided in this book over a series
of essays reprimanding various authors for failing to live up to this
exacting standard. Thus Edith Wharton is chastised for remaining "the
imperious, assured young Protestant" who lacked "a sense of . . . heaven
and glory," while the bitter satire of Sinclair Lewis is dismissed as making
"Creation a fairy story, the Incarnation an impossibility and the Redemption a joke." In place of these renegades, one of the contributors
to this volume proposed Robert Bowen's novel, *The Weight of the Cross,*
and Crawford Power's *The Encounter* as exemplifying appropriately
Christian "affirmations" of "the great fact of the universe" rather than
the "counsels of despair."[39] But here we come back to T. S. Eliot's essay
"Religion and Literature" which claimed that the great Christian writers
are Corneille, Racine, and Baudelaire; Eliot shrewdly remarked that
though he himself enjoyed the novels of G. K. Chesterton, "when the
same effect is aimed at by zealous persons of less talent than Mr. Chesterton the effect is negative."[40] The work of Robert Bowen and Crawford
Power is indeed "negative," in Eliot's acid phrase, because its narrowness
of perspective and lack of textual density have the effect of denying access

39 Harold C. Gardiner, S.J., "A Christian Appraisal: The Point of It," in *Fifty Years of
the American Novel: A Christian Appraisal,* ed. Harold C. Gardiner, S.J. (1951; rpt. New
York: Gordian, 1968), pp. 1, 4; Anne Fremantle, "Edith Wharton: Values and Vulgarity," in *Christian Appraisal,* pp. 29, 31; C. Carroll Hollis, "Sinclair Lewis: Reviver
of Character," in *Christian Appraisal,* p. 90; Nicholas Joost, "'Was All for Naught?':
Robert Penn Warren and New Directions in the Novel," in *Christian Appraisal,* pp. 289–
91.
40 T. S. Eliot, "Religion and Literature," p. 392.

to more complex cultural forces beyond the range of the author's own consciousness or personality.

Eliot, then, was concerned to reconcile ethics and aesthetics, to work through formal properties toward larger cultural questions. In contemporary literary and cultural criticism, attempts to "empower" minority traditions often seem to involve overthrowing not only the narrowly established boundaries of a literary "canon" but also aesthetic values of every kind. Following Northrop Frye's argument in *Anatomy of Criticism* that "archetypes are most easily studied in highly conventionalized literature: that is, for the most part, naive, primitive and popular literature," there have been several studies of Catholic literary institutions at various points in history, demonstrating how the machinery of reading unions, fraternal associations, and publication societies produced a ready-made readership for self-justifying and self-congratulatory Catholic novelists, the Maurice Francis Egans, the Jedediah Vincent Huntingtons.[41] Yet while Egan and Huntington may be "archetypal," in Frye's structuralist sense, they rarely introduce into their texts any real artistic substance, and so these novels tend merely to reinforce the rigid distinction between spiritual and secular worlds rather than collapsing it. The believer accepts Huntington's premises; the nonbeliever does not. The most interesting writers, though, always manage to imply a complex world whose ramifications expand beyond the limitations of one individual author's vantage point: Georg Lukács said that Balzac's texts tell the reader a great deal more about the historical processes of capitalism in nineteenth-century France than one would have gained from an interview with the arch-reactionary novelist himself, and similarly the novels of Mary McCarthy or Flannery O'Connor tell us a considerable amount about the development of twentieth-century Catholicism in the United States precisely because of the density and indeterminacy of these texts.[42] Although Flannery O'Connor herself may have adhered to the same theological principles as Robert Bowen and Crawford Power, her fictional texts are infinitely more complex and challenging and avoid being oppressed by the same deadweight of premature thematic closure. Despite Frye's formulation, the most typical writers (in the sense of telling us most about a common culture) are nearly always the best writers, not the worst.

This does not mean we should necessarily accept received opinions of what constitutes the best or worst within any given tradition. Indeed,

41 Northrop Frye, *Anatomy of Criticism: Four Essays* (Princeton: Princeton Univ. Press, 1957), p. 104.
42 Georg Lukács, *The Historical Novel*, trans. Hannah and Stanley Mitchell (Lincoln: Univ. of Nebraska Press, 1983), pp. 81–5.

one of the consequences of this project will be to problematize that rigid affiliation between American literature and an ideology of romanticism, an affiliation institutionalized by critics from F. O. Matthiessen to Douglas Robinson. Robinson, for whom American literature is "definitively Romantic" even in its "deviations" from romanticism, nominates the "unquestionably mainstream" American tradition as Emerson ("our greatest Romantic apocalyptist"), Poe, Hawthorne, Melville, Twain, James, Faulkner, West, Ellison, and Barth.[43] One could, though, establish a competing antiromantic "Catholic" tradition comprising Brownson, Santayana, Dreiser, Farrell, Fitzgerald, Tate, Berryman, Frank O'Hara, Flannery O'Connor, and Barthelme. It would be a mistake to claim the latter is in any way more valid than the former: that would be simply to replicate Robinson's unexamined assumption. But it would also be a mistake to dismiss aesthetic values as irrelevant because all aesthetic values must to some extent be ideologically determined. Melville is a great writer, Jedediah Vincent Huntington is not, and to attempt to validate a "Catholic" tradition by trumpeting Huntington and disparaging Melville would be highly foolish. What would be more reasonable to assert is that some complex and interesting "Catholic" writers in America have received less than their critical due because they are alleged not to fit in with this mythical "mainstream" of Protestant romanticism. By exposing the implicit ideological bias in any critical reading of texts, it is possible to open up new angles of perception and turn the whole idea of a literary canon into a culturally relative phenomenon rather than an absolute truth. Without at all waging war on Emerson, it is important to recognize that not all American literature conforms to the premises of the Emersonian tradition.

Much has been written about the history of immigration to the United States by the Irish, Italians, Poles, and others, and there has also been a good deal of analysis of the American Catholic Church's involvement in various social issues, from censorship, poverty, and crime through to the difficulties and prejudices faced by politicians like Al Smith and John F. Kennedy. All of this will be relevant to my arguments, and in fact one of the aims of this work is to locate those points where text and context come together, where social history intersects with modes of literary perception. But the significance of art, as opposed to history, is exactly in art's emphasis upon those "unexpected combinations" Iser talked about: fictional art can show us where religious sensibility lingers and manifests itself in less obvious, even strange and unpredictable ways. And that, of course, is where the real value of demystification and de-

43 Douglas Robinson, *American Apocalypses: The Image of the End of the World in American Literature* (Baltimore: Johns Hopkins Univ. Press, 1985), pp. 28, 3.

construction emerges. Anyone can recite immigration statistics, but to apprehend those silent areas where religion flies free of rigid conceptual pigeonholes and begins exerting pressure in a more intangible fashion seems a more interesting and valuable task.

Two potential hazards of this study are overgeneralization and reductivism. These (interlinked) dilemmas are an issue Edward Said addressed in *Orientalism*, in which he maintained that cultural studies focusing upon the Orient tend to produce a reified version of the East through a process of "synchronic essentialism," the quasi-scientific view "that the whole Orient can be seen panoptically." This view, wrote Said, denies the conception of historical progression that a more narrative framework would provide: "Narrative, in short, introduces an opposing point of view, perspective, consciousness to the unitary web of fiction; it violates the serene Apollonian fictions asserted by vision."[44] In Said's caution, we may detect a reaction against what John Higham has called "the more grandiose pretensions of intellectual historians" of the 1940s and 1950s, with their large-scale holistic theories about Puritanism, antiintellectualism, or whatever. As Laurence Veysey wrote in 1979: "The healthiest trend in the writing of intellectual history during the past two decades has been the move toward greater modesty in defining social aggregates. ... Generalizations, in other words, to be credible, must be extremely hard earned. They require far more arduous preparation, far more careful spadework, than many of our predecessors a generation ago were aware."[45]

Evidently, it is necessary here to beware that individual texts are not violently wrenched or distorted to fit some abstract, synoptical account of "Catholic" cultural patterns. At the same time, one feels the kind of intellectual puritanism that insists upon viewing the object itself untainted by any kind of parallel or analogy is itself an ideological value judgment that does not necessarily comprise a universal truth. In fact, the epistemological status of analogy is itself a highly complex issue. In *The Order of Things*, Foucault traced three fundamentally different modes of Western knowledge: the networks of similitudes and resemblances that appertained until the end of the seventeenth century, when all cognition was predicated upon analogical addition to what was already known and language itself was a "ternary system," simultaneously describing word, object, and metaphysical meaning; the shift toward classical represen-

44 Edward Said, *Orientalism* (1978; rpt. Harmondsworth: Penguin, 1985), p. 240.
45 John Higham, Introd., *New Directions in American Intellectual History*, ed. John Higham and Paul K. Conkin (Baltimore: Johns Hopkins Univ. Press, 1979), p. xii; Laurence Veysey, "Intellectual History and the New Social History," in Higham and Conkin, pp. 21, 23.

tation in the eighteenth century, when language aspired to the scientific ideal of neutrally describing the object in and for itself, without other-worldly or analogical impediments; and then the problematization of representation in the early nineteenth century, when the status of language itself became an object of intellectual scrutiny. In Foucault's account, those who purported to perceive analogical resemblances in the post-Renaissance era were peremptorily dismissed as madmen: within the Cartesian *episteme* of order and analysis, similitude became relegated – as Francis Bacon put it – to the level of a charming fantasy that had not yet attained the age of reason. We know the early American Puritans read Bacon, and the style of American thought since the seventeenth century has, not surprisingly, tended to avoid the earlier models of analogy and to develop instead from those post-Renaissance categories of knowledge outlined by Foucault. It is not such a huge distance from John Cotton's seventeenth-century assumption that "all delight springeth from correspondency between the faculty and the object" to William Carlos Williams's twentieth-century maxim: "No ideas but in things."[46]

This is not to suggest the earliest American philosophers were able entirely to evade the configurations of medieval thought. As Perry Miller put it: "Though Puritan literature abounds with condemnations of scholasticism, almost no limits can be set to its actual influence"; seventeenth-century Puritan thought was embroiled within the frameworks of philosophical analogy whether it liked it or not.[47] Later on, I shall suggest how distinctive Puritan conceptions of language gradually introduced a perspective different from that produced by earlier aesthetic conventions, but here I want simply to note the centrality of analogy to Catholic modes of thought in themselves. As Peter Berger has said, the Catholic doctrine of *analogica entis,* with its insistence upon substantive links between heaven and earth, reveals itself through the elaborate networks of intercession that bind the Catholic faithful to an invisible world through emphasis upon saints, departed souls, transubstantiation, and so on.[48] This analogical impetus descends in a direct line from Aquinas's understanding of the universe as an organism whose constituents are in harmonious proportion and whose relationships are based on substantial compatibilities. Though the issue need not detain us here, there are large disputes within Catholic theology about whether Aquinas was proposing

---

46 For the Puritans and Bacon, see Perry Miller, *The New England Mind: From Colony to Province* (Cambridge, Mass.: Harvard Univ. Press, 1953), p. 12; Cotton quoted in Perry Miller, *The New England Mind: The Seventeenth Century* (New York: Macmillan, 1939), p. 259; William Carlos Williams's phrase appears in *Paterson* (New York: New Directions, 1963), p. 9.

47 Miller, *The New England Mind: The Seventeenth Century,* p. 104.

48 Berger, *Sacred Canopy,* p. 111.

a metaphysical and ontological rationale for these structures of analogy – whether he saw analogy as the essential key to the universe – or whether he simply understood analogy to be a convenient metaphorical vehicle for his philosophical explanations.[49] However that may be, it is the latter idea that will be the focal point of this book: analogy not as theological "truth" but as a methodological style, "a language of ordered relationships articulating similarity-in-difference," to use David Tracy's definition. Tracy, a contemporary Catholic theologian, distinguished this "analogical" imagination more characteristic of Catholic thought from a "dialectical" impulse more typical of Protestantism. These tendencies, for Tracy, constitute different "families" of theological discourse: analogy involves the manifestation and likeness of God within nature, while Protestant dialectics imply a radical disjunction or unlikeness between the divine and human worlds.[50] It will be my contention that this predilection for analogy reveals itself, often in obscure ways, within the form and style of modern "Catholic" literary works. Likewise, this book will itself be constructed upon an analogical principle, comparing different authors to discover points of resemblance, and one of the reasons for considering a large number of authors is to emphasize aspects of creative similitude (despite manifest differences as well) across a broad range of historical contexts. To select six or seven authors and show how Catholicism has "influenced" their work would have been easy enough, but ultimately predictable and unsatisfactory. More illuminating is to conceive of a long tradition of American Catholic fictions, where texts analogically intersect and shed light upon each other, compositely forming a critique of some of the dominant modes and patterns within the American literary consciousness.

This process of analogy leads naturally into a universalist perspective, gathering up heterogeneous strands into one all-encompassing whole, but my hope is that the Catholic assumptions underlying this project will be worked through in a self-aware and indeed self-reflexive sense. Unlike Foucault, I do not see the analogical impulse as having been simply overtaken by the march of human thought, but I would suggest that analogy be reworked not as a philosophical principle but as a trope of fictional style. For instance, Marshall McLuhan's ideas in the 1960s about

49 For instance, William F. Lynch, S.J., asserted that "analogy is a metaphysical explanation of the structure of existence, indeed of all that exists"; whereas David Burrell, C.S.C., maintained that Aquinas employed analogy only in a provisional, self-reflexive sense. See Lynch, *Christ and Apollo: The Dimensions of the Literary Imagination* (New York: Sheed and Ward, 1960), p. 149; Burrell, *Analogy and Philosophical Language* (New Haven: Yale Univ. Press, 1973), pp. 119–22, 168–70.
50 David Tracy, *The Analogical Imagination: Christian Theology and the Culture of Pluralism* (New York: Crossroad, 1981), pp. 405–8.

the electronic global village betray a misguided attempt to elide Catholic analogical fictions into the ideal realm of a transcendental signified. One of the most debilitating aspects about McLuhan's desire for what he called a "Pentecostal condition of universal understanding and unity" was his apparent failure to recognize how these universalist modes of thought were particular to his own Catholic heritage.[51] A greater sense of provisionality could have rendered McLuhan's tone less messianic and so allowed more attention to be focused upon his (often interesting) perceptions about the impact of new technology. This is, perhaps, one of the advantages of studying Catholic universalism within a specifically American context: because American Catholicism is a minority culture, there is less temptation toward any form of proselytizing or delusion that the Catholic discourse in the United States is the only language available. We also uncover the agreeable paradox of analyzing an absolutist universalist movement within relativistic and historical terms, an irony which will facilitate the kind of demystification with which this book is concerned.

So while this project has in some ways been foreshadowed by the reconceptualization of literary studies through the perspectives of racial and other minority groups that has become widespread recently – and particularly by the recognition of how ideology affects the language and formal properties of these works, as Myra Jehlen has noted – nevertheless, the tradition here differs from that of black or feminist writing insofar as blacks and feminists tend to emphasize the role of difference, while the stress here is on similarity.[52] Blacks and women point to how their modes of existence, thought, and language diverge not only from central American mythologies but also from any kind of systematization. As Toni Morrison said in 1983: "Our interests have always been, it seems to me, on how un-alike things are rather than how alike things are. Black people always see differences before they see similarities, which means they probably cannot lump people into groups as quickly as other kinds of people can. They don't tend to say all Polish people are such and such."[53] But if blacks exert pressure toward the recognition of difference, Catholics exert pressure toward the recognition of similarity, analogy, universalism. Thus the danger of Said's "synchronic essentialism" is less

51 Andrew Ross, *No Respect: Intellectuals and Popular Culture* (New York: Routledge, 1989), p. 118.
52 See Myra Jehlen, "Introduction: Beyond Transcendence," in *Ideology and Classic American Literature,* ed. Sacvan Bercovitch and Myra Jehlen (Cambridge: Cambridge Univ. Press, 1986), pp. 1–18.
53 Claudia Tate, ed., *Black Women Writers at Work* (New York: Continuum, 1983), pp. 123–4.

pronounced here, because an ideology of synchronic essentialism is precisely the mode with which Catholic cultural texts are working.

The other major hazard is taking an excessively reductive approach to individual literary works. No doubt Mary McCarthy, for instance, would protest against being explained away as a "Catholic" novelist: the category would seem altogether too limiting. This book is not, however, concerned with that old-fashioned kind of biographical approach that seeks to domesticate texts through relating them to the events of one author's individual life. More pertinent here are influences the authors themselves would not necessarily have acknowledged or, in some cases, have vociferously rejected as part of the abandoned debris of childhood. The purpose is rather to analyze texts in terms of a wider cultural pattern, to indicate how cultural materials affect artistic composition in ways the author would probably not recognize, and hence to elaborate the unconscious sediments of artistic production. We should not of course be bound by the intentional fallacy: it may be interesting to hear Mary McCarthy's memories of her Catholic girlhood, but, rather than simply projecting this biography forward into her later novels, it will be more important to determine how less overt transformations of religion emerge within her writing. So while freely accepting that critical "justice" is not being done to any given author, I would also dispute the idea that such "justice" can ever be done under any circumstances. All critical readings are necessarily partial and ideologically determined, and the only difference here is that the central ideological constituents are explicit and self-conscious rather than implicit and unconscious. Deconstruction not only licenses the plurality of the text, it also denies that anything other than plurality is possible. The work of art, in Roland Barthes's famous epigram, is not a nut to be cracked but an onion to be peeled.

In recent critical theory, religion has usually been associated with what Paul de Man called "the dead-end of formalist criticism." De Man used this phrase to describe the yearnings of I. A. Richards to resolve textual tensions by a myth of origins and unity deriving ultimately from a Christian source. In "The Death of the Author," Roland Barthes similarly designated the desire for final meaning a "theological" impulse. Jacques Derrida himself, in *Writing and Difference,* used the same metaphor in asserting that chimeras of literary "truth" and "reality" are a derivation from "the theological certainty of seeing every page bind itself into the unique text of the truth."[54] Derrida related this "theological certainty"

---

54 Paul de Man, *Blindness and Insight: Essays in the Rhetoric of Contemporary Criticism,* 2nd ed. (London: Methuen, 1983), pp. 229–45; Roland Barthes, "The Death of the Author," in *Image-Music-Text,* trans. Stephen Heath (Glasgow: Fontana-Collins, 1977), p. 146; Jacques Derrida, *Writing and Difference,* trans. Alan Bass (London: Routledge and Kegan Paul, 1978), p. 10.

to nostalgia for the unfallen world, for some metaphysical point of origin prior to the infinite deferrals and displacements of language. However, no such opposition between literary signifier and theological signified is proposed here. On the contrary, this book is concerned with how Catholic theology itself might be seen to function as a fluctuating signifier, a series of fictional constructions. Such theological tropes set up a discourse with which "Catholic" poetics engage in a map of misprision, a more or less rebarbative intertextual relationship.

Part I

Old Icons in a New Land

2

Stereotypes, Inheritances, and Immigrants

From the start, the United States was geographically bounded by Catholic empires: Spanish territory in Central and South America, and "New France" to the north. Spanish and French influences can be seen on these borders in the sixteenth century: the first Catholic parish to be established within the present-day United States was set up at Saint Augustine, Florida, in 1565, while French Catholics also instituted early settlements in the towns of Saint Louis and Detroit. Within the locale of New England itself, progress was slower. Various antipriest laws throughout the American settlements were reinforced by the penal laws approved by William and Mary, after the downfall of King James II in 1688. These penal laws subsequently became applicable to all papists within the colonies, with the result that imprisonment and execution became fairly commonplace, and the early eighteenth century was a particularly difficult time for the Catholic church in America. In addition, there was here a great deal of residual hostility toward Catholicism, the original enemy of Anne Bradstreet and the cause of her exile from Lincolnshire, as she lamented in "A Dialogue between Old England and New," where the New Englanders are said to "hate Rome's whore, with all her trumpery." Increase Mather in 1669 similarly identified the Catholic church as a "Roman Anti-Christ"; while in 1757, Edward Wigglesworth – a theological "liberal" within the terms of the New England debate – was still continuing to lambaste Catholicism's association with "Heresies, Superstitions, Cruelties, Idolatries, and other crying Wickednesses." Even when theology had to some extent been supplanted by politics in the more cosmopolitan atmosphere of the late eighteenth century, such a plainspoken atheist as Thomas Paine nevertheless found it natural to inscribe political processes within religious metaphors: the corrupt institution of monarchy was, he said, "the Popery of government."[1]

1 *Poems of Anne Bradstreet,* ed. Robert Hutchinson (New York: Dover, 1969), p. 102;

35

The point here, of course, is that theology never was altogether supplanted. As Sacvan Bercovitch has argued, the early Puritans' conception of exodus, an errand into the wilderness, eventually reworked itself into a figurative interpretation of secular history, so that the doctrine of free enterprise became invested with elective grace, social progress aligned with the chiliad, American nationalism conflated with biblical typology. "To be *self-made* in America was more than to make one's fortune," noted Bercovitch. "It was to embody a cultural metaphysics."[2] We see clearly enough an interaction between empirical fact and religious vision in John Winthrop's double-edged notion of a "city on a hill"; yet Bercovitch suggested this kind of interpretative strain should not be seen as a phenomenon confined merely to the early American Puritan environment, for it has become transformed throughout later American history into a mode of perpetual jeremiad, where the emphasis falls upon radical prophecy, the allegorical rather than literal meaning of the present. George Washington was not simply George Washington but, for those reading the War of Independence in the shadow of biblical typology, Moses leading his people to freedom.

All this, however, is something quite alien to American Catholic modes of thought. It is true that some early medieval theologians, such as John Scotus Erigena, were similarly concerned to interpret nature as if it comprised an intricate network of symbols aspiring to rise above their gross material status. But the theologian who most influenced subsequent Catholic thought, Thomas Aquinas, imagined earthly affairs in firmly Aristotelian rather than Platonic categories. For Aquinas, the world was a concrete and natural entity, not a typological narrative; God was to be found within nature, not beyond it. Thus the crucial religious authority was not the prophet but the priest, not some charismatic figure foreshadowing a millennial future but a mediator capable of sacramentally consecrating human space and time. It was a priest who could infuse bricks and mortar with the spirit of God, turn earthly seasons into liturgical cycles, transubstantiate bread and wine into the actual body and blood of Christ. In Aquinas's eyes, the natural world could offer proof of God's existence, but the erratic events of worldly history could not. "Strictly speaking," he wrote, "every science which has been invented by human industry yields a literal meaning only." Typological parallels between George Washington and Moses would have seemed to Aquinas

Mather and Wigglesworth quoted in Howard Mumford Jones, *Belief and Disbelief in American Literature* (Chicago: Univ. of Chicago Press, 1967), p. 7; "Common Sense," in *The Complete Writings of Thomas Paine,* ed. Philip S. Foner (New York: Citadel, 1969), I, 12.

2 Sacvan Bercovitch, *The American Jeremiad* (Madison: Univ. of Wisconsin Press, 1978), p. 157.

highly speculative, if not absurd. As Umberto Eco wrote in his description of *The Aesthetics of Thomas Aquinas:*

> There is no spiritual sense in secular history, nor in the individuals and events of the natural world. There is no mystical significance in what has happened since the Redemption. Human history is a history of facts, not of signs. . . . Universal allegory is thus liquidated. Mundane events are returned to their natural status. If they have a meaning, they have it only in the eyes of a philosopher, who sees them as natural proofs of God's existence, but not as symbolic messages. With Aquinas, we witness a kind of secularization of postbiblical history and the natural world.[3]

One consequence of this worldliness was a cautious skepticism among American Catholics toward all the figurative rhetoric promulgated by the first settlers and leaders of the early Republic. The various apocalyptic prognostications of an "end" to history, an imminent day of doom, were viewed askance by Catholics; so were the equally frequent trumpetings of a new beginning, a great awakening, a nation born again. This kind of cultural antagonism was highlighted in a comment made by Increase Mather, when, amid his zest for "the Delectable Study of the Prophecies," he observed triumphantly that "but few Papists have been Chiliasts."[4]

Any attempt to make categorical distinctions between Puritan and Catholic styles of thought in early America must, however, be especially wary of two things. In the first place, as we have already noted, Puritan scholars were themselves deeply indebted – albeit sometimes unconsciously – to medieval scholastic modes of thought, and they were just as familiar with the conceptions of Aquinas as with those of Calvin. Secondly, much recent work on American Puritanism has emphasized the plurality of its intellectual perspectives: despite Perry Miller's monumental endeavor to codify the first three generations of New England intellectual life as expressing "almost unbroken allegiance to a unified body of thought," subsequent research has uncovered all kinds of tensions and inconsistencies that make it difficult to point definitively to any clear "Puritan" outlook.[5] Nevertheless, it is possible to identify certain tendencies in the American Puritan manner that distinguish it from Catholic alternatives. For instance, the Puritan reliance upon the authority of the

3 Umberto Eco, *The Aesthetics of Thomas Aquinas,* trans. Hugh Bredin (Cambridge, Mass.: Harvard Univ. Press, 1988), p. 152.
4 Perry Miller, *The New England Mind: From Colony to Province* (Cambridge, Mass.: Harvard Univ. Press, 1953), p. 187.
5 Perry Miller, *The New England Mind: The Seventeenth Century* (New York: Macmillan, 1939), p. vii.

Bible as internalized by each individual reader led to a prioritizing of that individual spirit's relationship with his or her maker and a consequent elimination of all intermediaries between the human soul and divine being. This in turn valorized the contractual nature of the relationship between man and God: rather than the Catholic notion of mere *assensus* or passive obedience to authority, Puritanism demanded a free and voluntary movement toward belief on the part of the human subject. Hence the frequently cataclysmic images of religious conversion in Puritan narratives: whereas Catholics saw grace as inhering naturally within the material world, Thomas Hooker, for example, looked upon grace as involving rather "a holy kind of violence," an irruption of spirit into the fundamentally empty world of matter.[6] Such upheavals brought into play once again that apocalyptic temper so alien to a Catholic experience. Because the Reformers rigorously disavowed the efficacy of the sacraments – which Calvin had described as inclining man, already "naturally too much inclined to the earth . . . to rest in the exhibition of a corporeal object rather than in God himself" – these Puritan believers focused their attention instead on a distant *Deus Absconditus,* the absent God who chose to reveal only part of his divinity in the Bible and to reserve his essential being for a sphere quite beyond human comprehension.[7] It is this ontological division between spirit and matter that Puritan discourse could hope to bridge only by the violent energy of a conversion experience or by the tortuous rhetoric of apocalypse.

David Tracy has distinguished between the Catholic doctrine of analogy or "manifestation," whereby spirit and matter are said to be ironically joined together by the bonds of transubstantiation and intercession, as opposed to the Puritan style of "proclamation," which is grounded upon a series of divisions and dialectical absences wherein one side of the conceptual equation fails to coincide with the other.[8] However much the Puritans may have fabricated typological parallels between human and divine creation, argued Perry Miller, they always maintained a sense of the asymmetrical nature of these equations, an awareness of how in the final analysis part of God must remain "entirely incomprehensible to man."[9] As the older scholastic influences began to fade around the end of the seventeenth century, this theological division between spirit and matter began to feed into the increasing emphasis upon a demystified and secular worldly logic: if no access to other worlds was linguistically or philosophically feasible, then an absolute dualism could be posited

6 Ibid., p. 28
7 Miller, *The New England Mind: From Colony to Province,* p. 83.
8 David Tracy, *The Analogical Imagination: Christian Theology and the Culture of Pluralism* (New York: Crossroad, 1981), pp. 376–89.
9 Miller, *The New England Mind: The Seventeenth Century,* p. 10.

between a literal-minded rationalism on the one hand and an altogether invisible world of spirit on the other. Again, such a dichotomy works against the Catholic principle whereby the visible world is potentially infused with "sacramental" power and hence exists on an analogical as well as a logical plane. For the Puritans, though, this essential fissure between spirit and matter became paradigmatic of other kinds of fissure: between revealed truth and worldly logic, between the purity of good and the blackness of evil, between the ideal aspirations of the soul and the gross material condition of the body. Such dualisms can readily be recognized in the Puritans' captivity narratives, for instance, where we see an urgent quest to exorcize the forces of diabolical darkness by a process of regenerating, and hence liberating, the imprisoned spirit.[10]

It was, then, the metaphorical and ideological as much as the legislative structure of early America that worked to marginalize the Catholic community. In political terms, though, the Catholic situation improved after the revolutionary war at the end of the eighteenth century. Following the institutionalization of religious tolerance in the American Constitution, John Carroll was appointed the first American Catholic bishop in 1790. The whole question of religious pluralism was to become a thorny issue for subsequent generations of American Catholics, who were to have difficulty reconciling this national ideology of religious freedom with a Catholic insistence upon itself as the one true universal Church. At this time, however, John Carroll was understandably reluctant to engage in complex theoretical debates around this theme. Carroll jumped at the chance to establish American Catholicism on a sounder basis and attempted to avoid controversy by acquiescing in the notion that all churches were equal before the law.

It was in the light of these new ideals of religious freedom that the Jesuit-educated Frenchman St. Jean de Crèvecoeur produced in 1782 his *Letters from an American Farmer,* applauding America as a land of "religious indifference" where Catholic and German Lutheran could coexist peacefully with their personal religion being "nobody's business." Crèvecoeur prophesied that "in a few years, this mixed neighbourhood will exhibit a strange religious medley, that will be neither pure Catholicism nor pure Calvinism," and he accordingly invented that famous metaphor whereby "individuals of all nations" were to be "melted into a new race of men."[11] Crèvecoeur's presence in the United States implies the more aristocratic influences at work in American Catholicism during this period: Crèvecoeur, like John Carroll, was an educated product of the

10 This is analyzed in Richard Slotkin, *Regeneration through Violence: The Mythology of the American Frontier, 1600–1860* (Middletown, Ct.: Wesleyan Univ. Press, 1973), p. 148.
11 Hector St. Jean de Crèvecoeur, *Letters from an American Farmer* (London, 1782), pp. 61, 64, 65, 55.

Enlightenment who brought a high-minded and flexible intellect to bear upon the problematical issues of church and state. Maryland, America's leading Catholic stronghold, had in fact been founded in 1632 by an English nobleman and courtier who converted to Catholicism – Baron Baltimore – and the Louisiana Purchase of 1803 also brought the French upper classes of New Orleans within this framework of noblesse oblige. We see a representation of this aristocratic sensibility in Willa Cather's historical novel *Death Comes for the Archbishop* (1927), in which the high-born French clergymen Bishop Latour and Father Vaillant gradually come to adapt themselves to life in the Southwest of the United States, skillfully insinuating themselves into the roughneck native culture so as to propagate their faith, with only an occasional bout of nostalgia for the European world of ecclesiastical politesse they have left behind.

By 1790, however, Crèvecoeur was safely back on his native French estates, and his vision of religious tolerance in America was hardly to be borne out by the events of the subsequent century. Although French collaboration with America in the revolutionary war against Britain helped in the late eighteenth and early nineteenth centuries to ease some of the old tensions between American Puritanism and Catholicism, the dream of reason enshrined in the Enlightenment rhetoric of the Constitution was soon under heavy pressure from the more emotive and irrational forces of entrenched religious traditions. In the nineteenth century, what radically changed both the internal structure of American Catholicism and external attitudes toward the church was immigration, especially immigration from Europe. This became particularly marked after the Irish famines of the 1840s: the Catholic population grew from 650,000 in 1840 to 1.6 million by 1850, and thence by 1900 to 12 million, of whom it was estimated that 5 million were first-generation immigrants.[12] Naturally enough, most immigrants found themselves on the bottom rung of the social ladder, and though there was a certain amount of upward mobility as the nineteenth century wore on – with the lace-curtain Irish gradually becoming as familiar a stereotype as the shanty Irish – nevertheless, Catholicism at this time came to be identified as an essentially lower-class phenomenon. In some ways, the American church gained in strength from its increased membership, and the first national council of its hierarchy took place in Baltimore in 1852, but in other areas the influx of immigrants created problems. There were many disagreements among the various national immigrant factions about the best way to organize the Church: the well-educated French often failed

---

12 Statistics from Will Herberg, *Protestant–Catholic–Jew: An Essay in American Religious Sociology*, 2nd ed. (New York: Anchor-Doubleday, 1960), p. 140; and John Tracy Ellis, *American Catholicism*, 2nd ed. (Chicago: Univ. of Chicago Press, 1969), p. 88.

to concur in outlook with the more proletarian Irish, for instance. Yet it was populist Irish Jansenism, with its strict emphasis upon orthodoxy and obedience, that came to have the greater long-term influence; the Jesuits' emphasis on personal freedom and intellectual training of the human will became confined to a much smaller band of upper-class American Catholics. The Irish were also looked down upon by the large German Catholic population, which was prominent particularly in the Midwest, while a massive influx of Italian immigrants at the end of the nineteenth century further complicated the situation. Ethnic antagonisms within the American Catholic church were exacerbated by the immigrants' different native languages, which created many difficulties in ecclesiastical administration.

After these nineteenth-century arrivals, American Catholicism came to be identified more and more as an urban phenomenon, necessarily distancing itself from the Edenic gardens and pastoral imperatives sanctified by American Puritanism since the time of the pilgrim fathers. It came as well to be seen as a "religion of the masses" rather than of any social elite: Tocqueville's traveling companion, Gustave de Beaumont, writing in 1831, contrasted Protestant and Catholic congregations by remarking that while the Protestants generally originated from the same social rank or class, the Catholic parishes received indiscriminately persons of all conditions in society. Tocqueville himself advanced for this a theological as well as a sociological explanation. Protestantism, explained Tocqueville, was designed to foster independence, whereas Catholicism stressed human equality:

> In the Catholic Church the religious community is composed of only two elements: the priest and the people. The priest alone rises above the rank of his flock, and all below him are equal. On doctrinal points the Catholic faith places all human capacities upon the same level; it subjects the wise and ignorant, the man of genius and the vulgar crowd, to the details of the same creed. . . . Reducing all the human race to the same standard, it confounds all the distinctions of society at the foot of the same altar, even as they are confounded in the sight of God.[13]

This recognition of social class as a purely secular and therefore arbitrary category has influenced the curiously parodic representation of class distinctions in many American Catholic fictions, as we shall see later. It is precisely because Jay Gatsby or even villains like Rico in Mervyn Le Roy's 1930 film, *Little Caesar,* have such profound disrespect for the tacit assumptions and conventions of polite society that they plot to take it by storm and so win some of the spoils for themselves. For Gatsby and

13 Alexis de Tocqueville, *Democracy in America*, ed. Phillips Bradley (New York: Knopf, 1945), I, 300–1.

Rico, social superiority does not in any sense betoken ethical or spiritual superiority; as de Tocqueville implies, from the viewpoint of Catholic theology the notion of civilized breeding or good "taste" becomes a pure irrelevance.

It follows from this that any idea of human betterment is also, theologically speaking, a profound self-delusion, where the temptation is the danger of conflating any social or intellectual improvement with heightened grace in the sight of God. As most nineteenth-century Catholics steered well clear of such temptations, the feeling grew among some sections of the American population that these Catholics were not only ignorant but actually gloried in their ignorance. This acquiescence to an unenlightened state was particularly characteristic of the dogmatically Jansenist temper of nineteenth-century American Catholicism, which had scant conception of Luther's notion of *sola scriptura,* whereby an individual soul would become his own church for the purpose of seeking salvation, or indeed of the Emersonian emphasis upon *sola natura,* man's grand isolation within nature and "original relation to the universe." On the contrary, Tocqueville found American Catholics to be "very submissive and very sincere," unwilling to challenge established authority.[14] This again helped to create a stereotype of Catholicism as an undemocratic and authoritarian system unfriendly to free intellectual enquiry, contemptuous of Enlightenment rationalism, and hostile to social reform. The liberal optimism that induced northern abolitionists to exert pressure for the freedom of black slaves also caused them to cast a disapproving eye upon the various forms of bondage appertaining to the Church of Rome. In turn, Catholics were generally hostile to the abolitionist movement, partly because they feared competition from blacks for their jobs, but partly also out of an ingrained preference for the authority of the social status quo. There were exceptions to this position, of course; but the *Baltimore Catholic Mirror* summarized the more widespread opinion when it wrote in 1863 that "there was not a happier people on earth than the slaves" and that emancipation would be "fatal."[15]

Ironically, it was left to Frederick Douglass in his *Life of an American Slave* (1845) implicitly to politicize the Catholic position by associating the Catholic struggle for civil rights in Ireland with black struggles in the New World. Douglass pays tribute here to Daniel O'Connell and to Sheridan's "mighty speeches on and in behalf of Catholic emancipation,"

14 Ralph Waldo Emerson, "Nature," in *The Complete Works* (Boston: Houghton Mifflin, 1903), III, 3; Tocqueville, *Democracy in America,* II, 28. For the affiliations between Luther and Emerson, see Sacvan Bercovitch, *The Puritan Origins of the American Self* (New Haven: Yale Univ. Press, 1975), p. 152.

15 James Hennesey, S.J., *American Catholics: A History of the Roman Catholic Community in the United States* (New York: Oxford Univ. Press, 1981), p. 147.

a "bold denunciation of slavery" which, says Douglass, "gave tongue to interesting thoughts of my own soul."[16] Yet even though it would seem they had little to lose in social and economic terms at this time, it is noticeable that such notions of being an oppressed minority were rarely voiced by American Catholics themselves. Indeed, rather than complaining about political injustices, much popular Catholic literature of this time cautioned against the dangers of material prosperity, which was said too often to involve dangerous associations with Protestants or even a sinful marriage to one of them. Colleen McDannell has written of how, for novelists like Maurice Egan and Mary Sadlier, "wealth and virtue were almost mutually exclusive."[17] In Sadlier's *The Blakes and the Flanagans* (1853), Catholic Mr. Blake's upward mobility receives its sharp comeuppance when his son performs such ungodly acts as attending Columbia University, joining the Masons and marrying a non-Catholic.

In this turning away from social and political aspirations, we see clearly the concrete effects of theological ideas upon the material world. In a broad philosophical sense, the Catholic tendency to ignore liberalization programs signifies a more general lack of faith in the American dream of an earthly paradise. The optimism of abolitionist humanism, like the ebullience of transcendentalist vision, was rejected by Catholicism as not doing justice to the essentially squalid nature of man's tenure on earth. Traveling amid the material wretchedness and ubiquitous Catholic iconography of Mexico in the late 1930s, English novelist Graham Greene declared notions of "human dignity" and "progress" to be "great empty Victorian conceptions that life denies at every turn," and it is something of this spirit of *contemptus mundi* that permeated nineteenth-century American Catholicism. The idea of human progress, like the idea of social class, was seen as a chimera liable to deflect attention away from more eternal goals. A pastoral letter from American bishops in 1843 warned parishioners that "without faith it is impossible to please God" and sternly cautioned the faithful against "preferring in the least point the dictates of your erring reason." It was this underlying skepticism about the value of human autonomy that helped produce what Oscar Handlin called Catholics' "deep-rooted pessimism about the world and man's role in it."[18] This opposition between Catholic contempt for the world on one hand and the spirit of rational humanism on the other is given an unor-

---

16 *Narrative of the Life of Frederick Douglass, an American Slave,* ed. Benjamin Quarles (Cambridge, Mass.: Harvard Univ. Press, 1960), pp. 8, 66.
17 Colleen McDannell, "'True Men as We Need Them': Catholicism and the Irish-American Male," *American Studies,* 27, no. 2 (1986), 31.
18 Graham Greene, *The Lawless Roads* (London: Heinemann, 1978), p. 74; Oscar Handlin, *Boston's Immigrants: A Study in Acculturation,* 2nd ed. (1959; rpt. New York: Atheneum, 1976), pp. 128, 125.

thodox twist by Henry James in his 1886 novel *The Bostonians*, in which James continually associates (the Protestant) Olive Chancellor with a spirit of martyrdom and posturing self-sacrifice. Olive, who feels she was "born to lead a crusade" and who cherishes "the ecstasy of the martyr" at "the altar of a great cause," urges the young and innocent Verena Tarrant not to abandon her "divine" mission to campaign on behalf of women's rights. Without Verena's skills on the lecture platform, Olive feels, the "crusade would lack sweetness, what the Catholics call unction"; but the more worldly Verena eventually forsakes her consecration to this "holy office" in favor of a more humanistically satisfying marriage to the Mississippi conservative, Basil Ransom.[19] It is interesting to see how James's choice of metaphors in this novel implicitly associates Catholicism with a spirit of psychological excess which places it outside the main currents of American social life. The embittered celibacy which James attributes here to Olive Chancellor is consistent with a popular nineteenth-century view of Catholic priests and nuns as sexually repressed and prurient because of their eschewal of "normal" married life.

Besides perceiving its members as enmeshed in un-American pessimism, critics of American Catholicism also expressed doubts about the undemocratic constitution of the church itself. Many felt that the appointment of bishops and other church officials by the conclaves of Rome was despotic and contrary to the American way of democracy and free election. The larger issue arising out of this fear of the external authority of Rome turned upon the general question of whether or not Roman Catholicism was secretly plotting to take over the United States. Notwithstanding John Carroll's acceptance in the eighteenth century of the idea of religious pluralism, the feeling that Rome was simply biding its time to strike remained a powerful fear in the Protestant consciousness. In fact, there was at this time little agreement within the American Catholic hierarchy itself as to how the relationship between church and state should be defined. Liberal theologians like Cardinal Gibbons of Baltimore tended to take a fairly relaxed attitude and to welcome ways in which Catholicism was becoming assimilated into the mainstream of American life. Others, like Archbishop John Hughes of New York, took more of a hard line concerning Catholicism's revealed truths: Hughes fought hard and successfully for separatist Catholic parochial schools, thereby incurring the wrath of those who believed the nondenominational public-school system was an essential prerequisite for the instillation of American ideas of democracy. It was this uneasiness about sinister if not subversive foreign influences that helped to motivate anti-

19 Henry James, *The Bostonians* (New York: Modern Library-Random House, 1956), pp. 147, 172, 160, 158.

Catholic organizations such as the Know Nothing movement in the 1850s, the American Protective Association in the late 1880s and 1890s, and the Ku Klux Klan in the early twentieth century.

This specter of a foreign agency fitted with another religious stereotype: Catholics were thought to be devious and dishonest, in contrast to the Puritan paradigm of a straightforward plain-dealing people. We can see this theme going back to 1704, when Governor Seymour of Maryland, proclaiming himself "an English Protestant gentleman," declared that he was weary of the "gawdy shows and serpentine policy" of Catholic officials. Sir George Hardy, an eighteenth-century governor of New York, similarly warned his Pennsylvanian colleague Robert Morris to beware the "ingenious Jesuit" in Philadelphia.[20] Literary manifestations of jesuitical trickery occur right through the nineteenth century, from James Fenimore Cooper's 1827 novel, *The Prairie,* in which the subtle Spanish priest Father Ignatius wars against a pragmatic (and ultimately victorious) Yankee for the soul of the hero Middleton, up to Henry James's *The Golden Bowl* in 1904. In James's last great novel, the ethical sensibility of an American family, the Ververs, looks on helplessly as the Italian Prince Amerigo weaves his wicked spells of amatory intrigue. This Italian Prince conjures up the shade of Machiavelli, thought by the early American Puritans to be a profoundly evil man; and here James's fictional hero is said to be "somehow full of his race," with his actions showing "how little one of his race could escape after all from history." The Prince can talk quite seriously and intellectually about duplicity, whereas Maggie Verver simply puts up "the English, the American sign that duplicity, like 'love,' had to be joked about. It couldn't be 'gone into.'" It is James's favorite antithesis, of course: the Old World versus the New, corruption versus "innocence." Edwin Sill Fussell has suggested that the reason James went out of his way to make the Ververs, as well as Prince Amerigo, Roman Catholic was to reveal how nationality rather than religion is the "determinate" factor in moral behavior.[21] Yet it could, I think, equally well be argued that this novel implies that Maggie and Adam Verver themselves are not so morally pure, so "Adamic," as they might like to think: Maggie's emotional incest and "spiritual" adultery, like her father's lust for power and control, are but more genteel shadows of Prince Amerigo's rank licentiousness. In James, as in Cooper, Catholicism becomes almost inescapably associated with Old World patterns of Machiavellian corruption and guileful behavior.

20 Hennesey, *American Catholics,* p. 40.
21 Henry James, *The Golden Bowl* (New York: Scribner's, 1909), I, 16, 10, 15; Edwin Sill Fussell, "Henry James's Gentle Heretics and the Old Persuasion: Roman Catholicity in *The Golden Bowl,*" *Henry James Review,* 11 (1990), 39. On the Puritan view of Machiavelli, see Miller, *The New England Mind: The Seventeenth Century,* p. 467.

It is, then, not difficult to see how a stereotypical notion of American Catholics emerged during the course of the eighteenth and nineteenth centuries. They were seen as poor, lazy, ignorant, undemocratic, devious, psychologically intemperate, sexually perverse, and often drunk. Nor was this kind of image confined to extremist groups like the Know Nothings: in the early 1840s, Walt Whitman, then editor of the *New York Aurora,* manifested what Paul Zweig has called a "violently anti-Irish and anti-Catholic" streak. In 1842, Whitman published a tedious, sermonizing novel, *Franklin Evans,* designed to "rescue Young Men from the demon of Intemperance," as the publisher's announcement put it, and directed clearly (though not exclusively) at the excesses of the Irish.[22] In Henry David Thoreau's *Walden* (1854), Irish Catholicism more explicitly becomes synonymous with everything that Thoreau chooses to reject. Living in their squalid homes, their minds dominated by materialistic anxieties, the Irish appear emblematic of all those "ruts of tradition and conformity" from which Thoreau desires to escape. The Irish do not possess sufficient imagination to reinvent their own lifestyle. Inert and submissive, they exist simply so they can pay rent, drink, and eat. Thoreau plainly considers the mind of Irish farmer "John Field" to be beyond redemption: "The culture of an Irishman is an enterprise to be undertaken with a sort of moral bog hoe." This kind of slavish mental conformity is directly linked by Thoreau with the baneful influence of Catholicism, as we see when another visitor to Walden Pond is dismissed as having failed to achieve the dignity of full manhood because of the teachings inculcated in his youth:

> But the intellectual and what is called spiritual man in him were slumbering as in an infant. He had been instructed only in that innocent and ineffectual way in which the Catholic priests teach the aborigines, by which the pupil is never educated to the degree of consciousness, but only to the degree of trust and reverence, and a child is not made a man, but kept a child.[23]

In his later essay "Life without Principle" (1863), Thoreau further associates this sense of submission with the slick Catholic mechanisms for absolving sins: "In the Catholic Church, especially, they go into Chancery, make a clean confession, give up all, and think to start again. Thus men will lie on their backs, talking about the fall of man, and never make

22 Paul Zweig, *Walt Whitman: The Making of the Poet* (Harmondsworth: Penguin, 1986), p. 222. See also Thomas L. Brasher, ed., *Walt Whitman: The Early Poems and the Fiction* (New York: New York Univ. Press, 1963), p. 124.
23 Henry David Thoreau, *Walden,* ed. J. Lyndon Shanley (Princeton: Princeton Univ. Press, 1971), pp. 323, 205–6, 147.

an effort to get up."[24] Instead, Thoreau elects to prioritize full human independence and self-reliance. Indeed, in *Walden* he goes so far as to make these qualities synonymous with the idea of America itself. Rejecting John Field's materialistic concerns as unutterably trivial, Thoreau proceeds to assert that "the only true America is that country where you are at liberty to pursue such a mode of life as may enable you to do without these." It is significant, of course, that Thoreau chooses the Fourth of July as the first day of his personal independence.[25]

Thoreau's flight constitutes the American pastoral myth in its classic version, the escape from religious and social institutions into nature and into an idealized version of the self. Like Thoreau, Leo Marx, in his classic critical text *The Machine in the Garden* and elsewhere chose to align this pastoral mode with an image of the essential spirit of America; in a subsequent essay on "Pastoralism in America," Marx claimed that "the primary emotional thrust of our major literature is generated by sympathy with protagonists who are at odds with the dominant culture, and by sympathy with their quest, however unsuccessful, for an alternative way of life."[26] It is, however, important to realize that this myth originates from a specific historical and cultural setting and does not constitute a universal truth. Thoreau's kind of romanticism, with its emphasis upon individualism and escape from established authority, can be seen to emerge in a direct line from the Puritan temper of the early settlers. The attitude of these settlers toward social and political institutions was of course a complex question, with the Massachusetts Bay area generally placing more emphasis upon temporal authority than the numerous antinomian sects developing around this time. In specifically religious terms, though, all Puritans were agreed upon the need to distance themselves from the mediating systems established by Rome and hence to purify the relationship between individual man and his God. In this sense, the pastoral myth operated as a powerful metaphor for the Puritan project. Subsequent efforts to identify this pastoralism with a quintessentially "American" literary tradition have helped critically to hypostatize the language of romantic individualism, thus effectively validating writers like Thoreau. But to equate "major literature" with this notion of the purifying quest is instantly to designate Dreiser, Farrell, and others as "minor" literature, simply on (unwitting) ideological grounds. As be-

24 "Life without Principle," in *The Writings of Henry David Thoreau*, X (Boston: Houghton Mifflin, 1893), 261.
25 Thoreau, *Walden*, p. 205; see also Bercovitch, *American Jeremiad*, p. 186.
26 Leo Marx, *The Machine in the Garden: Technology and the Pastoral Ideal in America* (New York: Oxford Univ. Press, 1964); "Pastoralism in America," in *Ideology and Classic American Literature*, ed. Sacvan Bercovitch and Myra Jehlen (Cambridge Univ. Press, 1986), p. 53.

comes apparent in American Catholics' urban-centered literature of the twentieth century, such pastoral myths have little purchase upon their collective imagination because pastoralism's mode of idealistic withdrawal from a supposedly oppressive authority is antipathetic to a Catholic sensibility, which tends more to foreground conceptions of philosophical analogy, human similitude, and social order.

Thoreau's pastoral impetus is of course commensurate with that correlation between natural and social worlds institutionalized within the American Constitution, the notion that there is a law "higher" than mere legal codes, a "law under which a God of nature had given inalienable rights to individuals," as Catherine L. Albanese put it.[27] Such an affiliation between "nature" and individual liberty did not, though, carry much weight within American Catholic thought during the nineteenth century. In fact, the Jansenist mood of this time ensured that "nature" and individualism were more often perceived as threats to the unity and decorum of the church. Up until the 1830s, a more "garden of the soul" type of Catholicism had been widespread, placing a humanist emphasis upon the interior depths and sensibility of an individual's spirit; but the Church found it could cope with the huge waves of immigration in the 1840s only by falling back upon its more visible and immediate instruments of public authority, ritual, and conformity. The Catholic church in the mid-nineteenth century also found that it could use developments in the printing media to help spread the faith among these newer immigrant markets, and accordingly all kinds of new Catholic magazines began to spring up. This involvement in the processes of mechanical reproduction helps to explain why the movement toward greater industrialization and urbanization in late nineteenth-century America "seems not to have caused the same anguish for Catholic writers as it did for secular prophets like Howells, Norris, and Crane," as Paul R. Messbarger has noted.[28] As rural life occupied no especially privileged place within the American Catholic consciousness, its disruption caused no particular sense of loss.

The paradox here is that Thoreau's rebellious individualism and essentializing of "nature" becomes an orthodox and Constitutionally guaranteed form of behavior, while Catholic deference to authority comes to be seen as unorthodox and even threatening. It may be true to say that the centrality of this pastoral ideology to traditional lines of American

27 Catherine L. Albanese, *America: Religions and Religion* (Belmont, Ca.: Wadsworth, 1981), p. 273.

28 Jay P. Dolan, *The American Catholic Experience: A History from Colonial Times to the Present* (Garden City: Doubleday, 1985), pp. 211–12; Paul R. Messbarger, *Fiction with a Parochial Purpose: Social Uses of American Catholic Literature, 1884–1900* (Boston: Boston Univ. Press, 1971), p. 154.

thought has contributed more profoundly to the uncertain identity of Catholic culture within the United States than empirical factors concerned with social or economic status. By the turn of the twentieth century, at least, it was no longer true to say Catholics were heavily outnumbered in America: by 1920 one in six of all Americans had a Catholic background, a total in excess of seventeen million. Nor is it true to say Catholics were totally inconspicuous in the higher echelons of society: Catholic lawyer Charles O'Conor was the Democratic presidential candidate as early as 1872, for example. Yet the myth of Catholic impotence persisted. In 1922, Cardinal O'Connell of Boston was still claiming "America is a Protestant country, expressive of Protestant traditions, not Catholic," and even as late as 1967 Howard Mumford Jones was writing of how "from 1607 virtually into our own times the American tradition has been a Protestant tradition."[29]

It is true that some individual states preserved anti-Catholic constitutions until well into the nineteenth century: New Hampshire until 1877, for instance. However, a more important explanation for this assumption of Protestant cultural hegemony is the metaphorical implications of "manifest destiny," an idea which in one form or another continued to be powerful through the end of the nineteenth century. According to Daniel Dorchester's 1888 account, *Christianity in the United States,* while Catholic colonies "were successfully planted in some portions, the territory originally comprised within the United States was mysteriously guarded and reserved for another – a prepared people." Yet there is a telling note of defensiveness in Dorchester's argument, a sense that this "mysteriously guarded" territory may be in danger of finding itself overrun by hordes of unwashed Catholic immigrants. This tone is consistent with R. Laurence Moore's perception that every American religious group likes to imagine itself a threatened species because "outsiderhood is a characteristic way of inventing one's Americanness."[30] The American temperament, said Moore, thrives on believing itself to be in an embattled minority, even when the facts and statistics of the matter suggest otherwise. WASP groups have always fondly imagined themselves in imminent danger of being usurped by industrial development, immigration, war, or whatever, just as Catholic groups have happily invented the fiction of their own marginalization and inefficacy.

This fabrication of opposition as a means toward self-definition was in fact highly convenient for several different groups within the com-

29 Statistics from George C. Bedell, Leo Sandor, Jr., and Charles J. Wellborn, *Religion in America* (New York: Macmillan, 1975), p. 252; for O'Conor, see Hennesey, *American Catholics,* p. 181; Jones, *Belief and Disbelief in American Literature,* p. 2.
30 R. Laurence Moore, *Religious Outsiders and the Making of Americans* (New York: Oxford Univ. Press, 1986), pp. 10, xi.

munity. From the Protestant point of view, it afforded another version of their enduring pastoral myth. Pastoralism and social hegemony are, on the face of it at least, mutually exclusive categories, and one way to avoid becoming ensnared in the institutions of power is to imagine oneself always in purifying retreat. If one cannot always be fleeing from Old World decadence, one can at least discover new demons in the urban political and industrial worlds to escape from. As Moore put it: "If Catholic culture did not transform Protestant culture, it profoundly affected the myth of what American Protestant culture was supposed to be."[31] Similarly, from the Catholic point of view, the designation of themselves as a persecuted minority during the nineteenth century helped to shift attention away from the potentially corrupting pathways of material wealth and liberal reform and to divert attention instead toward more significant spiritual matters. By fostering the myth that Catholics were powerless anyway within the American social hierarchy, the clergy found it easier to succeed in their mission of encouraging the faithful to renounce the snares of this world in favor of the promises of the next. The situation was quite unlike that in Italy, or France, or Spain, where Catholicism was an established religion and the population would naturally be exposed to Catholic influences as they went about their normal everyday lives. Whereas in Italy intellectuals and other social climbers could find the church's influence operating at every level of society, in the United States to be upwardly mobile was to run the risk of moving away from the church's spheres of control because the secular influences of the United States pulled in directions quite different from those of Catholic authority. One result of this was stern invective by Catholic officials against those faculties of rational thought prized by the secular tradition: the bishops' pastoral letter of 1843 warning the Catholic population against "the dictates of your erring reason" was disseminated into a community underpinned by a "self-imposed ghetto mentality," as John Tracy Ellis called it, which scorned the use of the human intellect as untrustworthy.[32]

This Catholic myth of passive impotence, then, was the inverted correlative of that Protestant myth of active epic, pioneers engaged on a quest to create their own history and to discover new pastures away from the corruptions of civilization. Each myth depends upon the other, indeed each myth defines the other, which is one reason their cultural legacy persevered long after the facts of history began pointing in other, more complex directions. While romantics like Thoreau exploited Ca-

31 Ibid., p. 71.
32 John Tracy Ellis, "The American Catholic and the Intellectual Life," in *The Catholic Church, U.S.A.,* ed. Louis J. Putz, C.S.C. (Chicago: Fides Publishers, 1956), p. 355.

tholicism to emphasize more clearly the urgency of moral protest and dissent, Catholic thinkers exploited American romanticism to emphasize more clearly the urgency of moral conservatism. In 1848, as Thoreau was acting out the role of a charismatic biblical prophet in his denunciations of slavery, the *Boston Catholic Observer* was pointing to the folly of that romantic and revolutionary spirit currently abroad in Europe as it insisted upon "the necessity of subordination and obedience to lawful rulers."[33] As Max Weber once noted, extraordinary intellectual or charismatic powers exerted by particular individuals have never been welcomed wholeheartedly by the Church of Rome: the institution of Catholicism tends to regard with suspicion those "religious virtuosi" who "instead of relying on the capacity of the institutionalized church to distribute grace" rather "seek to attain grace by their own unaided power."[34] Within the context of artistic production, Catholicism maintains a similarly skeptical attitude toward the whole idea of lyrical or subjective intuition: the emphasis within traditional Catholic thought on a preexistent, objective world has ensured a profound incompatibility between Catholic aesthetics and the romantic view that art might involve some new type of knowledge. Thus Thoreau's prophecy, like Whitman's Song of Myself, was (and is) a tone unfamiliar to the Catholic sensibility. For Whitman, to compose was to create; from an orthodox Catholic point of view, though, any equation between artistic composition and original invention appears meaningless. To quote again from Eco's work on Aquinas:

> A great deal of modern aesthetics considers artistic forms to possess an ontological value superior to that of natural forms, just because it is a product of the human spirit. This view is quite different from the Thomistic conception of art. For Aquinas, artistic form is ontologically dependent; it possesses its own value, but it has no metaphysical autonomy, nor can it rival divine creation.[35]

The radical divergence between these different aesthetic and philosophical positions sets the framework for the quandaries and ambiguities of the American Catholic intellectual tradition. In his analysis of *Anti-Intellectualism in American Life,* Richard Hofstadter wrote that the apparent absence of any such tradition was a remarkable phenomenon, given the numerical presence of Catholics in the United States. Hofstadter blamed this deficiency largely upon the malignant influence of the immigrant Irish: "More than any other group, the Irish put their stamp on American

33 Handlin, *Boston's Immigrants,* p. 139.
34 Max Weber, *The Sociology of Religion,* trans. Ephraim Fischoff (London: Methuen, 1965), p. 187.
35 Eco, *Aesthetics of Thomas Aquinas,* p. 173.

Catholicism; consequently the American Church absorbed little of the impressive scholarship of German Catholicism or the questioning intellectualism of the French Church and much more of the harsh Puritanism and fierce militancy of the Irish clergy."[36] While such ethnic factors are not irrelevant to the composition of the American church, it is also significant here that Hofstadter synonymously aligned "intellectualism" with the adjective "questioning." It will be the contention of this book that there is, in fact, a viable American Catholic intellectual tradition – conceived in a widely cultural rather than theological sense – but that this tradition has been obscured from view precisely because it rejects the traditional American equation of intellectualism with "questioning" or with "nonconformity," in the broad sense of that term. In 1899, William James, writing in the aftermath of the anti-Dreyfus conspiracy, talked of how "we 'intellectuals' in America must all work to keep our precious birthright of individualism, and freedom from these institutions" of church, army, aristocracy, and royalty. "*Every* great institution," James went on, "is perforce a means of corruption – whatever good it may also do. Only in the free personal relation is full ideality to be found."[37] Here James echoes Thoreau in seeing institutions as per se corrupt and a threat to the life of the mind. In James's eyes, Catholicism is thus the most corrupting and intellectually deadening institution of all: those "very submissive" Catholics Tocqueville found in the United States would appear to have no part to play in the life of the national mind. Writing from Rome in 1900, William James described the Vatican as the "Mother of Harlots," epitome of everything "that was mean in life" and nothing that was "ideal."[38] To be an intellectual, from William James's perspective, was to be an outsider, an iconoclast, a quester. Once again, this is an archetypal romantic position which has its own cultural validity but which is not applicable as a universal philosophical truth.

It must be admitted, nevertheless, that an examination of Catholic literary culture in the nineteenth century would appear to bear out William James's argument about the deadening influence of institutional authority. Popular novelists like Jedediah Vincent Huntington, Charles Constantine Pise, and Maurice Egan preached a tedious conformity to hearth and home. Irish immigrant playwrights like Dion Boucicault and William Kelly produced theatricals featuring heartless landlords impeding the Irish struggle for freedom, spicing their dramas with popular reels and jigs to make the evening go with a swing: hardly the kind of fare,

36 Richard Hofstadter, *Anti-Intellectualism in American Life* (London: Cape, 1964), p. 138.
37 Ibid., p. 39.
38 See Van Wyck Brooks, *The Dream of Arcadia: American Writers and Artists in Italy, 1760–1915* (New York: Dutton, 1958), p. 168.

one would imagine, likely to have engaged the intellectual sympathies of William James. The most popular work of all was Cardinal James Gibbons's *Faith of Our Fathers,* first published in 1876 and reputed to have sold over two million copies. No wonder that even a sympathetic critic like Messbarger has concluded "the record of American Catholic literature of the nineteenth century is almost wholly bereft of serious artistic value."[39] Orestes Brownson, whose work I will examine in the next chapter, was in some ways an interesting exception. Still, it was not until the early twentieth century that more aesthetically complex and ambitious writers such as Theodore Dreiser, James T. Farrell, and Scott Fitzgerald began to emerge from within Catholic systems of thought. It is not so much that theology was simply superseded by fiction "as the most appropriate literary mode in an increasingly secular and antitheological age," as David Reynolds has suggested.[40] It is more a question of theology itself becoming secularized, transformed from an explicit dogma into an implicit and unconscious state of mind, but still maintaining itself as a cultural force with power to shape the direction of fictional texts.

39 Paul Messbarger, "The Failed Promise of American Catholic Literature," *U.S. Catholic Historian,* 4, no. 2 (1985), 147.
40 David S. Reynolds, *Faith in Fiction: The Emergence of Religious Literature in America* (Cambridge, Mass.: Harvard Univ. Press, 1981), p. 215.

3

Transcendentalism and "Catholicity": Orestes Brownson

While Thoreau was, as we have seen, frankly hostile to the systems of Catholicism, Ralph Waldo Emerson was – in abstract terms, at least – attracted by a notion of how individuality might interact with some form of universal design. In his 1846 poem "Each and All," Emerson celebrates a reciprocal interaction between his transparent eyeball and the all-embracing cosmos as he describes how "I yielded myself to the perfect whole." Likewise, the opening chapter of his *Representative Men* (1849) welcomes the idea of interpenetration between what is local and what is universal: he applauds ways in which "the individual . . . is ascending out of his limits into a catholic existence."[1] In Emerson's eyes, though, this catholic idea always remained firmly in its lowercase version. For Emerson, those correspondences and analogies that might bind the universe into an ideal form were made up of invisible threads, not visible phenomena. John Henry Newman suggested in 1864 that "the root of all controversies between the Catholic Church and Protestantism" lies in "whether it is of the essence of the church to be visible, i.e., to exist on earth in the form of sacraments and a divinely instituted ministry, or to be invisible, consisting solely in the union of its members with Christ through faith"; and in these terms, Emerson's style of transcendent vision bears more relation to the absent God of orthodox Protestant hermeneutics than to the sacramental materialism of Catholic thought.[2] Indeed, in his Divinity School Address of 1838, Emerson complained of how the ideal "doctrine of the soul" had degenerated into more mundane aspects of "the positive, the ritual." Hence, said Emerson, religion had become "petrified into official titles," a move which, so he claimed,

---

1 Ralph Waldo Emerson, *Poems and Essays* (Boston: Houghton Mifflin, 1889), p. 62; *Complete Works* (Boston: Houghton Mifflin, 1903), IV, 34.
2 John Henry Newman, *Apologia pro Vita Sua,* ed. A. Dwight Culler (Boston: Houghton Mifflin, 1956), p. 66.

"kills all generous sympathy and liking."[3] In this word "petrified," Emerson may have been referring covertly to the institution of Saint Peter, exactly the kind of ecclesiastical establishment that in his opinion would corrupt and ossify the spirit.

Another way to explain this might be to say Emerson's discourse fits with a tradition of American Protestant poetics that revolves upon an axis of conceptual dualisms: realist versus idealist, logical versus transcendent, visible versus invisible. Yet this dichotomy, institutionalized by William James in the twentieth century as the "tough" against the "tender," essentially involves two sides of the same coin: it posits a fallen and fragmented material world that can (possibly) be reconciled into an idealized, abstract unity only through the medium of some extraordinary prophetic power.[4] This tradition extends from John Winthrop's "Model of Christian Charity," which posits a typological interaction between earthly and heavenly cities, through to Whitman's attempt in *Song of Myself* to infuse material substances with ideal spirit. Like Emerson in his essay "The Poet" (and elsewhere), Whitman casts himself in a prophetic role as the reconciler of this postlapsarian world. The great fear for all of these seers is the threat of a loss of vision, the failure of the material world to conform to their transcendent aspirations. Again, this style of cultural poetics is predicated upon the Protestant notion of the *Deus Absconditus:* since God has withdrawn from the experiential world, the only possible way to bridge the vast chasm between matter and spirit is through the offices of prophecy. Robert Daly has written of how the early American Puritans cherished the idea of the poet as *vates,* seer, rather than *poeta,* maker; and Emerson similarly positions himself within an updated, secularized version of this vatic tradition.[5]

The Catholic style of discourse, however, is very different. Here the analogical potential of any given object is not dependent upon the gaze of some prophetic seer who might be able to endow it with an ideal status. Indeed, prophetic intervention may actually hinder the operation of Catholic sacramental analogy, for in the latter system the earthly object is inherently both itself and something other, as in transubstantiation. In this model, God is present, not absent; analogy is not a privileged or distant or faintly glamorous vision, but a brute material fact. In Protestant poetics, divine grace is an uncertain phenomenon whose presence cannot be relied upon, with the result that worldly logic, however ontologically imperfect, appears to be the best human beings can do. In Catholic

3 Emerson, *Complete Works,* I, 130–1.
4 William James's concepts of "tough-minded" and "tender-minded" come from his 1906–1907 lectures on Pragmatism.
5 Robert Daly, "Puritan Poetics: The World, the Flesh and God," *Early American Literature,* 12 (1977), 155.

poetics, though, the sacramental presence of divinity is assured, even if the mediating priest himself is foolish or wicked; and this means that, within a Catholic idiom, worldly logic – and, in fact, terrestrial systems of all kinds – are always problematized in a much more immediate way by the presence of analogy.

Hence to emphasize the importance of analogical imperatives within Catholic aesthetics is not to claim analogy has no significance within other cultural languages, but rather to suggest that Catholic poetics characteristically make analogy much more of a visible and material affair. As we shall see later, writers from an American Catholic background often recast analogical doctrines within worldly styles, displacing analogy's theological terms into secular equivalents. This works as a parallel to, and as a literary transformation of, the Catholic understanding of how analogical processes can be realized concretely within the everyday world. To take one example, the "Catholic" writer Jack Kerouac spends some time in *On the Road* celebrating the fact that Greyhound bus stations analogically resemble each other all over America. While Whitman, say, might conceivably have been moved to describe something similar, in Kerouac we find the poetic emphasis skewed toward celebrating these bus stations in themselves. Kerouac is not so interested in elucidating the abstract shape of an overall idealist design as he is in revealing what he takes to be the "grace" inherent within these mundane objects. To his mind, such "grace" is guaranteed by the way these worldly objects participate in the larger structures of analogy; yet this transubstantiative power ultimately resides not within those ideal structures but within the actual material objects. One of the reasons so many readers find difficulty with Kerouac is that his texts are less concerned with any form of abstract vision than with imposing a seemingly absurd value upon the most banal worldly goods. But this is because he seeks to describe those worldly goods within the cultural framework of Catholic analogy; unlike Whitman or Emerson, who present themselves as privileged seers prophetically empowered to perceive invisible resemblances, Kerouac styles himself as a surrogate Catholic priest in whose hands sacramental analogy becomes a materialized and worldly event.

Back in the nineteenth century, one significant challenge to this pattern of Emersonian idealism came from Orestes Brownson, a member of the transcendentalist circle who converted to Catholicism in 1844. Brownson wrote in a subsequent essay that while Emerson throughout his career had sought "unity and catholicity," his works had not succeeded in fully achieving this harmonious state because of Emerson's "great misfortune" of never having become a Roman Catholic. Although Brownson admired Emerson inordinately, he claimed the latter was "a poet rather than a philosopher," someone who had no sense of historical cause and effect but who preferred to transcend material circumstances and aspire toward an intuition of pure disembodied Being.[6] True to his Catholic outlook, Brownson opted for visible rather than invisible analogies, declaring his own preferred mode to be the doctrine of "communion." This asserted that man needs to communicate with the objective world of family, society, nation, in order fully to realize his latent humanity. Brownson thus rejected the ahistorical ideal of transcendentalism and placed his faith instead in the ways ideal being could be mediated through secondary, concrete forces within the immanent world. In this way, he was taking issue with the "perennial Protestant impulse toward unmediated communication with divinity" (in R. W. B. Lewis's phrase) that informed the mood of early American Puritanism as well as the individualistic impetus of nineteenth-century transcendentalism. Brownson insisted instead that man is "body as well as soul" and so needs to accommodate himself within the earthbound organization of the church. In his definition, the church thus became another version of "the real body of Christ, a real living organism, and in some sense a continuation of the Incarnation."[7] Just as Christ incarnated himself within historical time, so (according to Brownson) a human being should acquiesce in his provisional terrestrial status. He should not be forever desiring to transcend it, in Emersonian fashion, by the self-deluding ambition of attempting to intuit divine being.

In this sense, Brownson's essential philosophical doctrines remained fairly consistent throughout his career. Because his political persuasions did indeed change from radical to conservative while his religious creed oscillated from Presbyterian to Universalist to Unitarian to Catholic, Brownson has sometimes been written off as an opportunistic chameleon, most famously by James Russell Lowell in his 1848 poem *A Fable for Critics*:

> He shifts quite about, then proceeds to expound
> That 'tis merely the earth, not himself, that turns round.[8]

But while Brownson's political allegiances altered, the underlying conceptual framework that gave rise to these allegiances was not so turbulent. Brownson's notion that thought and existence always result from a co-

---

6 Orestes A. Brownson, "Emerson's Prose Works," in *The Works of Orestes A. Brownson*, ed. Henry F. Brownson (New York: AMS Press, 1966), III, 434, 433; "American Literature," in *Works*, XIX, 3.

7 R. W. B. Lewis, *The American Adam: Innocence, Tragedy and Tradition in the Nineteenth Century* (Chicago: Univ. of Chicago Press, 1955), p. 175; Brownson, *The Convert; or, Leaves From My Experience*, in *Works*, V, 167, 147.

8 *The Complete Poetical Works of James Russell Lowell* (Boston: Houghton Mifflin, 1897), p. 128.

operation or communion between a subjective self and an objective reality was not easy to assimilate within the rigid patterns of nineteenth-century thought, being as it was antipathetic both to scientific empiricists, who devalued the significance of subjectivity, as well as to the transcendental idealists who exalted it. Nevertheless, Brownson's early involvements with radical politics – his role in founding the Working-Men's party in Philadelphia in 1828, his quasi-Marxist views on the ownership of property put forward in an 1840 essay, "The Laboring Classes" – are substantially consistent with his advocacy of Catholic Christendom after his conversion in 1844. The social *ecclesia* modulates into a religious *ecclesia,* but the doctrine of communion persists, along with his continuing critique of the exclusively subjectivist proclivities of romanticism and transcendentalism.

All the gurus of romantic thought are lambasted in Brownson's later essays: the "shallow-pated Rousseau," the "shallow . . . and but too successful" Descartes, the perfidious Voltaire, the egocentric Kant, the treacherous Luther.[9] Yet it was as early as 1839, in a commentary on Emerson's "Divinity School Address," that Brownson criticized the transcendentalists as a narrow "literary caste," too much isolated from the wider community. Brownson took issue here with Emerson's heroic image of the scholar as "a solitary soul, living apart and in himself alone." He insisted instead that great writers emerge naturally out of their community. Great writers, Brownson claims, are not so much the active "central sun" inventing a culture as the passive "glass" through which any given culture expresses itself:

> This notion, which some entertain, that a national literature is the creation of a few great men, is altogether fallacious. Chaucer, Shakespeare and Milton, Spenser, Pope and Johnson are not the creators of English literature; but they are themselves the creatures of the spirit of the English nation, and of their times. . . . Great men do not make their age; they are its effect.[10]

While this is a specific rejection of Emerson's attempt to equate the spirit of America with individualistic heroism, it also shows Brownson's concern to detach himself from romantic ideals even five years before his conversion to Catholicism. After 1844, the transcendentalists quickly blamed Brownson's hostility to their doctrines upon his newfound religious faith, whereas it might plausibly be argued this faith was a product of his hostility rather than the other way around. It has been too easy for critics (then and now) to dismiss Brownson's critique of transcen-

9 "Philosophy and Catholicity," in *Works,* III, 182, 184; "A Letter to Protestants," *Works,* V, 250.
10 "American Literature," *Works,* XIX, 6, 17, 16.

dentalism as the rantings of a newly baptized Catholic, when in fact, as Brownson himself said in his 1857 autobiographical work *The Convert,* "I had, after all, less to change on becoming a Catholic than was commonly supposed at the time."[11]

Thus the division of Brownson's career into a phase of political activism before 1844 and a phase of religious conservatism afterward is far too simplistic. Brownson's philosophy appears erratic only if one takes the excessively narrow view that a sensibility of "Catholicity" necessarily involves strict adherence to Roman Catholic theological doctrine, for Brownson was concerned with "Catholicity" before his conversion as well as afterward. This is not to claim, as some Jesuit scholars have done, that Brownson's lifework was always tending inevitably toward its ultimate destination of the Church of Rome; it is simply to point out that there is a fundamental coherence about Brownson's persistent attempts to rework Emersonian idealism by attaching the spirit of America to immanent realities of social life. Brownson's official position may have shifted from that of being a rebellious member of the transcendentalists' "Hedge Club," which he attended in 1836, to being an equally rebellious, transcendentalist-oriented member of the church of "Catholicity"; but though the emphasis shifted, the components in this strange hybrid of American individualism and religious conformity stayed more or less the same. In 1842, Brownson's philosophy was, as he put it, "Catholicity without the papacy"; by 1844, it was Catholicity with the papacy. Yet he still remained, as Van Wyck Brooks said, "too Yankee for the Catholics" as well as "too Catholic for the Yankees."[12] Brownson fitted nowhere, and it is precisely because of this anomaly that he sheds important light upon the social and philosophical quandaries of American Catholicism in the middle of the nineteenth century.

One interesting point to note is that Brownson always used the word "Catholicity" rather than "Catholicism" or "Roman Catholicism." As we saw with Emerson, a "catholic" idiom, in the broadest sense of that word, was one of the general aims of the transcendentalists, who were attempting to expand their subjective perceptions of the world into concentric circles of universal phenomena. In a similar kind of way, Brownson seems keen to exploit the universalist implications of his term "Catholicity" without pinning the word down too narrowly to mean simply the theology of nineteenth-century Rome. Again, Brownson's "Catholicity" is consistent with his concern for the working masses and

---

11 *Works,* V, 90.
12 See Arthur M. Schlesinger, Jr., *A Pilgrim's Progress: Orestes A. Brownson,* 2nd ed. (Boston: Little, Brown, 1966), p. 149; Van Wyck Brooks, *The Flowering of New England 1815–1865* (New York: Modern Library, 1936), p. 248.

it reveals the same kind of democratic impulse evident in his social essays of the 1830s. Coming as he did from the unlettered Vermont frontier, Brownson was, as he put it in his 1843 oration "The Scholar's Mission," "no great believer in the superior capacities, or virtues, of what are called the upper classes." Indeed, one of the complaints Brownson made about Emerson's poems (and about the works of the transcendentalists in general) was that they were "addressed not to all men, but to a school, a peculiar school, a very small school, composed of individuals who, by nature or education, have similar notions, tastes, and idiosyncrasies." Brownson said that his concern as a scholar was for "all men, especially of the poorer and more numerous classes," and he found the universalist sympathies of "Catholicity" to be more in keeping with this broad aim than either transcendentalist exclusivism or Unitarian elitism.[13] The Unitarian scholar Andrews Norton's attempt to locate the precise historical truth of Christianity and to establish this as a basis for religious worship was, for instance, disparaged by Brownson: "This philosophy necessarily disinherits the mass," he said. "It denies to men all inherent power of attaining to truth." Norton's religious activities at Harvard seemed to Brownson altogether too narrow. In Brownson's eyes, only the democratic impulse of Catholicity, which neglects social distinctions and treats all human beings equally, could respond to the democratic energies of the new American Republic. In this way, he claimed, American civil life was fortunate enough to find itself "in strict accordance with Catholicity" because "here, for the first time in the history of Christendom, have we found a civil order in harmony, as to its principles, with the church."[14] America's political rejection of all those archaic social hierarchies of Europe is seen by Brownson as forming a parallel to the Catholic church's rejection of Protestant emphases upon social gentility and good taste. One of the commonest myths of Catholicism, as we see so often in the stories of Flannery O'Connor, is how the grace of the Catholic church knows no temporal boundaries and can work for everybody equally, be they pillars of the establishment or, as is more customary in O'Connor, disinherited social outcasts.

Given Brownson's equation of "Catholicity" with American democracy, it is particularly interesting to note Emerson's reaction in 1858 to the news that Anna Barker Ward had converted to Catholicism. In his patronizing way, Emerson had always been tolerant toward the Roman religion – "a dear old church," he wrote to Margaret Fuller in 1843, adding how much he had enjoyed the sensual and aesthetic experience

13 *Works,* XIX, 74, 87; "R. W. Emerson's Poems," in *Works,* XIX, 191.
14 See Perry Miller, *The Transcendentalists: An Anthology* (Cambridge, Mass.: Harvard Univ. Press, 1950), p. 208; Brownson, "Catholicity and Literature," *Works,* XIX, 452.

of Catholic Mass. Emerson later went so far as to suggest to Isaac Hecker that the latter must have joined the Catholic Church because of the immense beauty of its "art and architecture," to which the zealous Hecker's response was, not surprisingly, sharply in the negative. With Ward, Emerson similarly attributes the conversion to her "taste for historic splendor, and poetic and mannered style," though he insists that his own mature American way is to give priority to moral content: "To old eyes, how supremely unimportant the form, under which we celebrate the justice, love and truth, the attributes of the Deity and the soul!" Naturally enough, Emerson also views Catholicism as a threat to that newly discovered sense of American identity for which he has been campaigning so vigorously. "I must," he writes in a draft of his first letter to Ward after receiving the bad news, "lament the chance-wind that has made a foreigner of you – whirled you from the forehead of the morning into the medievals, again." Obviously this xenophobia – the word "foreigner" is significant – has a conceptual basis which is consonant with Emerson's declaration of American literary independence, but it also seems to contain a more emotive undercurrent, grounded perhaps upon Emerson's temperamental disdain for the Catholic clergy. Elsewhere in this letter, he writes of how "a priest, as we know him, is a hat and coat, of whom or of which very little can be said: usually an Irishman, though he comes to you from Rome."[15] For Emerson, the priest is not only a foreign import but also a dehumanized object: that "of whom or of which" is a euphemistic but distinctly hostile phrase, implying how these priests lack that full manly independence Emerson extolled. Driven as they are by slavish conformity to external authority, the Catholic clergy can have little interest in the cultivation of any inner, individual soul.

The point is that Catholicism ultimately becomes unacceptable to Emerson not only in a high philosophical sense but also, more covertly, in a low social sense. Emerson not only disagrees with Catholicism in principle, he also snobbishly excludes Catholics from his inner circle because they lack personal charm and sophistication. As Emerson wrote to Arthur Hugh Clough immediately after Ward's conversion in 1858: "I grieve that she has flung herself into the Church of Rome, suddenly. She was *born* for social grace, and that faith makes such carnage of social relations."[16] To upbraid a person for choosing a particular religion on the grounds that this religion lacks "social grace" might seem an odd comment from someone who ostensibly prided himself on deeming style

15 Richard D. Birdsall, "Emerson and the Church of Rome," *American Literature,* 31 (1959), 274, 279.
16 Ibid., p. 279.

and form "supremely unimportant" when compared with the central "attributes of the Deity and the soul." Yet Emerson's Neoplatonic impersonality was only ever a feigned impersonality: the limits of his alleged universalism are exposed when he confronts Catholicism, which can fit into his partial scheme of things only if it remains a strictly aesthetic phenomenon. Here again is the paradox R. Laurence Moore and others have noticed about the established circles of American religious and cultural life: independent nonconformity becomes socially acceptable, integration within an organization becomes socially uncouth. Brownson himself was marginalized by the transcendentalists after his conversion to Catholicism because his deference to an outside authority demeaned him in the eyes of those who placed priority upon more genteel forms of individual human spirit and "social grace." The perseverance of this New England cultural tradition has also adversely affected Brownson's subsequent critical reputation. Perry Miller, who admired Brownson, nevertheless could not help noting with a touch of disdain that Brownson "was not a Harvard man," that "there was always a kind of peasantlike crudity in him," and that this "instability" was "manifested in his histrionic conversions and retractions." It was Brownson's fate to be (in an intellectual sense) nouveau riche, and this pushiness did not endear him to the New England establishment. Brownson started out very much at the center of transcendentalist life, visiting Brook Farm and employing Thoreau as a live-in tutor for his children, but he ended up being seen "as a boorish, turncoat propagandist for a socially marginal church," as Lawrence Buell put it.[17]

Actually, though, Brownson never quite abandoned transcendentalism. The enduring theme of his later works is how "Catholicity" is entirely compatible with human individuality, worldly reason, and social progress. In his 1855 essay "Philosophy and Catholicity," Brownson quotes Aquinas on how "natural things" and the "things of grace" form two distinct realms and he goes on to rebuke "many Catholic writers" for "misapprehending the relation between the intelligible and the superintelligible." Such writers forget, says Brownson, that "the human race were left, as to the natural or intelligible order, to find out every thing by their own unassisted reason, to invent language, and to create for themselves all the moral and intellectual sciences." He castigates American Catholics for being apparently unable to "reconcile the immovable character of their church with what seems to them the progressive nature of man and society."[18] Yet such reconciliation, according

17 Miller, *Transcendentalists*, p. 45; Lawrence Buell, *New England Literary Culture: From Revolution through Renaissance* (Cambridge: Cambridge Univ. Press, 1986), p. 229.
18 *Works*, III, 190, 195, 196.

to Brownson, is or should be what "Catholicity" is all about. "The Catholic faith," as he writes in 1868, "is the reconciler of all opposites."[19] Authority is compatible with liberty, grace is compatible with nature, faith is compatible with reason, because in all of these cases one side of the equation operates in a quite distinct sphere of activity from the other side. Divine authority is superior to human liberty but it does not deny human liberty – within its own proper areas – the right to exist. In an 1861 essay, "Harmony of Faith and Reason," Brownson quotes "the Holy See" as insisting that "although faith is above reason, there is no dissension or discord between them."[20] Scientific laws and all the apparatus of nineteenth-century rationalism can operate quite independently from the higher wisdom of the church.

Brownson's elimination of allegorical or typological significance from mundane affairs is consistent with Aquinas's rejection of any figurative meaning for secular history. For Brownson, human beings are autonomous and independent when it comes to affairs of this earth. In an 1868 article "Nature and Grace," he asserts that "the law of nature and the law of grace really coincide" and that "grace neither annihilates nor supersedes or transforms our nature."[21] In *The Convert,* he reinforces this notion that "man was intended from the beginning to live simultaneously in two orders, the one natural and the other supernatural." Given this terrestrial self-sufficiency, the human consciousness is free to contrive its own schemes for social and political reform without fearing that it may be in any way impinging upon or usurping divine prerogatives. In this way, Brownson specifically reacts against the popular (Thoreauvian) image of Catholicism as involving the abrogation of human thought and "degrading intellectual bondage."[22] Such reaction is particularly noticeable in his 1862 essay "Slavery and the Church," which, contrary to most Catholic opinion during the Civil War period, takes the side of the Unionists. This essay was written, said Brownson, to dissociate the church from charges that it was in favor of slavery and to prove that Catholics had no essential quarrel with abolitionists or any other social reformers. While the explicit agenda here is the slavery of blacks in the South, the implicit agenda is the alleged slavery of Catholics within the Church of Rome. By denouncing the more open form of slavery, Brownson is obliquely denying the proposition that Catholicism itself necessarily involved intellectual serfdom.

Brownson's "Catholicity," then, is a sophisticated form of idealism

19 "Nature and Grace," ibid., 371.
20 *Works,* III, 268.
21 Ibid., 354, 367.
22 *Works,* V, 175, 176.

that attempts to reconcile various contraries within a vision of ultimate unity. It is this theological drive for unity that underpins and inspires his political positions. His analysis of the Civil War, for instance, is influenced by a theological universalism: he claims that "we need the Southern individualism to temper the New England socialism," so that in their quest for independence the southerners are "guilty of the precise error in regard to the nation that the Protestant or schismatical reformers in the sixteenth century were guilty of in regard to the church."[23] It is a grave mistake, in Brownson's view, for the southerners to believe their individualism could be fulfilled only by secession from the main body of the Union. Again, this desire to reconcile apparently disparate forces is not confined to the years after Brownson's conversion to the Catholic church. In his 1836 *New Views of Christianity, Society, and the Church,* as the author himself put it later: "I devoted myself to solving the problem of a religion which should be neither Protestantism nor Catholicity, but which should embody all that was true and holy in the latter, with the free spirit, the ideas and sentiments which had been developed by the former."[24]

Brownson, then, saw his task as to bring together the American, Protestant, quasi-transcendentalist emphasis on individual freedom and inner light with the older Catholic doctrines of social and ecclesiastical communion. This process inevitably led him into quarrels not only with the transcendentalists but also with American Catholic clergy, for whom at this time all notions of the "inner light" tended to be anathema. Brownson was vociferous in his rejection of the Jansenist heresy that matter is per se evil; indeed, he wrote in 1867 that "Jansenists are as much out of the pale of the church as are Calvinists or Lutherans themselves."[25] Unfortunately for Brownson, it was, as we have seen, the harsh, puritanical sensibility of Irish Catholicism that was dominating the American church at this time, and the clergy did not take at all kindly to Brownson's suggestion that they should be tolerant toward the merry-making peccadilloes of the material world. Brownson's claim that "not all imperfection is sin, and no man is bound to be perfect" was viewed askance by prelates like Archbishop Hughes of New York, who also had little time for Brownson's subtle differentiations between nature and grace.[26] In the austere minds of these clergy, human nature was at least potentially bad and, thus, much better off suppressed, with obedience to the dictates of the church greatly to be preferred to the vagaries of

23 "Reform and Reformers," *Works,* XX, 295. See also Carl F. Krummel, "Catholicism, Americanism, Democracy, and Orestes Brownson," *American Quarterly,* 6 (1954), 28.
24 *The Convert, Works,* V, 85.
25 "Rome or Reason," *Works,* III, 300.
26 "Catholicity and Literature," *Works,* XIX, 451.

human independence and liberty. This heavy stress on obedience was not, as Brownson imagined, simply a Jansenist conspiracy; it was also part of the institution's strategy for survival. In the Catholic hierarchy's eyes, Brownson's scholarly – though, perhaps, rather too ingenious – readings in Catholic theology failed to take account of the pressures on the church in a concrete historical situation where it found itself charged with the salvation of vast numbers of working-class immigrant families. In this environment, it was not surprising that discipline and conformity should be prioritized over explorations of human freedom; yet Brownson, ever the theorist, could never quite understand why the nineteenth-century church was so unresponsive to his philosophical speculations.

Brownson especially infuriated church officials by his 1859 essay "Public and Parochial Schools." Here he derogated the "narrow-minded bigotry" he associated with "some Catholics" in America and urged Catholic parents to send their children to public schools if they thought those schools offered a superior education:

> We are, and always have been, decidedly in favor of *really* Catholic schools, that is, schools in which our children are sure to be taught, and well taught, their religion . . . but we cannot favor, under pretext of providing for Catholic education, a system of schools which will train up our children to be foreigners in the land of their birth.[27]

Brownson is once again aligning the Catholic faith with his understanding of the word "catholic" to mean universal, all-embracing. This, he says, is what Catholic "really" means, not simply an acquiescence to the narrower Roman Catholic teachings. Such etymological dexterity was not, of course, a point Archbishop Hughes found himself admiring. Yet ironically enough, since the Second Vatican Council in the early 1960s "Catholic" rather then "Roman Catholic" has increasingly become the church's preferred mode of designation, and many contemporary Catholic intellectuals have moved closer to Brownson's way of thinking. In 1985, for instance, the American Jesuit scholar Avery Dulles produced a book entitled *The Catholicity of the Church,* whose view of Catholicism as grounded upon pluralism and universalist communion bears marked similarities to Brownson's philosophy.

Brownson did permit himself a brief period of relative theological quietism after receiving religious instruction from Bishop John Fitzpatrick of Boston prior to joining the church in 1844, but in general he often diverged from nineteenth-century Catholic orthodoxy in his views on papal infallibility, social reform, and other matters. He had an especially low opinion of immigrant Irish Catholics and, in an echo of

Thoreau, wrote in 1849: "Nobody can deny that in external decorum
and the ordinary moral and social virtues the Irish Catholics are the most
deficient class of our community." He consequently took great pains to
avoid identifying "Catholicity" with what he called "Irish hoodlumism,
drunkenness and poverty."[28] Like Thoreau again, Brownson disparaged
many of his fellow Catholics for being merely men of routine, creatures
of "secular habits, customs and usages" which they had unthinkingly
inherited from their ancestors, erroneously believing such habits to be
an essential component of Catholic worship.[29] The residual transcendentalist element in Brownson scorned mere obedience to custom or
authority and sought rather to put "Catholicity" into juxtaposition with
the American temper of self-reliance. We see this very clearly in his late
(1875) review of a Father Walter Hill's *Elements of Philosophy*, in which
Brownson attacks Hill for following Aquinas too slavishly and not being
imaginative enough "in translating [Aquinas's] sense, enveloped as it is
in medieval scholasticism, into the language of modern thought. . . . In
order to understand his solution of a problem, we must first solve it for
ourselves." This, of course, is classic transcendentalist doctrine: past texts
must be overhauled and renewed so as to bring them into the realms of
"perpetual modernness," as Emerson said of Plato's work.[30] The best
part of Aquinas's work, according to Brownson, is that it destroys itself.
He scorns to be Aquinas's mere follower, just as Whitman said he scorned
to be Emerson's.

Brownson had talked in *The Convert* of how he considered the "superannuated scholasticism" of Roman Catholic scholars to be "engrossed
with obsolete questions" and "wanting in broad and comprehensive
views."[31] Conversely, throughout his Catholic career Brownson was
repeatedly accused of the heresy of "ontologism," the idea that human
beings could directly intuit a knowledge of God as he manifested himself
within creation. Seven propositions concerning the intuition of God were
denounced by Pope Pius IX in 1861, as a prelude to the broader series
of papal assaults on all aspects of modernism that characterized the late
nineteenth century. Accordingly, both Brownson and his friend Isaac
Hecker, who had also converted to Catholicism in 1844, found some
difficulty in bringing their Americanist sense of subjective experience
into harmony with the more authoritarian demands of church orthodoxy.
Hecker, like Brownson, had been heavily involved with transcendentalist
circles: he resided for a while at the communes of Brook Farm and

28 In a letter to J. A. McMaster, 14 Mar. 1849. See Schlesinger, *Pilgrim's Progress*, p. 214.
29 "Present Catholic Dangers," *Works*, XII, 140.
30 *Works*, II, 487; Emerson, *Representative Men*, in *Complete Works*, IV, 45.
31 *Works*, V, 157–8.

Fruitlands, and when visiting Rome in 1857, he suggested to Pius IX that American democracy offered an excellent opportunity for the Catholic church to show it need not always exist in partnership with conservative and repressive political regimes. The Pope, however, remained unconvinced and told Hecker he thought the spirit of the United States worked toward "a too unrestricted freedom."[32] Much to Hecker's surprise and disappointment, Brownson himself also published an adverse review of Hecker's 1857 book, *Aspirations of Nature,* alleging that it had diverged too far from Catholic orthodoxy; Hecker was, Brownson said later, becoming "semi-pelagian without knowing it," indulging in a form of humanistic idealism that dangerously underestimated the power and significance of original sin.[33] Brownson and Hecker subsequently patched up their differences, but in 1899 Pope Leo XIII was more forthright, writing to Cardinal Gibbons that Hecker's reliance upon the inner light and the immanence of grace within nature was unacceptable and could not be tolerated by the Catholic church.

The overall significance of Brownson in relation to a wider tradition of American Catholic fictions lies precisely in the way he reinterprets the Old World faith through a New World perspective. Anticipating Max Weber's argument about the symbiotic relationship between a Protestant ethic and the spirit of capitalism, Brownson dismisses Protestantism as being too concerned with material goods and as engendering an ethic of unfettered individualism that results in social fragmentation and even, in the end, a "spirit of lawlessness."[34] In place of this subjectivist anarchy, Brownson posits the idea of a society framed by, but not totally dependent upon, the authority of the church. This emphasis on the importance of community principles is a trait Brownson shares with Aquinas. In the *Summa Theologiae,* Aquinas noted how "man is naturally a social and political animal" and advanced the theory that "men even in the state of innocence would have lived in society," firstly because that which constitutes the "common good" does not necessarily coincide with the desires of any given individual, and secondly because "if one man had a greater degree of knowledge and justice than others, it would be unfitting that these should not be used for the good of the others." Aquinas's view of salvation as a communal enterprise, in which social law impels a person "to proper actions in relation to his final end," exists in sharp contrast to the American pastoral programs of Emerson and Thoreau, in which every man was his own church and no person's

---

32 William L. Vance, *America's Rome* (New Haven: Yale Univ. Press, 1989), II, 35–41.
33 Joseph F. Gower and Richard M. Leliaert, eds., *The Brownson-Hecker Correspondence* (Notre Dame: Univ. of Notre Dame Press, 1979), p. 42.
34 "Protestantism in a Nutshell," *Works,* VI, 154.

"knowledge" was deemed inherently better than anybody else's.[35] Whereas for Aquinas human law was necessary for the common welfare, for Thoreau the law comprised a coercive realm to be evaded in the name of self-determination and freedom.

This is not to say that Brownson seeks simply to aggrandize the secular city of man into a mirror image of the city of God. Like Aquinas, Brownson cherishes an abstract conception of communal destiny rather than looking triumphantly to vindicate any particular community or political movement. Moreover, though Brownson admits to admiring the social organization of medieval times, he acknowledges that "it is impossible, even if it were desirable, to restore the mixture of civil and ecclesiastical governments which obtained in the middle ages." What he does urge upon his readers, though, is the compatibility of Catholic ideals with those of contemporary American democracy and the wisdom of a social order based upon metaphysical as well as positivistic principles. His 1866 treatise *The American Republic,* written in the aftermath of the Union's victory in the Civil War, involves a curious conjunction of Thomistic communitarianism with the millennial schemes of American romanticism. In an echo of the old "manifest destiny" idea, Brownson entertains a vision of the United States receiving "from Providence a special work or mission," the task of embodying and renewing Christian purposes within the historical world.[36] The essential difference here, of course, is that Brownson's manifest destiny involves a Catholic Christendom, not a Protestant utopia.

Brownson's new model of Christendom bears some resemblances to the idealized social networks proposed by later Catholic or neo-Catholic writers: Allen Tate's idyll of the Old South, for instance, or T. S. Eliot's "Idea of a Christian Society." Eliot himself did not discover Brownson's writings until 1955, subsequently writing to Russell Kirk about how it was "remarkable that a Yankee a century ago should have held such views as his, and depressing that he has been so ignored that most of us had never heard of him."[37] Eliot's own conception of a "Christian society" was, however, an impossibly hierarchical and feudalistic affair, while Brownson's modernistic reconciliation of the city of man with the city of God can be seen to operate in a much more ingenious fashion. In *The American Republic,* Brownson suggests that since the American state is inherently "organized in accordance with catholic principles, there

35 Mary T. Clark, ed., *An Aquinas Reader* (Garden City: Doubleday–Image, 1972), pp. 367, 360, 386.
36 *Works,* XVIII, 211; 199.
37 Russell Kirk, "Orestes Brownson and T. S. Eliot," in *No Divided Allegiance: Essays in Brownson's Thought,* ed. Leonard Gilhooley (New York: Fordham Univ. Press, 1980), p. 165.

can be no antagonism between it and the church." The aims of the church in a divine sphere are said to correspond so closely with the aims of the United States in a practical sphere that "what is called a state religion, would be an anomaly, or a superfluity."[38] Once more, we see Brownson inventing an analogy between the unifying forces of the United States and the unifying designs of universal Catholicism. This analogy enables him neatly to sidestep any theoretical problems that might have been created by the "syllabus of errors" enunciated in a papal encyclical of 1864, which roundly condemned, among other things, the separation of church and state. In the last chapter of *The American Republic,* triumphantly entitled "Destiny – Political and Religious," Brownson waxes lyrical about the "Mission" of the United States and its capacity to form "one grand nation, a really Catholic nation, great, glorious, and free."[39] Once more, we see Brownson's phrase "really Catholic" proposing an unorthodox interpretation of church affairs that would not generally have been welcomed by the more hardheaded Catholic prelates of this time.

This prophetic strain is always evident in Brownson's writing, from his 1836 *New Views of Christianity* onward. It is not coincidental that Brownson was, like Tate and Eliot, a religious convert who approached his newfound faith with much greater theoretical self-consciousness than the typical "cradle" Catholic intellectual. Brownson was intent upon anticipating Ezra Pound's injunction to "make it new": he aspired to renew Catholicism in the virgin land of America just as he had apocalyptically renewed his own life in terms of this particular Christian doctrine. Brownson claimed in an 1857 letter to Hecker that "the only men in the country who really understand the American people thoroughly are the converts": he seems to imply here this born-again sensibility is endemic to the American consciousness and that it is the stagnant, conventional Irish who are hopelessly out of touch with the ever-changing flow of the American dream.[40]

Brownson's questing spirit, energized by the impulses of romanticism, looks forward to one important strand within the American Catholic consciousness. This is the line that runs through Tate, Robert Lowell, Katherine Anne Porter, Walker Percy and is concerned with the ways in which the teachings of Catholicism stand as a challenge to the limitations of secular and "Protestant" thought. All of these writers, appropriately enough, are converts: for them, Catholicism constitutes (as it were) a superego rather than an id, a series of ideas and formulas to which they give conscious assent. There is, however, another tradition,

38 *Works,* XVIII, 211–12.
39 Ibid., 222.
40 Gower and Leliaert, eds., *Brownson-Hecker Correspondence,* p. 199.

equally prominent within American Catholic fictions, wherein religion operates as a more subliminal force dictating patterns of thought and behavior of which texts (and their authors) are not necessarily aware. This is the tradition emerging in Santayana, which runs through Fitzgerald, Farrell, Frank O'Hara, Barthelme, and others. Brownson did appreciate in a theoretical way how this subliminal impulse might function: in an 1847 essay "Religious Novels," he acknowledges that "a book may be recognized as Catholic by its spirit and temper . . . as well as by its formal teaching"; similarly, an article on "Catholic Secular Literature" two years later eschews the idea of "monastic discipline" for "seculars" and asserts that popular literature should "spiritualize the secular" rather than attempt the opposite process of forcibly inserting spiritual concepts into a secular sphere.[41] Again, the idea is that while "the religious state is far higher than the secular," nevertheless "the secular is not unlawful" and so salvation can be attained without the need to forsake this more mundane level.[42] Hence, says Brownson in 1873, Catholic literature should emerge "freely and spontaneously" as the expression of a broadly based, habitual Catholic atmosphere. It is wrong to suggest such literature "must be filled with arguments for the church, or have a good Catholic moral tacked on to the end."[43]

Brownson's own artistic efforts, however, signally fail to fulfill these admirable aesthetic designs. His whole style of writing is polemical and binary rather than universalist. Throughout his works he inveighs against Protestantism in its various guises, and such stylistic antagonism and repulsion serves to work against any doctrine of communal life, however much he may advocate that life as a conceptual ideal. Brownson's literary idiom remains essentially romantic and transcendentalist: he sings a "song of myself," he is always the hero of his own narratives, and because of this solipsism the social *ecclesia* he proposes remains altogether invisible. What the young Van Wyck Brooks said of Emerson's work, that it "has all the qualities of the typical baccalaureate sermon," and that its "persistently abstract" tone could not encompass "the whole welter of human history and social complexity," might actually be seen as a more pertinent critique of Brownson's writings.[44] Nor is this narrowness confined simply to his philosophical essays. Brownson admitted that "religious novels are usually wretchedly dull as novels," and of no text would this comment be more apt than the author's own *Charles Elwood, or The Infidel*

41 *Works,* XIX, 147.
42 Ibid., 298, 294.
43 "Religious Novels, and Woman Versus Woman," *Works,* XIX, 566; "Religious Novels," ibid., 147.
44 Van Wyck Brooks, "America's Coming-of-Age" (1915), in *Three Essays on America* (New York: Dutton, 1934), pp. 64, 60, 63.

(1840), a barely fictionalized account of his own religious torments. "I do not send it forth as a work of art," he says in the preface, never speaking a truer word.[45] Scarcely more of a case could be made for *The Spirit-Rapper* (1854), the "autobiography" of a fictional mesmerist. As the author's preface observes only too accurately, this text does not follow "any recognized rules of art": it is, says Brownson, not a novel, not a romance, not a biography, not an essay or treatise – "and yet it perhaps has some elements of them all, thrown together in just such a way as best suited my convenience, or my purpose."[46] But this aesthetic idiosyncrasy might be seen to be at odds with the theme of *The Spirit-Rapper,* which uses the self-absorbed figure of the mesmerist to lampoon precisely the kind of philosophical solipsism to which Brownson's text itself is prone. The reader is told in no uncertain manner that this spirit-rapper is but an emblem of the "Neoplatonists," the "false mystics," the visionary reformers, the Boston transcendentalists – all those who erroneously attempt to abstract the soul from the body by granting some form of autonomy to the human spirit. Yet Brownson's diatribe against idealism is itself couched in the most rarefied and disembodied form: his "novel" is populated not with people or places of substance but with such predictably thin conceits as "Mr. Increase Mather Cotton, a rigid puritan minister of high standing." Admittedly, *The Spirit-Rapper* does have a few agreeably acerbic moments, when Brownson's talent for not suffering fools gladly comes to the fore: Joe Smith, founder of the Mormon movement, is elegantly dismembered, as are those Scandinavian backwoodsmen said still to harbor a belief in the potency of Odin.[47] But these palpable hits score in a pugilistic rather than a descriptive or novelistic sense. Brownson was too much of a dogmatist to write good literary satire; he lacked the satirist's subtle gift of an imaginative empathy that might bring to light latent human weaknesses. On the contrary, Brownson's invective originates only too obviously in his own mind and is then simply projected upon the external lineaments of his stock fictional types.

It is this formalistic solipsism that compromises Brownson's attacks on conceptual solipsism throughout all of his writings. In his chapter on Brownson and Theodore Parker in *The American Adam,* R. W. B. Lewis chose to insert these writers into the "Party of Irony" on the grounds that their idealistic aspirations found themselves inevitably running up against a cognizance of disillusionment and evil in the second half of the nineteenth century. I think it could be argued, though, that a sense of irony is exactly what Brownson's writing lacks. Despite his attack on

45 "Religious Novels," *Works,* XIX, 146; *Works,* IV, 173.
46 *Works,* IX, 1.
47 Ibid., 17, 99, 109.

what he called the "goings-on at Brook Farm," Brownson's own essays read like an extended literary version of the Brook Farm project, as though the earthly manifestation of all these splendid ideals cannot be too far away: "If we proceed with singleness of heart, Almighty God will approve us, and give us success" in "the great work of reconverting society," he says with a hint of breathlessness in his 1855 article "Philosophy and Catholicity."[48] It is that apocalyptic, millennial strain so characteristic of the transcendentalists. In keeping with this tone of radical prophecy, Brownson blames the American Catholic population for being too self-indulgent when it comes to religious matters. "The mass of our Catholics," he writes to Hecker, "think only of enjoying their religion for themselves, and lack every thing like a Missionary spirit."[49] Brownson has little notion of the world as being stranded in medias res, at the midpoint of a long pilgrimage; on the contrary, he harbors a (very American) desire for the new order to manifest itself here and now. It has to be, as he puts it in an 1867 essay, "Rome or Reason," Catholicism or scientific atheism; for "thinking men," he claims, there can be no midway point between these alternatives. He deplores the tendency of the duplicitous French to think that people can simultaneously be Catholic in one department of life and atheistic in another. As Arthur Schlesinger, Jr., observed, Brownson was obsessed with a need "to reach the ultimate certitudes" and for him it was always a question of all or nothing.[50]

From one angle, this is the kind of philosophical rigidity characteristic of converts to any religion. Brownson's 1874 essay "Extra Ecclesiam Nulla Salus," in which he takes the doctrine that there can be no salvation outside the Church at its strictest and most literal level – rebuking any "tender-hearted theologians" who might think otherwise – demonstrates exactly this dogmatic tendency at work.[51] Yet in this inflexibility there is also something more puritanical than Catholic, more indebted to the spiritual culture of Brownson's early days than to the religion of his latter years. The French lay theologian Jean Guitton suggested in 1961 that "the essence of Protestantism lies in its *purity*": as a "religion of separation and transcendence," said Guitton, Protestantism cherishes "the desire never to resign itself to alloys or compromises. . . . Catholicism, on the other hand, although it is just as anxious to achieve complete purity,

---

48 *Works*, III, 184. Brownson's derogatory remarks about Brook Farm occur in his review of Hawthorne's *Blithedale Romance*, which Brownson thought was too lenient in its attitude toward the reformers. See Robert S. Levine, *Conspiracy and Romance: Studies in Brockden Brown, Cooper, Hawthorne, and Melville* (Cambridge: Cambridge Univ. Press, 1989), p. 148.

49 Gower and Leliaert, eds., *Brownson-Hecker Correspondence*, p. 201.

50 "Rome and the World," *Works*, III, 347; Schlesinger, *Pilgrim's Progress*, p. 282.

51 *Works*, V, 575.

accepts a provisional combination of the pure and impure. It is afraid of disturbing the indwelling presence of the good by detaching it too soon from the less good, and even the evil, which are bound up with it."[52] It is just that sense of provisionality and compromise that Brownson's work ignores. Like so many converts, he takes Catholic doctrine at its face value and thus neglects its deeply entrenched structural ironies. Scott Fitzgerald was making a typically "Catholic" statement when he said in 1936 that "the test of a first-rate intelligence is the ability to hold two opposed ideas in the mind at the same time, and still retain the ability to function"; but while Brownson was keen to make attempts to reconcile apparently opposing categories of spiritual and secular, transcendentalism and "Catholicity," he was never able to countenance the more elusive idea that such reconciliations might not be necessary.[53] In the idiosyncratic fashion of Catholic logic, for instance, a declaration of the temporal power of the pope can happily coexist with its exact opposite in terms of worldly circumstances. The church's paradoxes of divine grace are traditionally empowered to contradict and "redeem" the follies of the postlapsarian world without necessarily resolving that world's terrestrial muddle. But on this kind of issue, Brownson's rationalistic mind demanded closure, the matching of the idea with historical reality. He was not able readily to comprehend that kind of duplicity we see so often in medieval paintings, for example, where the "spiritual" iconography takes it upon itself to "transubstantiate" the most squalid empirical facts, leaving the work of art suspended indefinitely between the grace of heaven and the corruption of earth.

Nevertheless, Brownson's work is valuable in a negative, contradictory sense, in that it shows up the limitations of Emerson's universalist pretensions and reveals the narrow ideological basis of the transcendentalist movement. This is not, let us be clear, an attack upon the integrity of Emerson's work itself. Some old-style Catholic professors used to make Emerson and Whitman the targets of what Joseph X. Brennan called their "sacred rage"; the American romantics were abhorred for skepticism toward institutionalized authority, emphasis on Christ's humanity rather than his divinity, disbelief in original sin, and so on. This in turn led to nervous attempts to valorize Emerson by some Catholic scholars in the 1960s, who claimed that the increasingly "liberal" and "fluid" character of their church ensured it could now be more responsive

52 Jean Guitton, *The Church and the Gospel,* trans. Emma Craufurd (Chicago: Henry Regnery, 1961), pp. 224–5.
53 F. Scott Fitzgerald, "The Crack-Up," in *The Crack-Up with Other Uncollected Pieces, Note-Books and Unpublished Letters,* ed. Edmund Wilson (New York: New Directions, 1945), p. 69.

to the complexities of Emersonian thought.[54] The defensive and at times grudging tone of these essays seems to admit Emerson only on sufferance, however. My point is not that Emerson's writing is not brilliant, but that it is not ideologically all-encompassing, not even all-encompassing in an American context; yet the critical hypostatization of Emersonian paradigms has led toward the regrettable marginalization of other forms of American discourse. As early as 1836, Brownson criticized Emerson's *Nature* for being too "pantheistic," and the effort to exclude Brownson from the "canon" of American literature might be said to have begun at that point.[55] For Brownson, "the imperfect light of nature" was inextricably associated with "the darkness and corruption of heathenism," a doctrine antipathetic not only to Emerson and Thoreau but also to famous scholars like Perry Miller.[56] Miller, who liked to emphasize the cultural continuity between the Puritan pastoralism of early New England and nineteenth-century Prostestantism's sense of the natural man, wrote in 1955 that the United States might be seen as "Nature's nation" where "magnificent hymns to American Nature" could be found amongst the texts of evangelical and other Christian preachers as well as within the works of romantic poets.[57] Nor has this assumption that "nature" offers what Miller called "an assuaging of national anxiety" much abated. In his 1981 account of *Faith in Fiction,* David Reynolds aligned the developing "mainstream" of American literature in the nineteenth century with "a turning away from tangled metaphysical questions and an embrace of such real aspects of experience as nature, human feelings, and vernacular perspective." Nature once again is said to constitute a grand metanarrative within which all human problems can be resolved.[58]

Such "tangled metaphysical questions," however, were not to be disposed of quite so easily. The problem is, of course, that these conceptualizations of "human feelings" and the "vernacular" derived from an Enlightenment view of the "natural" world that was itself a metaphysical

54 Joseph X. Brennan, "The American Catholic and American Literature," *Emerson Society Quarterly,* 39 (1965), 88; Francis E. Kearns, "Emerson and the American Catholic Scholar," *Emerson Society Quarterly,* 39 (1965), 63–8.

55 Schlesinger, *Pilgrim's Progress,* p. 132.

56 "A Letter to Protestants," *Works,* V, 254.

57 Perry Miller, *Nature's Nation* (Cambridge, Mass.: Harvard Univ. Press, 1967), pp. 202–3. For this idea of cultural continuity, see also Miller's "Individualism and the New England Tradition" (1942), in *The Responsibility of Mind in a Civilization of Machines,* ed. John Crowell and Stanford J. Searl, Jr. (Amherst: Univ. of Massachusetts Press, 1979), pp. 26–44.

58 David S. Reynolds, *Faith in Fiction: The Emergence of Religious Literature in America* (Cambridge, Mass.: Harvard Univ. Press, 1981), p. 197.

and ideological issue. The parameters of "nature" and the general limitations of American romantic culture Brownson saw clearly enough. The creation of an American literature substantial and complex enough to offer a viable alternative tradition was, though, to be left to others.

4

Nineteenth-Century Myths of Catholic Europe

For Brownson and Hecker, then, the Catholic religion appeared primarily as an abstract idea that was connected only accidentally with the qualities of any particular geographical place. This sets them apart from the perspectives of Irish, Italian, and other nineteenth-century American immigrants, for whom Catholicism was intimately connected with their abandoned European homeland. This land often reappeared within the immigrants' collective imagination as a lost arcadia, a dream of green fields whence they had been expelled into the industrial wastelands of North America. For non-Catholic writers, though, nurtured as they were on the pastoral myth of the United States as a new Eden, Catholic Europe signified something quite different: corruption, oppression, Babylonian decadence. What is curious here is the extent to which American writers in the nineteenth century seem to be obsessed with the Old World. From Washington Irving to James Fenimore Cooper, from William Dean Howells to Henry James, nearly every major American author reveals a compulsion to rewrite the story of escape from European bondage. Sometimes the Reformation was dealt with literally, as in Cooper's *The Heidenmauer* (1832), set in sixteenth-century Europe, which chronicles the rise of Lutheranism as it affects two Benedictine monks in the Abbey of Limburg. At other times we see a revisionist Protestant version of Catholic history, as in Harriet Beecher Stowe's *Agnes of Sorrento* (1862), in which Savonarola is hailed as a proto-Puritan intent upon cleaning up the corrupt papal court of the Borgias.

Part of this obsession arose from the early-nineteenth-century image of Catholicism as a sinister, gothic phenomenon, full of devious monks and dark dungeons. The black romanticism of English novelists like Matthew "Monk" Lewis and Ann Radcliffe established a field of vision for texts such as Washington Irving's *Tales of a Traveller* (1824), in which Irving fancifully represents the Catholic church as both picturesque and ghostly, an emanation of the land of the living dead. The author talks of "the vast, deserted, melancholy Campagna with the Tiber winding through it, and St. Peter's dome swelling in the midst, the monument – as it were, over the grave of ancient Rome."[1] By implicitly associating this "monument" of St. Peter's with the "grave" and tombs of the ancient city, Irving is portraying the church as another kind of Rip Van Winkle, a colorful anachronism experiencing difficulty in coming to terms with the modern era. The reader senses both attraction and repulsion; on Irving's sentimental journey, Catholicism entails aesthetic thrills but also, potentially, a dangerous moral escapism. William Dean Howells encountered the same double bind in *Venetian Life* (1872), in which he describes how the Duomo contains "the horrible fascination of a dead saint's mortal part in a glass case": that phrase, "horrible fascination," aptly epitomizes one kind of ambivalence prevalent in nineteenth-century American writing. In a similar aesthetic vein, James Fenimore Cooper said he so much admired the "poetry" of Catholicism that he almost felt at times he could become a monk – provided, so he wrote, he were excused the "vigils and fasts," which he thought he had not been "created for." From this angle, Catholicism becomes associated with a prettified romanticism, attractive enough in formal terms provided its more substantive philosophies are kept safely at a distance.[2]

This kind of representation establishes the dichotomies that were to dominate nineteenth-century American versions of Europe. The aesthetic and "feminine" qualities of the European Catholic environment are played off against the sternly ethical and "masculine" virtues of Enlightenment logic and science. During his own spell as American consul in Venice, Howells admitted himself attracted to the beauty of the city, yet also noted with regret, "The charm of the place sweetens your temper, but corrupts you." It is this sense of a world charming but superannuated that pervades those novels by Howells set in Venice. For Mrs. Elmore in *A Fearful Responsibility* (1881), Venice is a "watery mausoleum."[3] For the American painter Ferris in *A Foregone Conclusion* (1874), the city's tone is one of "picturesque dilapidation," an environment that insidiously encourages idleness and loss of assertive male willpower. *A Foregone Conclusion* revolves around the character of Don Ippolito, a Venetian priest of scientific bent who devises a scheme for making breech-loading cannons that he would like to test in the American Civil War. Priesthood,

1 Washington Irving, *Tales of a Traveller, by Geoffrey Crayon, Gent.*, ed. Judith Giblin Haig (Boston: Twayne, 1987), p. 180.

2 William Dean Howells, *Venetian Life*, 2nd ed. (Boston, 1872), p. 187; Nathalia Wright, *American Novelists in Italy. The Discoverers: Allston to James* (Philadelphia: Univ. of Pennsylvania Press, 1965), p. 119.

3 See Wright, *American Novelists in Italy*, p. 170; William Dean Howells, *A Fearful Responsibility, and Other Stories* (Boston, 1881), p. 145.

he complains, involves "the life-long habit of a lie," fatally "leaving what you believe unspoken, what you will undone." Don Ippolito also manages to fall in love with the American girl Florida Vervain, and he hopes to become "a man" by renouncing his religious vocation and marrying Florida, a project he withdraws from, however, when he realizes Florida entertains only "an angel's heavenly pity" for him rather than a true "woman's love."[4]

It is an ideology of rationalist humanism that leads Howells here to criticize as "unnatural" Catholic notions of priestly celibacy: in an 1865 essay, "Marriage among the Italian Priesthood," Howells had condemned the celibacy requirement as "an ascetic superstition of the middle ages." In *A Foregone Conclusion,* Ferris directs a similar kind of ridicule toward the archaic practices of Venetian penitents "who think that they can get forgiveness for their sins by carrying a candle round the square!" Ferris sees these fetishistic performances as having barely emerged from the swamps of pagan ritual: "How far it is from Christ," he observes superciliously to Florida Vervain. The American painter is less cynical about his own cultural assumptions and projections, which involve reinventing heaven as an extension of the democratic political system enjoyed by the United States: "I imagine the kingdom of heaven is a sort of republic," says Ferris, "and that God draws men to Him only through their perfect freedom." This is his preferred model for Italy's political development as well; Ferris would like to see Italy rescued from the control of the Catholic church and transformed into a secular republic.[5]

Stowe's *Agnes of Sorrento,* although set in fifteenth-century Italy, is also located firmly within the discourses of humanism and science. For Stowe, science represents a crucial weapon in the evolutionary struggle by which the human race strives to better itself and move beyond the follies of its ancestors:

> The rosary, the crucifix, the shrine, the banner, the procession were catechisms and tracts invented for those who could not read, wherein the substance of pages was condensed and gave itself to the eye and touch. Let us not, from the height of our day, with the better appliances which a universal press gives us, sneer at the homely rounds of the ladder by which the first multitudes of the Lord's followers climbed heavenward.[6]

4 William Dean Howells, *A Foregone Conclusion* (Boston: Houghton Mifflin, 1902), pp. 103, 137, 190, 238.
5 William Dean Howells, "Marriage among the Italian Priesthood," *New York Times,* 19 Oct. 1865, p. 4; *Foregone Conclusion,* pp. 166–7.
6 Harriet Beecher Stowe, *Agnes of Sorrento* (Boston: Houghton Mifflin, 1896), pp. 96–7. Subsequent page references are given in parentheses in the text.

The tone is patronizing, of course, but also enjoyably comic. Stowe satirizes the childish quarrels of monks, the neurotic repressions of nuns who have not stepped outside convent walls since they were ten years old. Everything that purports to be religious ecstasy is scientifically demystified by Stowe's text. When scaling a mountain on retreat, Father Francesco thinks he has found God; but he "did not know," Stowe assures us, "that this high-strung calmness" was only a form of "nervous sensibility . . . as vividly susceptible to every mortal impression as is the vitalized chemical plate to the least action of the sun's rays" (242). Scientific empiricism, the evidence of the human senses, is given priority over traditional church teaching and authority. This is why Agnes herself, a "sweet image of perfect purity and faith" (105), embodies the ideal of the typical Stowe heroine. The spontaneity and sensible grasp of Agnes's childish wisdom apparently render all more abstract questions of philosophy and theology quite redundant.

The other heroes in *Agnes of Sorrento* are Savonarola and the "early Puritans" (257) of his Florentine community whose sense of personal religious integrity induced them to withdraw from the corrupt ceremonies of Alexander VI's papal court. Savonarola, like Agnes, is said to be a representative of "the True Invisible Church" predicated upon the "sustaining presence and sympathy of an Almighty Saviour" (315). It is this personal relation that is deemed to be the "substance" of Christianity, whether in the relation between an individual soul and Christ, or, on a more earthly level, the relationship between two human beings. Whereas the Catholic church has traditionally placed its highest emphasis on a state of celibacy, the Protestant Reformation discredited this ideal of virginity and elevated instead the moral status of the family; in Luther's opinion, nothing was more sustaining than a good marriage.[7] In eventually turning away from the convent to embrace her lover, Agostino Sorelli, Stowe's heroine is therefore conforming to the dictates of Protestant humanism.

The pattern in *Agnes of Sorrento* is that of binary opposition: Protestant spirit versus Catholic matter, purity versus corruption. Doubtless Stowe had in mind here an analogy with the American slavery issue, as Nathalia Wright has noted, and that would constitute another duality: the liberal, reforming North (of Italy/America) versus the backward South. Yet *Agnes of Sorrento* does not dismiss the religious machinery of Catholicism as altogether worthless. The idea of "an interceding Redeemer" is described as "far more consoling" than the "intense individualism of modern philosophy, which places every soul alone in its life-battle" (124); in

7 This is discussed in Jay Fliegelman, *Prodigals and Pilgrims: The American Revolution against Patriarchal Authority, 1750–1800* (Cambridge: Cambridge Univ. Press, 1982) p. 121.

this sense, the mediating iconography and ritual of Catholic Italy could be seen to soften the theological asceticism of New England Puritanism, to lend it more of a friendly human touch. (According to Wright, Stowe's subsequent shift from the Congregational to the Episcopal church was influenced by her acknowledgment of the human value of church ritual.)[8] There were other American writers of the nineteenth century whose rejection of Calvinist austerity led them toward greater sympathy with Catholic icons. Peter Gardella has commented upon how Pope Pius IX's 1854 declaration of the dogma of the Immaculate Conception, whereby the freedom of the Virgin Mary from original sin was made official Catholic doctrine, became conflated with American romanticism's increasing idealization of womanhood at this time, with the result that Mary became an object of reverence in the writings of Stowe, Longfellow, Hawthorne, James Russell Lowell, and Henry Adams. Even Emily Dickinson, in a few of her more picturesque poems, embraced the figure of the Madonna, though of course not so much for the Virgin's "immaculate" qualities as for her human and feminine sympathies. Such Mariolatry was not an indication of adherence to Catholic theology but rather implied the feminization of Protestantism, a break with stern Calvinist fathers, and an emphasis instead upon homely, domestic ideals and "the womanly in God."[9] This was all part of the popular nineteenth-century religion of brotherly love, whose icons naturally tended to be more recognizably human than invisibly transcended.

In this respect, American romanticism can be seen as an attack upon Calvinist patriarchy as well as desiccated positivism. Yet in the end these divergent impulses comprise two sides of the same coin. It is another version of what George Santayana was later to call the "genteel tradition" in nineteenth-century American culture: the "masculine" worlds of Calvinism or scientific positivism and the "feminine" world of human sympathy form a binary opposition, defining each other in terms of mutual exclusion.[10] Each term makes sense only by reference to the other. On one hand, as we have seen, European Catholicism was dismissed by

8 Wright, *American Novelists in Italy,* pp. 93, 89.
9 Peter Gardella, *Innocent Ecstasy: How Christianity Gave America an Ethic of Sexual Pleasure* (New York: Oxford Univ. Press, 1985), pp. 98–129. On "the womanly in God," see T. J. Jackson Lears, *No Place of Grace: Antimodernism and the Transformation of American Culture, 1880–1920* (New York: Pantheon, 1981), p. 242. For Dickinson, see Barton Levi St. Armand, *Emily Dickinson and Her Culture: The Soul's Society* (Cambridge: Cambridge Univ. Press, 1984), pp. 93–4. A wide-ranging treatment of this nineteenth-century shift to a "theology of feeling" can be found in Ann Douglas, *The Feminization of American Culture* (New York: Knopf, 1977).
10 See his 1911 lecture "The Genteel Tradition in American Philosophy," in George Santayana, *The Genteel Tradition: Nine Essays,* ed. Douglas L. Wilson (Cambridge, Mass.: Harvard Univ. Press, 1967), pp. 38–64.

American science as belonging to a puerile, inchoate state of civilization. On the other hand, when Catholicism was looked at more favorably by Stowe, Longfellow, Charles Eliot Norton, and other writers, they were interested not so much in the church itself as in those qualities it might contain that would differentiate it from Calvinist or positivist philosophies. Norton was less interested in Catholicism per se than in finding an environment away from the mechanistic operations of rationalism. Because of this reified dichotomy, Catholicism at this time became impaled upon a binary opposition where it was inexorably cast as the "feminine" side of the equation.

Those internal controversies about the direction of the church that so perturbed Catholic immigrants to America in the nineteenth century are, then, altogether absent from the work of American non-Catholics in their responses to Europe. Moreover, as T. J. Jackson Lears has said, for all their voluminous writing on medieval aesthetics there is hardly a mention here of the medieval Scholastic philosophers.[11] Saint Francis of Assisi is perhaps the most popular figure, because the Saint's innocent love of nature comes closest to the American romantic ideal of childish wisdom, as embodied in Agnes of Sorrento or in Louisa May Alcott's *Little Women* (1869). What we find instead is a cult of aesthetic experience, epitomized in Norton's book *Historical Studies of Church Building in the Middle Ages* (1880), his appointment to a Harvard professorship of fine arts, the establishment of a Dante Society at Harvard with Longfellow as its first president, and so on. James Russell Lowell, who was also part of this group, thought Catholicism the only "poet" among the churches but nevertheless found himself becoming "more and more persuaded" that "Romanism is a dead thing in Italy. . . . The Papacy lies dead in the Vatican, but the secret is kept for the present."[12] For Lowell, of course, this demise of church authority was far from being a matter for despair. On the contrary, being a man who on matters metaphysical found "no fault with a judicious shutting of the eyes," Lowell welcomed the abrogation of papal power and the way "Catholic" artists like Dante and Raphael could now be colonized by their true admirers, gentlemen of good taste such as himself.[13] A few American writers of this period did actually convert to Catholicism: Henry Harland joined the Church in 1897, after he had settled in London and worked with Aubrey Beardsley on the *Yellow Book*, while Italophile novelist Francis Marion Crawford, a political and religious conservative who considered Pope Leo XIII the

11 Lears, *No Place of Grace*, p. 142.
12 James Russell Lowell, *Fireside Travels* (Boston: Houghton Mifflin, 1887), pp. 291, 228–9.
13 The phrase comes from a letter to Leslie Stephen, 16 May 1874, in Charles Eliot Norton, ed., *Letters of James Russell Lowell* (New York, 1894), II, 125.

greatest man of the age, also took the Roman way. For most of these American literati, though, Catholicism constituted a supreme fiction rather than a theological imperative.

It has become customary in American literary history to disparage these "genteel" writers as the last gasp of a dying tradition. The socially aristocratic and aesthetically conservative temperament of men like Lowell and Norton was hardly conducive to the socialist, progressive outlook of critics such as F. O. Matthiessen, who naturally preferred to emphasize the more "democratic" American writers of this era. As Martin Green, Jane Tompkins, and others have pointed out, there is an issue of literary "canon" involved here: Hawthorne, for instance, who is most often championed today for being a follower of Melville's post-Calvinist "blackness," was in his own time praised more for his picturesque qualities and seen as closely affiliated with Longfellow's Harvard group, a circle with which Hawthorne did indeed have strong personal ties.[14] American critics from Matthiessen onwards have tended to be "passionately committed to the idea of American exceptionalism," as Joy S. Kasson put it, and consequently much more interested in "those aspects of American art and literature that set them apart from their Old World counterparts."[15] Because of this habitual obsession with American literature as an expression of American national culture, works looking back toward Europe have often been neglected as imitative and relatively uninteresting. But such an exclusive concern with literature as the projection of a democratic ideal ignores how the binary opposition of democratic positivism versus aristocratic aestheticism was not only mutually exclusive but also mutually defining. Like Hawthorne, William Dean Howells is more famous today for his quintessentially "American" themes, and it is no surprise to find Howells in *Venetian Life* disparaging all those sentimental, Byronic legends that have accumulated around the city and preferring instead to exercise his faculty of "democratic" realism by visiting "dirty neighborhoods that reeked with unwholesome winter damps."[16] Nor is it unpredictable that, like Margaret Fuller and Harriet Beecher Stowe, Howells should have been a keen supporter of Italian politicians such as Garibaldi and Mazzini who were trying to wrest Italy away from the temporal control of the papacy. The important thing to stress, though, is that Howells's disillusioned rationalism was entirely consistent with the Harvard group's version of Italy as a pleasing aesthetic

14 See Martin Green, *The Problem of Boston: Some Readings in Cultural History* (New York: Norton, 1966), passim; Jane Tompkins, *Sensational Designs: The Cultural Work of American Fiction, 1790–1860* (Oxford: Oxford Univ. Press, 1985), pp. 3–39.

15 Joy S. Kasson, *Artistic Voyagers: Europe and the American Imagination in the Works of Irving, Allston, Cole, Cooper, and Hawthorne* (Westport, Conn.: Greenwood, 1982), p. 3.

16 Howells, *Venetian Life*, p. 33.

phenomenon. Indeed, the mystique of Italian irrationalism might be seen as an indispensable counterpart to the forging of Howells's stylistic identity as an "American" writer. In 1870, Howells himself lectured at Harvard on "New Italian Literature," and in 1887 he published the study *Modern Italian Poets*. In his novels he represents Italy more as a legendary rather than a social or political phenomenon. Although skeptical of Italy's legends, he still prefers to write (iconoclastically) about these myths rather than dismiss them entirely, for his interest is still in the binary mode of opposing Italian romance to American realism.

There are few references to Italian politicians in Howells's 1886 novel *Indian Summer,* for instance. Colville and his American compatriots spend much time walking around Florence and comparing its artistic landscapes to the less picturesque world of Des Vaches, Indiana, where Colville used to work as a journalist. Sometimes Colville is nostalgic for the energy and expansiveness of Indiana, at other times he is content to cherish the "familiar monuments" of Florence.[17] It never occurs to Colville, however, to reject this simplistic antithesis, or to turn his attention to the business economy of Italy or the aesthetic heritage of America. Italy is art and America is business; for Colville, at least, never the twain shall meet. The rigid opposition of positivism versus aesthetics remains intact. Although characters like Colville can move from one side of the line to the other, they do not seem able to collapse the equation by handling both sides of it at once.

It was this bifurcation between science and art that ensured that many American writers of this time tended to perceive Europe within an educational idiom. Europe constituted the landscape of a "grand tour" whereby one could enlarge one's human experience by studiously annotating cultural differences. Sometimes this travel to Europe was overtly pedagogical, as in the case of Longfellow, sent to Europe by his father to prepare for a career teaching modern languages. In a more general sense, though, an ethic of cultural self-improvement underlay not only American tourism to Europe – by 1873, there were some twenty-five thousand visitors annually – but also the predilection for buying up European art and annexing it as part of one's own cultural heritage.[18] Edith Wharton was to become a big collector of Italian objects, while other American connoisseurs sought out the advice of Henry Adams on stained-glass windows and Charles Eliot Norton on rare editions of Dante. Yet, in spite of all this geographical mobility, most nineteenth-century Americans remained safely anesthetized to the more wide-

---

17 William Dean Howells, *Indian Summer* (Bloomington: Indiana Univ. Press, 1971), p. 8.
   Subsequent page references are given in parentheses in the text.
18 Statistics quoted from Lears, *No Place of Grace,* p. 186.

ranging implications of Catholic culture. Moral energy was back in grim New England; one traveled to Catholic Europe for a broadening humanist education or for aesthetic frivolity, a temporary flirtation with the exotic "Scarlet Woman" of Rome.

This idea of a clear-cut division between America and Europe owes something to the romantic aesthetics of Goethe and Ruskin, with their mythological distinction between the moral north and the sensual south. Ruskin, we know, was a great influence on Norton, who reworked Ruskin's philosophical antitheses into a perspective of Puritan America opposing the ardent charms of southern Europe. More importantly, though, this whole conception of division itself emerges from within the specifically romantic and Protestant doctrine of originality, originality that can (paradoxically) define itself only by insisting on what it is not. The pilgrim fathers' rejection of Europe in favor of America is mirrored not only by texts such as *Agnes of Sorrento,* which obviously plays off Old World corruption against Reformist zeal, but also more implicitly by works such as Howells's *Venetian Life,* which places morality and aesthetics in quite separate camps. This antithesis turns ultimately upon the idealization incumbent upon the intervention of "America" in world history, an intervention deemed comparable by American Reformers to the incarnation of Christ. Just as Christ brought about what Hans Robert Jauss called "the caesura in world history of *post Christum natum,* the sublation of the entire past through the new message of Christ," so American writers of the nineteenth century insist that Catholic Europe must have changed simply because Americans, the chosen people, are now observing it. This overhauling of the Old World involves a form of romantic or transcendentalist egoism: Europe is changed and remade by the advent of America. It is akin to the "model of the early Christian change in epoch, which sees the step from the old to the new as an act of conversion that demands the price of a rigorous repudiation of everything previous to it."[19] Following the example of Christ, Americans in Europe are determined to "make it new," as Ezra Pound was later to put it. James Fenimore Cooper and Charles Eliot Norton may be nostalgic for the beauties of Europe, but in the end they both conceive of themselves in quintessentially American Protestant fashion as new men, whose job is not simply to acquiesce in the old corruptions of Europe but to participate in a "myth of total renewal" whereby Europe can be colonized, remade, and reinvented according to the messianic destiny laid down for the United States.

This resistance to the premises of European Catholicism is also inherent

19 Hans Robert Jauss, "The Literary Process of Modernism from Rousseau to Adorno," *Cultural Critique,* No. 11 (Winter 1988-9), p. 31.

within the linguistic practices of the New World. Though the earlier American Puritans were necessarily caught up within inherited structures of medieval Scholasticism, Charles Feidelson argued later American Puritan divines made a "drastic break" with the Catholic assumption, deriving from Scholastic philosophy, that terrestrial incarnation might be analogically infused with divine presence. Whereas Aquinas imagined the human world and human language binding together many different modes of reality, literal and metaphysical, Puritans by contrast perceived language more as a logical sequence of cause and effect that could have only an arbitrary, figurative claim upon divine truth. Puritan discourse tended to be logical; Catholic discourse tended to be analogical. Medieval theologians stressed a form of transubstantial symbolism: God's presence could be revealed within earthly events. American Puritans stressed the mode of allegory: God's absence ensured that any human gesturings toward divine truth must remain provisional and ultimately self-canceling. In his essay "The Rhetoric of Temporality," Paul de Man maintained that whereas symbolism "postulates the possibility of an identity or identification, allegory designates primarily a distance in relation to its own origin" and operates by establishing "its language in the void of this temporal difference"; and in this sense, those distances and differences inherent within the structures of allegory might be seen as a tropological counterpart to that Puritan theological conception of the *Deus Absconditus,* the distant, absent God.[20] The crucial distinction here is between a Catholic universal vision, where every part of the world interpenetrates every other part, as opposed to a more atomistic (or allegorical) Puritan idiom where reason is divorced from transcendent truth and so can create only its own closed circle. In the universalism of Aquinas, language interpenetrates symbol, literal matter interpenetrates divine substance, and thus – by extension – Europe and America interpenetrate each other. For Aquinas, no part of the world can be closed off from any other part. In the sectarian outlook of Calvin, however, language is split off from divine being, just as the city of man exists in a state of fundamental disjunction from the city of God. Hence it was the theological and philosophical framework of Puritanism that helped to underpin and validate that rigid dichotomy whereby America could separate itself from Catholic Europe. While the language of Aquinas works to bring things together, the language of Calvin works to keep things distinctly apart.

*   *   *

20 Charles Feidelson Jr., *Symbolism and American Literature* (Chicago: Univ. of Chicago Press, 1953), pp. 84–6; Paul de Man, *Blindness and Insight: Essays in the Rhetoric of Contemporary Criticism,* 2nd ed. (London: Methuen, 1983) p. 207.

Here again it becomes important to find the distinguishing quality of good art. The most interesting American texts of this time that concern themselves with Europe do not just reproduce these dichotomies, but interrogate them. In Melville, Hawthorne, and James, in Twain, Adams, and (to some extent) Howells, we find a development of chains of ironies and paradoxes through which the simple Puritan opposition between Old World and New becomes increasingly problematized.

In *Benito Cereno* (1855), Melville takes the stereotype of European Catholic corruption and gives it a new direction by drawing implicit parallels with the corruptions of the New World, thus exploiting the imagery of Catholicism to subvert American pastoral idylls. In *Benito Cereno*, where we witness a mutiny by black sailors on board a Spanish ship, the rebels are said to be as "Black Friars pacing the cloisters," with one black servant described as "like a begging friar of St. Francis." The Spanish themselves resemble "a ship-load of monks," while their ships, "like superannuated Italian palaces," are also recast within Old World similes.[21] Through these linguistic metamorphoses, *Benito Cereno* associates the repressive American practice of slavery, which keeps blacks in bondage, with the various forms of submission demanded by Benito Cereno's Old World religion. The "attitude" of Melville's text toward Catholicism is, of course, complex and indeterminate. While Catholicism at this time was popularly imagined in the progressivist northern states as a tyrannical "slave power," nevertheless a deep-rooted uneasiness about the potentially destabilizing social consequences of liberation and mass exodus is also implicit in *Benito Cereno*. As Robert S. Levine has written, the American Captain Delano's metaphorical reconstitution of the black rebels as Catholic friars "exemplifies the way in which fears of Catholic immigrants and blacks permeated one another in the mid–1850s."[22] The crucial factor here is not that Melville is sympathetic toward either the organization of the Church or its individual members, but that his text undermines the antithesis of American purity against European corruption by defining a New World system of slavery within an Old World paradigm. We see a similar recognition of cultural miscegenation in *The Confidence-Man* (1857), which derogates "those Jesuit emissaries prowling all over our country," who, "the better to accomplish their secret designs . . . assume . . . the most singular masques."[23] As the novel progresses, however, we begin to appreciate how this apparent bifur-

21 Herman Melville, "Benito Cereno," in *The Piazza Tales and Other Prose Pieces, 1839–1860* (Evanston: Northwestern Univ. Press–Newberry Library, 1987), pp. 48, 57.

22 Robert S. Levine, *Conspiracy and Romance: Studies in Brockden Brown, Cooper, Hawthorne, and Melville* (Cambridge: Cambridge Univ. Press, 1989), p. 225.

23 Herman Melville, *The Confidence-Man, His Masquerade* (Evanston: Northwestern Univ. Press–Newberry Library, 1984), p. 92.

cation between Catholic jesuitry and Protestant plain dealing becomes undercut, for these elements of mask and disguise are subsequently revealed as integral to much wider currents of American culture. What appears at first to be an opposition between the Old World and the New turns out in the end to be an equivalence between them.

Hawthorne's *The Marble Faun* (1859) is one of the most famous nineteenth-century American disquisitions upon the cultural and psychological differences between Protestantism and Catholicism. The old stereotypes emerge once more: the American Kenyon follows the example of Ralph Waldo Emerson by preferring the "grand hieroglyphics" of nature to the crucifixes and visual icons of "priest-ridden Italy"; he declares his allegiance to "the broad and simple wisdom from on high"; he castigates his compatriot Hilda for her emerging interest in Catholicism.[24] The Old Church is associated with falsehood – "seldom an intolerable burthen to the tenderest of Italian consciences" (407) – a general lack of moral severity, and a warped obsession with the flesh antipathetic to humanist ideals of a flourishing sexuality:

> Here was a priesthood, pampered, sensual, with red and bloated cheeks, and carnal eyes. With apparently a grosser development of animal life than most men, they were placed in an unnatural relation with woman, and thereby lost the healthy, human conscience that pertains to other human beings, who own the sweet household ties connecting them with wife and daughter. (411)

Once again, however, this conception of Catholicism as an alien force is held in check by the psychological and conceptual equivalences that begin to manifest themselves. Hilda, who starts the novel convinced of her own quintessentially Protestant heritage, gradually begins to realize the connotations of Catholicism are not so irrelevant to her consciousness as she had originally imagined. Catholicism in *The Marble Faun* betokens the ubiquity of sin and guilt: Emersonian transcendentalism has often been criticized for its failure to admit the existence of evil, while conversely the notion of lost innocence, purity compromised, is one of the most familiar themes of American literature set in Europe. Hilda, while "disgusted with the pretence of Holiness and the reality of Nastiness" (326), nevertheless appreciates how the Italian landscape uncovers "that dismal certainty of the existence of evil in the world" (328); accordingly, she comes to have some understanding of the impulses through which "our heart-strings have mysteriously attached themselves to the Eternal City" (326). Like Dorothea Brooke in George Eliot's *Middlemarch*, Hilda

---

24 Nathaniel Hawthorne, *The Marble Faun; or, The Romance of Monte Beni* (Ohio State Univ. Press, 1968), pp. 258, 266, 368. Subsequent page references are given in parentheses in the text.

comes to believe, albeit unwillingly, in the validity of this picture presented by Rome, whose ancient ruins suggest the vast wrecking of moral ideals and the dignity of the human spirit.

Along with this acknowledgment of the universal Fall goes the supersession of autonomous individual consciousness. Hawthorne's characters are impelled toward a recognition of the universal thralldom of the human condition. As Miriam notes in chapter 13: "As these busts in the block of marble . . . so does our individual fate exist in the limestone of Time. We fancy that we carve it out; but its ultimate shape is prior to all our action" (116). The Emersonian belief in a human freedom to shape one's destiny is inverted into a recognition of the all-encompassing, interpellating power of original sin. Nevertheless, relinquishment of this self-reliant human spirit might also, for Hilda, become a means toward salvation. Recognizing Catholicism as "a faith which so marvellously adapts itself to every human need" (344) and acknowledging how its "mighty machinery" produces "a miracle of fitness for its own ends" (345), Hilda is tempted by the offer of the confessional that she "fling down the dark burthen at the foot of the Cross" (355), renounce all the self-imposed pressures of her own spiritual striving (as implied by the imagery of the angel, the white dove, and so on), and acquiesce instead in the Catholic church's impersonal mechanisms for the absolution of human guilt. In the end, though, the priest's devious attempts to convert Hilda repel her, and by the end of the novel her dovelike spiritual peace has begun to return, along with the more familiar attributes of Puritan self-reliance: "Her character had developed a sturdier quality, which made her less pliable to the influence of other minds" (375). The Protestant theologian Paul Tillich once wrote that a characteristic weakness of Catholicism is its tendency toward idolatry, what Tillich called "a sacramental objectification and demonization of Christianity" that borders on the magical, and it is the desire to resist such "objectification" that finally inspires Hilda's movement to reclaim her subjectivity.[25]

Still, her initiation into the mysteries of Catholicism does lead Hilda to the inference that her religious inheritance is a cultural difference rather than a simple moral imperative. Noting with approval a young Italian praying before the altar, she muses: "If this youth had been a Protestant, he would have kept all that torture pent up in his heart, and let it burn there till it seared him into indifference" (347). Henry James suggested that Hawthorne used the American Puritan heritage as an objectively transformed element in his work so that it constitutes his primary data,

25 Paul Tillich, *The Protestant Era,* trans. James Luther Adams (Chicago: Univ. of Chicago Press, 1948), p. 94. For a discussion of this point, see Avery Dulles, S.J., *The Catholicity of the Church* (Oxford: Clarendon Press, 1985), p. 155.

not his moral commitment, and from this perspective we can see *The Marble Faun* self-reflexively examining its own Puritan assumptions, playing them off against the claims of Catholicism and other cultural forces. Social conventions are reproduced textually in "unexpected combinations," as Wolfgang Iser would say, "so that they begin to be stripped of their validity" and "become objects of scrutiny in themselves."[26] In this light, I would want to qualify the suggestions of Robert S. Levine and Myra Jehlen that Hawthorne's texts implicitly participate in the anti-Catholic discourses of the mid-nineteenth century. Levine and Jehlen saw in Hawthorne an ideological representation of how the licentious energies of Catholicism pose a threat to the integrity of Puritan communities and to the principles of Reformation and Enlightenment. (Hester Prynne in *The Scarlet Letter*, like Zenobia in *The Blithedale Romance*, is notably tainted with the marks of Rome.) But it is not only that Hawthorne's novels are much more "complex and ironic" than nativist narratives, as Levine recognized, it is also that this very textual complexity and irony effectively subvert any aspiration toward authorial control. Hawthorne may very well have shared in the general American distaste for the papacy's political and military activities during the 1850s, as Levine suggested, but one of the strengths of *The Marble Faun* is that its narrative is too complex to be confined by such a narrow anti-Catholic perspective.[27] Just as Balzac's novels imply so much about the contradictions of capitalism in nineteenth-century France that the author's own philosophical outlook becomes suppressed – as Lukács noted – so Hawthorne's tales give us some glimpse of the deeper, less personalized ramifications of Protestant–Catholic tensions at this time.

To say Hawthorne simply "exposes" these cultural tensions would be to advocate an archaic myth of the author as omniscient seer; as Levine rightly noted, no work of art can evade being framed by the partiality of a particular historical perspective. Nevertheless, *The Marble Faun* is far from being the kind of allegory in which Protestant and Catholic temperaments remain mutually exclusive or even discrete categories. In fact, the book can be read as an allegory that also critiques its own allegorical premises, a text poised equivocally between the Old World and the New, for it establishes conceptual dichotomies only to subvert them. This formalistic ambivalence manifests itself not only in the text's

26 Henry James, *Hawthorne* (New York: Harper, 1880), pp. 57–60; Wolfgang Iser, *The Act of Reading: A Theory of Aesthetic Response* (London: Routledge & Kegan Paul, 1978), p. 61.
27 Myra Jehlen, *American Incarnation: The Individual, The Nation, and the Continent* (Cambridge, Mass.: Harvard Univ. Press, 1986), pp. 153–84; Levine, *Conspiracy and Romance*, p. 120, and "'Antebellum Rome' in *The Marble Faun*," *American Literary History*, 2 (1990), 25.

counterpointing of two European characters with two Americans, but also in its establishment of a narrative dialogue between internalized spirit and externalized iconography. The aesthetic counterpart to Catholicism's alleviation of the burdened personal soul is the visual imagery that permeates *The Marble Faun.* In chapter 7, Miriam seems to blend into Guido Reni's painting *Beatrice Cenci;* in chapter 15 she is shadowed in a drawing by the same artist; while of course the image of Donatello imitatively throwing himself into the posture of the *Faun,* a sculpture by Praxiteles, is the central and titular motif of the novel. The iconography acts to objectify Hawthorne's characters, to transpose them from free and autonomous agents into mere components of a long-established aesthetic and cultural landscape. In this respect, the pictorial imagery functions as a parallel to the theological operation of Catholicism, as perceived by Hawthorne, which "supplies a multitude of external forms, in which the Spiritual may be clothed and manifested; it has many painted windows, as it were" (344).

Catholicism has traditionally relied upon the allure of images – Madonnas, crucifixes, and so on – much more than Puritanism, which traditionally harbors a deep suspicion of the power of art and artifice. Colleen McDannell, in her study *The Christian Home in Victorian America,* has demonstrated that whereas nineteenth-century Protestant families sanctified the home through the provision of a "sacred time" for private prayer and meditation, Catholic families preferred to spiritualize their homes through the use of divine images: "What the Protestants did through reading, the Catholics did through seeing. Protestants sanctified their homes through utilizing the sacred word in home liturgies that emphasized Bible readings, prayers, and hymns. Catholics sanctified their homes with sacred images: the Sacred Heart picture, candles, crucifixes, and holy water fonts."[28] Nor was this use of iconography simply a populist phenomenon. Taking their cue from John Henry Newman, nineteenth-century Catholic intellectuals such as Hecker and George Tyrrell defended the use of images in religious worship by arguing that God speaks to mankind through all the human senses and bids mankind answer him back in his own tongue, as Tyrrell put it.[29] As we saw in Stowe's *Agnes of Sorrento,* this kind of visualization is often associated by American writers with a blind Catholic adherence to faith in contrast to the Protestant emphasis upon intelligent interrogation of superficial appearances. The narrator in *The Marble Faun* comments sardonically

28 Colleen McDannell, *The Christian Home in Victorian America* (Bloomington: Indiana Univ. Press, 1986), p. 106.
29 Dulles, *Catholicity of the Church,* p. 55.

upon how pictures form "the devotion of such as had not words for their own prayer" (346). It is noticeable also that when Hilda swings back toward her American roots, she begins again to detect "the large portion that is unreal, in every work of art.... She felt that there is something beyond almost all which pictorial genius has produced" (375).

What is fascinating about *The Marble Faun* is the way it reconstitutes this theological controversy in novelistic terms. On the one hand, all the painters and sculptors threaten to interpellate the Puritan freedom of spirit within an iconographic framework; but, on the other hand, the transparently allegorical nature of the "romance" (to use Hawthorne's favorite term) ultimately betrays the "Puritan" consciousness that informs the work. Just as Hilda detects what is "unreal, in every work of art," so Hawthorne is inviting the reader to do likewise; the self-conscious fabrications of the novel, "artfully and airily removed from our mundane sphere" (463), as Hawthorne puts it, persuade the reader to recognize both the text and the world as an illusion. Whereas the Italian Catholic temper extrapolates ideals from things of this world, the American Puritan mentality locates ideals within a transcendent, dematerialized sphere. Thus at the end of the novel, as the text openly confesses its own fictional status, we as readers put on the wings of the dove so as to ascend, like Hilda, toward a realm of pure intellect and disembodied spirit. Hawthorne's novel, like the Bible itself, is offered as valuable to us as readers for its purchase on our minds, not for allowing us to empathize with any literal social reality. In this way, the thematic conflict between Catholicism and Puritanism is replayed in the text's formalist oscillation between Catholic iconography and Puritan allegory or self-erasure. While in Catholic iconography literal and "divine" meanings interpenetrate each other, in the Puritan perspective language, like the terrestrial world itself, is merely a figurative instrument left to expose its own fallacious quality and to hint at intangible or "spiritual" qualities that can never be fully revealed.

The Wings of the Dove itself, published by Henry James in 1902, reveals a very similar sense of individual character finding itself potentially compromised by the icons of visual art. The American Protestant dove, Milly Theale, cherishes her sense of freedom and likes escaping to London's Regent's Park, where nobody knows who she is. When Lord Mark points out how Milly resembles a portrait by Bronzino hanging in his country home, James's heroine is mortified:

> The lady in question, at all events, with her slightly Michael-angelesque squareness, her eyes of other days, her full lips, her long neck, her recorded jewels, her brocaded and wasted reds, was a very great personage – only unaccompanied by a joy. And she was dead, dead, dead.

Milly recognized her exactly in words that had nothing to do with her. "I shall never be better than this."[30]

As in Hawthorne, the visualization moves toward deflating and even parodying the pretensions of the individual spirit. Through iconography, the romantic subject is transposed into an interpellated object. Of course, tensions between Protestantism and Catholicism form only one part of the mythological antithesis James is working with, the larger confrontation between the Old World and the New, but this religious dimension – usually transformed, in James, into secularized social forms – is one important aspect within his cultural equations.

This religious component becomes more explicit near the end of *The Portrait of a Lady* (1881) where we are told that "the old Protestant tradition had never faded from Isabel's imagination."[31] It is precisely this staunch, upright quality of Isabel's character that renders her vulnerable to the devious machinations of Madame Merle. In *Portrait,* Madame Merle and her daughter Pansy are subtly presented in an impersonal way, as though their sense of individual human identity has become attenuated: in her Italian convent, so we are told, Pansy is "evidently impregnated with the idea of submission, which was due to anyone who took the tone of authority; and she was a passive spectator of the operation of her fate" (I, 337–8). Isabel, though, cannot behold the nuns with such equanimity: the speech of the convent sisters "fell with a leaden weight on Isabel's ears" because "it seemed to represent the surrender of a personality, the authority of the Church" (II, 382). Similarly, Isabel's restless spirit perceives Madame Merle's social graces "as professional, as slightly mechanical" (II, 39); it is significant that on her first appearance in the novel Madame Merle has her "ample and well-dressed" back turned toward Isabel, who views it "for some moments with surprise" (I, 244). The moral imperative of impersonality inculcated into Pansy by the church is mirrored in this sense of impersonality enjoyed by Madame Merle, and again this objectification is externalized by a series of visual images. For Isabel, near the end of the book, "Madame Merle was already so present to her vision that her appearance in the flesh was like suddenly, and rather awfully, seeing a painted picture move" (II, 375).

As Leo Bersani has pointed out, it is true in a more general sense that "James's fiction is full of visual shocks which constitute crucial turning points for his heroes and heroines."[32] While not seeking exclusively to

30 Henry James, *The Wings of the Dove* (New York: Scribner's, 1909), I, 221.
31 Henry James, *The Portrait of a Lady* (New York: Scribner's, 1908), II, 349. Subsequent page references are given in parentheses in the text.
32 Leo Bersani, *A Future for Astyanax: Character and Desire in Literature* (Boston: Little, Brown, 1976), p. 133.

associate this pictorial consciousness with religious iconography, what we can suggest is that the visual dimension inherent within Catholicism (as we saw in *The Marble Faun*) reverberates formally and thematically in James's fiction to produce a sense of evil and betrayal, also linked, implicitly, with the Old World religious sensibility. The frozen tableaux of the narratives engender a Catholic understanding of the ubiquity and repetitive nature of sin. Take the famous moment in *The Portrait of a Lady* when Isabel sees Madame Merle with Gilbert Osmond and instantaneously realizes the duplicity to which she has fallen victim. The pictorial emphasis here usurps Isabel's spiritual strivings: the tableau draws Isabel into its old world of jealousies and betrayals, just as the sculpture by Praxiteles draws Hawthorne's Donatello into a cultural landscape that existed before his time. The visualization process transforms Donatello and Isabel Archer from subjective producers to objective products of their environment. Graham Greene noted that the recognition of evil in James's novels is always attached to the idea of betrayal by an intimate, but what we might suggest over and above this is that such recognition very often becomes attached also to ideas of impersonality, iconography, and Old World aesthetics.[33] On one level, there is a very traditional association here between Catholicism and Machiavellian corruption, but, as with Hawthorne, James is also implying larger issues about the relationship between the individual and his or her environment. The iconographic tableau usurps the romantic, typically American desire to gain mastery over an external, historical world.

In his travel writings, James allowed himself to be more relaxed and patronizing about Catholicism. Watching the cardinals flash their scarlet stockings at the basilica of Santa Croce in Rome, it is James the fastidious aesthete who contrasts the tawdry philistinism of the nineteenth century with this picturesque pageantry, which "makes you groan at the victory of civilization over colour."[34] Continuing toward Assisi on this 1873 tour, James again remarks upon how the local church agrees with his aesthetic sensibilities; it embodies, he says, "the very heart of Catholicism. . . . The tone of the place is a triumph of mystery, the richest harmony of lurking shadows and dusky corners, all relieved by scattered images and scintillations." Any moral or religious tone is significantly absent. James appreciates the building as a connoisseur, or even a voyeur. When an ethical note does begin to sound, we hear James's residual Protestant sensibility manifesting a suspicion of such grandiose artifacts:

---

33 Graham Greene, "Henry James: The Private Universe," in *Collected Essays* (New York: Viking, 1969), p. 24.

34 "A Roman Holiday," in Morton Dauwen Zabel, ed., *The Art of Travel: Scenes and Journeys in America, England, France and Italy from the Travel Writings of Henry James* (Freeport, N.Y.: Books for Libraries Press, 1958), p. 329.

> The frescoes, which are admirable, represent certain leading events in the life of St. Francis, and suddenly remind you, by one of those anomalies that are half the secret of the consummate *mise-en-scène* of Catholicism, that the apostle of beggary, the saint whose only tenement in life was the ragged robe which barely covered him, is the hero of this massive structure.[35]

The word "anomalies" is interesting. The grandeur of this monument materially symbolizes the spiritual grandeur of a man who was himself, in material terms, very poor. For some more literal-minded Americans this contradiction would have seemed mere hypocrisy, a typical machination of the Roman church, but the subtle imagination of James is aware of how "half the secret" of Catholicism turns upon just this kind of paradoxical displacement of one level of reality into another. Nevertheless, undertaking *A Little Tour in France* nine years later, James continues snobbishly to derogate the vulgarity of the shrine of Saint Martin at Tours. Setting out his stall for "the exquisite," James the ironic aesthete has no qualms about rejecting anything that smacks of Catholicism's lower-class elements. He is similarly patronizing about what he sees as the quaint ideas embodied in the sculpture at Bourges Cathedral:

> In the second frieze, stands the angel of justice, with his scales; and on either side of him is the vision of the last judgment. The good prepare, with infinite titillation and complacency, to ascend to the skies; while the bad are dragged, pushed, hurled, stuffed, crammed, into pits and caldrons of fire. There is a charming detail in this section. . . . These elaborate sculptures, full of ingenuous intention and of the reality of early faith, are in a remarkable state of preservation.[36]

Still, it is clear enough that James is highly sensitive to the cultural distinctions between Protestant and Catholic art. Coming across a work by Sir Joshua Reynolds at Montpellier, he describes it as "a picture suffused indefinably with the Anglican spirit" and Sir Joshua himself as "an eminently Protestant painter," with his decorous nudes and sense of the golden mean in all things.[37]

In these travel writings, James tended to stress the differences between Protestantism and Catholicism. This is, as it were, the Charles Eliot Norton side of Henry James, the upper-class dilettante who cherishes the aesthetics of Catholicism, the medievalist nostalgia of the Gothic revival, as an escape from the rude philistinism of middle-class life. Part of the fascination of James's best novels, though, lies in the ways in which such distinctions become increasingly problematized and more

---

35 "A Chain of Cities," in *The Art of Travel*, pp. 340, 342.
36 Henry James, *A Little Tour in France* (Harmondsworth: Penguin, 1985), pp. 16, 74–75.
37 Ibid., p. 157.

difficult to define. Recapitulating the pastoral myth, Richard Poirier wrote in *A World Elsewhere* that "the books which in my view constitute a distinctive American tradition . . . resist within their pages the forces of environment that otherwise dominate the world," although Poirier went on to acknowledge that such resistance to social "systems" usually proved to be, in the end, impossible.[38] Yet even this nostalgia for difference and escape, which certainly motivates the romantic quest of Isabel Archer, seems barely relevant to the tone of James's last novels. Here the metaphorical (as well as literal) journey is eastward, not westward; the cultural miscegenation of Old World and New denies the American soul freedom to resist that world within which he or she has been interpellated. In *The Ambassadors* (1903), Strether finds Notre Dame Cathedral in Paris a depersonalizing structure, "a refuge from the obsession of his problem"; and this sense of impersonality gradually comes to pervade the whole novel, for as Strether's visual imagination grows, so his sense of personal freedom seems to decline. By the end of the novel, he is moving "as in a gallery, from clever canvas to clever canvas," and he apprehends Chad's adultery with Madame de Vionnet as emerging from a Lambinet painting, as if these characters were merely objectified components of the old dance of intrigue and betrayal.[39] In his travel journalism, James wrote of Protestantism and Catholicism as sharply diverging traditions; but in his novels he shows, as Hawthorne shows in *The Marble Faun,* where points of crossover or equivalence occur and where the American idyll of individuality and innocence becomes compromised by the "mighty machinery" of a more impersonal Catholic world.

James was implicitly commenting upon this sense of crossover when he expressed in 1888 his weariness with the so-called "international" theme: "I can't look at the English and American worlds, or feel about them, any more, save as a big Anglo-Saxon total, destined to such an amount of melting together that an insistence on their differences becomes more and more idle and pedantic."[40] As his world becomes more complex, James not only critiques the American romantic temperament but also moves toward dissolving that formal antithesis, institutionalized by Puritanism, whereby European Catholicism is reified as the "other." Hints of this kind of "melting" permeate Howells's novels as well, though the typical response of Howells's characters to this perplexing ambivalence is to spend more and more time trying to pin down exactly what might constitute specific national or religious characteristics. The

38 Richard Poirier, *A World Elsewhere: The Place of Style in American Literature* (New York: Oxford Univ. Press, 1966), p. 5.
39 Henry James, *The Ambassadors* (New York: Scribner's, 1909), II, 3, 273.
40 In a letter to William James, 29 Oct. 1888. Leon Edel, ed., *Henry James Letters,* III (Cambridge, Mass.: Harvard Univ. Press, 1980), 244.

Americans in Florence in *Indian Summer* spend a great deal of time attempting analyses along these lines. Colville argues here for "the old national ideal" of American "girlish liberty," and when Mrs. Bowen disagrees with him, he tells her she has been "Europeanized" (37). Mrs. Bowen in turn asks Colville if he is becoming "Europeanized" because his social behavior appears increasingly conventional (111). The Reverend Mr. Waters proposes a gender division between the "masculine" energy of Protestantism and the "feminine" form of Catholicism: "Protestant systems are men's systems," he claims. "Women must have form. They don't care for freedom" (217). Waters later throws out a casual, unsubstantiated generalization about "the hysterical excess of Puritanism, in all times and places" (267). These increasingly desperate rationalizations seem to be a last-ditch attempt to hold together conceptual distinctions that are fast falling apart. Howells's text overtly organizes itself according to that dichotomy invented by the Puritans, the Old World versus the New; but it covertly subverts that dichotomy, as in its portrayal of the hybrid character of Madame Uccelli, an American woman married to an Italian: "She was supposed to be a convert to the religion of her late husband, but no one really knew what religion she was of, probably not even Madame Uccelli herself" (55).

As this myth of Catholic Europe as distinctly "other" becomes more and more difficult to maintain, so James and Howells find themselves confronting a situation that cannot be inscribed within traditional moral and cultural antitheses. The world, alarmingly, appears out of control, too wide and complex to be subsumed within the simplistic framework of "America versus Europe" that dominates James's early works. The American transcendental ego can no longer reinvent Europe, can no longer annex Europe as a projection of its own imagination, because the world becomes evasive and eludes such dogmatic impositions.

One of the ways this new complexity is characterized in James and Howells is by the representation of Europe as an intertextual phenomenon, where attempts at "pure" literal description can never do justice to the *mise-en-abîme* of cultural interpretation and reinterpretation that comprises Europe's elusive quality. In *Venetian Life,* Howells complains that "there would be nothing to say, after Mr. Ruskin, in praise or blame of the great monuments in San Giovanni e Paolo, even if I cared to discuss them."[41] Visiting Venice ten years later, Henry James wrote of the same sense of déjà vu and felt that the traveler was henceforth doomed always to experience Venice at second hand, through the refractions of innumerable books and photographs. In Howells's *A Fearful Responsi-*

41 Howells, *Venetian Life,* p. 164.

bility, Elmore tries to write the history of Venice, but fails, returning to his small American university town with the mission unaccomplished. The quandary encountered by Elmore here is a breakdown between American signifier and European signified. Venice cannot be inscribed by Elmore because the object is too tricky and chameleonic for his literal American mind to "capture." The devious complexities and multiple reflections of this watery city resist being subjugated by Elmore's innocent, egocentric romanticism.

In *Indian Summer,* Florence is another city described as "so well known that it affects one somewhat like a collection of views of itself" (8). The jaded behavior of Colville in his romance with Imogen similarly betrays the fictional hero's uneasy sense of having played a part in this kind of scene before. He declares to Imogen at one point "that if they loved each other they need not regard any one else," going on to remark to himself that this speech "did not strike him as of very original effect, and it was with a dull surprise that he saw it sufficed for her" (213–14). Colville's American romanticism manifests itself in the fact that his not being "original" is deeply disturbing to his sense of identity. But in Catholic Europe no individual can be wholly original; even sadness "lacks novelty" and is "a sort of plagiarism," as Ferris tells Florida Vervain in *A Foregone Conclusion.*[42] Various self-reflexive and intertextual references reinforce this sense of solid ground being cut from under the characters' feet. In *Indian Summer,* Colville and Mrs. Amsden wonder at one point whether they might be characters in a novel by James or Howells, while Imogen Grahame and Mr. Morton peruse a copy of Hawthorne's *Marble Faun,* as though their subjectivity were becoming transformed into an object emanating from within Hawthorne's text. In James's *The Sense of the Past,* Ralph Pendrel – who "wished he had been a Catholic" – also finds himself thinking back to *The Marble Faun,* and here this intertextual retrospection implies how the past becomes an active agent in determining the direction of present and future.[43]

What is lost in this hall of mirrors is the "aura" of self-validating presence. These authors, educated within a culture of romanticism, express frustration that art (and, by extension, life) can no longer bear that "original relation to the universe" Emerson eulogized; again, the old iconography of Europe has translated original subjects into plagiarized objects. This carries distinct resonances of those first complaints against Catholicism by Luther, Calvin, and other church Reformers: that its practices were too mechanical, that it did not allow enough scope for human originality and individual communication with God. The dilem-

42 Howells, *Foregone Conclusion,* p. 165.
43 Henry James, *The Sense of the Past* (New York: Scribner's, 1917), p. 89.

mas of the Reformation are reworked by these American authors not only in the foregrounding of themes about innocence and corruption but also through the more general representation (and problematization) of character and image.

Responses from American writers to this threat to spiritual freedom were various. When Edith Wharton discovered that the statues and build-ings of Italy had become "stiffened" and "conventionalized by being too long used as the terms in which Italy is defined," she comfortably as-sumed that the visitor could simply withdraw behind the "ornamental facade" of all these tourist attractions and seek refuge instead in *Italian Backgrounds* – the title of her 1905 travel book – where the country's true "enchanted spirit" and "imagination" were still to be found.[44] By shifting her attention from foreground to background, Wharton attempts to rein-vent Italy in the romantic image of arcadia, a rural paradise of humble stonemasons and village peasants. Yet there is an intimation in other American accounts of Europe around this time that Wharton's simple, pastoral strategy would no longer suffice. Several American texts of the late nineteenth century come to perceive resemblances between the im-personal structures of Catholicism and the modes of mechanical repro-duction demanded by industrial civilization. Indeed, the imagery of Catholicism is sometimes requisitioned as an expression of wider social and philosophical dilemmas introduced by the Gilded Age. Wharton's *Italian Backgrounds* suggests it is possible to avoid all this fakery and vulgarity by moving back from the city to the country, in a microcosm of the Puritans' original errand into the wilderness. For James and How-ells, though, these dislocated, disingenuous signifiers have become part of the larger quandary of the age.

Indian Summer affords a good example of this predicament. Colville laments here how the new economic climate in America has contributed to "the type of hard materialism which we produce in young girls, perfectly wide awake, disenchanted, unromantic, who prefer the worldly vanities and advantages deliberately and on principle, recognizing some-thing better merely to despise it" (29). These, of course, are just the kind of cynical and "unromantic" qualities that, according to American writ-ers, have been prevalent in Catholic Italy for centuries. But the national distinctions can no longer be maintained: Colville's American idealism has elided into a weary European acquiescence to cyclic repetition, just as in a wider conceptual sense the wealth and chicanery at the papal court of the Borgias have also turned full circle and manifested themselves within the materialistic climate of late-nineteenth-century America. In *Agnes of Sorrento,* Stowe played the purity of America off against the

44 Edith Wharton, *Italian Backgrounds* (New York: Scribner's, 1905), pp. 177–8.

decadence of the Borgias, but such a clear-cut bifurcation has now become untenable; the United States is forfeiting its myth of pastoral uniqueness and becoming incorporated within a world of universal repetitions and corruption. *Indian Summer* valiantly attempts to assert the differences between American romanticism and European Catholicism but is eventually obliged to acknowledge the underlying similarities as well. Catholicism is a "gilded religion for a gilded age," as T. J. Jackson Lears put it, no longer something for Protestants to define themselves against, but an image of the wealth and moral laxity in which they too have become ensnared.[45]

Thorstein Veblen's *Theory of the Leisure Class* was not published until 1899, but this fear of becoming strangled by decadent and "overcivilized" European traditions was widespread in the United States before then. Of course, this subversion of liberal optimism and the power of individual autonomy had many different causes: the growth of capitalist corporations, the rise of "naturalist" philosophies, and other factors all contributed at this time to what Alan Trachtenberg has called "the incorporation of America." Trachtenberg analyzed how a general sense of concern about the tentacles of "corporate power" began to throw into doubt the ideology of the self-made man: "The prospect of a mechanization of moral choice raised fears particularly among Americans clinging to a Protestant belief in free will, in the efficacy of human effort, and especially in the value of a properly trained and disciplined 'character.'"[46] What I want to suggest is not that the Catholic church was responsible for this displacement of subjectivity, but that it came in some texts to represent a rationalization of this sense of slippage the culture as a whole was experiencing. Disturbed at a world where behavior seemed increasingly determined by factors external to individual choice, American writers sublimated this general sense of anxiety by resurrecting the oldest symbol of oppressive impersonality in the national consciousness, the Catholic church. In the American imagination, Catholicism has traditionally represented everything that is the antithesis of individual liberty. Yet although Howells tries to use the church as an image of that from which America has escaped, he ends up using the church as an image of America itself. When he analyzes Colville's inability to represent his world literally in Florence, Howells is also implicitly expressing reservations about a failure to find points of literality or origin within the United States. He writes about Europe because Europe is where landscapes are traditionally overdetermined, elusive, difficult to pin down;

---

45 Lears, *No Place of Grace,* p. 193.
46 Alan Trachtenberg, *The Incorporation of America: Culture and Society in the Gilded Age* (New York: Hill and Wang, 1982), pp. 17, 45.

but his problem is that this sense of complexity is now also part and parcel of the United States.

As Howells himself associated his mode of realism with a common-sense, middle-class optimism, so the problematization of this realism raises doubts about the freedom of his characters to channel their lives along the lines of thrift, diligence, and "smiling" morality. Thus in *A Hazard of New Fortunes* (1890), we find New York City resisting representation: nobody can quite fathom what social and economic forces are driving the lives of these citizens and, as Amy Kaplan put it, Howells's text "exposes the drive toward moral unity in realism as a dream of mastery to compensate for the lack of control."[47] From this perspective, Basil March's visit to matins at Grace Church on Broadway becomes an image of withdrawal from these constantly frustrated aspirations toward rational "mastery." Although this is an Episcopalian church, it is associated by March with the "purely pagan impulse" he had experienced when visiting churches in Italy; March thinks he and his wife are visiting the church, with its "painted light" and "hallowed music," simply to "gratify an aesthetic sense, to renew the faded pleasure of travel for a moment, to get back into the Europe of our youth," yet the visit also symbolizes how March has become a compliant object interpellated within systems he cannot control.[48] Like Strether in Notre Dame Cathedral in James's *The Ambassadors,* the hero's subjugation by the overarching high church comes to imply his subjugation by overarching forces of other kinds.

A similar intimation of the collapse of subjectivism was to perturb Theodore Dreiser, when he visited St. Peter's Square in Rome as *A Traveller at Forty.* "It was really so large," he says, "and so tangled historically, and so complicated in the history of its architectural development, that it was useless for me to attempt to synchronize its significance in my mind. I merely stared, staggered."[49] Once again, the narrator finds he cannot dominate and overhaul the Catholic object within his own mind. As a lapsed Catholic himself, Dreiser's attitude to religious culture was interwoven with all kinds of bitter ambivalences, as we shall see later. Yet it is appropriate here to point out that in this travelogue Dreiser comes to perceive implicit parallels between the corruptions of the medieval papacy and the corruptions of modern America. He talks of the "cruelties of lust and ambition" prevalent within the courts of the Borgias, but while condemning the Church's "intellectual stagnation and

---

47 Amy Kaplan, "'The Knowledge of the Line': Realism and the City in Howells's *A Hazard of New Fortunes,*" *PMLA,* 101 (1986), 79.
48 William Dean Howells, *A Hazard of New Fortunes* (Bloomington: Indiana Univ. Press, 1976), p. 54.
49 Theodore Dreiser, *A Traveller at Forty* (New York: Century, 1923), p. 322.

pharisaism," he still cannot, he admits, also "help feeling the power and scope of this organization."[50] As William Vance has noted, the virtues and vices Dreiser "ascribes to the Borgias are recognizably those of his own ambiguous American hero, the financier, Frank Cowperwood."[51] That greedy desire for power so evident among the Italian aristocracy comes to foreshadow the mercenary social and economic creeds of the United States in the Gilded Age. "I think," says Dreiser, "we make a mistake when we assume that the manners, customs, details, conversation, interests and excitement of people anywhere were ever very much different from what they are now." Even more specifically, he claims that "there is close kinship between us and Italy" and that America has "rivaled [Italy] most closely in their periods of greatest achievement."[52] Not for Dreiser that "plain old Adam, the simple genuine self against the whole world" whom Emerson celebrated as an epitome of the new Eden.[53] Dreiser denies America's cultural originality, denies its fundamental innocence, denies to its people the possibility of romantic individualism.

One noticeable phenomenon is how these metaphorical representations of Catholicism suggest the apparent antithesis of Frederick Jackson Turner's famous "frontier thesis," first promulgated in 1893. Turner's emphasis was upon the "dominant individualism" of the American character, whose active engagement with the ever-changing frontier supposedly epitomized the national openness to psychological flexibility and cultural mobility.[54] Yet Turner's reconstitution of the archetypal American flight westward was itself a reaction to the increasingly uncertain identity of America in a time of growing urbanization, immigration, and "incorporation," and in this light we can see how the metaphorical reification of Catholicism within American discourse works in parallel with, not in opposition to, the Turner thesis. Both modes are responses to pressures on subjectivity and autonomy: Turner reacts by idealizing the West as a locus of freedom from the rigid structures of the East and Europe; other writers react by attempting figuratively to explain this new state of bondage in terms of the time-honored oppressions of Romanism. "Railway terminals and hotels are to the nineteenth century what monasteries and cathedrals were to the thirteenth," asserted the

50 Ibid., pp. 336, 347.
51 William L. Vance, *America's Rome* (New Haven: Yale Univ. Press, 1989), II, 45.
52 Dreiser, *Traveller at Forty*, pp. 386, 397.
53 See R. W. B. Lewis, *The American Adam: Innocence, Tragedy, and Tradition in the Nineteenth Century* (Chicago: Univ. of Chicago Press, 1955), p. 6.
54 Frederick Jackson Turner, *The Significance of the Frontier in American History*, ed. Harold P. Simonson (New York: Ungar, 1963), p. 57.

journal *Building News* in 1875.[55] By no means all Americans were happy with such widespread reemergence of monasteries and cathedrals, though, and the uneasy projection of Catholic icons in Howells, James, Dreiser, and other turn-of-the-century authors testifies to this general sense of cultural anxiety.

One response to this potential dissolution of American national identity was to go back to Europe, note all the demeaning corruption and slavery prevalent there, and escape from Europe once again in an action designed to recapitulate the flight of the first settlers. In the years immediately after the Civil War, when the foundational ideas of the United States seemed particularly unstable, Mark Twain tried to recharge the worn batteries of innocence in his enormously popular account *The Innocents Abroad* (1869), a book that sold some hundred thousand copies in its first two years of publication. Here the European traveler satirizes Catholic obsession with relics ("We could not bring ourselves to think St. John had two sets of ashes"), lampoons the "huge, coarse frescoes of suffering martyrs," and chastises the "useless trumpery of churches all over Italy" as being "one vast museum of magnificence and misery."[56] Twain reaches the familiar American conclusion that the ignorance and backwardness of European peoples derive to a large extent from the machinations of the church, which prefers to keep its subjects in intellectual darkness so that the importunities of reason might not disturb the serenity of blind faith: "The good Catholic Portugese crossed himself and prayed God to shield him from all blasphemous desire to know more than his father did before him. . . . It is in communities like this that Jesuit humbuggery flourishes."[57]

That more insidious sense of equivalence between European and American systems of oppression, such as Melville outlines in *Benito Cereno,* is taken up by Twain in his later work *A Connecticut Yankee at King Arthur's Court* (1889). In *Connecticut Yankee,* analogies begin to emerge between the European paradigms of ignorance and bondage (in this case, the feudal framework of medieval England) and those practices of racial slavery still prevalent within the nineteenth-century United States. Moreover, the sense of deceitfulness or duplicity Twain finds in Europe – symbolized most clearly by the Italian twins in *Pudd'nhead Wilson,* a perfect image of doubling and duplication – is itself paralleled by that paradoxical mirroring or twinning built into the very structure of Twain's language. To take just one example from *The Innocents Abroad:* "'See Naples and die.' Well, I do not know that one would necessarily die after merely

---

55 Trachtenberg, *Incorporation of America,* p. 120.
56 Mark Twain, *The Innocents Abroad* (New York: Harper, 1911), I, 218, 268, 329.
57 Ibid., 87, 89.

seeing it, but to attempt to live there might turn out a little differently."[58]
The comedy here operates on a principle of paradoxical reversal: Twain
takes delight in confounding the reader's normal expectations about Naples by bathetically shifting the possibility of death from a romantic to
a criminal context. Twain is iconoclastically inverting traditional notions
of Naples, of course, but the point is that his humor depends for its effect
upon our knowledge and recognition of those traditional ideas. In the
same way, the whole representation of Catholicism in *The Innocents
Abroad* could be said to depend upon this process of paradoxical reversal:
the comic satire is entirely dependent upon, and in thrall to, the object
it is satirizing. Twain's understanding of America is paradoxically dependent upon Europe, his conception of Protestantism dependent upon
a protest against Catholicism.

The inherently duplicitous nature of this invention of America, its
reflexive incarnation as "the Other's Other" as Leslie Fiedler put it, brings
about further complications in the American mythologizing of Catholic
Europe.[59] Duplicity or deceit is, of course, alleged to be a Catholic
characteristic – "it must be confessed that in Italy it does not seem to be
thought shameful to tell lies," complains Howells in *Venetian Life* – and
Howells's Italian texts are, like James's, scattered with images of this
endless dance of duplication and reduplication, which in Europe comes
to connote not only simple falsehood but also the mirroring or modu-
lation of one object into another.[60] To take one small but synecdochic
incident from *Indian Summer:* when Colville watches Effie and Mrs.
Bowen drive off in their carriage he sees "two pretty smiles, just alike,
from mother and daughter" (18). Everything in the Italian world appears
part of this landscape of fluidity and merging, the duplication of subjective, individualistic spirit into objective tableaux. This is why the Puritans
hated the production of mirrors during the Renaissance, as Sacvan Bercovitch has noted, because such processes of mirroring threaten to fracture the autonomy of the individual soul.[61] Yet in Howells this
duplication cannot be confined to the Machiavellian European world
because it comes also to infiltrate his own methods of artistic composition. Although Howell's texts generally contain many disparaging references to masquerades and fictions – particularly those texts set in
Venice, which he describes in *Venetian Life* as "to the other cities like
the pleasant improbability of the theatre to every-day, commonplace

58 Twain, *Innocents Abroad,* II, 30.
59 Leslie Fiedler, Afterword, *The Innocents Abroad,* by Mark Twain (New York: New
   American Library, 1966), p. 478.
60 Howells, *Venetian Life,* p. 361.
61 Sacvan Bercovitch, *The Puritan Origins of the American Self* (New Haven: Yale Univ.
   Press, 1975), p. 14.

life" – nevertheless the fundamental paradox of Howells's art is that he can manufacture his "realism" only by reproducing, and then parodying, those artificial stereotypes he so much despises. "Theatrical" is a derogatory adjective in Howells, betokening posturing self-indulgence; nevertheless, Howells can never quite manage to suppress the theatrical elements in his own fiction. The Catholic priest in *A Foregone Conclusion* complains of enduring "the life-long habit of a lie" in the profession of his faith, but Howells endures the lifelong habit of a lie in another way, by his career as a fabulist.[62]

In this way, Howells's technique of iconoclastic realism can be seen as a microcosm of the wider, paradoxical iconoclasm of Protestant culture: it must invent stereotypes to protest against, but in that very act of protest the text folds back upon itself and betrays the existence of those categories it had hoped to suppress. This is one reason for the repeated emphasis in Howells's novels upon the complexities and frustrations of artistic representation. In *A Foregone Conclusion,* Ferris tries to paint the priest Don Ippolito as he "really" is, but the artist finds himself unable to avoid confronting all those stereotypes and cultural assumptions that are necessarily brought to bear upon any given object: "It was the half expectation of coming sometime upon the lurking duplicity in Don Ippolito, that continually enfeebled the painter in his attempts to portray the Venetian priest."[63] What the narrator nostalgically hankers after is that point of pure origin, pure realism, which has become impossible to achieve, especially in the context of overdetermination that constitutes the condition of culture in the late nineteenth century. Through his critique of Ferris, Howells chronicles a desire for singularity and literalism, which, as his text implicitly recognizes, no longer seems available to the modern artist. Indeed, it is as though Howells tries to transfer the guilt of his own (inevitable) novelistic stereotypes by mocking the creation of artistic stereotypes by another fictional character within his novel. Just as the old device of a "play within a play" is supposed to lend greater verisimilitude to a theatrical experience, so Howells devises a "stereotype within a stereotype" in an ingenious but ultimately doomed attempt to cut away the layers of duplicity that enfold his art.

These negotiations with duplicity create a radically destabilized landscape where nothing can ever be quite what it seems. Again, Catholicism is not the only cause of this kind of irony, but the image of the church provides for American authors an external correlative to their sense of a world dislodged from local autonomy and comprised instead of multiple

62 Howells, *Venetian Life,* p. 10; *Foregone Conclusion,* p. 137.
63 Howells, *Foregone Conclusion,* p. 82.

interlocking strands. In the first years of the twentieth century, Henry Adams attempted to do justice to the universal complexity of this new industrial era by evoking elaborate parallels between modern America and medieval Catholicism. Adams disavowed the simple notion of ornate churches offering a comfortable retreat from the commercial and scientific cares of the Gilded Age. On the contrary, Adams's best-known image of Catholicism derives from his parallel between the Virgin and the dynamo: for early-twentieth-century man, says Adams, the dynamo is "a symbol of infinity," just as in medieval Europe "the Virgin had acted as the greatest force the Western world ever felt."[64] In his essay *Mont Saint Michel and Chartres* (1904), Adams complains that the unity of the twelfth century, symbolized by the Virgin Mary and epitomized by the popularity of the Crusades and the Song of Roland, has gradually disintegrated into the "complexity, multiplicity, variety, and even contradiction" of the present day.[65]

The posthumous discovery of manuscripts inscribed to the Virgin of Chartres has suggested to some Catholic historians that Adams may at some point have seriously considered converting to the Roman faith. Nevertheless, Adams's writing, like that of Norton and Henry James, usually preserves a detached and at times patronizing attitude toward the medieval church: "The twelfth and thirteenth centuries believed in the supernatural, and might almost be said to have contracted a miracle-habit, as morbid as any other form of artificial stimulant; they stood, like children, in an attitude of gaping wonder before the miracle of miracles which they felt in their own consciousness."[66] It is, however, a refusal fully to believe in the authenticity of these scenes he describes that constitutes the modernity of Adams's work. He paints an absurd picture of a world where every medieval nobleman and warrior "from the Welsh Marches to the shores of the Dead Sea" happily intoned the Song of Roland, but what prevents this vision from relapsing into facile nostalgia for an imaginary unity is Adams's self-conscious recognition of its fictional status. He openly acknowledges how this notion of social unity was a chimera even in the twelfth century: "We have got always to make allowances for what was going on beneath the surface in men's minds, consciously or unconsciously, and for the latent scepticism which lurks behind all faith," says Adams. "The Church itself never quite accepted the full claims of what was called Mariolatry."[67] By extension,

64 Henry Adams, *The Education of Henry Adams*, ed. Ernest Samuels (Boston: Houghton Mifflin, 1973), pp. 380, 388.
65 Henry Adams, *Mont Saint Michel and Chartres*, ed. Raymond Carney (Harmondsworth: Penguin, 1986), p. 357.
66 Ibid., p. 237.
67 Ibid., pp. 34, 95.

we are invited to deconstruct Adams's own picturesque fabrications and to uncover the "latent scepticism" underlying them. Being himself part of that confused and contradictory modern era which he describes, Adams admits (in *The Education*) that the historian must operate "without assuming anything as true or untrue, except relation." He goes on to insist: "One sought no absolute truth. One sought only a spool on which to wind the thread of history without breaking it."[68]

From this angle, the reader becomes free to reinterpret Adams's own fictions in a metaphorical or "relative" rather than literal sense. It then becomes apparent that, like James, Adams is fascinated by Catholicism as an image of displacement and impersonality. Visiting Rome in 1859, Adams notes that the city "dwarfs teachers"; like the character of Hilda in Hawthorne's *Marble Faun*, Adams's native Protestant soul is overwhelmed and not a little perturbed by this landscape of failed empires and the melancholy grandeur of ruined civilizations. "Rome could not be fitted into an orderly, middle-class, Bostonian, systematic scheme of evolution," he says. "No law of progress applied to it."[69] This reading of Rome in fact anticipates Adams's argument later in *The Education* about how, in the early twentieth century, individual willpower is necessarily becoming superseded by a more abstract conception of "force" or "energy": "Adams . . . began to mimic Faraday's trick of seeing lines of force all about him, where he had always seen lines of will."[70] The Bostonian emphasis upon individual self-improvement and moral freedom has become anachronistic. Like Henry James in his last great novels, Adams perceives the "mighty machinery" of the Catholic universe to be a mirror of that new, modernist world where energy must be understood within a relative and universalist framework. As in Aquinas, every object must be analogically related to a larger structure rather than seen simply in terms of its autonomous responsibility to itself.

All this constitutes a radical departure from the separatist logic of Protestant aesthetics. Perry Miller emphasized how the plain style of the early Puritans involved a rigorous attempt to "chain . . . language to logical propositions," or, as Michael Wigglesworth put it at the time, the propensity "readily to express in words what the mind in thought conceives."[71] Charles Feidelson, in his account of *Symbolism in American Literature,* similarly stressed how this Puritan temper tended to place emphasis upon carefully constructed ratiocination rather than the more speculative and insubstantial category of rhetoric. Calvinism's insistence

---

68 Adams, *Education*, pp. 435, 472.
69 Ibid., pp. 91–2.
70 Ibid., p. 426.
71 Perry Miller, *The New England Mind: From Colony to Province* (Cambridge, Mass: Harvard Univ. Press, 1953), p. 12.

upon rigid distinctions between the unspeakable realm of spirit and the purely demystified realm of matter formed a stark contrast to Catholicism's fanciful rhetorical analogies between these two spheres. This Calvinist logic of separation modulated in the nineteenth century into Protestantism's mental and linguistic "habit of picturing nature in atomistic form," in terms of strictly logical chains of cause and effect: Feidelson quoted A. N. Whitehead's observation on how this Protestant rationalism could be seen as a theological counterpart to the rationalizing impulses of modern science.[72] Again, an implicit religious ideology was in fact helping to define and support a supposedly neutral professional practice. For Henry Adams, however, the ultimate significance of the Madonna is precisely that she connotes a world beyond the confines of such Protestant reason and logic. Like a prototypic advocate of *écriture féminine*, the Virgin's intuitive and irrational sensibility disregards any law, dogma, or conventional morality she finds tiresome. The implication here is of an ontological incongruity between "divine" grace and human rationality, an incongruity that exposes the pitiful inadequacy of Bostonian moralists' attempts to aggrandize their own ethical imperatives into objectively verifiable truths. Like James in *The Golden Bowl* and *The Portrait of a Lady*, Henry Adams exploits Catholicism as an image of a world too subtle and intricate for Protestant ratiocination to gain mastery over.

It is apparent, then, that American non-Catholic writers of the nineteenth century mythologized Catholic Europe as something quite different from that everyday religion practiced by the lower-class masses of American Catholic immigrants. For the non-Catholics, the rationales of theology were more or less ignored; Adams is much less interested in Aquinas's Scholastic ideas than in the Church's irrational and illogical power, as revealed in the image of the Madonna. Catholicism also functions as the objective correlative of a world where everything has a double, or duplicitous, constitution: Adams's architectonic vision embraces man as both independent and dependent, both skeptical and believing. We see here an "acceptance of a fragmented self in a fragmented universe," in Lears's phrase, which moves away from humanist and meliorist versions of social progress, substituting instead the notion of man as an object interpellated within a world he can no longer fully control. Adams finds he cannot become the detached, transcendentalist seer of New England legend because he finds himself, as Carolyn Porter put it, "a participant in, as well as an observer of, the events whose progress he is designed to measure."[73]

---

72 Feidelson, *Symbolism and American Literature*, p. 86.
73 Lears, *No Place of Grace*, p. 296; Carolyn Porter, *Seeing and Being: The Plight of the*

It is this loss of Emersonian originality, this displacement of the romantic subject, that reestablishes conceptual ties between Protestant America and Catholic Europe. By problematizing the myth of individual selfhood, Catholicism operates also to interrogate received notions of American national identity with its supposed destiny of exceptionalism. The late nineteenth century was a time when the Old World and the New were being brought closer together not only geographically – thanks to more efficient modes of travel and telecommunications – but also metaphorically. Amid the corruptions of the Gilded Age, the time-honored corruptions of the Catholic church seemed to imply a world in which America was, ultimately, just the same as everywhere else.

Participant Observer in Emerson, James, Adams, and Faulkner (Middletown, Conn.: Wesleyan Univ. Press, 1981), p. 168.

Part II

The Ironies of Modernism

5

Modernism, Metaphor, and Ambivalence

In the nineteenth century, we can trace a fairly clear distinction between the beliefs of American Catholic immigrants and the views of those non-Catholic Americans who glamorously mythologized the Old World faith. In the early twentieth century, we find a similar dichotomy between writers for whom Catholicism constituted a native culture and those who viewed it, from an external perspective, as an interesting metaphorical concept. This division does not take as rigid a form as in the nineteenth century: many of the most significant early-twentieth-century writers from within a Catholic culture were apostates – Kate Chopin, Theodore Dreiser, Eugene O'Neill – while, conversely, some of those who mythologized Catholicism from outside (such as Hemingway) were tempted, at least temporarily, to embrace the content as well as the form of Catholic ideas.

Catholicism's cultural image in the early twentieth century came to be associated with that discomforting complexity thought to be characteristic of modernist miscegenation and ambivalence. One of the sharpest representations of this new stereotype appears in William Faulkner's *Absalom, Absalom!* (1936), where the "foreign and paradoxical" qualities of the mulatto Charles Bon, "a Catholic of sorts," pose a threat to the "fierce proud mysticism" of Henry Sutpen's "peculiarly Anglo-Saxon" and "puritan heritage."[1] Although Faulkner is concerned in this novel with exploring the limitations of Sutpen's Protestant sensibility, we see here a reworking of that intransigent nineteenth-century antithesis whereby Catholicism is positioned as a potential subversion of the autonomous Puritan spirit. The difference here is one of emphasis. In *Absalom, Absalom!* Charles Bon's sophisticated experience appears to mock Henry Sutpen's provincial innocence, and in this sense Faulkner's text reflects that widespread rebellion in the early twentieth century against

---

1 William Faulkner, *Absalom, Absalom!* (New York: Random House, 1936), pp. 108, 94.

III

the cultural values of Puritanism. The Victorian mythology that reified conceptions of Protestant optimism and independence in contradistinction to what Oscar Handlin called Catholicism's "deep-rooted pessimism about the world and man's role in it" becomes modified into a modernist division whereby Catholicism is envisioned as a welcome antidote to the philistine values of the "Booboisie," as H. L. Mencken called them.[2] This process of inversion manifests itself in some of John Steinbeck's novels as well: in the 1935 *Tortilla Flat,* for example, Catholicism is seen as an emblem of pastoral retreat from the repressive and self-righteous pieties of the Methodist community in Pacific Grove, which attempts to eradicate prostitution and other vices. By extension, this process of rebellion with which the text's "Catholicism" is associated also connotes a critique of the more general "Protestant" values of self-discipline and the work ethic. Steinbeck's fuzzy mysticism is designed to celebrate the sanctity of nature, as epitomized in Saint Francis, linked by the author with San Francisco. Since the Spanish and Mexican *paisanos* are considered closer to these elemental values than the more cerebral WASP Americans, Pilon's Latin incantation of the Hail Mary and Danny's role as "celebrant" at a party where red wine flows freely show Steinbeck transforming and domesticating religious motifs so as to eulogize the alleged glories of primitivism.[3]

According to Richard Hofstadter, it was this age of modernism, and especially the 1920s, that "proved to be the focal decade in the *Kulturkampf* of American Protestantism. . . . The older, rural and small-town America, now fully embattled against the encroachments of modern life, made its most determined stand against cosmopolitanism, Romanism, and the skepticism and moral experimentalism of the intellegentsia."[4] Small-town Protestantism was feeling itself on the brink of declining into a moral minority. In a statistical sense these fears were quite groundless, but the myth of infiltration by "Romanism" was a powerful one, inspired partly by the second great wave of immigration from Europe that reached its apogee between 1905 and 1910. In *The American Scene* (1907), Henry James portrays himself returning to inspect "the fine old disinterested tradition" of Boston, but being chastened to find the city now overrun with immigrants, or "saturated with the foreign mixture" as James puts it.[5] "No note of any shade of American speech struck my ear," he complains; "the people before me were gross aliens to a man, and they were in serene and triumphant possession." Here again we hear the

2 Oscar Handlin, *Boston's Immigrants: A Study in Acculturation,* 2nd ed. (1959; rpt. New York: Atheneum, 1976), p. 125.
3 John Steinbeck, *Tortilla Flat* (New York: Random House, 1935), p. 297.
4 Richard Hofstadter, *Anti-Intellectualism in American Life* (London: Cape, 1964), p. 123.
5 Henry James, *The American Scene* (London: Chapman and Hall, 1907), pp. 255, 232.

supercilious note typical of James's travel writing, although in bemoaning the loss of "'my' small homogeneous Boston of the more interesting time," the world of Emerson, Thoreau, and Longfellow that now seems to him "picturesquely medieval," James is implicitly ironizing his own narrative tone, enjoying the comic representation of himself as a hopeless old fuddy-duddy out of touch with these modern times.[6] Nevertheless, what was for James a disappointing if vaguely humorous tourist experience was for resident American citizens a concrete and at times intimidating social fact. In the year James published *The American Scene,* there were 1,285,000 immigrants to the United States.[7] Amid the rapidly expanding landscapes of urban, industrial, and cosmopolitan America, the old pieties of rural life seemed to be fading fast.

Out of this refurbished, cross-pollinated culture there arose new critical perspectives that rejected as anachronistic the narrower ranges of New England transcendentalism and Victorian idealism. In *The Wine of the Puritans* (1909), Van Wyck Brooks, himself of Irish ancestry, ridiculed the desiccated character and disembodied vision of nineteenth-century American writers who, according to Brooks, betrayed their Puritan ancestry by lacking any "vital connection" with the more robust, Rabelaisian realities of life.[8] In *America's Coming-of-Age* (1915), Brooks similarly celebrated American culture's emergence from those shadows of "delicate futility" and "unattached idealism" characteristic of the transcendentalists. In longer critical works like *The Ordeal of Mark Twain* (1919) and *The Pilgrimage of Henry James* (1925), Brooks continued to analyze what he considered to be the solipsism of the Puritan and romantic traditions, their loss of any sense of phenomenal objective reality.[9]

Another central figure in this cultural rebellion against Puritanism was George Santayana. Santayana was born in Madrid in 1863 of a Catalan mother and taken to New England when he was nine, but his Spanish Catholic heritage never found itself quite at home in the rationalist atmosphere of Boston. Despite his avowed atheism, Santayana's mind is typical of the American Catholic tradition in its intense sensitivity to tensions arising from an antagonism between his cultural inheritance and his patriotic allegiance. Santayana's antipathy toward the Protestant work ethic and liberal ideals of social progress caused him to enjoy a rebarbative relationship with Charles Eliot, the president of Harvard, where San-

---

6 Ibid., pp. 231, 245.
7 See Malcolm Bradbury and Howard Temperley, eds., *Introduction to American Studies* (Harlow, Essex: Longman, 1981), p. x.
8 Van Wyck Brooks, *The Wine of the Puritans: A Study of Present-Day America* (New York: Mitchell Kennerley, 1909), p. 130.
9 "America's Coming-of-Age," rpt. in *Van Wyck Brooks: The Early Years. A Selection from His Works 1908–21,* ed. Claire Sprague (New York: Harper, 1968), p. 118.

tayana taught philosophy. Indeed, around the turn of the century he wrote to William James complaining of "the years of suppressed irritation which I have passed in the midst of an unintelligible, sanctimonious and often disingenuous Protestantism, which is thoroughly alien and repulsive to me."[10]

One theoretical expression of this impatience is *Egotism in German Philosophy* (1915), in which Santayana echoes Brooks's complaint about the solipsism of romantic and transcendentalist modes of thought. In his chapter on "The Protestant Heritage," Santayana clearly links German philosophers' emphasis upon the subjective powers of the will with Protestantism's denial of established church authority:

> Kant was a puritan; he revered the rule of right as something immutable and holy, perhaps never obeyed in this world. Fichte was somewhat freer in his Calvinism; the rule of right was the moving factor in all life and nature, though it might have been betrayed by a doomed and self-seeking generation. Hegel was a very free and superior Lutheran; he saw that the divine will was necessarily and continuously realised in this world, though we might not recognise the fact in our petty moral judgments.[11]

Santayana suggests here that Protestantism's insistence on how "every individual must reinterpret the Bible and the practices of the church in his own spirit" has been inherited by German philosophy. These influences, he claims, have led toward the danger of "egotism," an "exorbitant interest in ourselves, in the medium of thought and action rather than in its objects." One side effect of this is the rejection of the whole notion of "happiness" as unworthy: "low, materialistic, and selfish."[12] Perpetual striving, rather than a contented acquiescing in the external world, is demanded by the tenets of German idealist philosophy. Santayana concludes by explicitly rejecting Kant's notion of the categorical imperative, which, he says, is "nothing but a private perspective"; he insists instead that "the will is absolute neither in the individual nor in humanity." Like Aquinas, Santayana prefers to assert the impersonal validity of the objective world: "Nature is not a product of the mind, but on the contrary there is an external mind, ages prior to any idea of it, which the mind recognises and feeds upon."[13] In his famous 1911 lecture "The Genteel Tradition in American Philosophy," Santayana had similarly associated

---

10 See Norman Henfrey, Introd., *Selected Critical Writings of George Santayana*, I (Cambridge: Cambridge Univ. Press, 1968), 7–8.
11 George Santayana, *The German Mind: A Philosophical Diagnosis* (New York: Crowell, 1968), p. 25. Santayana's *Egotism in German Philosophy* was given this new title for its second edition in 1939.
12 Ibid., pp. 26, 163, 152.
13 Ibid., pp. 167–8.

this "systematic subjectivism" of the German tradition with the Calvinist influences upon nineteenth-century American writers, from Emerson and Whitman through to William James.[14] It was this sense of being alienated from what he conceived to be the mainstream of American thought that led Santayana in 1912 to resign his teaching position at Harvard and to spend the remainder of his life in Europe searching for and analyzing the implications of his own cultural origins.

Santayana's only novel, *The Last Puritan* (1936), is a curious phenomenon that almost entirely eschews mimesis in favor of prolonged philosophical reflection and reverie on the part of its characters. The hero, Oliver Alden, is the "last puritan" of the title, an American youth whose "puritan virtues – his integrity, his courage, his scorn of pleasure, his material resourcefulness," together with his "truly clear and masterful will" – cause him also to become self-centered and unfeeling, especially where women are concerned.[15] Seeking to commandeer the world for his own purposes, Oliver "disliked to feel, and to be compelled to acknowledge, the existence of anything not to be dominated, and not relevant to his own life. Such things, his ego declared, had no right to be there: and yet they were!" (208). Visiting England, Oliver finds he prefers to inspect the historical monuments of Eton during the school holidays, when no rude human presence can disturb his solipsistic aesthetic musings. Conversely, Oliver is much moved by a visit to Emerson's Concord, because there the "pathetic inadequacy" of the "meagre" landscape seems to Oliver to suggest the splendor of "the spirit" that "had disdained to stop and to become material." Concord's "external humility and inward pride," concludes Oliver, are "much like his own" (404). His is a "Nordic" sensibility, a "monorail of sheer will" (18). Oliver equates his own puritan sensibility with the manifest destiny of the United States, which he applauds as having "been established in the full light of experience and reason, all the rubbish of ages cleared away, and all the superfluous fat of old human nature worked off and reduced to clean hard muscle" (237).

Set up against Oliver, we find his uncle Caleb Wetherbee, a Harvard philosopher who disparages Emerson's "self-worship" and subjectivist idea that "the world was . . . made to serve us by illustrating our philosophy" (186). We also encounter the fanciful figure of Oliver's cousin, Mario Van de Weyer, an Italian lapsed Catholic, who in his casual wom-

14 George Santayana, "The Genteel Tradition in American Philosophy," in George Santayana, *The Genteel Tradition: Nine Essays,* ed. Douglas L. Wilson (Cambridge, Mass: Harvard Univ. Press, 1967), p. 45.

15 George Santayana, *The Last Puritan: A Memoir in the Form of a Novel* (New York: Scribner's, 1936), pp. 225, 119. Subsequent page references are given in parentheses in the text.

anizing, love of art, and generally spontaneous behavior seems to embody everything Oliver tries to suppress. The reader also makes the acquaintance of Fraulein Irma Scholte, Oliver's German governess, whose eulogy to her native land's "spiritual grandeur" (542) and stretching of "eager hands for ever to the Beyond" (111) allows Oliver to produce a few barbed and very Santayana-like remarks about how the German military effort during the First World War has "faithfully . . . carried out the maxim of their philosophy: the categorical imperative, and the will to dominate" (542). All of these characters are rigid stock types, of course; Santayana was clearly no very brilliant novelist. Yet it is interesting to see how his thematic emphasis upon family ancestry and cultural roots shifts attention away from the freedom of individual character, away from that protoplasmic or "orphaned" quality that allows the liberty to reinvent personal identity, such as Twain describes in *Huckleberry Finn.* In *The Last Puritan,* on the contrary, everything is ancestrally predetermined – Oliver's scrupulosity of spirit is alleged to derive from a "ferocious Calvinist" grandfather (355) – and therefore, in one sense, the formal stereotyping of character becomes part of the meaning of the book.

The text eventually kills Oliver off in a motor accident and chooses to leave Mario victorious by saying that "any future worth having" will spring from men like him rather than from "weedy intellectuals or self-inhibited puritans" (600). Mario's ultimate triumph over Oliver clearly mirrors Santayana's own rejection of the will-to-power endemic in romantic philosophy. And yet the final word here points to cultural relativism: Mario suggests that all dogmatic philosophers should really be poets, for the cultural fictions they invent create their own internal validity without any claim upon the quality of objective truth. The trouble with philosophers, says Mario, is that they "insist on laying down the law for the universe" (602) rather than admitting the provisional and partial nature of their own idiosyncratic view of the world. This is another example of how "Catholic" culture within the United States, locked as it is within an oppositional status, comes to imply philosophical relativism rather than absolute solutions. It also sheds light upon the artistic constitution of *The Last Puritan,* for despite Oliver's final defeat he is much the strongest and most clearly defined character here; accordingly, within the internal structure of this novel, the pertinence of Oliver's view of the world cannot be simply canceled by the deus ex machina of a motor accident. Because Oliver is a more powerful character than Mario, Santayana's text implicitly gives at least as much weight to Oliver's arguments. Although Santayana's novel ends by ostensibly deriding the "long arctic night" (602) of Oliver's Nordic soul, it is, through its sympathetic representation of the hero, also covertly admiring that Nordic energy and willpower. In this sense, *The Last Puritan* is a novel of cultural ambivalence, which is, like Henry James's novels, delicately balanced between two worlds. The particular conclusion to this plot is less significant than the intricacy of the different forces played off within Santayana's narrative.

Santayana's work was a very considerable influence, both directly and indirectly, in the early twentieth century. Wallace Stevens, who was a student at Harvard in the late 1890s, came under his spell, being especially impressed by Santayana's *Interpretations of Poetry and Religion* (1900), in which he claimed that "religion and poetry are identical in essence" and that religious transubstantiation could be seen as analogous to the metamorphosing power of poetry, described by Santayana as "metrical and euphuistic discourse, expressing thought which is both sensuous and ideal."[16] Stevens celebrated the exiled Santayana in his late poem "To an Old Philosopher in Rome," and during his last illness in 1955 Stevens not only reminisced freely about Harvard and Santayana but, according to Anthony Sigmans, actually converted to Catholicism (although this is a controversial point – Stevens's daughter doubts that her father was ever converted.)[17] T. S. Eliot also heard Santayana lecture at Harvard and was impressed by his deviation from the long-dominant Harvard traditions of Protestant and Anglo-Scottish philosophy. Indeed, Eliot's doctrine of artistic impersonality – "not the expression of personality, but an escape from personality," as he put it in "Tradition and the Individual Talent" – has clear echoes of Santayana's rejection of German romanticism and "Egotism." Santayana's influence on the development of American modernism has generally been underestimated, partly because Harold Bloom and others have displaced Eliot's Anglo-Catholicism in favor of canonizing what Sanford Schwartz has called a "Romantic, radical, and Protestant tradition," supposedly epitomized by Wallace Stevens. While Stevens's work undoubtedly does possess this romantic side, it also embodies a more determinedly impersonal element – "Catholic," in Santayana's mythology – that contemporary American criticism has tended to downplay.[18]

Another American modernist writer who is rarely considered in a Catholic context is Ernest Hemingway. Everybody knows about Hem-

16 *The Works of George Santayana*, II (New York: Scribner's, 1936), 3, 200.
17 See Peter Brazeau, *Parts of a World: Wallace Stevens Remembered* (New York: Random House, 1983), p. 291.
18 For Eliot at Harvard, see Warner Berthoff, *The Ferment of Realism: American Literature, 1884–1919*, 2nd ed. (Cambridge: Cambridge Univ. Press, 1981), p. 175; T. S. Eliot, "Tradition and the Individual Talent," in *Selected Essays*, 3rd ed. (London: Faber, 1951), p. 21; Sanford Schwartz, *The Matrix of Modernism: Pound, Eliot, and Early Twentieth-Century Thought* (Princeton: Princeton Univ. Press, 1985), p. 72.

ingway the alienated tough guy and proto-existentialist, as John Killinger described him.[19] Yet, much to the disapproval of his Congregationalist parents back in Illinois, Hemingway became attracted to Catholicism under the influence of his second wife, Pauline Pfeiffer, whom he married in 1927. In January 1926, shortly before beginning his affair with Pauline, Hemingway wrote: "If I am anything I am a Catholic . . . am not what is called a 'good' Catholic. Think there is a lot of nonsense about the church. Holy Years, etc. What rot. But I cannot imagine taking any other religion seriously."[20] Hemingway's second and third sons were baptized as Catholics, but he himself renounced the faith during the Spanish civil war, partly because he detested the way the church allied itself with Franco. Still, in 1961, despite his suicide, Hemingway was given a Catholic burial. One of Hemingway's biographers, Jeffrey Meyers, followed the traditional critical line by indicating that the writer's relationship with Catholicism was purely superficial and expedient and that Hemingway's "works, during both the Protestant and the Catholic phases of his life, are consistently skeptical about religion and hostile to the Catholic Church." This, however, seems too simplistic. It is true, of course, that Catholicism was "a convenient accommodation that pleased Pauline," and it is also true to say Hemingway viewed with distaste the whole paraphernalia of saints and martyrs as well as the church's prohibitive attitude toward birth control. On the other hand, Hemingway's novels quite overtly display a yearning and "hunger for a Catholic completeness in life," as Flannery O'Connor said of Hemingway in a 1956 letter.[21]

For while Hemingway's heroes remain skeptical about the role of religion in this postwar world, they also regret that skepticism. The hard-boiled existentialist Robert Jordan, embroiled in the Spanish civil war in *For Whom the Bell Tolls* (1940), echoes T. S. Eliot's reworking of St. John of the Cross in "East Coker" as he muses on how "all we know is that we do not know." Strains of forfeited Catholicism similarly echo among the Spanish nationalists as a memento of the world they have lost. "Clearly I miss him, having been brought up in religion," laments Anselmo. "But now a man must be responsible to himself."[22] Another Hemingway hero who is, as he puts it, "technically" a Catholic is Jake

---

19 John Killinger, *Hemingway and the Dead Gods: A Study in Existentialism* (n.p.: Univ. of Kentucky Press, 1960), passim.

20 See Jeffrey Meyers, *Hemingway: A Biography* (London: Macmillan, 1985), p. 184.

21 Ibid., pp. 185–86; Sally Fitzgerald, ed., *The Habit of Being: The Letters of Flannery O'Connor* (New York: Farrar, Straus and Giroux, 1979), p. 130.

22 Ernest Hemingway, *For Whom the Bell Tolls* (New York: Scribner's, 1940), pp. 175, 41.

Barnes in *The Sun Also Rises* (1926). Barnes's sense of metaphysical displacement rises to the surface in a Spanish cathedral at Pamplona:

> At the end of the street I saw the cathedral and walked up toward it. The first time I ever saw it I thought the facade was ugly but I like it now. I went inside. It was dim and dark and the pillars went high up, and there were people praying, and it smelt of incense, and there were some wonderful big windows. I knelt and started to pray and prayed for everybody I thought of.

Barnes, though, finds himself obsessed with his own mundane problems and unable to concentrate on his prayers: "I was a little ashamed, and regretted that I was such a rotten Catholic, but realized there was nothing I could do about it, at least for a while, and maybe never, but that anyway it was a grand religion, and I only wished I felt religious and maybe I would the next time."[23]

In one sense, the ritual of bullfighting offers a potential compensation for the disappearance of this religious institution. Jeffrey Meyers claimed the fate of the matador both in this novel and in *Death in the Afternoon* (1932) works as a parody of the crucifixion, and so indeed it does; but what we also find here is a pattern very familiar within the Catholic tradition, whereby the earthly event parodies the divine image, but the divine image also, and at the same time, sanctifies the earthly event.[24] The bullfight ironizes the crucifixion, but the lurking memory of crucifixion also aggrandizes the bullfight into a memento of divine grace. It is the same kind of oscillation as in the form of mock-heroic, where the travestied ideal object actually elevates its parodic tormentor (Leopold Bloom is humanistically redeemed by Homer's Ulysses even as Bloom travesties him). This might be seen as a literary correlative of that theological conception of *analogica entis,* the analogical interaction between worldly and otherworldly states of being. This is not, of course, to claim that Hemingway was "really" a Catholic. It is simply to point out how the residual influence of Catholic culture continues to be an important determinant within his work.

The modernist movement rediscovered ritual and myth for many different reasons, of course. The widespread feeling after the First World War that the world was now "too huge and complex" for "individualism," which emerges in nearly all of the major writers of this time, could be seen in one way as a literal embodiment of Santayana's philosophical idea about the general inadequacy of "egotism."[25] Individualism,

23 Ernest Hemingway, *The Sun Also Rises* (New York: Scribner's, 1926), pp. 96–97.
24 Meyers, *Hemingway*, p. 186.
25 The phrase is from F. Scott Fitzgerald, *This Side of Paradise* (New York: Scribner's, 1953), pp. 228–29.

romanticism, and the puritanism of what William Carlos Williams was to call the "hard and little" soul all seemed out of date. In his idiosyncratic interpretation of American history, *In the American Grain* (1925), Williams sings the praises of seventeenth-century Jesuit missionary Père Sebastian Rasles, who sought, said Williams, "to hybridize, to crosspollenize" the environment of the pilgrim fathers by introducing influences from French Canada. Williams's denigration of what he sees as Protestantism's dehumanizing and repressive tendencies is very characteristic of this general rebellion against Puritanism in the 1920s: "The Puritan, finding one thing like another in a world destined for blossom only in 'Eternity,' all soul, all 'emptiness' then here, was precluded from SEEING the Indian. They never realized the Indian in the least save as an unformed PURITAN."[26] The hoarding of the English Puritans, both sexually and financially, forms for Williams a stark contrast to the more fertile French and Spanish influences. Whereas the Puritans were prohibitive and legislative toward both themselves and others, Catholics were more prepared to accept the established local culture on its own terms and to create a sense of community from that point of departure. No doubt this was all part of the subtle Jesuit plan to gain power by infiltrating pagan strongholds rather than attempting the more difficult feat of abolishing them entirely; nevertheless, according to Williams, it had the desirable consequence of a greater tolerance of local differences. "One should read [Rasles's] *Lettres Edifiantes*," he says, "I think one would understand better how much we are like the Indians and how nicely Catholicism fits us."[27]

Williams repeated this Catholic theme in a 1927 essay on Joyce's *Finnegans Wake*, which had by then just begun to be serialized in the Parisian magazine *transition*. Here Williams celebrates Joyce's dislocation of the "scientific" style, which supposedly offered clear and transparent access to the object of its contemplation. This redundant "scientific" style Williams associates with the asceticism of English Protestantism: "A full-dressed english which it must have been his delight to unenglish until it should be humanely catholic... The Catholic Church has always been unclean in its fingers and aloof in the head. Joyce's style consonant with this has nowhere the inhumanity of the scientific or protestant or pagan essayist."[28] Moreover, the idea of breaking down both conceptual and linguistic divisions so that the world appears to be "all one in the eyes of God – and man" appeals to Williams as working toward disrupting

---

26 William Carlos Williams, *In the American Grain* (London: MacGibbon and Kee, 1966), pp. 121, 113.
27 Ibid., p. 128.
28 William Carlos Williams, "A Note on the Recent Work of James Joyce," *transition*, no. 8 (1927), pp. 150, 152.

the divisive nature of individual identity. Once again, this process of unification was a central notion of the 1920s: "What we are after will be that certain bent which is peculiar to Joyce and which gives him his value. It is not that the world is round nor even flat, but that it might well today be Catholic; and as a corollary, that Joyce himself is today the ablest protagonist before the intelligence of that way of thinking."[29] There is an implicit equation here between Catholic and catholic. The new universalism of the 1920s, the insistence upon seeing people necessarily in relation to each other rather than as bound, like Hamlet, within their own individual nutshells produces a new sympathy for the idea of global unity (in one form or another). Williams – who had a Puerto Rican mother – is another American modernist writer whose work is not often examined in terms of a religious matrix, although in various reworked and secularized forms this religious matrix came to play a significant part in his thinking.

Williams's intertwining of Catholicism and catholicity also highlights the links between the universalist impulse of the Catholic church and the internationalist emphasis of modernism. As Malcolm Bradbury and others have emphasized, the innovative artistic spirit of modernism was designed to fly by the nets of national culture, to redirect attention away from local realism and toward more cosmopolitan, indeed, global perspectives. In this sense, modernism's hostility to the notion of separatist provincial culture could be seen as a correlative to Catholicism's universalist subversion of the idea of national identity. And from this angle Harold Bloom's attempt to exclude T. S. Eliot from the American "canon," like Philip Larkin's attempt to exclude Eliot and Ezra Pound from the "true" English heritage, might be interpreted as an effort to cling to chimerical conceptions of "genuine" national art in the face of all these radical aesthetic and philosophical cross-pollinations.[30]

This modernist desire to pass beyond what is merely local and contingent also led them toward the establishment of large-scale myths and legends of various kinds. These cultural fictions were supposed to alleviate the plight of alienated modern man, to impose some form of "shape" and "significance" upon the "futility" of modern civilization,

29 Ibid., p. 151.
30 Malcolm Bradbury and James McFarlane, "The Name and Nature of Modernism," in *Modernism, 1890–1930,* ed. Malcolm Bradbury and James McFarlane (Harmondsworth: Penguin, 1976), pp. 29–33; Philip Larkin, Preface, *Oxford Book of Twentieth-Century English Verse* (Oxford: Clarendon Press, 1973), p. v. Here Larkin boasts: "I have not included poems by American or Commonwealth writers, nor poems requiring a glossary for their full understanding." Hence he excludes Pound altogether and chooses nine poems by Eliot, the same number allowed to Edward Thomas.

as Eliot phrased it in his 1923 essay on Joyce.[31] Thus we find every form of idealized social synthesis being promulgated in this interwar period: Eliot's own Anglo-Catholic and royalist model, with its nostalgic vision of an organic Christian community; Yeats's feudal Ireland, staffed with obscure aristocrats from the Celtic twilight; Pound's fascist Italy; Marxist systems by the score; even technological paradises, as in the ascetic purity of Le Corbusier's architecture. All of these fictive utopias were driven by a desire for social and religious replenishment, the urge to invent a secularized modernist *logos,* which would have the power of "recreating God in the artist's image," as Frederick J. Hoffman described it.[32]

These proposed reorganizations of society appear contemporaneously with the widespread revival in Catholic theology of Thomas Aquinas's model for the harmonious restructuring of physical and metaphysical reality. After Pope Leo XIII's condemnation of modernist philosophy at the end of the nineteenth century, approved Catholic thinkers such as Etienne Gilson labored to reestablish and disseminate the doctrines of Thomism, which became institutionalized as the only proper mode of Catholic thought. The papacy continued to cling to these tenets of Scholastic philosophy through the first four decades of the twentieth century; as late as 1931, Pius XI promulgated the encyclical *Quadragesimo anno,* which poured scorn on newfangled ideas such as capitalism and socialism and harked back instead to the glories of medieval Christendom. In his first important work, *Art and Scholasticism,* published in the United States in 1930, French Catholic philosopher Jacques Maritain wrote of the Middle Ages as "the most *spiritual* period to be found in history," an era that offered "an example very nearly realised . . . of principles which the author believes to be true."[33] Maritain's search for what he termed "a truly Catholic, that is to say universal, synthesis," where everything in heaven and on earth would be in its appointed place, involved the imposition of intellectual order upon what he described as "the vast intellectual confusion bequeathed to us by the nineteenth century." Maritain's ambition to dissolve differences in what he called a "metapolitical" vision of universal harmony bears marked similarities to Eliot's classic modernist antithesis of "significance" against "futility," order against chaos.[34] The crucial point here is that despite all the fervent papal attempts to

---

31 "*Ulysses,* Order and Myth," in *Selected Prose of T. S. Eliot,* ed. Frank Kermode (New York: Harcourt Brace Jovanovich, 1975), p. 177.

32 Frederick J. Hoffman, *The Imagination's New Beginning: Theology and Modern Literature* (Notre Dame: Univ. of Notre Dame Press, 1967), p. 4.

33 Jacques Maritain, *Art and Scholasticism, with Other Essays,* trans. J. F. Scanlan (New York: Scribner's, 1930), p. 105.

34 Jacques Maritain, *The Things That Are Not Caesar's,* trans. J. F. Scanlan (New York: Scribner's, 1931), pp. 116, 64; *Art and Scholasticism,* p. 2.

dissociate Catholicism from the heresies of secular philosophy, this ideal-ization of the medieval order by Maritain, Gilson, and other Catholic scholars of this era can be seen as a counterpart to the idealized utopias concocted by Eliot, Yeats, Pound, and other poets and novelists. Gilson looked back to medieval times as the era when Scholasticism was, sup-posedly, incarnated within the structures of society, just as Yeats looked back to an archaic version of feudal Ireland where his mythological fan-tasies might be wedded to corporeal substance.

Whatever the status of these visions in historical terms, then, it is clear the neo-scholastics' dream of universal concord came to influence the thinking of Eliot, Allen Tate, Christopher Dawson, and other Christian litterateurs of the mid-twentieth century. Dawson, a British academic who was to become in 1958 the first professor of Roman Catholic studies at Harvard, produced books such as *Beyond Politics* (1939), in which he echoed the modernists by calling for a redemptive "national unity," an ideal synthesis that could not be achieved "by politics alone" but required the participation of the church to provide overarching symbolism and direction, such as (according to Dawson) the monarchy provides in Brit-ain.[35] Dawson's *Religion and Culture* (1948) is very reminiscent of Eliot's *Idea of a Christian Society,* which was published nine years earlier. Here Dawson advanced his theory of how "religion holds society in its fixed culture pattern" and how it is the "key of history," dictating "the inner form of a society."[36] Dawson perceptively described various ancient cultures to show how "the material and spiritual factors interpenetrate one another so completely that they form an inseparable unity"; however, not content to rest at the level of analysis, Dawson continued here with highly charged rhetoric imploring some new "synthesis," a "profound change in the spirit of modern civilization," a "return to unity," and "spiritual reintegration which would restore that vital relation between religion and culture" he claimed was so sadly lacking in twentieth-century America.[37]

From orthodox theological perspectives, one of the problems with Dawson's kind of imaginative (not to say fanciful) global synthesis was that it could become dangerously metaphorical, and hence heretical. It is not coincidental that Dawson and Allen Tate were both converts to Catholicism: their earnest, self-conscious conceptualization of Catholi-cism as a social construction is quite different in tone from the casual and sardonic acknowledgment of Catholicism as a fait accompli in the works of "cradle" Catholics like Dreiser and Scott Fitzgerald. Both Tate

35 Christopher Dawson, *Beyond Politics* (London: Sheed and Ward, 1939), p. 12.
36 Christopher Dawson, *Religion and Culture* (London: Sheed and Ward, 1948), p. 50.
37 Ibid., pp. 197, 217, 218.

and T. S. Eliot had much sympathy with Charles Maurras and his *Action Française* group, popularly known as the "Catholics without Faith," whose agenda of political and intellectual reaction included a plan not unlike Dawson's to exploit Catholicism as a symbol of social continuity and order: just as Dawson approved of the British monarchy, so Maurras and his followers planned to reinstall the French monarchy as a symbol of national hierarchy and unity. This movement was, however, condemned by Pope Pius XI when he peremptorily excommunicated Maurras in 1926. Maurras, an open agnostic, had strayed too far in the direction of Catholicism as metaphor; yet it was precisely these metaphorical aspects of religion that interested many intellectuals in the modernist era. Santayana and Hemingway, who were never consistent members of the church anyway, explored Catholicism's metaphorical and cultural implications without at all troubling themselves about reaction from Rome. Professed members of the faith such as Tate and Dawson trod a more wary line, attempting to ensure their speculative metaphorical signifiers did not altogether usurp the objective signified of Catholic "truth."

Yet even Maritain, who sought to delineate a purer kind of Thomistic synthesis, did not escape censure from other Catholics for the formalistic and therefore potentially self-referential aspects of his religious writing. In his early career Maritain was a friend of Maurras and was often praised by the *Action Française* group; consequently, Maritain became embroiled in the excommunication fracas of 1926, finding himself required solemnly to disavow any association with the banned group. Even then, however, churchmen's suspicions of Maritain's scholarly activities did not entirely abate. After Maritain's work had become well known to American Catholic intellectuals during the early 1930s, George N. Shuster, who was also prominent in these circles, suggested the precepts of this Thomistic revival might be all rather too rarefied: in particular, Shuster thought that Maritain's vision of universal order was too abstract, too unearthly, not sufficiently focused upon the *quidditas* of the concrete terrestrial object.[38] More recently, Umberto Eco has argued that Maritain's privileging of the "creative intuition" of an artist, whose "speculative intellect" might find "joy" in "the intuitive vision of the Divine Being," is a concept foreign to the objectivist aesthetics of Aquinas himself.[39] According to Eco, Maritain was refracting Scholastic thought through the idiosyncratic lens of Bergsonian modernism, a lens that offered greater

38 See William M. Halsey, *The Survival of American Innocence: Catholicism in an Era of Disillusionment, 1920–1940* (Notre Dame: Univ. of Notre Dame Press, 1980), p. 85.
39 Maritain, *Art and Scholasticism,* p. 5. See also Maritain's *Creative Intuition in Art and Poetry* (New York: Pantheon–Bollingen Foundation, 1953). For Eco's rejoinder, see *The Aesthetics of Thomas Aquinas,* trans. Hugh Bredin (Cambridge, Mass.: Harvard Univ. Press, 1988), pp. 60–3, 252.

license to the subjectivist proclivities of the artist as seer or "major man," in Wallace Stevens's unhappy phrase. Maritain's first book, published in 1913, was indeed an account of *La Philosophie bergsonienne,* and in the eyes of some Church theoreticians the affiliation between Maritain and these major men, the mythographers of modernist aesthetics, was rather too close for comfort.

Maritain was another convert to Catholicism, and in the self-consciousness of his efforts to establish a connaturality between the intuitive scope of the human sensibility and the qualities of divine grace we can hear echoes of the philosophy of Orestes Brownson, whose systems of belief were also perceived by the church as dangerously subjectivist and metaphorical. Again, just as Brownson offended church orthodoxy during the American Civil War by his support for the Union, so Maritain alienated many conservative Catholics during the Spanish civil war by his frequent expressions of animosity toward General Franco. Maritain refused to subscribe to the doctrine that only Franco could save Spain from godless communism; accordingly, he was attacked by traditionalists like Paul Claudel and Reginald Dingle, the latter writing that Maritain's philosophical views "hovered at times on the 'dangerous edge' of material heresy."[40] To be sure, Maritain's work was less ostentatiously provocative than Brownson's. Moreover, during the 1940s and 1950s, the period when Maritain was living and working in the United States, the American church itself was less Jansenistic in outlook, less inclined to treat human nature as inherently bad. Maritain lived to see the Second Vatican Council in the early 1960s, by which time his theological liberalism had been embraced by the institution in a way that Brownson's never was. Nevertheless, as with Brownson, some areas of intellectual tension still remained. Maritain's colleague Yves Simon wrote in 1963 that there had been "many conflicts throughout Maritain's career between his choice and his calling," Simon going on to count it a blessing that there had not been "a single case in which his calling was not preferred to his choice."[41] In a more general sense, though, this modernist ambivalence or incongruity between the "facts" of church dogma and the creative intuitions of human fiction was never quite resolved.

Before the Second World War, of course, these tensions and contradictions were more explicit. While the papacy was no friend of modernism, the whole notion of an American modernism was to add insult to injury as far as Rome was concerned. In the late nineteenth century,

---

40 Reginald P. Dingle, "French Catholics and Politics," *The Month,* no. 171 (Feb. 1938), p. 141.
41 Yves Simon, "Jacques Maritain: The Growth of a Christian Philosopher," in *Jacques Maritain: The Man and His Achievement,* ed. Joseph W. Evans (New York: Sheed and Ward, 1963), p. 24.

it was the "liberal" theological wing that controlled the American Catholic church, with leading ecclesiastical figures such as James Gibbons, John Ireland, and John Spalding attempting "to establish harmony between American institutions and Catholic ideology" by adapting the behavior of the church to the morals of a mobile, expanding American society. This was especially evident in the liberals' stress on individuality and freedom ("under the guidance of the Holy Spirit") as being the key to a contemporary Christian life.[42] While this new emphasis upon individualism fitted well with the American dream, it did not at all find favor with the Italian prelates Archbishop Satolli and Cardinal Mazella, who headed an investigation into the American church in the 1890s and whose advice led to Leo XIII's 1899 apostolic letter *Testem benevolentiae*, in which the pontiff chastised the American church for relaxing the ancient rigor of the faith and becoming too indulgent toward modern theories of individual freedom. This broadside was followed in 1907 by Pope Pius X's more wide-ranging encyclical *Pascendi Dominici Gregis*, which launched a scathing attack on all aspects of late-nineteenth-century learning: theories of evolution, "higher" biblical criticism, Kantianism, Hegelianism, and many other forms of subjectivist error were all to be classified, as far as Pius X was concerned, under the baneful title of modernism, "the heresy of all heresies."

Not surprisingly, "official" Catholic culture in America was cowed for a while by these papal denunciations. The intense theological controversies of the 1880s and 1890s regarding the dynamics of the relationship between Americanism and Catholicism were generally suppressed in favor of adherence to Scholastic orthodoxy. It is ironic that at a time when modernist art was subverting the metaphors of puritanism with metaphors of cosmopolitan catholicity, the American Catholic church itself was sanctioning a reworking of old-fashioned ideas of American "innocence." Michael Williams, who founded the Catholic magazine *The Commonweal* in 1924, attempted to rehouse nineteenth-century romanticism within the "organic reality" of Catholicism and to expel modernist alienation and skepticism in favor of Pollyanna optimism and moral confidence.[43] Some Catholics in the 1920s grasped at the "New Humanism" of Ivy League reactionaries like Irving Babbitt and Paul Elmer More as a bulwark against what they took to be the disintegrative tendencies of modern times. Yet the best authors, as always, refused to acquiesce slavishly in such narrow dogmas. As we have seen, some

42 R. Laurence Moore, *Religious Outsiders and the Making of Americans* (New York: Oxford Univ. Press, 1986), p. 57. The fullest account of this "Americanization" controversy within the Catholic church is Thomas T. McAvoy, C.S.C., *The Americanist Heresy in Roman Catholicism, 1895–1900* (Notre Dame: Univ. of Notre Dame Press, 1963).
43 See Halsey, *Survival of American Innocence*, pp. 20–65.

writers from within a Catholic context took no notice of the papal injunctions against modernism and continued to erect fictionalized myths and humanized rituals, like Hemingway's bullfighting or Joyce's sacramental metamorphoses of daily life, in competition with papal orthodoxies. Others, such as Santayana, were intent upon self-consciously exploring the metaphorical associations of particular religious heritages. Still others, such as Kate Chopin and Eugene O'Neill, played off this rebellious modernist impulse against the forces of Catholic conventionality, thereby setting up fascinating tensions in their work between what one might call – to use the Freudian terminology much in evidence around this time – a modernist ego and a Catholic id.

Kate Chopin's *The Awakening* (1899) is typical of one strand of early-twentieth-century "Catholic" writing in the way it affiliates religion with other repressive social forces that an enlightened individual should attempt to overcome. Chopin, née Katherine O'Flaherty, was born into a strongly Catholic family and educated at Catholic schools in St. Louis, Missouri, moving down to New Orleans in 1871 after her marriage to Oscar Chopin. Although Kate Chopin never publicly repudiated Catholicism, she did not practice it in adult life; nevertheless, traces of this inheritance remain as a significant component of her writings.[44] In *The Awakening,* Chopin carefully delineates the social framework of the Catholic Creoles of Louisiana, that group into which central protagonist Edna Pontellier has married, thereby renouncing the Presbyterianism of her childhood. The New Orleans of this novel is dotted with such curiosities as the Festival twins, "girls of fourteen, always clad in the Virgin's colors, blue and white, having been dedicated to the Blessed Virgin at their baptism."[45] Another strange inhabitant is the enigmatic "lady in black" (43), equipped with her Sunday prayer book and silver rosary beads, who functions as a symbol of that "stifling atmosphere" (36) from which Edna is trying to escape.

The intimate relationship between religion and the novel's thematic axis of repression and liberation becomes explicit when Edna joins a party sailing across the bay for mass at the *Chênière Caminada,* a "quaint little Gothic church of Our Lady of Lourdes." Edna finds this ceremony altogether too much for her to bear: "A feeling of oppression and drowsiness overcame Edna during the service. Her head began to ache, and the lights on the altar swayed before her eyes. Another time she might

---

44 See Paul R. Messbarger, *Fiction with a Parochial Purpose: Social Uses of American Catholic Literature, 1884–1900* (Boston: Boston Univ. Press, 1971), p. 165.
45 Kate Chopin, *The Awakening,* ed. Margaret Culley (New York: Norton, 1976), p. 24. Subsequent page references are given in parentheses in the text.

have made an effort to regain her composure; but her one thought was to quit the stifling atmosphere of the church and reach the open air" (36). For Edna, Catholicism comes to be associated with the world of her husband and therefore with all the more general disappointments of her marriage. Opposed to this suffocating milieu are all the clear vistas promised by her dream of a romance with Robert Lebrun.

It is "dream," though, that is the crucial word here. Lebrun is described by Edna in quasi-religious terms as "the unattainable" (88); she admits she feels closer to him when he is away in Mexico than when he physically presents himself in Louisiana. In fact, Edna is not so much interested in sexual fulfillment as in a form of spiritual fulfillment: she lauds Mademoiselle Reisz's music for its ability "to reach [her] spirit and set it free" (78), for instance; and when she abandons Pontellier, Edna experiences "a feeling of having descended in the social scale, with a corresponding sense of having risen in the spiritual" (93). Indeed, Edna seems willingly to embrace worldly defeat as a sure emblem of spiritual triumph: like the "great tragedian" (19) who haunted her imagination in youth, she yearns for defeat because this will guarantee her martyrlike triumph over the brutalities of material circumstances. Edna's stoic passivity – "she had abandoned herself to Fate, and awaited the consequences with indifference" (103) – is quite different in kind from that energetic, mercenary optimism we see in the feminist heroes of Mary Austin or Willa Cather. Whereas Olivia Lattimore, in Austin's *A Woman of Genius,* and Thea Kronberg, in Cather's *The Song of the Lark,* will their ultimate success, Edna wills her own ultimate failure. She gleefully immerses herself in the sea on the final page of the novel in an act of self-extinction that also symbolizes the rewards of baptism and new life. Again, the "spiritual" overtones in this scene seem more significant to Edna than the mere fact of bodily death. In this way, the Catholic context of Chopin's novel modifies its thematic pattern and compromises the freedom of its heroine.

It is noticeable as well how the language of Catholicism works its way into this novel's structural metaphors. Edna's flight for freedom is represented by a transformed image of the Holy Ghost ascending. Early in the book, Edna is ironically described as possessing "more wisdom than the Holy Ghost is usually pleased to vouchsafe to any woman" (15), and this image expands into the symbolism that serenades Edna's bid to escape from her sluggish social environment: "The bird that would soar above the level plain of tradition and prejudice must have strong wings" (82). Joyce was to use the symbolism of birds and flight in a similar (albeit more sophisticated) way seventeen years later in *Portrait of the Artist as a Young Man,* and conceptual parallels between *The Awakening* and *Portrait* are obvious enough as well. In both cases, we see an apostate modernist soul attempting to slough off the shackles of a repressive Catholic society. Their problem is, of course, that a clean break can never be made. Edna Pontellier's "bird" contracts "a broken wing" and comes "circling disabled down, down to the water" (113), just as the all-pervasive Catholic metaphors of *Portrait* ensure that Stephen Dedalus manifestly fails to fulfill his vow of flying freely away from the nets of the church.

The reasons for this are more than psychological; they have to do with both the generic nature of modernism and, in Chopin's case, the nature of that antithesis into which American Catholicism was locked in the early twentieth century. In the first place, modernism, like any kind of literary modernity, operates only paradoxically. As Paul de Man has said, in the very act of transgressing old boundaries and discarding anachronistic generic conventions, modernity implicitly, if reluctantly, admits its kinship with those antiquated models. Because no greater proximity to the elusive "reality of the moment" is ever possible, modernity will simply reform itself as a new system of signifiers bearing but a tangential relationship with the signified that it attempts to encode.[46] Modernism, that is to say, bears an intertextual and necessarily parodic relationship to writing that has gone before: Joyce and Chopin actually depend upon a Catholic environment so that their modernist freethinking can flourish. Freethinking can never exist in a vacuum, it must always engage in dialogue with the thinking that preceded it. Thus the works of Chopin, like those of Eugene O'Neill and James T. Farrell, are symbiotically intertwined with those very values they are inverting. Although Farrell's novels reject the idea of Catholicism, if Catholicism were to be taken out of them, they would disappear.

Secondly, this paradox can be applied to a more particular cultural situation, insofar as it becomes apparent in retrospect that the American modernist representation of Catholicism was "intertextually" dependent upon those old nineteenth-century stereotypes of Catholicism, whose premises modernism was overturning. That mythology opposing Protestant optimism and free will to Catholic passivity and pessimism is validated rather than interrogated by the plays of Eugene O'Neill, for example, in which the characters seem generally quite unable to escape from the circumstances of their environment or the psychological traumas of their upbringing. This gloom and inertia, which is set within a specifically Catholic milieu in *Long Day's Journey into Night* (1941), is also apparent in many of O'Neill's other plays: in the series of cyclic reflections and fatalistic repetitions underlying the trilogy *Mourning Becomes Electra* (1932), and in the Freudian patterns and obsessions of *Strange*

46 Paul de Man, *Blindness and Insight: Essays in the Rhetoric of Contemporary Criticism,* 2nd ed. (London: Methuen, 1983), p. 162.

Interlude (1928), in which Nina Leeds's compulsion to adhere to the dictates of "God the Father" is transferred from a religious to a psychoanalytical, father-fixated context.[47] O'Neill's leaden symbolism also effectively contributes to this air of claustrophobia: the persistent "fog in the harbor" of *Long Day's Journey* creates an atmosphere within which characters seem to overlap and merge into each other, as though unable to differentiate themselves from their surroundings.

The traditional social locations of Irish-American Catholicism are quite evident in *Long Day's Journey*. Here we find nostalgia for the European homeland, as evidenced by James Tyrone's having "several histories of Ireland" in his bookcase; attachment to the shaping spirit of ancestry, with Tyrone's wife, Mary, claiming "the past is the present isn't it? It's the future too"; a tendency toward alcoholism, manifested in their son, Jamie; a constant fear of poverty and the poorhouse; a consequent burning desire for respectability and social success (Mary boasts that Tyrone "made his way up from ignorance and poverty to the top of his profession"); and a perennial sense of breast-beating guilt for failure to live up to the rigid standards of behavior that their culture has imposed upon them.[48] Jamie and Edmund, especially, crucify themselves with maudlin, self-punishing confessions about their supposed derelictions of duty. In a bizarre kind of way, one feels *Long Day's Journey* could have been written by Thoreau, so precisely does it appear to fulfill his nineteenth-century vision of Protestant will power and originality opposing Catholic stagnation and conventionality. O'Neill inverts Thoreau's value judgments insofar as the playwright approaches his characters with intuitive "pity and understanding and forgiveness," as he himself wrote in the play's prayerlike dedication; yet this image of Catholicism as the province of social outsiders has still not been broken. Like *The Awakening, Long Day's Journey* embodies the modernist double bind wherein Catholicism is something to be escaped from but can never be escaped from. Edmund's Nietzschean declaration that "God is dead" is promptly contradicted by the sense of sin that pervades the play.[49] The illnesses and other calamities that befall the Tyrone family are implicitly attributed by them, in their guilt-ridden way, to the abandonment of divine protection; Mary reminisces mournfully about her bright, clear days of faith back at convent school.

As William Halsey has pointed out, Catholics themselves have often been "irritated by O'Neill's fatalism," and certainly the playwright's

47 *The Plays of Eugene O'Neill*, I (New York: Random House, 1951), 199.
48 Eugene O'Neill, *Long Day's Journey into Night* (London: Cape, 1956), pp. 34, 9, 75, 52.
49 Ibid., pp. 5, 67.

emphasis upon the darker landscapes of the subconscious mind is very much at odds with the kind of optimstic messages emanating from *Commonweal* circles in this interwar period.[50] It is, however, wrong simply to envisage O'Neill's dramas as "realistic" portrayals of immigrant communities. What O'Neill is offering through his focus upon passive martyrdom is not social mimesis but a more abstract expression of wider modernist fragmentation, an intimation of insecurity that is refracted here through images of his native Catholic environment. Hence for Catholics to claim their social culture was no longer "like that" is in many ways beside the point; although O'Neill's dramas are based upon a particular cultural situation, he exploits that situation to imply metaphysical rather than social bondage. Hence the traumas of the Tyrone family are not to be assuaged merely by upward social mobility: I would not wish to advocate the kind of reading of O'Neill where all the symbolic cycles of Greek fate might be seen as mere subterfuges to express the harder, more material fate of immigrant displacement, since O'Neill's work resists being limited by that kind of positivistic explanation. In 1932, O'Neill himself described "the one true theater" as "a Temple where the religion of a poetical interpretation and symbolical celebration of life is communicated to human beings, starved in spirit by their soul-stifling daily struggle." He also disparaged "most modern plays" as concerned simply "with the relations between man and man," adding: "That doesn't interest me at all. I am only interested in the relation of man and God."[51] For O'Neill, this "God" was not necessarily a Christian entity; indeed, he compared his own theatrical rituals to those worshipping the god Dionysus in ancient Greece. Nevertheless, O'Neill's plays echo and re-echo with the implication that a purely secular environment is insufficient, that it necessarily betokens a world of loss. Hence the suffering in these dramas arises partly out of a very modernist despair at the apparent absence of a benevolent God, and partly out of a sense of limitation deriving from Catholic eschatology, a force that cuts deeper than the more immediate pleasures of social good cheer much vaunted by *Commonweal* Catholics at this time. This is the eschatology Scott Fitzgerald was expressing when he wrote to his daughter that "life is essentially a cheat and its conditions are those of defeat": Fitzgerald did not mean that defeat was inevitable on a literal, everyday level, but that no ultimate transcendence of life's circumscribed conditions is possible.[52] It is classic

50 Halsey, *Survival of American Innocence*, p. 125.
51 Louis Sheaffer, *O'Neill: Son and Artist* (Boston: Little, Brown and Co., 1973), p. 404; Benedict Nightingale, "Why O'Neill's Ghosts Haunt Us Still," *New York Times*, 12 June 1988, Sec. 2, p. 14.
52 In a letter of 5 Oct. 1940. Scott Fitzgerald, *Letters to His Daughter*, ed. Andrew Turnbull (New York: Scribner's, 1965), p. 156.

Catholic antiromanticism; Emerson, one feels, would not necessarily have agreed. Within this ideological framework, then, O'Neill draws upon the expressionist techniques of modernist drama so as to undercut the bland optimism of quotidian life. His images of social and economic defeat stand as metaphors for that final sense of metaphysical defeat Fitzgerald was talking about.

O'Neill himself abandoned churchgoing at the age of fifteen, two years after his Catholic confirmation. In 1929, however, at the age of forty-one, he was still writing of how "the sickness of today," as he perceived it, was "the death of an old God and the failure of science and materialism to give any satisfactory new one for the surviving religious instinct to find a meaning for life in, and to comfort its fear of death with."[53] O'Neill did in fact later write one overtly religious play, the expressionist drama *Days without End* (1932). Before the script of this play was published, O'Neill went so far as to ask Catholic churchmen Martin Quigley and Daniel Lord, S.J., to review the manuscript. O'Neill declared himself gratified by their generally favorable response and subsequently wrote to Quigley that he hoped there was "enough strength and conviction in the play to overcome the pseudo-intellectual pose of New York critics . . . that religious faith is an outmoded subject," though to another correspondent he insisted this was "a play about a Catholic" and "not Catholic propaganda."[54] In *Days without End,* the character of John Loving confronts a cynical, Nietzschean alter ego who dismisses religion as one of the "superstitions" of childhood. But while John meditates upon his own socialist and atheistic past, he is assured by the Catholic priest Father Baird of "the secret longing of your own heart for faith," and the play ends with the Nietzschean alter ego put firmly in its place and John kneeling at the foot of the cross in "ecstatic mystic vision."[55] The play's religious implications are not unambiguous, insofar as it is hinted that the desire to embrace God, like the contrary desire to embrace death that John displayed previously, could be seen in a psychological sense as a self-fulfilling prophecy, thus making religious belief a form of psychotherapy rather than theology. Nevertheless, however one reads it in a "spiritual" sense, this play is certainly notable for its analysis of the tentacular power of religion as a cultural inheritance: "The road finally turns back toward home," crows Father Baird as he guides John Loving back to the flock.[56]

This cultural inheritance, though usually more muted, is still implicit

53 Frederick J. Hoffman, *The Twenties: American Writing in the Postwar Decade,* 2nd ed. (New York: Free Press–Macmillan, 1965), p. 256.
54 Halsey, *Survival of American Innocence,* p. 126; Sheaffer, *O'Neill: Son and Artist,* p. 426.
55 *The Plays of Eugene O'Neill,* III (New York: Random House, 1970), 544, 560, 566.
56 Ibid., 504.

in O'Neill's more ambitious and famous works. In *Long Day's Journey into Night,* the characters find the psychological force of their ancestral religion impairs their full assimilation within the dominant framework of American society. Likewise, the dramatis personae of *The Iceman Cometh* (1947) are trapped within the past, although here the sense of personal failure becomes extended into a more general metaphor for the failure of a society constructed upon the pipe dreams of capitalism. O'Neill's early affinities with anarchism and the Provincetown Players lurk beneath the surface of *Iceman,* though his typically Catholic lack of faith in the ultimate triumph of any human form of paradise led the playwright to doubt the efficacy of the utopian socialism offered by many of his bohemian colleagues as a political panacea. In *Iceman,* Larry Slade, "one time Syndicalist-Anarchist," attributes the revolutionary movement's lack of success to its all too fallible human base: "The material the ideal free society must be constructed from is men themselves," he complains, "and you can't build a marble temple out of a mixture of mind and manure."[57] Once again, an abstract conception of human freedom finds itself annulled by the psychological complexity that underlies and circumscribes it. The dream of reason is held in check by a sense of man's irredeemable limitations. The future is locked in bondage to the past.

57 Ibid., 570, 590.

6

Isolation and Integration: Theodore Dreiser and James T. Farrell

The impending fatalism in Eugene O'Neill's dramas, then, arises not so much from any Calvinistic notion of mankind's "Innate Depravity" – the phrase famously used by Melville to describe the sense of sin in Hawthorne's writing – but rather from the cultural conditioning emerging out of one particular section of society. It has often been noted how the lingering shade of Calvinistic necessity transformed itself during the nineteenth century into that tone of philosophical determinism that haunts the patterns of late-nineteenth-century fiction, especially in the naturalist period.[1] But whereas the focus of Melville and Norris (for example) is upon a psychological darkness, the demonic undercurrents within the human psyche that work to subvert the forces of light, such tensions between freedom and determinism in O'Neill, Theodore Dreiser, and James T. Farrell have more to do with a clash between individual exceptionalism and social conformity. It is true that the characters of O'Neill and Farrell internalize this pressure toward conformity, so that the struggles of these characters to escape from the shackles of their environment also become internal struggles to escape from the shackles of their own psychological compulsions. Nevertheless, what we often find in these American "Catholic" fictions of the modernist period is the representation of a homogeneous ethnic and religious community that makes great efforts to preserve its own self-replicating similarity by suppressing any threat of difference.

---

1 Herman Melville, "Hawthorne and His Mosses," in *The Piazza Tales and Other Prose Pieces, 1839–1860* (Evanston: Northwestern Univ. Press–Newberry Library, 1984) p. 243. On Calvinism and naturalism, see for instance Eric J. Sundquist's essay "The Country of the Blue": "Naturalism dramatizes the loss of individuality at a physiological level by making a Calvinism without God its determining order and violent death its utopia." Introduction to *American Realism: New Essays,* ed. Eric J. Sundquist (Baltimore: Johns Hopkins Univ. Press, 1982), p. 13.

134

The idea of a world linked together by bonds of analogical similitude can sometimes be exhilarating, as it is in the poetry of Frank O'Hara, for example, where all the disparate objects on the New York streets merge into each other in a kind of ecstatic communal dance. In Dreiser and Farrell, however, this sense of similitude more often betokens a gloomy, stifling conformity. Leo Bersani has aligned this kind of repressive social conformity with the turgid realism of many nineteenth-century novels, whose perennial urge toward "coherence," said Bersani, "involves a serious crippling of desire." Sexual desire, with all its connotations of risk and loss, is marginalized (if not altogether eradicated) by the "ordered significances of realistic fiction," which strive to reflect and bolster the supposedly ordered significances of society.[2] One example of how Bersani's theory might be applicable within a Catholic context is Kate Chopin's *The Awakening,* where the differences of desire are necessarily expelled by a society that demands conformity and similarity. As we shall see, the worlds of James T. Farrell's fiction also revolve around a fight between individual desire and the pressures of a smothering community, a community whose inexorable homogeneity is mirrored by the seemingly inevitable repetitiveness of Farrell's sledgehammer style of literary realism.

This emphasis upon the styles of conformity demanded both by social communities and by the socialized *ecclesia* of the Catholic church necessarily places the American "Catholic" novel outside that "tradition" of romance as outlined by Richard Chase in 1957. Chase's *The American Novel and Its Tradition* is an excellent book, which scrupulously acknowledges the limitations and debatable points of its own argument and is careful to stress that its conclusions reflect general tendencies rather than absolute truths. Nevertheless, nearly every category Chase defined as exemplifying "the originality and 'Americanness' of the novel" is scarcely relevant to the "Catholic" idiom as it appears not only in Dreiser and Farrell but also in later exponents such as Mary McCarthy, Flannery O'Connor, and Donald Barthelme. Chase distinguished between the "formal abstractness" of American romance as against the "solid moral inclusiveness" of the English social novel; however, as Chase said, this notion of "abstractness" arises to a large extent out of a Puritan dialectic between good and evil, a dialectic that has never had much purchase upon the Catholic literary (or cultural) imagination. Chase claimed that in Calvinist mythology such a dialectic verged at times toward a "kind of Manichaean demonology," the conception that the power of evil and

---

2 Leo Bersani, *A Future for Astyanax: Character and Desire in Literature* (Boston: Little, Brown, 1976), pp. 6, 61.

the power of good are categorically distinct and equipotential.[3] In Christian terms, this idea is, of course, heretical; as Jay Fliegelman noted, all colonial Protestantism ostensibly avoided the "simplistic clarity of Manichaeanism" and steadfastly denied the possibility of "any independent agency of evil in the world."[4] Nevertheless, it is true to say the literary styles of later eras that were influenced by the American Protestant heritage have tended to move closer to these Manichaean antitheses than those conceived within a Catholic cultural tradition. The Puritan conflicts of the light and the dark, the elect and the damned, which Chase found replayed in Melville, Twain, and Faulkner bear little relevance to the Catholic worlds of Dreiser, Farrell, and Fitzgerald, where all morality is a more mixed, purgatorial affair. These theological differences were succinctly described during the nineteenth century by John Henry Newman:

> Calvinists make a sharp separation between the elect and the world; there is much in this that is cognate or parallel to the Catholic doctrine; but they go on to say, as I understand them, very differently from Catholicism, – that the converted and the unconverted can be discriminated by man, that the justified are conscious of their state of justification, and that the regenerate cannot fall away. Catholics on the other hand shade and soften the awful antagonism between good and evil, which is one of their dogmas, by holding that there are different degrees of justification, that there is a great difference in point of gravity between sin and sin, that there is the possibility and the danger of falling away, and that there is no certain knowledge given to any one that he is simply in a state of grace, and much less that he is to persevere to the end.[5]

In the Catholic milieu, therefore, the secular power of romantic idealism is displaced by a contrary emphasis upon the inherent conditions of terrestrial imperfection. Within this human world, neither ultimate regeneration nor any kind of "certain knowledge" of heavenly preferment appears possible. In these circumstances, the only viable option becomes to wait patiently for the advent of "divine" grace.

Nor has the quest for "pastoral idyls," inspired by a nostalgia for simpler agrarian or frontier pasts, been of any great consequence as far as Catholic writers are concerned.[6] Again, Chase laid stress on the pastoral mode as characteristic of American romance, but, as Ellen Moers noted,

3 Richard Chase, *The American Novel and Its Tradition* (Garden City: Doubleday-Anchor, 1957), pp. vii–viii, 11, 202.
4 Jay Fliegelman, *Prodigals and Pilgrims: The American Revolution against Patriarchal Authority, 1750–1800* (Cambridge: Cambridge Univ. Press, 1982), pp. 158–9.
5 John Henry Newman, *Apologia pro Vita Sua,* ed. A. Dwight Culler (Boston: Houghton Mifflin, 1956), p. 26.
6 Chase, *American Novel,* p. 1.

Dreiser is unusual in American terms in the way he accepts urban situations "as the norm" without indulging in any pastoral retrospection.[7] American Catholic writers have tended to be urban not only because the city was where immigrant communities happened to congregate, but also because the kind of idealized metaphors endemic to the pastoral genre generally seem irrelevant to a Catholic view of the world. For a Catholic sensibility, everyone and everything on earth is subject to ontological limitations sub specie aeternitatis, and therefore the kind of pastoral apotheosis described by Chase would appear to be simply self-delusion. In the universalism of the Catholic mind-set, the fundamental conditions of life are the same in the most pleasant green pastures of the country as in the most squalid urban jungles of the city. The secular Enlightenment ideal of close proximity to "nature," so powerful a meta-narrative within the American consciousness, has not been something Catholic writers have very often aspired to. For Catholics, "nature" is just as likely to be destructive as redemptive, and the urban world just as likely to be redemptive as destructive.

Thus the desire for transcendence, which Chase saw as central to the American tradition of romance, has little meaning within a Catholic context where ultimate idealism is impossible and the material conditions of reality constitute a fait accompli. Those "radical disunities" Chase cherished in Melville and Faulkner as proof of an heroic straining against the confines of society are denied by the environment of Dreiser, where everything is on the contrary solid, homogeneous, universal.[8] However much Dreiser's characters move geographically from one part of the country to another, the problems they encounter are always essentially the same. In Dreiser, the obstacles of life remain obstinately in place: those dematerializing and melodramatic figures of Hawthorne and Brockden Brown, designed to rise above the circumscribed and restricted life of any particular community into the more airy realms of eternal truth, give way in Dreiser and Farrell to an emphasis upon the corporeal, the substantial, the down-to-earth. The transcendent hero outside society becomes supplanted by an immanent group of characters within it. Novels written from a position within a specific social group – the "novel of manners," as Chase termed them – were disparaged by him as being more characteristic of the middlebrow traditions of English fiction: "In America, with the exception of Henry James, the novelists of manners are among the writers of second or third rank: Edith Wharton, Ellen Glasgow, Howells, John O'Hara, J. P. Marquand, Sinclair Lewis, Scott Fitzgerald. The great writers, such as Melville, Hawthorne, or Faulkner,

7 Ellen Moers, *Two Dreisers* (New York: Viking, 1969), p. viii.
8 Chase, *American Novel*, p. 7.

sometimes approach the novel of manners . . . but it is not their natural style." For Chase, Faulkner, "a more universal genius," is the prophet who perceives those high abstract patterns that Fitzgerald vitiates by incorporating them into social situations, just as in the naturalist mode Frank Norris is the seer and Dreiser the journeyman who performs the "considerable service" of redesigning naturalism for a social setting.[9]

Chase's agenda is in the end, of course, not "universal" but narrowly ideological. His book, brilliant though it is, constitutes an attempt to equate the New England Puritan legacy with an exclusivist myth of the United States itself. His idealization of allegorical "romance" derived in a direct line from the apocalyptic modes of Puritan typology, where every worldly event hovered on the brink of becoming dematerialized into its biblical correlative; it altogether ignored the view of Catholic philosophy that human history since the Redemption should be seen as a demystified, substantially secular affair. This attempt to define a heritage of separatist "Americanness" by prioritizing allegorical romance and disparaging secular realism led Chase to relegate novels "of manners" to a secondary position within the canon, and therefore to underestimate writers such as Wharton, Fitzgerald, and John O'Hara. Nevertheless, it is true that no American novelist has been able to perceive society as immutable or authoritative, as it tends to appear in the English model. For Trollope, or for George Eliot, or even for Kingsley Amis, English society forms an objective reality, a given landscape against which the author's fictional characters must perform. For Farrell and Dreiser, by contrast, the constructions of society take on a provisional quality even in their most obstinate and repressive manifestations. Although for Farrell's heroes the social and religious *ecclesia* is an intimidatingly obvious presence, there is always a sense that Danny O'Neill (or another hero) could dissolve this world simply by moving away from it. This is rarely the case in English fiction: characters are, of course, exiled from the main currents of English society, either by choice or compulsion, but those main currents still flow remorselessly on. While it is true that Farrell, Dreiser, and Fitzgerald can never altogether transcend their social group in the approved fashion of American "romance," neither can they accept their external social circumstances as a fully naturalized legislative power, as in the English mode. The behavior of Farrell's characters, like Trollope's, is patterned by the customs of the social world they inhabit; but, unlike Trollope, Farrell conceives these customs to be provisional and susceptible to historical change.

In American Catholic fiction of the modernist period, then, one of the central tensions we see emerging is between pressure to adhere to the

9 Ibid., pp. 157–8, 204.

standards of a particular ethnic or religious society and pressure to escape. It is the dilemma of Joyce's *Portrait* and Chopin's *Awakening* over again: modernist rebellion confronts the rigid demands of "common sense," in the strict sense of that phrase, the moral standards of a common or communal group. The ordinary makes attempts to chasten and domesticate the extraordinary; the extraordinary aspires to fly free of such restrictions. This situation is complicated further within the American cultural tradition by the fact that, in Richard Chase's terms, it is the extraordinary that becomes ordinary. The desire to secede from the restrictive boundaries of any given community becomes the surest way to assimilate oneself into the ever-mobile flow of the American Dream; while, paradoxically, conforming too slavishly to community life involves alienating oneself from the norms of American romanticism and individualism. There is of course nothing essentially "natural" about this urge to conform by rebelling; on the contrary, the ideological directives underpinning the idea of flight from social and legalistic restrictions seem clear enough. However, what we characteristically find in American Catholic writers is a conflict between a desire for integration and a compulsion toward isolation: between an urge on the one hand to collapse the old ethnic order and work one's way into American society by adopting the conventional behavior patterns of energetic individualism, and a residual sentiment on the other that insists these secular and materialistic values are not "genuine" and never can be. That equation made by the Calvinists between material wealth and spiritual well-being has rarely been available to the more ironic Catholic temperament. It was this dubious sense of alienation from the values of American society that induced several Catholic modernist writers to assume an ambiguous if not openly hostile attitude toward the ebullient optimism of the American Dream.

This dilemma of Catholic writers poised between integration and isolation can be seen to operate as a parallel to the social and theological controversies within the Catholic church around the turn of the century concerning the issue of "Americanization." There was intense debate at all levels about how far Catholicism should support the American capitalist system and how far it should oppose it. In the nineteenth century, when Catholics were generally outside the mainstream of American life, poverty and self-denial were held up to be the paradigms of a truly Christian life, and many immigrants found themselves dependent upon charitable organizations to help them out of material hardship. Around the 1880s, however, the American labor movement began to gather force, and as so many of the immigrant workers were Catholic, the church naturally looked upon their efforts with some sympathy. In 1887, Cardinal Gibbons, newly appointed archbishop of Baltimore, vigorously and successfully defended to Rome the establishment of a Catholic workers' association, the Knights of Labor, Gibbons's fear being that if the Knights were banned many Catholics would leave the church and seek refuge in godless left-wing political organizations. At this time, the hierarchy of the American church was attempting to demonstrate sympathy with the impoverished lot of its parishioners without licensing what it conceived to be the atheistic and materialistic philosophy of socialism.

Some Catholic clergymen, not surprisingly, were forthright in their denunication of the labor movements. Bishop James Quigley in 1902 condemned social democracy as a "recent importation from continental Europe" marked "by unbelief, hostility to religion and hatred of the Catholic Church"; while Archbishop John Ireland openly denounced the strikes of the 1890s and declared the church to be "the great prop of social order and law."[10] There was clearly no unanimity of approach, but it would be fair to say that there was generally cautious support among American Catholic clergy at this time for various forms of social activism. Pope Leo XIII's 1891 encyclical *Rerum novarum* had trod a fine line between emphasizing the inviolability of private property and urging the state to help relieve social distress by instituting eight-hour days, compulsory Sunday rest, and so on, and this sense of preserving a delicate balance between conservatism and liberalism characterized the attitudes of the American Catholic leadership between 1880 and 1914. After the First World War, though, the tentative support for reform became more clear-cut. In 1919 the National Catholic Welfare Council was established, an advisory body that was instrumental in producing in the same year a pamphlet entitled *Bishops' Program of Social Reconstruction*. This document, composed largely by Monsignor John Ryan and signed by four bishops, called for legislation on health and old-age insurance, unemployment, the right of workers to organize, and the establishment of minimum wages. The council's belief was that squalid material living conditions would hinder the development of spiritual qualities; in a pastoral letter of 1919, the American bishops affirmed their conviction that industrial stability was contingent upon ownership being shared with workers "as rapidly as conditions will permit." A few years later, Pope Pius XI's 1931 encyclical on reconstructing the social order, *Quadragesimo anno,* also insisted that workers were entitled to wages of "ample sufficiency," although the pope here sharply distinguished his sanction of the idea of justice for the individual working man from any wider approval of systems of socialism or capitalism.[11] Pius XI, like Pope Leo

10 See Aaron I. Abell, *American Catholicism and Social Action: A Search for Social Justice, 1865–1950* (Garden City: Hanover-Doubleday, 1960), pp. 150, 86.
11 Ibid., pp. 211, 237.

XIII before him, was loath to relinquish Rome's old dream of a neo-medieval social order.

This new affinity between American Catholicism and radical social programs reinforced traditional fears within the United States about the subversive and un-American leanings of Catholic ideology. These fears were fueled by the various other Catholic organizations dedicated to social reform that flourished between the wars and especially in the 1930s: the Catholic League for Social Justice, founded in 1932; the Catholic Worker Movement, headed by former communist Dorothy Day, which was set up in 1933; the Association of Catholic Trade Unionists, established in New York in 1937, and so on. These institutions were, on the whole, gradualist in tendency and again were designed partly to combat the influence of godless communism by showing that commitment to economic reform did not necessarily involve abandoning the Catholic faith. Nevertheless, the emergence in the early twentieth century of Catholicism as a significant oppositional force in a social and political context is important. While in the nineteenth century Catholicism signified an estranged and alien "other," supported only by faith and charity, in the first four decades of this century it came to be recognized as an alternative to the older American traditions in a sociopolitical, psychological, and aesthetic sense.

James Terence Fisher has argued that Dorothy Day and her *Catholic Worker* movement were in fact still deeply attached to those idylls of worldly failure and deferred, otherworldly gratification that had characterized the American Catholic mentality during the nineteenth century. The *Catholic Worker*, said Fisher, was grounded upon "a univocal rhetoric of suffering, martyrdom, and self-abnegation," and its utopian experiments – such as the workers' commune at Newburgh, New York – were almost willful disasters.[12] Fisher linked this oppositional "counterculture" with the Catholic theological concept of society as a "Mystical Body," a doctrine that was becoming increasingly popular in the 1930s and was formally promulgated in Pope Pius XII's 1943 encyclical *Mystici Corporis Christi*. The purport of this for the devout Catholic was that by immersing himself in work for the "Mystical Body" of society, he was automatically, at the same time, immersing himself in Christ. Hence, Dorothy Day, Peter Maurin, and their colleagues on the *Catholic Worker* were devoted not so much to the general improvement of social conditions as to a form of passive, self-mortifying "antitriumphalism," an obsession with "self-dissolution," which "carried a powerful erotic

12 James Terence Fisher, *The Catholic Counterculture in America, 1933–1962* (Chapel Hill: Univ. of North Carolina Press, 1989), p. 76.

charge."[13] It is interesting to consider this kind of compulsion alongside the various tendencies toward self-immolation we see in the texts of Eugene O'Neill, Scott Fitzgerald, James T. Farrell, Martin Scorsese, and others. What I would argue, though, is that rather than simply reflecting psychic masochism, these more sophisticated Catholic authors reflect upon it as an integral part of the cultural matrix from which their work emerges. Farrell's texts, for example, train their deconstructive light upon the idea of passive suffering; yet by transferring this oppressive weight from the realm of religious doctrine or subliminal psychological conditioning into that of aesthetic play, his texts allow for the possibility of "reorganizing" these social conventions so "they begin to be stripped of their validity" and "become objects of scrutiny in themselves," as Wolfgang Iser put it.[14] Once "self-dissolution" is acknowledged as an arbitrary rather than inevitable event, its radical transformation becomes possible.

In retrospect, this perseverance of a separatist Catholic "counterculture" can be seen as an ironic fulfillment of Leo XIII's directive in his 1899 apostolic letter, which instructed the American church to maintain its separate identity and resist any compromising integration with the freewheeling life of the United States. Although no papal decree was going to prevent Catholics in the early twentieth century from moving more toward the center of society, nevertheless, this sense of an oblique, quizzical, and at times openly antagonistic attitude toward American institutions lingered at least up until the Second World War. Whereas the pope's reservations about the United States concerned its theological inadequacies, however, American Catholics of the early twentieth century just as often disapproved of their native land because of the inadequacies of its social system, especially as this system related to their own economic positions. The Vatican was alienated from the United States because the country was too materialistic; American Catholics were alienated from the United States because their lives were not materialistic enough. Hence, of course, the vast popularity amongst lower-middle-class Catholics of Father Charles Coughlin's radio broadcasts in the 1930s, during which Coughlin launched tirades against the "evils" of the banking system.

This underlying hostility and suspicion can be seen in the work of three novelists born into Catholic environments who were deeply involved with the society of their time: Theodore Dreiser, James T. Farrell, and Scott Fitzgerald. In each of these writers, as in Eugene O'Neill, there are conflicting pressures between a longing to crack the code and "make

13 Ibid., pp. 50, 163, 80.
14 Wolfgang Iser, The Act of Reading: A Theory of Aesthetic Response (London: Routledge and Kegan Paul, 1978), p. 61.

it" on the one hand and an irredeemable sense of alienation on the other. These pressures work in different ways, of course: Farrell pushes his sense of separatism through into a flirtation with political Trotskyism, while Fitzgerald metamorphoses his role as the eternal parvenu into an ironic celebration of the American Dream. Still, this quandary of being caught between two positions, neither fully isolated nor fully integrated, is one that recurs persistently in their novels.

Theodore Dreiser is the first major American author to emerge from within Catholic culture and also, as Ellen Moers noted, "the first whose people were not only poor, but unrespectable."[15] While Emerson and Thoreau possessed no great riches, they were, as T. S. Eliot said, products of a world of high culture and leisure, terms that certainly could not be applied to Dreiser's German Catholic home in Terre Haute, Indiana. Dreiser's father, a first-generation immigrant, was a zealous adherent of Catholicism who insisted upon sending his son to a parochial school, where the nuns reinforced the speech Dreiser had heard at home by teaching him the German language before English. Like his great contemporary Joseph Conrad, who switched from Polish to English, and like (as we shall see later) Jack Kerouac, whose native tongue was French, the style of Dreiser's texts always preserves a hint of something foreign. In a similar way to Conrad and Kerouac, Dreiser defamiliarizes the English language, uses it in a willful and self-conscious rather than instinctive manner; it seems to be for him not something acquired naturally but something learned, perhaps awkwardly. All the Germanic circumlocutions of his prose also work subliminally to reemphasize one of the central themes of his novels, which is the intense difficulty of expression, the painful stress involved in trying to match concrete facts with their verbal equivalents.

In 1964, Irving Howe claimed that "Dreiser has dropped out of the awareness of cultivated Americans."[16] This may not be as true today as it was in the period after the Second World War, when the New Critical advocacy of textual finesse held sway, as did a widespread abhorrence of intellectuals tainted by communism; still, it is probably the case that Dreiser has not been as widely read as his importance would merit. One reason for this, as Larzer Ziff has suggested, is that Dreiser "is a literary radical in the basic sense of the word, for he plants new roots, not as an act of rebellion, for this argues an understanding of the bases of society, but as an act of creation, as if the society he portrays had never been

---

15 Moers, *Two Dreisers*, pp. xiv–xv.
16 Irving Howe, "An American Tragedy," in *Critical Essays on Theodore Dreiser*, ed. Donald Pizer (Boston: Hall, 1981), p. 292.

portrayed before."[17] Dreiser does not react against previous literary conventions, he simply ignores them. The etiolated idealist aspirations of an Emerson and the provincial scrupulosity of a Sarah Orne Jewett are equally alien to his universalist, materialist, Catholic way of thinking. His texts represent the world in fragments, as Ziff said, because in terms of a fully embodied "Catholic" tradition in American literature there had been nothing like it before: Dreiser had to invent his own genre.

Appropriately enough, in a 1915 essay for *The Nation* Stuart Sherman suggested that "Mr. Dreiser's field seems curiously outside American society" and that the "barbaric naturalism" of Dreiser's characters could be attributed to the fact their author was not of Anglo-Saxon origin. Dreiser's texts sound, said Sherman, "a new note in American literature, coming from the 'ethnic' element of our mixed population."[18] The old restrictive tone of the "genteel tradition" was no more an option for Dreiser than it was for Joyce, who was to say a few years later that if *Ulysses* was not fit to read then life was not fit to be lived. In both cases, we see an all-inclusive, global sensibility attempting to collapse the effete and repressive pieties of a previous literary tradition. (William Dean Howells, not surprisingly, found Dreiser offensively vulgar and always preferred to give him a wide berth.)[19] No more than Joyce could Dreiser dissolve the smells and substance of material society into those melodramatic idylls or allegorical conflicts between the light and the dark that we see in the "tradition" of American romance recommended by Richard Chase. Indeed, in what is probably his greatest novel, *An American Tragedy* (1925), Dreiser deliberately subverts the Manichaean boundaries between good and evil by his emphasis upon the confused and unfathomable motives underlying human behavior. Disembodied patterns of good and evil may be all very well, but Dreiser's writing implies that in the fallen human world everything is a good deal more complex and mixed-up than that.

This is not, of course, to assert that Dreiser was a "Catholic" writer in any narrowly orthodox or intentional sense. In *Dawn* (1931), the first volume of his autobiography, Dreiser follows the modernist line by playing off the old superstitions he knew in the Germanic community of his childhood against the scientific knowledge and freedom of the brave new American world. Dreiser officially abandoned the Catholic church after his mother's death in 1890, when he was nineteen; as Sarah

17 Larzer Ziff, *The American 1890s: Life and Times of a Lost Generation* (New York: Viking, 1966), p. 338.

18 See Thomas P. Riggio, "Theodore Dreiser: Hidden Ethnic," *MELUS,* 11, no. 1 (1984), 55.

19 Richard Ellmann, *James Joyce,* 2nd ed. (New York: Oxford Univ. Press, 1976), p. 551; Ziff, *American 1890s,* p. 341.

Dreiser, a Catholic by marriage, had been erratic (and reluctant) in her church attendance, the local Chicago priest raised doubts as to whether she could properly be buried in consecrated ground. Although the priest did eventually allow the interment to take place, the embittered Theodore finally chose to take flight from what he called "the numskull state of mind that faith in the Catholic Church represents."[20] *Dawn*, however, describes this hostility as emerging at an earlier stage of Dreiser's life. Portraying himself as a child "wild for anything that represented the opposite of what I had" (69), Dreiser proceeds to pour scorn upon "the intellectual dry-rot of the Middle Ages, the horrible charnel-house of mediaeval ideas, as represented by my father's church" (557). Catholic priests are dismissed as "sacrament and indulgence salesmen" intent upon corrupting children "with unverifiable dogma or just plain lies," as opposed to those more worthy scientists "who have labored and meditated on behalf of reality" (26). Escaping from the "outrageous" Catholic parochial schools of Indiana into the modernistic world of Chicago, Dreiser exults: "I think my young American soul gave one bound and thereby attained to the meaning of freedom" (191–2).

The vitriol Dreiser directs toward Catholicism here is comically effective but psychologically unconvincing. While protesting vigorously against the folly and stupidity of the church, *Dawn* implicitly reveals that Dreiser's rebellion is not as unambiguous as he himself appears to think. Like Joyce, Dreiser admits to "admiring" the rituals of Catholicism as an "artistic spectacle" (480). After the family's move to Chicago, Dreiser talks of how his father's search for a new church "irritated and at the same time interested me, for much as I might dislike the routine of the Catholic Church, it was ever of interest to me as a spectacle, and I was never weary of comparing a new church and its priests with those of some other" (166). The young Dreiser of *Dawn* also harbors a Stephen Dedalus–like interest in the dynamics of flight: wondering why he cannot "rise in the air and fly or float like a bird or a cloud," he yet insists, with a fervent secularism, that this dream "had no relation to any of the woody or plastic angels of the Catholic Church" (60).

Throughout *Dawn,* in fact, Dreiser protests just too much about the redundancy of the church to his way of thinking. Sometimes his observations appear blatantly self-contradictory:

> By then I was so weary of these things that the mere thought of them was torturing. Yet at the elevation of the Host, so cowed was I by dogma that I invariably knelt, not because I felt it to be so sacred or spiritual a moment but because of the fear that if I did not I might die

---

20 Theodore Dreiser, *Dawn* (New York: Liveright, 1931), p. 481. Subsequent page references are given in parentheses in the text.

in the act of committing a mortal sin and so be consigned to eternal fire. (129)

But if he was frightened of "eternal fire," he must necessarily, even if unconsciously, have perceived this ritual of transubstantiation as sacred; the statement is a non sequitur. An odd perspective begins to manifest itself in the reading of *Dawn,* because it becomes apparent that the narrator is not only fallible but actually self-deceiving and that he is conflating different eras of his life, retrospectively reinterpreting the past in the light of the present. A few pages into the book, Dreiser describes his father as a man "obsessed by a religious belief" and solemnly avows: "I looked on him as mentally a little weak" (6). But when did he? At the age of two or three, which is the point at which *Dawn* opens? In the same way, despite all the splenetic wrath directed toward Catholicism during the narrative, the end of *Dawn* finds the author still regularly performing his religious duties. Calling to mind his brother Al, he remarks: "We practically agreed that there was little or nothing to Catholicism. Yet believe it or not, we went to church" (358). It might be possible to attribute this sense of confusion to Dreiser's technical clumsiness as a writer, his inability to organize a plausible impression of historical chronology. But the confusion seems to betoken a more radical contradiction within the text: despite Dreiser's conscious dissociation of himself from the religion of his upbringing, his unconscious mind is still enmeshed within its cultural mythologies. Dreiser bewildered a Quaker audience in 1939 by telling them that "up until I was forty years of age I believed fully that the world belonged to the Devil." As if to make quite sure Satan would be kept eternally at bay, the supposed atheist Dreiser received Holy Communion on Good Friday 1945, a few months before he died.[21]

One obvious result of Dreiser's Catholic inheritance is an inclination toward the use of metaphors culled from religious liturgy. In *Dawn,* girls become a "seraphic" vision (459) and his mother's misery a "crucifixion" (22), just as in his 1914 novel, *The Titan,* the hero Cowperwood is said to see "clearly, as within a *chalice-like* nimbus, that the ultimate end of fame, power, vigor was beauty" (my emphasis).[22] Not surprisingly, though, the more general representation of Catholicism within Dreiser's novels is unflattering. There is a sardonic comment upon its dogmatic tendencies toward the end of *An American Tragedy,* where Mrs. Griffiths, trying to raise money for an appeal against her son Clyde's death sentence, decides not to bother asking Catholics because "the mercies of Christ as interpreted by the holder of the sacred keys of St. Peter, as she knew, were not for those who failed to acknowledge the authority of the Vicar

---

21 Moers, *Two Dreisers,* p. 296.
22 Theodore Dreiser, *The Titan* (New York: Lane, 1914), p. 470.

of Christ."[23] There are several other unfriendly portraits of Catholics in Dreiser's novels: in *Jennie Gerhardt* (1911), Lester Kane embodies the kind of conformity and allegiance to his family background that one would expect from the scion of a wealthy Irish-Catholic clan. "Born a Catholic," Kane is now "no longer a believer in the divine inspiration of Catholicism"; nevertheless, with Letty Gerald to act as his "confessor," Kane eventually chooses to appease his family by abandoning the disreputable Jennie Gerhardt and marrying instead the eminently respectable widow Mrs. Gerald in a Catholic church: "He was an agnostic, but because he had been reared in the church he felt that he might as well be married in it."[24] Pressures of Catholic family life also impose themselves upon Aileen Butler, the Irish-American second wife of Frank Cowperwood, financier, titan, and stoic. Aileen runs into the most severe opposition from her father, Edward Butler, when she initially plans to marry Cowperwood in *The Financier* (1912): Edward Butler forbids the marriage on account of Cowperwood's earlier divorce – "It's me duty to be hard. It's me obligation to you and the Church" – but this has no effect on Aileen, who simply sidesteps Catholic prohibitions by announcing that she does not "believe in any religion any more."[25] Nevertheless, when Aileen finds out in *The Stoic* (1947) about Cowperwood's affair with Berenice Fleming, her outrage is still couched within a religious idiom, as she "repeated to herself, like a rosary of trebled length, all of the ills which she could conjure." Despite her avowed atheism, the religion of her childhood continues to be one determining influence upon Aileen's behavior. When her husband is dying, "her thoughts wandered back to the extreme religiosity of her parents," and she permits an Episcopalian minister to pronounce the last rites over Cowperwood.[26]

Another significant Catholic figure is John J. McKenty in *The Titan* (1914), "brought from Ireland by his emigrant parents during a period of famine" and now a wheeler-dealer of great virtuosity, "patron saint of the political and social underworld of Chicago."[27] One central theme of Dreiser's work, which is crystallized in McKenty, is that of the outsider, the immigrant striving to "make it" in a foreign country. This notion of the poor boy envious of the moneyed folk he sees around him recurs throughout Dreiser's texts, as does the fear of poverty and failure; indeed the word "failure" always falls with an ominous lead weight in

23 Theodore Dreiser, *An American Tragedy* (New York: Boni and Liveright, 1925), II, 359.
24 Theodore Dreiser, *Jennie Gerhardt* (New York: Harper, 1911), pp. 133, 337, 390. Subsequent page references are given in parentheses in the text.
25 Theodore Dreiser, *The Financier* (New York: Harper, 1912), pp. 531–2.
26 Theodore Dreiser, *The Stoic* (Garden City: Doubleday, 1947), pp. 257, 271.
27 Dreiser, *The Titan*, p. 84.

Dreiser's novels, as in *An American Tragedy*, where Walter Dillard is described as "most anxious to attain some sort of social position" for himself because his father had been "a small town dry goods merchant before him, who had failed." Dreiser was, as Irving Howe said, "the kind of writer who must keep circling about the point of his beginnings, forever stirred by memories of his early struggles and preoccupations," and it is not difficult to relate this form of social insecurity to a typically ethnic sense of being marginalized by the institutions of society.[28] Dreiser is explicit about this fear in *Dawn:*

> Because of the various events I have narrated . . . I became mentally colored or tinged with a sense of poverty and defeat and social ill-being in connection with our family that took me years and years, and then only in part, to overcome, and traces of which I still find darkly ensconced in certain corners of that subconscious which is a part of the deeper and more mysterious self of me. For years, even so late as my thirty-fifth or fortieth year, the approach of winter invariably filled me with an indefinable and highly oppressive dread, and that at periods when I needed not to be in dread of anything that winter and poverty, or the two of them together, could do to me. (107)

While this is remarkable in its tribute to the coercive influences of a particular environment, it is similar in kind to that nervous sense of outsiderhood expressed by other "cradle" Catholics such as O'Neill, Farrell, and Fitzgerald. It helps to account for that frantic urge for success we find in the novels of Dreiser and Fitzgerald, coupled with the semiconscious belief of both writers that failure and defeat are the proper stations for their characters. As F. O. Matthiessen observed, Dreiser "was the outsider, with an intense desire to move *up* and *in*," but he was also the marginalized political radical exposing and fighting social injustice.[29] It is this polarity that brings forth the characteristically Catholic tension in his work between conformity and alienation, between integration with society and opposition to it. This polarity also helps to account for the behavior of individual characters within Dreiser's novels: one of the reasons Lester Kane chooses to marry Mrs. Gerald rather than Jennie Gerhardt is that he and his Catholic family fear their social status is so tenuous that one step out of line could jeopardize the fortune old Mr. Kane has accrued since his immigration from Ireland. Lester does not have the comfortable confidence and sense of cultural security to act purely out of his own volition.

This supersession of individual volition by more impersonal social and

28 Dreiser, *An American Tragedy*, I, 201; Irving Howe, Afterword, *An American Tragedy*, by Theodore Dreiser (New York: New American Library, 1964), p. 820.
29 F. O. Matthiessen, *Theodore Dreiser* (London: Methuen, 1951), p. 38.

philosophical mechanisms is, in fact, another crucial Dreiser theme that can be related to his Catholic consciousness. In his 1920 essay "The Essential Tragedy of Life," Dreiser declared this tragedy to consist in the fact that man is conscious of the immense forces beyond his control, but conscious also of the basic fact that he cannot use these forces but is instead used by them. We see this conception restated in "The Myth of Individuality" (1934), in which Dreiser asserted that "man is not living, but is being lived by something which needs not only him but billions like him in order to express itself."[30] Of course, this shift from an active to a passive voice can be linked up with the naturalist movement in literature, the influence of Darwin and Herbert Spencer, and so on, and it is by no means the intention here to offer Catholicism as any kind of "explanation" for Dreiser's analysis of the insufficiency of human freedom. Nevertheless, as Ziff said, there are ways in which the universalism of Spencer's ideas dovetailed neatly with the universalist language inculcated in Dreiser's youth: "Spencer operated for Dreiser as a choric explanation of experience, a worldly-wise replacement for the Roman Catholicism of his childhood."[31] Moreover, in a passage that foreshadows Oscar Handlin's comments on how many nineteenth-century Catholic immigrants tended to acquiesce in the poverty of their social circumstances as a divinely ordained and apparently immutable fact, Dreiser himself in Dawn draws a parallel between psychological passivity and religious indoctrination:

> If some persons take to drink and others to drugs, a far greater number become addicted to religious formulae, and with equally fatal results. Their brains simply ossify, since independent inquiry is no longer needed, and their natural emotions, being vainly rejected as sinful, transform themselves into a single aspect or expression, and they are forever on their knees before an immense and inscrutable something which cares no more for their adoration or supplications than it does for those of an expiring beetle. (349)

That beetle is interesting, coming so clearly as it does from the menagerie of naturalism, like Frank Norris's octopus, or like the symbolic lobster and squid of Dreiser's The Financier. One inference to be drawn here is that religion, like money and lust, is another of those impersonal forces that reduce human characters to a state of animalistic anonymity. Another inference, though, may be that Dreiser's particular refraction of natu-

---

30 Theodore Dreiser, "The Essential Tragedy of Life," in Hey, Rub-A-Dub-Dub! A Book of the Mystery and Wonder and Terror of Life (London: Constable, 1931), pp. 246–59; Matthiessen, Theodore Dreiser, p. 239.
31 Ziff, American 1890s, p. 336.

ralism can be read in some ways as a transformed version of Catholic mythology.

This parallel between naturalism and Catholicism is developed in an interesting way in *Jennie Gerhardt*. The familiar naturalist ideas about fate are described here through the imagery of a chess game: Lester tells Jennie that "all of us are more or less pawns. We're moved about like chessmen by circumstances over which we have no control" (401). But this metaphor of the black and white chessboard is recapitulated in the final scene of the novel, which describes Lester's funeral service in a Catholic church. Here we are told that "a white shroud bearing the insignia of suffering, a black cross, was put over [the coffin], and the great candles were set beside it" (428). This last tableau is designed to act as a kind of masque or summary of the novel, with the symbolism of the shroud and cross mirroring that of the chessboard, and it makes explicit the ways in which a subterranean current of "Catholic" thought in Dreiser becomes aligned with his social philosophy. This ritual of the church so much impresses Jennie that "she was suffused with a sense of sorrow, loss, beauty, and mystery. Life in all its vagueness and uncertainty seemed typified by this scene" (427); and it is because she is so charmed by "the sense of infinite loss" (428) this scene embodies that Jennie herself comes to believe "she had evidently been born to yield, not to seek" (430). The assurance that misery is inevitable becomes for Jennie a welcome relief; for her, renunciation and defeat appear to be the deepest truths of life. One could, no doubt, invoke the old stereotype of Catholic masochism here. Yet this representation of the displacement of individuality through the imagery of Catholicism was also, as we saw earlier, prevalent in the texts of Howells, James, and Adams. Catholicism is exploited by these turn-of-the-century writers as the symbol of a world where individual autonomy has, for various reasons, found itself superseded by universal dependence. Dreiser reinforces this equation of dependency and religious feeling in *Dawn* when he talks nostalgically about his desire for "some definite universal heart of whom the declaration 'Come unto me, all ye that are weary and heavy-laden, and I will give you rest,' were true" (124).

In this sense, as Roger Asselineau has argued, Dreiser should be seen not just as a naturalist but also as a "belated transcendentalist": his concern is with the world of spirit, even in its absence, as much as with the world of matter.[32] If we were to follow Mikhail Bakhtin's notion of the "dialogics" of literary texts, we would say that in Dreiser's work the conflicting pressures of physical and metaphysical are held in open,

---

32 Roger Asselineau, "Theodore Dreiser's Transcendentalism," in *Critical Essays on Theodore Dreiser*, ed. Pizer, p. 102.

unresolved opposition rather than being forced dialectically into any final truth. Certainly the residual metaphysical undercurrents of Dreiser's writing remain strong: *Sister Carrie* (1900) was originally entitled "The Flesh and the Spirit" and allotted chapter titles like "The Spirit Awakens: New Search for the Gate"; *Jennie Gerhardt* talks of how "the spirit of Jennie" is "caged in the world of the material" and how "such a nature is almost invariably an anomaly"; while later in the same novel the narrator comments on how "we live in an age in which the impact of materialized forces is well-nigh irresistible; the spiritual nature is over-whelmed by the shock." The particular social form of this metaphysical idealism varies: it becomes Lutheran in *Jennie Gerhardt,* Quaker in *The Bulwark* (1946), Oriental in *The Stoic* (1947). But the underlying premise remains the same: the pattern is of a fall into the corrupt material world, the collapse of the soul into an inferno of money and what Dreiser charmlessly calls "the sex force."[33] Thus Dreiser's "naturalism" is never grounded upon the self-enclosed empiricism of a natural world, but should be seen rather as an unveiling or iconoclastic dismantling of a latent realm of the spirit. Rather than being any kind of photographic replication of "real" life, Dreiser's work forms one side of an equation that is setting itself in intertextual opposition to what it conceives to be a failed idealism.

This failed idealism should not be seen simply as deriving from Cath-olic sources. According to Ellen Moers, Dreiser was "a child of two very different religious traditions," who, toward the end of his life especially, revealed more sympathy with his mother's Anabaptist spirituality than with the more tangible substances and practices of his father's Catholi-cism. Interestingly enough, Dreiser in later life criticized Catholicism (and other institutionalized religions) for becoming excessively "pow-erful and wholly practical and political organizations," which, he feared, would turn Christianity into "a great, solid, material-seeming affair."[34] The churches, according to Dreiser, were becoming too much a part of the American capitalist and corporate world. As we saw earlier, this kind of parallel is very obvious in *A Traveller at Forty* (1923), in which Dreiser implicitly aligns the "accentuated craft, lust, brutality and greed" at the court of the Borgias with the unscrupulous manners of modern American financiers, a parallel that serves to reemphasize the comparisons within his own fiction between the pressures of religious subjugation and those of industrial dehumanization.[35] In an attempt to overcome this unhappy situation, Dreiser's later works experiment with various shades of meta-

---

33 Theodore Dreiser, *The Bulwark* (Garden City: Doubleday, 1946), p. 33.
34 Moers, *Two Dreisers,* pp. xiii, 293.
35 Theodore Dreiser, *A Traveller at Forty* (New York: Century, 1923), p. 336.

physical idealism in the hope of incorporating a more redemptive sense of New Testament "spirit." In his plays, strange abstract characterizations like "The Shadow" (in *The Blue Sphere*) and "The Rhythm of the Universe" (in *Laughing Gas*) testify to the redundancy of the autonomous human being, but they also try spiritually to transform this landscape of despair by invoking the mystical selflessness and ecstatic anonymity of Oriental religions. In Dreiser's posthumous novel *The Stoic*, we find Dreiser's metaphysical bent once again inserted into the context of Eastern thought, as Berenice becomes committed to the philosophy of the Bhagavad Gita, with its doctrine of how "the limited thought of the self ... was lost in the larger thought of the not self that brought about forgetfulness of self in the nervous person, and so health."[36] It is, moreover, not difficult to see parallels between these various forms of monism and Dreiser's own literary style. The obtrusive symbolism of his novels – the rocking chair in *Sister Carrie*, the lobster and squid in *The Financier* – becomes another aspect of Dreiser's universalist determinism, because each part of the novel becomes synecdochic of every other part: the fraction implies the whole. The dominant symbols within each novel internally determine its action and allow as little scope for random fluctuations in a textual sense as Dreiser's abstract philosophy allows in a conceptual sense. Each novel becomes a series of claustrophobic parallels and mirroring devices that offer no way out of the cage.

It is this sense of fatality, coupled with the poor immigrant boy's urgent desire for social success, that gives rise to an irreparable contradiction in Dreiser's work. The individual is desperate for achievement in the conventional American way, but the destiny of that individual is not within his or her own hands. The Horatio Alger game is accepted, but the premises upon which that game is constructed are inverted. This is why Dreiser, like Farrell and Fitzgerald, comes so close to parodying the American Dream. In *An American Tragedy*, Clyde Griffiths is not in any sense a rugged nonconformist, on the contrary, he wholeheartedly subscribes to the values of upward mobility propagated by his culture; but then he finds the ideology of the self-made man exposed as a chimera by the events on the boating lake, when Roberta Alden somehow tumbles into the water. It is not only legal notions of "justice" that are portrayed by Dreiser here as being fraudulent: the law clearly supposes a person to be freely responsible for his or her own actions, but so does the idea of social justice institutionalized by the United States's democratic dream of freedom of opportunity. In *An American Tragedy* and *Sister Carrie*, Dreiser establishes the conventional frameworks for material success but then, by refusing to deliver the goods of materialism, frustrates the great

36 Dreiser, *The Stoic*, p. 277.

expectations that these circumstances would normally imply. As with Farrell and Fitzgerald, Dreiser's inheritance of the mythology of Catholicism places him in an uneasy relationship with the central premises of American society, for while his national culture emphasized personal freedom, his religious inheritance did not.

Toward the end of Dreiser's life, he was selected as a surrogate literary father by James T. Farrell, who wrote of how in his youth Dreiser's name had the same "magical effect" for him as that of baseball stars like Joe Jackson and Ty Cobb.[37] Dreiser subsequently became an admirer of Farrell's work and in fact sought Farrell's advice on the manuscript drafts of his last novels, *The Bulwark* and *The Stoic*. Both men shared similar immigrant family backgrounds and both flirted for a while with communism, though they generally believed the muddy mixture of human nature to be fundamentally at odds with the perfectionist impulse of Marxist rationalism. Just as Dreiser and Farrell could never commit themselves altogether to rationalism, so they were never fully fledged materialists; although many critics have linked Dreiser and Farrell together under the banner of "naturalism," Farrell himself always resisted this label both for himself and for his friend. Recalling how he advised Dreiser not to modify the "mystical and religious overtones" in *The Bulwark,* Farrell observed: "I had been aware that Dreiser was not the thoroughgoing determinist and naturalist which many of his critics have described him to be."[38] In an interview a few years before his death, Farrell remarked upon something similar in his own work: "Of course I've always thought there's multiple causation. That is, I didn't think that economic causation was always the decisive factor, but that there's multiple causation." For both authors, the matrix of Catholicism, in various unorthodox and modified forms, is one "causation" that competes with other more obvious and immediate factors within their texts. Emile Zola's claim that "metaphysical man" was dead is not borne out by the complex medley of forces we see operating here.[39]

The quintessentially Irish-Catholic context of Farrell's works hardly needs emphasizing. In the Studs Lonigan trilogy (1932–5), set in a lower-middle-class Chicago community between 1916 and 1931, religion is a determining influence upon Studs both consciously and unconsciously: "He didn't know that he bowed his head when he muttered the Lord's

37 James T. Farrell, *Reflections at Fifty and Other Essays* (New York: Vanguard, 1954), p. 128.
38 Ibid., p. 137.
39 Dennis Flynn and Jack Salzman, "An Interview with James T. Farrell," *Twentieth-Century Literature*, 22 (1976), 6; Marcus Klein, *Foreigners: The Making of American Literature* (Chicago: Univ. of Chicago Press, 1981), p. 208.

name, just as Sister Cyrilla had always taught them to do."[40] Within the claustrophobic environment of St. Patrick's parish, inexorable racial differences appear to testify to the redundancy of Crèvecoeur's idyllic melting-pot myth. In her contention that "the public schools ain't no place for Catholic children" (*YL* 46), Studs Lonigan's mother displays an attitude the most staunchly separatist Catholic clerics would have been proud of. Moreover, the general hostility to "niggers and kikes" (*YL* 19) throughout this trilogy is very marked. "Hook-nosed, bow-legged" Davey Cohen (*YL* 29) earns widespread ridicule for his dedication to learning and the life of the imagination, while in *Judgment Day* Studs's father bemoans how the neighborhood is being dragged down by other immigrant groups: "What with the Jew international bankers holding all the money here, and the Polacks and Bohunks squeezing the Irish out of politics, it's getting to be no place for a white man to live" (*JD* 306). The Catholic milieu is explicit also in Lonigan's admiration for the defeated 1928 presidential candidate, Al Smith – "If there hadn't been such a dirty A.P.A. anti-Catholic prejudice against Al Smith, he would have been elected" (*JD* 419) – in Studs's dedication to the Order of Christopher where he develops a "zeal for martyrdom" (*JD* 150), and in the general hostility toward art, education, or indeed any form of secular idealism that might direct attention away from those religious "truths" vested within the landscapes of Studs's childhood. Patrick Lonigan informs his son that "you're better off without an education, and a lot of book-learning" (*JD* 53), not that there is much chance of Studs falling victim to those particular vices.

Catholicism is implicit, though hardly less apparent, in the attitude of Studs and his friends toward women. Religious prohibitions lead to a mixture of obsessive fantasy coupled with intense fear of the opposite sex, resulting in male bonding and an emergence of the familiar madonna–whore complex. In *Young Lonigan,* Studs's childhood dream girl, Lucy Scanlan, appears as "something different and purer" and women generally as "higher creatures that a guy just couldn't understand, no matter how much he tried" (*YL* 107). Meanwhile, Studs's own mundane body, with its "aches and dirty thoughts" (*YL* 111) is viewed by him as an object merely of contempt. By the time of his *Young Manhood,* Studs is foolish enough to take the "cherry" of Nellie Cullen after a dance, an indulgence that leaves him with a "dose," thus rendering him unfit to squire Lucy Scanlan around the night spots of Chicago: "And it made

40 James T. Farrell, *Studs Lonigan: A Trilogy Containing Young Lonigan, The Young Manhood of Studs Lonigan, Judgment Day* (New York: Random House – Modern Library, 1938), p. 9 of *Young Lonigan.* Subsequent page references are given in parentheses in the text. *Young Lonigan* is abbreviated as *YL; The Young Manhood of Studs Lonigan* as *YM; Judgment Day* as *JD.*

him feel like a louse, him still not completely cured from the dose that little bitch from Nolan's had given him, taking Lucy out when he had a dirty disease. He felt as if he wanted to crawl before her on his hands and knees, and kiss the hem of her dress" (*YM* 278). Open violence toward women is not uncommon. In *Judgment Day*, Studs views with approval a film wherein Joey Gallagher chastises his girlfriend by "planting his foot into her buttocks," a gesture welcomed by Studs as "the way to treat a high-hat broad like that" (*JD* 66–7).

In the time-honored fashion of poor, claustrophobic Catholic communities, however, both madonnas and whores must compete for the hero's attention with the incestuous claims of his own beloved mother: Mrs. Lonigan kisses Studs well into his late teens, declaring that he "would always be her baby" (*YM* 155). Nor is Studs averse to taking an interest in female family members of his own generation: with Frances, "dirty thoughts rushed to his head like hot blood. He told himself he was a bastard because... she was his sister" (*YL* 62). The Italian-American hero Tony Camonte in Howard Hawks's 1932 film *Scarface* finds himself in a similar familial quandary. The incestuous atmosphere developed among the immediate family is, in one sense, another version of the more conceptual kind of incest suggested by the church: Mother Church refuses to surrender her children and demands that they be faithful to her rather than move out into a potentially dangerous world of confusion and difference.

The clannish and separatist nature of Studs's environment is, then, fairly obvious, and one might suggest this environment is reflected in the tortuous, muddied locutions of Farrell's prose. The "gracelessness," as Alfred Kazin noted, seems so methodical that it becomes "a significant style in itself": the reader feels himself wading through a heavy linguistic swamp in the same way as Studs becomes bogged down in the mire of social and economic poverty around St. Patrick's parish.[41] Nevertheless, played off against the separatism of Studs's "old, not-belonging feeling" (*YM* 252), we find various strands in this trilogy that signify the way Catholic communities in the early twentieth century were becoming more "Americanized," were seeking to integrate themselves within the dominant frameworks of cultural life. The theme of patriotism remains strong throughout, with the Lonigan family wholeheartedly joining in celebrations of "the President and the Flag." At the beginning of *Young Manhood*, Studs, praying at the stations of the cross, displaces his desire for martyrdom into a wish to die for his country during the First World War: "If he was killed in action," he thinks, "it would be a hero's death"

41 Alfred Kazin, *On Native Grounds: An Interpretation of Modern American Prose Literature* (New York: Harcourt, Brace and World, 1942), p. 381.

(*YM* 7). Studs aims to imitate Christ's passage to Calvary by an act of self-sacrifice through which he can demonstrate his patriotism: "Old Glory that had never kissed the dust in defeat. . . . Old Glory! His Flag! Proudly he told himself: I'm an American" (*YM* 36). Curiously enough, a great many American flags tend to be waved around in the work of Catholic authors – one thinks of all the icons of national myth in Robert Altman's films – and while this might be attributed partly to the insecurity of aliens wishing urgently to display their patriotic allegiance, it may also be the case that Catholics tend to have a cultural predilection for seizing upon and investing significance in emblems of communal iconography. Studs Lonigan and his companions rally around the American flag in the same way they rally around their church monuments. For Studs, the nation of the United States itself becomes an extended *ecclesia*, a social institution to be explained not so much by reference to its inner meanings as by its external badges of membership.

The Lonigans, then, are essentially conformists. They conform to the demands of their church and the demands of their country, and this temperament is reflected also in their acquiescence in the social status quo. It is because of the strength of this conventional outlook that in *Judgment Day* the Lonigans find the Great Depression of the 1930s so hard to fathom. Patrick Lonigan, who has always been implacably opposed to trade unions, now finds himself unable to afford an oxygen tent for his stricken son; while Studs himself, who insists on rejecting "the Bolsheviks" as "against the country and the church" (*JD* 182), finds himself unemployed and without enough money to marry Catherine Banahan. Inevitably the blame falls upon the "Jew international bankers" (*JD* 306): Patrick hopes they will soon be able to get "a strong man . . . like Al Smith or Mussolini" into the White House, "that'll make America a country for Americans only" (*JD* 76). Patrick Lonigan instinctively assumes that he himself is a true, assimilated American, whereas the Jews are not. This kind of anti-Semitism was also a feature of Father Coughlin's infamous radio broadcasts during the 1930s; Coughlin's enthusiasm for public ownership and his loathing of financial fraud led him into a crazed hatred for what he took to be the usurious practices of Jews, a hatred that struck a chord in many Catholic blue-collar homes at this time.

It is this odd mixture of alienation on the one hand and conformity on the other that produces metaphors of the fight and the game, two of the dominant images in American Catholic fiction of the twentieth century. In the Lonigan trilogy, there is a great deal of casual violence, with street fights and gang warfare reflecting the social environment within which Studs is brought up; but, more than this, the fight becomes symbolic of the struggles Catholics think they must undertake to be successful within the American social system. Because they are conformist, they believe in the value of society's conventional prizes; but because they are alienated, these prizes do not come naturally to Farrell's Catholics, so they have to fight harder to achieve them. When Studs boasts "I'm small but I'm awfully tough" (*YL* 69), we should see the smallness as a social as well as a physical inferiority and the toughness as a direct response to both. Fittingly, Studs admires boxers like Jack Dempsey and Terry McGovern, whose "fighting heart that only an Irishman could own" (*YL* 97) is a crystallized image of the immigrant underdog fighting his way to success and fame. After suffering various economic setbacks in *Young Manhood,* Studs starts thinking "of himself as a prizefighter or some kind of an athlete putting himself in condition to come back" (*YM* 230). As in some of the films of Martin Scorsese – *Raging Bull,* for instance, which focuses upon the career of the boxer Jake La Motta – this intense drive to "make it" proves to be disorienting for the protagonists in a psychological sense, for the perpetual desire to "beat" people begins to result in the development of violent and sadistic attitudes within personal relationships.

This tension also, in Studs's case, leads to an obsession with the idea of the game. Studs is very proud of his high-school football triumphs and is constantly yearning to repeat them, vainly hoping in this way to impress potential girlfriends. The game signifies for him an arena of clear-cut rules, a place where cerebral doubt and ambiguity are irrelevant and pure force can win the day, a situation that obviously suits Studs down to the ground. But the image of the game also connotes for Studs that larger field of American capitalist society, where there are winners and losers and the essential thing is to fight one's way to triumph. The important point here is how social and economic success is equated with technical expertise, not with moral superiority. It was in the first decade of this century that Weber made his famous parallel between the "Protestant ethic" and "the spirit of capitalism," suggesting how under Protestantism the making of money becomes an ethical imperative in itself and not simply a means toward a further end. As Weber argued, for the Protestant temperament economic success has traditionally been associated with ethical excellence, the paradigm of this in the United States being the Benjamin Franklin model of thrift, diligence, and self-discipline. Protestantism's emphasis on worldly zeal and energetic individuality was contrasted by Weber with the more disdainful approach to terrestrial success epitomized by Thomas Aquinas, who declared himself in favor of work only for the maintenance of self and the community. Where this end is achieved, said Aquinas, the precept ceases to have any meaning.[42]

42 See Max Weber, *The Protestant Ethic and the Spirit of Capitalism,* trans. Talcott Parsons (New York: Scribner's, 1958), p. 159.

American Catholicism has tended to follow Aquinas rather than Franklin by firmly dissociating secular and commercial from moral ideals. The moral ideals of Farrell's characters are rooted in another area of existence altogether. While these characters certainly welcome economic power, they see its acquisition as an ethically neutral technique, like the skill needed to win a game. In Studs's mind, success is symbolically associated with the art of playing pool: "He remembered the feeling of power he had had, running the table, his eye, brains, arm, all of himself concentrated on the balls, all clicking together like a coordinated machine, and the thrill that went with each shot as the balls were smashed, cut, banked, eased into the pockets" (YM 166–7). These images bring to mind two other Scorsese films. In the prologue to The Last Waltz (1978), members of The Band play a pool game called "cutthroat," clearly envisioned as a parallel to the savage competition in the rock music industry that this film goes on to chronicle. The object of cutthroat, explains Rick Danko in answer to a question from Scorsese, is to keep your balls on the table while knocking everybody else's off. And in a later film, The Color of Money (1987), Scorsese's heroes conquer American society by quite literally achieving wealth on the pool table. The urban, lower-class Italian–Catholic world of Scorsese's early films is very similar in tone to Farrell's world, not only in its landscapes and themes but also in its metaphors of alienation, struggle, and success.

The corollary to this dissociation of social achievement from moral prowess is that success inevitably becomes something of a lottery. If success is not something one inevitably deserves, it might be something one can help to induce by skill or determination, but elements of luck and chance will almost certainly be involved as well. Hence life appears to Studs as not only a game but also a gamble, where the greatest asset is not Franklinesque zeal but simply being dealt a good set of cards. Brooding in Judgment Day on his misfortune in being caught up in the depression, Studs thinks of how "all along, always during the old days, he had felt that somehow, some day, he was going to pull a royal flush out of the deck of life," and this belief in the efficacy of chance leads him to hope that "in the morning, maybe it would all pass away, the market would start going up" (JD 209). In Religion and the Decline of Magic, the historian Keith Thomas wrote of how the heathen concept of fortune continued to be a powerful idea for Christians during the Middle Ages, but how it was later repudiated by Tudor theologians like Bishop Pilkington, for whom "the very idea of Fortune was an insult to God's sovereignty." According to the Puritan ideology of divine providence and divine retribution that developed in Tudor times, the "course of worldly events could... be seen as the working-out of God's judgments."[43] This faith in providence became, of course, an official tenet of Puritan America, with Catholic sympathy for the goddess of fortune becoming channeled into a subversive, oppositional framework.

As Thomas noted, there is also a more mundane social context for this devotion to fortune: "The worship of the goddess Fortune began in the classical world, where the social system gave little opportunity for hard work to reap its own reward. In modern times the gambling complex – seeing life in terms of 'the lucky break' – remains the philosophy of the unsuccessful."[44] Thus in Farrell, as in Robert Altman's film *California Split* and Mario Puzo's account *Inside Las Vegas,* there is a fascination with the roulette wheel, and with gambling generally, as the means by which underdogs might break into the worlds of success offered by American society. Yet these empirical observations on the role of fortune remain insufficient unless they are also informed by a framework of (displaced) theology. By declining to equate material and spiritual well-being, the American Catholic heritage refuses to view the typically strenuous business life as a guarantee of, or even a pointer toward, eternal salvation, and this deprives the nation's commercial culture of that spiritual ambience with which it is invested by the Protestant tradition. The central emphasis of so many short stories by Flannery O'Connor is upon how the impoverished outcast or rebel can be nearer to divine grace than the smug patriarch encompassed by all the usual commodities and rewards of an arduous secular life. Within the American Catholic tradition, capitalism is denied any aura of mystification, and so the American Dream is often represented in its barest functional outlines: as a game, a boxing ring, a football pitch, a pool hall, a gambling table.

The other central way in which the Studs Lonigan trilogy reveals its displaced Catholicism is in the hero's lack of any cohesive center of self. I suggested in the introductory chapter that Althusser's conception of "interpellation" could be seen as a transformed version of Catholic philosophy, and of no sequence of novels is "interpellation" a more appropriate term than these three. Studs is caught up in a world of cinematic sequences, fantasies of success in war, sport, and so on, to such an extent that the distinction between phantasmal and literal reality often becomes blurred for the reader. It is also noticeable how often Studs perceives himself from the outside, seeing himself as he thinks others see him. Not only does he abnegate his ego by projecting it into an empathy with film stars on the silver screen, he also compromises his sense of emotional selfhood by concentrating upon his external image as viewed through

43 Keith Thomas, *Religion and the Decline of Magic: Studies in Popular Beliefs in Sixteenth and Seventeenth Century England* (London: Weidenfeld and Nicolson, 1971), pp. 79, 89.
44 Ibid., p. 111.

the eyes of others: "Studs felt a thrill of pride as he signalled the readiness of his team; hundreds of people were watching, saw that he was captain" (*YM* 122). It is the antithesis of Emerson's self-reliant man, the romantic soul with an "original relation to the universe." All Studs's relations to the universe are inherited, and he acts as he thinks he ought to act: "Would it or wouldn't it be a good idea to get married? Everybody did, and had kids. He guessed that maybe you couldn't help yourself about it when the right broad came along. That was what love was" (*YM* 159). It is the traditional and indeed stereotypical idea of Catholic passivity that social historians such as Oscar Handlin discovered among the immigrants in nineteenth-century Boston. This denial of free will accounts, of course, for the stagnant state of life Studs finds himself in, and for his inability to remake himself in terms of either psychology or environment. He is trapped within, to quote the title of a later Farrell novel, "A World I Never Made."

This air of fatalism also pervades Farrell's later Danny O'Neill pentalogy, though here the author succeeds more in critically distancing himself from his material so that the sense of claustrophobia is balanced by a tone of ironic humor. This is particularly true of the comic representation of Grandmother O'Flaherty, with her rigid insistence that "we must all bend ourselves to the will of God," her implicit trust in the distribution of holy water as a remedy for every catastrophe, and her repressive attitude toward her unfortunate middle-aged son Al, whom she vows to "take . . . over me knee" should he ever think of abandoning her by getting married.[45] Incest is brought to the surface openly in the first novel, *A World I Never Made* (1936), when Margaret O'Flaherty's friend, Martha, complains of having been raped at the age of thirteen by her father; indeed, the O'Neill-O'Flaherty novels generally rotate upon the repetitive axis of "sin," guilt, beatings, violence, and recrimination, a cyclic psychological process mirrored by the economic imprisonment of these Catholic families. Jim O'Neill, for example, unluckily finds he has sired too many offspring for his limited financial resources to cope with, and so his son Danny is sent off to live with his cousins, the O'Flahertys. Protestants are as absent from these novels as (say) whites are absent from the world of Toni Morrison, which is why it is such a surprise when a group of charitable Baptists and Presbyterians visit the O'Neills after Jim's stroke in *Father and Son* (1940). The visitors here are made to feel emphatically unwelcome – "may they burn those ugly faces of theirs in the fires of hell," cries Jim's wife Lizz – for Jim prefers to suffer by perceiving his fatal illness as "punishment for his sins," in the

45 James T. Farrell, *No Star Is Lost* (New York: Vanguard, 1938), pp. 620, 444. Subsequent page references are given in parentheses in the text following the abbreviation *NS*.

same way Margaret O'Flaherty masochistically courts misery in her frustrated adulterous relationship with Lorry Johnson.[46] Unconsciously believing her sorrow to be appropriate retribution for her sense of sin, Margaret dramatizes to herself her own unhappiness – "Heavy the cross. Miserable the road" (NS 272) – and finds a kind of perverse sensuality in humiliation.

Margaret is an interesting character because on the surface she is involved in energetic rebellion against the manners and morals of her family – she engages in a violent spitting match with her "dirty old Irish" mother in A World I Never Made.[47] Yet in the subsequent No Star Is Lost, fantasies of guilt continue to haunt her mind – "Devils wearing green lights danced in Margaret's head" (NS 379) – and her desire for existential freedom is eventually defeated by the umbilical cord that, as she imagines, ties her to the O'Flaherty family: "It's because of the way I was treated when I was a little girl. I was beat so, that's why I have my nerves" (NS 394). In his 1936 essay "Social Theories in American Realism," Farrell described what he took to be a shift in fiction away from an emphasis upon autonomous personal consciousness, which he associated with Henry James, toward the Dreiserian idiom where "characters take on coloration of the environment."[48] Certainly within Farrell's own Catholic landscapes the environment tends to determine character rather than the other way around. We see this determinism working also upon Margaret's brother Al, whose emphasis upon the sanctity of the home and implicit confidence in the sportsmanlike American system – "You got to play the game according to the rules to get anywhere" (WNM 104) – echoes the kind of conformity that pervades the Studs Lonigan trilogy. In A World I Never Made, shoe-shop assistant Al is quite content with his own social position; he enthusiastically endorses Leo XIII's encyclicals condemning socialism as being "against the home and the family and religion" (WNM 177).

The only character here who does eventually rebel against the constrictions of his past and turn to socialism is Farrell's alter ego, Danny O'Neill. Initially Danny, rather like Studs Lonigan, interests himself in a kind of martyrological meritocracy, courting pain and glory on the football field – "If you loved football, any sacrifice for it was justified" (FS 411) – and planning in Father and Son to become the first American

46 James T. Farrell, Father and Son (New York: Vanguard, 1940), pp. 454, 404. Subsequent page references are given in parentheses in the text following the abbreviation FS.
47 James T. Farrell, A World I Never Made (New York: Vanguard, 1936), p. 330. Subsequent page references are given in parentheses in the text following the abbreviation WNM.
48 Quoted in Alan M. Wald, James T. Farrell: The Revolutionary Socialist Years (New York: New York Univ. Press, 1978), p. 123.

saint. However, during his spell at the University of Chicago he loses his religious faith and takes up socialism instead. It is significant that Danny begins to see himself as less American and more Irish as the sequence develops. At the beginning of *My Days of Anger* (1943), Danny's friends view him as an Horatio Alger figure, "a child of success in an age of success"; but as his oppositional temper increases, so does his sense of ethnic identity and consequent social displacement: "He was Irish. Not a drop of any other blood in him for generations."[49] William Boelhower has suggested that chronicles of American immigrant life are often cast in the form of trilogies, or other sequences of novels, to reflect the "perspectival system inherent in the immigrant experience, which is patterned on the spatial shift from Old World to New World and is naturally concerned with the attempt to establish a trajectory of continuity out of what might be called a catastrophic act of topological dislocation."[50] While this may be generally true, the Danny O'Neill sequence works in exactly the opposite way to this, because here the hero comes to feel less "continuity" and more of a sense of difference and alienation as he goes along. In his case, the quest for psychological coherence and ultimate assimilation into American life does not reach a grand climax as the sequence of novels ends. On the contrary, Danny's religious and ethnic inheritance is found finally to be incompatible with the passage of natural development Boelhower's formula would imply.

Ethnic divergence from WASP assumptions is consistently associated by Farrell with political radicalism. The Jewish union organizer Levinsky in *A World I Never Made* and the communist Bernstein in *My Days of Anger* both define themselves in opposition to the views epitomized by the stock figure "A. Lincoln Jones" in the latter novel, who solemnly praises the "Anglo-Saxon American system of ideas of self-government and initiative" (*DA* 142). In Farrell's later trilogy centered upon the character of Bernard Carr, the radical Carr is so interested in Irish culture that he plans to write a study of it. Carr and Danny O'Neill are haunted by anxieties about not belonging in America, and so they invent this legend of Irish cultural roots in an attempt to recover for themselves a reassuring sense of plenitude and identity. Michael M. J. Fischer has written recently of how "ethnicity" itself is an unstable concept that is necessarily refracted through the vagaries of human memory and should, therefore, be seen as a psychological rather than sociological phenome-

---

49 James T. Farrell, *My Days of Anger* (New York: Vanguard, 1943), pp. 54, 100. Subsequent page references are given in parentheses in the text following the abbreviation *DA*.

50 William Boelhower, "Ethnic Trilogies: A Genealogical and Generational Poetics," in *The Invention of Ethnicity,* ed. Werner Sollors (New York: Oxford Univ. Press, 1989), p. 158.

non: "It is often transmitted less through cognitive language or learning," said Fischer, "than through processes analogous to the dreaming and transference of psychoanalytic encounters."[51] This is exactly what we find with Farrell's characters: their self-defined "Irish" ethnicity is not so much an anthropological awareness as a fictive mask they create within their minds in an effort to alleviate their own psychic confusion. This assumption of ethnic identity also helps them to rationalize situations in which they find themselves marginalized by intangible forces governing the social and economic structures of society. It is undoubtedly true that the nostalgia of Farrell's characters for their Irish "roots" is, in a strictly theoretical sense, a doomed project; no ultimate point of ethnic origin is conceivable, all categories are fluctuating and mixed. It is true as well that this image of society's "mainstream," which Bernard Carr and Danny O'Neill define themselves against, is itself an evanescent, if not entirely insubstantial, fiction. Fischer noted that the contemporary ethnographer must avoid the simplistic process of "comparison by strict dualistic contrast," but this theoretical pitfall is not one that Carr and O'Neill manage to avoid.[52] The idea that American society was dominated at this time by a homogeneous Protestant establishment is demonstrably false; the crucial point, however, is that Farrell's characters firmly believe this conspiracy theory to be true. They project a monolithic conception of WASP hegemony from within their own minds to explain away their material poverty and psychological insecurity.

The pattern of myth making here is the same as that by which Studs Lonigan hankers after the impossible plenitude of the past, "some supposed status-quo-ante when the tribal institutions were harmonious with life," as Marcus Klein put it.[53] The immature Studs is of course neurotically terrified by the prospect of change and difference; yet this fear of loss, which he so naively embodies, is the same kind of fear that, in less brutal forms, works its way through most of Farrell's fiction. One of the reasons his characters constantly invent legends and fantasies about their lives is that they hope subliminally to erase existential anxieties and complexities by transposing them into the charmed circles of self-engendered myth. Farrell's literary style is sometimes flat and monotonous not because of any lack of sophistication on the author's part but because his texts are concerned with reflecting the thought processes of people who would prefer to suture the inevitable contradictions of ex-

51 Michael M. J. Fischer, "Ethnicity and the Post-Modern Arts of Memory," in *Writing Culture: The Poetics and Politics of Ethnography* (Berkeley: Univ. of California Press, 1986), pp. 195–6.

52 Ibid., p. 201.

53 Klein, *Foreigners*, p. 214.

istence with wooden obsessions, rather than confronting these difficulties with an open intelligence.

It is through this kind of psychological transference that Danny O'Neill is bound not to the practices of Catholicism but to its memory. Despite his atheism, Danny cherishes the myth of Catholicism as a refuge from social alienation and epistemological uncertainty. On one level, this is the same irony of apostasy we saw operating in the character of Margaret O'Flaherty. Danny is entwined with the idea of the church even as he attempts to evade its clutches precisely because of the ways in which metaphors of religion have conditioned his sensibility: "'Goddamn you, you non-existent God!' he flung to the star-filled sky" (DA 249). Danny's feelings of religious guilt at having consorted with a prostitute are also all too evident: he feels "soiled" (DA 261) because "sin was so casual" (DA 312). Yet Danny's attachment to Catholicism is more self-conscious than Margaret's, and there is a feeling that, despite his reading of Nietzsche, he secretly nurtures the prohibitions of the church as lending spice and meaning to his life. When he takes a girl back to a hotel after a party, Danny humorously signs the register "Mr. and Mrs. Baude-laire," for it is Baudelaire's poetry of "vice, sin, and evil" (DA 312), together with Joyce's Ulysses, that now becomes his favored reading. Danny realizes he is still carrying the "ghosts" of his former selves with him, and while he is determined politically to "do battle so that others did not remain unfulfilled as he and his family had been," he is still aware that he will always carry with him these "scars and wounds" of his Catholic past (DA 401).

The problem here from a political point of view is that this compulsion to dive back into the past diverts attention from the socialist struggle for a better future. Farrell's next persona, Bernard Carr, ultimately discovers that the agenda of social radicalism is not compatible with the anguish of his lapsed Catholicism. Carr marches in the 1932 communist May Day parade and he flirts with the party throughout The Road Between (1949) and Yet Other Waters (1952). In these novels, he finds himself aesthetically and emotionally moved by the "Internationale" and the "Marseillaise" in much the same way as he is moved by Gregorian chants and Chartres Cathedral. But in the end these irrational attachments are overcome by a sense of rational detachment; Bernard comes to believe that communists and Catholics are both engaged upon the kind of "quest for certainty" he has spent the latter part of his life trying to avoid.[54] The writings of American communists come to seem to Bernard "ab-

54 James T. Farrell, Yet Other Waters (New York: Vanguard, 1952), p. 88. Subsequent page references are given in parentheses in the text following the abbreviation YOW.

stract, formal, even Jesuitical."[55] Of his own fictional hero Paddy Stanton, Carr remarks that "Paddy wants Communism to be a materialized Holy Trinity. He wants the Revolution to be a kind of virgin birth of history" – which is, says the skeptical Carr, "just the opposite of me" (*YOW* 88).

Farrell explicitly equated Catholic and communist martyrologies in some of his nonfiction essays during the 1950s, and in fact the situation readers find themselves confronted with in the Carr novels is a Philip Roth–like *mise en abîme* of authorial alter egos. Like Bernard Carr, Farrell himself experimented with communism in the mid–1930s and was particularly attracted to Trotsky's theories of art; but, as with Carr, Farrell's association with communism was a rebarbative one, with the author's attacks on what he conceived to be the excessive narrowness of Marxist aesthetic theory infuriating nearly everybody else in the party. However, like the fictional Carr's own fictional hero Patrick Stanton, both Carr and Farrell are themselves clearly enchained to the past and held in check by its psychological and cultural legacies. In this trilogy, Carr's process of existential self-definition gradually inverts itself into an obsession with time past as the hero plunges back into the South Side of Chicago, where he moons after his lost childhood love, Elsie Cavanagh. Carr's excuse for this is his belief that "there's continuity in everything, there's an individual continuity of past, present, and future in everybody's life" (*YOW* 79). Not surprisingly, though, Carr's vow to discover "my own continuity" does not find favor with the Marxist critics portrayed in *Yet Other Waters*, who dismiss Carr's new novel *A Boy's World* on the grounds that in this text-within-a-text "religion" is "treated with sympathy." "He has begun to burn incense and swing literary censers to yesterday," they complain (*YOW* 387).

Yet Carr's retrospective repining mirrors Farrell's own compulsion to repeat the past. Directly after completing the Carr trilogy with *Yet Other Waters,* Farrell looked back to his own earlier fictional world and produced *The Face of Time* (1953). Less a sequel than a prelude to the Danny O'Neill novels, *The Face of Time* focuses upon the lingering death from stomach cancer of Danny's grandfather Tom O'Flaherty, with Danny himself depicted here as a young child. The literary model for this "recherche du temps perdu" is clearly Proust, whom Farrell considered to be the greatest twentieth-century novelist and to whom he explicitly paid tribute in the essay "How *The Face of Time* Was Written."[56] Indeed, a Proustian sense of the inexorable passing of time works its way into

---

55 James T. Farrell, *The Road Between* (New York: Vanguard, 1949), p. 66. Subsequent
    page references are given in parentheses in the text following the abbreviation *TRB*.
56 Farrell, *Reflections at Fifty*, pp. 39–40.

many of Farrell's novels, which very often feature a long drawn-out death both as an ontological memento mori and as a sacrificial offering to the gods of the historical clock: Jim O'Neill in *Father and Son,* Grandmother O'Flaherty in *My Days of Anger,* Bernard Carr's father in *The Road Between,* and Carr's mother in *Yet Other Waters.* Farrell himself, in a 1977 interview, related this necrophilia to "the teaching and dogma of the Catholic Church" of his childhood, which firmly impressed upon him "the idea that the purpose of life was death" and that his own life existed in a brief "span . . . which must come to an end."[57] Again, we see the Catholic consciousness expressing human limitation, rather than those more familiar American horizons of infinite potential. However, in Farrell this sensitivity to the burdens of human mortality operates in tandem with an authorial yearning for the compensations of artistic immortality. Carr's fictional creation Patrick Stanton is said to write "so he might be important to posterity," a wish associated by Carr with his own (fictional) mother's ardor for a religious heaven (*TRB* 151). Farrell's fictional creation Bernard Carr wants to "try to write a book that would live as long as the Church, if not longer" (*TRB* 229). In the same way, Farrell himself openly admitted in interviews that the desire for posthumous fame was a primary motive behind his writing.

All of these characteristics – submission to the past, a sense of mortality, a longing for eternal life – emerge partly out of Farrell's Catholic inheritance. It would of course be absurd to claim that a longing for eternal life is confined only to Catholic culture; but it would be equally absurd to deny that a suitably transformed version of this religious idea is one component, among many others, in Farrell's work. In *Yet Other Waters,* Bernard Carr castigates his hero, Paddy Stanton, for failing to perceive the link between his discarded "Catholic absolutism" and his present-day adherence to communist orthodoxy: "He doesn't know a damned thing about his own emotions and drives," remarks Bernard scornfully (*YOW* 89). The implication is that self-conscious awareness of personal impulses and motivations constitutes a road to freedom, and Carr takes pride in the fact that this is the path he has embarked upon. Yet the texts of Farrell's novels do not altogether support this existential optimism. As we have seen, mythologies of Catholicism, albeit renegotiated and sublimated in various ways, deeply influence the structure and direction of Farrell's writing in a far more profound and wide-reaching way than Carr's easy parallel between Catholicism and communism would imply. It is not only the themes of these novels but also their shape and formal constituents that bear material traces of a particular cultural environment.

57 See Robert James Butler, "Christian and Pragmatic Visions of Time in the Lonigan Trilogy," *Thought,* 55 (1980), 462.

A less complex version of Farrell's kind of "Catholic" realism is the work of Pietro Di Donato, whose most famous novel *Christ in Concrete* was published in 1939. As with Farrell, Di Donato's narrative proceeds in a lumbering, mechanical prose style that is in fact mimetic of the world it describes, in this case the world of Italian Americans working in the New York construction industry. Di Donato is building blocks of prose, as it were, to recapitulate formally the crushing of human individuality by the brutal economic and industrial forces of America. Several of the characters in this novel are also crushed literally by buildings falling on top of them, a grim train of events that allows scope for Catholic patterns of martyrdom to reinvent themselves in a socioeconomic context: Annunziata reconciles herself to her husband's accidental death on the building site by reminding herself that "we live and suffer not in vain, and our reward awaits."[58] As with Farrell again, there is some impulse to break out of this cycle of passive suffering, for as the novel progresses Annunziata's son Paul begins to view matters from a more hard-headed political perspective. Di Donato himself subsequently followed the familiar modernist pattern by substituting communism for his lapsed Catholicism on the grounds that "I couldn't live without an ideal," and he later became enamored of Che Guevera and what he called Che's "society of brotherhood."[59]

Conversely, though, there is another sense in which the characters of *Christ in Concrete* appear to be deeply attached to, and protective of, their rituals of suffering. One of the reasons this novel is finally less satisfactory than Farrell's work is that Di Donato represents Italian immigrant life as locked away in a self-congratulatory and self-perpetuating world of its own, so that the ethnic wedding feasts and other activities seem to take place in an impossible historical vacuum. It is true that many of Farrell's characters also try to separate themselves from the rest of the world, but Farrell arranges his texts in such a way that the reader is able to apprehend how these characters who float between an imaginary ethnic past and an intimidating American future come to invent self-deluding fantasies to appease their cultural insecurity. In Farrell, the pressures of history impinge upon and therefore ironize the subjectivity of his characters, but in Di Donato this ironic, reflexive narrative stance is altogether less apparent. Whereas Farrell's texts reflect upon and interrogate the whole conception of ethnic identity, Di Donato tends to represent ethnicity as a simple and relatively unproblematical category.

Nevertheless, Di Donato's understanding of the novel as a medium

---

58 Pietro Di Donato, *Christ in Concrete* (Indianapolis: Bobbs-Merrill, 1939), p. 303.
59 Dorothée von Huene-Greenberg, "A MELUS Interview: Pietro Di Donato," *MELUS*, 14, nos. 3–4 (1987), 44, 50.

of incarnation does exemplify one important shift in emphasis in the collective imaginations of Dreiser, Farrell, and other Catholic modernist novelists. *Christ in Concrete* is structured upon a series of analogies between God and man: Paul, as an "artist of brick and mortar," is said to be following in the footsteps of Christ as a "poor carpenter," and Paul extends these materialized analogies by the way he envisions his late father, Geremio, informing him that this family of construction workers represents "Christ in concrete." Thus by coming "to crucified rest in the concrete forms," this Italian-American family is analogically imitating the crucified life of Christ, the implication being that God himself is present by transubstantiation within the human world.[60] The point here is that the concrete, incarnational, and fully embodied mode of "Catholic" fiction is different in emphasis from that more abstract, disembodied "Protestant" genre of American romance analyzed by Richard Chase. Protestant romance dissolves the mundane world into a more lucid spiritual allegory; Catholic realism invests the mundane world itself with sacramental significance. It would of course be foolish to claim that "realism" itself comprises a "Catholic" literary form. Yet this divergence from allegorical conflicts of good and evil in Dreiser and Farrell, together with their rejection of any idealistic "world elsewhere" or pastoral idyll, betokens a sharp withdrawal from the American tradition of Enlightenment humanism. Dreiser and Farrell are locked into a mode of imitation, not innovation; their texts prostrate themselves before the preexistent world rather than seeking romantically to transcend or redesign it. Their concentration on the mixed and unadulterated stuff of quotidian reality strikes a new note in American literature by its insistence upon the obduracy of material circumstances and upon the impossibility of any apocalyptic reordering of these circumscribed conditions of life.

60 Di Donato, *Christ in Concrete*, pp. 96, 84, 297.

7

Conformity and Parody: Scott Fitzgerald and *The Great Gatsby*

At the beginning of his writing career, Scott Fitzgerald made the apparently odd remark that he considered "H. L. Mencken and Theodore Dreiser the greatest men living in the country today." F. O. Matthiessen admitted to finding Fitzgerald's praise for Dreiser surprising, and certainly the cumbersome circumlocutions of Dreiser's prose are, in a stylistic sense, worlds away from Fitzgerald's grace and charm.[1] Nevertheless, as we shall see, the outlooks of Dreiser and Fitzgerald are not altogether dissimilar, in that both men perceived themselves as outsiders in American society, partly by virtue of their Catholic upbringings. It is true that Fitzgerald's family origins in the Catholic strongholds of Maryland and Saint Paul, Minnesota, were more upmarket than Dreiser's; nevertheless, the simple fact that both his parents were practicing Catholics placed Fitzgerald (so he thought) in a tense relationship with the institutions of society. As he wrote later in his notebook: "When I was young the boys in my street still thought that Catholics drilled in the cellar every night with the idea of making Pius the Ninth autocrat of the republic."[2] These general insecurities would not have been diminished by the fate of his father, fired from his job as a salesman for Procter and Gamble at the age of fifty-five and, according to André Le Vot, a man who had "a singular capacity for failing in everything he undertook." Again, one can see a link with Dreiser's father, the hapless John Paul Dreiser, who lost all his property to what the family called "Yankee trickery."[3] Fitzgerald's obsession with smart Princeton clubs and other emblems of social acceptability no doubt derived in part from this sense of outsiderhood implanted in his youth.

1 See F. O. Matthiessen, *Theodore Dreiser* (London: Methuen, 1951), p. 187.
2 See Joan M. Allen, *Candles and Carnival Lights: The Catholic Sensibility of F. Scott Fitzgerald* (New York: New York Univ. Press, 1978), p. 21.
3 André Le Vot, *F. Scott Fitzgerald,* trans. William Byron (Harmondsworth: Penguin, 1985), p. 6; Matthiessen, *Theodore Dreiser,* p. 5.

Fitzgerald remained a practicing Catholic at Princeton and it was not until 1918, at the age of twenty-one, that he confided to his journal this would be his "last year as a Catholic." Then, however, he turned to an enthusiastic apostasy, displaying open contempt toward the piety and bigotry of the Irish with whom he had come in contact in his hometown. Nor was Fitzgerald enamored of the religious fervor he encountered on a trip to Rome in 1925, declared a Holy Year by Pope Pius XI, or "Pope Siphilis the Sixth and His Morons" as Fitzgerald vengefully named the papal entourage.[4] Leslie Fiedler has in fact claimed that Fitzgerald's books "have no religious insights, only religious décor" and that in Fitzgerald we see how the "sensibility of the Catholic in America becomes, like everything else, puritan." Fieldler's implicit equation of "religious insights" with some "profound sense of evil or sin" seems again to prioritize the kind of dualistic, Manichaean impulse that is more relevant to Poe or Melville than to the analogical, integrative sensibility of the "Catholic" Fitzgerald.[5] Nevertheless, it is true there is more than a touch of traditional American Puritanism about the sexual attitudes within Fitzgerald's novels. As Joan Allen said, for a writer proclaimed in his youth as risqué and shocking, Fitzgerald is remarkably squeamish about all aspects of sexuality. Pristine purity is the preferred mode, as in *The Beautiful and Damned* (1922) where Gloria admires the "Films Par Excellence" studio because it is so clean and new, so unlike the "heavy closeness" and the "scent of soiled and tawdry costumes which years before had revolted her behind the scenes of a musical comedy." This is, as Allen noted, the familiar Augustinian dichotomy of spirit and matter transferred into contemporary terms. Visiting General Lee's old home at Arlington, Gloria is outraged by a "Ladies' Toilet" sign, a memento of the gross requirements of the flesh.[6]

The corollary of this Augustinian antithesis is the traditional madonna–whore complex, with which Fitzgerald's texts are also richly stocked. *The Beautiful and Damned* jokily meditates on how Anthony and Gloria are souls made for each other in heaven, and Anthony is said to admire the aptly named Gloria precisely because she rises above the realms of the corporeal. Another familiar Fitzgerald idea emerging from this dualistic outlook is the way a spiritually intact man is helped on his path to destruction by a predatory, devouring female. Toward the end of *Tender*

---

4 Matthew J. Bruccoli, *Some Sort of Epic Grandeur: The Life of F. Scott Fitzgerald* (New York: Harcourt Brace Jovanovich, 1981), pp. 52, 89; Le Vot, *F. Scott Fitzgerald*, p. 180.
5 Leslie Fiedler, *An End to Innocence: Essays on Culture and Politics* (Boston: Beacon Press, 1955), p. 181.
6 Allen, *Candles and Carnival Lights*, pp. 44–5; F. Scott Fitzgerald, *The Beautiful and Damned* (New York: Scribner's, 1922), pp. 398, 166. Subsequent page references for *The Beautiful and Damned* are given in parentheses in the text.

Is the Night (1934), Nicole is represented as becoming more and more "evil-eyed," increasingly concerned to emasculate Dick's professional ambition: "Naturally Nicole, wanting to own him, wanting him to stand still forever, encouraged any slackness on his part."[7] D. S. Savage saw it as a fault of *Tender* that the narrative is told too much from the hero's point of view, exposing all of Nicole's flaws but none of Dick Diver's own; yet the structure of this novel is surreptitiously and subtly arranged to mirror that old medieval myth whereby a depraved woman leads a priestly man astray and deflects his attention from higher, disembodied ideals.[8]

Fiedler's thesis about the author's concern for religious decor rather than religious substance might also be borne out by a reading of Fitzgerald's first novel, *This Side of Paradise* (1920). Here emphasis falls upon a rejection of scientific positivism, the kind of intertwining of poetic and religious intensity Santayana and his circle at Harvard promulgated in the first decade of this century. Thus in Fitzgerald the "tall golden candlesticks and long, even chants," which Amory Blaine associates with the more glamorous kind of Catholicism espoused by Monsignor Darcy, become transformed into an apotheosized version of Princeton as a heavenly city, with "halls and cloisters . . . outlined each by myriad faint squares of yellow light."[9] We hear also of choral singing that "drifted over the campus in melancholy beauty" (59), and of the spiritualizing effect of the university's "Gothic architecture," whose "chastity of the spire" symbolizes its "upward trend" (60). (In one of his letters from Princeton, Fitzgerald described the college football players as "consecrated and unreachable – vaguely holy.")[10] The character of Monsignor Darcy in this novel is based upon Father Sigourney Webster Fay, whom Fitzgerald knew at Newman Academy in New Jersey, and who revealed to Fitzgerald a glittering and cosmopolitan new version of Catholicism quite different from the leaden dogmatism he had found within the Irish community of Minnesota. The "Swinburnian" Monsignor Darcy similarly convinces Amory Blaine of the intellectual superiority vested within this world of dazzling golden beauty, even though Amory regretfully recognizes how the harsh realities of the First World War are undermining the vestiges of this sanctified realm. Still, Fitzgerald's first novel reveals the shade of what Le Vot has called "a luminous oneness, the glittering

7 F. Scott Fitzgerald, *Tender Is the Night* (New York: Scribner's, 1934), p. 170. Subsequent page references are given in parentheses in the text.
8 D. S. Savage, "The Significance of F. Scott Fitzgerald," *Arizona Quarterly*, 8 (1952), 205.
9 F. Scott Fitzgerald, *This Side of Paradise* (New York: Scribner's, 1953), pp. 176, 59. Subsequent page references are given in parentheses in the text.
10 Le Vot, *F. Scott Fitzgerald*, p. 46.

lost paradise that haunts the fabric of his great works like a memory."[11] This elegiac sense is evident again in *The Beautiful and Damned:* here Anthony Patch is engaged in writing essays about the Renaissance popes, and he is also a devotee of the Middle Ages, much to the disapproval of his sternly commercial grandfather who believes the Middle Ages are better off left where they are. This is the same kind of antithesis between demystified positivism on the one hand and religious aesthetics on the other that we saw worked out in the thought of Charles Eliot Norton and other gurus of the nineteenth century.

While religious themes and images are evident enough on the surface of Fitzgerald's texts, then, the more problematical question is to what extent a Catholic cultural inheritance significantly modifies the wider directions of Fitzgerald's writing. One of Fitzgerald's biographers, Matthew J. Bruccoli, has denied that any important religious associations are to be found after the author's early maturity; Bruccoli claimed Fitzgerald simply abandoned his faith "without a backward glance," that there is no Catholicism in *The Great Gatsby,* and that Zelda subsequently replaced the church in the author's affections.[12] This, however, would surely postulate too cataclysmic a fissure in Fitzgerald's consciousness. For one thing, it seems clear that his religious inheritance caused these texts to be permeated with "guilt of a very Irish Catholic order," as Anthony Burgess put it.[13] Throughout Fitzgerald's novels runs the idea that, in a secular rather than a theological sense, the beautiful are necessarily the damned: one side of the equation implies the other. Anthony Patch, for instance, is oppressed by "a sense of waste" (54), a general feeling that he has not made the most of his opportunities. In his own eyes, so we are told, he "seemed to have inherited only the vast tradition of human failure" (218). Anthony parallels his own disasters with those he fancifully imposes upon his apartment's night elevator man, whose "air of being somewhat above his station . . . made him a pathetic and memorable figure of failure" (299). Dick Diver in *Tender Is the Night* is similarly obsessed with his increasingly inevitable dive into alcoholism, divorce, and professional obscurity, and it seems to be some latent sense of the ontological insufficiency of his own individual character that produces this guilt-ridden, masochistic streak in Diver's character. Like Farrell's heroes, Diver feels his sense of selfhood to be compromised by something he cannot control: "Dick was paying tribute to things unforgotten, unshriven, unexpurgated" (91). The word "unshriven" is significant: Dick is, as Fitzgerald wrote in his original plan for the book, a "spoiled priest,"

11 Ibid., p. 26.
12 Bruccoli, *Some Sort of Epic Grandeur,* p. 96.
13 Anthony Burgess, "Scott on the Rocks," *Observer Review,* 8 Apr. 1984, p. 22.

priestly in his various forms of idealism, but priestly also in his remorse at the necessary failure of that idealism within a corrupt world that appears to be, quite literally, beyond redemption.[14]

Ernest Hemingway once muttered scornfully about Fitzgerald's "cheap Irish love of defeat," and he was equally hostile to those introverted, confessional essays such as "The Crack-Up" which Fitzgerald produced in the 1930s to analyze the "sodden-dark" quality of his own "self-immolation," as he described it.[15] These essays are, as Andrew Turnbull said, "the work of a lapsed Catholic for whom confession was a rhythm of the soul."[16] What should be stressed, though, is that this sense of decline and fall in Fitzgerald is never merely a personal predicament but involves, in a larger way, a mordant perception of the irredeemably flawed and fragmented nature of human existence. Even in minor short stories like "Three Hours between Planes," which concerns the fleeting reunion of old childhood playmates, or "The Bridal Party," at the end of which Michael sees Rutherford and Caroline "recede and fade off into joys and griefs of their own, into the years that would take the toll of Rutherford's fine pride and Caroline's young, moving beauty" – in these stories, the perennial elegiac strain is not associated simply with personal failure but with the necessarily melancholic operation of time sub specie aeternitatis.[17] Many readers have failed to appreciate that Fitzgerald's remarks in "The Crack-Up" about "the futility of effort" and "the inevitability of failure" refer not to his own alcoholic and economic traumas in the 1930s but to what he was thinking back in the mid 1920s, at the height of his fame and fortune:

> Life, ten years ago, was largely a personal matter. I must hold in balance the sense of the futility of effort and the sense of the necessity to struggle; the conviction of the inevitability of failure and still the determination to "succeed" – and, more than these, the contradiction between the dead hand of the past and the high intentions of the future.[18]

This is just the same kind of "contradiction" we find in the texts of Dreiser, Farrell, and Eugene O'Neill. The craving for material success is held in check by knowledge of the ultimate provisionality and futility of all material concerns, knowledge that emanates from the residual

14 See Appendix B in Arthur Mizener, *The Far Side of Paradise: A Biography of F. Scott Fitzgerald* (Boston: Houghton Mifflin, 1951), p. 307.
15 Le Vot, *F. Scott Fitzgerald*, p. 300; F. Scott Fitzgerald, *The Crack-Up*, ed. Edmund Wilson (New York: New Directions, 1945), p. 81.
16 Andrew Turnbull, *Scott Fitzgerald* (Harmondsworth: Penguin, 1970), p. 274.
17 *The Stories of F. Scott Fitzgerald: A Selection of Twenty-Eight Stories*, ed. Malcolm Cowley (New York: Scribner's, 1954), p. 286.
18 Fitzgerald, *Crack-Up*, p. 70.

Catholic sensibility within specific social communities. It is not that Fitzgerald's orientation is definably "Catholic" in a theological sense, any more than Dreiser's or Farrell's is. The crucial point is that these metaphysical leanings modulate into secular forces that materially affect the texts of writers emerging out of that particular historical context. Like Dreiser and Farrell, Fitzgerald is locked in by what he called "the dead hand of the past": not by any otherworldy conception of religion, but by its detached, floating signifiers that transfer themselves into more amorphous forms of psychoanalytical resonance.

It is this crucifying contradiction between a desire for success and a sense of the inevitability of failure that produces in these texts the constant impulse of secularized martyrdom. "Nothing succeeds like failure" in Fitzgerald's work, said Leslie Fiedler, because his novels are constructed upon "The Christian paradox of the defeated as victor."[19] In *The Beautiful and Damned,* Gloria lies awake at night "making a likeness of Anthony akin to some martyred and transfigured Christ" (361). Furthermore, Anthony Patch himself internalizes this image by becoming possessed of Christ's grand sense of *contemptus mundi:* for Anthony, endowed with a sense of the vanity of all things, "all efforts and attainments were equally valueless" (93). Because his relatives had tended to die young, Anthony is constantly aware of the proximity of death; indeed, he imagines the grim reaper to be waiting for him at every corner. This death wish also dominates *Tender Is the Night,* with its Keatsian account of oblivion as tender, welcoming, a consummation devoutly to be wished. Dick Diver again imitates Christ in his denial of that demarcation of the self characteristic of a humanist idiom and in his ambition instead to encompass the world within an all-embracing, universalist style. As a psychoanalyst, Dick Diver is concerned with trying to allow others to live through him: he becomes a surrogate confessor to the sick and disturbed, and thoroughly enjoys his priestly function of absolving his patients, granting them new life. At the start of the novel, Dick blithely acts out his role of omniscience and omnipotence, skillfully controlling the social life around him: "That one could parade a casualness into his presence was a challenge to the key on which he lived" (87). At first, then, Dick appears "Godlike" (104) to Rosemary Hoyt and the other denizens of the French Riviera; but, as the novel progresses, Nicole develops into an autonomous person who no longer needs to be saved, while Dick becomes older and increasingly incompetent in his various different spheres of activity. By the end, his grand sacramental impulse has reduced itself to that maudlin gesture of a "papal cross" by which Dick "blessed the beach" on the penultimate page of the novel (314). Nevertheless, this

19 Fiedler, *An End to Innocence,* p. 175.

is the Christ-complex manifesting itself once again: Dick has sacrificed his own life so that Nicole may live. The worldly defeat is· covertly presented as a quasi-divine triumph.

Another motive for Dick's blessing of the beach is that he desires to project himself into a close empathy with the lifestyle of his particular generation. Fitzgerald said in "The Crack-Up" that he had "a tendency to identify myself, my ideas, my destiny, with those of all classes that I came in contact with," and this process of intense identification necessarily undermines the stability of the subjective self by turning it into an object judged in terms of its relation to others.[20] As we have seen, Catholicism has always emphasized the idea of community life, the social *ecclesia,* rather than an individualistic search for salvation, and in Fitzgerald's wide-angle focus upon his peer group we witness a transformed and secularized version of this externalized *ecclesia.* Despite the many unusual psychological characteristics of Fitzgerald's dramatis personae, they all, curiously enough, seem to emerge as the inevitable products of their surrounding circumstances. Character functions as a mirror of the times, and there is little sense of an individual soul protesting against or alienating itself from this given environment. Amory Blaine embodies the brash iconoclasm of the post–1919 generation; Gatsby typifies the capitalist opulence of the mid 1920s; Dick Diver dives in accordance with the Wall Street Crash. We find throughout Fitzgerald's work that it is the typical rather than the idiosyncratic attributes of any fictional person that receive greater emphasis: Nicole Diver, for instance, is said to imply "the essence of a continent" (136). Indeed, it is the task of Dick as a psychoanalyst to relieve his patients of their individual eccentricities so as to enable them to rejoin the paradigms of orthodoxy and normality sanctioned by society.

In *This Side of Paradise,* Amory Blaine tells Monsignor Darcy how much he enjoys making lists and asks Darcy if he can explain this phenomenon, to which the priest replies: "'Because you're a medievalist . . . we both are. It's the passion for classifying and finding a type'" (114). This love of classification works its way through all of Fitzgerald's work. Malcolm Cowley said Fitzgerald lived in a world "of clocks and calendars," taking delight in chronicling the pop songs and fashions of each passing year, and the effect of these lists and calendars is to ritualize particular times by transforming characters and scenes into emblems of one specific historical era.[21] In *The Beautiful and Damned,* for instance, there is one chapter set in November 1913 in which Richard Caramel is

20 Fitzgerald, *Crack-Up,* p. 71.
21 Malcolm Cowley, *A Second Flowering: Works and Days of the Lost Generation* (Harmondsworth: Penguin, 1980), p. 30.

said to be wearing "one of those knee-length, sheep-lined coats . . . that were just coming into fashionable approval" (32). This is a secular equivalent to the ritualization of time in the annals of the Catholic church through its cyclic pattern of feast days and ecclesiastical seasons such as Lent and Advent. Whereas the characters of Dreiser and Farrell find their fate circumscribed by upbringing and environment, Fitzgerald's characters find their destiny inexorably bound up with the movement of the calendar, but in all these cases the external forces produce a similar passivity within the sensibility of the central characters. The fictional heroes are represented as glass figures through which social forces are refracted; contrary to Richard Chase's definition of American romance, there is general reluctance here to propose any fugitive quest away from society or any radical act of protest and alienation. The pastoral mode is supplanted by an inescapably social mode. In this way, Dick Diver's blessing of the beach at the end of *Tender Is the Night* could be seen as a self-reflexive gesture, insofar as the text itself is concerned to sanctify the actions of one particular generation, to encapsulate the forms of their grandeur and folly within the high ceremonies of art. By this strategy of categorizing and universalizing, Fitzgerald was implicitly displaying his affinities with the Universal Church.

It is, though, *The Great Gatsby* (1925) that is Fitzgerald's most profound yet, at the same time, most enigmatic meditation upon the mythologies of Catholicism. This is the novel that seems finally to disprove Leslie Fiedler's argument that Catholicism provides only a superficial "décor" in Fitzgerald's texts. Although it lacks the explicit religious iconography of Monsignor Darcy's medieval candlesticks or Anthony Patch's Renaissance popes or Dick Diver's papal cross, nevertheless Catholic ideology is "secularly" resonant in *The Great Gatsby* in two significant ways: first, in its contemplation of the power or powerlessness vested within symbolic metamorphoses of various kinds; and second, in its inclination toward becoming a parody of the American Dream.

Initially, moreover, *The Great Gatsby* did in fact begin with a strong "Catholic element," as Fitzgerald himself put it, in that the tale "Absolution" originally comprised the first chapter of *Gatsby*, before being rewritten by Fitzgerald as an independent short story.[22] In "Absolution," Jay Gatsby is revealed in his first incarnation as "Rudolph Miller," and this original opening chapter described how as a boy the hero chose to reject Christianity as a framework for his imaginative designs. "Absolution" depicts the rite of passage whereby Rudolph Miller is filled with "exultation" as he realizes he will no longer put the "abstraction" of

22 Allen, *Candles and Carnival Lights*, p. 103.

Catholic religious duties "before the necessities of his ease and pride." Miller, like Gatsby after him, grows to feel there must be "something ineffably gorgeous somewhere that had nothing to do with God."[23] The most obvious traces of Catholicism in the final published text of the novel are to be found in the way Gatsby's aspirations toward "something ineffably gorgeous" take the form of a spiritualization of earthly matter. As Giles Gunn said, Gatsby appears like "a grotesque parody of some high priest or shaman who is continually dispensing holy waters, con- secrated food, and other elements of the sanctified life to whatever as- pirants he can gather around him."[24] Moreover, the white purity of Gatsby's clothes is an emblem of his reluctance to soil his "immortal" love for Daisy Buchanan with the rude detritus of the terrestrial world: the clock, of course, has symbolically stopped when Gatsby encounters Daisy again at Nick Carraway's house. Gatsby carries with him an aura of transcendence as he moves within his landscape of "enchanted ob- jects," as Carraway calls it, and one of the curious things about the novel is that this transcendence is not, finally, undermined by Gatsby's financial criminality or by his neurotic insecurities and jealousies.[25] In one of his typical stylistic paradoxes, Carraway oxymoronically contrasts Gatsby's worldly "corruption" with the hero's "incorruptible dream": "I thought of the night when I first came to his ancestral home, three months before. The lawn and drive had been crowded with the faces of those who guessed at his corruption – and he had stood on those steps, concealing his incorruptible dream, as he waved them good-by" (154–5).

In this way, as André Le Vot put it, "the corrupt means Gatsby uses to achieve his ends have not altered his fundamental integrity, his spiritual intactness." This recognition of the ends justifying the means is a familiar old Jesuit ploy, and that sense of corruption and idealism being sym- biotically entwined and rotating together upon the same axis may help to account for the sense of shifting perspectives we constantly experience in *The Great Gatsby*. To quote Le Vot again, "two modes, satiric and lyric, dominate the book";[26] Gatsby's follies are clearly exposed, but at the same time Carraway elevates Gatsby into transfigured splendor by those famous parallels with Columbus and the early settlers: to Nick, "Gatsby's wonder when he first picked out the green light at the end of Daisy's dock" is comparable to that "transitory enchanted moment" when the Dutch sailors first became aware of the "fresh green breast of

23 Cowley, ed., *Stories of F. Scott Fitzgerald*, pp. 167, 171.
24 Giles Gunn, *The Interpretation of Otherness: Literature, Religion, and the American Imagi- nation* (New York: Oxford Univ. Press, 1979), p. 208.
25 F. Scott Fitzgerald, *The Great Gatsby* (New York: Scribner's, 1925), p. 94. Subsequent page references are given in parentheses in the text.
26 Le Vot, *F. Scott Fitzgerald*, p. 144.

the new world" (182). The structural ambiguity introduced by this deployment of Carraway as a detached, ironic narrator clearly adds to our
sense of a double perspective, so that the text consists of something like
a series of Chinese boxes, an infinite spiral of ironic mirrors where nothing is allowed to stay undisturbed by its contrary and where no view of
Gatsby himself can ever be considered a "final" one.

All of this is familiar enough, of course. My argument, however, is
that this ambivalence should be seen not just as a formalistic phenomenon, but also as a textual stress emanating from specific pressures that
can be located within the context of a religious culture. One of the reasons
for this chameleonic nature of Gatsby's representation lies in the text's
double-edged attitude toward the appurtenances of the American Dream,
an ambivalence that can be related to the uncertain social status of American Catholicism at a particular moment in history. The Great Gatsby is
poised equivocally at the frontier of social conformity, being (like Carraway) "within and without, simultaneously enchanted and repelled" by
the world it describes (36). This flirtation with the Janus-like form of
parody, whereby the novel is lyric and satiric at one and the same time,
can be seen as a parallel to those tensions within American Catholicism
in the early decades of this century arising from the issue of "Americanization," when theologians were debating whether the church should
maintain a sense of separation from mainstream American ideals, or
whether it would be best served by moving toward assimilating itself
within the dominant patterns of American cultural life. As we have seen,
clerics with more conservative or separatist tendencies (such as Archbishop John Hughes of New York and later Michael Corrigan, Bernard
McQuaid, and Anton Walburg) were staunch advocates of parochial
education and other forms of dogmatic orthodoxy, and they feared that
the integrity of the church would become compromised by a too free
and easy interaction with the secular optimism and commercial framework of the United States. Concurrently, however, more "liberal" prelates like James Gibbons and John Lancaster Spalding wanted American
Catholicism to emerge out of the constrictive confines of its oppositional
ghetto and to play a more central role in the development of American
society. Gibbons and Spalding thought the church would never reach its
full potential for growth in the United States if it remained locked into
the role of a refuge for impoverished immigrants seeking escape from
the pressures of harsh Protestant materialism.

By reason of that ubiquity of ideological influence that frames the
production of literature, one can see these conflicts refracted in Fitzgerald's own life and art. He was himself by no means a ghetto child (there
is a statue of Fitzgerald's ancestor Francis Scott Key, author of the "Star-
Spangled Banner," in the public square at Baltimore); nevertheless, the

fact that he came from a devout Catholic family at a time when the institution of Catholicism was hovering uneasily on the margins of American society ensured that Scott was placed in an awkward relationship with his confreres. Fitzgerald analyzed his own sense of social insecurity in a 1933 letter to fellow outsider and Catholic apostate John O'Hara:

> I am half black Irish and half old American stock with the usual exaggerated ancestral pretensions. The black Irish half of the family had the money and looked down upon the Maryland side of the family who had, and really had, that certain series of reticences and obligations that go under the poor old shattered word "breeding" (modern form "inhibitions"). So being born in that atmosphere of crack, wise-crack and countercrack I developed a two cylinder inferiority complex. So if I were elected King of Scotland tomorrow after graduating from Eton, Magdalene, the Guards with an embryonic history which tied me to the Plantagonets [sic], I would still be a *parvenue*.[27]

Thus Fitzgerald himself, while aspiring toward social conformity and acceptability, nevertheless finds himself in some ways irredeemably alienated. The more crucial point, however, is that these cultural tensions, of which Fitzgerald's own life offers a microcosm, substantially affect the implicit direction of his novels. In *The Great Gatsby* elements of Catholic assimilation combine with elements of Catholic alienation. It is the desire for assimilation that induces Jay Gatsby to compose his *Hopalong Cassidy* notebook in imitation of Benjamin Franklin's *Autobiography*: Gatz seeks to "read one improving book or magazine per week" (174) and to follow an elaborate series of strenuous mental and physical exercises in the hope that this Franklinesque zeal will be the way to wealth, as indeed it duly turns out to be. In this sense, then, Gatsby acts out the American dream of upward social mobility. Yet it is the religious-oriented sense of alienation that deprives Gatsby of the Protestant spirit that underpinned Franklin's dedication to self-improvement and the work ethic: in *The Great Gatsby* any moral equation between the acquisition of wealth and inherent virtue is noticeably absent. Here again we see the relevance of Max Weber's distinction between Protestant and Catholic attitudes toward "the spirit of capitalism." In his account of *The Self-Made Man in America*, Irvin G. Wyllie confirmed how this theological and cultural distinction became a historical reality in the late nineteenth and early twentieth centuries, with Catholics forming a very small percentage of the American "business elite" and Catholic leaders "standing

27 Bruccoli, *Some Sort of Epic Grandeur*, p. 25.

aloof from the glorification of wealth," choosing instead to uphold "their church's traditional indictment of materialism."[28]

By the mid 1920s, as we have seen, circumstances had changed, and American Catholicism was no longer so much centered in immigrant ghettos. Nevertheless, a note of estrangement continues to sound throughout *The Great Gatsby*. While Gatsby partially assimilates himself within the accepted idiom of material success, he himself places little value on that success except insofar as it enables him to become a more respectable suitor for Daisy; in addition, the ironic distance preserved by Carraway's detached, quizzical narrative further ensures that the reader does not empathize with Gatsby's social and economic success in the way he more readily does with the narrator's aspirations in Franklin's first-person *Autobiography*. Moreover, apart from a few mysterious telephone calls during his party, we never see exactly how Gatsby has made his pile. Whereas Franklin provides us with details of his successful accomplishments, Gatsby jumps straight from being a young soldier embarking for the war in Europe to his status as a Long Island magnate equipped with a vast number of "beautiful shirts" (93) and a state-of-the-art orange squeezer. The novel, like Daisy's voice, is "full of money" (120), but it is bereft of the industry that produces money. As a result, the book enters an ambiguous cultural area; for, by celebrating American wealth but not the moral basis usually associated with the development of such wealth, *The Great Gatsby* veers toward becoming a parody of those traditional American narratives of economic success.

Parody is a double-edged form, depending both upon implicit recognition of a model or archetype and also upon a sense of ironic dissociation from its assumptions – which is precisely what we find in *Gatsby*, where the outward emblems of social conformity are contradicted by the inner sense of psychological disjunction Gatsby experiences. Unlike Weber's Lutherans and Calvinists, Gatsby sees no essential value in accumulating wealth for its own sake: for him, business life is no more than a game or sport, a playful facade, like the extravagantly superficial re-creation within his Long Island mansion of Merton College Library, a perfect image of parody's doubling and duplicity, its strict observation of formal signifiers even as it radically voids itself of substantive signifieds. As Catholics became increasingly Americanized, they began to play the games of society without believing in their ultimate spiritual significance – an idiom replicated in the way Gatsby's library contains books whose significant content is canceled by their uncut pages. Thus the persistent irony in the novel can be read not just as a narrative and

28 Irvin G. Wyllie, *The Self-Made Man in America: The Myth of Rags to Riches* (New Brunswick: Rutgers Univ. Press, 1954), p. 57.

structural irony, but as irony embedded within a particular form of cultural process.

The religious context of the book, then, helps to account for its oblique stance toward the American business world. In 1957, the Catholic critic Walter J. Ong, S.J., wrote that the American Catholic mentality was gradually developing away from its oppositional status and beginning to celebrate the mass consumer markets of the United States, idealizing the *Reader's Digest* and Coca-Cola advertisements, as if in recognition that Catholicism is "a tradition capable of penetrating indifferently all cultures, and, indeed, designed by God to do precisely this."[29] Something of this same sensibility is anticipated in *The Great Gatsby,* which invests Gatsby's yellow Rolls-Royce and motorboats and gorgeous buffet tables with an aura that is vaguely metaphysical. The parodic element persists, though, precisely because it is a consumer culture that is being sanctified, rather than traditional Puritan ideas of thrift and production. Fitzgerald eulogizes the spending, not the getting, of money.

In this way, Fitzgerald's famous comment in "The Crack-Up" that "the test of a first-rate intelligence is the ability to hold two opposed ideas in the mind at the same time, and still retain the ability to function" can be applied to *Gatsby*'s own ambiguous situation between the pressures of assimilation and the pressures of alienation.[30] It is this ambiguity that leads the novel toward that dualistic form of parody whereby the text itself is "within and without," situated equivocally on the borders of social conformity. Gatsby himself is not exactly an upright Hopalong Cassidy hero, but neither is he simply a Prohibition-era criminal. Carraway's complex, bifurcated narrative denies us the security of any one perspective on the hero, and this formal ambivalence can be related, in part at least, to Fitzgerald's Catholic inheritance, which renders him unable to accept the nostrums of American social life without maintaining his sly distance from them. In "The Crack-Up," Fitzgerald wrote of how his "old dream of being an entire man" involved "a sort of combination" of John Pierpont Morgan and Saint Francis of Assisi, a remark that illuminates how the figure of Gatsby is attempting to hold both sides of this equation, worldly attachment and worldly detachment, in a delicate balance.[31]

Parody is also a form of dualism that presupposes a difference between the objective signification and its subjective re-creation; and this cultural dualism integral to Fitzgerald's Catholic discourse can be seen to exist

29 Walter J. Ong, S.J., *Frontiers in American Catholicism: Essays on Ideology and Culture* (New York: Macmillan, 1957), p. 2.
30 Fitzgerald, *Crack-Up,* p. 69.
31 Ibid., p. 84.

alongside (and in parallel to) the various linguistic dualisms and series of differences that arise in the novel. *The Great Gatsby*'s meditation upon the power of analogy, metaphor, and metamorphosis is also a disquisition upon the Catholic theme of transubstantiation: can the timeless come into contact with time, can the icons be transformed into real flesh, or are they doomed to remain simply icons? In a transformed version of Catholic idolatry, Gatsby worships Daisy's image with what the narrator calls "unwavering devotion" (110): he hoards newspaper clippings about her and reinvents her character to fit with the "creative passion" of his "dreams" (97). Gatsby's quandary, however, is that he can never be certain that his adoration will be repaid with an appropriate response from Mrs. Tom Buchanan.

We see a prime example of this ambivalence at the end of chapter 6, after Carraway has reintroduced Gatsby to Daisy:

> His heart beat faster and faster as Daisy's white face came up to his own. He knew that when he kissed this girl, and forever wed his unutterable visions to her perishable breath, his mind would never romp again like the mind of God. So he waited, listening for a moment longer to the tuning-fork that had been struck upon a star. Then he kissed her. At his lips' touch she blossomed for him like a flower and the incarnation was complete. (112)

The religious connotations here are self-evident. Gatsby's aspirations toward transcendent divinity ("the mind of God") seem in one way to be compromised by Daisy's appearance as a real live human being, whose "perishable breath" betokens mutability and mortality. Still, the word "incarnation" has obvious Christian overtones, as if Daisy, like Christ, might be a God made flesh who does not necessarily forfeit her divine status by manifesting herself in a human guise. Again, Carraway's narrative preserves its double-edged, elusive quality: the beginning of this paragraph implies the collapse of Gatsby's dream is imminent, but the end of the paragraph suggests its embodiment is "complete."

Also noticeable here is the use of the word "vision" to describe Gatsby's rapture. The visionary aspects of Gatsby's "religious" enterprise are interpreted to the reader through the frequent use of visual images and symbols, which play a very prominent role in the novel: the advertising hoarding of Dr. Eckleburg's eyes, the color symbolism of Gatsby's "blue lawn," the "green light at the end of Daisy's dock" (182), and so on. Indeed, Le Vot's researches have shown that in the early manuscripts *Gatsby* was even more heavily laden with symbolism and that concessions to verisimilitude came at a relatively late stage of composition.[32] Fitz-

32 Le Vot, *F. Scott Fitzgerald*, p. 148.

gerald's use of such iconography recalls that affiliation between visual substance and Catholic culture explored in the writings of Hawthorne and Henry James. Actually, though, in the final text of *Gatsby* it is the continual transmutation of realism into symbolism, the circular interplay between Daisy and the green light (for example), that functions as a corollary to that sense of evanescence which is one of Fitzgerald's main themes in the novel. The perpetual dialogue between realism and symbolism, between physical and "metaphysical," ensures that, for the reader as well as for the narrator, objects in the text come to seem "inessential" and begin to "melt away" before our eyes.

Just as at the end of the novel Long Island metamorphoses itself for Carraway into the "fresh green breast of the new world . . . that flowered once for Dutch sailors' eyes," just as Gatsby throughout the book seeks to cancel the past and metamorphose Daisy Buchanan into the Daisy Fay redolent of Malory's Arthurian legend, so Fitzgerald's archetypal images cause the world under scrutiny to slide, to become dislocated, to metamorphose itself into a phantasmagoric hall of mirrors whose meaning is something other than a literal representation of the material world. In turn, this process of dematerialization becomes an analogue to the elegiac sense of loss Fitzgerald is writing about: the use of symbolism causes the scene to evaporate in the same way as the passing of time brings about the final evaporation of Gatsby's grand design. Such evaporation occurs ultimately because of a gap between object and symbol that comes to prove irredeemable. If Daisy Fay could remain a fairy-tale enchantress like Morgan le Fay – her punning distant relation in *Morte d'Arthur* – Gatsby's dream would remain inviolable; his problem comes when he must actually kiss Daisy's flesh and bring their relationship into the terrestrial world. When Gatsby actually makes his move with Daisy, he exposes himself to all the vulgar muddle, jealousy, and accident that eventually brings about his demise, although it is his grandeur, in Carraway's eyes, that he never in fact renounces belief in "the colossal vitality of his illusion" (97).

Nevertheless, concludes Carraway, Gatsby must have felt he had "paid a high price for living too long with a single dream" (162). Daisy refuses to become transubstantiated into the golden princess of legend; she obdurately remains the self-interested and self-preserving wife of Tom Buchanan. The worldly object cannot become correlated with the divine symbolism Gatsby attempts to impose upon it, and so the world lapses like the summer into casual mutability with "that obliging and indifferent sea" (178) sweeping all its worldly refuse away. Throughout the text we find a range of metaphors postulating the metamorphosis of the fallen world into a more sublime model: Gatsby regards "the silver pepper of the stars" (21), Carraway talks about the "long white cake of apartment-houses" on 158th Street (28), and so on; but the novel also implicitly acknowledges that these transmutations are arbitrary and provisional rather than sanctioned by any valid form of idealism.

There is a revealing instance of this in the first chapter, when Daisy says to Carraway:

> "I love to see you at my table, Nick. You remind me of a – of a rose, an absolute rose. Doesn't he?" She turned to Miss Baker for confirmation: "An absolute rose?"
>
> This was untrue. I am not even faintly like a rose. (15)

Carraway's disillusioning mind holds in check those equivalences and analogies that the other characters are intent upon fabricating. This is not to deny that Carraway himself indulges in these linguistic games from time to time, but he generally recognizes them as purely fictional constructions: the structural irony of his narrative role ensures Carraway's distance from the more extravagant phantasms of Gatsby's imagination. Carraway knows he is not a rose, that there is an irreparable difference between the analogical pretensions of the signifier and the mundane reality of the signified; moreover, especially toward the end of the novel, the text of *Gatsby* is haunted by a sense of the vacancy surrounding the icons it has established.

As we have already seen, notions of the materialization of analogy are crucial to Catholicism in a theological sense. The Catholic insistence upon conceptual links between heaven and earth manifests itself within the complex networks of intercession that bind the city of God to the city of man through emphasis upon such mediating forces as saints, departed souls, transubstantiation. Although the idea of analogy is not in itself a specifically Catholic phenomenon, one of the crucial distinctions to be made between the material analogies of Catholic discourse and the analogical mirrors of Puritan typology is that the latter tended to involve a strict reliance upon literal biblical hermeneutics. It was essential, said Samuel Mather in 1683, that religious interpreters find a close correlation between worldly event and biblical prototype and not go gadding about rhetorically inventing farfetched anagogical or tropological meanings: "But for men to set their Fancies a Work to extract Allegories out of every Scripture-history, as the Popish Interpreters use to do, is not safe nor becoming a judicious Interpreter. Luther called such Allegories *Spumam Scripturae,* they beat the Scripture into froth by allegorizing all things."[33] Thus the biblical typology of the Puritans became a way of prophetically envisioning terrestrial affairs as the direct products, albeit

---

33 Quoted in Karen Rowe, *Saint and Singer: Edward Taylor's Typology and the Poetics of Meditation* (Cambridge: Cambridge Univ. Press, 1986), pp. 8–9.

seen through a glass darkly, of a higher transcendent order. Catholic fictions, by contrast, find no such clear typological correlation: for Aquinas, as we will recall, human history was an entirely secular matter. Nevertheless, since in the Catholic view God is present within nature, the worldly experiences and imaginative capacity of artists become valid media for the elucidation of "divine" reality. Whereas stricter Puritan minds were in awe of God's inscrutable silence and so chose to adhere cautiously to the words of the Bible, Catholic writers found themselves more free to illuminate creatively the links supposed already to exist between earth and heaven.

It is for these reasons that Puritan sensibilities have generally viewed the idea of metaphor with the gravest suspicion, as something like a literary equivalent of the metamorphosis inherent in transubstantiation. In his poem "Meditation 22 (First Series)," Edward Taylor found it a cause for self-congratulation that his "Quaintest Metaphors are ragged Stuff / Making the Sun seem like a Mullipuff"; similarly, in his influential treatise of 1649, *The Saints' Everlasting Rest,* Richard Baxter summarized the Puritan hostility toward anthropomorphic allegory:

> But what is my scope in all this? is it that we might think Heaven to be made of Gold and Pearl? or that we should picture Christ, as the Papists do, in such a shape? or that we should think Saints and Angels do indeed eat and drink? No, not that we should take the Spirit's figurative expression to be meant according to strict propriety: or have fleshy conceivings of spiritual things, so as to believe them to be such indeed: But this; to think that to conceive or speak of them in strict propriety, is utterly beyond our reach and capacity: and therefore we must conceive of them as we are able.[34]

For Baxter, then, allegory of this kind was a regrettable pragmatic necessity not to be confused with ultimate truth, because, unlike the Puritan type, it was validated by no clear metaphysical authority.

In subsequent centuries, Jonathan Edwards and Ralph Waldo Emerson both came to envision nature itself as a system of elaborately organized analogies. However, they were both still writing within a Puritan cultural framework and were consequently concerned to secularize this idea of typology by replacing biblical authority with a transcendent Christian or Neoplatonic ideal. Accordingly, earthly nature was redefined in their eyes as a series of fallen fragments that might become holistically reunified by an act of heroic human prophecy. In Emerson's texts, the prophet is no longer an exponent of biblical hermeneutics but a seer capable of

34 *The Poems of Edward Taylor,* ed. Donald E. Stanford (New Haven: Yale Univ. Press, 1960), p. 37; Baxter quoted in Robert Daly, "Puritan Poetics: The World, The Flesh, and God," *Early American Literature,* 12 (1977), 156–7.

elucidating those invisible analogies binding the universe into an ideal harmony. Nevertheless, as Sacvan Bercovitch remarked in an illuminating aside: "It was in the Puritan image that Emerson . . . cast his great essay on *Nature* (1836) – though not explicitly, of course."[35] In this way, we can see how Emerson transforms Puritanism into an implicit secular philosophy, just as in the next century Fitzgerald was to transform and secularize the impulses of Catholicism.

In "Protestant" literature, of course, the notion of a miraculous series of material interactions or visible analogies between secular and divine spheres has always seemed quite impossible. Indeed, theologian Paul Tillich defined "the Protestant principle" as a rigid refusal to absolutize things worldly and finite: Protestantism, said Tillich, insists instead "that the sacred sphere is not nearer to the ultimate than the secular sphere; both are infinitely distant from and infinitely near the Divine."[36] In "Catholic" writing, however, there has often been an emphasis upon some form of transubstantiation between physical and "metaphysical" realms. Gerard Manley Hopkins's technique of "inscape" is one modern example of this, and the idea also occurs within the more secularized aesthetic form of Joyce's "epiphanies," which derive ultimately from Thomas Aquinas's apprehension of how commonest objects might become radiant. Scholastic philosophy held that common earthly material participates in God's grace through the bonds of analogy that bring about a continuous interpenetration between human and divine worlds; hence, said Aquinas, every historical existence simultaneously participates in primary spiritual essence: "Being is one in all by analogy," since each part of God's creation embodies a "dynamic tendency towards the Absolute."[37] The Catholic sociologist Andrew Greeley has claimed that the "anthropology" of this "analogical imagination" works its way so deeply into a Catholic person's consciousness that it comes to be taken "for granted, and it rarely occurs to us that others totally disagree with it, do not find it as reasonable, as plausible, and as self-evident as we do."[38] However that may be, it is just this analogical imagination that fires the mind of Gatsby in his attempts to transubstantiate Daisy and defy the limitations of linear history by mingling her worldly existence with a timeless essence. In his blithe assumption that it is possible to "repeat

35 Sacvan Bercovitch, *The Puritan Origins of the American Self* (New Haven: Yale Univ. Press, 1975), p. 158

36 Paul Tillich, *Christianity and the Encounter of the World Religions* (New York: Columbia Univ. Press, 1963), p. 47.

37 Mary T. Clark, ed., *An Aquinas Reader* (Garden City: Doubleday–Image, 1972), pp. 44, 36.

38 Andrew Greeley, "Why I Remain a Catholic," in *Why Catholic?*, ed. John J. Delaney (Garden City: Doubleday, 1979), p. 65.

the past" (111), Gatsby seeks to redeem the accident of Daisy's time on earth by infusing her with a "spiritual" substance that epitomizes a higher, "divine" grace.

This is not to say Gatsby "believes" in God, any more than Fitzgerald himself did. Nor, of course, does *The Great Gatsby* accept this doctrine of analogical transubstantiation at face value but rather – through the narrative of Carraway – skeptically interrogates the power of analogy, playing it off against the demystifying forces of deconstruction and difference. Nevertheless, it is a Catholic framework that provides one of the crucial terrains upon which this conflict of belief and skepticism works itself out, and to ignore the submerged religious context of the novel is not simply to miss a few abstruse theological refinements but the cultural base of the text itself. Writing can be substantially affected by other than self-evidently substantial things, and the intangible forms of religious apostasy provide part of the cultural matrix from which Fitzgerald's fiction emerges.

This is not, of course, to echo the regrettably partisan and reclamatory approach too often mooted in any discussion of Fitzgerald's Catholicism. The Jesuit Harold Gardiner, to take one example, wrote in 1951 that the "real reasons" for Fitzgerald's "rootlessness" lay in his abandonment of the One True Faith.[39] Gardiner's convictions about "real reasons" may strike us as less than fully convincing, not least because a wide-ranging and amorphous sense of "rootlessness" was part of the experience of that entire 1920s generation. To reiterate, it is not my intention here to offer Fitzgerald's Catholicism as any kind of monolithic explanation for the tensions and complexities of his work. What we can say, though, is that the implicit discourse of Catholicism produces cultural undercurrents that pull his text in directions it might not otherwise have taken: toward forms of ritualism; toward a parodic oscillation between the pressures of social assimilation and ironic alienation; toward images of idolatrous analogy that in the end find themselves stranded without metaphysical guarantees. It is also important to recognize that although these tendencies are more overt in Fitzgerald's early fiction, they do linger in unexpected and subterranean ways within his later work. If the art of Fitzgerald's contemporary, Ernest Hemingway, was one of personal "grace under pressure," so in a wider conceptual sense might this phrase apply to the dynamics of *The Great Gatsby*.

39 Harold C. Gardiner, S.J., "A Christian Appraisal: The Point of It," in *Fifty Years of the American Novel: A Christian Appraisal,* ed. Harold C. Gardiner, S.J. (1951; rpt. New York: Gordian, 1968), p. 8.

Part III

Poetry of Confession and Apostasy

8

The Analogical Imagination:
Allen Tate

In Allen Tate, Robert Lowell, John Berryman, and Frank O'Hara, the twentieth century has produced some extraordinary poets who were writing within the cultural framework of Catholicism, thereby challenging many of the familiar ideological paradigms of American literature. So narrow, however, is the traditional definition of "religious" aesthetics that the most famous American Catholic poet of this century is probably Thomas Merton.

Merton, a flamboyantly contemplative monk most famous for his prose autobiography, *The Seven Storey Mountain* (1948), was, as Robert Lowell said in 1945, "a modest, not altogether satisfactory minor writer," better known as a phenomenon than as a poet.[1] Merton's verse is that of a poor man's Gerard Manley Hopkins. Infused like Hopkins with the spirit of the thirteenth-century theologian Duns Scotus, to whom he dedicated one of his numerous poems, Merton strives through alliterative intensity to reveal the sacramental grace of God that he considers to be immanent within the *haeccitas* or individuating property of each created object:

> Striking like lightning to the quick of the real world
> Scotus has mined all ranges to their deepest veins:
> But where, oh, on what blazing mountain of theology
> And in what Sinai's furnace
> Did God refine that gold?
>
> ("Duns Scotus")[2]

The tense monosyllables and staccato rhythm ("where, oh, on what . . . ") make this stanza almost pastiche Hopkins. Merton's central theme here as elsewhere is transformation: how God "Buries His thought

1 Robert Lowell, "The Verses of Thomas Merton," *Commonweal*, 42 (1945), 240.
2 *The Collected Poems of Thomas Merton* (New York: New Directions, 1977), p. 164. Subsequent page references are given in parentheses in the text.

too vast for worlds / In seed and root and blade and flower"; how "The Sowing of Meanings" – to quote the title of the poem in which these latter lines appear – is uncovered by the "clean, transforming fire" of religious insight (188). It is a poetic version of the theological idea of transubstantiation; appropriately enough, in "After the Night Office – Gethsemani Abbey," the poet expressly welcomes "The truth that transubstantiates the body's night" (109).

In artistic terms, though, these redemptive visions become – as they rarely do in Hopkins – predictable and even sentimental because of the lack of any kind of internal dialogue within the poetry itself. Take, for example, "Carol":

> Eternal Peace is sleeping in the hay,
> And Wisdom's born in secret in a straw-roofed stable.
>
> (89)

The triumph of "Eternal Peace" here is altogether too easy. There is no genuine interplay between the security of faith and the insecurities of the outside world, as there is in Eliot's religious poetry, for example. Instead, Merton's happy revelations seem to exist in a self-created vacuum. Merton converted to Catholicism in 1938 and, as William Everson said, there is something in his religious verse that remains "convert-like, pedantic, pedagogical."[3] Later in his life, Merton turned more toward social protest and vented his spleen against what he took to be the dehumanizing technologies of the modern world, as in "Why Some Look Up to Planets and Heroes":

> What next device will fill the air with burning dollars
> Or else lay out the low down number of some Day
> What day? May we consent?
> Consent to what? Nobody knows.
> Yet the computers are convinced
> Fed full of numbers by the True Believers.
>
> (306–7)

In this guise, Merton cultivates a Zen-like miniaturism designed to stand in opposition to the march of science. His "political" poetry is, however, once again locked into a world all its own; like his devotional offerings, these protest poems are of little interest to anyone who shares an opposing point of view.

Allen Tate's work is much broader in intellectual scope, and in Tate's poetry we find all the taut and tense qualities Merton's verse so noticeably lacks. "Tension," in fact, is a key word in Tate's artistic vocabulary: in

---

3 See James Terence Fisher, *The Catholic Counterculture in America, 1933–1962* (Chapel Hill: Univ. of North Carolina Press, 1989), p. 243.

a 1938 essay, "Tension in Poetry," he talked of how a poem should become the site for an interaction of different meanings and metaphors, rather than simply relapsing into that vague "affective state" characteristic of romantic hyperbole.[4] Tate's own work fulfills this program exactly. His poetry is "metaphysical" in the seventeenth-century sense, poised on the paradoxes of faith and doubt, the Incarnation and the world. Tate's only familial link with Catholicism was a maternal grandfather from Maryland – his father was Episcopalian, his mother Presbyterian – but Tate's participation in the modernist quest for order led him to flirt with Catholicism for over twenty years before finally converting on 22 December 1950. His poem "The Cross," written in 1928, is a good example of how Tate expands an overtly religious symbol so that it takes on more complex cultural connotations:

> Long ago
> Flame burst out of a secret pit
> Crushing the world with such a light
> The day-sky fell to moonless black,
> The kingly sun to hateful night.[5]

The cross here becomes not only a crucifix but also that crossing or conjunction of opposites suggested by the icon of the "blinding rood." Cross symbolism, with its implications of the reconciliation of contraries, goes back long before the advent of Christianity, and Tate here is drawing upon these primeval associations as he incorporates the tension of opposites ("light," "night") within his poem.

The crossing of meanings inherent within Tate's very frequent poetic paradoxes is, then, a formal analogue to the cross of Christianity that hangs heavily over his work. Paradox, the interaction between logical and apparently illogical levels of meaning, is a characteristic technique of such diverse "Catholic" authors as Joyce, Chesterton, and Buñuel. It was also characteristic of the analytical methods of New Criticism, that movement with which Tate was associated in the years immediately after the Second World War. For a while, it was thought that Tate, Cleanth Brooks, R. P. Blackmur, John Crowe Ransom, and the other New Critics were intent upon analyzing poems as "a structure of complex tensions cut loose from the flux of history and authorial intention, autotelic and unparaphrasable," as Terry Eagleton put it. Nothing, though, could be more misleading. As Eagleton, Frank Lentricchia, and others have shown, the New Critical movement was in fact bound upon the wheels of the ideological conservatism operating in the early cold war

4 Allen Tate, *Essays of Four Decades* (Chicago: Swallow Press, 1968), p. 57.
5 Allen Tate, *Collected Poems, 1919–1976* (New York: Farrar, Straus and Giroux, 1977), p. 33. Subsequent page references are given in parentheses in the text.

years, because the conception of an impersonal or scientific "autonomy" for the poem advanced in parallel with the increasing emphasis on impersonal, scientific data within the culture of that time. Poetry, like science, became the prerogative of technocrats: just as experts on atomic fission dutifully suppressed their subjectivity to participate in larger corporate projects, so experts on poetry attempted to suppress their personal idiosyncrasies in order to focus upon the linguistic and technical intricacies of poetic texts. One consequence of this was that the values of the larger project were rarely challenged: "In response to the reification of society," commented Eagleton, "New Criticism triumphantly reified the poem."[6] The American world, like poetry itself, was assumed to be an ultimately harmonious and integrated structure; indeed, the "organic" work of art demanded by the tenets of New Criticism implicitly mirrored the (supposedly) organic and unified nature of this society.

By a similar intersection of text and context, the New Critical fascination with pun and paradox can be seen not just as a dedication to the independent artistic artifact but also as the functioning of a specifically Christian cultural ideology. Brooks, Ransom, and many other New Critics besides Tate were practicing Christians, and their aesthetic forms circuitously reflect this religious framework. Tate deploys the duplicitous trope of paradox to imply a material world reduplicated and twinned with its spiritual counterpart, as in his poem "The Buried Lake":

> living we have one way
> For all time in the twin darks where light dies
> To live.
>
> (139)

The "*twin* darks," an image taken up later in "the *double* of our eyes" (my emphases), mirrors that familiar Christian paradox whereby "light dies / To live" and terrestrial death becomes spiritual renewal. Wit is used here to forge a bridge between material and immaterial, between Lucy and Saint Lucia; the paradox of this poem's final line – "I knew that I had known enduring love," where the past tense of "known" contradicts the meaning of "enduring" – points to the necessary irony of attempting to encapsulate divine truths within the limited secular conditions of poetry (140). All of these ironies are, of course, finally predicated upon the central Christian paradox of incarnation, "The living wound of love" as Tate oxymoronically describes it in "Seasons of the Soul" (118). In another paradox, the poem "Sonnet to Beauty" inverts the standard images of human beauty by proclaiming "the doctrine of

---

6 Terry Eagleton, "The Idealism of American Criticism," *New Left Review,* no. 127 (May–June 1981), pp. 53–4.

the incorporate Word" as revealing "true," that is Christian, beauty in the apparently humdrum image of "The mortal youth of Christ astride an ass" (28).

Another overlap between technique and ideology in Tate's poetry emerges in his use of artistic order as a formal corollary to ideas of social and religious order. In "To the Romantic Traditionists," Tate's self-consciously "crabbed line" stands as a rebuke to the more extravagant outpourings of the Whitmanian tradition (81). In "The Twelve," he invokes "that promontory Form / Whose mercy flashed from the sheet lightning's head," where the capitalized "Form" suggests poetic form (punningly fitting with the "sheet" on which this text appears) as well as the personal form or shape of Christ. Moreover, it is interesting to note that this poem, whose "Twelve ragged men" obviously connote the twelve apostles, is itself almost – but not quite – in a regular twelve-syllabic meter, as though the poem were searching for the secure promontory of its own form just as the disciples sought out the redemptive vision of Christ:

> Now the wind's empty and the twelve living dead
> Look round them for the promontory Form
> Whose mercy flashed from the sheet lightning's head;
> But the twelve lie in the sand by the dry rock
> Seeing nothing.
>
>   (44)

In his preface to the 1936 *Reactionary Essays,* Tate talked about "the art of apprehending and concentrating our experience in the mysterious limitations of form," and that word "mysterious" is interesting, suggesting as it does a correlation between artistic order and something intangible and unknowable.[7] This places Tate's perspective in sharp contrast to that of traditional classical humanism, which associates formal control with what is eminently knowable and so susceptible to human reason.

In "Sonnets at Christmas," Tate further associates the formal, regular pattern of the sonnet with the regular rebirth of the seasons guaranteed by the passage of nature. This, in turn, becomes equated with the promised rebirth of Christ:

> The going years, caught in an after-glow,
> Reverse like balls englished upon green baize –
> Let them return, let the round trumpets blow
> The ancient cradle of the Christ's deep gaze.
>
>   (103)

7 Tate, *Essays of Four Decades,* p. 613.

A similarly comforting pattern can be observed in poems such as "Seasons of the Soul" and "Causerie," where the rejuvenation of the natural (and especially Southern) landscape forms an analogy to the concept of Christian resurrection. In "Seasons of the Soul," every stanza within each section ends on one specific word – "jaws," "hall," "love," "silences" – which conveys the impression of an essential stillness underlying this apparent rotation of the earth, a sense of heterogeneous variety coming down finally to one ultimate truth (114–22). It is an ingenious poetic reworking of that medieval notion of an interpenetration between divine essence and earthly accident. The singular climactic word appears to summarize and harmonize the plural, disconnected events of this artistic and natural landscape.

The villains of the piece, for Tate, appear within the tradition of unfettered poetic and philosophical romanticism. Emerson is summarily dismissed in one critical essay as "the Lucifer of Concord . . . the light-bearer who could see nothing but light, and was fearfully blind." The onanistic Whitman is described in one poem as the stuff of a "False Nightmare."[8] Another work, "Retroduction to American History," castigates that romantic individualism where "every son-of-a-bitch is Christ, at least Rousseau" (11). Even Tate's friend Robert Penn Warren does not escape this particular lash: in his early (1924) poem "To a Romantic," Tate chastises Warren for the arrogance of holding his "eager head / Too high in the air" and turning to the "impermanent" landscape of the "vagrant West" rather than disciplining his mind through the classical fixity of permanent truth (7). One of Tate's best-known poetic statements of this antiindividualist theme is "Last Days of Alice," which uses Carroll's *Through the Looking Glass* as a metaphor for what Tate sees as the narcissistic self-indulgence inherent within the necessarily solipsistic idiom of romanticism. Alice exists in a world of dreamy theoretical abstraction, a world deprived of that social *quidditas* and sense of otherness Tate takes to be a precondition for the existence of morality in the world:

> . . . she broke, plunged through the glass alone
>
> Alone to the weight of impassivity,
> Incest of Spirit, theorem of desire,

---

8 Tate, "Emily Dickinson," in *Essays of Four Decades,* p. 284. "False Nightmare" was omitted from Tate's 1977 *Collected Poems;* it can be found in *Poems by Allen Tate* (New York: Scribner's, 1960), p. 56. Conversely, Whitman himself declared the idea of formal verse to be as outmoded as sacraments or dogma. See F. O. Matthiessen, *American Renaissance: Art and Expression in the Age of Emerson and Whitman* (New York: Oxford Univ. Press, 1941), p. 590.

Without will as chalky cliffs by the sea,
Empty as the bodiless flesh of fire.

(38)

Alice's world of self-reflexive emptiness is the Derridean heaven of an infinitely mirrored *mise en abîme*. Tate, however, perceives this as a dangerous landscape where all sense of demarcation and limitation has been lost:

heaven is a dayless night,
A nightless day driven by perfect lust
For vacancy.

(39)

Rather than this ludic reduction of everything to an extension of the protagonist's ego, the poet yearns for a sense of evil, of sinister otherness, so as to jolt the world out of its amoral complacency:

O God of our flesh, return us to Your wrath,
Let us be evil could we enter in
Your grace, and falter on the stony path!

(39)

Such knowledge of evil was, of course, what Tate claimed Emerson and other romantic writers so fatally lacked.

Tate's most complete prose statement attacking this kind of subjectivism is to be found in "The Angelic Imagination: Poe as God" (1951), written shortly after his formal conversion to Catholicism, where Tate draws upon the ideas of Jacques Maritain as he upbraids Poe's attempts to usurp the divine prerogative of creation. Tate had met Maritain at Princeton in the 1940s, and, as we have seen, the Frenchman was at the center of the "Thomistic Revival" in the middle years of the twentieth century, when attempts were made to revive Thomas Aquinas's proposed reconciliation of Christian thought with a philosophy of the natural world. In *The Dream of Descartes* (1944), Maritain lamented the way Cartesian rationalism sought to divide spirit from body, mind from matter. Such dualism, said Maritain, had fostered the regrettable tendencies of romanticism whereby Promethean man sought to cancel his lower being and soar upward toward the heavens, failing however to understand that God had specifically created man to act out his existence within the sphere of terrestrial limitation and that God's presence is to be found within, rather than beyond, the natural world. In Maritain's eyes, the "cultural significance" of Cartesian idealism was that "it carries along with it a sort of anthropocentric optimism of thought" that ignores the fact that human reason can never achieve perfect autonomy but needs always to be informed by divine grace.[9] For Tate, Poe had similarly erred because of his "catastrophic acceptance" of Cartesian principles and his refusal to acknowledge limitations of any kind. Instead, Poe conceived "of human language as a potential source of quasi-divine power"; but, said Tate, "when neither intellect nor will is bound to the human scale, their projection becomes godlike, and man becomes an angel."[10] Tate's use of the word "angel" clearly signals his debt to Maritain and other neo-scholastic philosophers of this period, who used the "angelic" imagination as a derogatory phrase to describe the human intellect's tendency to divorce itself from the natural world and set itself up as autonomous and entirely self-referential. This was a concept that, as we shall see later, also profoundly affected Flannery O'Connor, Walker Percy, and other Catholic writers in the middle part of the twentieth century.

The various alternatives to this "angelic" state of affairs, alternatives that Tate sought throughout his life, centered upon communal mythologies of the South as well as mythologies of Catholicism. A quest for the security of father figures who might alleviate the burden of existential self-reliance and alienation is implicit throughout his poetry: in "Emblems," for example, he laments how "Unkempt the fathers waste in solitude / Under the hills of clay" (36). This yearning for paternalistic authority becomes explicit in Tate's 1938 novel, *The Fathers,* a narrative set in nineteenth-century Virginia. Tate's relationship to the South is, however, a complex matter. While he wrote biographies of Stonewall Jackson and Jefferson Davis and was heavily involved in the Agrarian movement of the 1930s, he lived most of the latter part of his life in Minnesota, ridiculing those who claimed his dearest wish was to be a Confederate general. In fact, it seems that Tate was attracted to the loss of the old South as much as to the old South itself: he wrote to John Peale Bishop in 1931 that his ambition was "to live a life of failure" because "the significance of the Southern way of life, in my time, is failure."[11]

Yet from Tate's point of view the fall of the South, like the collapse of classical civilizations, ironically clears the way for the intervention of divine grace. It is the paradox of *felix culpa,* the fortune of man's original expulsion from Eden, an event that allows the possibility of redemption. In "The Mediterranean," Tate seems to equate pagan and Edenic worlds as he reconstitutes a prelapsarian country "out of time's monotone" (66); in "Causerie," though, the poet's spirit of *contemptus mundi* implies that

9 Jacques Maritain, *The Dream of Descartes,* trans. Mabelle L. Andison (Port Washington, N.Y.: Kennikat, 1969), p. 171.
10 Tate, *Essays of Four Decades,* pp. 412, 408, 411.
11 See Richard Gray, *Writing the South: Ideas of an American Region* (Cambridge: Cambridge Univ. Press, 1986), p. 122.

only through the "wreck" of human civilization can man hope to attain
God:

> In Christ we have lived, on the flood of Christ borne up,
> Who now is a precipitate flood of silence,
> We a drenched wreck off an imponderable shore.
>
> (14–15)

If the South is "the country of the damned," as Tate says in "To The
Lacedemonians" (87), then the existence of damnation permits the possibility of its reversal into redemption, just as hell implies heaven and
evil implies good. In *Christ and Apollo* (1960), a book much admired by
Tate, the Jesuit critic William Lynch wrote of how a person must first
descend into experience and accept the fact of the fallen human condition
before being able to rise and proceed to a higher order, and elements of
this theological argument are evident in Tate's approach to the South,
which he perceives as something that has to be lived through before it
can be ultimately transcended. Tate's accounts of the lives of Confederate
heroes like Jackson and Davis are circumscribed in advance by the smell
of inevitable defeat; but, as in all martyrology, the fated worldly demise
becomes a "spiritual" triumph, actually paves the way for this nobler
victory, because only through the collapse of the material world can a
higher vision be gained. Tate's novel *The Fathers* does not consist of
simple nostalgia for the antebellum South, and indeed the feudal rigidities
of the Buchan family are portrayed in this text with a mixture of sympathy and irony not too dissimilar from the novel's attitude toward its
romantic, radically disruptive hero, George Posey. Posey is "a man without people or place," a character of flexible intelligence but uncertain
personal identity, whose mode of heroic anarchy is compared by narrator
Lacy Buchan to the buccaneering Jason on his quest for the golden
fleece.[12]

Tate's sensibility was in many ways close to that of the deracinated
George Posey, and in his contribution to the Agrarians' manifesto *I'll
Take My Stand* (1930) Tate is quick to point out that for him the South
constitutes a provisional metaphor rather than a geographical or historical
fact: not so much a "particular house," he says, as "the house of a spirit
that may also have lived elsewhere."[13] The idea of a Southern civilization
restored to its antebellum glories operated for Tate as a necessary myth,
a fiction; moreover, one of the most significant aspects of this myth was
that it formed a counterpart to his conception of a worldly civilization
irradiated by divine grace. In his 1952 essay "The Man of Letters in the

12 Allen Tate, *The Fathers* (Denver: Swallow, 1960), p. 179.
13 Allen Tate, "Remarks on the Southern Religion," in *I'll Take My Stand: The South and
the Agrarian Tradition, by Twelve Southerners* (New York: Harper, 1962), p. 155.

Modern World," Tate spoke of his desire to "think of society as the City
of Augustine and Dante, where it was possible for men to find in the
temporal city the imperfect analogue to the City of God," and in this
idealistic vision of an (approximate) "analogue" between earth and
heaven we see how much Tate's dream of universal order was based
upon metaphysical premises.[14] He was not so much concerned with the
empirical realities of the South as with its figurative connotations, the
ways in which, even within its framework of political instability and
decline, it might operate as a memento of the celestial city. In keeping
with this outlook, Tate's 1964 essay "The Uniliteral Imagination" redefines T. S. Eliot's notion of modern man's "dissociation of sensibility"
as a bifurcation between "the external world" and "the interior world
of the mind" – rather than, as Eliot had suggested, a split between interior
feeling and interior thought.[15] For Tate, the quandary of the twentieth
century was not so much the psychological issue of emotions having
become separated from intellect as the social and religious issue of individual man having become separated from his environment. Uprooted
from his "natural" home and from his religious *ecclesia,* unhoused modern
man is left to face the world alone, a particular quandary for Catholic
writers bearing in mind the church's traditional emphasis on communal
salvation and the interdependence of self and society.

Much of Tate's work can be seen as a reaction against, and an attempt
to compensate for, this typically modernistic sense of alienation. In *The
Fathers* the continual insistence upon family titles ("Brother George,"
"Brother Charles," and so on) has the curious effect of introducing
religious overtones into this secular society, as if the characters were all
"brothers" in some ecclesiastical order, or maybe even in some higher
spiritual sense. The frequent invocation of "brothers" in the long poem
"Sonnets of the Blood" creates a similar impression. In his contribution
to *Partisan Review*'s 1950 symposium "Religion and the Intellectuals,"
Tate also displays considerable admiration for Charles Maurras, the
French intellectual who, as we saw earlier, sought to justify the institution
of religious order as a means toward social cohesion rather than as a basis
for theological faith. Maurras had been excommunicated back in 1926,
but Tate continued to manifest sympathy: "Countless are the roads to
genuine belief. Historical insight is one of them, even though it is not
in itself genuine belief. In many ways today it has *directed the attention* to
spiritual possibilities which our pervasive naturalism had obscured; and
thus it has discovered a hitherto unexercised gift of faith."[16] For Tate, it

14 Tate, *Essays of Four Decades,* p. 6.
15 Ibid., p. 460.
16 Allen Tate, "Religion and the Intellectuals," *Partisan Review,* 17 (1950), 252.

was crucial that the social and historical circumstances of the external world should provide a context within which the interior world of belief could appropriately function. Tate followed Maurras in cherishing this notion of a reciprocal interaction between social order and Christian salvation, but he was also shrewd enough to recognize that this "perfect traditional society . . . has never existed, can never exist, and is a delusion." Nostalgia for the perfect order of medieval Christendom was, for Tate, historically unjustifiable. And in the contemporary era, especially, the idea of a Christian society was to be found only as an abstract and imaginative conception, "an imperative of reference," a perennial "moral ideal" rather than "an absolute lump to be measured and weighed."[17]

Nevertheless, this postulation of an "analogue" between the worlds of subjective consciousness and objective society forms a parallel to those analogues between literal and "spiritual" significations that, as we have seen, Tate contrives in his poetry through metaphysical wit and paradox. His 1951 essay "The Symbolic Imagination: The Mirrors of Dante," a companion piece to his attack on Poe's penchant for "angelism," stated the theoretical bases for these processes of analogy by way of an analysis of The Divine Comedy: "To bring together various meanings at a single moment of action is to exercise what I shall speak of here as the symbolic imagination. . . . The symbolic imagination conducts an action through analogy, of the human to the divine, of the natural to the supernatural, of the low to the high, of time to eternity." Dante, said Tate, uncovers "a coherent chain of analogies" and thus reveals, through imagery of multiple mirrorings, how "the entire natural world is a replica in reverse of the supernatural world."[18] Dante's poetic architecture carries reverberations in terms of Tate's own poetic practice, of course. As Ferman Bishop has said, Tate's covert exploitation of the etymological origins of Latinate words works to create a kind of transubstantiative oscillation between different verbal levels, a process that imitates the revelation of an immanent divine presence within mundane affairs: in the "Spring" section of "Seasons of the Soul," for instance, "combustible juice" yields up its Latin origin of "comburo," to consume by love.[19] This is, in fact, the same kind of uncovering of hidden grace we saw in a far more labored way in Thomas Merton. Tate, like Dante, reads the world as a text, and seeks, as he said the Florentine poet was seeking, "the key to the resemblances of things."[20]

What is most significant for us here is to apprehend how this emphasis

17 See John L. Stewart, The Burden of Time: The Fugitives and Agrarians (Princeton: Princeton Univ. Press, 1965), pp. 332–3.
18 Tate, Essays of Four Decades, pp. 427, 428, 441.
19 Ferman Bishop, Allen Tate (New York: Twayne, 1967), p. 150.
20 Tate, Essays of Four Decades, p. 430.

upon analogy materialized within the terrestrial world works as a specifically Catholic cultural phenomenon. Catherine Randall Coats has written of how a "Protestant consciousness," by contrast, tends to experience "a rupture between Word and world due to the Protestant rejection of secular existence and to their emphasis on the transcendence of the Bible." The Protestant sensibility, said Coats, takes to heart Saint Paul's warning that while the Word giveth life, the letter killeth; and this leads to "the Protestant writer's highly ambivalent, extremely self-conscious relationship to his text," where he always fears the act of writing will violate his spiritual integrity.[21] The Catholic writer, on the other hand, places more faith in the phenomenal world, whose ultimate validity it sees as guaranteed by the Incarnation: Tate would have approved of the twelfth-century theologian Hugh of St. Victor, who asserted that "this whole visible world is a book written by the finger of God, that is, created by divine power." As Gabriel Josipovici has said, the medieval church did not talk of the human imitation of Christ, but of the human reenactment of Christ; it was not until 1418 that Thomas à Kempis produced *Imitatio Christi,* which was predicated upon the essential difference between Christ and man and consequently upon man's need for "a studied conformity of the spirit" to find salvation.[22] But Tate's mentors are Saint Augustine and Dante, who find more direct analogies between the city of God and the city of man. For Dante, man does not simply follow God but embodies God: the Incarnation provides an assurance that human nature, when fulfilling itself as human nature, is concurrently participating in divine being. The earthly accident is transubstantiated into divine essence, so that it can be, like Tate's puns, two things at once; again, we see here the literary consequences of a Catholic mode predicated upon similarity rather than difference. In this light, it is also significant that Tate should have singled out for praise Dante's mastery of pictorial imagery, for faith in the phenomenal world justifies the whole idea of art as visualization. Earthly vision becomes a key to analogous forms of divine vision: "It was scarcely necessary," said Tate, for Dante to have read, though he did read, the *De Anima,* to learn that sight is the king of the senses and that the human body, which like other organisms lives by *touch,* may be made actual in language only through the imitation of *sight.*[23] We have already seen the ideological connotations of visual imagery in novelists such as Hawthorne, James, and Fitzgerald, and Tate reinforces this sense that iconography is asso-

---

21 Catharine Randall Coats, "Dialectic and Literary Creation: A Protestant Poetics," *Neophilologus,* 72 (1988), 161.
22 Gabriel Josipovici, *The World and the Book: A Study of Modern Fiction* (Stanford: Stanford Univ. Press, 1971), pp. 29, 43.
23 Tate, *Essays of Four Decades,* p. 424.

ciated with the phenomenal Catholic letter rather than with an internalized Protestant spirit.

This Catholic ideology is also fairly explicit in Tate's critical pronouncements. Dante's claim in *De Vulgari Eloquentia* that the true poet "is he who can free himself from the chance whims of a private language and write a poem not from his own but from God's point of view" finds an echo in Tate's continual pummeling of nineteenth-century romanticism. Romanticism, claimed Tate, is merely a poetry "of communication" that seeks to transmit vague personal emotions rather than concentrating upon that artistic order, proportion, and radiance consequent upon the idea of the poet as a surrogate version of the divine maker.[24] In "The Uniliteral Imagination," Tate defined Shelley's angelic alienation from nature in specifically religious terms: it is, he said, a style of "Godwin-Methodism," a self-scourging search for transcendental meanings and "impossible attempts at human perfectibility" based upon the "Manichean heresy" of disgust with the reality of the human condition. Tate was, however, less explicit on religious philosophy when commending to his audience "The Severed Head," the "great poem" by Robert Lowell with which he concluded this paper. He omitted to mention that, by contrast with Shelley, Lowell's work appeared "great" to him precisely because it too is predicated upon the Catholic impulse of analogy. "John Donne would have understood it," proclaimed Tate triumphantly, as though this were itself the final imprimatur; whereas in fact Donne was another Catholic writer who happened to share a very similar kind of Metaphysical sensibility.[25]

The problem here is that all these illuminating critical and creative ideas have become entangled with the impossible question of truth or falsity. Tate clearly believed Dante was a "truer" poet than Shelley. Sister Mary Bernetta, O.S.F., similarly praised Tate for his adherence to Catholic "truth" and his rejection of attempts "to reach salvation by secular means alone." (Sister Bernetta vouchsafed to us along the way her opinion that excessive reliance upon these secular ideals constitutes "a prime fallacy of the present era.") Vivienne Koch, by contrast, believed Tate's religious tendencies are entirely regrettable and that he wrote his best poetry when he succeeded in eluding that dogmatic straitjacket.[26] One would not wish either to prescribe or to proscribe any particular kind of critical perspective, of course, nor to insist upon a similarly limited philosophy of universal skepticism. But the difficulty with the aesthetic

24 Tate, "Tension in Poetry," in ibid., p. 58.
25 Tate, *Essays of Four Decades*, pp. 460–1.
26 Sister Mary Bernetta, O.S.F., "Allen Tate's Inferno," in *Allen Tate and His Work: Critical Evaluations,* ed. Radcliffe Squires (Minneapolis: Univ. of Minnesota Press, 1972), p. 267; Vivienne Koch, "The Poetry of Allen Tate," in ibid., pp. 253–64.

requirements of Sister Bernetta, Koch, and indeed Tate himself is that they elide philosophical assumptions into literary judgments without knowing it. Their competing philosophies are seen not as competing philosophies but as absolute truths, with their opinions on literature emerging as a by-product of these deeply held but unstated beliefs. It is of course inevitable that judgments on literature should be inextricably bound up with matters of ethical and epistemological belief, but it is unhelpful for literary critics simply to apportion praise or blame according to their own particular metanarrative impulses. Such a process is, as Derrida described it, the "phallogocentric" fallacy, the insertion of a critical master "key" into all texts equally so as to "unlock" their "meanings" according to the tenets of one given viewpoint.[27] Within the framework of literary criticism, the contest between Dante and Shelley can be referred only to ideological paradigms, not to moral or metaphysical verities.

Although Tate criticized Shelley's aspirations toward "human perfectibility," strong residual elements of a similar kind of idealism manifest themselves in Tate's own writing. What Jean Guitton called the Catholic genius for "alloys or compromises . . . a provisional combination of the pure and impure" was as foreign to Tate as it was to Orestes Brownson.[28] Indeed, in terms of the promulgation of Catholic dogma, the dilemma of Tate was similar to that of Brownson: there was always an unwillingness or an inability to relinquish some last layer of romantic purity. Tate, like Brownson, desired so firmly to project a sense of ordered control over his material that there is in these texts an absence of any self-reflexive irony that might balance this romantic urge for perfection against an acknowledgment of the limitations, imperfections, and discontinuities of the fallen world. In this sense, Tate gives an odd impression of having mastered the teachings of Catholicism just too carefully. He has taken the neo-scholastics' views on the analogical imagination too much at face value, with the result that he goes back through the annals of literature awarding plus or minus marks according to whether or not any given author conforms to the "analogical" Catholic pattern. In its newfound religious zeal, Tate's work actually interprets the analogical imagination in what William Lynch would have called a "univocal" or monolithic way. Tate lapses into a form of solipsistic "angelism" that ensures the form of his writing moves toward contra-

---

27 See Derrida's critique of Jacques Lacan, "The Purveyor of Truth," *Yale French Studies*, 52 (1975), 31–113.
28 See Jean Guitton, *The Church and the Gospel*, trans. Emma Craufurd (Chicago: Henry Regnery, 1961), pp. 224–5.

dicting all those multiple and impersonal transformations of analogy that constitute the central theme of his later creative and critical endeavors.[29]

This is not, of course, simply a fault of Tate's own intellect or imagination; it reflects a more general predicament of Catholic culture within the United States, where Romanist aesthetics and ideology have never quite meshed comfortably with the American structures of society. Maritain's *Art and Scholasticism* talked nostalgically of how in medieval times the artist was "ranked simply as an artisan" and supposed to concern himself merely with practical problems of form and technique, not with moral themes or judgments. The medieval artist, said Maritain, was so much at home within the culture of Christendom that he was not perturbed by that "inner vexation of spirit" consequent upon the post-Renaissance disjunction between inward aspiration and external phenomenon.[30] George N. Shuster, in his 1930 book on *The Catholic Church and Current Literature*, argued that while the medieval artist was not looking for "what we should term 'original creations,'" the modern religious writer by contrast has to present his vision of the world knowing full well a large part of his audience will be "utterly incredulous."[31] Whereas the text of a medieval writer consciously or unconsciously reflects a framework of communal faith, the modern writer is obliged to project that faith through the force of his or her own personal will. In his "Remarks on the Southern Religion" in *I'll Take My Stand,* Tate suggested that loyalty to a tradition must be "spontaneous" and "automatically operative before it can be called tradition," and in these terms neither the old South nor modern America in general could possibly be seen as lands of Christian tradition, much as Tate always wished that they might have been.[32] While seeking the repose of an impersonal Christian tradition, he ironically recognized that, within modern America, Christianity could exist only as an internalized (and therefore quasi-romantic) form of belief.

If the situation of the Christian in America was difficult, the situation of the Catholic Christian was doubly difficult. The Catholic, said Shuster, finds that amid "the overwhelmingly Protestant character of the scene," he has only a "bare and commonplace" cultural tradition to fall back upon. In Shuster's eyes, the Catholic writer in America must acknowl-

29 William F. Lynch, S. J., *Christ and Apollo: The Dimensions of the Literary Imagination* (New York: Sheed and Ward, 1960), pp. 107–52.
30 Jacques Maritain, *Art and Scholasticism, with Other Essays,* trans. J. F. Scanlan (New York: Scribner's, 1931), pp. 21, 15.
31 George N. Shuster, *The Catholic Church and Current Literature* (New York: Macmillan, 1930), pp. 25, 30.
32 Tate, "Remarks on the Southern Religion," p. 162.

edge there can be no kind of harmony between the devout individual and the secular community, no "spirit of affection which breeds the masterpiece." Accordingly, that "serenity" and spontaneity of allegiance to Catholic traditions, which in the neo-scholastic view a religious artist should naturally seek, is forever denied to New World authors.[33] The neo-scholastic view of art as an instinctive "habit" – Maritain's word – placed emphasis upon beauty rather than didacticism, poetry rather than apologetics. Tate, however, found himself confronted with the perennial problem faced by an orthodox Catholic writer in a predominantly secular culture: the force of this "Catholic" beauty and poetry will not emerge on its own but requires the supporting pressures of didacticism and apologetics to propel it into the light of day. (For the "almost-blind," as Flannery O'Connor put it, "you draw large and startling figures.")[34] So far from achieving the artistic goal of blessed impersonality, then, Tate – like Brownson – spends so much of his textual energy negotiating negative reversals of Protestant and romantic ideologies that his anti-romantic impulse becomes not a form of classical serenity but, ironically, a crusading, romantic gesture in itself.

This is one reason Tate became so fascinated by the ghostly image of his southern "cousin" Edgar Allan Poe, for Poe's form of solipsistic alienation was, potentially, a mirror image of Tate's own. Poe's "angelism" may be the formal antithesis to Dante's "symbolism," but in Tate's own literary consciousness these angelic and symbolic sensibilities become insidiously combined. This conflict is replayed within the very syntax of Tate's poetry, whose most distinctive quality is a taut, rebarbative, and argumentative language that openly flaunts its intellectual acidity and challenges the reader to unpack the text's paradoxes, as in "Sonnets of the Blood":

> What is the flesh and blood compounded of
> But a few moments in the life of time?
> This prowling of the cells, litigious love,
> Wears the long claw of flesh-arguing crime.
>
> (49)

That adjective "flesh-arguing" epitomizes how, within Tate's work, one concept argues against another in a jagged, quizzical, discordant fashion. And yet the ultimate aim of his poetic style seems to be to reach a classical grandeur and resonance, as at the end of the ninth section of this poem:

33 Shuster, *The Catholic Church and Current Literature*, pp. 100, 99, 53.
34 Maritain, *Art and Scholasticism*, pp. 9–12; Flannery O'Connor, *Mystery and Manners: Occasional Prose*, ed. Sally and Robert Fitzgerald (New York: Farrar, Straus and Giroux, 1969) p. 34.

Whether by Corinth or Thebes we go
The way is brief, but the fixed doom, not so.

(53)

The pattern of syntactical differences in this poem reworks the same dichotomy as we saw in *The Fathers:* a statuesque, classical fixity is played off against a disruptive, rebellious, constantly interrogative force.

This statuesque quality in Tate's writing arises partly out of a modernist infatuation with order and the quest for absolutes. The Jesuit literary critic Calvert Alexander advised his readers in 1935 that the twentieth-century "loss of faith in the old secular world would mean a renewed faith in the new supernatural world . . . or abysmal despair." A similar kind of stark antithesis was postulated by Middleton Murry, who claimed the choice of modern man lay between Catholicism and communism, and also by Evelyn Waugh, who said in 1930 that his choice of faith had been between Rome and Moscow.[35] In Waugh's novels, as in the work of other English Catholic writers of this modernist epoch – Belloc, Chesterton, Compton Mackenzie – such a quest for order tends to resolve itself into a supercilious form of high satire where the Catholic sensibility looks down as from a great height upon the comic follies of the fallen world. In Tate, though, Catholic modernism redefines itself as an eccentric version of American pastoral: the cramped, constricted shape of his poetic lines comes to imply the defensive shape of a moral and social world where the dominant pattern is one of withdrawal and where men seem to "huddle in humble communal enclaves, protecting themselves against the paradoxes imposed by an angry and demanding God," as Charles Altieri put it.[36] Indeed, the elliptical, enigmatic style of Tate's poetry seems mimetically to reflect an intimation of a world beyond this world: in Tate's work not everything is obvious at first sight, and this "invisible" quality comes to imply a further arena (of words or meanings) transcending the text's difficult surface. In this way, Tate reworks the standard American modernist language of alienation to imply, particularly in his later poems, a radical sense of alienation from the things of this earth.

For critics in the late twentieth century, modernism is as difficult a subject to discuss as were eminent Victorians for Lytton Strachey back in 1918. The modernists are neither our contemporaries nor yet historical figures. They currently exist in a limbo where an audience does not feel the need to make those radical adjustments necessary for reading Freneau

35 Calvert Alexander, S. J., *The Catholic Literary Revival: Three Phases in Its Development from 1845 to the Present* (Port Washington, N.Y.: Kennikat Press, 1968), pp. 11, 6.
36 Charles Altieri, *Enlarging the Temple: New Directions in American Poetry during the 1960s* (Lewisburg: Bucknell Univ. Press, 1979), p. 55.

or Whitman, say, but where it is equally clear that these writers' concerns do not exactly coincide with our own. The oedipal temptation simply to slay the father, as Strachey did, is apparent enough, but in the end too obvious and therefore unsatisfactory. Yet when we take a step back and examine Tate's modernist creations from a detached perspective, it becomes apparent how many intellectual artifices and puzzles are involved here. To say there is an element of fakery about Tate's poetry is not to disparage it but to suggest that his texts are, like those of W. B. Yeats, knowingly taking upon themselves the masks of modernism, juggling philosophical traditions and abstract associations as in some elaborate cerebral exercise. When Robert Lowell said he found in Tate's verse "the resonance of desperation, or rather the formal resonance of desperation," that latter qualification is significant.[37] Tate's poetry seems to become abstracted into a formal replica of itself, relocating concrete object as disembodied concept, fact as dogma.

Again, part of the reason for this may be that Tate, coming to the church by the intellectual route of conversion, took neo-scholastic dogma too seriously. Although the neo-scholastic revival was originally promoted by Pope Leo XIII and others as a bulwark against the atheistic misdeeds of secular modernism, neo-scholasticism eventually came to offer its own parallel version of modernism. Neo-scholasticism created an architectonic system, the so-called Thomistic synthesis, whose conceptual nodes ("angelism" versus "symbolism") can be seen to function as a counterpart to all those binary oppositions (order versus chaos, classical versus romantic, Rome versus Moscow) cherished by a modernist aesthetics. In both cases, we find a "blessed rage for order" attempting to resolve all disparities, to anneal all contradictions. In their obsession with systems of corporate belief, Catholic philosophers of this era such as Gilson, Maritain, and Dawson were the church's counterparts to the totalizing modernist imaginations of Yeats, Stevens, and Hart Crane. It was this neo-scholastic and modernist pressure for unity that directed Tate toward the impossible task of trying to reconcile things that stoutly refused to become reconciled. Rather than letting his analogical Catholic imagination cooperate casually with the free-flowing impetus of American romanticism, Tate always attempted to suppress his own romantic or "angelic" inclinations in favor of some putative social and religious harmony. This quest for harmony was all the more hopeless because Tate himself was quite well aware, as we have seen, that the neo-scholastic idealization of a "harmonious" medieval Christendom was the purest fiction; yet, true to the dictates of his church, he

---

37 See Albert Gelpi, *A Coherent Splendor: The American Poetic Renaissance, 1910–1950* (Cambridge: Cambridge Univ. Press, 1987), p. 390.

still felt himself obliged to choose between the heretical angelic imagination and the divinely sanctioned symbolic imagination. This self-imposed circumscription of his own poetic possibilities probably contributed to the artistic drought of the last twenty years of Tate's life. After his conversion in 1950, he wrote only a few poems, some in Latin, some composed in a pattern strictly imitating Dante's medievalist style of terza rima. The rest was silence.

Poets write what they write, of course, and it is a critical absurdity to suggest they could or should have written in any other way. Tate's poetry has its own idiosyncratic genius that would have been vitiated had he attempted to adopt other standards. But the development of Tate's poetic career may not exactly have been helped by the directions of early twentieth-century neo-scholastic philosophy. In her essay "The Catholic Novelist in the Protestant South," Flannery O'Connor suggested that one result of the Counter-Reformation for the Catholic imagination had been an "overemphasis on the legal and logical and a consequent neglect of the Church's broader tradition."[38] As we shall see later, the more open poetry of Berryman, O'Hara, and (to some extent) Lowell was able to reinvent what O'Connor commended as the "concrete reality" of the twentieth-century American environment in terms of a radically challenging "Catholic" aesthetic ideology, whereas Tate's religious strictness eventually came to ensure the alienation of his art from the main currents and energies of American life. In this way, Tate was implicitly adhering to the kind of religious agenda outlined in 1935 by Calvert Alexander, S.J., who inveighed sternly against "a certain type of bourgeois Catholicism" that had been too eager to cooperate with the "prosperous humanistic" world of the United States.[39] Tate allowed these ingenious but archaic theories from the Thomistic revival to exert enormous influence over his own poetic output, and of all Catholic writers it is perhaps Tate who most scrupulously followed Pope Leo XIII's line about the need to suppress the errors of "Americanism." Lapsed Catholic writers like Fitzgerald and Berryman did not care in the slightest for what Pope Leo had to say, but Tate the faithful convert did, and it was this final acquiescence in church dogma that led him further away from the material landscapes of America and into a disembodied realm of the spirit.

38 O'Connor, *Mystery and Manners*, p. 205.
39 Alexander, *The Catholic Literary Revival*, p. 13.

9

Interiorization of Theology: Robert Lowell

While Allen Tate moved into Catholicism in the latter part of his career, Robert Lowell's overtly religious phase occurred relatively earlier. Lowell was twenty-three years old when he converted in 1940. He subsequently spent a year working in New York for the Catholic publishers Sheed and Ward, recalling later that at this time he was "more interested in being a Catholic than in being a writer."[1] As with many Catholics of this era, one of the motives for Lowell's religious ardor was a fear of the postwar world becoming dominated by what he called "a universal materialistic state."[2] After the Stalinism of the 1930s, the totalitarian constitution of Nazism, and the ominous symbolism of the 1939 Nazi-Soviet pact, Marxism came to have considerably less attraction for intellectuals in the immediate postwar period. The implicit modernist affiliation between Catholicism and communism was on the wane; in the West, at any rate, absolutism of all kinds became increasingly unpopular. Perhaps no longer feeling any pressure to appease the church's demoralized radical wing, Pope Pius XII declared in 1949 a general excommunication for all those who "defend the materialistic doctrines of communism" or sought to establish communist governments. Here, as elsewhere during the late 1940s, it became a case of us against them; the Vatican entered the cold war with a vengeance.[3]

Tate was in fact an early friend and admirer of Lowell, writing the introduction to Lowell's first collection, *Land of Unlikeness,* in 1944 and, as we have seen, extravagantly complimenting "The Severed Head," from Lowell's 1964 collection *For the Union Dead.* Lowell returned the

---

1 Sue Mitchell Crowley, "Mr. Blackmur's Lowell: How Does Morality Get into Literature?" *Religion and Literature,* 19, no. 3 (1987), 30.
2 James Terence Fisher, *The Catholic Counterculture in America 1933–1962* (Chapel Hill: Univ. of North Carolina Press, 1989), p. 67.
3 James Hennesey, S.J., *American Catholics: A History of the Roman Catholic Community in the United States* (New York: Oxford Univ. Press, 1981), p. 289.

favor by looking upon Tate as his poetic "father" and sometimes even addressing him as such.[4] Tate's commendations, though, were not entirely unequivocal. In his 1951 essay "The Symbolic Imagination," Tate accused Lowell of being one of those poets who had lapsed into an "angelic" sensibility:

> The Catholic faith has not changed since Dante's time. But the Catholic sensibility, as we see it in modern Catholic poetry, from Thompson to Lowell, has become angelic, and is not distinguishable (doctrinal differences aside) from poetry by Anglicans, Methodists, Presbyterians, atheists. . . . Catholic poets have lost, along with their heretical friends, the power to start with the 'common thing': they have lost the gift for concrete experience. The abstraction of the modern mind has obscured their way into the natural order.[5]

It is doubtful that Tate's strictures would by this time have had any immediate effect upon Lowell's poetic practice: 1951 also saw the publication of the last of Lowell's three overtly "religious" collections, *The Mills of the Kavanaughs*. Nevertheless, it is interesting that by the time of *Life Studies* in 1959 Lowell had moved toward the kind of poetry that, in its concentration upon the "common thing" and "concrete experience," was ironically moving in the direction Tate thought "Catholic" poetry should take. Indeed, in this focus upon "the natural order" Lowell's later verse embodies Tate's conception of a "Catholic sensibility" more precisely than any poetry Tate himself ever wrote.

By the time of *Life Studies,* Lowell had of course ceased to be a practicing Catholic. Lowell's Catholicism is usually explained in psychological terms as a temporary resting place amid the swings and roundabouts of his manic-depressive cycles. These cycles emerged out of the erratic pattern of rebellion against a liberal aristocratic Boston childhood, followed by sympathy for the southern Agrarians, support for Franco, and the Catholic period of the 1940s; then, in the 1950s – after the traumatic experience of his mother's death – a recuperative period on the West Coast, where Lowell's development of more relaxed and "natural" forms of free verse paralleled his escape from constricting religious dogmas. The early collections, *Land of Unlikeness* and *Lord Weary's Castle* (1946), feature surrealistic juxtaposition – or "farfetched misalliance," as the poet himself later described it – of the mundane and the sacramental.[6] In "Christmas at Black Rock," we witness "drunken Polish night-shifts walk / Over the causeway" as "their juke-box booms / *Hosannah in*

---

4 Stephen Matterson, *Berryman and Lowell: The Art of Losing* (Totowa, N.J.: Barnes and Noble, 1988), p. 4.
5 Allen Tate, *Essays of Four Decades* (Chicago: Swallow Press, 1968), pp. 429–30.
6 Robert Lowell, *Day by Day* (New York: Farrar, Straus and Giroux, 1977), p. 121.

excelsis Domino"; while in "The North Sea Undertaker's Complaint,"
the narrator describes a grotesque situation in which he hears:

> our dumb
> Club-footed orphan ring the Angelus
> And clank the bell-chain for St. Gertrude's choir
> To wail with the dead bell the martyrdom
> Of one more blue-lipped priest.[7]

As Albert Gelpi has said, the figurative constructions in *Lord Weary's
Castle* often resemble those in Flannery O'Connor's stories in that they
focus upon a "moment of violence as the moment of grace," with that
violence implying the necessary "contradictions inherent in temporal
existence," the conflict between banal secular experience and a divine
presence.[8] In addition, these early poems are bestrewn with metonymical
icons of Catholic ritual – papal bulls, gold chalices, and so on – as if to
signify the austere impersonality of the religious system that promises
redemption.

Lowell's first title, *Land of Unlikeness,* derives from a phrase used by
Catholic neo-scholastic philosopher Etienne Gilson, who was himself
drawing upon Saint Augustine's conception of "regio dissimilutidinis,"
the world of those without a sense of God.[9] Whereas Tate fabricated
analogies between the city of God and the city of man, Lowell suggests
that no such congruent "likenesses" are available in twentieth-century
America. For Lowell, the old South can by no conceivable stretch of the
imagination become a likeness of the divine kingdom. This is why his
early poems must attempt so violently to wrench divine grace through
this dark land of nonanalogy and unlikeness. It accounts also for the
turbulence of the poet's rhetoric, rhetoric most critics have found disturbingly hyperbolic. The usual response here is that Lowell's language
appears both extravagant and unnaturally elliptical; consequently, in the
eyes of many readers it seems too artificial, rather like the gamey wordplay of Shakespeare's earliest plays.

Life Studies is normally seen as a welcome retreat from this kind of
clotted style. Steven Gould Axelrod invoked Philip Rahv's "seminal"
essay "The Cult of Experience in American Writing" as he sought to
incorporate "Lowell's Poetry of Experience" into the "basic theme and

---

7 Robert Lowell, *Lord Weary's Castle* (New York: Harcourt, Brace and Company, 1946),
   pp. 6, 33. Subsequent page references are given in parentheses in the text. If the location
   of the poem is not clear, the page reference follows the abbreviation *LWC*.
8 Albert Gelpi, "The Reign of the Kingfisher: Robert Lowell's Prophetic Poetry," in *Robert
   Lowell: Essays on the Poetry,* ed. Steven Gould Axelrod and Helen Deese (Cambridge:
   Cambridge Univ. Press, 1986), p. 54.
9 Matterson, *Berryman and Lowell,* p. 18.

unifying principle" of American writing, that is, the "affirmation of individual experience." From Hester Prynne to Huckleberry Finn to Jake Barnes, explained Axelrod, "the principle is always the same, the growth of consciousness and the deepened sense of personal identity resulting from immersion in firsthand experience," so that "in the radically experimental and existential qualities of his [later] poetry, Lowell continues the central quest of the American imagination."[10] The unwitting partiality of this "world elsewhere" approach, with its unself-conscious attempt to make "central" the culturally specific ideology of Protestant pastoral, hardly needs further emphasis. Any attempt simply to invert this ideological stance, however, remains equally problematical. Taking the heterodox stance that "the early works of [Lowell's] 'Catholic' period constitutes his principal claims to a lasting poetic achievement," Gelpi went on to analyze how in these early poems Lowell's exultant rhetoric transforms "the limited perception of the sense phenomena into awed apprehension of the absolute."[11] This move to redefine the Lowell canon usefully reveals the hidden ideological agenda whereby Lowell is normally considered in quite other ways, in terms of a development of "personal identity"; but if one critic prefers *Lord Weary's Castle* while another prefers *Life Studies,* does that reveal more about the philosophical and cultural perspectives of any particular reader than about the inherent merits of Lowell's two collections?

What I would like to suggest, though, is that this accepted division of Lowell's career into "religious" and "secular" phases may actually be misleading as well as critically unhelpful. Lowell himself did not see such a clear-cut division between the two styles. As he said to Frederick Seidel in 1961: "There is a question whether my poems are religious, or whether they just use religious imagery. I haven't really any idea. My last poems don't use religious imagery, they don't use symbolism. In many ways they seem me more religious than the early ones, which are full of symbols and references to Christ and God."[12] Lowell made these remarks despite the fact that by the early 1950s he had divorced Jean Stafford and left his Catholic theology behind. He told Ian Hamilton in 1971 that Catholicism now seemed "unbelievable," though he added: "I don't believe, but I am a sort of gospeller, I like to read Christ's words."[13] Lowell also enjoyed a curious relationship with the Episcopal church, which he reentered in November 1955, and from which (at his own

10 Steven Gould Axelrod, *Robert Lowell: Life and Art* (Princeton: Princeton Univ. Press, 1978), pp. 8–9.
11 Gelpi, "The Reign of the Kingfisher," pp. 51, 56.
12 *Robert Lowell: Collected Prose,* ed. Robert Giroux (New York: Farrar, Straus and Giroux, 1987), p. 250.
13 Ibid., p. 277.

request) he was buried in 1977. In the light of Lowell's own metaphysical interests and his startling assertion that the poems of *Life Studies* might be "more religious than the early ones," we should perhaps interrogate the conventional wisdom whereby this 1959 volume is considered to be the great turning point in the poet's career, "a departure from his religious view," dividing readers into either the Catholic camp or, more frequently, the liberal humanist camp.[14] On the contrary, in many ways Lowell's later work may be a natural development from, or even an embodiment of, his earlier poetic premises.

One of the important sources for *Lord Weary's Castle* was E. I. Watkin's book *Catholic Art and Culture*. This was published by Sheed and Ward in 1944, a couple of years after Lowell had worked as an editorial assistant there, so it is possible Lowell knew of Watkin's work before it appeared in final book form. In his prefatory note to *Lord Weary's Castle*, Lowell acknowledged the "Our Lady of Walsingham" section of "The Quaker Graveyard in Nantucket" as "an adaptation of several paragraphs" from Watkin; but these paragraphs appear in the very last pages of the book as a culmination of Watkin's overall thesis, the whole argument of which repays further inspection. Watkin began with a tribute to the famed "medieval synthesis," its ideal blend of worldly and otherworldly knowledge, as epitomized in Aquinas's *Summa* and the "literary cathedral" of Dante's *Divine Comedy*.[15] He went on to trace the declining secular influence of Catholicism and its reemergence in a more spiritualized form within the art of the Counter-Reformation and baroque periods. In the final chapter, in which the Walsingham discussion appears, Watkin said that "the death of historic Christendom" is an accomplished fact and that, rather than lamenting the divorce of church and state, Catholics should look for more "contemplative interiorisation" in "the kingdom of the Holy Ghost": "Religion must be revived and upheld by the free co-operation of men and women who hold it with a strong and intelligent conviction because they see its truths from within and who draw, from the profound sense of supernatural life, strength to resist the force of a natural vitalism patronised by the state."[16] Watkin's rejection of state patronage would have appealed to the antitotalitarian impulse in Lowell. Unlike many Catholic writers of this time, Lowell had little nostalgia for the corporate identity of a medieval state; indeed, he found external conformity to any social system to be anathema, much preferring the cultivation of an inner garden of the soul. In 1945, the year after Watkin's

---

14 Matterson, *Berryman and Lowell*, p. 55.
15 Edward Ingram Watkin, *Catholic Art and Culture* (New York: Sheed and Ward, 1944), pp. 60, 65.
16 Ibid., pp. 215–16, 145, 204.

book was published, Lowell himself wrote of how he saw "American Catholic culture" as being "in a relatively receptive state of transition," more welcoming to the enlightening forces of art and imagination.

Consequently, the poet would have been impressed by Watkin's description of the shrine of Walsingham as embodying "an inner beauty more impressive than outward grace," and would have been generally enthused by the way Watkin perceived this as emblematic of the increasing interiorization of Catholicism, its contemporary shift from icon to spirit.[17] In "The Quaker Graveyard," Lowell reworks Watkin's analysis as the poem sets about firmly dissociating religious devotion from slick anthropomorphism:

> Our Lady, too small for her canopy,
> Sits near the altar. There's no comeliness
> At all or charm in that expressionless
> Face with its heavy eyelids. As before,
> This face, for centuries a memory,
> *Non est species, neque decor,*
> Expressionless, expresses God.
>
> (13)

True to Watkin's thesis, the status of the icon becomes problematized. It is the very "Expressionless" inadequacy of the image that betokens a spiritual power beyond.

Watkin's emphasis on "interiorisation" needs to be borne in mind when considering the Catholic theology framing "The Quaker Graveyard" and other poems in *Lord Weary's Castle*. At Walsingham, said Albert Gelpi, God is "all inscrutable transcendence" and "inhuman otherness," a tendency he associated with "the Puritan cast of Lowell's Catholicism," which gave the poet a "fevered and chaste" disdain for the human body and thus an inability to conceive of salvation in terrestrial terms.[18] This is the same kind of criticism Allen Tate made of Lowell's "angelic" proclivities, his modernistic tendency to perceive the world too much in abstract terms. Unable to give imaginative credence to the idea of the concrete Incarnation, so the argument goes, Lowell's residual Puritanism directs him toward believing that God must enter the material world only in order to obliterate its innate depravity.

Now, it may well be true that in *Lord Weary's Castle* Lowell's overt Catholic theology confronts the resistance of a covert Puritan sensibility, and the tensions Gelpi identified certainly play a significant part in the poem. It is, however, also important to note that this relocation of divine

17 Robert Lowell, "The Verses of Thomas Merton," *Commonweal*, 42 (1945), 240; Watkin, *Catholic Art and Culture*, p. 213.
18 Gelpi, "The Reign of the Kingfisher," pp. 63, 58.

truth within the internal rather than the external world was increasingly an important aspect of certain strands of Catholic thinking, especially American Catholic thinking, around the time Lowell was writing. Lowell's poetry follows Watkin by groping for some new form of religious experience, a quest that necessarily involves a movement away from architectonic Thomistic harmonies or facile "likenesses." Just as the modernist idealism of Yeats and Eliot was effectively blasted by the Second World War, so the parallel systems of Thomism were appearing increasingly implausible within that fragmented, postwar, postmodern world from which Lowell's poetry began to emerge. In this light, the assumptions behind R. P. Blackmur's infamous early review of *Land of Unlikeness* also seem anachronistic:

> Lowell is distraught about religion; he does not seem to have decided whether his Roman Catholic belief is the form of a force or the sentiment of a form. The result seems to be that in dealing with men his faith compels him to be nearly blasphemous. By contrast, Dante loved his living Florence and the Florence to come and loved much that he was compelled to envisage in hell, and he wrote throughout in loving meters. In Lowell's *Land of Unlikeness* there is nothing loved unless it be its repellence; and there is not a loving meter in the book.[19]

Here Blackmur was implicitly subscribing to that neo-scholastic myth of the medieval age of faith – "Dante loved his living Florence" – a myth the papacy disseminated at the beginning of the twentieth century in order to combat the subversive influences of modernism and Americanism. But, argued Watkin, that kind of age of faith was no longer a viable proposition. If, as Watkin said, "every genuine art is the organic expression of a culture," then the art of the twentieth century, where "spiritual" revelation can only be an oblique and difficult event, must be more faithfully served by Lowell's tortuous and internalized rhetoric than by any easy nostalgia for "loving meters."[20] The highly wrought tension of Lowell's early verse reflects the difficulty of Christian belief in a post-Christian age.

It does not, though, seem true that Lowell entirely rejects worldly attachments and pleasures in *Lord Weary's Castle*. "Between the Porch and the Altar," from this collection, takes its title from the Ash Wednesday epistle: "Let the priests serve the Lord between the porch and the altar, weeping and saying, Be favorable, O Lord, be favorable unto thy people: let not thine heritage be brought to such confusion, lest the heathens be lords thereof." Yet the poem goes on to mingle its religious

19 R. P. Blackmur, *Form and Value in Modern Poetry* (New York: Doubleday–Anchor, 1952), p. 335.
20 Watkin, *Catholic Art and Culture*, p. 122.

imagery with "heathen" situations and it ends up equivocally celebrating profane as well as sacred love. This is why the poem's title is particularly appropriate: Lowell's text negotiates an ambiguous space "between" the human porch and the divine altar, neither quite in this world nor quite out of it. In fact, I would argue that these earlier poems are less monolithically religious, and the later poems less monolithically secular, than has usually been thought. Certainly it is Christian teaching that provides the framework for the first collections, just as the more hedonistic affairs of human life provide a framework for the poems written in the 1960s and 1970s, but in every phase of Lowell's artistic career we find human sensuality competing with a lurking epistemological uneasiness. The moods of his poetry always swing between belief and unbelief.

The central image in "Between the Porch and the Altar" is that of the snake, a figure that coils and recoils throughout all four sections of the poem. In the first part, "Mother and Son," it betokens the metamorphoses of time:

> Meeting his mother makes him lose ten years,
> Or is it twenty? Time, no doubt, has ears
> That listen to the swallowed serpent.
>
> (41)

Later on, the snake becomes associated with human sexuality, the sin of adultery and the Fall of man:

> When we try to kiss,
> Our eyes are slits and cringing, and we hiss;
> Scales glitter on our bodies as we fall.
>
> (42)

This idea of a fall permeates the entire poem: "I am a fallen Christmas tree," declares the narrator in the last section, "At the Altar" (45). However, one power that might stand as a bulwark against these serpentine forces of time and sexuality is the Catholic church:

> I eye the statue with an awed contempt
> And see the puritanical facade
> Of the white church that Irish exiles made
> For Patrick – that Colonial from Rome
> Had magicked the charmed serpents from their home,
> As though he were the Piper.
>
> (42)

Just as Saint Patrick exercised control over these "charmed serpents," so throughout this poem the subversive snake is played off against various bastions of order and control: this white "puritanical" church, the "black-windowed blocks" of a "Gothic church" in "At the Altar" (45), the

"Black nuns" who "stand on guard" in the third part, "Katherine's Dream" (43), as well as the maternal tyrant of the first section. At the end of the poem, the protagonist describes how the Lord "watches me for Mother" (45), as though the Word of God were itself a displaced form of this oedipal authority.

John Berryman thought that Lowell uncompromisingly "damns the mother-fixed adulterous drunken protagonist" of this narrative, and most other critics have agreed that the work is a Christian satire on the carnal appetites of a fallen New England.[21] That reading, I think, may be too simplistic, for the imagery here tends toward deliquescence and uncertainty, and whether or not these old authoritarian legislators are withering away remains an open question:

> The Farmer sizzles on his shaft all day.
> He is content and centuries away
> From white-hot Concord, and he stands on guard.
> Or is he melting down like sculptured lard?
>
> (42)

Time and motion, as epitomized by the figure of the snake, seem to be undermining the moral and aesthetic "guard" of transcendentalist Concord. As the old standards are "melting down" and can no longer be maintained, Lowell's poem chooses to reincarnate the Christian spirit amid the sensual delights of a big-city restaurant:

> I sit at a gold table with my girl
> Whose eyelids burn with brandy. What a whirl
> Of Easter eggs is colored by the lights.
>
> (45)

The Christian resurrection of "Easter" is now recast within a secular context. The religious altar has transformed itself into a "gold table" where human rather than divine intercourse can take place.

It is true that at the end of "At the Altar" we have to reckon with divine retribution, the apocalyptic lightning of *Dies amara valde,* an exceedingly bitter day. Yet even this intervention is not without its ambiguities:

> *Dies amara valde.* Here the Lord
> Is Lucifer in harness: hand on sword,
> He watches me for Mother, and will turn
> The bier and baby-carriage where I burn.
>
> (45)

21 John Berryman, "Robert Lowell and Others," in *The Freedom of the Poet* (New York: Farrar, Straus and Giroux, 1976), p. 289.

Perhaps, in the best Puritanical fashion, the burning sexual desires of this licentious sinner will cause him to burn in hell. But the equation here between "Lord" and "Mother," and the establishment of an alliterative parallel between "bier" and "baby-carriage," suggest that this baby carriage may itself be another kind of bier or coffin, a form of death. The son is being buried alive because he cannot escape from psychological dependence upon his mother. This refers back to the opening lines in "Mother and Son," where we are told that meeting his mother makes the hero regress twenty years; it also, incidentally, anticipates the theme of many of the *Life Studies* poems, which lament the pernicious and pervasive influence of familial authority. I am not claiming this as a first meaning for Lowell's poem; it may not even be a conscious one. But there are in "Between the Porch and the Altar" threads of radical disjunction, a barely suppressed sense of psychological issues unresolved. The text is normally read simply as indicating that spiritual death is a function of excessive emotional self-indulgence, but it can also be read in a contrary light, as if to imply how emotional death may be a function of moral infantilism and religious guilt.

This kind of density and complex overdetermination is one of the aesthetic attractions of Lowell's poetry. In this poem, we can see the shadow of what Michael Riffaterre has called a "ghost text," where the semiotic play of Lowell's language swings in an opposite direction to that of the poem's carefully constructed syntax:

> One
> Must have a friend to enter there, but none
> Is friendless in this crowd, and the nuns smile.
>
> (43)

In terms of representative mimesis, these nuns are smiling; but the homophones "nuns" and "none" create what Riffaterre called a "dual sign" whereby the semiotics of the text implicitly pull us in another direction. "[N]one / Is friendless": nuns are indeed usually thought of by the laity as lonely and "friendless" because they have sacrificed human attachments for the sake of God. Within the context of this poem, the semiotic double play hints that while Kathleen is in some ways keen to come closer to the welcoming nuns and confess her sexual transgressions, she also fears relinquishing human contact for a more austere and isolated spiritual piety. This is not formal "ambiguity" in the strict New Critical sense because Lowell's syntax here is clear enough, but that destabilizing "semantic pendulum," in Riffaterre's phrase, is symptomatic of the way this poem slides uneasily between two poles: an overt religious piety, as opposed to a covert hostility to asceticism and a desire for worldly pleasures.[22]

Lowell's work, then, is fiercely resistant to simple thematic paraphrase because it is grounded upon a style of linguistic and metaphysical transformation. Apart from this sense of a "ghost text," the language also comes to have multiple significations because words and images merge by analogy into each other, as Lowell wrestles heroically with the attempt to discover some form of coherent teleology within these landscapes of apparent unlikeness. In this sense, his verbal transformations can be seen as a literary correlative to the transformations of divine grace inherent within the Catholic sacrament of confession, a sacrament described by Kathleen in the third part of this poem:

> good people go
> Inside by twos to the confessor. . . . I begin
> To cry and ask God's pardon of our sin.
> Where are you? You were with me and are gone.
> All the forgiven couples hurry on
> To dinner and their nights, and none will stop.
>
> (43)

Confession has always been one of the hardest Catholic practices for non-Catholics to understand, because the sacrament seems to dispense redemptive grace in an impersonal, automatic, even slick fashion and not to trouble itself too much about the sincerity or otherwise of the suppliants' repentance. As (lapsed Catholic) Pietro Di Donato put it:

> With us you could kill someone, rape your mother, and go to the priest that same day and be absolved, as long as you did not leave the Catholic religion, because we are imperfect. So you see there was redemption available at all times, or purgation – whatever you want to call it. This is a magical power because you could always change your life from one hour to another or one day to another. You could reform the way Augustine did and many illustrious fathers of the Church.[23]

Having received forgiveness here, Lowell's adulterers "hurry on / To dinner and their nights," eager to start up the old cycle of sin and repentance once again. Yet such acquiescence in a fallen world is not necessarily, in Catholic terms, a cause for despair. "Between the Porch and the Altar" has too frequently been viewed through the lens of its final Puritanical apocalypse, when actually that apocalypse is, as we have seen, double edged, and the poem generally more willing than is usually ac-

---

22 Michael Riffaterre, *Semiotics of Poetry* (London: Methuen, 1978), pp. 90–1.
23 Dorothée von Huene-Greenberg, "A MELUS Interview: Pietro Di Donato," *MELUS*, 14, nos. 3–4 (1987), 42.

knowledged to locate itself within the limitations of the carnal world. Indeed, the text surreptitiously suggests how divine grace can immanently manifest itself within these earthly festivals of eating, drinking, and sex. Again, one of the strengths of this poem is the way it remains verbally and conceptually open to transformation and refuses to lock itself into any rigid mode of "logical" dogma. Similarly, the protagonist's conclusion that "the Lord / Is Lucifer in harness" (45) is a rejection of the Puritan or Manichaean conception of evil being radically disjunct from and antagonistic toward the forces of good. Lowell's poem opts instead for the more flexible Catholic notion of evil being a subset of good, a mere "removal of good" or "perversion of the will," as Saint Augustine put it.[24]

Di Donato, as quoted above, looked upon the *Confessions* of Saint Augustine as a paradigmatic example of how divine grace can (apparently) transform evil into good, and in fact Lowell's disavowal of New England Puritanism in *Lord Weary's Castle* and his later works has much in common with Augustine's gradual denial of Manichaeism in the *Confessions*. In this fifth-century text, Augustine favors God with an explanation of how he came to reject the idea of "two masses of good and evil." It was, he says, because "it became obvious to me that all that you have made is good, and that there are no substances whatsoever that were not made by you."[25] Cheering himself with the thought of God's declaration that he had made the world and found it good, Augustine then proceeds to chronicle his share of "hell's pleasures," confident that his lusts and jealousies will be redeemed by the bounty of God's grace: "I acknowledge that it was by your grace and mercy that you melted away my sins like ice . . . compared with my guilt, the penalty was nothing. How infinite is your mercy, my God!"[26] If evil is nothing but the absence of good, as this treatise claims, then evil can be comfortably subsumed into good by an infusion of divine spirit. Hence the importance, for Augustine, of the literary form of confession: simply by admitting and recounting his sins, he is opening the way for an accession of redemptive grace. By the same process, the adulterous penitents in "Between the Porch and the Altar" find that Catholic confession permits a relatively easy assuagement of sin because evil is not such a threateningly alien force as it appears in Puritan theology. Whereas Puritanism, like Manichaeism, is predicated upon what Herman Melville called the "power of blackness," sin in the Catholic church is an altogether more

24 Saint Augustine, *Confessions,* trans. R. S. Pine-Coffin (Harmondsworth: Penguin, 1961), pp. 63, 150.
25 Ibid., pp. 106, 148.
26 Ibid., pp. 43, 51, 58.

venial affair, a mere imbalance of the scales between good and evil.[27] This is why "At the Altar" declares God to be "Lucifer in harness": the seemingly profane and sensual images in that poem can actually operate as a mirror of divine glory, just as in earlier baroque art, according to Watkin, "the erotic emblem" became a reflection of a more exalted love:

> Images of earthly passion, never coarse or suggestive but conceived according to the mythological fancy of late antiquity, symbolise every phase and aspect of love, sacred and profane. . . . [Baroque art] will teach us how to be free without being lawless, to be humanist without being secular, to rise high yet range far, to live a life with Christ, yet regard no human interest as alien.

This is, as Watkin put it, the "horizontal" force of immanence that balances the "vertical" power of transcendence. Acknowledgment of the way God reveals himself within the world is a vital counterpart to the apprehension of God's distant grandeur, notwithstanding the fact that "Christianity hitherto has preeminently represented transcendence . . . with a relatively inadequate appreciation of immanence."[28]

It was this "relatively inadequate appreciation of immanence" that Lowell's poetry set out to correct. "At the Indian Killer's Grave," from *Lord Weary's Castle,* ends with a physical, indeed erotic, image of the Madonna that fuses sexual with sacred love:

> Gospel me to the Garden, let me come
> Where Mary twists the warlock with her flowers –
> Her soul a bridal chamber fresh with flowers
> And her whole body an ecstatic womb.
>
> (57)

Similarly in "Where the Rainbow Ends," the last poem in this collection, the narrator sees an image of the Last Judgment descending upon Boston, but then – crucially – walks away from it. The apocalypse of the "black and white sky" gives way to a "marriage feast" complete with "At the high altar, gold / And a fair cloth." Again, the stern dualism of black and white, evil and good, has been superseded by images of a more humane warmth:

> What can the dove of Jesus give
> You now but wisdom, exile? Stand and live,
> The dove has brought an olive branch to eat.
>
> (69)

27 Herman Melville, "Hawthorne and His Mosses," in *The Piazza Tales and Other Prose Pieces, 1839–1860* (Evanston: Northwestern Univ. Press–Newberry Library, 1984), p. 243.
28 Watkin, *Catholic Art and Culture,* pp. 149–50, 212.

"Stand and live": which is exactly what Lowell chose to do, exiling himself from Puritan New England so as to eat freely from the olive branches of sanctified sensual pleasure.

Life, then, becomes an embodiment of the divine spirit. Lowell made this point explicitly in his 1944 essay "Hopkins and Sanctity," in which he emphasized the "heroic sanctity" of the Jesuit's life, rather than his art, and asserted that Hopkins "would have been a saint had he written nothing." Enthused with the Catholic theological concept of "substantial action," Lowell sought here to undermine any firm distinction between life and art: "Writings as well as writers should be judged in terms of substantial action," he said. "For writings are dependent on writers . . . all his writing is just what he is: the work of his unique personality and holiness."[29] Nor is this perspective confined to Lowell's early Catholic years. A passage on Thoreau, drafted in the late 1960s and revised shortly before Lowell's death, places exactly the same emphasis upon moral and "substantial action" rather than artistic achievement: "He had the shy, brief, ascetic life of Hopkins. . . . Thoreau, no Christian, and unaware of any quarrel with God, is *the* New England saint."[30] This biographical approach may contain elements of critical naïveté, never seen to worse advantage than in the 1961 interview with Frederick Seidel when Lowell alleged that "Macbeth must have tons of Shakespeare in him."[31] The point here is not Lowell's perspicacity, but his continual stress on a writer's life and actions as the foundation for his art. This emphasis can be related not only to the Catholic concern for substantial action but also to the Augustinian idea of autobiographical confession betokening a venial human nature which allows for the intercession of divine grace: the ragged imperfection of life, rather than the formal perfections of art, was Lowell's chosen métier. Also implicit here is Watkin's notion of a contemporary shift from "theocentric" to "anthropocentric" Christianity, as the kingdom of God descends to man on earth to become "the kingdom of God in man, the kingdom of a deified humanity."[32]

Thus "Beyond the Alps," the opening poem in *Life Studies,* which is often said to signify Lowell's rejection of Catholicism, needs to be read with care. "Ultramontane" is a term for the doctrine of papal supremacy – it was used in a derogatory sense by French theologians during the controversy over papal infallibility – and as the poem is set on a train journey from Rome to Paris, most critics have had no problem in postulating Lowell's brisk rejection of the city of God for the city of the

29 *Robert Lowell: Collected Prose,* pp. 167–8, 170.
30 Ibid., p. 192.
31 Ibid., p. 246.
32 Watkin, *Catholic Art and Culture,* p. 215.

artists. Lowell himself, however, expressed more doubt: "I've always regarded the poem as a declaration of my faith or lack of faith, and what it means theologically I think is impenetrable."[33] The poem is set in 1950, "the year when Pius XII defined the dogma of Mary's bodily assumption," as the epigraph informs us:

> The lights of science couldn't hold a candle
> to Mary risen – at one miraculous stroke,
> angel-wing'd, gorgeous as a jungle bird!
> But who believed this? Who could understand?
> Pilgrims still kissed Saint Peter's brazen sandal.
> The Duce's lynched, bare, booted skull still spoke.[34]

Just as "Between the Porch and the Altar" has been read as a specifically religious poem, "Beyond the Alps" has been read as a specifically anti-religious poem; but here again there is a sense of uncertainty and lack of closure – "Who could understand?" – that has been generally overlooked. The Italian crowds still submissively kissing Saint Peter's sandal have not comprehended the spiritual (as opposed to literal) meaning of Mary's assumption, the way it connotes the immanent glory of bodily existence. Nor does the papacy, represented here as a fitting successor to the fascist dictatorships of Caesar and Mussolini, desire to enlighten them. For the Holy Father, the dogma of the Assumption is a politically expedient measure enabling the public image of the Catholic church to compete with the insurgent kudos of positivistic science. The narrator, however, turns his mind to another exiled poet:

> I thought of Ovid. For in Caesar's eyes
> that tomcat had the Number of the Beast,
> and now where Turkey faces the red east,
> and the twice-stormed Crimean spit, he lies.
>
> (12)

Ovid, dispatched to the Black Sea by Augustus Caesar on account of the supposed immorality of his *Ars Amatoria,* acts here as a parallel to Lowell, in self-imposed exile from the papal city on account of his propensity for the sensual life. This poem implies that the true meaning of the Assumption may be a paean to the life of a sexual human body, but that this significance has been suppressed by the Machiavellian author-

33 Lowell made this remark in a taped television interview, "Robert Lowell: A Mania for Phrases," *Voices and Visions,* dir. Peter Hammer, New York Center for Visual History Production, 1988.
34 Robert Lowell, *Life Studies,* 2nd ed. (London: Faber, 1972), p. 11. Subsequent page references are given in parentheses in the text. If the location of the poem is not clear, the page reference follows the abbreviation *LS.*

itarianism of the papacy, so that, "Much against my will" (11), Lowell
must take his leave of Rome.

Still, this rejection of the more external, iconographic, and conformist
aspects of Catholicism does not necessarily indicate disavowal of its spirit
of "contemplative interiorisation," to come back to Watkin's phrase.
Rather, the imagery of unscaled peaks, of Everest still unconquered and
the "mountain-climbing train . . . come to earth" (12) may signify, in
Watkin's terminology, the shift from divine transcendence toward
earthly immanence, from the impersonal toward the personal. Like Orestes Brownson, another Yankee who converted to Catholicism, Lowell
was wary of the catechistic dogma of the church and attempted instead
to reinvent the Catholic tradition through the characteristically American
lens of romantic subjectivism. Lowell of course formally left the church,
while Brownson never did. Yet many Catholic philosophers of this postwar era from Watkin to Eugene Kennedy were also drifting away from
Thomism, suggesting as they did so that the institution should place
more emphasis on the spirit rather than on what Kennedy in 1988 called
the "concrete, literalist" letter of church law.[35] From this perspective,
Lowell's work was more consonant with some strands of Catholic thinking in the second half of the twentieth century than Brownson's was
with official doctrines of a hundred years earlier.

I do not want to insist upon this parallel too rigidly. I am not trying
to assert that Lowell always "really" remained a Catholic; I am simply
pointing out that some of the developments in Lowell's writing mirror
developments in the Catholic church around this time. The poet's mind,
if not his soul, was attuned to a "Catholic" conceptual matrix. In 1958,
one year before *Life Studies* was published, the conformist zeal of Pius
XII was succeeded in the Vatican by the reforming programs of Pope
John XXIII, whose spurning of old-style triumphalism might be seen as
a curious correlative to Lowell's dismissal of his own earlier rhetorical
liturgies. *Life Studies* focuses clearly enough upon earthly matters and
the personal life; however, the text does not simply recapitulate that
personal life in a haphazard way but, not unlike Augustine's *Confessions*,
studiously analyses the life as an embodiment of particular epistemological theories. In appropriately tricksy fashion, the very title of the collection is a virtual oxymoron. In his 1971 conversation with Ian
Hamilton, Lowell noted that "Catholicism notices things, the particular,
while Calvinism studies the attenuated ideal," and this is what we find
in *Life Studies,* where an emphasis on the *quidditas* of particular objects

35 Eugene Kennedy, *Tomorrow's Catholics/Yesterday's Church: The Two Cultures of American
   Catholicism* (New York: Harper and Row, 1988), p. 22.

is a sign of the poet's continued cultural rebellion against Boston.[36] This
tendency to subvert New England dualism by translating abstract conceptions into physical entities operates all through Lowell's work – we
see it in the earlier poem "Mr. Edwards and the Spider," where an actual
living spider intrudes into Jonathan Edwards's sermonizing abstraction
about God dangling spiders over the pit of hell – but in *Life Studies* this
tendency becomes much more marked. It is, of course, naive to suppose
that Lowell here offers us "maskless confessions," as M. L. Rosenthal
supposed: the "I" of *Life Studies* remains a fictional creation.[37] But the
important thing, as James Merrill remarked of confessional poetry generally, is that it all sounds as if it were true: by his illusion of a true
confession, Lowell creates an impression of concrete immanence, like
the girl in a Vermeer painting "solid with yearning" who is celebrated
in "Epilogue," one of his last poems.[38] This is actually a very familiar
American pilgrimage, the course taken by Henry James at the end of the
last century, away from New England idealism into the supposedly more
generous sensuality and sensibility of the Old World. "Waking in the
Blue," in *Life Studies,* associates "Mayflower screwballs" with an obsessed examination of Harvard professor I. A. Richards's book *The Meaning of Meaning,* which in turn becomes affiliated with the neurotic
narcissism of potential suicides, the old-timers holding their locked razors
(96); while a later poem, "Harvard," juxtaposes the "black rag" and
"thick arctic snow" of Boston with a more exuberant scene where
"Chaucer's old January made hay with May."[39]

This sense of escape from New England culture was especially important to Lowell because it promised relief from the solipsistic romanticism he associated with the Puritan legacy. In his last volume, *Day by
Day* (1977), the poetic narrative recounts the quotidian rituals of life in
Kent, England; Lowell's designation of this existence as an "Afterlife"
(in the titles of two poems from this collection) suggests how for him a
religious impulse – in the broadest sense of that term – was intimately
linked to a desire for personal psychological stability. Whereas Allen Tate
rejected romanticism on purely intellectual and theological grounds,
Lowell's reactions to his native heritage rarely have the same kind of
philosophical objectivity. In *Lord Weary's Castle,* he rages against Concord and the mercantile greed of the Quakers with the fervor of someone

---

36 *Robert Lowell: Collected Prose,* p. 278.
37 M. L. Rosenthal, *The Modern Poets: A Critical Introduction* (New York: Oxford Univ.
    Press, 1960), p. 228.
38 Donald Sheehan, "An Interview with James Merrill," *Contemporary Literature,* 9 (1968),
    1–2; Lowell, *Day by Day,* p. 127.
39 Robert Lowell, *For Lizzie and Harriet* (New York: Farrar, Straus and Giroux, 1973),
    p. 21.

fatally implicated within the sins of his fathers. Indeed, the trauma of a Faustian hell in "Skunk Hour" – "I myself am hell, / nobody's here" (*LS* 104) – may be a counterpart to the crazed empathy with Hitler and Napoleon that Lowell experienced in his manic phases. This nightmare vision of an absolutist, all-embracing ego is an exaggerated version of the transcendentalists' tendency to deny the validity of the empirical world except insofar as it appeared reflexively within their own consciousness. In "The Quaker Graveyard," one line describes how "night / had steamed into our North Atlantic Fleet" (*LWC* 8): most people would see the fleet steaming into the night, but the Puritans, who overhaul the world as an extension of their own ego, perceive it the other way around. Significantly, in his sonnet sequence *History* (1973) Lowell is unimpressed by the "solipsism" of Bishop Berkeley, which he parallels with the romantic dreams of Whitman. He is also especially hard on Napoleon, who, the poem tells us, had more power to hurt people:

> ... three million soldiers dead,
> grand opera fixed like morphine in their veins.
> Dare we say, he had no moral center?

Lowell prefers the "humor" and "good health" of Goethe, who "loathed neurotics for the harm they do" and whose "artist's germ of reckless charm" was directed more toward the irrational and inconsistent world outside of himself.[40]

All of Lowell's poetry, in fact, can be read on one level as an attempt to evade the prisons of narcissism. His erection of elaborate systems of otherness – his "imitations" of other poets, his invocation of ancestors and descendants – are indications of a desperate flight away from the confines of the self. *Land of Unlikeness* also works in this way, of course: like Tate in his religious poetry, Lowell is concerned with the tortuous process of inserting the individual ego into a wider matrix of belief. Here the skillfully contrived mirrors between Lowell's poems and the forms of famous earlier works – the way "The Quaker Graveyard" almost exactly reflects the structure of Milton's "Lycidas," for example – testify to the poet's concern to represent himself as the imitator of a preexistent universe rather than as the romantic creator of a world ex nihilo.

As he retreats into these impersonal structures, though, the poet seeks at the same time also to preserve a sense of risk-taking existential freedom. There is a perennial dialogue in Lowell's poetry between fate and fortune, between the predestined forms of a "Lycidas" or a classical sonnet and the loose, colloquial rhythms of an individual speaking voice. In "The Charles River," Lowell asks: "who / can hope to enter heaven with clean

40 Robert Lowell, *History* (New York: Farrar, Straus and Giroux, 1973), pp. 72, 77, 80.

hands?" In the 1973 collection *The Dolphin,* grace is said to inhere not in strict allegiance to any system but in trusting to the imperfect fluctuations and surprises of fortune:

> My Dolphin, you only guide me by surprise,
> a captive as Racine, the man of craft,
> drawn through the maze of iron composition
> by the incomparable wandering voice of Phèdre.[41]

Yet at the same time the overall impersonal structure, the "iron" regularity of Racine's alexandrines, is just as important to Phèdre's identity as her eccentric singularity. The overarching structure frames her existential individuality, just as her individuality humanizes the overarching structure; the interpenetration works both ways.

It is just this kind of interpenetration that also determines the "religious" context of Lowell's last poems. There is indeed, as Gelpi noted, a "recoil from prophecy" here; but rather than simply lapsing into tired irony and weary routine, it could be argued that these later volumes delineate a careful immanence where the lived life of the world embodies rather than contradicts what Lowell conceives as the essence of the modern religious spirit.[42] This casual and apparently inconsequential chronicling of life "Day by Day" exactly fulfills Tate's prescription for the best Catholic poetry, that it should start with the "common thing" and "concrete experience"; accordingly, from this perspective, the low-key and mundane nature of Lowell's later poetry delineates a careful "religious" vision. It is, of course, a surprise in *History* to see Lowell iconoclastically personalizing people like Allen Tate and Dante, whom we normally associate with a more impersonal idiom, and Lowell's judgment on *The Divine Comedy* – "All comes from a girl met at the wrong time" – hardly seems an adequate account of Dante's enterprise.[43] But the religious imagery throughout *Day by Day* is persistently humanized rather than negated or satirized. We see this interpenetration between physical and "metaphysical" in "The Withdrawal":

> One wishes heaven had less solemnity:
> a sensual table
> with five half-filled bottles of red wine
> set round the hectic carved roast –
> Bohemia for ourselves

41 Lowell, *For Lizzie and Harriet,* p. 19; *The Dolphin* (New York: Farrar, Straus and Giroux, 1973), p. 78.
42 Gelpi, "The Reign of the Kingfisher," p. 65.
43 Lowell, *History,* p. 56.

and the familiars of a lifetime
charmed to communion by resurrection.[44]

This is clearly not a strictly Catholic Holy Communion, but in its exploitation of religious imagery to sanctify the sensual world it nevertheless engenders a genuine form of "communion" and "resurrection." It is the same kind of location of sensual human experience within a divine framework that we saw back in "Between the Porch and the Altar."

Lowell is of course more openly agnostic in *Day by Day*. In "Off Central Park" he observes how the works of Catholic theology in his bookcase are "still too high for temptation" (with a pun on "high": too theologically as well as too physically high). In "Home," he admits to a sense of loss arising out of this renuciation of Catholicism:

The Queen of Heaven, I miss her,
we were divorced. She never doubted
the divided, stricken soul
could call her Maria,
and rob the devil with a word.[45]

Nevertheless, as the 1970 poem "Flight in the Rain" puts it, "prayer can live without faith." Caught on a terrifying airplane journey, God may seem "*déjà vu*," but he is still privy to Lowell's "*Deo gracias* on the puking runway."[46] Similarly, in "Return in March" (from *Day by Day*) the appearance of spring in Boston is poetically heralded by a puff of white smoke, the image traditionally associated with the Vatican's signal of the election of a new pontiff:

a brick chimney tapers and points a ladder
of white smoke into the blue-black sky.[47]

This is more than simply a mythologization of the secular world by the exploitation of images culled from religious iconography; it is also a suggestion that natural physical life has countermanded spirit and is in fact now the true religion. In "Our Afterlife I," the narrator encounters two apparently ageless Tennessee cardinals, eminences whom he punningly contrasts with his own advanced age, "an eminence not to be envied"; nevertheless, he says, to be aware of years passing is at least to be "active in flight" and so cognizant of the time "when Cupid was still the Christ of love's religion." For Lowell, the immanent, incarnated world has become more crucial than the transcendental.[48]

44 Lowell, *Day by Day*, p. 72.
45 Ibid., pp. 44, 115.
46 Lowell, *History*, p. 161.
47 Lowell, *Day by Day*, p. 95.
48 Ibid., p. 21.

In his *Life Studies* poem "For George Santayana," Lowell describes the American philosopher as a "free-thinking Catholic infidel" who was convinced "'There is no God and Mary is His Mother.'" The same paradoxical phrases could be applied to Lowell's own work. In Lowell's affectionate tribute, though, there is also a hint of impatience with Santayana's "boyish shyness," his temperamental pusillanimity, his scholarly withdrawal from the world:

> you died
> near ninety,
> still unbelieving, unconfessed and unreceived,
> true to your boyish shyness of the Bride.
> Old trooper, I see your child's red crayon pass,
> bleeding deletions on the galleys you hold.
>
>   (65)

Lowell's own life as a "Catholic infidel" was more robust. Like his fictional "Mermaid," his concern was to translate souls into soles, spirit into matter, the distant abstractions of scholarship into the more immediate pleasures of daily life.[49] "Risk was his métier," says Lowell of another of his fictional heroes, Ulysses, and the poet imitatively established his own life on this principle of existential hazard, rejecting the New England Puritanism of his ancestors to flirt with the Old World faith.[50] While Lowell clearly did not remain a Catholic in any formal sense, I would argue that the familiar critical idea of *Life Studies* as a "watershed" in his personal and artistic development is not entirely accurate. As we have seen, Lowell's later poems embody perceptions of the immanent "common thing" and move away from angelic abstraction, as the neo-scholastics recommended, more completely than the earlier ones.

This dialogue between American subjectivism and Catholic orthodoxy, which is as old as Orestes Brownson, is of course one of the reasons for continuing tensions between American Catholicism and the Vatican. James Terence Fisher has written of how in this era American Catholic writers like Thomas Merton and Jack Kerouac were attempting to reconcile their religious heritage with what Fisher called an idiom of "personalism" predicated upon the American romantic drive for freedom. According to Fisher, Merton and Kerouac were aspiring to create new literary styles of self-expression and hence "a new Catholic identity in which the story of one's soul could be told as part of an American adventure."[51] Lowell's story of his own soul is not too far removed from

49 Lowell, *The Dolphin*, p. 35.
50 Lowell, *Day by Day*, p. 8.
51 Fisher, *The Catholic Counterculture in America*, p. 204.

this model. Although Lowell resolved his personal tensions by leaving Rome, in the light of his reading of Watkin we can see how closely his work approximates to this desire to align the vagaries of personal biography with a sacramental system of values. R. P. Blackmur, using Reinhold Niebuhr's phrase, wrote of Lowell as a "post-Christian" Christian; yet the term need not be a derogatory one, for despite Lowell's agnosticism his poetry makes a genuine attempt to redefine the essence of religious faith through studies of human life.[52]

52 R. P. Blackmur, "Religious Poetry in the United States," in *Religious Perspectives in American Culture,* ed. James W. Smith and A. Leland Jamison (Princeton: Princeton Univ. Press, 1961), II, 273, 280.

10

The Weight of the Cross: John Berryman

Whereas Tate and Lowell were both converts, John Berryman was a "cradle Catholic" – an expression Berryman himself denounced as "truly *disgusting* . . . like 'let it all hang out' – image of testicles dangling through zippers."[1] This different inheritance is reflected in the different stances of their poetry. For Tate and Lowell, Catholicism is a product of willed choice and consequently a mode of Apollonian order. For Berryman, religion is far less systematic, far more emotive, and in psychological terms comes to constitute one aspect of an inchoate, Dionysiac anarchy. Berryman's Dream Song 188 says of "Cal" Lowell:

> Cal has always manifested a most surprising affection
> for Matthew Arnold, – who is not a rat but whom
> I can quite take or leave.[2]

Berryman's reckless roughing-up of the psyche left him without much patience for Arnold's liberal humanism, and here he manifests obvious surprise at the relative traditionalism of Lowell's taste. Whereas Berryman sought out disintegration, eventually coming to see disintegration as a divinely ordained moral imperative, Lowell generally sought to buttress his unwilling crack-ups by a cool study of life and an affirmation of humanistic or Episcopalian reason. There are many important links between Berryman and Lowell, of course: they shared personal friendship, a Catholic cultural legacy, a "confessional" poetic style. Berryman suggested emendations when Lowell was writing *Lord Weary's Castle,* and Lowell was generous in his praise of Berryman's poetry, especially the late work *Eleven Addresses to the Lord,* which, wrote Lowell to Berryman in 1970, is a "marvelous prayer" that will be seen as "the crown

---

1 John Berryman, *Recovery* (New York: Farrar, Straus and Giroux, 1973), p. 122.
2 John Berryman, *The Dream Songs* (New York: Farrar, Straus and Giroux, 1969), p. 207.
  Subsequent page references are given in parentheses in the text, following the abbreviation *DS.*

of your work."[3] After Berryman's death, though – as we shall see later – Lowell's enthusiasm for the self-immolating excesses of this religious narrative became more muted and he said it was not his "favorite side" of Berryman's work. Alleń Tate, although a colleague and protector of Berryman at the University of Minnesota, was even further away temperamentally, disliking *The Dream Songs* and abhorring what he took to be the exhibitionism and self-indulgence of Berryman's 1970 volume *Love and Fame*.[4]

Berryman was brought up in Oklahoma as a very strict Catholic, serving as an altar boy at the six o'clock mass every morning between the ages of eight and twelve. Berryman said later that Father Boniface, the Belgian priest whom he assisted at these masses and who makes sporadic appearances in Berryman's later poetry, influenced his childhood more than anyone else except for his own father. After the latter committed suicide in 1926, Berryman's mother married John Angus Berryman, who promptly introduced his new wife and stepson to the Episcopalian church. Berryman's Jesuit education was consequently interrupted; but after being dispatched to an Episcopalian boarding school in Connecticut, he assured his mother: "I find this church almost identical with the Roman Catholic Church – prayers and all; in some respects I like it even better."[5] Although the substance of Berryman's Christian faith eventually became more and more problematical, his psychological incarceration within the structures of religious discipline always remained very obvious. On the eve of his first marriage, to a practicing Catholic, Berryman lamented how "the empty sky . . . tricks men" when "there is not a shred of reason for believing Anything or Anyone is there"; but he still urged the "Spirit sitting in the empty skies" to bring "happiness and peace" to "Your faithful daughter Eileen Mulligan, Your *good* daughter who believes in You." Similarly, after failing to get his teaching job at Harvard renewed, Berryman spent the summer of 1943 selling encyclopedias in New York City, an "experience of despair" he nevertheless ebulliently reckoned to have been "given me as a penitence – a *good* – to clear my soul." The Baudelaireian pose of the martyred *poète maudit* was always an image of himself Berryman enjoyed: "I am fitted to suffer more acutely than others," he proudly declared at this time.[6]

3 Stephen Matterson, *Berryman and Lowell: The Art of Losing* (Totowa, N.J.: Barnes and Noble, 1988), p. 8.
4 *Robert Lowell: Collected Prose,* ed. Robert Giroux (New York: Farrar, Straus and Giroux, 1987), p. 117; John Haffenden, *The Life of John Berryman* (Boston: Routledge and Kegan Paul, 1982), p. 394.
5 Haffenden, *Life of John Berryman,* pp. 18, 41.
6 Ibid., pp. 138, 149, 155.

Berryman's early poetry is centered around the idea of the Fall and "The epistemology of loss," as "The Ball Poem" puts it.[7] In "The Black Book (i)," the primal Fall of man recapitulates itself as the lapse of "solemn and high bells" into "Hell's / irritable & treacherous / despairs" (155). "New Year's Eve" laments the passing of old liturgical comforts – "Our loss of Latin fractured how far our fate" (63) – while the landscape of "The Dispossessed" is shot through with images of absence set amid the "evil sky":

> The race
> is done. Drifts through, between the cold black trunks,
> the peachblow glory of the perishing sun
>
> in empty houses where old things take place.
>
> (67)

In "The Song of the Demented Priest," God has shrunk, like the re-visited landscape of childhood, into an object surprisingly "small," and the diminished priest here finds himself impaled upon a manic pun: "I wonder" (50). Does the cleric wonder, awestruck, at the power of God, or does he wonder skeptically whether God exists at all? These early poems are riven with violent contradictions of this kind. In "Not To Live," such contradiction takes the form of an incongruous juxtaposition of spiritual significance with material metaphor: "I cannot wring, / like laundry, blue my soul" (157). The way this ethereal "soul" is eccentrically envisioned within the image of mangled laundry implies the competing tensions by which these poems are assailed.

Berryman's Sonnets, a volume first published in 1952, equally clearly exemplifies the theme of rebellion that dominates Berryman's first major phase. He rebels against the church and against fathers of all kinds and he delights in representing grand systems sliding into a state of collapse; yet, by a familiar paradox, that process of collapse can be cherished only if the lineaments of the original system linger sufficiently strongly to generate a satisfactory friction. The sonnet is an ideal form in which to express this kind of antagonism, because the classical shape of the sonnet produces a fixed pattern for Berryman's erratic syntax to crash up against. The deliquescence of mental breakdown, predicated upon the dislocation of conventional social paradigms, is mirrored in the linguistic dismemberment of the poised sonnet. Words merge into each other through onomatopoeia and enjambment:

7 John Berryman, *Collected Poems 1937–1971,* ed. Charles Thornbury (New York: Farrar, Straus and Giroux, 1989), p. 11. Subsequent page references are given in parentheses in the text.

> Burnt cork, my leer, my Grouch crouch and rush,
> No more my nature than Cyrano's: we
> Are 'hindered characters' and mock the time.
> (120)

Mocking the time, or immortalizing transitory events, is one traditional task fitted to the sonnet's formal regularity and numerological exactitude: "for short time an endless monument," as Edmund Spenser's *Epithalamion* sequence puts it. But in Berryman's Sonnet 20, we find that time rives art's immortal yearnings:

> (Secret, let us be true time crucifies.)
> (80)

These contrary impulses, between time and eternity, are envisaged as a cross, a crucifix, upon which the earthly lovers are martyred or maybe even damned:

> Time, time that damns, disvexes. Unman me
> (123)

Gliding about his satanic "metamorphosis" (Sonnet 95), the poet self-consciously translates the old courtly forms into mocking quotation marks, but he cannot quite bring himself finally to reject them:

> A 'broken heart' . . . but *can* a heart break, now?
> Lovers have stood bareheaded in love's 'storm'
> Three thousand years, changed by their mistress' 'charm'.
> (122)

The crucifix, in fact, becomes an apt emblem for this sonnet sequence, because the narrator finds himself engulfed by apparently irreconcilable forces that threaten to tear him apart. He can achieve no coherent philosophy, no calm synthesis; instead, he is racked and pulled between time and eternity, between human sexuality and divine grace:

> Squalor and leech of curiosity's truth
> Fork me this diamond meal to gag on love,
> Grinning with passion, your astonished martyr.
> (77)

As we saw, Robert Lowell's crafty half-fictions experience relatively little difficulty in elevating erotic passion to a new, more humanistic form of religion; but for the cradle Catholic Berryman, a sense of "incurable sins" (Sonnet 8) is much stronger. In the prologue to this sequence, the author cites Jacques Maritain as he broods upon how, or indeed whether, original sin is susceptible of earthly redemption:

> *The original fault*
> *will not be undone by fire.*
>
> *The original fault was whether wickedness*
> *was soluble in art. History says it is,*
> *Jacques Maritain says it is,*
> *barely.*

Because of this abiding guilt, the *Sonnets* are riddled with Berryman's compulsion to shrive himself of his sins. He confesses his failure to reply to a letter from his grandmother, now dead (Sonnet 114). He deplores his own envy (Sonnet 32) and lust (Sonnet 111). At the same time, pulling against these hellish landscapes we find images of "birds / Antiphonal at the dayspring" (91) and of angels and sacraments:

> Our Sunday morning when dawn-priests were applying
> Wafer and wine to the human wound, we laid
> Ourselves to cure ourselves down.
>
> (106)

It is a world where the spiritual is counterpointed with the secular, where Christian eschatology and symbolism are played off against philosophical agnosticism:

> Nothing there? nothing up the sky alive,
> Invisibly considering? . . . I wonder.
>
> (88)

He has, says Sonnet 102, not been to mass for eight hundred weeks.

Nevertheless, despite this lack of clear faith, the tone of these poems is one of self-scourging piety, as if Berryman were yearning to perceive and arrest something that lies just beyond the purview of poetic jurisdiction. It is not unlike Gerard Manley Hopkins's technique of alliterative inscape, seeking to burrow deep inside the poem, as it were, so that the mere language falls away as the poet drives forward on a savage quest for the original silence:

> Faiths other fall. Afterwards I kissed you
> So (Chris) long, and your eyes so waxed, marine,
> Wider I drowned . . . light to their surface drawn
> Down met the wild light (derelict weeks I missed you
> Leave me forever) upstreaming; never-seen,
> Your radiant glad soul surfaced in the dawn.
>
> (104)

Consummate human love, like divine love, resides in a state of imaginary plenitude on the other side of the mirror. To use Derrida's terms, writing itself constitutes for Berryman a form of "disruption" set against "the encyclopedic protection of theology and of logocentrism": Berryman's text strives to tear down delusive literary words in order to incorporate the primal silence of the Word.[8] This is why in "The Facts & Issues," the penultimate poem of the posthumous collection *Delusions, Etc.* (1972), the author's final lines appear to be a form of celebration:

> I am so happy I could scream!
> It's *enough!* I can't BEAR ANY MORE.
> *Let this be it.* I've *had* it. I can't wait.
>
> (263)

By killing himself shortly after completing this poem, Berryman succeeded in eradicating crucifying worldly tensions and regaining instead a paradisiacal silence.

While this original silence may constitute the ultimate end of Berryman's mission, his textual enterprises necessarily locate themselves within the lapsed and uncertain terrestrial world. Indeed, such is the force of these irreconcilable tensions in Berryman's life and art that the whole question of religious "belief" or "disbelief" becomes scarcely relevant to any discussion of Berryman's epistemology. Christopher Ricks reckoned *The Dream Songs* to be "a theodicy" – "a vindication of divine providence in view of the existence of evil" – while other readers, such as Douglas Dunn and Gary Q. Arpin, have found in Berryman's major work "an absence of faith" and the lack of "a positive religious attitude."[9] But the paradoxes of genuine blasphemy are entwined in such a complex way within these poems that Berryman's language seems to exempt itself from even a putative purchase on final meaning or "truth." The textual significations are so dense, multivalent, and indeed contradictory that it would be not only reductive but actually impossible to collapse their complexity in the name of any one systematic doctrine. *The Dream Songs,* as Berryman stated in his 1971 *Paris Review* interview, are by no means a consistent exposition of some "religious or philosophical system." When the interviewer asked about Ricks's idea of a theodicy, Berryman himself expressed uncertainty: "It's a tough question. The idea of a theodicy has been in my mind at least since 1938. . . . I simply don't know. I put my stuff, in as good condition as I can make it, on the table, and if people want to form opinions, good, I'm interested in the opinions."[10]

8 Jacques Derrida, *Of Grammatology*, trans. Gayatri Chakravorty Spivak (Baltimore: Johns Hopkins Univ. Press, 1976), p. 18.

9 Christopher Ricks, "Recent American Poetry," *Massachusetts Review*, 11 (1970), 336; Douglas Dunn, "Gaiety and Lamentation: The Defeat of John Berryman," *Encounter*, 43, no. 2 (Aug. 1974), 72–3; Gary Q. Arpin, *The Poetry of John Berryman* (Port Washington, N.Y.: Kennikat, 1978), p. 70.

10 Peter A. Stitt, "Interview with John Berryman," in *Writers at Work: The Paris Review Interviews*, 4th ser., ed. George Plimpton (New York: Viking, 1976), pp. 308–9.

Many writers, of course, decline to comment too explicitly on their work, but Berryman's indecision here exactly mirrors the theological bewilderment that pervades *The Dream Songs* themselves. There is, as Berryman observed, "a lot of theology" in *The Dream Songs;* indeed, he said in 1971 that "I have been interested not only in religion but in theology all my life."[11] Yet the end result is that there is no end result, for on religious matters *The Dream Songs* are not only inconclusive but actually confusing:

> Hankered he less for youth than for more time
> to adjust the conflicting evidence, the 'I'm
> immortal-&-not' routine,
> Pascal, Spinoza, and Augustine,
> Kafka and all his tribe, living it out alone,
> Mary Baker Eddy's telephone.
>
> in her vault with a direct line to the *Monitor:*
> it ain't rung yet, pal, nor has Christ returned,
> according to the *World Almanac*
> which I read less for what it say than for
> what's missing: the editor of the *Atlantic* burned,
> for instance, and Christ came back.
>
> (*DS* 369)

We are none the wiser. The beginning of the second stanza seems to suggest that though Christ has not returned "yet," his nonappearance does not necessarily signify nonexistence, it merely means his return has not yet been documented by the *World Almanac*. The poem is in a process of adjusting "the conflicting evidence" and does not achieve, nor perhaps even seek, finality. Appropriately enough, Pascal, with his "cagey bets" (*DS* 251), is one hero of *The Dream Songs,* the philosopher who reckons there is no harm in divine belief even if his rational mind cannot altogether countenance it.

Some of the most barbed comments in these poems are reserved for Protestant theologians and philosophers. Dream Song 254 ridicules "Luther, who undone / the sacramental system & taught evil / is *ingrained*" (*DS* 273); while Song 294 chastises the New England sage of Concord for the way his disembodied, angelic intellect betokened a lack of common human sympathy: "Emerson's insufferable essays, / wisdom in every line, while his wife cried upstairs" (*DS* 316). Even though Henry, Berryman's alter ego, may hedge his Pascalian bets around the question of the actual existence of the Almighty, the creed he lives by is firmly grounded upon Catholic theological principles. Unlike Luther, Henry

11 *Paris Review Interviews,* 4th ser., pp. 301, 320.

welcomes human sin as an opportunity for the intervention of divine grace:

> We hear the more
> sin has increast, the more
> grace has been caused to abound.
> (DS 22)

This validates Henry's delight in the "adventure of sin" (DS 360) and his being "prepared to live in a world of Fall / for ever" (DS 84). It is an extreme form of the doctrine of immanence, the idea that by living fully in the world a fallible human being can participate in God's "sacramental" grace. Berryman suggests in one of his last poems, "Unknowable? perhaps not altogether," that this God is not the shadowy distant spirit of transcendentalism but an amalgam of intellect, laughter, and imagination. Hence by imitating these latter qualities, so the poem maintains, men can claim "we're trans-acting with You" (258). This is envisioned as another version of the Catholic belief in transubstantiation: God is deemed by the poet to be knowable and present within the world. It also explains why Henry has no time for Emerson's idealistic ruminations or for Luther's Puritan piety. *The Dream Songs* imply that humans can come closer to God by fulfilling themselves through ordinary sinful human activities.

This is also why Berryman was so enthusiastic about the early Christian philosopher Origen's doctrine of *apocatastasis,* whereby at the end of time every human being would become reestablished in Christ. "Resolve to know that in you there is a capacity to be transformed," Origen urged his audience in the *Dialogue with Heracleides.* For Origen, as for Berryman, the human body was not a lamentable prison for the spirit, but provided an opportunity for creative tension between soul and flesh. The human body was "the appropriate 'sparring partner'" God assigned to each Christian on his own individual journey toward salvation. Origen thus saw the corporeal nature of human incarnation as "a temporary staging point along the spirit's progress back to a former harmony with God," as W. H. C. Frend put it.[12] In this way, Origen took issue with the received Christian notion that earthly matter was the cause of evil and sin. As the theologian Karl Aner explained:

> For Origen sin was fundamentally something οὐκ ὄν, something ἀνυπόστατον, something unreal, because it was only a transitory condition; for none of the rational souls was evil when it came from the hands of

12 W. H. C. Frend, "The Devil and the Flesh," *New York Review of Books,* 2 Feb. 1989, p. 40.

the creator, and at the end they would all return to God. Divine providence had created the world of experience as a place of purification for
the spirits who, before the beginning of time, had fallen into the misuse
of their freedom to develop, and had been incorporated in more subtle
or more coarse matter according to the extent of their fall into sin.[13]

Berryman's *Dream Songs* recognize that such a vision of the world as a
place where matter is gradually, but inevitably, infused with spirit would
render the idea of hell redundant. In Origen's eschatology, hell is, quite
literally, empty:

> Hell is empty. O that has come to pass
> which the cut Alexandrian foresaw,
> and Hell lies empty.
> Lightning fell silent where the Devil knelt
> and over the whole grave hath settled awe
> in a full death of guilt.
>
> (*DS* 63)

Origen's philosophy would bring about the "death of guilt," as this
poem suggests, and the ultimate abolition of evil. Hardly a notion to
appeal to Luther or the Puritans, of course, with their more scrupulous
quest to separate the light from the dark; indeed, it was also too strong
for the Catholic church, whose Fifth General Council in 553 condemned
as heretical Origen's principle that evil could eventually disappear altogether. Berryman's poetry, however, continues to toy with this notion
that the living human being might become a vessel of divine grace, that
"Heaven is here / now, in Minneapolis" (*DS* 136), that the earthly delights of literature and adultery could in themselves be sanctioned by a
divine benevolence.

Amid the more immediate terrestrial struggles of *The Dream Songs,*
though, such divine harmonies seem a long way off. These poems are
torn with the kind of struggle between spirit and matter that we saw in
Berryman's Sonnets. The author wrestles with the corporeal world and
aspires to storm his way into a higher realm of the spirit:

> there are secrets, secrets, I may yet –
> hidden in history and theology, hidden in rhyme –
> come on to understand.
>
> (*DS* 178)

In keeping with this urgent hermeneutic quest, the book's very title, *The
Dream Songs,* suggests displacement and transfiguration of vision:

---

13 Karl Aner, "Sin and Guilt," in *Twentieth Century Theology in the Making,* ed. Jaroslav
Pelikan, trans. R. A. Wilson (London: Collins-Fontana, 1970), II, 186.

"'Unam Sanctam' was my other dream," says Henry in Dream Song 322, after musing on yet another of his women (344). This conception of the dream's ability to metamorphose the mundane world parallels the transformational function of song: "Where the word stops," noted Aquinas in a commentary on the psalms, "there starts the song, *exultation of the mind bursting forth into the voice.*"[14] The Dream Songs, then, imply a world of apotheosized vision, although the irony is that this spiritual impulse is forever running aground on the drab world of matter:

> I consider a song will be as humming-bird
> swift, down-light, missile-metal-hard, and strange
> as the world of anti-matter . . .
> but can Henry write it? . . .
> Therefore he shakes and he will sing no more.
>
> (DS 120)

The incongruity of this violent juxtaposition between dream and reality, song and prose, is highlighted by the often comic intrusion of a choric "O" into segments of verse that seem the least susceptible of being endowed with graceful harmonies:

> Blind his assistants, some in the Old Bailey,
> some at the Waldorf Towers, the Pump Room,
> trying their best O.
>
> (DS 193)

This structural irony leads toward imagery of crack-up, as the material object is unable to bear the extravagant euphony with which it is charged:

> I will have more to say at a later time
> with my whole cracked heart, in prose or rhyme
> of this lady of the northern sea.
>
> (DS 311)

This potential crack-up extends also into the religious field:

> Father Hopkins, teaching elementary Greek
> whilst his mind climbed the clouds, also died here.
> O faith in all he lost.
>
> (DS 399)

Here the syntax itself has become fragmented into a fatal ambiguity: does Hopkins have faith in a lost world, or has he lost faith in everything? The very process of signification has become riven apart.

Burdened by these irreconcilable contraries, Henry defines himself as

---

14 Quoted in Jacques Maritain, *Creative Intuition in Art and Poetry*, (New York: Pantheon–Bollingen Foundation, 1953), p. 251.

a martyr, taking up "the weight of the cross" (*DS* 118) and identifying himself with Saint Stephen (*DS* 7) as well as Christ (*DS* 145). Indeed, the narrator seems to seek out pain as a guarantee of the authenticity of his personal experiences. Compare Saint Augustine in the *Confessions:*

> Men even procure for themselves the pleasures of life by means of pain, not unexpected pain which comes upon them uninvited, but pain which they deliberately induce for themselves. There is no pleasure in eating and drinking unless it is preceded by the discomfort of hunger and thirst.[15]

This masochist's charter is taken up by Berryman in Dream Song 113:

> That isna Henry limping. That's a hobble
> clapped on mere Henry by the most high GOD
> for the freedom of Henry's soul.
>
> (*DS* 130)

Henry also aligns himself with the martyred John F. Kennedy (*DS* 219) as well as "Connolly & Pearse" and other "hero-martyrs" of the Irish Nationalist movement (*DS* 283, 331). Also, of course, Berryman cherishes the pain and suicides of his literary colleagues – Schwarz, Jarrell, Blackmur, Plath, Hemingway – as confirmation of the messianic torture of his profession.

Berryman said in 1971 that Saint Augustine was "a particular interest of mine," and Augustine's life was a topic he used to lecture on frequently at the University of Minnesota.[16] It is, in fact, possible to perceive more elaborate parallels between *The Dream Songs* and Augustine's *Confessions*. In Book 10 of the *Confessions*, there is an extended passage on the use and power of memory: mind and memory, Augustine says, are one, because the mind engages in conceptualization only by recalling events from memory, so that "the memory is a sort of stomach for the mind." The importance of this is that it historicizes the mind, referring intellectual categories to man's actual experience of living as well as to traditional Neoplatonic abstractions; and this provides a justification for the literary genre of Augustine's *Confessions*, in which he deploys his personal biography as an exemplum of the human situation. (Augustine deplores, of course, the "abominable arrogance" of those who "want to be light, not in the Lord, but in themselves"; he would have hated Rousseau.)[17] Berryman's use of personal memory to underpin and vindicate his poetic themes works in a similar way. In *The Dream Songs*, disparate times are

15 Saint Augustine, *Confessions*, trans. R. S. Pine-Coffin (Harmondsworth: Penguin, 1961), p. 162.
16 *Paris Review Interviews*, 4th ser., p. 300.
17 Saint Augustine, *Confessions*, pp. 220, 173.

all jumbled together and circle around haphazardly, as out of sequence as the erratic poetic syntax. As with Augustine, the crucial connecting factor is memory: Berryman's use of "Henry" as a narrative alter ego allows the author to introduce complex shifting perspectives between the "I" of now and the remembered "Henry" of then, as in this 1968 poem from *Henry's Fate:*

> Long (my dear) ago, when rosaries
> based Henry's vaulting thought, at seven & six,
> Henry perceived in the sky
> your form amidst his stars
>
> ....
> I was *the* altar-boy he depended on
> on freezing twilit mornings, after good dreams.
> Since when my dreams have changed.[18]

Also in keeping with Augustine's emphasis on memory is the way associative rather than rational links become an aesthetic imperative in Berryman's poetry. In Dream Song 186, he is rude to the logical Jesuits who are blind to the world's sacramental ecstasies: "The parking-lot tilted & made a dance, / ditching Jesuits" (*DS* 205). In a later poem, "A Usual Prayer," he similarly describes "men's thinking" as "being eighteen-tenths deluded" (259). This discrediting of the power of objective rational thought provides increased scope for the flourishing of idiosyncratic subjective associations; as with Augustine, Berryman's confessional style implies, not a romantic idiom of individual autonomy, but an admission of the necessarily fractured and fallible state of human consciousness sub specie aeternitatis. The irrationalism of Berryman's poetry reveals the triviality and inadequacy of human schemes of rationality in the sight of "God."

Thus despite Henry's bravado about God being his "enemy" (*DS* 15) and his consequent willed "assault on immortality" in the surrogate forms of love and fame, there is in fact a profound sense of self-rupture within *The Dream Songs*, which is consistent with the overtly religious poems of Berryman's last phase.[19] The prayer sequences at the end of *Love and Fame* and throughout the posthumous *Delusions, Etc.* are not so much evidence of "a new style in architecture," as Helen Vendler suggested, but imply rather a development out of the earlier work.[20] To be sure, Berryman was by this time under the influence of his much publicized "conversion" by the "God of rescue" who called upon Berryman while

18 John Berryman, *Henry's Fate and Other Poems* (London: Faber, 1978), p. 14.
19 Ibid., p. 40 ("The assault on immortality begins").
20 Helen Vendler, *Part of Nature, Part of Us: Modern American Poets* (Cambridge, Mass.: Harvard Univ. Press, 1980), p. 336.

the poet was in the hospital undergoing treatment for alcoholism.[21] His posthumous novel *Recovery* (1973) makes an equation between recovery from alcoholism and recovery from religious despair, and, according to his biographer John Haffenden, Berryman professed a regular Catholicism throughout the final year of his life. Nevertheless, as Robert Lowell saw, these last poems "are a Roman Catholic unbeliever's, seesawing from sin to piety, from blasphemous affirmation to devoted anguish. . . . This is a traditionally Catholic situation, the *Sagesse,* the wisdom of the sinner, Verlaine in jail. Berryman became one of the few religious poets, yet it isn't my favorite side."[22] Not Lowell's "favorite side" because his own humanism preferred an existentialist self-reliance rather than this kind of "religious" surrender.

The eschatology of hell, purgatory, and heaven manifests itself openly at the end of *Love and Fame,* as the poet moves from a mental hospital in "The Hell Poem" to a singing cardinal at Seville Cathedral in "Heaven." But these poems reveal anything other than Christian orthodoxy. "Eleven Addresses to the Lord" denies a belief in hell – "Rest may be your ultimate gift" (218) – and more generally scorns any prospect of life after death (215). The Second Coming is also viewed as an improbable future event:

> One sudden Coming? Many so believe.
> So not, without knowing anything, do I.
>
> (217)

"The Facts and Issues," in *Delusions,* again finds the poet-theologian in a quizzical mood:

> I feel pretty sure that evil simply ends
> *for the doer* (having wiped him out,
> by the way, usually) where good goes on,
> or good *may* drop dead too: I don't think so.
>
> (263)

Again, doubt rather than closure is of the essence. There is, as Douglas Dunn observed, "a nervous edge, an incompletion" about these poems, and the language is "'mixed' and quirky."[23] One of the notes in *Recovery* talks about the fictional hero's "hostility . . . against the gabbled masses" of Catholic church services, and this narrative alter ego also declares himself "hostile to Trinity – dubious of X [Christ], hostile to BVM [Blessed Virgin Mary] – anti-Pope."[24] Indeed, Berryman at various

21 *Paris Review Interviews,* 4th ser., pp. 317, 319.
22 Haffenden, *Life of John Berryman,* p. 384; *Robert Lowell: Collected Prose,* p. 117.
23 Dunn, "Gaiety and Lamentation," p. 77.
24 Berryman, *Recovery,* pp. 240, 72.

points in his life actively considered converting to Judaism, believing the
Jewish emphasis on a here and now rather than the life to come would
best suit his immanentist convictions. A story entitled "The Imaginary
Jew," which he published in a 1945 issue of the *Kenyon Review,* outlines
his cultural preference for Judaism over what he conceived to be the more
bigoted aspects of Irish Catholic culture.

Exactly what Berryman "believed" is a meaningless question; all we
can say is that there are certain recurring patterns of belief and nonbelief.
Origen's proposition that "Hell is empty" is mooted once more in
"Compline," one of the *Delusions* poems (235). More important than
any specific creed, though, is the overarching Catholic cultural context
of Berryman's poetry. One epigraph to *Delusions* is from Paul Claudel:
"On parle toujours de 'l'art réligieux.' L'art est réligieux" (223). Berryman's opus testifies to the truth of this remark, at least as far as his
own work was concerned. This is not, though, the narrower sense of
"religious art" Claudel would have had in mind. Berryman's poetry is
"religious" not because it adumbrates religious principles but because it
is inextricably entwined with the residual material of a particular religious
inheritance. Berryman is, as he puts it in "Sext," "obedient to disobedience" (231); the rejection of the altar boy's creed involves, not its
obliteration, but its paradoxical inversion. Thus the words of the "Hail
Mary" – "pray for us now and at the hour of our death" – become
reconstituted in "Nones" as "pray with me now in the hour of our
living" (231). This life, rather than the next, became Berryman's métier.

In this secular perspective, the narrator in *Recovery* gratefully observes
that while he had always preserved faith in God as "Creator and Main-
tainer," the dramatic coup staged by the "God of rescue" permitted him
to see how the Almighty was also a sympathetic existentialist "interested
in the individual life in the ordinary way." This new sense of God's
humanity would have reinforced the analogies Berryman intuited between his *Dream Songs* and the structure of the Gospels. Henry, like
Christ, and like Augustine in the *Confessions,* was supposed to be a man
leading an exemplary life. In *Recovery,* we are told of the hero, Berryman's fictional self-replication, that "New Testament criticism . . . constituted his only hobby."[25] Berryman himself was especially fascinated
by Philip Carrington's 1960 commentary *According to Mark,* in which
Carrington demonstrated how Mark's story of Christ carefully rear-
ranges events to fit in with the cycle of Jewish fasts and feasts, thus
emphasizing Mark's power as a "rudely Semitic and popular" fiction
writer.[26] Carrington's point is that Christ, like any other literary hero,

25 Ibid., pp. 49, 233.
26 See John Haffenden, *John Berryman: A Critical Commentary* (New York: New York

is subject to the whims of narrative design; the Gospels were not engraved on divine tablets of stone, but are the fallible record of an ordinary man's life. The historical character of Christ is transliterated into a fictional figure made out of words, just as Berryman's own life becomes transliterated into the persona of Henry. In his poem "The Search," Berryman outlines his own (abortive) plans for a historical study of the Gospels (199–200); while, according to Haffenden, toward the end of his life Berryman was planning to write a new biography of Christ himself. "The evil in me was foul," declared Saint Augustine, "but I loved it"; the ineradicable humanity of God and the saints establishes an analogue that is used to justify the venial excesses of Berryman's narrative heroes and to demonstrate that, despite their foibles, these heroes can participate in the rewards of grace.[27]

Unlike Lowell, though, Berryman was never able finally to rest content with this idea of anthropocentric humanism; he was always more attracted to literary works that challenge or radically undermine the limitations of an individual, worldly self. He wrote an admiring introduction to the 1952 Grove Press edition of Matthew Lewis's eighteenth-century extravaganza *The Monk,* where, as Berryman said, "the point is to conduct a remarkable man utterly to damnation."[28] In a 1946 essay for the *Kenyon Review* Berryman also extolled *The Great Gatsby* as "a masterpiece," wherein Fitzgerald's genius was said to reside in describing "a beauty and intensity of attachment, which his imagination required should be attachment to something inaccessible."[29] In *Recovery,* the hero, Alan Severance, talks of God as making "Himself available to certain men and women in terms of inspiration – artists, scientists, statesmen, the saints of course, anybody in fact – gave them special power or insight or endurance – I'd felt it myself: some of my best work I can't claim any credit for, it flowed out all by itself, or in fact by His moving."[30] This "special power or insight," whether into damnation like Lewis's hapless monk, or into areas of the unattainable like the equally unhappy Gatsby, became for Berryman the creative basis of his art. The collapse of the self, like the collapse of formal poetic structures, becomes a guarantee of "divine" inspiration.

This is why Berryman hurled himself against life, desiring to make love to every woman he met, to read every book he came across, to

Univ. Press, 1980), p. 135; Philip Carrington, *According to Mark: A Running Commentary on the Oldest Gospel* (Cambridge: Cambridge Univ. Press, 1960), p. 6.

27 Saint Augustine, *Confessions,* p. 47.
28 John Berryman, "The Monk and Its Author," in *The Freedom of the Poet* (New York: Farrar, Straus and Giroux, 1976), p. 131.
29 Berryman, *The Freedom of the Poet,* pp. 198, 200.
30 Berryman, *Recovery,* p. 49.

undertake the doomed enterprise of knowing everything. He was a self-confessed masochist; in the *Paris Review* interview, he famously asserted: "Among the greatest pieces of luck for high achievement is ordeal. . . . My idea is this: The artist is extremely lucky who is presented with the worst possible ordeal which will not actually kill him. . . . I hope to be nearly crucified."[31] Such crucifixion would, thought Berryman, verify his artistic sainthood. Jacques Maritain, again promulgating his controversial notion of the metaphysical status of "creative intuition," wrote in 1953 that as "art continues in its own way the labor of divine creation," it is therefore "true to say with Dante that our human art is, as it were, the grandchild of God."[32] Berryman seemed determined to follow Maritain's attempt to reconcile Catholicism and romanticism by forging close familial alliances between himself and the Holy Trinity. God, he says at the end of *Love and Fame,* is "a delicious author / rational and passionate," the same kind of scribe as Berryman aspired himself to be; while, quoting Hopkins, he declares that Christ is the only true literary critic (221). Whatever the directions of Berryman's spiritual beliefs, then, the aesthetic structures of his work were substantially determined by his Catholic heritage. The end of his life brings forth another of those paradoxical, irreconcilable contraries that dogged Berryman's enterprise: the profession of religious faith clashes against the mortal sin of suicide. But then, as Berryman told the *Paris Review* in 1971, he considered himself to be a Catholic but not a Christian.[33] While the religious framework of his art embodies a crucial pattern on the level of cultural materialism, it resists being subsumed within any kind of theological certainty.

31 *Paris Review Interviews,* 4th ser., p. 322.
32 Maritain, *Creative Intuition in Art and Poetry,* p. 65.
33 *Paris Review Interviews,* 4th ser., p. 320.

11

The Dialogue of Blasphemy: Frank O'Hara

Frank O'Hara was born into an Irish–Catholic family in Baltimore in 1926 and brought up in Worcester, Massachusetts, where he attended parochial schools. O'Hara's father was a strict Catholic and the poet's memories of this time were so unfavorable that, as an adult apostate, Frank O'Hara disliked to talk about his family upbringing. He made a brief exception to this in *Autobiographical Fragments:*

> I had rather summarily deduced that my whole family were liars and, since our "community" consisted of a by and large very mixed national descendency it couldn't be that they were Irish liars, they must be Catholic liars. Had I been a French child I probably would have simply become an anticleric; as it was, I blamed almost everything onto the Catholic Church, which they all talked about in the most revoltingly smarmy way (a priest once later said, trying to win me over, that I had been overparochialized!).[1]

O'Hara's poetry has the reputation of being loose, colorful, anarchic, as if to reap the benefit of this rejection of religious institutions. He is, said Marjorie Perloff, a poet of "indeterminacy," an heir of the Rimbaud–Stein–Williams tradition in which fields of continuous flux and process predominate, rather than a product of the symbolist and modernist quest for ulterior structures Perloff traced through Baudelaire to Eliot and Stevens, and thence forward to Lowell and Berryman. Helen Vendler has similarly asserted that O'Hara "genuinely has no metaphysical baggage": he appears to have freedom to move in whatever direction his long, sinuous lines take him.[2] In Charles Altieri's eyes too, O'Hara de-

---

1 Frank O'Hara, *Standing Still and Walking in New York,* ed. Donald Allen (San Francisco: Grey Fox Press, 1983), p. 30.
2 See Marjorie Perloff, *The Poetics of Indeterminacy: Rimbaud to Cage* (Princeton: Princeton Univ. Press, 1981), passim; Helen Vendler, *Part of Nature, Part of Us: Modern American Poets* (Cambridge, Mass.: Harvard Univ. Press, 1980), p. 192.

248

lineates a brilliant "landscape without depth," a "demystified" world "stripped of... ontological vestments." The names and places in his poetry, as Perloff pointed out, have no "inner reality": one cannot annotate O'Hara in the way one annotates *The Cantos* or *The Waste Land*, bringing to bear an external system of reference that explains and enriches the poem.[3] In O'Hara, all is there on the dazzling surfaces; and that, it would seem, is all there is there.

But while O'Hara was not in any sense a consistent thinker, to talk, like Vendler, of "his utter absence of what might be called an intellectual syntax" is misleading.[4] O'Hara's rich surfaces are never as self-sufficient and self-defining as he might like them to be; instead, they are constantly engaging in dialogue with the worlds of intellectual syntax he has rejected. This is to use "dialogue" in Mikhail Bakhtin's sense of a circuitous struggle between competing forces or ideologies, a struggle which can never be resolved within that grand final conclusion typical of dialectic, but which must remain forever beached upon the open-ended strands of the dialogic imagination where different voices perennially ebb and flow. For Bakhtin, writing comprises not one grand truth but many partial truths, and literary style – which is not mere abstract stylishness, but always "ideologically saturated" – is the crucial signpost revealing where these cultural tensions lie.[5]

In "Causerie de Gaspe Peninsula," for instance, O'Hara evidently seeks to reduce Catholic icons to nothing more than Firbank-like frivolities:

> "The king and his knights
>   went to the church under a ravishing mantle
> of blue all stitched with air currents. Mary Magdalene!
>   the boats were foundering in the banks." "I put down
> the towel and suddenly a hideous stain appeared
>   on the open pages of the book, it was *Inclinations*
> by England's famed Ronald Firbank and I read the legend
>   'Your name is mud.'"[6]

The desire here is to shock, to blaspheme against the divine substance of Mary Magdalene by transposing this religious symbol into no more than a two-dimensional aesthetic surface. The superficiality of the artistic image betokens, in O'Hara's eyes, the superficiality of religion itself, the

3 Charles Altieri, *Enlarging the Temple: New Directions in American Poetry during the 1960s* (Lewisburg: Bucknell Univ. Press, 1979), p. 110; Marjorie Perloff, *Frank O'Hara: Poet among Painters* (Austin: Univ. of Texas Press, 1977), p. 25.
4 Vendler, *Part of Nature*, p. 194.
5 Mikhail Bakhtin, *The Dialogic Imagination: Four Essays*, trans. Caryl Emerson and Michael Holquist, ed. Michael Holquist (Austin: Univ. of Texas Press, 1981), p. 269.
6 Frank O'Hara, *Poems Retrieved*, ed. Donald Allen (Bolinas, Ca.: Grey Fox Press, 1977), p. 97.

way religion is no more than a fanciful aesthetic phenomenon. Yet the
linguistic paradox here is that "Mary Magdalene" does not and cannot
exist simply in terms of this moment of instantaneous personal perception
that the poet wishes to illuminate for us. Like any signifier, Mary Magdalene carries connotations, cultural allusions, the residue of all that
"metaphysical baggage" Vendler claimed O'Hara had expelled from his
work. The poet may indeed have sought to expel it, but doing so is like
postulating a transcendent and dematerialized signifier: it is a pure
impossibility.

Following Vendler's argument, Charles Altieri suggested that whereas
Robert Lowell (for instance) is openly a "poet of nostalgia," hankering
after that "center or source of reference" that has traditionally informed
"Western poetry and metaphysics," O'Hara on the contrary attempts to
cancel this nostalgia, perceiving it as "purposeless." Altieri himself acknowledged that O'Hara does keep his reader "aware of the potential
nostalgia," even while refusing it; but, following Bakhtin's line, we can
go further than this and say that O'Hara is entrammelled in a dialogue
with this nostalgia, a nostalgia toward which his texts maintain a highly
equivocal attitude.[7] It is no coincidence that O'Hara, who was usually
very generous with praise for other writers and silent rather than openly
hostile if he disliked something, was unusually aggressive in his attitude
toward Lowell, whom he described as having "a confessional manner
which [lets him] get away with things that are really just plain bad but
you're supposed to be interested because he's supposed to be so upset."[8]
The explicit "nostalgia" and sense of metaphysical displacement in Lowell's poetry was, perhaps, too close to O'Hara for the latter to feel quite
comfortable. O'Hara in fact wrote a very funny parody of Lowell's early
style, "A Web of Saints Near the Sea," in which he ridicules Lowell's
tortured invocation of Catholic luminaries:

> Life sappeth the spirit; and given the will to Paul,
> I call upon Ignatius the Loyalist, the shriven of
> the Lord, to beat a tambourine for Mother Ursuline.[9]

Conversely, O'Hara in his professional occupation as a critic of visual
art was always very alert to the religious dimensions of iconography,
praising Francis Bacon, crucifixions and all, as "a magnificent artist" and
remarking of Andy Warhol's pictures: "Maybe they're not real icons,
but there's some sort of almost religious element in them."[10]

---

7 Altieri, *Enlarging the Temple*, p. 126.
8 O'Hara made this remark in an interview with Edward Lucie-Smith. See *Standing Still*,
  p. 13.
9 O'Hara, *Poems Retrieved*, p. 171.
10 O'Hara, *Standing Still*, pp. 10, 20.

This phrase, "some sort of almost religious element" could apply to O'Hara's own poetry as well. One critic, Anthony Libby, went so far as to find in this work a "complex luminosity" and "radiance" that suggests "the *claritas* of epiphany poetry." The tone of Libby's argument brings to mind the aesthetic outlook of liberal Catholics in the 1950s, who, strongly influenced by Maritain's *Art and Scholasticism,* entertained the notion that in their search for the "quiddities" of things artists might become Thomists without knowing it. But while O'Hara "frequently *sounds* visionary," as Libby said, we should remember that O'Hara's Christian images are always being reworked into iconoclastic patterns: O'Hara's project is to redefine spiritual grandeur in terms of material and physical life.[11] These celebrations of life in New York City draw upon a residue of religious imagery so as to bathe the mundane world in a radiant, "transubstantiated" light. The poetry does not, of course, advocate the literal "truth" of these otherworldly metaphors, but exploits their cultural connotations so as to reconstitute the material world within a form of apotheosized play. For instance, "Second Avenue," a paean to the Manhattan metropolis, embraces "heretics," "a nun trembling before the microphone," snakes, angels, "priests with lips like mutton," "drunken Magi," "spiritual contamination," "sainthood," "a rosary pressed in the shape of a tongue," and so on. Here the tongues of celestial fire have been reincarnated as tongues of erotic play, as the poet engages in the paradox of describing earthly bliss through metaphysical metaphors:

> it's heaven in Heaven! with the leaves falling
> like angels who've been discharged for sodomy.[12]

O'Hara's poetry usually gives the impression of being spoken casually by a narrator who could easily have chosen one phrase rather than another. But in fact apparently throwaway phrases like "it's heaven" or "To Hell With It" (the title of a later poem) often carry eschatological reverberations. The dialogue of blasphemy is implicit even in his use of these slang colloquialisms.

In O'Hara's early writing, though, the very frequent "religious" images tend to imply less a sense of exuberant and blasphemous parody than a heavy legacy of religious disquiet. Here the tone is one of – as O'Hara himself put it in a journal entry of 1948 – "guilt . . . passed down

---

11 Anthony Libby, "O'Hara on the Silver Range," *Contemporary Literature,* 17 (1976), 257, 261, 259.

12 *The Collected Poems of Frank O'Hara,* ed. Donald Allen (New York: Knopf, 1972), pp. 139–50. Subsequent page references are given in parentheses in the text.

generation to generation, like syphilis."[13] These early works are immersed in hostile images of chalices ("Sea Changes") and "holy water" ("The Man without a Country") and are staffed with characters like a "priestly transvestite" ("The Weekend") and sinister-looking nuns (about whom O'Hara seems to have had a particular phobia).[14] The aggression of these representations suggests how the poet is concerned to manipulate institutional stereotypes so as to gain some form of psychological revenge for his religious traumas. We see this again in "The Argonauts":

> The apple green chasuble, so
> cut with gold, spins through
> the altar like a buzz saw
> while nuns melt on the floor.
>
> (45)

The nuns here are said to be excited sexually by the priest's flowing vestments as he goes about his official business at the altar. As the title "Argonauts" implies, this poem is designed to uncover the subversive pagan impulses lurking within ostensibly Christian practices. The green and gold of this Christian ritual are linked with pagan or prelapsarian hedonism, that Edenic "apple" also bringing to mind the idea of sexual transgression.

While this sense of "genuine blasphemy," to use T. S. Eliot's term, is more clearly apparent in O'Hara's early phase of youthful rebellion, it also, less obviously, informs the whole structure of the poet's later work. Eliot's famous phrase appears in his 1930 essay on Baudelaire: "Genuine blasphemy, genuine in spirit and not purely verbal, is the product of partial belief, and is as impossible to the complete atheist as to the perfect Christian. It is a way of affirming belief."[15] It is these "paradoxical integuments," as he describes them, that O'Hara engages with in "Ashes on Saturday Afternoon," where he inverts the sacrament of the Eucharist by prescribing "vomit on Sunday after wafer and prayer" (77–8). Similarly, his poem "Easter" paradoxically celebrates the idea of resurrection in terms of a renewal of sexual rather than spiritual life:

> O sins of sex and kisses of birds at the end of the penis
> cry of a black princess whose mouth founders in the Sun.
>
> (98–9)

The very word "sins" gives it away: the poet continues to perceive terrestrial categories through a (partly) suppressed spiritual frame of ref-

---

13 Frank O'Hara, Early Writing, ed. Donald Allen (Bolinas, Ca.: Grey Fox Press, 1977), p. 99.
14 Ibid., p. 81; Poems Retrieved, p. 111.
15 T. S. Eliot, Selected Essays, 3rd ed. (London: Faber, 1951), p. 421.

erence. The object cannot be simply itself; it must also be *not* something else. Every proposition involves a rejection. Even O'Hara's lover, Vincent Warren, is celebrated in "Saint" for not being Saint Vincent de Paul: "he sleeps like a temple to no god" (332). Again, in the poem "St. Paul and All That," O'Hara draws upon – while, of course, inverting – the Pauline doctrine of a love that turns the world upside down and redeems the world through suffering (406). "Paul" was Vincent Warren's middle name, and for O'Hara acceptance of human love was always bound up with rejection of the divine.

O'Hara was, of course, a frank black atheist, and Eliot's phrase "partial belief" might not seem appropriate to this kind of avowed secularism. Nevertheless, as we have seen, "belief" is itself a slippery and, in literary terms, scarcely relevant category because it implies a subjective autonomy that is hardly available within the intellectual framework of the postmodern condition. It is the old "intentional fallacy" quandary in another guise: just as an author's texts carry no necessary identity with what he or she intended to create, so an author's (or indeed any person's) beliefs bear no necessary identity with what he or she intends to believe. By drawing upon Eliot's phrase "partial belief," I am not attempting to indicate O'Hara himself partially believed in God – in any case, an unanswerable and ultimately meaningless question – but to suggest how O'Hara's texts find themselves intertwined with the "paradoxical integuments" of Catholic culture. For if the language of O'Hara's poetry is predicted upon paradox, so is the overall movement and conceptual shape of his work. In his jokey "Personism" manifesto of 1959, O'Hara asserted: "I don't believe in god, so I don't have to make elaborately sounded structures."[16] Aesthetic closure and rationalist order are for him explicitly associated with what he calls (in "Ode on Causality") the "neurotic coherence" (302) demanded by divine projections: "A lot of people," he writes, "would like to see art dead and sure, but you don't see them up at the Cloisters reading Latin."[17]

Abandoning this "neurotic coherence" demanded by neoclassical art, O'Hara proceeds to manipulate parody and paradox so as to reinvent Catholic theology in terms of those subjectivist philosophies popular during the 1950s. In appropriate existentialist fashion, public creeds become private value systems, or, as O'Hara termed it, "personism." The impersonal nature of Christian grace, for instance, becomes translated into his personal friendship with the painter Grace Hartigan, upon whose name O'Hara puns inordinately. To take just one example, "In Memory

16 Reprinted in *The Selected Poems of Frank O'Hara,* ed. Donald Allen (New York: Vintage–Random House, 1974), p. xiii.
17 O'Hara, *Standing Still,* p. 128.

of My Feelings," which is dedicated to Hartigan, celebrates the poet's "Grace / to be born and live as variously as possible" (256). Obviously Grace Hartigan is the primary meaning here; equally obviously, no one fixed denotation is semantically possible and O'Hara's poem also draws upon the residual religious connotations of this word. Similarly, O'Hara creates a linguistic and thematic play around the Catholic doctrine of the Assumption:

> So this is the devil's dance? Well I was born to dance.
> It's a sacred duty, like being in love with an ape,
> and eventually I'll reach some great conclusion, like assumption,
> when at last I meet exhaustion in these flowers, go straight up.
>
> ("Poem," 244)

The ability to "go straight up" to heaven in bodily form was bestowed upon the Virgin Mary by the dogma of the Assumption, proclaimed in 1950. Here O'Hara reworks "assumption," in its lowercase form, as the existentialist "bet" outlined by Sartre, Camus, and others: that urge toward self-realization even in the midst of uncertainty, the kind of courage that must assume (said Camus) that Sisyphus, doomed to roll the boulder up the hill for all eternity, was, despite all evidence to the contrary, happy. In this context, "go straight up" becomes for O'Hara a human and specifically sexual rather than spiritual ascension. The Virgin Mary's elevation to heaven is transformed into a blasphemous image of erection.

Sexuality and scatology, in fact, become frequent sources of blasphemous wordplay in O'Hara's poetry. In "St. Simeon," the monk's cowl or habit becomes that more sinful and sexual habit – "does sin beg a habit from us?" – that brings forth a paradoxical "curse of joy."[18] In the 1961 poem "Shooting the Shit Again," erotic excitement is bound up with a perverse delight in dirt and transgression:

> oh god it's hard for anything to get dirty any more...
> oh god it's hard[19]

It is not the idea of impersonal posterity that excites O'Hara, but the personal posterior: "O my posterity! This is the miracle: that our elegant invention the natural world redeems by filth" ("Oranges: 12 Pastorals").[20] In this way, O'Hara equates redemption with "filth"; and in this devotion to the flowers of evil, his sexual "inversion," or homosexuality, becomes a counterpart to his textual delight in the rebellious linguistic practice of paradox, or turning things around the other way. In the prose

18 O'Hara, *Poems Retrieved*, p. 98.
19 Ibid., p. 205.
20 Quoted in Perloff, *Frank O'Hara*, p. 41.

poem "Episode," he gets in a dig at Gerard Manley Hopkins's theory
of how divine "inscape" reveals itself through poetry:

> the old ear and the young tongue going into it, and staying;
> or vice versa, and retrograde, crab-wise, inverse. I think
> inverse is ever so much better than inscape, and I wouldn't
> shit you.

O'Hara, as he says, prefers erotic "inverse" to religious "inscape."[21] By
a similar paradox, the suffering of Christian martyrdom, savagely
mocked for its self-importance in "My Heat" – "*Miserere, Domine,* / what
a grumbler!" (194) – becomes in "Colloque Sentimentale" the more
worldly mixture of pain and pleasure associated with sadomasochism:

> "what's
> most painful is most peaceful and I
>
> I must be punished because I'm popular.
> It's wet and your neck is knotted with mine."
>   (87)

The cultural residue of Catholicism in O'Hara's poetry, then, forms
an essential matrix for his work. As in "In Memory of My Feelings,"
the poetic voice frequently defines itself as a serpent or devil:

> And now it is the serpent's turn.
> I am not quite you, but almost, the opposite of visionary.
>   (256)

Vendler and Perloff both read this as implying that O'Hara is indeed the
very "opposite of visionary" and therefore a man firmly rooted in the
material world.[22] But, by a typically playful paradox on the author's
part, the phrase is ambiguous: another possible reading is that "almost"
refers forward as well as backward within the syntactical structure. The
poet is almost, but not quite, the opposite of visionary. He cannot quite
escape from a "visionary" idiom.

Cognizant of this "visionary" predilection induced by his own Catholic
culture, O'Hara correlates his own identity with that of the less reputable
characters from Christian tradition. In a Harvard journal entry for 1948,
he noted: "I am reading, slowly, Saint Jerome, and I know now that
Satan lives, and I have not yet made up my mind which side I am on."
But it was the archfiend who seems to have got the verdict, for in the
autobiographical piece "A Story Out Loud," O'Hara salutes the devil as
"an old carousing friend of mine;" while "In Memory of My Feelings"

---

21 O'Hara, *Poems Retrieved*, p. 174.
22 See Vendler, *Part of Nature*, p. 193; Perloff, *Frank O'Hara*, p. 145.

develops an elaborate metaphor of the narrator as serpent, "coiled around the central figure" (256), shedding skins and shifting his shape in response to the quick metamorphoses of city life.[23] The diabolic Al Capone is another who enlists O'Hara's sympathies, particularly in the gangster's ultimate sense of guilt and his good Catholic desire for eternal torment:

> Let us fall to our knees and,
> in the words of Al Capone
> perhaps? go straight to hell.
> ("Another American Poem")[24]

At the same time, though, O'Hara envisions himself also as a priest and martyr. In "Hatred," he suffers on the cross on account of his heroic desire to assume "black robes" and rejuvenate the "bored earth" by apotheosizing the secular world into new legends of sexual love:

> No revolutionary canticle broke the mist
> of that casque, and somewhere like a starry curtain
> we drifted towards the Outer, where new myths
> lay gasping at our white vanquished languor.
> As martyr I am able to whip the crowd into shape.
>
> (120)

In "For James Dean," the film star becomes for O'Hara the paradigm of this sanctified martyr, a spirit too good for this careless world and therefore "eager for the punishment / which is your only recognition." It is Dean's "final impertinence" which will "rebel / and enslave him": the masochism that results in earthly destruction will lead to Dean's ultimate transcendent glory among the "latter-day saints" (228–9).

Writing about modern art, O'Hara assumed the mantle of a tough materialist, praising Reuben Nahian (for instance) for being "unrepressed, unneurotic, unabashed in his approach to sexuality"; his work, said O'Hara, does not contain the "guilt or masochism" one finds in "most sexually oriented images in modern art, from Rodin to Andy Warhol."[25] O'Hara's own poetry, however, does not altogether correlate with this critical theory, for his poetry can never quite realize such tough-minded sensuality as a self-sufficient category. Instead, O'Hara oscillates between

> endless torment pretending to be the rose
> of acknowledgement (courage)
> and fruitless absolution.
>
> ("To Hell with It," 276)

23 O'Hara, *Early Writing*, pp. 98, 134.
24 Ibid., p. 88.
25 Frank O'Hara, *Art Chronicles 1954–1966* (New York: Braziller–Venture, 1975), p. 87.

Though he rationally recognizes the idea of absolution as "fruitless," his emotional sensibility still offers allegiance to metaphysical conflicts of the light and the dark, angels and demons. The religious sublime has merely contracted into a more limited terrestrial sublime:

> as the train bears Khrushchev on to Pennsylvania Station
>   and the light seems to be eternal
>   and joy seems to be inexorable
>   I am foolish enough always to find it in wind.
>   ("Poem," 340)

Wind, traditional symbol of the Holy Spirit, is here reimagined as an invigorating natural entity. It is human rather than theological geometry that can approach the "eternal":

> sick logic and feeble reasoning are cured
> by the perfect symmetry of your arms and legs
> spread out making an eternal circle together.
>   ("Poem A la Recherche de Gertrude Stein," 349)

On listening to Stravinsky, as we are told in the "Ode to Michael Goldberg":

>   I first recognized art
>   As wildness, and it seemed right,
>   I mean rite, to me.
>   (292)

Stravinsky's *Rite of Spring,* of course; but, in the pun's larger sense, also the idea of human art itself as a fitting and appropriate ritual.

So while it may be true that O'Hara aspires toward William Carlos Williams's poetic dream of the unencumbered concrete, "no ideas but in things," it is also true that O'Hara's work emerges out of a religious culture that propels his texts in quite another direction. Vendler asserted that O'Hara's work has "no religion, no politics, no ideology, no nothing"; but this apparently pleasing "tough-minded" idiom – to use William James's terms – can manifest itself in O'Hara's texts only through a dialogic inversion of what is "tender-minded."[26] And indeed it is within the interpenetration of these different forces, the conflict of these competing cultural systems, that many of the creative tensions of O'Hara's work are to be found.

These kinds of dialogue and conflict are essential to the overall form and structure of O'Hara's poetry as well as to its more overt imagery and themes. While these conflicts arise partly out of a religious inheritance,

26 Vendler, *Part of Nature,* p. 192.

their ramifications are, in aesthetic terms, considerably more wide-ranging. O'Hara expands the "paradoxical integuments" of his art to introduce what Bakhtin called a "double-edged discourse" of paradox and parody (Greek "para," at the side of) so as to write against all the dominant cultures within which he finds himself interpellated. As in Bakhtin's formula, the dialogue inherent within a parodic genre becomes a means of introducing competing discourses which rebel against the "hegemony of a single and unitary language." For Bakhtin, the "heteroglossia" to be found among "low genres" – street songs, buffoon spectacles, clownish parodies – can operate to decentralize and so demythologize the dominant "verbal-ideological world," thereby rendering it a relative rather than an absolute construction.[27] This subversive strategy is one of the functions of O'Hara's many literary parodies, in which he lampoons not only Lowell, but also Eliot – in "Mr. O'Hara's Sunday Morning Service" – Dickinson, Pound, Coleridge, Joyce, and others. (The Catholic apostate Joyce was, not surprisingly, an important figure in O'Hara's youth; O'Hara read *Ulysses* in high school and wrote as well in one of his memoirs: "Oh my God didn't *Portrait of the Artist as a Young Man* say everything? Should I send it to all my friends so they'd understand me?")[28] At Harvard, O'Hara also wrote "False Positions," an amusing prose dialogue between Christian and Greek gods, in which "Jesus Christ, realizing that he would soon be committed to the flesh, sought an interview with Pallas Athene... in order to brief himself on the human condition in general, and the course of action most advisable for himself in particular."[29] Like Joyce and other Catholic literary rebels, O'Hara turned to parodic iconoclasm as a weapon of vengeance against the idealistic metanarratives of his cultural and religious conditioning.

One of the crucial aspects of O'Hara's poetry, then, is that this emphasis on paradox and parody, which derives partly from an iconoclastic religious sensibility, also comes to carry wider significance within the broader context of his work. As with Joyce, O'Hara's lapsed Catholic idealism betokens a larger dialogue between presence and absence, plenitude and loss. Bakhtin himself maintained that the relativity of perspective introduced by Joyce's kind of parodic dualism could function properly only within the novel, where many voices can be heard all at once. In poetry, said Bakhtin, the multiplicity and variety to be found in novels necessarily become flattened out by one unitary narrative voice:

27 Bakhtin, *The Dialogic Imagination,* pp. 324, 358, 273, 368.
28 For O'Hara's parody of Eliot, see *Poems Retrieved,* p. 33; O'Hara, *Early Writing,* p. 116.
29 O'Hara, *Early Writing,* p. 137.

> Poetic style is by convention suspended from any mutual interaction with alien discourse, any allusion to alien discourse. . . . The language of the poet is *his* language, he is utterly immersed in it, inseparable from it. . . . The world of poetry, no matter how many contradictions and insoluble conflicts the poet develops within it, is always illumined by one unitary and indisputable discourse. Contradictions, conflicts and doubts remain in the object, in thoughts, in living experiences – in short, in the subject matter – but they do not enter into the language itself. In poetry, even discourse about doubts must be cast in a discourse that cannot be doubted.[30]

For Bakhtin, poetry is per se an authoritarian structure: while poetry is capable of engendering formal ambiguity, that does not disturb the text's essentially centripetal nature. It is, however, just that sense of overall poetic unity that O'Hara strives to break down. He undercuts traditional aesthetic order, not in the (impossible) hope of abolishing it, but out of a desire to subvert aesthetic order by instituting parodic dialogues with these rigid preestablished forms. In his prose poem "Schoenberg," O'Hara praises the German composer for "having slaughtered the false Florimells of harmonious thought and their turgid convincements"; and O'Hara's long, cataloguing lines, through which the aleatory debris of urban life forces its way into the closed "harmonious" structures of art, work as a parallel to Schoenberg's musical experiments in atonality.[31]

This atonality links O'Hara's New York as well with the images of vacant mechanical reproduction that appear in Baudelaire's Parisian poems. Walter Benjamin said of Baudelaire that the French poet's aim was "the creation of a cliché," the recording of modern city life in all its blankness and randomness, the annihilation of any idealistic meaningful "aura" in favor of the vagaries of kaleidoscopic chance. This is exactly what we discover in O'Hara's poetry, where material objects are positioned by chance and become entirely interchangeable with each other. "To perceive the aura of an object we look at," said Benjamin, "means to invest it with the ability to look at us in return"; whereas when Baudelaire looks at Paris, as when O'Hara looks at New York, the objects are enticing, maybe, but fundamentally inert, remote, and unresponsive.[32] O'Hara once wrote that in Jasper Johns's work, "the meticulously and sensually painted rituals express a profound boredom, in the Baudelairean sense, with the symbols of an oversymbolic society"; and that sense of the redundancy of "objective" rituals and symbolism,

---

30 Bakhtin, *The Dialogic Imagination*, pp. 285–6.
31 O'Hara, *Poems Retrieved*, p. 50.
32 Walter Benjamin, "On Some Motifs in Baudelaire," in *Illuminations*, trans. Harry Zohn, ed. Hannah Arendt (New York: Harcourt, Brace and World, 1968), pp. 194, 190.

and of the external world's failure to answer to the artist's private desires, permeates O'Hara's own work as well.[33] Like the lapsed Catholic Baudelaire, O'Hara perceives contingent city landscapes in terms of their absence from centers of symbolism and signification. This, incidentally, crucially distinguishes him from Whitman, in whose poetry the catalogues of urban life become animated as the responsive double of the man.

This effect of alienation is heightened by the recognition in Baudelaire and O'Hara of how aesthetic perception has been modified by the new technology of a modern era. Just as Baudelaire became fascinated by daguerreotypy, which he deemed "startling and cruel," so O'Hara is fascinated by the cinema.[34] In both cases, a process of mechanical reproduction divests empirical objects of any idealized autonomous "aura" and reinvents them instead as part of a terrestrial wheel of fortune. For Baudelaire, a photograph subverts the carefully arranged structures of painting by exposing "the passing moment in all its nakedness," while film, in O'Hara's world, subverts and parodies the structures of Catholic liturgy. We see this process most obviously in the poem "Ave Maria," where "the soul / that grows in darkness" is "embossed by silvery images" from the movies (372). It appears also in his testimony "To the Film Industry in Crisis":

> not to the Catholic Church
> which is at best an oversolemn introduction to cosmic entertainment,
> not to the American Legion, which hates everybody, but to you,
> glorious Silver Screen, tragic Technicolor, amorous Cinemascope,
> stretching Vistavision and startling Stereophonic Sound, with all
> your heavenly dimensions & reverberations & iconoclasms!...
> the heavens operate on the star system. It is a divine precedent
> you perpetuate! Roll on, reels of celluloid, as the great earth rolls on!
>
> (232–3)

Again, the significant point here is that a dialogue is established between primary theological ideal and secondary terrestrial parody. The film industry may be glamorized and partially apotheosized by this celestial analogy, but the analogy also functions by ironic negation. Technicolor and Cinemascope have in themselves no metaphysical sanction, and that absence is precisely what the poem is implying, just as Baudelaire's poems of urban spleen engage in dialogue with a lost religious ideal and signify the implicit absence of any "correspondence" between earth and heaven. Through his multifarious long lines, through his random, collage-like juxtapositions of personal perceptions and reminiscences, O'Hara violates

---

33 O'Hara, *Art Chronicles*, p. 11.
34 Benjamin, "On Some Motifs in Baudelaire," p. 188.

the sacred order of artistic integrity, thereby allowing himself the space to work through a dialogic parody of Catholicism and other forms of established order. Although Bakhtin said the truly decentered "heteroglossia" would be impossible to embrace within poetic discourse, O'Hara's decentered and parodic verse, with all its accumulated heterogeneity of objects, does indeed incorporate poetry within a framework of the dialogic imagination.

This dialogue is not only between Catholicism and blasphemy, then, but also between presence and alienation in a more general sense. Although O'Hara's poetry chronicles the absence of coherent metanarratives, these landscapes of urban alienation nevertheless offer up the possibility of smaller, more localized moments of secular "grace." By a typical existentialist strategy, the networks of harmony, wholeness, and radiance become internalized, compressed into a private sphere. O'Hara's poem "The 'Unfinished'" prioritizes self-generating presence as an ethical imperative:

> so I will be as unhappy as I damn well
> please and not make too much of it because I am
> really here and not in a novel or anything or a jet plane

With this stress upon how it is "really here," the voice of the text goes on to ridicule nostalgia for absence as "the vat of longing" where the danger is we will "suffocate in its suet" (317). This, of course, is consistent with O'Hara's enormous thematic emphasis on friends, the here and now, and indeed the "personism" definition of poetry as nothing more than a personal communication, like using the telephone. This nostalgia for idealized presence manifests itself in O'Hara's art criticism as well as his poetry. Writing about Jackson Pollock, O'Hara praises the painter for perceiving the force of ritual in all its "original" and "legendary splendor" rather than through the secondary distortions of mythological or metaphorical perspective. In Friedrich Schiller's terms, it is a preference for the naive over the sentimental, for what Schiller alleged to be the "naive" or "Homeric" capacity to embody a natural object in itself rather than the merely "sentimental" feat of reconstituting this object through an act of the human imagination.[35]

So although O'Hara charts his own alienation from the plenitude of heaven, the paradox is that he urgently desires to recapture this plenitude within an earthly context. This is why O'Hara's fascination with material reality can never become simply a delight in the world's multifarious surfaces; instead, he seeks to replenish the lapsed symbolism of divine

35 O'Hara, *Art Chronicles*, p. 22; Friedrich Schiller, *On the Naive and Sentimental in Literature*, trans. Helen Watanabe-O'Kelly (Manchester: Carcanet, 1981), p. 38.

presence with an idealized embodiment of human persons. Moreover, as Mutlu Konuk Blasing has written, one of O'Hara's putative replacements for these bifurcated ironies of metaphysical loss is an articulation of the human body itself in all its polymorphous and "infantile wholeness." Attempting to overcome that necessary absence or "fatal alienation at the core of writing," O'Hara piles up alimentary and other physical images in an effort to convince himself, as well as the reader, that this human person is indeed "really here," present in the flesh.[36] Again, the pattern is to attempt to transubstantiate the existential into the essential, to elevate pure physical process into the status of categorical "truth." In his criticism of Lowell, O'Hara said "I don't think there is such a thing as a bad line if it's true."[37] This reverence for "truth" on O'Hara's part reveals more than a trace of nostalgia for dimensions of imaginary plentitude and unified presence.

O'Hara's "personism," then, is not so much a rejoicing in the casual and accidental as an attempt to infuse the accidental with a force that is essential. This, however, highlights another of those paradoxes central to O'Hara's writing. O'Hara is in many ways a poet of pure contingency, junk art, random urban intersections. Nevertheless, as we have seen, he seeks to infuse these accidental landscapes with what Charles Altieri called a metaphysic of *"radical presence,* the insistence that the moment immediately and intensely experienced can restore one to harmony with the world and provide ethical and psychological renewal." O'Hara, suggested Altieri, participates in the Heideggerian "challenge . . . to imagine non-Christian sources of immanent value."[38] In this sense, O'Hara's essential idea of "personism" might be seen as a transformed version of phenomenological idealism, where the creative mind invents its own self-validating presence through its engagement with the processes of eternal creation and re-creation. Yet it is also true – and this is the crucial point – that O'Hara's style, in its emphasis upon broad communion rather than inner solipsism, is too "Catholic" to perceive any kind of subjectivism as an entirely self-sufficient category. Unlike Kant or Heidegger, O'Hara cannot rest content within a romantic universe of his own making. The self-validating world of existentialist presence is always, at the same time, implicitly acknowledging the wider circumference of Baudelairean alienation. Indeed, the significance of O'Hara's work lies precisely in this "dialectic between presence and alienation," as Altieri put

---

36 Mutlu Konuk Blasing, "Frank O'Hara's Poetics of Speech: The Example of 'Biotherm,'" *Contemporary Literature,* 23 (1982), 53, 59.
37 O'Hara, *Standing Still,* p. 13.
38 Altieri, *Enlarging the Temple,* pp. 78–9.

it, in the recognition that phenomenological idealism finds itself inevitably compromised by the empty but ineradicable world of matter.[39]

The semantic dimensions of paradox and parody also work against this nostalgia for Heideggerian unity, because paradox and parody are predicated upon a form of doubling and division, the very kind of bifurcation O'Hara's phenomenological idealism would like ideally to avoid. In this sense, paradox and parody act as tropological emblems of the frustrating ironies inherent within O'Hara's aesthetic enterprise. While his texts aspire to reincorporate themselves within the real presence of "personism," they find themselves interpellated instead within linguistic forms grounded upon division and therefore alienation. O'Hara, one feels, would like to cancel language altogether and regain the idealized presence (and silence) of "personism," just as he would like to cancel Catholicism and regain the idealized nonbelief of a secular state. Both aspirations, however, appear impossible; his poetry is doomed forever to negotiate the uneasy spaces between language and presence, between Catholicism and atheism. In this way, O'Hara's dialogue of blasphemy becomes a metonymical replication of the larger duplicities within his work, for the manner in which his texts become embroiled within the divided discourses of paradox and parody comes to reflect that double bind whereby his poems blasphemously free themselves from the constraints of Catholicism, but in the end can never quite free themselves. These poems find themselves bound to reflect back upon systems they have ostensibly rejected.

Given this fact that O'Hara's texts participate, albeit unwillingly, within a Catholic discourse, we can extend our range of reference to see how the secularized aesthetics of Catholic culture work their way into the more abstract directions of O'Hara's writing. As I suggested earlier, an ideology of transformed Catholicism is implicit within O'Hara's interrogation of the limits of romanticism and of subjective consciousness. Catholic philosophy, as outlined by Aquinas, has traditionally rejected the dichotomy of subject/object, signifier/signified, insisting instead that "because being is the formal object of human knowing, no thinking takes place that is not thinking of something ... consciousness is always consciousness *of* something."[40] This is why Catholic theology has always abhorred Descartes, because the French philosopher posited human reason as an autonomous entity entirely abstracted from the world of matter. But for O'Hara, as for Aquinas, the creator's mind interpenetrates that world of matter, revealing through this process of intercommunication

39 Ibid., p. 112.
40 Mary T. Clark, ed., *An Aquinas Reader* (Garden City: Doubleday–Image, 1972), p. 36.

a primary and essential "truth." The shaping human will is, for O'Hara, by no means a Promethean or even an independent faculty. On the contrary, it is represented within his poetry as a relatively insignificant phenomenon, just as Kant and the whole Kantian tradition of romanticism was marginalized by Catholic thought because the Church has always given precedence to the faculty of understanding (God) over the faculty of reshaping oneself or the world: precedence, that is to say, to the human intellect over the human will. Aquinas states this quite explicitly in the *Summa Theologiae*. Defining the intellect "as apprehending universal being and truth," Aquinas goes on:

> So that if we compare the intellect and will in regard to the universality of their objects . . . then the intellect is, speaking absolutely, higher and more excellent than the will. And if we consider the intellect according to the universal nature of its object, and the will as a particular kind of power, again the intellect is higher and prior to the will because the will itself, its act, and its object are included within the notion of *being* and *truth,* which the intellect perceives. So the intellect knows the will, its act, and its object just as it knows other things, such as wood or stone falling under the universal idea of *being* and *truth.*[41]

The power of will, that is to say, is subservient to the intellect, because the intellect perceives how the will is one object among many others within the universal scheme of things. Human will cannot stand outside or dominate the world in Cartesian fashion, for it is implicated within the very world it describes.

It is true that this displacement of Cartesian consciousness is a familar aspect of much postmodernist poetry. Yet here again, O'Hara's slant upon the "death of the subject" takes an idiosyncratic turn. In John Ashbery and Adrienne Rich, for example, we find a decentering of the poetic voice, so that the romantic subject becomes – as it were – marginalized by its own discourse. In Ashbery's "Self-Portrait in a Convex Mirror," we witness a reinterpretation of American romanticism, a rewriting of Whitman's *Song of Myself* from a post-Cartesian point of view. In O'Hara's poetry, though, this Cartesian point of view is much less prominent, in fact barely visible even in shadow form. It is not simply that the Cartesian sensibility finds itself marginalized, as in Ashbery; in O'Hara, the shaping, Cartesian consciousness does not exist in the same way, because the antisubjectivist slant of O'Hara's work has little correlation with that tradition of romanticism which Ashbery is (adding to and) subverting. At Harvard, O'Hara took two poetry composition classes from John Ciardi, the Italian-American poet well known for his translations of Dante's *Divine Comedy,* and a curiously Dantesque tone

41 Ibid., pp. 290–1.

of creative impersonality can be seen lurking within O'Hara's subsequent writing.[42] Just as Dante effaced himself before thirteenth-century Florence, so O'Hara effaces himself before twentieth-century Manhattan.

If it evades the tenets of egocentric romanticism, O'Hara's writing also eludes the more empiricist orthodoxies of objectivism. As Thomas Meyer noted, the fluctuating spirals of objects in O'Hara's texts are not consistent with that hard empirical specificity of the image we associate with the "concrete" poetry of Charles Olson or William Carlos Williams:

> When is it important the sandwich in a poem be liverwurst *qua* liverwurst and when could it be egg salad or ham as long as it's definitely nominated one or the other? This rather strange consideration crops up all over O'Hara's poems. How is it the specific creates an interchangeability that undercuts our trust in specificity as the very quality of uniqueness?[43]

While Meyer chose to relate this regrettable "interchangeability" back to "the facelessness and soullessness plaguing our late, modern world," that does not seem to do justice to the tone of exuberance that pervades O'Hara's poetry, even amidst these landscapes of "lurking emptiness," as Altieri called them.[44] In O'Hara, specificity and interchangeability do not necessarily seem to be mutually exclusive categories. His objects possess an irreducibly concrete element that makes every individual thing different from every other, but such particularity by no means involves a secession from the larger structures of analogical patterning or universal form.

My point is that O'Hara, with his Catholic cultural legacy, radically diverges from that romantic tradition of American poetry sanctioned, even in its reconstituted postmodernist form, by Ashbery and Olson. O'Hara conforms more to the archetype of the "southern" artist, as outlined by John Ruskin in his 1851 book *The Stones of Venice*. For Ruskin, the northern, romantic, "Protestant" imagination works to create a new world of its own, but the temperament of the southern, neoclassical, "Catholic" artist is content to imitate a world that is already there. In this sense, O'Hara's poetic anonymity is not simply a function of the postmodernist displacement of romanticism but is, on the contrary, an integral and primary part of his aesthetic framework. Furthermore, the external objects in O'Hara's texts flow into each other not simply because of soulless impersonality – although that kind of alienation is certainly part of O'Hara's terrain – but because from another perspective

42 See the course descriptions in O'Hara, *Early Writing*, pp. 150–1.
43 Thomas Meyer, "Glistening Torsos, Sandwiches, and Coco-Cola," *Parnassus*, 6 (1977), 245–6.
44 Altieri, *Enlarging the Temple*, p. 114.

these objects are all, as Aquinas would say, analogically interchangeable with each other, all part of that interpenetrating process of creation. The liverwurst sandwich and the ham sandwich correspond to each other because they are both accidents that, in Aquinas's terms, participate in the one "universal idea of being" – in this case, the idea of New York fast food, or, more generally, the life of Manhattan. O'Hara's long kaleidoscopic lines mimetically demonstrate these objects fluctuating and merging into each other, and so the form of his poetry reveals precisely this Catholic principle of materialized analogy at work. It is, of course, a secularized form of analogy: these objects bound together by fast-food similitude are not sanctioned by any final metaphysical divinity. Nor, though, do these objects seem to rely for their validity merely upon the shaping spirit or artistic will of the poet. O'Hara is by no means within the vatic Emersonian tradition that aspires prophetically to envision analogies that are invisible to the naked eye. Quite the opposite: O'Hara frequently renders himself almost anonymous, immersing and submerging himself within material creation so that, as Charles Molesworth said, he "often loses domination of himself to the surrounding objects."[45]

Molesworth offered R. D. Laing's "ontological insecurity" as an explanation of this phenomenon, but again that does not seem altogether adequate. O'Hara's best work seems to expand outward rather than contract inward: it is concerned with a heterogeneous view of the external world, not with the eccentricities of private psychology. Indeed, it is another of the paradoxes of O'Hara's work that this poet of "personism" is one of the least personal of all American poets. He does not parade himself, but annuls himself, smothering his ego in the face of creation in a way curiously similar to that of another, more orthodox Catholic poet, Gerard Manley Hopkins. Nor is it coincidental that, like Hopkins, O'Hara was (carefully and deliberately) careless about publication. In both cases, a radical piety worked against the poet's arrogant vaunting of himself as a "maker." Hopkins would have said his poems were authored not by himself but by God; O'Hara would have said his poems were authored not by himself but by the material world, especially by the material world of Manhattan.

This kind of impersonality is unusual within the American poetic heritage. Warner Berthoff said that "O'Hara's verse, even at its best, was deliberately 'minor'"; but it only seems to be "minor" because the poet – "deliberately," as Berthoff perceptively observed – refused to conform to that model of the "strong" individual voice that has become a pre-

45 Charles Molesworth, "'The Clear Architecture of the Nerves': The Poetry of Frank O'Hara," *Iowa Review*, 6, nos. 3–4 (1975), 63.

requisite for admission into the pantheon of American romanticism.[46] (This is one of the reasons Allen Tate's poetry is also so alien to many American ears.) Conversely, however, O'Hara's kind of willed will-lessness has long been a central plank in the Catholic artistic tradition. Jacques Maritain contrasted what he conceived as the villainous Rousseau's "self-centered ego" with the "spiritual communication" favored by Catholic work, where a "creative self" gains access through art to the larger world of "abundance and magnanimity" characteristic of God's universe. Whereas the romantic idiom of Rousseau expresses only himself, said Maritain, the ego of the Catholic artist "dies" so that the artist can live within his work "humbly and defenselessly." For O'Hara, rational ideas of order, whether social or aesthetic, would at best be an arbitrary construction. In his view, therefore, art can never be an absolute or closed phenomenon because, as Maritain said, anything totally perfect on earth would be "lacking a lack": "A totally perfect finite thing is untrue to the transcendental nature of beauty. And nothing is more precious than a certain sacred weakness, and that kind of imperfection through which infinity wounds the finite."[47]

This carefully manipulated "imperfection" and lack of closure in O'Hara's work leaves his poetry open to the irruptions of "sacramental" grace: that "Grace / to be born and live as variously as possible," as "In Memory of My Feelings" puts it (256). "Grace does not abolish nature," said Aquinas, "but sustains and perfects it"; and – ironically, for such a keen atheist – that statement from the Angelic Doctor might almost function as the motto of O'Hara's poetry.[48] For he is, as Perloff said, clearly a poet of "immanence rather than transcendence," a poet dedicated to celebrating the graceful abundance of the natural environment rather than troubling himself with any romantic ideal of the poet transcending nature through his status as prophet or quasi-divine seer.[49] Indeed, O'Hara's comic mockery is employed not just to make fun of others but also to make fun of any pretension he might cherish of himself as an artistic "maker"; he specifically refuses to play the role of a godlike artist standing outside his texts so as to place himself in a position of mastery over his work and the world. O'Hara once wrote of the painter Franz Kline that Kline manipulated parody, paradoxes, and theatrics to hold "at bay all possibilities of self-importance, pomposity, mysticism and

46 Warner Berthoff, *A Literature without Qualities: American Writing since 1945* (Berkeley: Univ. of California Press, 1979), p. 165.

47 Jacques Maritain, *Creative Intuition in Art and Poetry* (New York: Pantheon-Bollingen Foundation, 1953), pp. 195, 142, 144, 167.

48 Quoted in Jaroslav Pelikan, *The Riddle of Roman Catholicism* (New York: Abingdon Press, 1959), p. 147.

49 Perloff, *Frank O'Hara,* p. 130.

cant which might have otherwise interfered with the very direct and personal relation he had to his paintings and their content."[50] The same thing is true of O'Hara's own poems, in which self-parodic comedy operates to subvert the narrow impetus of human will and to expose his texts to the presence of ulterior (though demystified and secular) graces. From this perspective, the shadow that "double-edged discourse" of parody and paradox throws upon O'Hara's texts functions in a creative as well as a de-creative fashion. In its blasphemous dialogue with Catholicism, O'Hara's poetry employs parody not only to liberate itself from the repressions of religion but also to liberate itself from the prison of solipsism. Parody's ceaseless circulation between opposite poles, its perennial lack of closure, allows O'Hara to ironize Catholicism from the vantage point of "personism" at the same time as ironizing "personism" itself from the vantage point of a "Catholic" sensibility.

It is, then, an architectonic vision that we find in O'Hara's work, a world where, in the typical Scholastic manner, the powers of darkness are apprehended as a subset of the great world of good rather than a direct challenge to it. Orthodox Catholic thought has considered evil to be a mere absence of good rather than, as in the Puritan idiom, its polar opposite; as Aquinas said: "An evil thing is good through its essence but evil through the goodness it lacks."[51] Thus O'Hara's apparent sense of poetic irresponsibility and his refusal to discriminate between worldly objects is, in the end, a metaphysical statement. His universalist idiom implies that the power finally to control and judge is not within a human purview. O'Hara once wrote of Scott Fitzgerald's Jay Gatsby and Rosemary Hoyt that they "are quickly fixed by events in an airy space which belongs to no one, least of all them"; and it is a similar sense of being an objective participant in the world, rather than its subjective overseer, that irradiates O'Hara's poetry.[52] In the lapsed Catholic world of O'Hara, as in that of Fitzgerald, human beings merge with the immanent world; they do not, indeed cannot, transcend it.

So, in the final analysis, Vendler's comments on what she called O'Hara's "radical incapacity for abstraction" and how "like Byron, when he thinks he is a child" seem inappropriate. O'Hara did of course always scorn abstraction and allegory – "Lord! spare us from any more Fisher kings!" he said in an essay on John Rechy – but this scorn emanated from his Catholic consciousness, his submergence of the creative ego within a world of natural immanence and "grace."[53] Writing from within

50 O'Hara, Art Chronicles, pp. 52–3.
51 Aquinas Reader, ed. Clark, p. 54.
52 O'Hara, Standing Still, p. 180.
53 Vendler, Part of Nature, p. 179; O'Hara, Standing Still, p. 162.

the dominant intellectual tradition of American romanticism, Vendler instinctively associated the concept of "thought" with a form of abstract idealism O'Hara was never interested in. Yet Vendler's abstract idealism can itself be read as an ideological construction, no less than O'Hara's transformed Catholicism; in "Poem Read at Joan Mitchell's," O'Hara celebrates "happiness" as "the least and best of human attainments," a phrase in which we may hear a direct echo of Santayana's complaint against Kant and other German idealist philosophers for their disparagement of the goal of human happiness as "low, materialistic, and selfish."[54] Thus it is possible to see a generic coherence in the way American Catholic writing turns away from aspirations toward self-willed transcendence and acquiesces instead in the limitations of the grossly corporeal world: "for our symbol we'll acknowledge vulgar materialistic laughter," says O'Hara in "Ode to Joy" (281). It is not of course that one or the other of these perspectives is "true," it is simply that they are different, and one of the tasks of criticism is to recognize such differences.

In 1964, drawing upon Sartre's biography of Jean Genet, O'Hara suggested that the relation of George Spaventa's sculpture to his human figures could be seen as a parallel to Genet's attitude toward his dramatis personae, "in anxiety especially." Just as Sartre said that Genet's outlook had been shaped by the old paradigms of Catholicism, so in Spaventa's sculpture, said O'Hara, it is "as if metaphysics were to be felt emotionally."[55] Metaphysics felt emotionally is the grand paradox upon which Frank O'Hara's poetry rotates.

54 George Santayana, *The German Mind: A Philosophical Diagnosis* (New York: Crowell, 1968), p. 152.
55 O'Hara, *Art Chronicles*, pp. 131, 133.

Part IV

Iconography and the Cinema of Catholicism

12

The Allure of Iconography: Andy Warhol and Robert Mapplethorpe

In attempting to discover analogies between writers of literature and authors in the visual arts, we necessarily confront the fact that each artistic medium possesses its own history, separate from that of any other medium. Indeed, some formalist critics (such as René Wellek and Austin Warren in their *Theory of Literature*) maintain that the differences between each art are so irreconcilable that it is impossible for criticism to draw appropriate homologies from among the various cultural fields. However, as Mario Praz pointed out in his discussion of parallels between literature and the visual arts, the same doubt might be raised about different genres within literary tradition. Can one reasonably talk about a poem by Dryden in comparison with a play by Dryden, bearing in mind the radically divergent forces of production that bring these texts to birth?[1]

Again, the problem seems to persist only if we indulge our nostalgia for the final all-encompassing "meaning" of a literary work. To discuss *Absalom and Achitophel* alongside *All for Love* would certainly be to blur various issues about the distinctive genres into which Dryden's work fits, but it would also provide another (contextual) angle that might be neglected if *Absalom and Achitophel* were to be studied only as an example of "Augustan" poetry alongside, say, *The Rape of the Lock*. Similarly, to analyze Robert Altman alongside Scott Fitzgerald and Frank O'Hara is not to "explain" any of them, but to offer a further elucidation, a new angle of illumination. This seems a particularly relevant undertaking in the case of film studies, which over the last few years has tended to retreat into a hermetic world of its own, encased in a psychoanalytic (especially Lacanian) discourse, which, while often brilliantly executed, has often failed to address the broader cultural areas that might be considered in

---

1 Mario Praz, *Mnemosyne: The Parallel between Literature and the Visual Arts* (London: Oxford Univ. Press, 1970), p. 40.

273

film study. There is a parallel here, perhaps, with those "New" critics of literature in the 1950s, whose pyrotechnic skill with poetic wordplay deflected their attention from wider issues. As Robert Phillip Kolker has written recently, it is necessary now "not merely to reduce film to abstract generic patterns, but to open up the sealed spaces and weave together the loose ideological pieces of film, literature, television (advertising, religion, photography, painting, politics) – our entire cultural discourse – in order to find out what in the world we are talking about."[2]

Clearly film is dependent upon the visual faculty, and this in itself places the medium in a tense relationship with some of the dominant ideas within American culture. We have already noted the deep suspicion of iconography institutionalized by the Puritan heritage emerging out of the seventeenth century and seen how the deployment of visual images within texts by Hawthorne, James, Fitzgerald, and others is often associated with a specifically Catholic sensibility. In her book *The Interpretation of Material Shapes in Puritanism,* Ann Kibbey quoted John Calvin as scorning "the incomparable boon of images, for which there is no substitute, if we are to believe the papists." "Whatever men learn of God from images is futile, indeed false," Calvin went on. "We see how openly God speaks against all images, that all who seek visible forms of God depart from him." Kibbey suggested that Calvin conceived of Catholic visual art as existing in opposition to those living icons, Protestants themselves, who constituted the proper visual art of Christianity. From this perspective, what Kibbey called "literal-minded realism" and a concentration upon the common stuff of quotidian reality were considered superior to papist icons which tended to lead in the direction of superstitious ritual and fetishistic adoration.[3] Hence most of the earliest painting in the United States consists of portraits of local worthies and other living, everyday icons. In accordance with this Puritan code, James Fenimore Cooper's pastoral idealization *The Pioneers* (1823) significantly employs the word "film" in a derogatory sense to imply unwelcome interference and illusion: "It may be humbly hoped that the film which has been spread by the subtleties of earthly arguments will be dissipated by the spiritual light of Heaven."[4]

The Jewish cultural legacy has very often preferred a similar kind of detachment from graven images. To take one example, Mary Antin's autobiography *The Promised Land* (1912), which chronicles her experi-

2 Robert Phillip Kolker, "On Certain Tendencies in American Film Criticism," *American Quarterly,* 38 (1986), 332.
3 Ann Kibbey, *The Interpretation of Material Shapes in Puritanism: A Study of Rhetoric, Prejudice, and Violence* (Cambridge: Cambridge Univ. Press, 1986), pp. 45, 49.
4 James Fenimore Cooper, *The Leatherstocking Tales,* I (New York: Library of America, 1985), 128.

ences as a Jewish child in Russia before her family immigrated to the United States, notes with distaste how "in every Gentile house there was what they called an 'icon,' which was an image or picture of the Christian god, hung up in a corner, with a light always burning before it." The Christian god, says Antin, appeared to be "nothing but images," whereas "the Jew was conscious that between himself and God no go-between was needed." It may not be too great a leap from Antin's sensibility to the films of Woody Allen, which pride themselves on their idiosyncratic and highly literate Jewish culture and which, in their systematic demystification and parody of mass iconography, move closer to a "cinema-without-images" than anything the (mainstream) American film industry has yet produced.[5]

Conversely, "Catholic" writers have tended to be more sympathetic toward the pictorial projections of the cinema. Frank O'Hara was infatuated with the film industry, as we have seen. John Berryman wrote to Robert Penn Warren as early as 1937 that "competent recognition, in *The Southern Review,* of the film as a formidable or legitimate art-form would, it seems to me, be worth any trouble or breach of policy."[6] Robert Lowell's 1970 panegyric to "Harpo Marx" insists that "The movie's not always the sick man of the arts," and, like O'Hara's "To the Film Industry in Crisis," conceptualizes the cinematic immortality of the silver screen as a secular equivalent to the eternity of Christian heaven:

> Harpo Marx, your hands white-feathered the harp...
>   Harpo, your motion picture
> is still life unchanging, not nature dead...
> Movie trucks and five police trucks wheel to wheel
> like covered wagons. The crowd as much or little.
> I wish I had knelt.... I age to your wincing smile,
> like Dante's movie, the great glistening wheel of life.[7]

In Lowell's vision, the angelic harp becomes conflated with the human Harpo, a secular icon before which the poet feels a compulsion to kneel. In the same way, the wheels of the police truck become an analogical mirror of the film's "wheel of life," the cyclic immortality of the spinning reels of celluloid, which is itself a transformed version of Dante's "wheel that spins with even motion" at the end of the *Paradiso*. Rather than the discordant "Land of Unlikeness," which characterized his tortuous early

5 Mary Antin, *The Promised Land* (Boston: Houghton Mifflin, 1912), pp. 6, 39. Compare Roland Barthes's phrase "religion-without-images" in *Camera Lucida: Reflections on Photography,* trans. Richard Howard (New York: Hill and Wang, 1981), p. 75.
6 John Haffenden, *John Berryman: A Critical Commentary* (New York: New York Univ. Press, 1980), p. 86.
7 Robert Lowell, *History* (New York: Farrar, Straus and Giroux, 1973), p. 143.

verse, Lowell here uses the cinema as an image of likeness or analogy: as a human figure, Harpo becomes like – but not exactly the same as – the character he portrays. The approximation of human actor to his cinematic incarnation works as a parallel to the "likeness" Lowell seeks to establish between harp and Harpo, the city of "God" and the city of man. His "Catholic" style of literary analogy is appropriate for film subjects because cinematic icons function crucially as a displaced mirror, reflections as seen through a glass darkly, of actual human identities. The analogical structures of neo-scholastic theology operate in the same way: if they were literal equivalents to divine truth, there would be no reason for their existence; but if they bore no relation to divine truth, they would be irrelevant. The power of traditional Catholic theology, like the power of cinema, lies in its ceaseless aspiration – never finally resolved – to work transformations upon the ironies of difference.

It is important here to beware of cultural overgeneralizations, and it would of course be absurd to associate the American film industry merely with the idiosyncrasies of "Catholic" culture. Yet one could hardly imagine (say) the New England temperament of Robert Frost reconciling itself to the antics of Harpo Marx in an equally compliant fashion. In fact, Frost's famous hymn to thrifty self-sufficiency "Provide, Provide" specifically scorns the beautiful woman who was once "The picture pride of Hollywood," taking a grim delight in her fall from fame and fortune. So it is surely not coincidental that the growth of the cinema in the 1910s and 1920s coincided with a cultural rebellion against residual Puritanism both in its rural Yankee form, such as we see in Frost, and in its more genteel manifestations, as evidenced by E.E. Cummings's famous satire on "the Cambridge ladies who live in furnished souls."[8] In the popular mythology of this time, the equation between films and Catholic ritual did indeed become commonplace: movie houses were known as "cathedrals," with the darkened auditorium and organ music for silent films all adding to the atmosphere of liturgical devotion. Equally important were the "gods" and "goddesses" on the silver screen, the Valentinos and Pickfords who engendered just the kind of mass, fetishistic adoration that would have made John Calvin shudder. As Tom McDonough put it: "The movies' most profound power is their power to make us feel ecstastically smaller than what we see, to share in their bigness so that we feel heroically adjusted to our place in the big picture. It's a religious effect – what the good sisters used to call 'pagan awe.'" Given the potential power of these icons to compromise the inner directions of an

8 *The Poetry of Robert Frost: The Collected Poems, Complete and Unabridged,* ed. Edward Connery Lathem (New York: Henry Holt, 1979), p. 307; E. E. Cummings, *Complete Poems, 1913–1962* (New York: Harcourt Brace Jovanovich, 1972), p. 70.

individual soul, it is not surprising that "some more fundamentalist Protestant religionists forbid movie-going to their congregants," as Warren
Susman noted.[9] However, William Carlos Williams's 1923 poem "Light
Becomes Darkness" takes a more sympathetic point of view toward the
movie houses by equating the "catholicity" of their mass iconography
with social "progress":

> The decay of cathedrals
> is efflorescent
> through the phenomenal
> growth of movie houses
>
> whose catholicity is
> progress.

Movies, thought Williams, betokened a welcome development away
from that "biblical rigidity" through which "light" and "darkness" constituted a "schism" that seemed "adamant" – a pun, of course, on the
sin of Adam. Rather than this irreparable and zealous distinction between
right and wrong, the "universality" of the movies would come to imply
a "moral force" that would facilitate social contentment.[10] Movie houses
would help to alleviate the old Puritan burden whereby absolute responsibility used to devolve upon the soul of each isolated, guilt-ridden
individual.

Besides this visual impetus, the ambiguous status of film as a popular
form was another reason for its being handled gingerly by the cultural
establishment. As a mass art, film was inevitably engaged from the first
in a dialogue with more senior institutions. As Fredric Jameson has
remarked, it is not enough simply to recover the sociological context of
any popular culture without recognizing the antithesis that designates
popular culture as "popular," the (implied) cultural hegemony with
which pop art enters into a dialogue.[11] This is especially important when
considering "Catholic" art, most of which has originated from outside
the dominant ideologies and institutions of American culture. In James
T. Farrell's novels, for instance, pop art becomes one of the central
principles of composition; as Blanche Gelfant has noted, the prevalence
of newspapers, films, and pulp magazines indicates the new kinds of

---

9 Tom McDonough, "That Great Blank Page, the Screen," *New York Times Book Review*,
   15 Nov. 1987, p. 42; Warren I. Susman, "'Personality' and Twentieth-Century Culture," in *New Directions in American Intellectual History*, ed. John Higham and Paul K.
   Conkin (Baltimore: Johns Hopkins Univ. Press, 1979), p. 224.
10 *The Collected Poems of William Carlos Williams: Volume 1, 1909–1939*, ed. A. Walton
   Litz and Christopher MacGowan (New York: New Directions, 1986), 213–14.
11 Fredric Jameson, *The Political Unconscious: Narrative as a Socially Symbolic Act* (Ithaca:
   Cornell Univ. Press, 1981), pp. 85–6.

ways in which Farrell's characters perceive their world.[12] Farrell is engaged not in naive, naturalistic mimesis, but in examining how images of the mass media have shaped his heroes' angles of perception. There is inevitably an ideological and a class issue involved here: when Walter Allen talked of the "seedy violence" of Farrell's world, "the great barren urban agglomerations from which the things of beauty that should surround the child are so strikingly absent," Allen was betraying his own distaste for the social milieu within which Farrell's characters necessarily live out their lives. Economically impoverished classes tend to feed on popular art rather than high culture, and as Catholic communities within America were usually part of this less affluent society – up until the Second World War, at least – so they would find themselves surrounded by the more accessible icons of a mass consumer market. Justifying his obsession with cinema rather than literature, Martin Scorsese recalled that "I grew up in a house without books, and basically everything I learned was visual."[13]

Gelfant compared Farrell's work to that of Andy Warhol in its probing examination of the psychological effects of popular culture, and, perhaps more clearly than that of any other artist, the iconography of Warhol pursues the implications of a Catholic spirit in modern American film and photography. Warhol himself came from a blue-collar Czech-Catholic family in Pittsburgh, where his father was an immigrant coal miner, and the way in which "from the beginning, Warhol craved fame with a thirsty, calculated desperation" (Stephen Koch) can, on one level at least, be traced back to this impoverished social background.[14] Like Gatz transforming himself into Gatsby, Andrew Warhola remade himself into Andy Warhol, seeking celebrity and fortune to assure himself of escape from these obscure origins. As he remarked with a slightly plaintive air in *Exposures,* a 1979 collection of his celebrity portraits: "When I was a kid not growing up in Pittsburgh, I saved my pennies, wolfed down my salt and pepper soup, and ran downtown to see every Judy Garland movie. That's why it's so great to be good friends with her daughters, Liza Minnelli and Lorna Luft."[15] It is true, as Bradford R. Collins has said, that Warhol never quite relinquished this ghetto per-

12 Blanche Gelfant, "Realism and Naturalism: Representation in Farrell's *Studs Lonigan,*" MLA Convention, San Francisco, 28 Dec. 1987.

13 Walter Allen, *Tradition and Dream: The English and American Novel from the Twenties to Our Time* (London: Phoenix, 1964), p. 149; David Thompson and Ian Christie, ed., *Scorsese on Scorsese* (London: Faber, 1989), p. 145.

14 Stephen Koch, *Stargazer: Andy Warhol's World and His Films* (New York: Praeger, 1973), p. 20.

15 Andy Warhol, *Andy Warhol's Exposures* (New York: Andy Warhol Books–Grosset and Dunlap, 1979), p. 182.

spective. In his panegyrics to Coca-Cola, and in his awestruck celebrations (written and visual) of "the best country in the world" in his 1985 book *America,* Warhol sounds like an immigrant just off the boat who is enchanted with the new wonders he sees around him.[16]

As with Gatsby, however, Warhol's relationship with the American success story is by no means unproblematical. The very fact that Warhol's representations of Marilyn Monroe, Elvis Presley, and other American "stars" have produced such conflicts of critical interpretation is one indication of these tensions. For Collins, Warhol openly celebrates the glories of capitalism. In Robert Hughes's view, though, the artist cynically and meretriciously exploited the publicity media for his own shallow interests. By contrast, for many Italian and German critics – notably Rainer Crone – Warhol is a skillful satirizer of American mass markets, an artist in the political tradition of Bertolt Brecht and Walter Benjamin, who exposes the contradictions of capitalism by mirroring its assumptions and holding them up for public examination.[17] This extreme divergence of views is exacerbated by the fact that Warhol's style underwent many changes: the pop artist of the mid 1960s was a rather different figure – more socially and politically aware, some would claim – from the Reaganite party goer of the 1980s. Nevertheless, even back in 1964 Philip Leider was writing of how Warhol had created "art that may be a mockery or may not be a mockery ... most a mockery when most fashionably accepted, most subversive when most a fad."[18] There is in all of Warhol's output a sense of something slippery, an elusiveness that can perhaps be related to the same kind of parodic sensibility we saw at work in *The Great Gatsby.*

For, like Fitzgerald, Warhol came from an immigrant background where he was neither fully assimilated into America nor entirely alienated from it. While lauding all the conventional accoutrements of the American Dream, Warhol's Catholic sensibility could never quite buy into that dream as an absolute or final reality. Warhol looks at Monroe and Presley through a pair of quizzical metaphysical spectacles that acknowledge how these American icons are like Catholic saints, but in the end really aren't. His works aggrandize American popular culture but also

16 Bradford R. Collins, "The Metaphysical Nosejob: The Remaking of Warhola, 1960–1968," *Arts Magazine,* 62, no. 6 (Feb. 1988), 49; Andy Warhol, *America* (New York: Harper and Row, [1985]), p. 17.

17 Robert Hughes, "The Rise of Andy Warhol," *New York Review of Books,* 18 Feb. 1982, pp. 6–10. For discussions of these disagreements surrounding the political status of Warhol's art, see Thomas Crow, "Saturday Disasters: Trace and Reference in Early Warhol," *Art in America,* May 1987, p. 128, and Brian Wallis, "Absolute Warhol," *Art in America,* March 1989, p. 27.

18 Philip Leider, "Saint Andy," *Artforum,* 3, no. 5 (Dec. 1964), 27.

ironically detach themselves from their own (supposedly celebratory) premises. This is the sense of uneasiness that we find in many American Catholic fictions, a residual jokey quality that ensures the audience does not know whether to take the text at face value or not. It is what the Jesuit critic William F. Lynch called an "ironic imagination," which works to "de-absolutize" worldly objects by implying that they possess only a provisional quality in the light of higher truths.[19]

None of this is necessarily conscious or intentional in Warhol's work, of course, but intentional fallacies should not concern us unnecessarily here. Warhol's place within a cultural tradition signifies more than any particular formulations he may have made about his own art. Even in an overt sense, though, Catholicism remained a powerful influence upon Warhol up until the end of his life. He attended mass at least three times every week; in 1978, he planned to have a cross blessed and installed in his studio to ward off further fires; in 1980, he sought out an audience with the pope in Rome.[20] Moreover, traces of Catholic liturgy in Warhol's art are not hard to find. "Warhol's icons are kin to sacred relic," wrote Robert Pincus-Witten: Jacqueline Kennedy and Presley become objects of "transubstantiation," oscillating between human and quasi-divine status.[21] Robert Hughes made a similar point when he said that in its identification of the earthly film star with the divine Madonna, Warhol's 1962 work *Gold Marilyn Monroe* suggests "Genet in paint."[22] Other paintings feature altarpiece-like diptychs, or, in the case of *The Last Supper* (1986), a variation on more ostensibly Christian iconography. This latter work derives from a silk-screened blowup of Leonardo's original painting, which Warhol has subdivided into segments and rearranged in a random order, some panels appearing upside down. At work here is a kind of "anti-idealism or antitheology" that can neither give full allegiance to modernist ideals of art and religion nor entirely abandon them.[23] Instead, Warhol reworks the Catholic icons of high art into a form of postmodernist aesthetic kitsch.

Of equal significance, though, is the way Warhol's Catholic mind-set becomes a more implicit, subliminal force within his artistic operations.

19 William F. Lynch, S.J., *Images of Faith: An Exploration of the Ironic Imagination* (Notre Dame: Univ. of Notre Dame Press, 1973), p. 102.
20 *The Andy Warhol Diaries,* ed. Pat Hackett (New York: Warner, 1989), pp. 109, 275, 439.
21 Robert Pincus-Witten, "Pre-entry: Margins of Error. Saint Andy's Devotions," *Arts Magazine,* 63, no. 10 (Summer 1989), 58–9.
22 Robert Hughes, "The Best and Worst of Warhol," *Time,* 13 Feb. 1989, p. 95; for *Gold Marilyn Monroe,* see Carter Ratcliff, *Andy Warhol* (New York: Abbeville Press, 1983), p. 31.
23 Seth Edenbaum, "Parody and Privacy," *Arts Magazine,* 62, no. 2 (Oct. 1987), 45.

His Campbell soup cans and other famous images from pop culture replicate themselves ad infinitum into a universality that aspires to replicate the universal structures of Catholicism. As Pincus-Witten put it: "Through the ritual of art, Warhol proclaims their glory through a mass of detail, monotonously intoning their holy names even unto the heavenly infinity inherent in the grid or serial format. The same thing, over and over again, in whatever the direction, stretching away, infinitely."[24] Warhol in fact devoted his whole life to these frameworks of incessant repetition, eating the same lunch for twenty years, watching television game shows back to back and remarking how "it would be terrific if everybody were alike."[25] In Warhol's world, of course, they are exactly that. This environment where everything is the same as everything else not only annuls any possibility of subjective freedom for the human spirit but also compels the artist to relinquish his familiar role of prophet or seer. The whole notion of "personal" art, like "personal" feelings, is abandoned; Warhol represents the Catholic rejection of romanticism at its most extreme. In this blithe insouciance toward everything that is "just personal" (in Jay Gatsby's dismissive phrase), and conversely in his intense adoration of the impersonal mechanisms of mass iconography, Warhol stands at the opposite end of the popular culture spectrum from the Jewish spirit of Woody Allen, whose work always prioritizes the value of individual feeling and seeks to rebel against the restrictions and compromises demanded by the corporate world. After viewing Louis Malle's film *My Dinner With André* in 1982, Warhol confided to his diary that "I fell asleep, it was so boring. Hippie talk. I guess the kids are thinking this is intellectual because it talks about feelings."[26]

In this sense, Warhol's view of himself as a businessman was not simply cynicism but might be seen as a return to an older social and aesthetic tradition. Just as in medieval times the artist was an anonymous servant of his ecclesiastical patrons, dutifully celebrating an impersonal and not a personal vision, so Warhol manufactured an anonymity that enabled him to reflect the wider culture his texts serve – in his case, the materialism of American business culture. Warhol's dictum that "real art should be commercial" was not so much a mercenary statement as a form of conceptual burlesque: art only has a commercial value because no higher human endeavor can have any meaning.[27] The whole notion of a "higher" individual sensibility was, for Warhol, meaningless: "Once you see emotions from a certain angle," he claimed, "you can never think of them

24 Pincus-Witten, "Pre-entry: Margins of Error," p. 58.
25 Quoted in Koch, *Stargazer*, p. 23.
26 *The Andy Warhol Diaries*, p. 445.
27 Warhol's 1970 remark is quoted in Emile De Antonio and Mitch Tuchman, *Painters Painting* (New York: Abbeville Press, 1984), p. 119.

as real again."[28] It is a formula of monastic discipline and impersonality; everyone and everything must be reduced to the same level, no rebellious desire for "a world elsewhere" can possibly be allowed.

Thus Warhol's appropriation of the stars of New York high society possesses a double-edged significance. On one hand, like Gatsby, Warhol cherished this company not on account of its inherent interest or worth but rather as an act of personal revenge: to show that he was as "good," that is, as socially acceptable, as any of them. Yet on the other hand Warhol also resembles Gatsby in that this self-conscious display of his own superficial motives and behavior implicitly comments on the equal superficialities of "established" society. By infiltrating these smart social circles, Warhol was engaging in an act of insidious parody that reveals the hollowness of any claims by art or society to depth, permanence, or "natural" significance. Truth, for Warhol, was in the care of God, not liberal humanists. Any aspiration toward "truth" in this world must inevitably be superficial and trashy. Art cannot be a repository of wisdom; it can only reflect, travesty (and enjoy) the world it finds itself surrounded by. This, incidentally, accounts for some of the oppositional energy critics like Thomas Crow and Rainer Crone have found in Warhol's visions of American life. The silk screen photographs of the electric chairs are indeed gruesome, but they are sinister precisely because America's notion of its own ethical "justice" conflicts with the self-consciously aesthetic, colorful, and superficial images Warhol has created.[29] The American political and cultural system attempts to naturalize what is in fact an arbitrary phenomenon, and it is precisely those pretensions to moral depth that Warhol's texts ironically detach themselves from.

When he turned his attention to film, Warhol's ironic conjunction of icon and iconoclasm functions in a similar way. His achievement here was to incorporate into art the boredom, the "everyday banality" that, as Carter Ratcliff said, "even high art tends to censor."[30] By logging the eight-hour (non-)development of the Empire State Building, by chronicling for fifty minutes a lovers' kiss, Warhol's films make their audiences uneasy and disrupt familiar viewing habits. Through frustrating these desires for more orthodox entertainment, the films bring into sharp relief the fact that what we think of as "normal" cinema in fact consists simply of narrowly constructed hermeneutic and cultural codes. Again, the effect is to burlesque traditional culture, to uncover and make fun of – without necessarily satirizing – society's implicit assumptions.

28 *The Philosophy of Andy Warhol: From A to B and Back Again* (London: Picador, 1976), pp. 32–3.
29 Mike Weaver, ed., *The Art of Photography, 1839–1989* (New Haven: Yale Univ. Press, 1989), no. 461.
30 Ratcliff, *Andy Warhol*, p. 103.

Warhol's most famous film, *The Chelsea Girls* (1966), directs this burlesque toward a specifically Catholic context. Here the male character (played by Ondine, one of Warhol's retinue) fancies himself in the role of father confessor and tries to persuade a young girl to confess she is a lesbian and to tell him about her first sexual experiences. Rather like Joyce's Stephen Hero trying to persuade his girlfriend Emma Clery to "go to confession" to him so he can hear her "sins," Warhol's ritual operates as a parody of the power structure inherent in the Catholic sacrament of confession: Ondine's overt prurience and voyeurism supposedly shed light upon the covert prurience of more established priests.[31] Later in the film, Ondine, having now elevated himself to the status of pope, chooses to beat up one of his penitents after she has confessed to sexual misdeeds. It is a scabrous anticlericalism worthy of Buñuel, a spoof designed to expose what the film conceives to be those sadistic and masochistic impulses that disguise themselves in the altruistic cloaks of Catholic liturgy. Still, as with so many rebellious Catholic artists, one can detect a note of traditional devotion alongside the biting satire. Ondine goes on to assert that the Catholic church has disappeared and been replaced by Greenwich Village, where, he says, his flock consists of "homosexuals, perverts of all kinds, criminals of all kinds." These are the people who "really care," says Ondine, and he professes nothing but contempt for those others who think they are doing good. Despite its heterodoxy, this is in fact the same kind of radical piety that we find in the novels of Genet or even Flannery O'Connor: the thief, the outcast, conscious of his worldly powerlessness, can be closer to God's grace than the smug social philanthropist. Reworking Eliot's famous phrase about "genuine blasphemy" being an "affirmation of belief," we could say that awareness of genuine damnation becomes an affirmation of the possibility of redemption.

Warhol's works maintain an ambiguous attitude toward the dogmas of Catholic faith, and it would be reductive (if not actually impossible) to attempt to establish, in a biographical sense, what Warhol "really" believed. What we can say, though, is that his works never for one moment subscribe to those doctrines of good taste that characterize the American Protestant social ethos and aesthetic norm. "Protestantism, when it fades," wrote John Updike, "leaves behind a fuzzy idealism; Catholicism, a crystalline cynicism."[32] Warhol is certainly in the latter camp, as were many other lapsed Catholics in Warhol's circle: Brigid Polk, Viva, Jack Smith, Paul Morrissey. After 1968, all of the films

---

31 James Joyce, *Stephen Hero* (London: Granada-Panther, 1977), p. 139. *Stephen Hero* is the first draft of *Portrait of the Artist as a Young Man*.
32 John Updike, "Fast Art," *New Republic*, 27 Mar. 1989, p. 28.

produced by Warhol were actually directed by Morrissey, a Fordham graduate. In their version of *Dracula* (1974), Morrissey chose to switch the locale to Catholic Italy, where the subversive count amuses himself by preying upon the scions of an aristocratic Italian family, which prides itself upon strict fidelity to the Roman faith.

Another lapsed Catholic on the fringes of Warhol's group was Robert Mapplethorpe, a staff photographer for Warhol's magazine *Interview* in the 1970s and a great admirer of Warhol's work. In fact, Warhol as a youth in the 1940s was the subject of Mapplethorpe's first artist-celebrity portrait in 1971. Another portrait by Mapplethorpe, created shortly after Warhol's death in 1987, locates its subject within a clearly defined Catholic framework. Here Warhol's white hair is surrounded by a luminous silver halo, as though he were a saint. To emphasize this saintliness still further, the photograph is set off by a black frame in the shape of a cross.[33]

Mapplethorpe was brought up as a practicing Catholic in the suburbs of New York and remembered how he "went to church every Sunday," adding: "A church has a certain magic and mystery for a child. It still shows in how I arrange things. It's always little altars. It's always been this way – whenever I'd put something together I'd notice it was symmetrical."[34] Mapplethorpe's negotiations with his Catholic heritage are apparent in early works such as the 1969 *Tie Rack,* where an image of the Virgin Mary is defaced with scratchings and neckties, and in his more respectful 1971 portrait of Jesus (20). More crucially, though, Catholicism also underlies his general obsession with evil in its various forms. The recognition of evil qua evil is of course dependent upon the inversion of an initial framework of orthodox belief, and Mapplethorpe's famous 1978 portrait of himself with a whip protruding from his rear end like a devil's tail readily testifies to his devotion to the art of genuine blasphemy (75). Mike Weaver has also shown that the logo of the pentagram, which pervades Mapplethorpe's photography, was deployed in a nineteenth-century occult revival led by Eliphas Levi, where the triangle combined five times connoted diabolical homosexuality. Mapplethorpe's bodies are often shaped in the form of pentagrams – as in a 1986 portrait of *Thomas,* for instance (161) – thus implying Mapplethorpe's concern to reflect the

33 Richard Marshall, ed., *Robert Mapplethorpe* (New York: Whitney Museum of Modern Art, 1988), pp. 23, 173. Subsequent page references to prints in this catalog are given in parentheses in the text.
34 Quoted in Ingrid Sischy, "A Society Artist," in *Robert Mapplethorpe,* ed. Marshall, p. 82.

rituals of this occult magic.[35] In similar satanic vein, Mapplethorpe also provided photogravures for Paul Schmidt's 1986 translation of Rimbaud's *A Season in Hell,* wherein Mapplethorpe not only represented various scenes of debauch and suffering but also created a portrait of himself as the devil, with horns protruding from his forehead.

The last illustration in *A Season in Hell* is of a cross, with the picture itself split between black and white, shadow and light. This emphasis on what Richard Howard has called the "architecture of antitheticals" is one of the dominant motifs throughout Mapplethorpe's work.[36] Like the Catholic boy infatuated with the symmetry of "little altars," the structural patterns of much of Mapplethorpe's photography can be seen to resolve themselves into dialogues between spiritual white and diabolic black. In his series on *Lady Lisa Lyon,* for instance, a portrait of the heroine in a white veil is balanced by one of her in a black veil, just as a depiction of Lyon dressed in white and singing angelically from a hymnbook is played off against photographs where she is wearing a black leather outfit. Even more startlingly, Mapplethorpe's 1985 book of portraits, *Certain People,* features on its front cover a self-portrait of the artist in a tough, leather-clad guise, while in the photograph on the back cover Mapplethorpe is represented vulnerably and effeminately, with a naked torso, facial makeup, and lady's wig.

The ramifications of the bifurcations that permeate his work – between decadence and purity, black and white, obverse and reverse sides of the human personality – are sometimes extended by the way Mapplethorpe's work integrates reflecting mirrors within the picture frame itself. In the 1979 *Easter Lilies with Mirror,* for instance, the spectator not only sees these lilies arranged in the shape of a cross, but also necessarily inspects his or her own face in the mirror located at the center of the work (67). We, too, are entrammelled and incorporated within these dark lilies of death. Like Baudelaire, Mapplethorpe challenges the audience with his flowers of evil, defying the "hypocrite lecteur, mon semblable, mon frère" to deny that in these images of death and violence he can see his own image reflected. As Susan Weiley has written, Mapplethorpe's photographs constitute "indictments of our innocence. We are all implicated."[37] It is the absolute antithesis of Protestant pastoral: in Mapplethorpe's enclosed space, no possibility of change exists; no

35 Mike Weaver, "Mapplethorpe's Human Geometry: A Whole Other Realm," *Aperture,* no. 101 (Winter 1985), pp. 42–51.
36 Richard Howard, "The Mapplethorpe Effect," in *Robert Mapplethorpe,* ed. Marshall, p. 159.
37 Susan Weiley, "Prince of Darkness, Angel of Light," *Art News,* 87, no. 10 (Dec. 1988), 109.

"world elsewhere," either naturalistic or psychological, seems to be viable. Another 1986 portrait, *Thomas,* in which a man's body strains against the black circle surrounding him, suggests how Mapplethorpe's crucial theme is metaphysical as well as sexual bondage (170).

In this way, Mapplethorpe's portraits tend to work against the radical, transforming styles of American romanticism. Mapplethorpe is concerned not so much with finding new worlds as with mirroring and rediscovering worlds that are already there and, according to the terms of these photographs, always have been. As many critics have pointed out, there is a statuesque, immobile quality about most of Mapplethorpe's subjects, a quality that can no doubt be traced back to his early days as a sculptor but that also signifies the revelation of some essential form, which merely random or contingent motion tends to conceal from human view. In a 1987 *Vogue* portrait, for instance, Mapplethorpe transposes his model into the embodiment of a devil with horns: the woman is looking on anxiously as a pair of black feet above her head pull her hair out into a satanic shape, and those feet stand as an image of how this woman herself has been conceptually overturned, inverted from sublime angel to sinister devil (figure 1).[38] Similarly, in a portrait of Betsey Johnson from Mapplethorpe's 1989 collection *Some Women,* we see a similar kind of pattern whereby historical time and personal individuality become inverted by the timeless, immutable force of mortality (figure 2). Just as in the *Vogue* portrait the white angel reverses itself into a black devil, so here we find life reversing itself into death. The laugh on Johnson's face looks almost exactly like a grinning skull: the temporal accident of bodily incarnation is stripped away to reveal the metaphysical infrastructure underlying the provisional conceits of the human flesh. The way this photograph foregrounds the artificiality of Johnson's lipstick and her painted nails gives it an even more uncomfortable tone, as if to point out the grotesquely superficial quality of these fashionable allurements.[39]

Mapplethorpe develops this resistance to historical contingency and individual psychological complexity until it becomes a deliberate and systematic critique of that old aesthetic whereby portraiture was associated with illumination of an inner spirit. Mapplethorpe's work is concerned more with structural impersonality, or essential timelessness, a timelessness that deconstructs human identity and social meaning, rendering them arbitrary and therefore laughably provisional. The patterns of Mapplethorpe's photography are in fact curiously reminiscent of the

38 "Expo: Robert Mapplethorpe," *The Face,* Mar. 1988, p. 90.
39 Robert Mapplethorpe, *Some Women* (Boston: Bulfinch–Little, Brown and Company, 1989), p. 85.

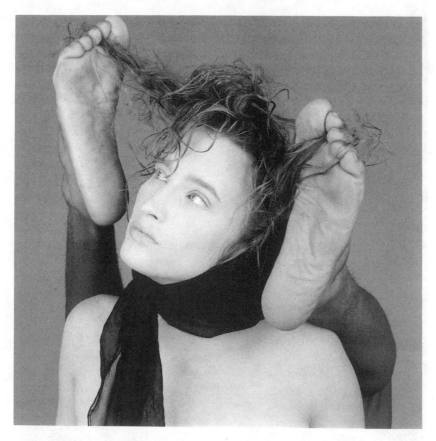

Figure 1. Italian Vogue, © 1987, The Estate of Robert Mapplethorpe

gestures within Hawthorne's novel *The Marble Faun,* where, as we saw earlier, visitors from America find the autonomous independence of their romantic soul becomes more and more compromised as their bodies find themselves imitating the preexisting patterns of Old World sculpture. Like the characters in Hawthorne's novel, Mapplethorpe's subjects oscillate between individual identity and abstract substance, and so the sense of frozen immobility here is not just a formalistic phenomenon but also epistemologically relevant: Mapplethorpe's subjects are locked, like Hawthorne's, within old patterns from which they cannot escape. In this connection, it is significant also to note that Mapplethorpe began experimenting with photographs of actual statues toward the end of his career. While the live human figures in Mapplethorpe's photographs are given an impersonal, sculptural quality, conversely these sculptures are animated, endowed with something like a human identity, so that, as

Figure 2. Betsey Johnson, © 1985, The Estate of Robert Mapplethorpe

Bill Berkson noted, there is a continuous interplay between ideas of "flux and fixity" in process here. For instance, in *Italian Devil* (1988) the sculptured face of a devil as it appears in this sinister close-up photograph seems to merge into the image of a living human person (figure 3).[40]

Because of its uncompromising rejection of "world elsewhere" ro-

40 Bill Berkson, "Robert Mapplethorpe at Robert Miller," *Art in America,* Apr. 1989, p. 258.

Figure 3. Italian Devil, © 1988, The Estate of Robert Mapplethorpe

manticism, Mapplethorpe's work always suggests a sense of imitation, of déjà vu. Roland Barthes implicitly criticized this lack of contingency in Mapplethorpe's work when he claimed that the old ghost of painting, with all its overtones of the stylized aesthetic pose, still haunts these photographs.[41] But Mapplethorpe's language of déjà vu actually works in a more complex way than this: we find this consistently deadpan ambience because his photographs deny the possibility that anything else exists or ever can exist. Like Warhol, Mapplethorpe eradicates from his photographs any internalized "aura," thereby annulling the idea of the photograph as a memento of a supposed lost plenitude. It makes no sense here to talk of fleeting transcendental visions or "decisive moments" of the kind invoked by Alfred Stieglitz or Henri Cartier-Bresson. In Map-

41 Barthes, *Camera Lucida,* p. 30.

plethorpe, there is no ideal space of which the photographs stand as a regrettable secondary replica. On the contrary, these pictures embody a timeless vision, or rather a dark mirror abstracted from time.

Yet though no radical or pastoral transformation of human destiny seems to be available within this world, Mapplethorpe's work also contains a radical political agenda in terms of its challenge to social attitudes and taboos, its dissolution of gender boundaries, its interrogation of racial and sexual stereotypes. While his photography may be epistemologically conservative, it can also be socially radical. It is this social radicalism that has, of course, received most critical attention, especially the notorious homosexual and sadomasochistic scenes, which are, as Stephen Koch has said, fueled by a vicious circle of guilt: religious and sexual guilt leads toward these rituals of violence, and this in turn engenders the guilt that accompanies participation in such rituals.[42] Nevertheless, while the sexual scenes obviously imply the acting out of these "sinful" tendencies, they also imply a move to redeem this guilt by hauling the darkness of transgression into the light of art. From this perspective, Mapplethorpe transubstantiates the fallen human body by investing it with a frozen form variously described as "sculptural," "liturgical," infused with "quiddity."[43] Mapplethorpe removes his material from the accidents of everyday life by his idiom of "the looking-glass layer," which transposes his posed subjects into a realm of pure, essential form epitomizing what Koch called a state of "secular grace."[44] Many of Mapplethorpe's photographs aspire to transcend a merely human context; as Richard Howard has said, the fact that impersonal facial masks so often take precedence "over individuality, over the personal" suggests how this quest for "ecstasy" and "the apparatus of the sacred" is predicated upon a search for something that the incomplete human realm (supposedly) tends to conceal.[45] In this sense, sexuality for Mapplethorpe is associated with a dark wizardry, the metamorphosing power of magic. It is also true, however, that the intermingling of light and dark in some of these photographs focuses our attention upon the perennial quandary of the flesh, the fact that the perfect symmetry of spirit is weighed down by the heavy shadow of the body. One of the portraits of Lady Lisa Lyon presents an extreme

42 Stephen Koch, "Guilt, Grace and Robert Mapplethorpe," Art in America, Nov. 1986, p. 150.
43 Alan Hollinghurst, "Robert Mapplethorpe," in Robert Mapplethorpe 1970–1983, ed. Alan Hollinghurst and Stuart Morgan (London: ICA, 1983), p. 8; Bruce Chatwin, Introd., Lady Lisa Lyon, by Robert Mapplethorpe (New York: Viking Press–Studio, 1983), p. 9; Susan Sontag, "Sontag on Mapplethorpe," Vanity Fair, July 1985, p. 72.
44 Sischy, "A Society Artist," p. 87; Koch, "Guilt, Grace and Robert Mapplethorpe," p. 149.
45 Howard, "The Mapplethorpe Effect," pp. 157, 159.

close-up of her legs covered with sand, making the body seem strange and grotesque, a cumbersome burden of terrestrial incarnation.

It could also be argued that in some of his more sardonic pieces – the 1978 self-portrait with the whip, for instance – the imagery seeks to aestheticize evil, to strip it of its association with moral degradation by turning "evil" into no more than a jokey series of fetishes. This is Mapplethorpe the terrorist, as he represents himself in another self-portrait of 1982, intent upon the decontextualization and violent parody of religious iconography (109). In this guise, the burden of Mapplethorpe's art becomes metonymical rather than metaphorical, for he takes standard religious and cultural meanings only to diminish them, to imply they mean less than they seem. One of his 1975 self-portraits suggests a pose of crucifixion, but parodically keeps its distance from cross symbolism by the amused smirk on Mapplethorpe's face (73). Also parodic here is the decentering of the human subject's image, its expulsion to the very margins of the photograph (figure 4). Although Mapplethorpe is teasing his audience with the metaphorical weight of the cross, he is reinventing this image within the metonymical confines of sexual fetishism: the afterthought, the fragment, becomes more significant than any supposed symbolic center. The process is similar to that in Mapplethorpe's last self-portraits where, dying of AIDS, he presents himself in an ornate dressing gown and fancy slippers as if to conjur up a world of 1890s decadence, the camp and artificial world of Aubrey Beardsley and Oscar Wilde, with all the connotations of moral outrage and opprobrium traditionally invoked by that scene.[46] By portraying himself within this environment, Mapplethorpe sardonically challenges his audience with the idea that the fatal sickness he embodies is deserved. Again, though, Mapplethorpe's black humor is concerned with problematizing all these religious, moral, and metaphorical associations, querying his audience's culturally conditioned equation of bodily illness with various forms of immorality and decadence. Whereas Scott Fitzgerald's novels internalize the conception of martyrdom at a literal and emotional level, Mapplethorpe's last photographs jokily toy with these familiar religious metaphors but, in the end, coolly and rationally refuse to participate within that discourse of the scourged, sanctified loser. In this sense, the ice-cold perfection of Mapplethorpe's photographic technique stands as its own rebuke to the vagaries of religious mythology.

Attempting to systematize Mapplethorpe's work into a coherent Catholic theology (or antitheology) would, therefore, be a counterproductive exercise. Some of his photographs aspire to reconcile a corporeal, fallen

46 Dominick Dunne, "Robert Mapplethorpe's Proud Finale," *Vanity Fair,* Feb. 1989, p. 133.

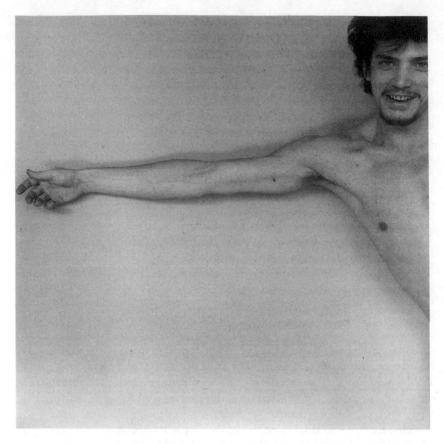

Figure 4. Self Portrait, © 1975, The Estate of Robert Mapplethorpe

human world with the grace of essential form. Others place more emphasis upon a chasm between the bondage and decadence of bodily existence as opposed to a realm of pure light. Still others wittingly mock the premises of religious belief and take pleasure in their own iconoclasm. Mapplethorpe's New York apartment contained a crucifix on the wall as well as a pet snake, and his work reflects a similarly incongruous juxtaposition of divinity and demon. So it is not the internal consistency of Mapplethorpe's "thought" that is significant here, but the ways in which his iconography, like Warhol's, emerges out of and implicitly reflects the residual material of Catholic culture.

Like Warhol, Mapplethorpe was an expert game player in the politics of the art world, manipulating its market in jesuitical fashion so as to secure for himself the maximum prices and publicity. The more general charge against Warhol has also been leveled at Mapplethorpe: the notion that the artist's cynical, fashion-oriented sensibility has the effect of turning style into substance. The point made by Andy Grundberg and others is not that style is necessarily bad in itself, but that by essentializing style Mapplethorpe voids his pictures of any "center" of "moral gravity."[47] It is this ethical insouciance that has perturbed so much of Mapplethorpe's audience: the most subversive aspect of his work is not so much its thematic content as the fact that these pictures seem to take no moral attitude toward their own themes. The 1979 photograph of Brian Ridley and Lyle Heeter, for instance, shows this gay sadomasochistic couple encased in leather and chains, but posing nonchalantly in a living room surrounded by humdrum ornaments and books carefully arranged on the coffee table (55). The most shocking aspect here is that the scene is depicted as not shocking. There have always been photographers who have chosen to dwell upon sex and violence – Brassai and Weegee come to mind. But in Brassai and Weegee, the camera (and hence the viewer) is positioned as a voyeur, safely detached from the scene being peered at: Brassai's murky, enigmatic Parisian nightlife and Weegee's violent world of New York crime both possess a lurid, gothic quality that serves to place a barrier between the object and the spectator. Mapplethorpe's photographs, however, look at the spectator with a blank, amoral gaze. Here violence has become domesticated and ordinary, not self-evidently extraordinary, and it is precisely this erasure of moral perspective that has made Mapplethorpe so controversial an artist.

This flattening approach might of course be attributed partly to the milieu of fashion, and partly also to the political desire to disturb received attitudes and images concerning race and sexuality. Stuart Morgan has written of how Mapplethorpe's more controversial photographs function in the same way as Warhol's, by mirroring the social codes of their audience and holding up implicit assumptions and prejudices for thoughtful inspection. Yet the "visual democracy" in Mapplethorpe, which Morgan also talked about, the way his "level gaze" turns away from a hierarchy of aesthetic or moral meanings, is also reminiscent of Warhol, and it is a phenomenon that can be related to the Catholic temperament they shared.[48] By removing human spirit from his photographs, Mapplethorpe, like Warhol, evades ethical judgments by refusing to enter into the "soul" of his models. Instead, he prefers to treat them as objects, patterns, bodies. That romantic freedom and individual autonomy cherished by Protestant culture is trumped by a "Catholic" system where "inner light" is less significant than one's assigned place within an overall

47 Andy Grundberg, "The Allure of Mapplethorpe's Photographs," *New York Times*, 31 July 1988, Sec. 2, p. 30.
48 Stuart Morgan, "Something Magic," *Artforum*, 25, No. 9 (May 1987), 122.

structure of meaning. Even in the frozen white tableau representing *Princess Gloria von Thurn und Taxis* (1987), we see the statuesque woman with her eyes closed; the windows to her soul have been obliterated, and she resembles a human corpse as much as a divine angel (197). In Mapplethorpe's world, as in Warhol's, everyone is equal in the sight of "God": by eradicating the nonconformities and eccentricities of spirit and abolishing the superficial differences of earthly categories, both artists bring all human subjects down to the same conceptual level. Social status is only provisional; moral viewpoints as contrived by human beings are inevitably flawed; aesthetic hierarchies are irrelevant. The camera does not look up to kings and down to paupers, as John Berger claimed is typically the case, but rather examines everything with the same cool, level, nonjudgmental gaze.

Unlike film, which deals with an illusory fictional world, photography has succeeded in occupying an important place within the American artistic tradition because its promise of representing an unmediated "reality" is consistent with that familiar urge of American romanticism to bypass artificial (especially European) artistic conventions in favor of representing a more primary "truth." In the transcendental ambition of Stieglitz's "Equivalents" sequence, for instance, we see a desire to find parallels within the unmediated natural world to exalted states of the human spirit. In the social realism of Paul Strand and Walker Evans, emphasis is placed upon undercutting the old boundaries of stylized art so as to embrace all types of landscape, all classes of people. By contrast with these expansive tendencies, the subject matter of Warhol and Mapplethorpe might seem narrow and mean spirited and their methods unduly contrived. Yet these are just the same accusations that were leveled against Henry James by American realist novelists at the end of the nineteenth century. It is true that Warhol and Mapplethorpe's celebrity portraits, tinged as they are with artifice and decadence, differ radically from the austere romanticism of Strand and Stieglitz; but austere romanticism is not the field these portraits work within, any more than it was the chosen terrain of Henry James. Exemplars of "Man in the Open Air" (F. O. Matthiessen's Whitmanian phrase for his preferred heroic and naturalist type of American culture) Warhol and Mapplethorpe are not.[49] They resemble more a pair of louche papal courtiers at one of the more lenient times in the Curia's history.

Holding that the religious significance of any given work is more

---

49 F. O. Matthiessen used Whitman's phrase as the title of the concluding section to *American Renaissance: Art and Expression in the Age of Emerson and Whitman* (New York: Oxford Univ. Press, 1941). At one time, Matthiessen considered also using this phrase as the title of the book itself.

important than what its creator happened to believe – what, after all did Leonardo or Raphael "believe"? – the Roman church has never been shy about requisitioning artists' work for its own ideological uses. The Collection of Modern Religious Art in the Vatican Museums currently boasts theologically unorthodox paintings by John Sloan (*Indian Religious Dance*), Graham Sutherland, and Francis Bacon, as well as ceramics by Picasso. One wonders how long it will be before Warhol and Mapplethorpe find their way into this elevated company.

13

Ritual and Burlesque:
John Ford and Robert Altman

The standard screen representation of Catholicism is not an issue that need long detain us. Just as we saw earlier how the ethnic and religious stereotypes reproduced by mediocre fiction provide such a paucity of information that the messages emerging from these texts become repetitive and predictable, so we are not primarily concerned with films that categorize Catholics according to the familiar patterns described by Les and Barbara Keyser: "Catholics are immigrants; they live in crime-ridden ghettoes; they are desperately trying to be assimilated; their parents cling to traditional values; their women are conscience-stricken virgins with repressed sexual desires; and their religion demands ritual, statues, penance, and unnatural postures."[1] The authors here were explicitly referring to the representation of Catholics in D. W. Griffith's *Intolerance* (1916), but we encounter similar reifications in films such as the famous gangster movies of the early 1930s, which feature various kinds of nefarious activity among Catholic ethnic groups. Edward G. Robinson's Rico in *Little Caesar* (1930) and Paul Muni's Tony Camonte in *Scarface* (1932) – both Italian-Americans – along with Jimmy Cagney's Irish-American Tom Powers in *The Public Enemy* (1931) present personifications of heroes at once glamorous, sinister, and doomed. Circumscribed both by censorious prolegomenas insisted upon by federal authorities, which pedantically outline the "evils associated with Prohibition," and also by dramatic finales in which the villains reassuringly receive their bullet-ridden comeuppance, these steely outsiders were nevertheless attempting to crack the American system and "be somebody," as Rico puts it.

The tough charisma of these antiheroes induced admiring empathy from some of their fellow Catholics, for whom the gangsters offered

---

1 Les and Barbara Keyser, *Hollywood and the Catholic Church: The Image of Roman Catholicism in American Movies* (Chicago: Loyola Univ. Press, 1984), p. 10.

296

superbly insouciant paradigms of social vengeance. In John O'Hara's *BUtterfield 8* (1935), Jimmy Malloy cherishes the idea of his physical resemblance to Jimmy Cagney as an emblem and guarantee of his aggressive detachment from what he calls the "upper crust" of American society. The magnetism of these cinematic "big shots" for culturally disenfranchised Catholics is attested to in James T. Farrell's introduction to the 1944 edition of *The Young Manhood of Studs Lonigan*. As Farrell said, the gangsters "were business men, engaged in illegal activities for profit"; they pursued the American dream of individual ambition and economic laissez-faire to its logical conclusion, to an area where the conception turned around and became a crazy parody of itself.[2] Fitzgerald's Jay Gatsby and, later on, William Kennedy's 1975 portrait of "Legs" Diamond also fit into this Catholic celebration of the modernist gangster as parodic outsider, a hero who overcomes his marginal social status to construct for himself a darker version of the traditional rags-to-riches story, so as to gain access to the rewards of American society.

This image of Catholicism as embodying disturbingly foreign tendencies recurs in many different guises in later films. In *The Exorcist* (1973), the church offers an occasion for unwelcome cases of diabolism; in *Looking For Mr. Goodbar* (1977), it provides a context for extreme sexual repression and subsequent hysteria; in Sidney Lumet's 1982 film *The Verdict,* written for the screen by David Mamet, the jesuitical hypocrisies and duplicities of the Catholic hierarchy in Boston are routed by the all-American heroism of Paul Newman, who eventually proves the clergy have been trying to cover up a case of negligence at a hospital under their jurisdiction. The conventions here are not dissimilar to those in popular English novels of the late eighteenth century – Ann Radcliffe's *The Italian* and *A Sicilian Romance,* for instance – in which Catholic functionaries prowl through Gothic caverns, their dark deeds providing lurid entertainment that is, in the end, comfortably suppressed and repressed by Radcliffe's middle-class Anglo-Saxon society.

Not all cinematic accounts of Catholicism were as hyperbolic as this, of course. Bing Crosby's priests in *Going My Way* (1944) and *The Bells of St. Mary's* (1945) were just the kind of cosy, domesticated clerics one would welcome along for a familial white Christmas. Indeed, in Frank Capra's *It's a Wonderful Life* (1946), James Stewart's George Bailey is cheered by seeing that *The Bells of St. Mary's* is showing at his local cinema rather than the squalid sex shows his archenemy, the ambitious businessman Mr. Potter, would have preferred. But this scene – and

---

2 John O'Hara, *BUtterfield 8* (New York: Harcourt, Brace and Co., 1935) p. 69; James T. Farrell, Introd., *The Young Manhood of Studs Lonigan* (Cleveland: World Publishing, 1944), pp. 7–8.

indeed the whole film, in which a "guardian angel" is standing by on Christmas Eve to forestall Bailey's suicide by demonstrating to him how much good he has done in the world – epitomizes the streak of "populist sentimentality" that, according to Andrew Sarris, Capra was sometimes prone to fall into. Capra was born in Sicily, immigrated to the United States at the age of six, and described himself in adult life as a "Christmas Catholic."[3] We can see in Capra's films (as in those of his fellow Sicilian-American, Martin Scorsese) displaced images of the immigrant's urgent striving for social acceptability: lower-class Clark Gable forcing his way up the social scale by marrying Claudette Colbert in *It Happened One Night* (1934), or the small-town boys seeking their fortunes in the big city in *Mr. Deeds Goes to Town* (1936) and *Mr. Smith Goes to Washington* (1939). We also infer from these films a sense of what Capra conceives to be the snobbery of the establishment upper classes. The focus in Capra's work consistently emanates from a point of view outside charmed social circles, and (as with John Ford) there is a frequent propensity to burlesque the pomp and pretentiousness of the rich.

Capra's sentimentality is often brilliantly produced and it gives his films many of their most effective moments, just as all those Cagneyesque priests, martyrs, and gangsters from films like *Angels with Dirty Faces* (1938) and *On the Waterfront* (1954) are not only memorable in their own right but also tell us something about how Catholicism was perceived in the United States during the first half of the twentieth century. Yet in the end these stereotypes still remain stereotypes, unsatisfactorily uncomplicated images. I would argue that it is the more unorthodox and sophisticated films of directors such as John Ford, Robert Altman, Alfred Hitchcock, and Martin Scorsese that actually provide more insight into how Catholicism has operated in modern times as an implicit ideological aesthetic that continues to have psychological and cultural relevance.

This leads inexorably into the auteurist controversy currently besetting film studies, the problem of whether one can talk about Ford as the "author" of *The Searchers* or whether this is a naive, "literary" treatment that fails to take into account the film's generic conventions, conditions of production, relation with the institutions of Hollywood, and so on. This is surely, though, not a question simply of one thing or the other. It is true that the *Cahiers du Cinéma* group of the 1950s, reacting against what they took to be the industrial homogeneity of Hollywood and anxious to establish film as a valid "art," discussed with what now seems to us a certain amount of romantic naïveté the authorial "vision" of

3 Andrew Sarris, *The American Cinema: Directors and Directions 1929–1968* (New York: Dutton, 1968), p. 87. For an account of Capra's Catholicism, see Charles J. Maland, *Frank Capra* (Boston: Twayne, 1980), pp. 91–2.

individual "geniuses" like Howard Hawks or Alfred Hitchcock. But the essence of the auteur theory is not in fact dependent upon the idiosyncratic genius of the individual auteur: one can acknowledge the significance of the studio system and other commercial institutions to the production of Ford's films without thereby claiming that Ford's films turn out the same, or on the same artistic level, as those of (say) Andrew V. McLaglen. Ford's films must of course negotiate the preexistent conventions of the Western genre; they are not simply envisioned and authored by one individual person. But it is within this very process of negotiation and dialogue that the exceptional quality of Ford's films emerges: his films play with and sometimes parody the legends of the West so that his audience can reexamine these generic clichés in a new light. This process is, in fact, the same as for an author in any other artistic medium. A critic in the 1990s should not neglect the institutions framing Shakespeare's modes of production, but that does not mean he or she should therefore treat Shakespeare's plays as being equivalent to those of Thomas Kyd, for whom the modes of production were very similar.

Naturally, one would not wish to relapse into the more old-fashioned type of auteurist idea that privileged thematic content over form and apprehended "mere" technique as incidental to what the author had to "say." The skills of how the cinematic representations are created signify precisely what they have to say. This is why it is so crucial to attend to the specific nature of film language, as engendered by actor, studio, director, or whoever, or whatever; indeed, it is one of the general contentions of this book that no text is ever dreamed up by an individual author out of nothing, but can always be related back to the wider cultural forces that helped shape it. Nevertheless, we come back to the fact that films made by certain directors tend to have more complex information, more "unexpected combinations" as Wolfgang Iser would say, than those made by other directors. John Ford is not the sole author of his films, but the films in which he has a share of authorship are different from other people's: Ford enjoys what Althusser would call "relative autonomy," even though admittedly working within a given set of conventions.[4] Just as Scott Fitzgerald had a genius for putting words together, so the works of Ford and Robert Altman reveal a genius for the texture and language of the moving camera that most films simply lack. Critics never quite agree on the relative merits of film directors, of course, any more than they agree on the relative merits of writers. Nevertheless, by general consensus, Ford is among the major directors in the history of

4 Louis Althusser, "Ideology and Ideological State Apparatuses (Notes towards an Investigation)," in Lenin and Philosophy and Other Essays, trans. Ben Brewster (London: New Left Books, 1971), p. 137.

cinema; while at least one critic – Pauline Kael – has claimed that Altman made five or six films in the early 1970s whose quality has never been equaled in modern times.[5]

John Ford's biography clearly testifies to his intense involvement with the Catholic church. Ford's father was born in Galway and immigrated to Portland, Maine. Ford himself was in his youth a member of the Knights of Columbus and, like his father, a lifelong active supporter of the IRA.[6] His nephew, John Feeney, actually became a priest, eventually presiding over the multiple masses that smoothed Ford's passage from this world to the next; indeed, the film director died with rosary beads in his hands.[7] Within Ford's work, overt representations of Catholicism in both its social and political aspects are not hard to find. *Mary of Scotland* (1936), for instance, somewhat sentimentally outlines the doomed history of Mary, Queen of Scots, following the Stuart-Catholic party line whereby Mary herself (Katharine Hepburn) never stoops to a scheming thought. Mary here is portrayed as heroically steadfast in her loyalty to the "old faith," whereas the invidious Queen Elizabeth (Florence Eldridge) appears as a cheap opportunist who transfers her allegiance from Catholicism to Protestantism when it is politically expedient to do so. Some of the film's best moments come from Moroni Olsen's comic turn as a long-bearded John Knox, waxing lyrical about the "old faith" as "the work of Satan" and precipitating Mary's final martyred walk to the scaffold.

Another of Ford's representations of Catholics as beautiful losers occurs in *The Informer* (1935), from a novel by Liam O'Flaherty, where Ford portrays the cowardly betrayal of Sinn Fein worker Frankie McPhillip (Wallace Ford) by Gypo Nolan (Victor McLaglen), who turns informant so he can claim reward money from the police and emigrate to America. The epigraph to this film – "Then Judas repented himself and cast down the thirty pieces of silver and departed" – makes it clear enough where the director's sympathies lie. In an embodiment of this biblical motto, the last scene features Nolan, who has been punitively shot by the IRA, struggling into a church to beg forgiveness of Frankie McPhillip's mother before expiring ecstatically in an apotheosis of confession and redemption. In this final shot, Mrs. McPhillip (Una O'Connor) looks down upon the penitent Nolan like a benign Madonna.

The Fugitive (1947), from Graham Greene's novel *The Power and the*

5 Pauline Kael, "Current Trends in Films," Portland State Univ., 20 Oct. 1989.
6 Tag Gallagher, *John Ford: The Man and His Films* (Berkeley: Univ. of California Press, 1986), pp. 26, 29.
7 Joseph McBride and Michael Wilmington, *John Ford* (New York: Da Capo, 1975), pp. 9–11.

Glory, is an even more overtly Christian work that focuses on a vagrant priest (Henry Fonda) reenacting the ritual of crucifixion as he flees from oppressive anticlerical authorities in Mexico. "The following photoplay is timeless," intones a voice-over at the beginning of the narrative, preparing the audience for the radical abstraction of the film's style, with its anonymous characters – "A Fugitive," "A Sergeant of Police," and so on – and its allegorical chiaroscuro, its interplay of black and white shadow and light. Ford, who spent a whole year making this picture, called *The Fugitive* his only "perfect" film, and in this opinion he differed interestingly from his critics, most of whom have found the film's unusually expressionistic and highly ritualized style to be at odds with the more squalid and credibly human world of Greene's novel.[8] Ford, however, remained devoted to *The Fugitive:* it is as if the film constituted for him an idealized masque, a revelation and apotheosis of the spirit in a world from which mundane human tensions have (temporarily) been erased.

One of the important things about Ford's more celebrated films, though, is that this sense of apotheosis – which shines through unobstructed in *The Fugitive* – subsequently comes into significant conflict with a more recognizable human environment, so that dialogues are established between worlds of spirit and matter, plenitude and loss. Loss, in fact, is a central theme of Ford's work. The emphasis falls on how green "was" my valley, as in the 1941 film of that name, which chronicles the dispersion of a Welsh coal-mining community as its children emigrate to Canada, New Zealand, and other parts of the globe. Likewise, in *The Quiet Man* (1952), John Wayne's Sean Thornton yearns to reinsert himself into the small Irish community from which his family has been exiled, and he recommends himself to Mary Kate by participating in Catholic church services, something to which he is also a stranger. *The Quiet Man* is not so much a sentimental film as a film about how such sentimentality operates. Thornton explains to the Widow Tillane (Mildred Natwick) that ever since he was a boy "Innisfree has been another word for Heaven to me"; but though the lush green cinematography on one level validates Thornton's idyll, he (and the viewer) soon come to realize that life with Maureen O'Hara's cantakerous Mary Kate will consist of anything other than easy pastoral nostalgia. In this sense, mystification in Ford tends to be accompanied by demystification; plenitude disappears even as it is inscribed. The process is akin to what William Boelhower has called "ethnic semiosis," whereby the inevitable displacement and absence of ethnic origins lapses into the circulation of signs rotating around the

8 Gallagher, *John Ford,* p. 234.

chimera of an imaginary center.[9] *How Green Was My Valley* follows this pattern by foregrounding the way in which its Edenic society is reconstituted in memory: "Who shall say what is real and what is not?" asks the narrator at the beginning of the film, describing his dead friends as a "living truth within my mind."

In other films, this dialectic between presence and loss, the "spiritual" and the material, occurs in a more sudden and unpredictable fashion. In *Rio Grande* (1950), Victor McLaglen, Ford's perennial good-hearted Irishman here impersonating "Sergeant Quincannon," comically pauses to genuflect before the altar while rescuing a small girl from a bullet-ridden church in Mexico. In the jungle of *Mogambo* (1953), Ava Gardner's Eloise Kelly suddenly takes time off from stalking Clark Gable to confess her sexual misdemeanors to a priest. The point is not that these are not "genuine" expressions of religion, but rather that they are both unexpected, and hence both are trading off an incongruity between the emblem of piety and that unsympathetic world surrounding it. Whereas in *The Fugitive* the psychology of the priest is comfortingly externalized by the formalized cinematography, in most of Ford's other films noble or "spiritual" impulses find themselves colliding with a careless secular world.

It is this sense of disjunction that helps to bring about the idea of martyrdom that echoes throughout Ford's cinema, not only in religious contexts (*Mary of Scotland*) but also in films celebrating wartime heroics, such as *The Battle of Midway* and *They Were Expendable*. *They Were Expendable* (1945) focuses upon America's worst wartime defeat, in the Philippines. Against a backdrop of fatalistic and religious music, including a muted version of "For Those in Peril on the Sea," Jack Holt's General Martin affirms to his men: "Our job is to lay down that sacrifice. That's what we were trained for and that's what we'll do. If any individual boat runs into trouble, it will have to be considered expendable." At the end of the movie, after the inevitable naval catastrophe has taken place, General Martin insists upon flying the more valuable officers back to the United States so they can help build up new reserves and continue the struggle. The price of this, however, is that the luckless bosun's mate, "big Mick" Boots Mulcahey (Ward Bond), is left behind in charge of a crippled band of men for whom there is no room on the airplane to Australia, and consequently no hope. The film closes with a rousing chorus of "Glory, Glory Hallelujah," with the sailors seeing the glory of the coming of the Lord in compensation for their grisly terrestrial end. It is the old Catholic pattern of "Victory through Defeat" translated

9 William Boelhower, *Through a Glass Darkly: Ethnic Semiosis in American Literature* (New York: Oxford Univ. Press, 1987), p. 132.

into a wartime context. Similarly, in *The Long Voyage Home* (1940), from four one-act plays by Eugene O'Neill, Irish crew members on board an English navy vessel lie on deck with their bodies in the shape of a crucifix, ruminating upon exile from their native land, before enemy bombers approach to dispatch these sailors on their terminal voyage rather sooner than they had anticipated. This interest in martyrology also helps to lure Ford's sympathies in the direction of Confederate armies: in his references to the Civil War in *The Horse Soldiers* (1959) and elsewhere, the fated imminent demise of the South appears to be one of the qualities that attracts Ford's attention.

Ford was also drawn toward the South in reaction against what his films take to be the mean, cerebral narrow-mindedness at the centers of federal power. In *Rio Grande,* Wayne's Kirby Yorke complains bitterly about the State Department's ignorance of local conditions and its failure to provide him with enough troops to combat the Indians. In *Fort Apache* (1948), the same Wayne character comes into conflict with Henry Fonda's Owen Thursday, a theoretician of war who hankers after the politesse of the military academy and plans his assault on the Comanches along the lines of battles fought back in 1221. When the Irish-American soldier Michael O'Rourke (John Agar) takes Thursday's daughter off riding within range of the Comanche camp, he is scorned by Thursday as behaving like an "uncivilized Indian." One idea relevant here is Boelhower's tracing of a dichotomy in the theory of American identity between the universalizing structures established by the Enlightenment, which sought to impose a rational grid upon the land, as opposed to those ethnic, aleatory, and therefore oppositional energies implied by Indian culture: "a mobile, shifting semantics, a performative discourse that made no sense outside of its own local context."[10] If we follow this pattern, it is not hard to see how Ford identifies his own Irish-Catholic ethnicity with the Indian's traditional role of disenfranchised outsider. Indeed, toward the end of his life Ford himself stated:

> More than having received Oscars, what counts for me is having been made a blood brother of various Indian nations. Perhaps it's my Irish atavism, my sense of reality, of the beauty of clans, in contrast to the modern world, the masses, the collective irresponsibility. Who better than an Irishman could understand the Indians, while still being stirred by the tales of the U.S. Cavalry? We were on both sides of the epic.[11]

Ford's Catholicism becomes a lowercase catholicity, a delight in the ethnic cross-fertilization that disrupts the rigidly dualistic mentality associated in his films with the Yankee outlook. *Cheyenne Autumn* (1964)

10 Boelhower, *Through a Glass Darkly,* pp. 46, 63.
11 Gallagher, *John Ford,* p. 341.

resists the reification of Indians as the "other" in its depiction of the Cheyennes' flight from Oklahoma to the Yellowstone country, while the boisterous John Wayne character in both *She Wore a Yellow Ribbon* (1949) and *The Searchers* (1956) also comes to experience an unusual sense of empathy with Comanche culture. *The Grapes of Wrath* (1940) shows similar sympathy for outsiders forced into the experiences of displacement and exile, and in fact Ford later drew a parallel between *Grapes of Wrath* and the Irish famine of the 1840s, which induced his own father to flee to America.[12]

At the same time, it is essential to recognize that the status of problematic outsiderhood enjoyed by the Indian is not something that could satisfy Roman Catholic culture in the United States. One central paradox of American Catholicism is its aspiration toward universalism – "holy Catholic, apostolic, and universal Church" – in a country where it has traditionally represented a minority interest. In historical terms, this paradox produced the theological controversy in the early decades of this century around the issue of "Americanization": as we have seen, Catholic thinkers debated whether the Church should fight to maintain a separatist identity, or whether its long-term welfare would be better served by a closer integration within the dominant patterns of American cultural life. It was a sense of being situated within these conflicting pressures, between an inheritance of alienation on the one hand and an impulse toward assimilation on the other, that led Ford to take a double-edged attitude toward American mythologies, which he himself recognized when he said, "We were on both sides of the epic." I am talking here, of course, about subconscious cultural forces that operate in a subliminal way, as in Michael Fischer's model of how modern ethnicity functions within a transformed and amorphous idiom of consciousness, "through processes analogous to the dreaming and transference of psychoanalytic encounters."[13] But, in however circuitous a form this might emerge, it is partly because of his ethnic and religious background that the notion of the "frontier" in Ford becomes a self-reflexive trope indicating a radical ambivalence toward an American society where he, as an Irish Catholic, lives on the border.

The frontier in Ford's cinema, then, is not only a geographic place but also a psychological state of mind. Throughout his films we see an emphasis on the establishment of shared myths and community feeling, as in the weddings, the burials, the frequent renditions of "Shall We

---

12 Peter Bogdanovich, *John Ford* (London: Studio Vista, 1968), p. 76.
13 Michael M. J. Fischer, "Ethnicity and the Post-Modern Arts of Memory," *in Writing Culture: The Poetics and Politics of Ethnography* (Berkeley: Univ. of California Press, 1986), p. 196.

Gather at the River": these are the "sacramental" moments, engineered
by deep focus and wide-angle shots, and embodying the full potential
of comic ritual, that rhythm Susanne Langer described as "heightened
vitality, challenged wit and will, engaged in the great game with
Chance."[14] Indeed, it is one of the extraordinary aspects of Ford's pictures
that they possess an uncanny ability to mythologize events even as they
record them, so that the action seems to take place on two different levels
at once. At the same time, though, there is a knowingness about how
such myths are often invented specifically to serve the needs of a particular
community. *She Wore a Yellow Ribbon,* for example, is a patriotic epic
Western about the foundation of a society – "Wherever they rode and
whatever they fought for," declares a final voice-over, "that place became
the United States" – but at the same time the film's implicit identification
with Indians and with the unnamed, inglorious masses of slaughtered
cavalry soldiers reveals a more problematic side to this conservative
myth. Similarly, in both *Young Mr. Lincoln* (1939) and *Fort Apache* we
find a double perspective operating whereby the image Henry Fonda
will bequeath to posterity becomes more important to him, and to us,
than his incarnation as an individual person. In *Young Mr. Lincoln,* the
hero spends a lot of time inspecting his own image in the mirror and
the film's last shots are of statues of Lincoln, as if to signify his transposition from a historical to a symbolic entity. This myth-making process
is even more explicitly foregrounded in *The Man Who Shot Liberty Valance*
(1962), whose initial shot of a puffing steam engine introduces the film's
central smoke screen whereby the legend that it was James Stewart's
Stoddard – rather than, as was actually the case, John Wayne's Doniphon
– who disposed of Lee Marvin's dastardly Valance enables Stoddard to
embark upon his popular career as a senator and help transform the
wilderness of the West into a garden.

It is the fact that myth is intertwined with knowing irony in Ford's
cinema that produces, as Joseph McBride and Michael Wilmington noted,
an "odd synthesis of anarchism and authoritarianism which makes his
work equally attractive to those on both extremes of the political spectrum."[15] The ideological situation of Ford's cinema is notoriously difficult to pin down, because order is balanced off against anarchy to
produce films that, in their ambivalence, verge toward becoming parodies of the American Western genre. Ford's American Catholic sensibility, poised equivocally on the frontier of social conformity, produces
films that are both inside and outside the myth of the pioneering West:

14 Susanne Langer, *Feeling and Form: A Theory of Art* (New York: Scribner's, 1953),
   pp. 348–49.
15 McBride and Wilmington, *John Ford,* p. 21.

the ethnic expression here becomes a formalistic ambivalence. This merging of romanticism and irony is reflected in the mise-en-scène of Ford's cinema: in that frequent disjunction of perspective whereby an interior space or charmed circle (a church, a dance, a home) is played off against an all-encompassing view of wide open space surrounding it; and also in Ford's preference for neutral, distancing shots rather than over-the-shoulder angles, which might invite an audience to identify with one individual character. In *The Searchers,* we do not look with John Wayne at the Indians, we look at Wayne looking at the Indians. Characters are positioned within a structured space and become components of the landscape from which they emerge. In this sense, the vast rocks of Monument Valley operate as an essence around which the individual characters circulate as accidents, temporary embodiments of a changeless theme: "You said that tower over there looked like a cathedral back in Santa Fe," says Sandy (Harry Carey, Jr.) to Travis (Ben Johnson) on the journey westward in *Wagon Master.* The way in which Ford tended to use the same actors over and over again reinforces this impression of mere personal identity becoming tangential to wider issues of repetition and ritual.

As Northrop Frye pointed out, this form of ritual, which can contain and overcome an individual tragedy within itself, is most closely associated with the genre of comedy, whose etymological origins – Greek *komos,* revel or feast – indicate the traditional affiliation between comedy and social harmony.[16] In comedy, attention tends to be deflected away from personal suffering and focused instead upon the functioning of the group as a whole. Not for Ford the existentialist individualism of *High Noon;* rather, his films subvert individual dignity and propose an idiom of what we might call ontological burlesque, something that becomes fundamental to Ford's perception of human existence in the world. This ontological burlesque is intimately linked to Ford's residual Catholicism. G. K. Chesterton, a more theologically minded Catholic, expressed a similar notion when discussing cinema in his 1936 collection of essays *As I Was Saying:*

> merely lowbrow films seem to me much more moral than many of the highbrow ones. Mere slapstick pantomime, farces of comic collapse and social topsy-turvydom, are, if anything, definitely good for the soul. To see a banker or broker or prosperous business man running after his hat, kicked out of his house, hurled from the top of a skyscraper, hung by one leg to an aeroplane, put into a mangle, rolled out flat by a steam-roller, or suffering any such changes of fortune, tends in itself rather to edification; to a sense of the insecurity of earthly things and

16 Northrop Frye, *Anatomy of Criticism: Four Essays* (Princeton: Princeton Univ. Press, 1957), p. 175.

> the folly of that pride which is based on the accident of prosperity. But
> the films of which I complain are not those in which famous or fash-
> ionable persons become funny or undignified, but those in which they
> become far too dignified and only unintentionally funny.[17]

Chesterton's emphasis here is intently metaphysical: he believes the reversals of comic farce epitomize how men are all on the same level in
the sight of God, which is why slapstick is, in his view, "good for the
soul" (my emphasis). Ford shares this cast of mind: one hardly sees a
conscious theological impulse in those rough-and-tumble whisky drink-
ers scattered through his films who link his cinema with the Irish-
American vaudeville tradition of the nineteenth century; still, these
ragamuffins always operate as a threat to the pretentiousness of those
"far too dignified" characters (in Chesterton's phrase) who believe in
their own elective superiority. There is in Ford's moviemaking a touch
of gentle sadism that enjoys ridiculing his characters and witnessing their
indignity. One classic confrontation of this kind is in *Donovan's Reef*
(1963), where John Wayne, impersonating the Irish soak Michael Patrick
Donovan, mocks and finally quite literally upends Elizabeth Allen's Bostonian snob. Similarly, in *Seven Women* (1966) the more earthy Dr. Cart-
wright (Anne Bancroft) witnesses the psychological breakdown of the
narrow-minded Protestant missionary Miss Andrews (Margaret Leigh-
ton), who babbles on irrelevantly about sins of fornication and unclean-
liness when the more urgent issue of plague is gathering about her. The
wandering burlesque troupes in *My Darling Clementine* (1946) and *Wagon
Master* (1950), which produce parodic versions of Shakespeare and other
plays, might be understood in this light as offering self-reflexive comments upon Ford's cinematic enterprise as a whole. In *Clementine*, the
company led by Graville Thorndyke (Alan Mowbray) proceeds from
"The Convict's Oath" (a "Blood Chilling Drama") to a jokey version
of *Hamlet*, with Thorndyke's recitation of Hamlet's famous soliloquy
seeming to lampoon that nervous Protestant spirit by which the Dane
was agitated.

   In Ford's movies, then, everything is brought down to the same irredeemably comic level. Ford himself said toward the end of his career:
"I feel I'm essentially a comedy director, but they won't give me a
comedy to do" – though we should qualify this by adding that Ford's
films always reveal the comic elements inherent within any given situation.[18] As Constance Rourke has noted, this burlesque sensibility is
characteristic not only of American humor but of the American national

17 G. K. Chesterton, "About the Films," in *As I Was Saying* (Freeport, N.Y.: Books For
   Libraries Press, 1966), pp. 187–8.
18 Gallagher, *John Ford*, p. 269.

spirit generally, with its inclination to overturn the Old World vices of pomp and pretentiousness; moreover, Ford's predilection for deflation is also especially appropriate to the psychology of the West, whose vast landscapes dwarf and ridicule the more formalized, genteel manners of the Eastern seaboard.[19] But Ford's lingering Catholicism is also a significant component in this cultural matrix. We may recall how Tocqueville designated Catholics "the most democratic class in the United States" because, he said, their religion "subjects the wise and ignorant, the man of genius and the vulgar crowd, to the details of the same creed . . . reducing all the human race to the same standard, it confounds all the distinctions of society at the foot of the same altar, even as they are confounded in the sight of God."[20] The Catholic conception of democracy was, for Tocqueville, not so much a political as a theological idea. It revolved, as Chesterton similarly noted, around an intuition of the theological irrelevance and indeed farcical nature of human distinctions sub specie aeternitatis. It is this sense of the ridiculous that Ford's cinema also shares, a commitment to ritual involving a rigorous undermining of human vanity. For Ford, burlesque becomes a moral imperative.

Though Robert Altman's work shares some of Ford's characteristics, it is more elusive to analyze in terms of Catholic patterns. Altman was born in 1925 into a Catholic family in Kansas City, where his father and grandfather were both very active in church affairs. The family was of German ancestry – its original name was "Altmann" – and in the emphasis on festival and ritual within Altman's cinema we may detect a trace of that "folk flavor" of Midwestern German Catholic culture, whose "love of music, relaxed observance of the Sabbath, and opposition to the temperance movement," as Catherine Albanese has written, were very much at odds with the more ascetic attitudes of the immigrant Irish. In later life, Altman enigmatically described himself as a "closet German."[21]

Although Altman's children were baptized as Catholics, he himself is, unlike Ford, an apostate, having left the church about the same time as he joined the army in 1943. Gerald Plecki epitomized the attitude of most critics when he remarked of Altman that "religion never affected his life

19 Constance Rourke, *American Humor: A Study of the National Character* (Garden City: Anchor–Doubleday, 1955), p. 232.
20 Alexis de Tocqueville, *Democracy in America,* ed. Phillips Bradley (New York: Knopf, 1945), I, 311.
21 Catherine L. Albanese, *America: Religions and Religion* (Belmont, Ca.: Wadsworth, 1981), p. 74; Patrick McGilligan, *Robert Altman: Jumping Off The Cliff* (New York: St. Martin's Press, 1989), p. 25.

very much."[22] Certainly the religious culture is more subdued here, except perhaps for M*A*S*H (1970), which makes fairly clear analogies between the church and the army. As Altman said later: "Catholicism to me was school. It was restrictions; it was things you had to do. It was your parents. It was Mass on Sunday and fish on Friday. And then when I got out of that I got into the army. It was the same thing – you had to have a pass to get out."[23] Hence M*A*S*H satirizes oppressive military systems by comparing them to oppressive systems of religion. The film's mock version of "Onward Christian Soldiers" signifies how the army attempts to equate itself with Christianity as an institution demanding loyalty and obedience, but in M*A*S*H both forces fail miserably. Altman's compulsion here is to lampoon religion itself as much as the U.S. army. When the Painless Pole (John Schuck) finds himself the victim of sexual impotence and plans to commit suicide, Catholic priest Dago Red (René Auberjonois) worries anxiously about whether or not he is allowed to give absolution to a man about to end his own life; but this vexed question happily proves redundant as the Painless Pole's vital member enjoys a "mock resurrection" when Jo Ann Pflug's Lieutenant Dish comes on the scene.[24] M*A*S*H also includes a parodic version of the Last Supper, where the Holy Eucharist becomes equated with sexual potency (figure 5). The gleeful profanity here operates on the Joycean principle whereby satire of religion often implies an obsession with the forms and meanings of the religion being satirized.

This loss and absence of religious belief is a theme that manifests itself explicitly in two of Altman's later films. In the 1970 science fiction world of Quintet, Paul Newman's Essex finds himself stranded in an ice age city presided over by the autocratic figure of "Saint Christopher" (Vittorio Gassman). Saint Christopher wears crucifixes and mumbles Latin prayers; he also harps on about "the geometric shape of the universe," which he declares to have five stages – birth, maturing, living, aging, and death – with an empty "void" at the center. He advises Essex to while away the time in this godforsaken city by playing the game of quintet, the pattern of which reflects Saint Christopher's gloomy image of life. Indeed, quintet is compulsory in this city: "limbo" has been redefined as the name of a zone on the quintet playing board. Saint Christopher, who believes "hope is an obsolete word," is a high priest of the metaphysical vacuum that surrounds this desolate arena; his cassock is white rather than black, as if to mirror the frozen wastes outside. But Newman's Essex finally decides to reject these rigid structures, and at

22 Gerald Plecki, Robert Altman (Boston: Twayne, 1985), p. 1.
23 Alan Karp, The Films of Robert Altman (Metuchen, N.J.: Scarecrow Press, 1981), p. 5.
24 Keyser, Hollywood and the Catholic Church, p. 190.

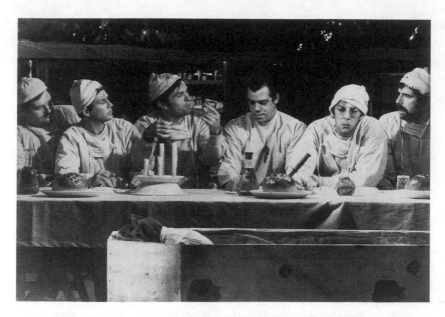

Figure 5. Robert Altman's parody of the Last Supper in *M*A*S*H*

the end of the film he leaves the city to set out on a lone voyage "north," opting for the more dignified and heroic gesture of self-extinction.

As in *M*A*S*H*, religion in *Quintet* connotes oppression and suffocation. It produces the kind of environment toward which the only appropriate response is rebellion. However, in *Come Back to the Five and Dime, Jimmy Dean, Jimmy Dean* (1982), based upon a play by Ed Graczyk, Altman's interrogation of the psychological complexities of belief moves into a more equivocal area. This film rotates around the myth of James Dean, which swiftly becomes conflated with the martyrdom of Christ: a song asking "Must Jesus Bear the Cross Alone?" plays under the opening sequences, together with pictures of Dean and Christ, and later one image of Dean appears to be bleeding, like Christ crucified. The scene takes place at a reunion of "the Disciples of James Dean" twenty years to the day after the star's fatal accident, with the past lives of the Texas "Disciples" being acted out behind a two-way mirror. Sandy Dennis's Mona suffers here from what Cher's Sissy calls a "Mona Magdalene" complex: Mona believes she was the one chosen "from everybody else to bring his child into this world" – Dean's child, that is, not Christ's – and she is decidedly reluctant to face up to the fact that the night of love she spent twenty years ago was with a local lad who recommended himself to her because of a physical resemblance to Dean. "Believing is so funny isn't it," muses the cranky old storekeeper Juanita, "when what you believe in doesn't even know you exist." Dean, like God, is an absent deity, a shadow who haunts their lives without ever revealing himself. Juanita (Sudie Bond) appears as a Bible Belt fundamentalist cherishing the image of her late husband, Sidney, hobnobbing in heaven with the Almighty, but Jo (Karen Black) destroys her illusion by un-covering how Sidney was actually an alcohol-sodden wretch who kept a bottle under the counter and died of a decayed liver. Juanita finds her worldview shaken: "I wonder why it was that my God turned away from me like that?" "I just think," replies Sissy, "that there's so many people in the world nowadays that it's hard for him to give the personal attention that he used to." As a special concession to relieve some of this divine burden, Sissy reveals that "I don't pray no more, I gave it up for Lent."

Just as Christianity in *M★A★S★H* and *Quintet* is represented as foolishly authoritarian, so Altman commented that he saw *Come Back to the Five and Dime* as an attempt "to undo this God thing, to find out the truth. I don't like the idea of superstars – they're an excuse for the masses not to think about their own problems."[25] But the paradox in this film is that the characters continue urgently to seek some form of belief, which has become an emotional and psychological necessity long after any rational justifications for such belief have evaporated. Indeed, much of Altman's cinema has focused upon ways in which popular myths or media legends might operate as surrogate systems of communal faith in a postreligious era. James Dean was in fact also the subject of one of Altman's first films, a documentary made in 1957 that balances skeptical demystification with covert worship of its idol. "We weren't as tough on him as we originally had intended to be," remarked Altman later. In similar fashion, Altman attacked Tom Laughlin, the (allegedly) egotist-ical star of his 1957 movie *The Delinquents,* on the grounds that Laughlin suffered from a "big Catholic hang-up," a sense of guilt that he had not become a priest, and what Altman revealingly called a "James Dean complex." As we saw earlier, Frank O'Hara was also obsessed with the legend of the self-punishing Dean, a legend O'Hara's residual Catholic sensibility implicitly admired even as his tough materialism explicitly rejected it. In Altman's careful alienation of himself from the institutions of Hollywood and in his proclivity to court financial disaster in the service of personal artistic ideals, Altman's biographer, Patrick McGilligan, has suggested there has been more than a touch of Dean-like martyrdom about the film director's own career.[26]

We find in Altman, then, a profound ambivalence toward social cus-toms. On one hand, his films cherish the rebellious outsiders, the alien-

25 Quoted in Robert Self, "Robert Altman and the Theory of Authorship," *Cinema Journal,* 25, no. 1 (Fall 1985), 8.
26 McGilligan, *Robert Altman,* pp. 124, 111, 201.

ated, those on the margins of sanity and respectability: Susannah York's obsessed, enigmatic character in *Images* (1972), the schizophrenic heroines of *Three Women* (1977), Richard Nixon on the edge of a nervous breakdown in *Secret Honor* (1983). On the other hand, though, the Catholic communitarian spirit of Altman is, as William Parrill remarked, concerned with "the public groupings that hold men together" and so is always ensuring these isolated individuals somehow become related back to the manners of the larger world they have spurned.[27] Philip Baker Hall's Richard Nixon in *Secret Honor* is a good example of this, for although Nixon is the only character in the film and speaks to the camera in a frenzied private monologue, he must also exist simultaneously within the framework of his public image and legend, as the plethora of television and video screens on the walls of his White House office indicate. Similarly, in the underestimated *O. C. and Stiggs* (1987), the anarchic impulses of the rebellious teenage heroes are played off against the self-advertising television rhetoric of Randall Schwab (Paul Dooley), an insurance magnate in Phoenix, Arizona, whose gloriously vulgar, nouveau riche wedding party for his daughter is spoofed – but not altogether satirized – by the youthful pair. The protesters must always have something to protest against.

Other Altman representations of popular myths include Robin Williams self-consciously cherishing his media stardom in *Popeye* (1981) and Dick Cavett playing himself as a famous talk show host in *Health* (1982). Altman's best-known celebration of secular ritual, though, is *Nashville* (1975), where the audience's attention is directed toward such corporate mythologies as the institution of country and western music, the race for the presidency, and the impending bicentennial celebrations. Significantly, all these public images are filmed in Altman's characteristic style: refracted and reproduced through glass doors, mirrors, advertisements, television newscasts. *Nashville* is not so much concerned with defining these icons in and for themselves as in apprehending how they are perceived within the modulations of the wider world. These myths of society become explicitly equated with the rituals of Catholicism when the film focuses upon several statues of Madonnas in the bedroom of Sueleen Gay (Gwen Welles), an apprentice country singer who worships Ronee Blakley's Barbara Jean and who tries (ineptly) to emulate her idol, practicing her imitative act in the dressing table mirror. Moreover, during the movie we look in upon Catholic, Baptist, and Black Revivalist church services; sacred symbols of old merge into sacred symbols of the new, as secular

27 William Parrill, "Robert Altman," in *Religion in Film*, ed. John R. May and Michael Bird (Knoxville: Univ. of Tennessee Press, 1982), p. 136.

society becomes apotheosized. Caught up within these redemptive mythic structures, the characters eulogize their own loss of individual freedom: "You may say / That I ain't free / But it don't worry me" runs the film's final song. Altman's frequent trick of sudden jump cutting at unorthodox moments, with its consequent defiance of the conventional logic of narrative, implies how any dramatic closure will be avoided here and how the epic institution of "Nashville" will simply roll on and on.

As Fredric Jameson has pointed out, in any textual narrative the "formal processes" become "sedimented content in their own right . . . carrying ideological messages of their own, distinct from the ostensible or manifest content of the works."[28] As the ideology of religion is no exception to this rule, it is crucial to recognize how a residual Catholicism is embedded in the formalistic patterns of Altman's movies as much as in their "manifest content," such as statues of Christ and the Virgin Mary. It may not be too fanciful to draw a parallel between Frank O'Hara's long, kaleidoscopic poetic lines and the sweeping, panoramic style of Altman's wide-angled cinema: in both cases there is a desire to reveal the arbitrariness of hierarchies, both aesthetic and social, and to focus instead upon the immanent glories of natural creation. The French filmmaker Eric Rohmer, a strict practicing Catholic, has theorized this particular kind of formal artistic language with some precision. Rohmer, crucially influenced by his fellow French Catholic and friend André Bazin, argued in 1951 that the cinema is uniquely able to capture reality and to communicate a faithful vision of the world because the camera offers a direct mimesis of the external world: not a literary description of the object, but the object itself. For Rohmer, the filmmaker can thus introduce the dimension of Christian morality by suppressing his own personal fantasies and instead focusing faithfully upon what is impersonal and "God-given":

> The task of art is not to confine us in a hermetic world of its own making. Born of things, it brings us back to things . . . curing the artist of that self-love which everywhere is destroying him. . . . Fascinated by his model, the artist forgets the order he had intended in his arrogance to impose on it, and in so doing, reveals the true harmony of nature, its essential unity. The song becomes a hymn, a prayer.[29]

Rohmer's thesis should not be seen as universally valid, of course; it is an ideological aesthetic emerging specifically from the tenets of Cathol-

28 Fredric Jameson, *The Political Unconscious: Narrative as a Socially Symbolic Act* (Ithaca: Cornell Univ. Press, 1981), p. 99.
29 Eric Rohmer, "Vanité qui la peinture," *Cahiers du Cinéma*, no. 3 (Aug. 1951), p. 28. Translated in C. G. Crisp, *Eric Rohmer: Realist and Moralist* (Bloomington: Indiana Univ. Press, 1988), p. 4.

icism. Nevertheless, it is this kind of aesthetic that Altman (and Frank O'Hara) share: a disavowal of personal "liberty" and subjectivity, a suspicion of the "arrogance" of self-expression, a preference for collapsing conventional aesthetic proportions and exposing texts to the impersonal largesse of the wide, wide world. Although the stress laid by Bazin and Rohmer on cinema's access to an unproblematical "reality" might now seem somewhat dated and theoretically unsophisticated, Altman's consistently parodic impulse actually operates with very similar motives, for its purpose is to subvert the mechanical clichés of Hollywood cinema so as to infuse these stereotyped images with a sense of the unpredictable, off-balance contingencies of human life. Altman's style of realism works in a different way from Rohmer's, but the essential strategy of impersonality derives from kindred cultural sources.

Pursuing further Jameson's line about the symbiotic interaction of ideological form and content, we can see that the idea of ritual dominates *A Wedding* (1978) not only in its thematic analysis of marriage and representation of the Episcopalian Brenner and Italian-American Catholic Corelli families, but also in the film's visual composition, which is designed to twin everything with its contrary. The groom, Dino Corelli (Desi Arnaz, Jr.), has a twin sister; a shot of men rushing for the lavatory is intercut with a shot of women rushing for the lavatory; the symbolic rebirth of marriage is twinned with the adjacency of death, as the groom's aged grandmother (Lillian Gish) chooses this celebration as an appropriate place in which to expire. The film describes an interpenetrating simultaneity depriving characters of individual dignity by a process of comic ritual that twins everybody with his neighbor in a ritual of consumption and excretion, life and death. As the Brenner bedrooms all have mirror-covered walls, the reduplication of these characters in the glass also acts as a formal correlative to this sense of splitting and entwinement.

My point is that these "formal processes" arise out of a culture of transformed Catholicism. As we have seen, many Catholic philosophers have stressed the significance of "analogy" and the "analogical imagination," the "key to the resemblances of all things," as providing "a metaphysical explanation of the structure of existence, indeed of all that exists."[30] This concept, deriving ultimately from Aristotle and Aquinas and disseminated after the Second World War by Catholic intellectuals such as Jacques Maritain and William F. Lynch, holds that each part of God's creation exists in a state of continuous interaction with the essential

30 William F. Lynch, *Christ and Apollo: The Dimensions of the Literary Imagination* (New York: Sheed and Ward, 1960), p. 149.

whole, or "primal cause" as Maritain put it.[31] In the "analogical order," said Lynch, we find an "*interpenetration* of unity and multiplicity, sameness and difference."[32] It is a reworking of Aquinas's argument in the *Summa Theologiae* about how the existence of earthly accident is always contingent upon God's essential being, so that any terrestrial incarnation can always be referred back to the divine center by means of what Maritain called the "infinite mirrors of analogy."[33] According to Catholic thought, the opposite to this analogical imagination is the "univocal," a romantic or solipsistic cast of mind that "wishes to reduce and flatten everything to the terms of its own sameness," exactly the kind of cinematic style critiqued by Rohmer and Altman. The neo-scholastics, we will recall, associated this univocal imagination with "angelism," the doomed attempt on man's part to elevate himself to the status of a quasi-divine being by aspiring to "shut himself off in solitude from man and God in order that he may stand brilliantly on his own."[34]

Now, it is by no means the intention here to suggest that Altman's films carefully follow the dictates of neo-scholastic dogma; but this system of thought, transferred from a theological to a culturally materialist context, affects the work of Altman in the same way as it affected the fictions of James Joyce, Luis Buñuel, and other Jesuit-educated lapsed Catholics. Just as *A Wedding* formalistically and thematically emphasizes analogies and resemblances among heterogeneous groups of people, so the central theme of *Brewster McCloud* (1970) is the communal nature of social life, the necessary sharing and indeed interchangeability of human characteristics. In this film, the hero's Faustian ambitions and efforts to fly are burlesqued by a system of analogies between birds and human beings, so that a series of linguistic and conceptual puns is established whereby human and animal behavior become interchangeable. The lecturer on ornithology – who begins visually to resemble a bird himself – orates on how "among forms of behavior which show great stereotypes are those that have to do with care of the body surface," while the frequent interruptions of bird droppings are analogically mirrored by Suzanne's discussion of how she gets diarrhea whenever she eats Mexican food. Scatology, indeed, plays a dominant role in the movie: there is even a plan at one point to call in a "scatologist" from the University of Houston to help the Texas police solve the murders that in fact Brewster has been committing. The scatology here signifies a desire to pour

31 Jacques Maritain, *Creative Intuition in Art and Poetry* (New York: Pantheon–Bollingen Foundation, 1953), p. 127.
32 Lynch, *Christ and Apollo*, p. 141.
33 Maritain, *Creative Intuition in Art and Poetry*, p. 128.
34 Lynch, *Christ and Apollo*, pp. 107, 80.

dirt on everybody. Everything is mocked and debunked: even the police lieutenants are deprived of their Steve McQueenesque glamor and reduced to reading "Captain America" comics, for Altman's film is designed to demonstrate how American society forms one mad, mutually interdependent circus, whose components are all punningly entwined with each other.

This is why Bud Cort's Brewster crashes dead at the end of the narrative. By attempting to fly, he was aspiring to transcend the communal funhouse, whose social unity is celebrated at the beginning of the film by a version of "Stars and Stripes." In M★A★S★H, the ubiquity of sexual desire invalidates the army's supposedly higher purpose; in Brewster McCloud, it is the universality of bodily functions that links the social fabric together. In the terms of Catholic theology, Brewster is a univocal character who, despite himself, becomes assimilated within an analogical order. This order is explicitly illuminated in one scene where Brewster has taken Suzanne's car by mistake, confusing it for his own, whereupon he notes that she has a statue on the windscreen exactly resembling the one belonging to him. "That's the Virgin Mary," replies Shelley Duvall's Suzanne, "that used to be really popular a long time ago." In Brewster McCloud, the universalism of religion has been transformed into the universalism of scatology, sexuality, and media mythologies – appropriately enough, the temple in the Houston amusement park has been renamed the "Shirley Temple" – but the emphasis is still upon what is "popular" and accessible to the whole of society. The romantic hero finds himself trumped by the infinite mirrors of analogy.

Some feminist critics have complained about Altman's degrading representations of women in M★A★S★H, Brewster McCloud, and other films, but for Altman, as for Ford, that touch of sadism implicit in burlesque humor becomes a moral imperative. Just as G. K. Chesterton deemed "comic collapse" to be "good for the soul," so the Jesuit critic William Lynch declared comedy to be the most ethical of artistic forms:

> It gets below all the categories within which the most of life is spent and destroys the most of these categories (the rich, the proud, the mighty, the beautiful, the style, the Joneses) in its descent. . . . Comedy is perpetually reminding the uprooted great man that in some important sense he was once, and still is, a bit of a monkey.[35]

Or, as Altman himself once put it, "Can you find somebody who isn't somewhat of a fool?"[36] We saw how back in the nineteenth century Orestes Brownson was often accused by the Catholic hierarchy of "on-

35 Ibid., pp. 91, 97.
36 Judith M. Kass, Robert Altman: American Innovator (New York: CBS–Popular Library, 1978), p. 230.

tologism," the notion, heretical within orthodox Catholic theology, that man could come to an intuitive knowledge of God by apprehending him directly through his worldly creations. For the Scholastics, this conflation of God with the natural world verged dangerously upon pantheism. But Altman, reckless of theological "truth" and in no sense a religious philosopher, curiously imitates Brownson by hinting, through his cinematic mode of ontological burlesque, at an intuitive knowledge of "sacred" presence. One of the oddest contributions to a 1979 volume on why public figures profess Catholicism featured an essay by journalist John Deedy, where Deedy claimed that his lapsed faith had been restored to its former serenity by a screening of *Nashville:* "I shouldn't confess it, but this is the way I got my handle on my Catholicism . . . it was a wonderfully diverting film, and for me it was more. . . . It's the shallowest of reasons for being Catholic, very likely, but there it is."[37] Deedy was quite unable to conceptualize why this film should have exercized such a profound effect on him, but his reaction does serve to emphasize how Altman's form of comedy, with its emphasis on analogy and burlesque, emerges to some extent from a latent metaphysical framework.

The Long Goodbye (1973) perfectly illustrates William Lynch's thesis of the "analogical order" being the "home of the comic," especially in its depiction of the sorry plight of Sterling Hayden's blocked writer, Roger Wade.[38] *The Long Goodbye* is, as Pauline Kael remarked, a veritable *Finnegans Wake* of the media world, piling allusion upon allusion. The figure of Elliott Gould's Philip Marlowe recalls many earlier screen actors, from Humphrey Bogart onwards; Marlowe's final comic waddle back through the alley after murdering Jim Bouton's Terry Lennox (to the strains of "Hooray for Hollywood") echoes both Carol Reed's famous film *The Third Man* and the ending of many Chaplin movies; similarly, for his portrayal of the rogue psychiatrist, Dr. Verringer, Henry Gibson intertextually trades off his role in the 1960s television comedy *Rowan and Martin's Laugh-In*.[39] There are any number of other examples. However, this "bisociative" technique, as Alan Karp has called it, does not constitute merely a tricksy collection of cinematic *hommages;* rather, it induces a universe of moral reflection, emphasizing the same kind of mirroring and interchangeability that we saw in *Brewster McCloud*.[40] The film is constructed upon Maritain's "infinite mirror of analogies," and though Hollywood here has superseded God as the prime cause, never-

37 John Deedy, "Why Catholic? Why Not?," in *Why Catholic?*, ed. John J. Delaney (Garden City: Doubleday, 1979), p. 40.
38 Lynch, *Christ and Apollo*, p. 108.
39 Pauline Kael, "Movieland – The Bums' Paradise," in *Reeling* (Boston: Little, Brown and Co., 1976), p. 187.
40 Karp, *Films of Robert Altman*, p. 45.

theless this oscillation between essence and accident – Hollywood archetype and its contemporary existential incarnation – is a fictional replication of those philosophical structures recommended by the Jesuits. Instead of an analogical order between human and divine, Altman posits an analogical order between human and Hollywood.

It is just this world of analogical reflection Roger Wade attempts to escape from. "I'm a man cannot stand confinement" thunders Wade, with the kind of crazed, phallic romanticism that refuses any acquiescence in human limits. "When a writer can't write," he says, "it's like being impotent." Wade is another version of Brewster McCloud, someone determined to dominate and overhaul the world in his own outsize person; but this individualism turns to frustrated alienation, and then to suicide as Wade drowns himself in the Pacific Ocean. Even in his death, however, Wade is deprived of sublimity: when he sets off into the ocean it is in a remote corner of the frame, while the camera focuses on Marlowe conversing with Wade's wife in the foreground. Moreover, in this grand gesture of suicide Wade still finds himself compromised by the mirrors of irony, for Wade is in fact only reflecting the fate of Norman Maine, who took a terminal stroll into the sea several years earlier in *A Star Is Born*. Roger Wade is a prime example of the "univocal" or "angelic" mind posing as the exclusive interpreter of an uncertain world and attempting to translate the energy of the human will into a form of infinity. As always with Altman, there is some sympathy for the eccentric and anarchic outsider; yet the comic and parodic structure of Altman's film ultimately denies Wade his cherished romantic singularity and instead places Marlowe in his traditional role of moral arbiter. Whereas Wade attempts to eradicate analogical irony, Marlowe thrives upon it. Because he knows he is only playing a role in an old movie, a role that has been acted out before, Marlowe does not trouble himself with internalized psychology: "Do you ever think of suicide, Marlowe?" Wade asks. "Me, I don't believe in it," replies Marlowe. Accordingly, the private eye contents himself with the surfaces of Los Angeles and with witty impersonations of the parts he has to play. While Wade attempts to accommodate the universe to his private dreams, Marlowe seems to welcome his fragmented self and his incarnation as the secondary accident of some primary, preexistent essence. Remarks made about *The Long Goodbye* by Altman himself shortly after completing the film are, unbeknown to the director no doubt, Erasmus-like in their disdain for romantic heroism and their rigorous praise of folly: "Most people who are considered heroes are always to be found messing about in someone else's affairs, and I don't think that's very heroic. I guess I have a great deal of affection for fools. I consider myself one. . . . I think being a fool is the only way to be."[41]

41 Jan Dawson, "Robert Altman Speaking," *Film Comment,* 10, no. 2 (1974), 41.

None of this, of course, is to imply that Altman should be seen as a "Catholic" filmmaker in the narrow sense. Indeed, there is a double deconstruction of theology at work here. In the first place, Altman exploits the cultural patterns of Catholic thought without paying any attention to the metaphysical origins by which these patterns are supposedly sanctioned. In the second place, we can see that even the moral imperatives established by this cultural language are in fact codes deriving from one particular and limited ideology. William Lynch asserted that the analogical imagination is "right" and the univocal imagination "wrong," but there is no attempt to make such clear-cut judgments in this analysis; we are concerned simply with how these fictions of theology have worked their way into Altman's imagination.[42] Compare Lynch's prospectus for "what makes a playwright" –

> He should know a great deal, and this in terms of his own blood stream, about the dance and ritual in the oldest and widest senses of these terms. . . . He should be a man who delights in the coronation of a queen or the inauguration of a President, who delights generally in a public style of life for man. He should know history and not think that his private mind can alone create a theatre.

– with Altman's insistence of filmmaking as:

> a collaborative art. I set a boundary line and framework, but I don't try to fill it all in. If I tried to put in the middle of it everything that was in my imagination, it would be simply that. It would be a very sterile work. So I try to fill it with things I've never seen before, things that come from other people.[43]

Like John Ford, Altman opens out his films to the wide screens of ritual and areas of public belief that expand beyond his own personal concerns. Both Ford and Altman veer toward analogical universalism in their work, the paradox being that these universalist tendencies can be related back to a very specific cultural inheritance. Altman is indeed a director who "delights in . . . the inauguration of a President," as we see not only from *Nashville* but also from the television series *Tanner '88*, created jointly by Altman and Jules Feiffer, which charts the progress of a fictional candidate during the 1988 presidential contest.

One consequence of this representation of politics as ritual is that the mode of Altman's fictions is, characteristically, disinterested irony rather than polemic or satire. For instance, as Leonard Quart has noted, in Altman's 1974 film *Thieves Like Us* the depression of the 1930s is never invoked as a cause underlying the behavior of outlaws Bowie (Keith

42 Lynch, *Christ and Apollo*, p. xiii.
43 Lynch, *Christ and Apollo*, p. 182; Altman quoted in Jonathan Rosenbaum, "Improvisations and Interactions in Altmanville," *Sight and Sound*, 44 (1975), 92.

Carradine) and Keechie (Shelley Duvall).[44] In the original 1937 Edward Anderson novel, their criminality is blamed on an inequitable social system; in Nicholas Ray's 1949 version of the story, Bowie and Keechie emerge as sanctified loners, tense and brooding rebels without a cause who devote themselves to protest against the world of social convention; but while Ray's version is protest-ant, Altman's is catholic, for Altman's thieves are antiheroic comedians content to play games of bank robbery in parody of the institutionalized thievedom they see around them. As T-Dub (Bert Remsen) puts it, "them capitalist fellows are thieves like us." Altman's Bowie and Keechie violate the first principles of a successful criminal career by deliberately seeking publicity and delighting to read about their own exploits in the newspapers. Whereas Nicholas Ray's characters scrupulously alienate themselves from the world, Altman's thieves desire to infiltrate society and become celebrities, listening to tales of "Gangbusters" and the "International Secret Police" on the radio and validating themselves by their proximity to this glamorous model. *Thieves Like Us* represents another example of Altman's universalism: omnipresent throughout the mise-en-scène are the modern madonnas of Coca-Cola advertisements – even the Mississippi State Penitentiary sign is flanked by Coca-Cola motifs – and, true to their interpellation within these corporate structures, all of Altman's characters dutifully respond by calling for ice-cold Cokes.

This absence of a social polemic in *Thieves Like Us* can also be located within the context of Catholic theology. One of the reasons Catholicism favors a ritualistic universalism is that its creed pays relatively little attention to the problems of human ugliness or evil. As we have seen, the Puritan sensibility is much closer to the Manichaean notion of evil being equally as powerful a force as good; but Thomas Aquinas observed that "the existence of *all things* derives from divine beauty" (my emphasis) because evil, according to Aquinas, betokens nothing more than a lack of the appropriate divine harmony and does not constitute any form of autonomous energy. As Maritain summarized the argument: "There are things deprived in some respect of due proportion, radiance, or integrity, but in which Being still abounds, and which keep on pleasing the sight to that very extent. For a pure intellect, everything is a kind of spatio-temporal number, as Pythagoras saw it."[45] Therefore for Altman the foolish or the stupid or even the immoral are essential numbers in a wider geometric pattern. In *Thieves Like Us,* he is not so interested in opposing capitalists to proletariat as in demonstrating the resemblances of these

---

44 Leonard Quart, "On Altman: Image as Essence," *Marxist Perspectives*, I, no. I (Spring 1978), 121–2.
45 Maritain, *Creative Intuition in Art and Poetry*, p. 164.

two groups, how they are both part of the same all-inclusive system. Similarly, in *Nashville,* the dim-witted song of Haven Hamilton (Henry Gibson) about how the United States "must be doing something right to last two hundred years" is hilarious, but not necessarily satirical. Altman deconstructs American myths and implies how they are brought into being, but, as he stated in a 1976 interview, he does not seek to annul these categories: "My attitudes and my political statements . . . aren't nearly as harsh as people seem to think. When *Nashville* came out, there was this wild reaction: 'Oh, what a terrible view of America!' It's a view of America, all right, but I don't agree that it's terrible. I'm not condemning America." Altman went on to say that he opposed "complacency" and "the feeling that any way we do things must be the right way."[46] But that is a long way from what Robert Phillip Kolker deemed Altman's "fundamentally desolate vision," his "bitter observation of domination and passivity, of assent to ritual and assumption of cultural myths," or from James Monaco's assertion that "Altman's people are universally addicted to an American mythos . . . to which their own reality never measures up. Altman doesn't seem to want to let them take action, and that is a major and unavoidable criticism of the theory of his work."[47]

While such political criticism may be valid enough in its own way, it does not seem to recognize the culturally specific ethos of Altman's cinema. Rather than confrontations of good and evil, the primary concern of Altman's films is to delineate landscapes of community and ritual where events unfold with a random contingency that is never purely aleatory but rather imbued with a kind of zany inevitability, as the hazards of existence are reflected back by the "infinite mirrors of analogy" to an essential whole. Whereas Kolker complained about the compulsive ritual and "passivity" in Altman's work, Andy Warhol gleefully seized upon a kindred spirit, noting in his diary how much he approved of the plotless format of *A Wedding* and observing that "Altman's doing all the things we tried to do in the late sixties and early seventies."[48] Nor is it coincidental that, as with Warhol, several of the acolytes in Altman's circle have come from a Catholic background. Scriptwriter Brian McKay, for instance, who worked with Altman on several early films, remarked on how the Jesuit education that he and Altman experienced may have been "the bond we had without ever discussing it."[49]

46 "The *Playboy* Interview: Robert Altman," *Playboy,* Aug. 1976, p. 55.
47 Robert Phillip Kolker, *A Cinema of Loneliness: Penn, Kubrick, Coppola, Scorsese, Altman* (New York: Oxford Univ. Press, 1980), pp. 323, 338; James Monaco, *American Film Now* (New York: Plume–New American Library, 1979), p. 326.
48 *The Andy Warhol Diaries,* ed. Pat Hackett (New York: Warner, 1989), p. 56.
49 McGilligan, *Robert Altman,* p. 244.

This passivity and political indeterminacy is another aspect linking Altman's cinema with John Ford's work. Ford's acknowledgment of how he was "on both sides of the epic" is reconstituted in Altman's stance as "simultaneously contemptuous and in love with his America," as Leonard Quart put it.[50] As we have seen, there is a specific social context for this, insofar as Ford's films operate within forms of gentle parody, poised in that familiar American Catholic way between the pressures of assimilation and the pressures of alienation, a pattern Altman's pictures take up as well. But there is also a transformed theological context at work here, as both Ford and Altman reject the dialectic of good and evil, opting instead for an all-embracing universalism. Their styles of filmmaking, with a heavy emphasis on ritual and a consequent tendency to disrupt and dislocate the solipsistic vision of any one individual character, operate in tandem with this thematic impulse. The frequent dances and hymn singing in Ford's films can be seen as a parallel to the overlapping dialogue and almost continuous use of panning in Altman's work.[51] Both directors describe wide open landscapes where characters merge and overlap, bound together as contingent components of secular (and, in Ford's case, religious) myths. Altman once said: "It's an impression . . . of total character and total atmosphere that I am in. What happens because of what." Both that sense of totality, and also the idea of things existing not as isolated objects but in terms of their relation to one another – "What happens because of what" – are crucial to the work of Ford as well as Altman.[52] Both filmmakers secularize the Catholic conception of materialized analogy, which emphasizes visible resemblances between disparate entities; and as a result of this they both discover a moral imperative in the form of comedy, through which social distinctions are obliterated as the structure of burlesque ensures that everybody comes to resemble everybody else in the sight of that entity Derrida would term (God).

This appearance of a religious heritage in Ford and Altman's work does not, of course, in any way undermine their status as "American" artists. As Werner Sollors has argued, distinctions between "ethnic" and "American" artists have historically tended to be far too simplistic. Just as the works of Eugene O'Neill, Carl Sandburg, Vladimir Nabokov, and many other "American" authors possess a latent ethnic component that coexists simultaneously with American idioms, so in the cinema of Ford and Altman we can perceive residual forms of religious ethnicity

50 Quart, "On Altman," p. 118.
51 Commenting on Altman's use of panning, Michael Tarantino has estimated there are no more than twenty static shots in the entire 111 minutes of The Long Goodbye. See "Movement as Metaphor: The Long Goodbye," Sight and Sound, 44 (1975), 98.
52 Kass, Robert Altman, p. 21.

operating in subtle and "unexpected combinations" that materially affect the texts' final shape.[53] Catholicism does not provide any underlying "explanation" of these filmmakers' work; but a religious ideology, often transferred from a metaphysical to a materialist context, is, for Ford and Altman, one force that illuminates their vision.

53 Werner Sollors, *Beyond Ethnicity: Consent and Descent in American Culture* (New York: Oxford Univ. Press, 1986), pp. 241–3.

14

Guilt and Salvation: Alfred Hitchcock and Martin Scorsese

Like John Ford's, Alfred Hitchcock's career in the filmmaking business began in the era of silent movies and spanned some fifty years. Like Ford's again, Hitchcock's family background was Irish Catholic. He attended St. Ignatius College in London and in later years would reminisce fondly about the ingenious methods of corporal punishment devised by the Jesuit fathers, who would make their victims wait in lengthy, torturous suspense before meting out the allotted sentence. Hitchcock's relationship with the Catholic church in his adult life is less easy to determine. We know he regularly attended mass in England before his emigration to the United States in 1939, though Donald Spoto has suggested this may have been simply a demonstration of piety to appease his mother and other family members. We know as well that Hitchcock's daughter Patricia was raised a Catholic. By the end of his life, though, Hitchcock's faith seems to have been practiced less diligently and he became very wary of priests. "I have a conscience with lots of trials over beliefs," he remarked enigmatically.[1] When asked by François Truffaut in 1966 how he felt about "being labeled a Catholic artist," Hitchcock's response was equally shifty:

> That's a rather difficult question, and I'm not sure I can give you a precise answer. I come from a Catholic family and I had a strict, religious upbringing. My wife converted to Catholicism before our marriage. I don't think I can be labeled a Catholic artist, but it may be that one's early upbringing influences a man's life and guides his instinct. . . . I am definitely not anti-religious; perhaps I'm sometimes neglectful.[2]

1 "Hitchcock: Part One," dir. Tristram Powell, *Omnibus*, BBC Television, 26 Sept. 1986; Donald Spoto, *The Dark Side of Genius: The Life of Alfred Hitchcock* (New York: Ballantine, 1984), pp. 129, 590.
2 François Truffaut, *Hitchcock*, 2nd ed. (New York: Simon and Schuster, 1984), pp. 316–17.

324

However "neglectful" he may have been, Hitchcock's 1980 funeral in Beverly Hills was presided over by his long-standing Jesuit friend Father Thomas Sullivan, who had served as theological adviser on Hitchcock's only explicitly religious film, *I Confess,* made in 1952.[3]

Hitchcock occupies a unique place within the framework of this study in that he is the only artist to be considered here who was born outside the United States. He was in fact born in Leytonstone, England, in 1899; he came to America at the age of thirty-nine and subsequently took American citizenship in 1955. Despite Hitchcock's English origins, there is general agreement it is the American films in the period between *Shadow of a Doubt* (1943) and *The Birds* (1963) that constitute the director's claim to greatness. Robin Wood has said that although the earlier British films have "a freshness and spontaneity that the far more carefully composed later films lack," nevertheless the latter "are characterized by a creative intensity that makes a preference for the British films analogous to preferring *The Comedy of Errors* to *Macbeth.*"[4] In part, this may be a result simply of artistic maturation; yet it may be as well that America helped Hitchcock to develop and sophisticate his peculiar cinematic vision. Leytonstone in the early twentieth century might almost have counted as an ethnic community, so heavy was its preponderance of Irish Catholic families who blended comfortably into that atmosphere of sharp cockney humor and criminal – or at least quasi-criminal – activities prevalent in London's East End. In Hitchcock's earliest films, we sometimes get the feeling crime is a familiar way of life, connected not so much with "evil" as with a marginalized community's desire to express its resentments against the dominant social order. (It is exactly this impulse toward vengeance that energized the vituperative black comedies made at Ealing Studios in the late 1940s and 1950s.) Hitchcock himself later expressed a sense of this narrowness when he described Britain as "insular" and "class-conscious" and its humor as "superficial" and "limited." By moving to the United States, however, Hitchcock shifted his attention away from social realism toward what Truffaut called the more "metaphysical anxieties" of fear, sex, and death.[5] Whereas a film like *The Lady Vanishes* (1938) features a cast of cosily eccentric Englishmen desperate to find out the latest cricket scores, Hitchcock's American films tend to be more austere and impersonal, more detached from immediate social mimesis; and this lack of easy processes of identification adds to their enigmatic, reverberative power.

We might draw a helpful parallel here with the work of Vladimir

---

3 Gene D. Phillips, *Alfred Hitchcock* (Boston: Twayne, 1984), p. 180.
4 Robin Wood, *Hitchcock's Films* (London: Zwemmer, 1965), p. 29.
5 Spoto, *The Dark Side of Genius,* p. 205; Truffaut, *Hitchcock,* p. 319.

Nabokov. The novels Nabokov wrote after his exile to America are much more effective than his earlier Russian books precisely because in this later American phase Nabokov's Old World sophistication comes into mordant collision with the Eisenhowerian blandness of small-town innocence. Hitchcock films like *Shadow of a Doubt,* set in Santa Rosa, California, and *The Trouble with Harry* (1955), which takes place in prim New England, exploit an ironic, Nabokov-like disjunction between the sunny facades of American social life and those less innocent activities lurking just out of sight. Moreover, Hitchcock's texts, like Nabokov's, have a remarkable eye for the icons of Americana: the white steeple of the New England church in *The Trouble with Harry* is filmed in a cool, detached style, which both admits the American landscape's picturesque quality yet simultaneously and surreptitiously hints at how this picture may not embody exactly those qualities it purports to embody. Hitchcock's gaze, like Nabokov's, often lingers on objects under scrutiny just a shade too long, so that they are taken out of their conventional situation and defamiliarized. We look at the church to admire its obvious beauty; but when Hitchcock's camera makes us keep looking at it longer than we need to, we begin to wonder uncomfortably what else might be there.

As many critics have noted, the dominant theme of Hitchcock's cinema is guilt, not only the guilt of the guilty but also the guilt of the apparently innocent. One recurring pattern is for a blameless bystander to seem, from surface appearances, a more likely criminal than the person who actually committed the unlawful act. It is this transfer of responsibility that comes to signify the "interchangeable guilt of all mankind," as Eric Rohmer and Claude Chabrol described it. Writing in 1957, Rohmer and Chabrol postulated the theory of Hitchcock as "a Catholic auteur" who delineates allegories of universal sin and the Fall of mankind.[6] Although Cary Grant's Roger Thorncliff in *North by Northwest* (1959) has not actually committed any worldly crime and is simply the victim of the CIA managing to bungle two different identities, Thorncliff gradually comes to believe that he might in fact be guilty after all; indeed, in an ontological sense, perhaps Thorncliff's former beliefs about his own sanctimonious innocence were a form of naïveté and self-delusion. Thorncliff's profession is advertising, and a man who trades upon the general preference for illusory images rather than solid truths here finds himself hoist by his own petard. Writing in 1984 in the Catholic magazine *America,* Robert E. Lauder followed Rohmer and Chabrol's Catholic argument by calling Thorncliff "a self-centered, mother-dominated, twice-

---

6 Eric Rohmer and Claude Chabrol, *Hitchcock: The First Forty-Four Films,* trans. Stanley Hochman (New York: Ungar, 1979), pp. 149, 25.

divorced irresponsible man who refuses all commitment." In Lauder's eyes, Thorncliff is, through the course of the narrative, "stripped" of "all his securities" until his moral education enables him "to make a commitment to another person." "Most significantly," concluded Lauder, "the only possession that he still has is a small cross around his neck."[7]

This is the reading of Hitchcock as a consciously Catholic artist, a moralizer concerned to probe beneath the deceptively innocent surfaces of the world so as to discover how all mankind participates in Original Sin. It is certainly true there is a compulsion in Hitchcock to undercut the authority of events as they appear on the glittering surface and to find out what dark truths lie underneath. In cinematic language this would appear to be a contradiction in terms because, as Geoffrey Hartman has written, the medium of film signifies a "central blank or zero," a denial of the "myth of depth"; but one of the intriguing things about Hitchcock's films is the way they strain to overcome that inevitable sense of absence and displacement upon which, as Christian Metz has argued, the flickering celluloid images of cinema are always predicated. (In theater, the actors are always physically present; in cinema, they are always physically absent.)[8] Somewhat in the manner of Flannery O'Connor, Hitchcock displays a fascinated disgust with the medium in which he works. For him, the necessarily superficial, two-dimensional images of the camera indicate exile from a universe of moral unity and a subsequent lapse into the world of confusion, muddle, and deceptive appearances. When Hitchcock undertakes his frequent exploration of a situation where all is not what it seems and the wrong person is indicted, we find an analogy operating between the camera and the false world: both are, in different senses, "framing" the victim. But these different senses then come to be equated, because the medium of film itself is necessarily implicated in the worldly deception. Yet, as a moralist, Hitchcock insists upon attempting to resolve these dilemmas in ethical terms. Turning back upon themselves to expose their contempt for those gratuitous glossy images they themselves have produced, Hitchcock's films attempt finally to save the good (or relatively innocent) man, to tear down the curtain and glimpse what truth exists behind it. This is why the victim, the falsely charged man, is often portrayed as being martyred; there appears to be enough of a moral center in these films to make sense of the idea of martyrdom. Hitchcock admitted to Truffaut that in hand-

7 Robert E. Lauder, "Alfred Hitchcock: A Film Maker of the Conscience," America, 4–11 Aug. 1984, p. 52.
8 Geoffrey H. Hartman, "Plenty of Nothing: Hitchcock's North by Northwest," Yale Review, 71, no. 1 (1981), 17; Christian Metz, "The Imaginary Signifier," Screen, 16, no. 2 (1975), 62–3.

cuffing the hero of *The Lodger* (1926) to a railing, he was consciously attempting to evoke the figure of Christ; while in *The Wrong Man* (1957), the innocent Henry Fonda not only murmurs prayers in front of holy pictures but, as Rohmer and Chabrol pointed out, his "face and Christ-like postures in his cell recall the iconography of the Stations of the Cross."[9]

Hitchcock often used the medium of black and white photography to externalize these moral themes into a pictorial universe of the dark and the light. In *Shadow of a Doubt,* he went to great lengths to contrast the clouds of black smoke when malevolent Uncle Charlie (Joseph Cotten) arrives at the Santa Rosa train station with that final puff of white smoke that celebrates the villain's departure from this world. Significant also is the fact that although he had released his first color film, *Rope,* in 1948, Hitchcock chose a stark, expressionistic black and white four years later to shoot his most obviously Catholic work, *I Confess.* In this film, the screenplay for which was written by Catholic novelist Paul Tabori, Montgomery Clift's priest helps to frame himself in the eyes of the police by refusing to divulge information given to him by a murderer during confession. Hitchcock later came to believe the film should never have been made, however, because it depends too much upon recognition of an abstruse theological principle. "We Catholics," Hitchcock told Truffaut, "know that a priest cannot disclose the secret of the confessional, but the Protestants, the atheists, and the agnostics all say 'Ridiculous! No man would remain silent and sacrifice his life for such a thing.'"[10] Robin Wood also found *I Confess,* with its blatant visual analogies between Clift's martyrdom and Christ's crucifixion, to be a touch pretentious, and Wood used the example of this film to underline the inadequacies of Rohmer and Chabrol's narrow approach to Hitchcock as an orthodox Catholic allegorist. For Wood, these more ostentatiously "Catholic" themes of guilt and redemption were not where Hitchcock's strange genius lay, nor did they comprise the sum total of the director's "metaphysical" proclivities. "That Hitchcock's Catholic background has relevance to the assumptions about the universe that underlie his films I would not deny," concluded Wood, "but it seems to me an indirect relevance."[11]

It is this "indirect relevance" I am especially concerned with here. Following Wood's analysis of the flaws in the Rohmer/Chabrol thesis, it has become customary in Hitchcock criticism either to neglect the

9 Truffaut, *Hitchcock,* p. 47; Rohmer and Chabrol, *Hitchcock,* p. 148.
10 Truffaut, *Hitchcock,* pp. 154, 204.
11 Wood, *Hitchcock's Films,* pp. 40, 44.

Catholic context as scarcely relevant biographical background or, alter-
natively, to associate it with a rigid form of patriarchy that the more
turbulent and powerful energies of these films are intent upon challenging. Thus, in one of the many recent feminist readings of Hitchcock,
Tania Modleski drew upon Julia Kristeva's assertion that "phobia and
the phobic aspects of religion are all ultimately linked to matrophobia."
She went on to argue that in these films we find "male symbolic systems
and masculine notions of identity and order" coming into conflict with
the "pollutant" of the feminine – the swamping mother, the "abject"
sexually active female – all of which constitute a threat to the autonomy
and independence of the male subject. In Modleski's eyes, Hitchcock's
residual Catholicism operates as a repressive and misogynistic structure
that compels his films to "enact 'rituals of defilement,' evoking and then
containing the fear of women that lies at the heart of these rituals."[12]

Now, it may very well be true that there is a deeply entrenched fear
of women within Hitchcock's cinema. The supposedly "castrating"
mother in *Psycho* (1960) and other films, together with the sexually predatory blondes who stalk through these movies undermining the strength
and equanimity of the male heroes, testify to such an apprehension of
the feminine as a dislocating and subversive power. In this sense, the
murderous violence visited upon women in films such as *Frenzy* (1972)
could be seen as a desperate attempt to forestall this power, to reassert
masculine control. Yet, as Modleski has suggested, these sexual politics
can be read in two ways: either as cinematic sadism pure and simple, or
as part of Hitchcock's "thoroughgoing ambivalence about femininity"
in an environment where attraction and repulsion have become intimately
intertwined. In this latter interpretation, argued Modleski, Hitchcock's
films take "the form of a particularly lucid exposé of the predicaments
and contradictions of women's existence under patriarchy": Hitchcock
deconstructs the power structures implicit within gender relations to
highlight the boundaries of conventional social respectability and "good
taste."[13] And I would argue that Hitchcock uses religion in just the same
way, to expose the limitations of a smug and self-satisfied society. Like
sexuality, religion for Hitchcock signifies a deviant force that can disturb
the comfortable ethics of middle America. Rather than being aligned
with Rohmer and Chabrol's theological orthodoxy or with Kristeva's
"male symbolic systems" of authoritarian domination, I would suggest
that the culture of Catholicism in Hitchcock's American films promotes

12 Tania Modleski, *The Women Who Knew Too Much: Hitchcock and Feminist Theory* (New
   York: Methuen, 1988), pp. 107–8.
13 Ibid., pp. 3, 27.

the representation of a world dangerously out of control, propelled as it is by the vertiginous desires of sex, crime, and metaphysics, all of which transgress the boundaries of small-town decorum and innocence.

For the perennial problem in Hitchcock is that rational orders and explanations do not, in the end, succeed in circumscribing the irrational terrors these films have raised. This, of course, is precisely why Hitchcock's works are so genuinely frightening. The eminently reasonable speech of the psychotherapist at the end of *Psycho* cannot succeed in repressing the ghastly terror of Norman Bates's final crazed expression, which defies closure and opens the film up to a whole series of chilling enigmas that reverberate long after the closing titles. Here, one feels, is where Rohmer and Chabrol's neat thesis about Hitchcock's institutional Catholicism falls into disrepair: "In the midst of chaos," they claim, "this Unity is always discernible and provides a source of light that plays some of its most beautiful rays over the somber facets of Evil."[14] While Hitchcock's texts might aspire toward this moral closure and religious "unity," there are many films, such as *Psycho,* in which that reassuring sense of overall coherence is denied.

In *Vertigo* (1958), to take another example, all the characters are searching for rational solutions to the problems that beset them. A California coroner briskly explains away Madeleine's fall from a church tower as the result of Scottie's negligent failure to keep a close watch on her. A doctor opines that James Stewart's Scottie is suffering from "acute melancholia, together with a guilt complex." His plain girlfriend, Midge (Barbara Bel Geddes), bracingly recommends Mozart "to sweep the cobwebs away"; while Scottie himself, trying to assure himself "there's an answer for everything," searches for the "key" that will enable him to unlock the mystery of Kim Novak's disappearance as "Madeleine" and her reemergence as "Judy." The film's plot moves toward resolving these dilemmas, a resolution that is in fact – as Edmund Wilson said of detective stories generally – the most banal area of the movie: the Kim Novak character turns out to have been involved with Gavin Elster (Tom Helmore) in an elaborate scheme to kill his wife. But the film's duplicitous ambiguities are far more resonant than its simple hermeneutic explanations. Madeleine's attempt at suicide by jumping into San Francisco Bay and her constant fear that she is walking down a long corridor toward the darkness of death are later dismissed by her as a mere counterfeit and part of Elster's criminal plan. Nevertheless, just as Madeleine's feigned love for Scottie proves in the end to be "real," so her skillfully contrived death wish ("I don't want to die, but there's something within me which says I must die") is also transferred from imitation to substance, for, in the final scene, Scottie and Judy are surprised at the top of a church tower by a nun emerging out of the shadows, whereupon Novak's character does indeed, and for the last time, plunge to her death. Perhaps an idea of retributive punishment for the sins of lust and murder is implied by this setting of the old Spanish mission in California: one scene early in the film is actually shot inside the church, as if to establish the religious ambience. Hitchcock himself downplayed the significance of these Catholic church scenes, suggesting they were simply a residue of the original Boileau-Narcejac novel from which the story derived, though by way of self-contradiction the director added that he "simply couldn't see anyone jumping from the tower of a modern Protestant church."[15]

The final moments of *Vertigo,* then, feature this intrusive nun crossing herself and tolling the church bell to announce Judy's death. Robin Wood interpreted the nun's appearance as "a symbol of Scottie's illumination," a sign that the murder mystery has been solved and resolved.[16] Yet, despite all this pressure for rational and religious closure, the viewer's overall impression is of a vertiginous *mise-en-abîme* which disallows all the claims of literal or recognizable reality. There is a double movement here, one toward empirical explanation, the other toward irrational terror. Scottie's vertigo, arising from an earlier brush with death when he nearly fell from a rooftop while chasing a criminal, signifies a fear of heights, a preference for standing on solid ground; but the terror of Hitchcock's film is that it ultimately denies him, and the viewer, any solid ground upon which to stand. Thus the "vertigo" of this film operates partly through the viewer's disorienting experience of the narrative, in which it becomes difficult to work out what is the past and what the present, what is "real" and what illusion. The fact that Hitchcock's dream sequences occasionally remind the audience that this is ultimately all illusion, all a fictional film event, only adds to the viewer's sense of vertiginous limbo. This kind of vertigo also enters the experience of Hitchcock's dramatic protagonists, caught up as they are in an unstable cycle of lust, crime, and death: Gavin Elster's murders, Scottie's sexual infatuation with Madeleine, Madeleine's own obsession with mortality all betoken the irruption of "uncanny" metaphysical components that create fissures within the film's literalistic surface. At several points in the narrative, Hitchcock's camera introduces a Chinese box of mutually reflecting objects so as to create the illusion of an infinite abyss: we see this in the geometric spirals of the title sequences and in the stairwell of the church tower, as well as in Madeleine's dream of walking along a mirrored corridor with darkness at its end. In *Vertigo,* none of those

15 Truffaut, *Hitchcock,* p. 317.
16 Wood, *Hitchcock's Films,* p. 98.

involved – not the audience, nor the dramatis personae – seem to know exactly where they are.

As with *Psycho,* then, neither institutional Catholicism nor ideas of moral unity seem sufficient to explain away this film's enigmas. As she makes the sign of the cross in the final frames, the nun may actually be redeeming the Novak character rather than attempting simply to ward off evil: "God have mercy," says the nun as Judy plunges to her death. As Donald Spoto has said, some of Hitchcock's films toy with the idea, familiar from Graham Greene and other Catholic writers, that "one can, in the last analysis, be freed from corruption only by guilt"; and, from this angle, the intensity of erotic desire so prominent in these films could be seen as analogous to that sense of displacement characteristic of religious experience and, more precisely, of the idea of redemption.[17] Both desire and redemption necessarily involve a movement beyond the banal, self-protective conventions of everyday life into an awareness of something strange and unfamiliar. *Vertigo* makes no glib moral judgments; in this respect, at least, Hitchcock refuses to usurp the prerogative of God. Nevertheless, there is in this film a suggestion of that old Catholic paradox whereby the rank black sinner, the person who is horribly aware of the awful potential of damnation, can be closer to redemptive grace than the honest citizen who has never troubled himself about anything beyond his or her own domestic affairs. Again, one thinks here of Flannery O'Connor, another Irish-American artist who flirted with a Jansenistic notion of the sanctity of crime, the ways in which recognition of the existence of evil could become a tortuous acknowledgment of the extrarational qualities of divine grace. It is within this paradoxical equation that Hitchcock's emphasis upon the irrational terrors of sex and crime may project a dark shadow of his Catholic heritage.

In this way, the intrusion of Hitchcock's sinister formulas into these safe, dull, repressive American communities actually comes to be – as it does in O'Connor – a moral imperative, a (parodic) replication of the disturbance of these secular havens by divine powers. Hitchcock himself said that a theme of *The Birds* (1963) is "complacency," and the dark crows poised to invade this genteel California community clearly suggest the dangerous irruptions of alien sexual impulses.[18] Here Rod Taylor's pusillanimous Mitch Brenner must fight off – in his own mind, at least – the claims of his possessive mother (Jessica Tandy) before being able to satisfy his erotic desires with Tippi Hedren. The fact that Hedren's Melanie appears in this film as the mirror-image of Mitch's mother, Lydia, is a visual indication of how Mitch subliminally interprets sex-

17 Spoto, *The Dark Side of Genius,* p. 15.
18 Wood, *Hitchcock's Films,* p. 128.

uality as an uncomfortable assault upon his idyll of childish dependence and virtuous family life.

Rather than conforming to the legalistic dictates of Catholic doctrine, then, Hitchcock's films, it would be truer to say, institute a paradoxical, yet no less "Catholic," morality of evil. *Rear Window* (1954) finds James Stewart's L. B. Jeffries substituting his telephoto lens for a penis and finding more delight in spying voyeuristically on sex and evil than in developing his relationship with Grace Kelly's Manhattan princess, Lisa Fremont. When Truffaut pointed out to Hitchcock that this kind of prurient curiosity is a sin in the eyes of the church, the director gruffly dismissed the criticism by saying "my love of film is far more important to me than any considerations of morality." Revealingly, Hitchcock also took violent exception to the London *Observer* reviewer who had declared "*Rear Window* was a horrible film because the hero spent all of his time peeping out of the window. What's so horrible about that?" demanded Hitchcock. "Sure, he's a snooper, but aren't we all?"[19] The effect here is something like that ontological burlesque we saw in Ford and Altman: whereas Ford and Altman use comedy to bring everything down to the same level, Hitchcock uses sex, voyeurism, and murder. Hitchcock hated the *Observer*'s criticism because it proposed exactly the kind of moralistic high-mindedness *Rear Window* itself is designed to subvert. Significantly Lisa Fremont eventually endears herself to Jeffries by participating wholeheartedly in the murder inquiry, showing great enthusiasm for the idea of a dismembered corpse. By the end of the film, she has abandoned her starchy Park Avenue fashions in favor of blue jeans, a sure sign, especially in these early days of teenage culture, of greater sexual daring.

So Hitchcock's comedy, like Ford's, is designed to shatter social complacency and pretentiousness and to reveal the essentially ignominious nature of human circumstances sub specie aeternitatis. This is why Hitchcock's films resist categorization in terms of conventional morality, Christian or otherwise. Lesley Brill recently offered a version of "The Hitchcockian Romance" wherein heterosexual love was said to emerge as a secular equivalent to Christian virtue: "True heterosexual love between well-matched partners approaches divine grace in many of Hitchcock's films," claimed Brill. "Deviance, therefore, is generally demonic; and it is artistically consistent that Hitchcock's villains often show signs of sexual perversity."[20] The problem with such an argument is that Hitchcock's heroes, even the best intentioned of them, often show "signs of sexual perversity" as well. We see this in *The Paradine Case* (1947), in

19 Truffaut, *Hitchcock,* pp. 319, 216.
20 Lesley Brill, *The Hitchcock Romance: Love and Irony in Hitchcock's Films* (Princeton: Princeton Univ. Press, 1988), p. 10.

which Gregory Peck's brilliant and happily married lawyer, Anthony
Keane, becomes attracted, despite himself, to the murderous Mrs. Paradine (Valli) precisely because of her association with evil and sexual
transgression. Ironically, however, it is Keane's intuitive sympathy with
Mrs. Paradine that leads him to probe more deeply into the secrets of
this dark mystery and to uncover the true circumstances of the affair.
Keane's obsession with evil becomes, paradoxically, a vehicle for moral
retribution, for it becomes the means through which Mrs. Paradine's
crime is revealed and punished; equally paradoxically, this obsession is
also shown as the road toward Keane's own "salvation," for his public
humiliation in court chastens the insouciant, chameleonic – even, perhaps, satanic – style of lying that Keane as a professional lawyer had
perfected, and so makes him subsequently less willing to deceive his
faithful wife. Good comes from evil, evil from good; last judgments are
not available within the imperfect rational order of the human world.
Motives in Hitchcock are invariably mixed, indeed unknowable; Robin
Wood noted that Hitchcock's films interweave good and evil so they are
"virtually inseparable," while his work "insists on the existence of evil
impulses in all of us." As Hitchcock himself said, responding to criticisms
of Psycho: "There's a devil in every one of us."[21] For Hitchcock, everyone
is a voyeur, everyone a potential murderer; and in exploiting his audience's fascination with this lubricious subject matter he was, in effect,
proving his point. Hitchcock told one of his actors, who had complained
about the director's notoriously sadistic practical jokes on the film set,
that the "whole point of comedy is to reduce dignity": as with Ford and
Altman, that reduction of dignity for both actors and audience comes to
imply in Hitchcock's world a profound (though not necessarily conscious) ontological purpose.[22]

   One of Hitchcock's projects that never came to fruition was a Gothic
nightmare entitled The Blind Man to be set in Disneyland, a plan ter-
minated by an outraged Walt Disney who refused to let the director of
Psycho befoul his amusement park.[23] This incident does, however, highlight Hitchcock's compulsion to expose the ideological limitations of the
most cherished, sanitized icons of American life. Uncle Charlie says to
his niece (Teresa Wright) in Shadow of a Doubt: "You're just an ordinary
little girl living in an ordinary little town... and I brought you night-
mares." The fact that the niece here is also called Charlie underlines the
ubiquity of this sense of sin, the way those who are apparently virginal
and innocent become implicated in the misdeeds of the guilty. It is true

21 Wood, Hitchcock's Films, p. 22; Spoto, The Dark Side of Genius, p. 536.
22 Spoto, The Dark Side of Genius, p. 142.
23 Ibid., p. 471.

that Hitchcock's religious sensibility does not permit good and evil ultimately to be equated in these films, but the recognition of what is good
and what evil tends to be an extremely complex and problematical issue.
So for Rohmer and Chabrol to insist upon how the "essentially Catholic
nature of his work" is endowed with the "bitterness of the moralist"
seems misleading. In *Rear Window,* for instance, Rohmer and Chabrol
talked about the hero's "moral solitude, conceived as the punishment for
that hypertrophy of desire"; whereas, as we have seen, the hero's sexual
desire as well as his ethical impulses – he actually saves people's lives –
are in fact brought out, not suppressed, by his voyeuristic activities.[24]
Hitchcock's project was more akin to that of Baudelaire, whom Hitchcock heralded in 1961 as "the French Edgar Allan Poe."[25] Like Poe and
Baudelaire, and indeed like Robert Mapplethorpe, Hitchcock tears the
veil from worldly appearances to uncover those flowers of evil that lurk
within the heart of even the most liberal-minded moviegoer, "hypocrite
lecteur, mon semblable, mon frère." Hitchcock, like Mapplethorpe, reminds the viewers of how they can never quite remove their metaphysical
handcuffs. His Catholicism was neither assiduous dogma nor diligent
moralizing but a subversively supernatural style of filmmaking induced
partly by his particular cultural inheritance.

Not even Hitchcock, however, makes the Catholic framework of his
films so crucial to their meaning as does Martin Scorsese. Like Hitchcock,
Scorsese underwent a Jesuit education; unlike Hitchcock, he also cherished ambitions of becoming a priest, an idea he abandoned only when
bad high school grades caused him to be rejected by Fordham University's divinity program. Having been an altar boy in his youth, Scorsese
officially left the church in the mid 1960s after hearing a priest in the
pulpit eulogize the American involvement in Vietnam as "a holy war."
Although he subsequently designated himself an agnostic, Scorsese has,
as he himself admits, "never gotten over the ritual of Catholicism." In
a 1988 interview, he ambiguously stated: "I'm a believer, but I'm
struggling."[26]

Scorsese's first script, "Jerusalem, Jerusalem," which centered upon a
three-day retreat at a Jesuit house, remained unfilmed. His first substantial
work, *Who's That Knocking on My Door?* (1968), examines without a
great deal of subtlety how the Catholic upbringing of Harvey Keitel's
J.R. engenders sexual guilt and psychological tensions in his relationships

24 Rohmer and Chabrol, *Hitchcock,* pp. 25, 32, 126.
25 Spoto, *The Dark Side of Genius,* p. 41.
26 Dian G. Smith, *American Filmmakers Today* (New York: Messner, 1984), pp. 116–17;
   "The *Sunday Times* Profile: Martin Scorsese," *Sunday Times* (London), 21 Aug. 1988,
   Sec. A, p. 12.

with women. Icons of the Madonna frown down from above the bed where J.R. gets up to no good with his unnamed girl (Zina Bethune). J.R.'s anonymous fiancée undertakes a reading of Fitzgerald's *Tender Is the Night,* another story about Catholic guilt, presumably in an effort to understand her obsessed lover; but J.R.'s description of her as a "broad" and "whore" unsurprisingly fails to endear him to the mysterious woman, and when he offers to "forgive" her for not being a virgin she pulls out of the relationship, leaving a relieved J.R. to hurry off to the priest and confess his own sexual impurity. Scorsese has said that the "religious stuff" in this film and *Mean Streets* (1973) is "just so personal" that he finds it difficult to review these works. He also claimed, though, that they had to be made "whether it's embarrassing to me or not. Because it's like a purging – it's got to be done, and you just have to be honest with yourself."[27]

In *Who's That Knocking,* the persistent imagery of mirrors reminds the audience of how J.R.'s mind is bifurcated between his secular and religious selves: it is, as Michael Bliss has said, God knocking importunately on the door as far as J.R. is concerned.[28] *Mean Streets* begins in a similarly metaphysical vein with a voice before the opening titles announcing: "You don't make up for your sins in church; you do it in the streets, you do it at home. The rest is bullshit and you know it." The rest of the film proceeds to act out the implications of this epigraph, with Harvey Keitel's Charlie seeking painful "crucifixion" on the mean streets of Little Italy as a guarantee of eternal redemption in the hereafter. The proximity of urban gangsters and priests has been a motif of the American cinema since the days of *Angels with Dirty Faces,* in which the villainous Jimmy Cagney and the saintly Pat O'Brien both appear as marginal characters who locate their ambitions outside the patterns of mainstream society; and the apparent authenticity of the torment Charlie experiences on these New York streets would seem to offer him a golden opportunity to avoid the need for subsequent detention in purgatory. Analogies between material and spiritual landscapes begin to develop in Charlie's mind: Tony's bar is bathed in a hellish red light; the fire of a cooking hamburger turns into a memento of Satan's eternal grill; the bright lights of the sex shops become a demonic inversion of the bright lights of a Catholic church service that appear at the beginning of the film. Scorsese's handheld camera shots add to the psychological anguish of these scenes, be-

27 Mary Pat Kelly, *Martin Scorsese: The First Decade* (Pleasantville, N.Y.: Redgrave, 1980), pp. 19–20.
28 Michael Bliss, *Martin Scorsese and Michael Cimino* (Metuchen, N.J.: Scarecrow Press, 1985), p. 47.

cause they give us the illusion the scenes are not staged or arranged in any way, thus making the tone seem nearer to documentary than to classical cinema. "I think the documentary is far superior to the dramatic film," Scorsese has said. "In the documentaries there's more of a truth that you get at. Something happens that you can't really do in dramatic films."[29]

In iconographic terms, Scorsese's religious sensibility often expresses itself through the colors of chiaroscuro. In *Alice Doesn't Live Here Anymore* (1974), the dark world of Phoenix barrooms is modified by the rays of sunlight shining through the window; but, by keeping his camera underexposed, Scorsese presents to us the image of a shadowy woman who seems to develop a golden halo, to become sanctified, when she starts to perform. *Taxi Driver* (1976) similarly rotates upon an axis of the light and the dark, with Cybill Shepherd's white madonna being contrasted with Jodie Foster's teenage whore. Some of the aesthetic and ideological tensions within this latter film arise from the fact that it was scripted by Paul Schrader, who grew up in the Christian Reformed church, a zealous splinter of Calvinism, such a strict organization that Schrader was not allowed to see a film until he was seventeen. Scorsese, unusually for him, barely modified his writer's script, and both he and Schrader later observed that in *Taxi Driver* there is, as Scorsese put it, "a clash between the Calvinist ethos and . . . a decadent vision of Catholicism." In other words, Scorsese's cinematography produces lush visual imagery that tends to glorify what Schrader's hero, Travis Bickle (played here by Robert De Niro), affects to despise. Schrader described Protestantism as having "a more individualistic, solipsistic, righteous quality" that is concerned to set itself apart from Catholicism's "emotional, communal flurry," and it is precisely that dichotomy Scorsese's film negotiates: Bickle is solipsistically obsessed with a drive for purity and engineers his apocalyptic cleanup of the prostitution racket for that end, whereas the director's camera work seems rather to luxuriate in images of the city's decadent mean streets, content to accept the Baudelairean premise that genuine blasphemy is a way of affirming belief.[30] Here, as in the 1985 *After Hours*, Scorsese specializes in what Robert Phillip Kolker has called the technique of "defamiliarization," employing rapid intercutting and "fragmentary, off-center editing," so as to make New York City appear strange and unknowable and therefore "a realm

29 Kelly, *Martin Scorsese: The First Decade*, p. 103.
30 Scorsese quoted in Peter Occhiogrosso, *Once a Catholic: Prominent Catholics and Ex-Catholics Discuss the Influence of the Church on Their Lives and Works* (Boston: Houghton Mifflin, 1987), p. 101; Richard Thompson, "Screenwriter: *Taxi Driver's* Paul Schrader," *Film Comment*, 12, no. 2 (1976), 13.

of distortion and threat."[31] This is the Hitchcockian mode that subverts the comfortable realism of naturalistic landscapes so as to hint at an uneasy, unassimilable metaphysical element.

The social milieu of Scorsese's films usually revolves around an outsider trying to "make it" and become an insider. Rico's injunction in *Little Caesar* to "be somebody" reechoes through the consciousness of Scorsese's gallery of Italian-Americans and other tough characters struggling to rise to the top of their respective fields: boxing in *Raging Bull*, singing in *Alice Doesn't Live Here Any More*, popular music in *New York, New York*, television in *The King of Comedy*, pool in *The Color of Money*. Again, it would not be difficult to see an autobiographical element involved here. Scorsese himself compared the actions of De Niro's Rupert Pupkin in *The King of Comedy* (1983) to his own desperate desire for success as a filmmaker: "Rupert's an extension of me inasmuch as he'd do *anything* to get what he wanted. . . . Rupert reminds me of the hunger I had in the sixties."[32] But, more importantly, the ambiguous circumstances of this drive for success can be viewed as a specifically Catholic cultural phenomenon, the same kind of situation as we saw in the novels of Scott Fitzgerald and James T. Farrell. Success in Scorsese's films is less a reward for industry than for good luck, less an indication of moral worth than the sign of a particular skill or technical expertise. Like Farrell, Scorsese cherishes the idea of American society as a game, a sport, where victory is dependent upon a strong nerve but also upon a lucky spin of the roulette wheel. In the epigraph to *The Color of Money* (1986), Scorsese's voice is heard before the opening credits explaining to the audience the rules of nine-ball pool: "Luck plays a part in nine-ball," he admits, "but for some players, luck itself is an art." Paul Newman's Eddie Felson does indeed keep trying to turn luck into an art by reiterating throughout the film his belief in an "area of excellence." "Pool excellence is not about excellent pool," he tells his young protégé. "It's about becoming somebody."

The Color of Money moves toward its grand final tableau of a pool championship in the gambling mecca of Atlantic City, but Eddie's addiction to gambling in fact reveals itself all the way through this film: he places bets on how soon people will leave the bar, for instance. "Money won is twice as sweet as money earned," Eddie tells Tom Cruise's Vincent, in a statement that directly inverts the values of the Protestant work ethic. As we have seen, the early American Puritans regarded gambling as sacrilegious and believed that God allotted worldly

31 Robert Phillip Kolker, *A Cinema of Loneliness: Penn, Kubrick, Coppola, Scorsese, Altman* (New York: Oxford University Press, 1980), pp. 229, 218, 230.
32 Smith, *American Filmmakers Today*, p. 127.

reward and punishment according to his predestined plan of the elect
and the damned; but for Scorsese, it is luck, and the cultivation of skill
to make that luck count, which is one of the sacred ideas capable of
saving his heroes from the poverty of their native environment. Scorsese's
heroes, like those of Fitzgerald, do not equate worldly success with divine
approval; on the contrary, it is worldly failure that seems more often to
meet with the sanctification of martyrdom. But if social triumph depends
upon an arbitrary and chancy system rather than one metaphysically
validated or ethically consistent, then Scorsese's heroes – like Fitzgerald's
Jay Gatsby – feel compelled to do everything in their power to make
sure the dice roll in their favor.

   Mean Streets, said Scorsese, "dealt with the American Dream," but it
is an oblique Catholic reworking of the American Dream.[33] The character
of Charlie goes so far as to bless his pool balls, making the sign of the
cross above them before he starts to play. All of the street people in this
film, in fact, are constantly turning to games like pool or blackjack in
an attempt to change their luck. Even more obtrusively, the representation here of the San Gennaro feast (to celebrate Saint Jannarius, patron
saint of Sicily) features a shot of a large wheel of fortune, as if to demonstrate how these immigrant communities in *Mean Streets* perceive their
life in the New World to be largely a matter of chance. "Luck is being
a Vanderbilt or Carnegie," declares Bill Shelley (David Carradine) in
Boxcar Bertha (1972), an earlier Scorsese film that focuses upon another
group of outsiders – the unemployed of the 1930s – and again shows the
characters wistfully gambling and throwing dice to while away the time.
It is noticeable as well that the dispossessed characters in *Boxcar Bertha*
seek simple power rather than any conceptual ideal of social justice. The
apogee of vengeance as far as Bertha (Barbara Hershey) is concerned is
to humiliate the bowler-hatted railroad chiefs by putting them through
a series of demeaning exercises at gunpoint. She then infiltrates a smart
party and, in a parody of a polite society announcement, informs the
gathering that this is a stickup. Like Farrell's early heroes, Scorsese's
personae have an innate conservatism and a desire to play the game
according to the rules. Although Bertha's friends operate on the margins
of society, they generally remain loyal to its values; they just want the
"luck" that would transfigure them into Vanderbilts or Carnegies. Appropriately enough, the band at the San Gennaro procession in *Mean
Streets* is patriotically playing the "Star Spangled Banner." Again, Scorsese's own professional ambition is a clear correlative to these immigrants'
drive for social acceptability and material success. Acknowledging in

33 David Thompson and Ian Christie, eds., *Scorsese on Scorsese* (London: Faber, 1989),
    p. 47.

1987 how his films to date have been critical rather than great commercial successes, Scorsese admitted that with *The Color of Money* he had deliberately set out "to have a picture that makes $150 million. It's one level of success I haven't had."[34] (In this sense, *The Color of Money* could also be said to be about the color of money Scorsese hoped to gross at the box office.)

Because worldly success is portrayed as being so much a question of chance, some of Scorsese's films drift toward that familiar Catholic pattern of becoming a parody of the American Dream. Rupert Pupkin in *The King of Comedy* hardly impresses with his maturity or sophistication, a thirty-four-year-old man still living with his mother who hopes to wow a woman by telling her she received his vote for prettiest cheerleader fifteen years ago. Nevertheless, Pupkin's bedroom fantasies of a "big break" eventually do come true, for he ends up on the cover of *Time, Newsweek,* and *Rolling Stone* and as the author of a best-selling book, *King for a Night,* which is promptly turned into a successful motion picture. By hijacking the television show of Jerry Langford (Jerry Lewis), Pupkin suddenly brings himself to the attention of 87 million Americans, and two years in prison is a small price to pay for his subsequent wealth and fame. Before his success Pupkin tended to conflate fantasy with reality, and *The King of Comedy* does nothing to distinguish between these two categories by presenting the fantasy sequences as though they were occurring naturalistically. The overall impression we are left with is that "illusion" cannot be separated out as a discrete category, that the whole world is comprised of shadowy reflections and images, that Pupkin is in fact as good a television talk show host as anyone else. Once again, success is a matter of pure chance. Similar kinds of irony attend the end of *Taxi Driver,* where Travis Bickle, having wreaked a violent, apocalyptic vengeance upon his own television set earlier in the narrative, finds himself turned into a media hero by the publicity machines of corporate America for his supposed act of heroism in rescuing the Jodie Foster character from a life of vice. As Michael Bliss put it, in Scorsese's films "the outsider is integrated into the prevailing social structure, which is shown to be adaptive enough to accommodate even the most outlandish forms of aberration."[35] His heroes are never represented purely as romantic outsiders; even the most alienated individuals, as in *Mean Streets,* are viewed implicitly through the lens of some corporate structure, so that each character is referred back to his or her relationship with a larger group. In Scorsese's early films, this "group" tends to be a narrow ethnic

34 Bart Mills, "Raging Back," *Guardian,* 20 Jan. 1987, p. 27.
35 Bliss, *Martin Scorsese and Michael Cimino,* p. 119.

unit; in his later work, though, it increasingly takes the form of a wider
national or mythic community.

So fame and material success are seen in these films as a gamble,
welcome enough when they arrive, but by no means a guarantee of
"spiritual" worth. The cautious conservatism of the immigrant temperament, allied to a strong sense of the world's inherent superficiality, leads
to an interesting quandary in Scorsese's work. As he himself put it in a
1987 interview: "How do you live a spiritual life, how do you live a
good life, when the system is just the opposite?... There's got to be
a way to do it in modern life, there has to be a way. I mean, living
spiritually."[36] One way is the martyrdom of Bill Shelley, who sacrifices
himself for the labor movement and finishes up crucified on a wagon
wheel at the end of Boxcar Bertha. Another way is that of Robert De
Niro's Jake La Motta in Raging Bull (1980), whose last defeat in the
boxing ring points him in the direction of ultimate spiritual triumph. La
Motta attributes the decline of his fighting ability not to the natural
processes of aging, but rather to his own self-indulgence and overeating.
His pride leads toward the hubris of believing his body immortal, and
he cherishes the brutal punishment he receives in and out of the ring as
welcome retribution for the guilt he is continually experiencing. During
a 1957 spell in jail for illicit activities with fourteen-year-old girls in his
Miami nightclub, La Motta pummels his head against the walls of his
cell and hammers the bars with his fists, as if protesting violently against
the physical condition in which he finds himself entrapped. The prison
cell operates as an extension of La Motta's own loathsome carcass from
which he yearns to escape, and the film's camerawork brilliantly captures
the fallibility of man's corporeal state through its mordant focus upon
La Motta's flesh. The fight sequences, for instance, were filmed not with
many cameras but with just one, a move that allowed Scorsese to eschew
visual detachment and instead work his way in close enough to produce
horrific magnifications of La Motta's pummeled body (figure 6).[37] The
film in fact defamiliarizes the human body, compels us to inspect the
status of man's fleshly incarnation as if for the first time. At the opening
of the film, La Motta appears slim, tough, and athletic; toward the end
of his career in the ring, we can see that the years of mortification of the
flesh have taken their toll; and by the end of the film the retired boxer
is grotesquely overweight, his stomach sagging in a morass of corruption.
The cycle of the film thus constitutes a memento of the fateful processes
of aging and decay. As Mark Le Fanu observed, the subject of Raging

36 "How Do You Solve a Problem Like Maria?," dir. Anthony Wall, Omnibus, BBC
    Television, 27 Mar. 1987.
37 Richard Combs, "Hell Up in the Bronx," Sight and Sound, 50 (1981), 132.

Figure 6. Robert De Niro as Jake La Motta in *Raging Bull*

Bull is in fact "nothing other than the limits of the human body, and the soul's imprisonment in its mortal frame . . . observed . . . under an intensity of pressure that can only properly be described as religious."[38]

By the end of his life, however, La Motta has become more reconciled to the loss of his former dominance and to his inevitable status as a

38 Mark Le Fanu, "Looking for Mr. De Niro," *Sight and Sound,* 55 (Winter 1985–86), 49.

human animal whose raging excesses can never release him from the prison of his declining, bull-like body. In his nightclub dressing room, he rehearses a routine in which he goes through Marlon Brando's famous self-lacerating speech from Elia Kazan's 1954 film, *On the Waterfront:* "It's like a peak you reach and then – downhill ... I could'a had class. I could'a been a contender. I could have been somebody. Instead of a bum, which is what I am." La Motta, of course – unlike the Brando character – once was a genuine "contender," and his sentimental embracing of failure here reveals some of that Catholic masochism we associate with characters like Fitzgerald's Dick Diver. Yet in acknowledging the inevitability of his own earthly defeat, La Motta succeeds, said Scorsese, in "redeeming himself."[39] The final words of the film, from the Book of John, are projected silently onto the screen: "Once I was blind and now I can see." By a familiar Catholic pattern, worldly defeat has turned itself into spiritual triumph. Pride in the triumph of sheer human force, and even – as Robert Casillo has argued – aspirations on La Motta's part toward a kind of "divine" impenetrability have given way to a paradoxical sense of triumph in the deliquescence of the human body, with the consequent religious illumination this fall entails.[40] Previously, La Motta had preserved a fierce independence, scorning hangers-on like Tommy Como (Nicholas Colasanto) for being mere entertainers and pimps who were dependent upon others; but in the end Scorsese's hero is brought to an understanding of the essential nature of his own human limitations.

Raging Bull was the winner of a poll conducted among critics by *American Film* magazine to determine the best film of the 1980s, and it is a magnificent work of art by any standards. Although its ethnic focus is not so narrow as *Mean Streets,* many of the social predicaments it portrays still arise out of tensions located within the confines of an idiosyncratically Italian-Catholic culture. La Motta's attitude toward women in this film is only slightly less aggressive than his attitude toward the boxers in the ring; indeed, in terms of sexual politics Scorsese's films continually hark back to the primitivist quandaries of *Who's That Knocking on My Door?* La Motta first sees the blonde Vickie (Cathy Moriarty) through a wire fence at the public swimming pool, where he looks up to her from street level; and this camera angle reflects La Motta's subliminal conceptualization of Vickie as an inaccessible, Madonna-like figure, an image that continues to haunt their relationship later. In an effort

39 Thomas Wiener, "Martin Scorsese Fights Back," *American Film,* Nov. 1980, p. 31.
40 Robert Casillo, "Catholicism and Violence in the Films of Martin Scorsese," in *Support and Struggle: Italians and Italian Americans in a Contemporary Perspective,* ed. Joseph L. Tropea, James E. Miller, and Cheryl Beattie-Repetti (Staten Island: American Italian Historical Association, 1986), p. 289.

to compensate for this sense of insecurity, La Motta feels compelled to visit upon Vickie some of the same violence with which he attacks Sugar Ray Robinson, and he ends up beating both of them. There is a hint in the film that Vickie herself may not at first be averse to a little rough treatment within their marriage, but later the situation becomes intolerable and she seeks a divorce. La Motta's brother (Joe Pesci) tries to placate Vickie, assuring her that her husband has "just been a contender too long"; but the situation is beyond repair, for in Scorsese's old-style Catholic world women tend to be perceived as mere adjuncts to male prowess. Eddie Felson in *The Color of Money* envisions a similarly subservient role for Vincent's girlfriend, Carmen (Mary Elizabeth Mastrantonio): "We've got a racehorse here, a thoroughbred," he tells her. "You make him feel good, I teach him how to run." De Niro's Irish-American Jimmy Doyle in *New York, New York* (1977) is another rowdy bull in a china shop who attempts to dominate Liza Minnelli's Francine Evans, although Francine succeeds here in resisting the submissive role. Jimmy's male pride is tormented by Francine's professional success as a singer, and he is outraged that she is willing to have their small child looked after by the Decca record company. It is Francine's scorn for Jimmy's implicit acceptance of traditional familial and ethnic roles that eventually leads to their separation.

In Scorsese's early films, as Michael Bliss has noted, we often come across homophilia pure and simple.[41] In *Mean Streets*, Charlie shares a double bed with Johnny Boy (De Niro) and scrupulously heeds the warnings of his local bosses to keep away from his (supposedly) unstable girlfriend, Teresa (Amy Robinson). As Charlie's lovemaking with Teresa was full of crucifix-ridden anguish anyway, this may not have been too great a hardship for either of them. What we find in Scorsese's later and more sophisticated films, though, is an attempt not simply to reflect these ethnic and gender stereotypes but to reflect upon them, to interrogate the conditions that produce such cultural and ideological assumptions. In this sense, *Alice Doesn't Live Here Any More* represents an interesting attempt to move away from the more rigid kinds of claustrophobic ethnic psychology. The overt subject of this film is change, change in a mental as well as a geographical sense, with Ellen Burstyn's Alice gratefully abandoning the world of New Mexico after her violently aggressive husband has been killed in a truck crash. The film chronicles Ellen's subsequent search for fulfillment both as a professional singer and in terms of a less antagonistic relationship with a man. For Scorsese, too, the film seems at times almost a deliberate inversion of his earlier preoccupations, implying as it does a determination to train his camera upon something new and different. But the irony here is that Alice's idea of a husband, as she says, is still the "strong and dominating" man she associates with her innocent, repressive past. The film begins in imitation of *The Wizard of Oz* by peering through a window at images of "Alice as a young girl"; in fact, *Alice* mirrors the *Oz* paradigm all the way through, for by finally kissing Kris Kristofferson's David alongside a fence that is an exact replication of the fence outside Alice's childhood home, the heroine has succeeded in getting back to where she started from. The end of her quest is not, ultimately, radical change but the recapture of innocence. Alice dreams not so much of independence but of a comfortable subservience; when her "ship comes in," she proclaims, she plans to equip herself with a fancy negligee and high-heeled gold slippers.

This correlation between *Alice* and *The Wizard of Oz* also introduces the question of the role of popular mythology in Scorsese's cinema. As in John Ford, we find a constant oscillation between myth and empirical reality, with quotidian life continually eliding into a mythic status that in Scorsese's case often appears as the world of the cinema and its legends. The frequent mirrors within the mise-en-scène of *Alice Doesn't Live Here Any More* reflect this dichotomy, with characters fragmented between their individual and mythic incarnations. At the end of the film, Alice decides to abandon her fantasy of getting to Monterey and opts instead to content herself with daily life in Tucson, with the sign "Monterey" outside her Arizona café signifying a metonymical diminution of her California dreaming. But this conclusion is itself another echo of *The Wizard of Oz,* which at the end of the narrative is exposed as merely a movie, simply someone rolling a film. In both cases, the dream is deconstructed, the idealistic vision acknowledged as too farfetched and so collapsed into a more homely sign; accordingly, by her final renunciation of mythic transcendence Alice is ironically fulfilling *The Wizard of Oz*'s mythic pattern. As in Altman's cinema, myth in Scorsese provides a structure of determinism and a circumscription of the characters' individuality, but it also produces a sanctification of mundane everyday reality. Indeed, Scorsese's use of the patterns of cinematic myth operates in a very similar way to his manipulation of Catholicism in the earlier films, for it emerges as an overarching but latent structure, forever knocking on the characters' psychological doors. Although these self-conscious cinematic parallels function in a more complex way in works like *Alice,* this intertextual style can be seen in embryo as far back as Scorsese's first films. There are many references to Ford's *The Searchers* in *Who's That Knocking on My Door?* – J.R. and his girlfriend have a long talk about the movie at one point – and in *Mean Streets* Charlie and Teresa actually go to see Ford's film. Even more aptly, Robert Phillip Kolker has convincingly argued that *Taxi Driver* should be seen as a conscious parody of *The Searchers:* Travis Bickle has come to believe quite literally in the myths of purity and heroism propagated by John Wayne, and in his final blitzkrieg – "somewhere between Charles Manson and Saint Paul," as Scorsese himself put it – Bickle is imitating Wayne's propensity to stand no nonsense from uppity Comanches.[42] Kolker's point is that the very form of parody, predicated upon doubling and reflection, works to deny that crazed individuality Bickle cherishes: cinematic myth here becomes an objectifying force that reveals how Bickle's psychopathic solipsism has failed to accommodate itself to the social and corporate environment. Bickle is, as Scorsese remarked, one of the world's "false saints," a character whose rigid idealism is not tempered by any awareness of the need to enter negotiations with a preexistent community.[43]

In *New York, New York,* we similarly find constant references back to old Hollywood musicals, a link strengthened by the starring role of Liza Minnelli, with her natural "intertextual" reference back to her mother, Judy Garland. Many critics have noted that the intrusions of banal reality here ironize and subvert the glamorous myths of Hollywood, which is true, but it is important to appreciate how the process also works in the opposite direction, with banal reality becoming irradiated or transubstantiated by the formal splendor of myth. In Scorsese, there is a continuous reciprocal interaction between these two levels. There are no location shots in *New York, New York,* and by emphasizing the artificiality of his hermetic cinematic environment Scorsese is not only commenting on the "star-making" ideology inherent in the genre of musical but also, by extension, engaging in a wider critique of the effort to "be somebody" within American society. In ideological terms, the musical has traditionally been the most conservative film genre because of its implicit belief in the ultimate inevitability of health, wealth, and happiness: as Rick Altman has written, the show's musical harmonies become associated with the thematic "harmony" of "romantic resolution," a strategy designed to consolidate that model of success the film stars simultaneously guarantee and incarnate.[44] By self-reflexively foregrounding the arbitrary nature of cinematic codes, Scorsese problematizes the musical genre's apparently effortless equation between sexual and economic gratification. *New York, New York* is by no means satirical in tone, and it does not seek to annul these generic assumptions; nevertheless, the du-

42 Kolker, *Cinema of Loneliness,* p. 239; Michael Rye and Lynda Myles, *The Movie Brats: How the Film Generation Took Over Hollywood* (London: Faber, 1979), p. 213.
43 Chris Hodenfield, "Martin Scorsese: The Art of Noncompromise," *American Film,* Mar. 1989, p. 48.
44 Rick Altman, *The American Film Musical* (Bloomington: Indiana Univ. Press, 1987), p. 51.

plicitous irony of Scorsese's movie works to interrogate such assumptions, reframing them in a quizzical style. Once again, the text veers toward that familiar American Catholic mode of parody, neither quite in this world nor quite out of it.

In Scorsese's first films, then, his characters live almost exclusively amid the iconography of religion, while in his later work they live amid the iconography of secular myth. Indeed, it is one of the formal characteristics of Scorsese's best work that he opens up his cinematic space to tap into the choric energies of myth. We see this in *The King of Comedy*, where Rupert Pupkin's success in mythologizing himself leads him onto the covers of *Time* and *Newsweek*; in the "Happy Endings" sequence of *New York, New York*, where Francine Evans and Jimmy Doyle finish up as famous musicians featured in *Variety*; in *Raging Bull*, where Jake La Motta's boxing triumphs are reported televisually, set within a framework of 1950s advertisements for Pabst beer. *Boxcar Bertha*'s opening credits are also in the style of television, with newsreel pictures of the 1930s merging into popular myths about Roosevelt that overlook the film. Scorsese's cinema has an almost McLuhanite feel for the images and icons of mass society, and these secular rituals tend to deflect the center of attention away from merely individual characters toward the social environment as a whole. The idiom shifts from uppercase Catholicism to lowercase catholicity, catholicity predicated upon a universalizing, all-encompassing strategy that develops out of, but modifies, the earlier religious purpose. In *Mean Streets*, the constant intercutting of spoken dialogue with raucous pop music creates a polyphonic effect where the focus is not on any one person but upon a multitude of different things happening all at once. The style here is, as Pauline Kael said, "operatic," a communal idiom where pop music (like the movies and the church) infiltrates the lives of these characters and comes to set the terms within which they see themselves.[45] Scorsese further explored his interest in music's mythic, choric potential both as an editor for *Woodstock* (1969) and as director of *The Last Waltz* (1978), a film that chronicles The Band's last concert. The Band's performance of "The Weight" here is celebrated by a puff of incenselike smoke, while Bob Dylan's leading of the company in "I Shall Be Released" seems reminiscent of the singing of an old school song, a plaintive celebration of the communal memory of one particular era.

In Scorsese's later films, therefore, we find realism and ritual interpenetrating each other as theology relocates itself within the vagaries of national myth. In this light, *The Last Temptation of Christ* (1988) is a

45 Pauline Kael, "Everyday Inferno," in *Reeling* (Boston: Little, Brown and Co., 1976), p. 169.

throwback to Scorsese's early work, not a surprising circumstance considering it took him some seventeen years to bring the project to fruition. The conflict between flesh and spirit, so apparent in *Who's That Knocking* and *Mean Streets,* becomes in this text a subject of torment for Christ himself. The film reeks of corporeality: animal flesh is roasted and consumed, human flesh is tortured and flayed. Like Charlie in *Mean Streets,* Scorsese's Christ (Willem Dafoe) searches with anguish for the spiritual life, and this quest ultimately leads him to reject the temptation of a normal domestic (and sexual) life and to opt instead, like so many of Scorsese's central characters, for the painful heroism of crucifixion. This antagonism between physical and spiritual substance is replicated here in the artistic difficulty of embodying abstract spiritual ideas within the physical limitations of the cinematic medium. The apparent absurdity of some scenes – such as the temptation in the desert, where Satan takes on the disguises of lions and snakes in stunts too obviously deriving from Hollywood's box of tricks – could be seen as a corollary to the film's central dilemma of the relationship between spirit and matter. The paradox of incarnation for Christ becomes the paradox for Scorsese of reincarnating the Bible within a form of contemporary art. In this sense, David Bowie's star turn as Pontius Pilate exemplifies the film's jokey self-reflexivity, its postmodernist recognition that all these images are, finally, nothing but a fabrication. Yet by foregrounding his fiction-making devices in this way, Scorsese surreptitiously directs his audience's attention to what he conceives to be the more profound issues behind the film, those religious implications that are signposted by the colorful events upon the screen but are not, in the end, to be confused with them. Like Hitchcock, Scorsese seeks to undermine the glamorous power of his own camera, to recover the moral and religious vision underlying all these deceptive facades and framings of the celluloid world.

The Last Temptation of Christ is, though, entirely consistent with Scorsese's long-standing project of attempting to achieve an interpenetration between spiritual and secular worlds, to "keep the supernatural on the same level as the natural" as he himself put it.[46] Christ's fluctuation between humanity and divinity is analogous to the way the gangsters of *Mean Streets* try to work out their salvation within the urban squalor of Little Italy. In Scorsese's own description:

> You don't practice penance in the church, you don't hide out in the church, you don't hide out in a monastery like a monk. You gotta live amongst the people and change life that way or help people reach salvation *in the street,* through day-to-day contact. . . . It's like a religious vocation. That's where I think a lot of my passion switched over from

46 *Scorsese on Scorsese,* p. 143.

the priestly vocation, when I decided that wasn't the right way for me to act out these things. Mine was harder: I had to do it in the street. . . . That's the sense of it all in terms of this Catholic thing we're talking about.[47]

Scorsese's sanctified secular rituals of television, pop music, and Hollywood musicals are all testimony to this desire to apotheosize the mundane world, to find salvation within the "day-to-day" events of the streets. The transubstantiation of Jimmy Doyle's life from empirical fact to Hollywood ritual in *New York, New York* is a correlative to Christ's descent from celestial to human status in *The Last Temptation*. Scorsese's films, balanced between mythic spirit and human flesh, function as cinematic equivalents of Catholic transubstantiation in that they aspire to describe two different levels of reality at once.

It is this kind of doubling and duplicity that links Scorsese's Catholic style with Hitchcock's. In Hitchcock, as in Scorsese, cinematic events exist in two realms simultaneously: on the immediate surface of the world, but also within a realm of "divine" truth, or demonic evil (Hitchcock), or secular myth (Scorsese). Nothing is ever quite what it seems, or all that it seems. Both directors subvert the blander conventions of American social life to reveal a sense of evil – and possible redemption – which derives from a strictly metaphysical perspective and has no connection with that kind of amiable blathering about "moral regeneration" with which political candidate Charles Palantine (Leonard Harris) regales his audience in *Taxi Driver*. Pauline Kael has suggested that *Mean Streets* embraces "a thicker-textured rot and violence than we have ever had in an American movie, and a riper sense of evil": whatever Scorsese's characters choose to do, their actions, like the actions of Hitchcock's characters, seem to be fraught with sin.[48] Scorsese himself saw the menacing atmosphere of *After Hours* as "to some extent a parody of Hitchcock's style," adding of Hitchcock that "over the years his films have become more emotionally meaningful for me."[49]

So the paradoxical, disturbing, defamiliarizing cinema of Hitchcock and Scorsese works to uncover areas of crime and guilt that resist explanation purely in terms of secular humanism or liberal optimism. These forces derive instead from traditionalist Catholic culture, with its less idealistic understanding of the parameters of the human spirit. In his 1891 essay "Criticism and Fiction," William Dean Howells argued that Dostoyevsky would never gain general acceptance in the United States because he ignored "the more smiling aspects of life, which are the more

47 Occhiogrosso, *Once a Catholic*, p. 92.
48 Kael, "Everyday Inferno," p. 169.
49 *Scorsese on Scorsese*, p. 101.

American," and we can be certain Howells would have felt equally uneasy about the sinister, foreign tendencies of Hitchcock and Scorsese.[50] Howells's attitude might seem absurdly anachronistic, of course; yet complaints from critics about the violent, unpleasant, even perverse sensibilities of these film directors are still very frequent in America today. Such criticisms may not be invalid in themselves, but they carry less weight if they ignore the ideological aesthetics of Catholicism and the displaced metaphysical contexts within which these films are working.

50 William Dean Howells, *Criticism and Fiction, and Other Essays,* ed. Clara Marburg Kirk and Rudolf Kirk (New York: New York Univ. Press, 1959), p. 62.

Part V

Postmodernism and the Novel of Displacement

15

The Rewriting of Theology: Katherine Anne Porter, Flannery O'Connor, Walker Percy, Donald Barthelme

In examining the work of three southern Catholic novelists whose religious beliefs were of a more traditional order, we will be able to see a
development from modernist to postmodernist conceptions of literature
and theology. Katherine Anne Porter, born in Texas, is firmly within
the modernist framework, even though her most famous work, *Ship of
Fools,* did not appear until 1962; Flannery O'Connor, from Georgia, and
Walker Percy, from Louisiana, both negotiate that postmodernist fragmentation and discontinuity more characteristic of the post-1945 era.
The relationship of Donald Barthelme both with the South and with
religion is more problematical, but many of the dilemmas and paradoxes
in his fiction bear interesting resemblances to theological paradoxes that
resonate in these more orthodox Southern writers.

For Katherine Anne Porter, Catholicism operates as an aesthetic fiction,
a beautiful idea, just as it did for earlier modernist writers such as Henry
Adams and Hemingway. She was brought up in a Methodist family and
was baptized a Catholic in 1910, shortly before her twentieth birthday.
These facts came to light only relatively recently; some earlier critics had
assumed from her fictional representations of Catholic families that Porter
was born Catholic. In her long-standing reticence about her own biography, one might see an element of wish fulfillment at work: loathing
what she later termed the "petty middle class puritanism" of her Texas
home, Porter participates in that familiar modernist rebellion against the
narrow cultural codes of the Protestant "booboisie," as H. L. Mencken
called it. Porter told Rhea Johnson she was "charmed" by Catholicism.[1]
She loved the dramatic and aesthetic qualities of High Mass, she looked
forward to the psychological catharsis of confession, and as she later told
Enrique Hank Lopez, she viewed the hereafter as "one of the most

---

[1] Joan Givner, *Katherine Anne Porter: A Life* (New York: Simon and Schuster, 1982),
pp. 185, 508.

charming ideas that man ever invented," adding that "it would be perfectly wonderful if it were true." With her attachment to these ceremonial aspects of Catholicism, Porter not surprisingly abhorred the "modernization of church ritual" proposed by the Second Vatican Council in the early 1960s. "I am," she said, "frankly appalled by the prospect of hearing High Mass in low English."[2]

Religious devotion in the literal sense was not a central part of Porter's intellectual constitution. In her twenties, she moved away from the church for several years; even after her reconciliation with the faith she was not, she said, "a regular churchgoer" but rather one of the "Easter and Christmas Catholics" – a visitor on special occasions.[3] Her essays reflect this sense of detachment. In a 1923 piece on "The Fiesta of Guadalupe" – a festival commemorating Juan Diego's vision of Mary on the hillside and the initiation of Mexico into the "mystic company" of the church – Porter finds that "the sight of men dancing in a religious ecstasy links one's imagination, for the moment, with all the lives that have been." The crucial word here is "imagination": as for Santayana and Wallace Stevens, religion appears to Porter as a supreme fiction, an event accessible to the higher powers of human fancy. Her spectatorial position gives Porter a patronizing superiority over the Mexicans' "awful hands of faith, the credulous and worn hands of believers; the humble and beseeching hands of the millions and millions who have only the anodyne of credulity."[4] This is a demonstration of what Robert Penn Warren's famous essay on Porter described as "irony with a center," the underlying skepticism that marks her work. This kind of irony was a crucial component of Porter's religious outlook as well. She loathed the dogmatic, an-ironic tendencies of T. S. Eliot's writing after his conversion to Christianity, for instance, while in 1963 she described the tradition of dissent as "a kind of church itself, with its leaders, teachers, saints, martyrs, heroes."[5]

When she wrote fiction about the South, Porter maintained this attitude of distance and superiority toward Catholicism by affiliating it with the Edenic, but necessarily spoiled, innocence of childhood and the old southern order. In her story "The Old Order," Porter's heroine remembers her grandmother's "feast-day voice" as "the only reality to them in a

2 Enrique Hank Lopez, *Conversations with Katherine Anne Porter, Refugee from Indian Creek* (Boston: Little, Brown and Co., 1981), pp. 22–3.

3 Ibid., p. 22.

4 *The Collected Essays and Occasional Writings of Katherine Anne Porter* (New York: Delacorte–Seymour Lawrence, 1970), pp. 395; 397–8.

5 Robert Penn Warren, "Katherine Anne Porter (Irony with a Center)," *Kenyon Review*, 4 (1942), 29–42; Katherine Anne Porter, "On a Criticism of Thomas Hardy," in *The Days Before* (London: Secker and Warburg, 1953), p. 26.

world that seemed otherwise without fixed authority or refuge"; but, as time has passed, so this imaginary plenitude and security has inevitably become disrupted by the changes of the modern world.[6] This is one of the most familiar equations within Porter's short stories: the pastoral idyll of the past is forfeited in favor of experiential journeys toward freedom, yet this past recurs in memory as something to which the characters remain emotionally attached, even though intellectually they have detached themselves from its premises. In "Old Mortality" (1936) and other stories, Porter's favorite heroine, Miranda, attempts to break away from her claustrophobic southern heritage and discover some form of existential self-definition, but her autonomy is continually being compromised by confrontations with elderly relatives such as Cousin Eva, whose hold on Miranda's psyche is irrational but insidiously pervasive. This pattern is repeated in Porter's larger representations of Catholicism, which, in typical modernist fashion, tends to be seen as emotionally desirable but philosophically dubious.

This leads Porter's texts into the realm of paradox, where we find her characters experiencing a perverse attachment to the bondage of a past they no longer believe in. Cousin Eva's persistent threat to chastise the twenty-two-year-old Miranda is a counterpart to the oppressive Mexican landscape of "Hacienda" (1934), in which those who "feel the whip know they suffer but do not know why."[7] "Hacienda" turns upon a dichotomy between archaic Catholic rituals in Mexico and the way these rituals – the candlelight processions, and so on – are reflected and reproduced by a modern Russian film crew. Although contemporary technology (and, by extension, literature) can reconstitute these old Catholic practices only in a detached, voyeuristic way, the concern of Porter's text is with how these sacrificial "moments of violence" produce for the inhabitants of Mexico themselves a "senseless excitement," how their traditional culture encourages an "almost ecstatic death-expectancy."[8] "Hacienda" is obsessed both with Catholic ritual in itself and also with the necessary failure of the modernist text to participate fully in these sacramental ecstasies. In the light of this kind of ambivalence, it is particularly apposite that Porter's fiction should be permeated stylistically with paradoxes and oxymorons: "The Old Order," for instance, talks of how a circus crowd "roared with *savage delight,* shrieks of *dreadful laughter* like devils in *delicious torment*" (my emphases). These self-contradictory tropes could be seen as analogues to the moral paradoxes around issues of repression and

6 *The Collected Stories of Katherine Anne Porter* (New York: Harcourt, Brace and World, 1965), pp. 322, 324.
7 Ibid., p. 142.
8 Ibid., p. 143.

freedom, plenitude and lack, that work through Porter's art. The bondage of the old faith, like that of the old Texan order, appears to absolve and to imprison in equal measure. (Harold Bloom has suggested that Porter's "truest contemporary, in the sense of a profound affinity in art" was Hart Crane, and Crane delighted in linguistic and thematic paradoxes of a similar kind.)[9] Catholicism, then, appears in Porter's work as a form of cultural and psychological conditioning, while also being an aesthetically attractive but irredeemably marginalized force within contemporary secular society. Characteristic of this process is Porter's 1931 story "The Cracked Looking-Glass," in which the Dublin-born Rosaleen has come to regret her migration to New York to live with her drab American husband, Dennis. Though she yearns after the green fields of County Sligo, which she had known in her youth, the cracked looking glass of the title implies that the fracturing of this pastoral inheritance is an inevitable phenomenon; in Lacanian terms, the symbolic order of the adult world is nostalgic for an imaginary plenitude of childhood that is impossible to recover. Expelled from her youthful Eden, Rosaleen can resort only to the consolatory formal gesture of lighting a candle in a Boston Catholic church.[10]

In Porter's last and longest piece of fiction, *Ship of Fools* (1962), religion in its theological conception has been almost entirely superseded by religious-based cultural traditions, and the narrative spends much time meditating upon the differences between Protestant and Catholic societies. On a ship called the *Vera* sailing from Mexico to Germany in 1931, we find established a (fairly simplistic) binary opposition between the sense of festive community enjoyed by impoverished Cubans, Spaniards, and other Latins and the rigid individualism and will-to-power favored by the ship's German crew. It is the same dichotomy Santayana outlined in *Egotism in German Philosophy* (1915), and the same dichotomy Porter herself wrote about during a 1931 visit to Berlin: "Nietzsche is dangerous," she said, "because his mind has power without intelligence; he is all will without enlightenment. His phrases are inflated, full of violence, a gross kind of cruel poetry – like Wagner's music."[11] Predictably enough, the German students on this fictional *Ship of Fools* revere Nietzsche, Goethe, Kant, Hegel, and Schopenhauer, philosophers who are also implicitly admired by the ship's stern German officers. Captain Thiele's "perfectly symmetrical morality" is said to loathe Catholics "on prin-

9 Ibid., p. 345; Harold Bloom, Introd., *Modern Critical Views: Katherine Anne Porter*, ed. Harold Bloom (New York: Chelsea House, 1986), p. 4.
10 *Collected Stories*, p. 125.
11 *Collected Essays*, p. 443.

ciple," and he views the squalling Latin passengers as "rabble."[12] The Lutheran Wilhelm Freytag's strict purity similarly gives him a "moral aversion to poverty, an instinctive contempt and distrust of the swarming poor" (63). Professor Hutten, former head of a German school in Mexico, is another stock figure who applauds the "old Germanic spirit" (342) of Kantian dualism, where a willed and transcendent "good" can separate itself off from tawdry human failings.

Contrasted with all of these Germanic types, we find the chronically ill Bavarian Catholic Doctor Schumann, a man whose closeness to death reinforces his sense of the limitations of any human endeavor. Watching a band of Latin dancers, the Catholic Schumann follows Aquinas by denying that good and evil are essentially distinct categories: "The gauzy glittering surface of gaiety lay lightly over the foulest pools of evil," thinks Schumann, "God bless the comedians just the same – are we not all sinners?" (349). Circuses and vaudeville acts cheer Schumann because they epitomize his intuition that the human race is not divided dualistically into devils and angels, but that evil is rather a subset – or, as Aquinas said, an absence – of good. Denying the possibility of pastoral innocence and idealism, Schumann also rejects the excesses of individualism; the self-indulgent, self-pitying alienation of his fellow passenger, La Condesa, is made to seem absurd by the fact that everyone here is, quite literally, in the same boat. The literary form of Porter's novel trumps the Germans' aspirations toward transcendence by reminding them that they too are necessarily participating in communality. On board this ship of fools, everyone is an object rather than a subject, a simple voyager on a journey between two cities: Vera Cruz and Bremerhaven, this world and the next. So in Porter's last novel Catholicism functions primarily as a form of cultural rebellion and antithesis. Just as her stories of the 1930s rebel against small-town Texas Methodism, so *Ship of Fools* rebels against a Germanic romanticism that becomes explicitly equated with Nazi ideals in the figure of Herr Rieber, a man who entertains plans to exterminate Jews as well as defective infants and any other impediments to the grand National Socialist design. Porter seems to have believed these racial characteristics were ingrained and timeless rather than historically constructed, remarking of the Germans in 1962 that "they are just as dangerous as they were, and the moment they get back their power they are going to do it again."[13]

12 Katherine Anne Porter, *Ship of Fools* (Boston: Little, Brown and Co., 1962), pp. 427, 172–3. Subsequent page references are given in parentheses in the text.
13 Quoted in William L. Nance, S.M., *Katherine Anne Porter and the Art of Rejection* (Chapel Hill: Univ. of North Carolina Press, 1963), p. 70.

The hostility of *Ship of Fools* to what Santayana called "the German mind" bears interesting resemblances to Alfred Hitchcock's 1948 film *Rope,* where James Stewart's Rupert Cadell acts as a moral agent to undermine the Nietzschean fantasies of two of his former pupils. One of these pupils, Brandon (John Dall), is a great believer in the "superior" people who are beyond good and evil and he opts for a lifestyle based upon stylish narcissism and fantasies of "the perfect murder." Stewart's character, though, explicitly associates this kind of Faustian amorality with the activities of Hitler and asks Brandon by what right he thought he could judge somebody "inferior." "Did you think you were God?" demands Stewart scornfully. Many such anti-German sentiments were echoed in the days immediately after the Second World War, of course. Yet the particular intellectual twist offered by Hitchcock, whose film specifically castigates the premises of German romanticism, reveals his affiliation with the tradition of Catholic thought extending from Santayana through Katherine Anne Porter. For these American Catholics, the German will is seen not just as politically dangerous but also as philosophically corrupt, attempting as it does to deny the communality of the human condition and to erect instead illusory paradigms of individualistic power and freedom.

Both Flannery O'Connor and Walker Percy engage more centrally than Katherine Anne Porter with Catholic theology. Indeed, in his nonfiction work, *Lost in the Cosmos* (1983), Percy specifically ridicules Porter's kind of modernist predilection for admiring, in detached fashion, the more superficial aspects of Catholic ritual, what is called here the "esthetic of the spectacle":

> The attraction between the noughted self and the fiesta (quite literally a feast for the starved vacuole of self) exists on a continuum of affinities: at one end, say, the serious yet finally hopeless nostalgia of Henry Adams at Mont-Saint-Michel, at the other the more comprehensive delectation of, say, Oppenheimer and Lawrence at a Pueblo festival in New Mexico which, with its outlandish mixture of Catholic and pagan rites, allows the self the best, it thinks, of both worlds: to keep its distance and at the same time savor the esthetic of the spectacle.[14]

Percy's novel *The Second Coming* (1980) similarly mocks the type of "present-day unbeliever" who transposes *The Divine Comedy* from ethics into aesthetics and "reads Dante for its mythic structure"; while *Lancelot* (1977) makes fun of the idea of a "Lowell Professor of Religion at Har-

---

14 Walker Percy, *Lost in the Cosmos: The Last Self-Help Book* (New York: Farrar, Straus and Giroux, 1983), p. 149.

vard."[15] In the same vein, Flannery O'Connor had little time for Evelyn Waugh, an Anglo-Catholic aesthete who, she said, "has too narrow a definition of what would be a Catholic novel."[16] Also in sarcastic tone is her 1958 story "The Enduring Chill," which satirizes the pretensions of Asbury, an artist manqué returned from New York to the South to die. Once again, Asbury is someone who hankers after the ornaments of religion rather than its spiritual essence. In the throes of his terminal illness, Asbury disdains the "literal mind" of his mother and tells the local Catholic priest he would prefer a conference with a Jesuit "man of culture" on the subject of Joyce, to which the cleric's bewildered response is that "Joyce" is someone he has never met.[17]

The fact that O'Connor's fiction is created out of a clearly defined framework of belief hardly needs emphasis here. Most of her close friends were Catholics – including Allen Tate's wife, Caroline Gordon, who converted to Catholicism in 1947 – while O'Connor's letters are strewn with theological references of the most erudite kind. Many critics have described how her fiction aspires toward the final apotheosis of divine revelation, and there is no need to go over that ground here. At the same time, O'Connor was, as she said in a 1955 letter, "a Catholic peculiarly possessed of the modern consciousness, that thing Jung describes as unhistorical, solitary and guilty"; and it is this sense of the incongruity between Catholic faith and a secularized modern world that brings about many of the tensions within O'Connor's texts.[18] For O'Connor, as for Percy, there is no self-evident social context with which Christian "truth" can intermesh, and this creates a sense of incongruity highlighted further by the especially anomalous juxtaposition of American Catholicism with the Bible Belt of the Deep South. Thus for Percy and O'Connor, Catholic faith must come to terms not only with a typically modernistic sense of philosophical exile and displacement, but also with the geographic displacement bound to be experienced by American Catholics in this particular region. The freak, said O'Connor in one of her essays, is an emblem of this displacement: only a person alienated from the smugly secular and humanist world could become an appropriate vessel for the

15 Walker Percy, *The Second Coming* (New York: Farrar, Straus and Giroux, 1980), pp. 189–90; *Lancelot* (New York: Farrar, Straus and Giroux, 1977), p. 138. For both novels, subsequent page references are given in parentheses in the text.
16 Sally Fitzgerald, ed., *The Habit of Being: The Letters of Flannery O'Connor* (New York: Farrar, Straus and Giroux, 1979), p. 236.
17 Flannery O'Connor, *Everything That Rises Must Converge* (New York: Farrar, Straus and Giroux, 1965), pp. 118, 126–7, 131.
18 *The Habit of Being: The Letters of Flannery O'Connor*, p. 90.

infusion of divine grace.[19] We see this pattern of dislocation in the 1954 story "The Displaced Person," where the vagrant Pole, Guizac, disrupts the comfortable and complacent farming world of the materialistic Mrs. McIntyre. Again in "Good Country People" (1955), the con man, Pointer, may be nearer to God than Joy Hopewell, the spinster with a wooden leg who prides herself upon her superior knowledge and her doctorate in philosophy. Who, this story asks us, are in fact the "good" country people? "I believe," said O'Connor in a 1955 letter, "and the Church teaches that God is as present in the idiot boy as in the genius." Hence for O'Connor all conceptions of individual autonomy and worldly dignity are subverted. Hers is a world where "The Lame Shall Enter First," where even a ne'er-do-well like Hazel Motes in the 1952 novel *Wise Blood* may achieve a surprising grace: Motes is, remarked O'Connor, "too wise . . . ultimately to deny Christ."[20]

Given her concern with how metaphysical "truths" can undercut life's social surfaces, O'Connor's radical piety clearly distances itself from secular mythologies of all kinds. The southern myth of nostalgic plenitude, which so enticed Katherine Anne Porter, carried as little weight with Flannery O'Connor as the northern myth of liberalism and social progress. "The topical is poison," she wrote, "I say a plague on everybody's house as far as the race business goes."[21] O'Connor favored the fictional forms of Gothic – or, as she preferred to call it, the grotesque – precisely to overturn the banal complacency of a literalist style. She conceived the formal shattering of "realism" by the shocking and grotesque to be a formal correlative to the shattering of bourgeois complacency by an unhoused religious vision. O'Connor was familiar with Mario Praz's 1933 book *The Romantic Agony,* in which Praz analyzes a similar pattern of literary subversion, in this case the subversion of Victorian poetic realism by various forms of dark Gothic sexuality.[22]

Yet O'Connor's use of the grotesque engages her texts in an interesting tension with the premises of neo-scholastic Catholic theology. As we will recall, at the beginning of the twentieth century Pope Leo XIII promoted the rationalistic mechanisms of Thomism as a reaction against the dangerous tendencies of modernist philosophy and science. By the 1950s, neo-scholasticism's effort to reconcile faith with reason reigned supreme in American Catholic colleges. This mode of thought was not, insisted Philip Gleason, simply a nostalgic or "Romantic medievalism,"

19 Flannery O'Connor, *Mystery and Manners: Occasional Prose,* ed. Sally and Robert Fitzgerald (New York: Farrar, Straus and Giroux, 1969), p. 44.
20 *The Habit of Being: The Letters of Flannery O'Connor,* pp. 99, 350.
21 Edward Kessler, *Flannery O'Connor and the Language of Apocalypse* (Princeton: Princeton Univ. Press, 1986), p. 44.
22 *The Habit of Being: The Letters of Flannery O'Connor,* p. 229.

which was "vaguely idealistic, intuitive, impressionistic"; indeed, it was "just the opposite – technical, bluntly realistic, discursive, precise, systematic and objective."[23] There are distinct traces of this neo-scholasticism in O'Connor's literary style: her texts are "bluntly realistic" and "precise" rather than "impressionistic" in their radical pruning of every romantic excess and in their aloof application of the letter of the Catholic law. But O'Connor's manipulation of the grotesque does to some extent problematize this neo-scholastic finitude, because the very nature of the grotesque genre inherently denies finality and closure. The traditional function of the literary grotesque is to rip things open, to render moribund systems vulnerable to the very forces they are seeking to exclude. In O'Connor's case, this is, as she said, the advent of "mystery" alongside "manners," the interruption of observable social reality by the latent force of divine truth. In a 1962 lecture, O'Connor remarked on how "what makes a story work" for her was:

> an action or a gesture which . . . would have to suggest both the world and eternity. The action or gesture I'm talking about would have to be on the anagogical level, that is, the level which has to do with the Divine life and our participation in it. It would be a gesture that transcended any neat allegory that might have been intended or any pat moral categories a reader could make.[24]

But by emphasizing the "anagogical level" rather than "any neat allegory," O'Connor's texts expose themselves to the vagaries of enigma and silence. No final aphorism directs the reader how to explicate "The Enduring Chill." Its "mystery" and lack of resolution may echo the mystery of divine grace within the terrestrial world; nevertheless, as with all mysteries, its precise location remains undefined. In O'Connor's world, it is not only a good man who is hard to find.

In many ways, though, it is this very sense of an irremediable gap or absence in O'Connor's writing that constitutes its artistic complexity. It is easy enough simply to "interpret" O'Connor's stories in the light of Thomistic theology, as Ralph Wood and other critics have done, but that does not seem to do justice to the full density of her material. This is not, of course, to deny the overarching theological framework of her fiction. But it is to suggest, like André Bleikasten, that the real interest of O'Connor's work lies in its representation of "the uncanny" – *das Unheimliche,* in Freud's term – "that disquieting strangeness apt to arise at every turn out of the most intimately familiar, and through which our everyday sense of reality is made to yield to the troubling awareness of

---

23 Philip Gleason, *Keeping the Faith: American Catholicism Past and Present* (Notre Dame: Univ. of Notre Dame Press, 1987), p. 23.
24 O'Connor, *Mystery and Manners,* pp. 153, 111.

the world's otherness." Bleikasten offers a Lacanian analysis of O'Connor's last story, "Parker's Back," and convincingly demonstrates that, rather than discovering here an "unequivocal transcendental signified equated with ultimate truth," the reader should rather be seeking "multiple meanings produced by the interplay of signifiers." The tattoo on Parker's back, the fictional hero's mordant desire to reject and artistically redefine his given body, is tentatively associated by Bleikasten with the guilty and potentially heretical business of creating art and artifice: "Writing, in the last resort, is perhaps little more than an elaborate and displaced form of tattooing, a sublimation of the tattooed body into the *corpus,* tomb and temple of the written self."[25] This argument would imply that – as with Gerard Manley Hopkins, Frank O'Hara, and other "Catholic" authors – O'Connor's texts betray an uncertainty about the extent to which the inherently transgressive and idiosyncratically subjective power of writing is able to reconcile itself with the dictates of objective "truth." Yet it is just this kind of potential ambiguity and excess of signification that rescues O'Connor's stories from being mere diagrammatic expositions of Catholic principles. The emphasis upon disruptive grotesque forms, a literary parallel to the conceptual gaps and mystery of theological anagoge, creates space for secular as well as sacred readings of O'Connor's fiction.

In this lurking sense of uncertainty and displacement, O'Connor's work strangely resembles that of Jean Genet. In Genet's world, as in O'Connor's, it is the villains and outlaws who become the true saints. The narrator of *The Thief's Journal* (1949) is in fact a genuine ascetic, "the humblest of the world's poor" as he describes himself, who insists upon a self-discipline "similar to spiritual exercises," which enables him to "set poverty up as a virtue." Yet Genet's thief does not neglect to note that, when he happens upon (temporary) riches, he too enjoys strutting up and down vainly in front of the poor. In this self-flagellating way, Genet's hero seeks to excoriate every trace of personal pride; he denounces Saint Vincent de Paul, by contrast, for a lack of true penitence and for a narcissistic inclination toward self-conscious "saintliness": "He should have been willing to commit the galley slave's crime instead of merely taking his place in irons."[26] Genet, then, is an overtly secular author who can be given a sacred interpretation; O'Connor, likewise, is an overtly sacred author who can be given a secular interpretation. Because both writers are attuned to the paradoxes and complexity of Cath-

25 André Bleikasten, "Writing on the Flesh: Tattoos and Taboos in 'Parker's Back,'" *Southern Literary Journal,* 14, no. 2 (Spring 1982), 8, 10, 17.
26 Jean Genet, *The Thief's Journal,* trans. Bernard Frechtman (New York: Grove Press, 1964), pp. 77, 176, 213.

olic culture, ideas of "belief" or "disbelief" cease to be relevant as wholly distinct categories, for neither writer is susceptible of being finalized by theological proof. It would of course be an exaggeration to suggest that the Catholic psychologies of O'Connor and Genet are actually self-mirroring and interchangeable. Although O'Connor wrote in a letter of 1955 that "the operation of the Church is entirely set up for the sinner; which creates much misunderstanding among the smug," she also noted at the same time that "sin occasionally brings one closer to God, but not habitual sin and not this petty kind that blocks every small good."[27] Nevertheless, the fictional personae of both O'Connor and Genet inhabit landscapes of dramatic irony where mysterious external forces are operating to displace the characters' powers of freedom and autonomous moral judgment.

This sense of displacement, however, highlights another area of tension within O'Connor's work. In her letters and essays, she continually stressed how "the concrete" is the artist's "medium" and how "fiction is so very much an incarnational art" whose fundamental task is to incarnate and make visible what Aquinas said should be the central concern of all artists, "the good of that which is made."[28] In her essay "The Nature and Aim of Fiction," O'Connor categorically rejected the Manichaeans' separation of spirit and matter and their heresy that "all material things were evil"; in a letter of 1957, she remarked disapprovingly that Graham Greene's writing lapses into this kind of heretical mode, attempting dualistically to divide grace from nature.[29] It is because she cherished what she called "the Catholic sacramental view of life" that O'Connor felt all natural creation to be fit subject matter for the Catholic novelist, since divine grace is immanent everywhere. This is also why she was so scathing about Cardinal Spellman and other bad Catholic novelists who, she said, prioritize narrow forms of preaching and dogma rather than "the order, proportion and radiance of what they are making." The religious novelist, said O'Connor, should not attempt to "tidy up reality" but should attend to the revelation of divine mystery within nature as it actually is.[30] Again, it is clear here that O'Connor's theories of art and religion as rigorously objective phenomena were heavily influenced by the neo-scholastic philosophers: Maritain's *Art and Scholasticism* was "the book I cut my aesthetic teeth on," she remarked in a 1957 letter. In 1956, she similarly commended William Lynch's work on the "anagogical or Christian imagination" as "very valuable." That neo-

27 *The Habit of Being: The Letters of Flannery O'Connor*, p. 93.
28 O'Connor, *Mystery and Manners*, pp. 146, 68, 65.
29 Ibid., p. 68; *The Habit of Being*, p. 201.
30 O'Connor, *Mystery and Manners*, pp. 152, 175, 189, 178.

scholastic hostility to the spirit of romanticism that so affected Allen Tate
is highly visible in O'Connor as well: "Nothing is more repulsive to me
than the idea of myself setting up a little universe of my own choosing,"
she declared in a 1956 letter; while any tendency of the writer toward
an "overflowing ego" is peremptorily slapped down in her essay on
"Writing Short Stories."[31] O'Connor's problem, though, is that while
aspiring sacramentally to celebrate the "good of that which is made,"
she does not find an easy social context within which she can insert her
representation of manners and mystery. She disdains novelistic didacticism, which she associates not only with bad art but also with an excessive
emphasis upon the subjective consciousness of an individual author –
"angelism," in the neo-scholastics' term. Yet in turning outwards to the
landscapes of Georgia, she finds little that seems to correspond with her
Catholic sense of purpose. Therefore the perennial temptation for
O'Connor is to distort this nature, to rearrange it in terms of patterns
more in accord with her own theological beliefs. Yet of course such
distortion itself becomes a rebellion against the objective "good of that
which is made."

This is why we can often see a difference between O'Connor's aesthetic
theories, as propounded in her letters and essays, and what happens in
the actual practice of her art. It is also why Walker Percy suggested that
O'Connor's stories sometimes have more of a "univocal" tendency than
the author herself might have wished:

> She means that the reader is supposed to understand that an action of
> grace occurred, a supervention of grace, especially in "A Good Man Is
> Hard to Find," where the old lady embraces the Misfit. We're supposed
> to understand that she has seen the light, that this act shows grace.
> Well, I'm not sure you really see that . . . she sees her fiction in much
> more univocal, theological terms than I would see it. I think it works
> without that rather simple theological reading, and I think it had *better*
> work without that.[32]

On one hand, this implies the sense of creative slippage that we discussed
earlier: it is the fact that O'Connor's fictions mean more than she intends
them to mean that constitutes their very source of strength. On the other
hand, though, Percy's comment illuminates an unresolved contradiction
in O'Connor's texts between the univocal and the analogical, between
the transcendent and the immanent. Edward Kessler has written of how
O'Connor's work emphasizes displacement, irony, and revelation, the

31 *The Habit of Being: The Letters of Flannery O'Connor*, pp. 216, 132, 147; *Mystery and Manners*, p. 90.
32 Lewis A. Lawson and Victor A. Kramer, eds., *Conversations with Walker Percy* (Jackson: Univ. Press of Mississippi, 1985), p. 233.

violent and apocalyptic destruction of what Kessler called "the confines of the concrete, the dead end of *vraisemblance*." That shattering of materialistic complacency is certainly one side of O'Connor; it is a side highlighted, as Kessler noted, by O'Connor's foregrounding of her own figurative language, particularly the "as if" construction, as if to imply that fictional language, like the world itself, is but a prelude to some ulterior vision.[33] But the other, equally compelling, side of O'Connor's work is designed precisely to focus upon concrete and (supposedly) objective realities – indeed, in a Thomistic way, to perceive the concrete fact as an analogical incarnation of divine truth.

In theory, then, O'Connor was attached to the concrete, but in practice her fiction sometimes drifts toward the realm of disembodied revelation, such as Percy complained about in "A Good Man Is Hard to Find." It was perhaps her awareness of this anomaly that induced O'Connor, in her essay "Novelist and Believer," to lament the twentieth century's "broken condition." Here, in a tone of nostalgia quite uncharacteristic of her writing, she yearned for that chimerical notion of the medieval synthesis: "I don't believe that we shall have great religious fiction until we have again that happy combination of believing artist and believing society."[34] This vision of the Middle Ages as a time of utopian social unity was a standard feature of mid-twentieth-century Catholic thought, although it was becoming somewhat anachronistic by the 1950s as Walter J. Ong and others were beginning to propose new and more recognizably American paradigms of Catholic culture and society. Reading O'Connor from a later perspective, however, we can see that this polarity between neo-scholastic objectivity and grotesque displacement, a polarity at which she worries away throughout her writings, bears close resemblances to the subsequent examination in postmodernist Catholic theology of an unsettling tension between the forces of analogy and difference.

Various radical Catholic theologians in the late twentieth century have set about deconstructing the limits and limitations of allegedly "objective" neo-scholastic thought. Karl Rahner, said David Tracy, conceived his philosophical project as to "upset the clear and untroubled certainties of the neo-Scholastics with his daring retrieval of the forgotten in the excess of meaning in the texts of Thomas Aquinas."[35] In 1973, David Burrell similarly enunciated a desire to liberate the discussion of "analogous discourse" from "the confinement of a particular school" and to acknowledge how the texts of Aquinas self-consciously (and self-

---

33 Kessler, *Flannery O'Connor and the Language of Apocalypse,* pp. 84, 15.
34 O'Connor, *Mystery and Manners,* p. 168.
35 David Tracy, *The Analogical Imagination: Christian Theology and the Culture of Pluralism* (New York: Crossroad, 1981), p. 107.

reflexively) employ analogy in a metaphorical sense to "make true if inadequate assertions about God." Aquinas, according to Burrell, offers strategies for knowledge, not a "naive congruence theory of identity" between heaven and earth. The bond of being is not absolute dogma, as the neo-scholastics thought, but a provisional invitation "to a quality of self-awareness achieved only in the practice of it."[36] David Tracy, re-reading Aquinas through Rahner and Derrida, likewise stressed "the tensive power of the negative" implicit within Thomistic conceptualizations. The differences and dissimilarities between God and the world are, Tracy asserted, equally as significant as those similarities upon which the analogical traditions in Catholic theology have traditionally insisted. It is this power of difference, Tracy declared, that prevents the idea of analogy from degenerating into an excessively domesticated sense of philosophical coherence: "If that power is lost, analogical concepts become mere categories of easy likenesses slipping quietly from their status as similarities-in-difference to mere likenesses, falling finally into the sterility of a relaxed univocity and a facilely affirmative harmony."[37]

It is just this creative tension between analogy and difference that fires O'Connor's fiction. In her yearning after some medieval utopia where "believing artist and believing society" could exist in perfect parallel, O'Connor imitates that typical modernist nostalgia for a lost plenitude where all contradictions might be annulled: one thinks of Eliot's idea of a Christian society, or Hemingway's Edenic Michigan woods, or Katherine Anne Porter's old assured Texan order. The modernists are tantalized by a holistic vision whose embodiment is never quite achieved, even though its outlines remain teasingly apparent. But in O'Connor this modernist strain finds itself crossed with the absences and discontinuities of postmodernism, predicated as it is upon a world of philosophical fragmentation and difference. It is this paradoxical sense of incompleteness and displacement in O'Connor's writing that ensures her fiction comes to carry a larger aesthetic complexity and significance than the rigidity of the neo-scholastic dogma professed in her letters and essays might imply. David Tracy wrote of how the fusion of analogy with difference in postmodernist Catholic theory introduced the prospect of a reconciliation between theology and cultural pluralism, and the plurality of readings available to the student of O'Connor would support just such a hypothesis. O'Connor is, to be sure, a "Catholic" writer, but not just along the lines of narrower neo-scholastic orthodoxies, for the grotesque

---

36 David Burrell, C.S.C., *Analogy and Philosophical Language* (New Haven: Yale Univ. Press, 1973), pp. 9, 168, 176, 170.
37 Tracy, *The Analogical Imagination*, p. 410.

forms of her texts are charged also with the multiple uncertainties and discontinuities of postmodernist literary and theological thought.

Whereas Flannery O'Connor was brought up within the church, Walker Percy converted to Catholicism in 1946, at the age of thirty, after a prolonged convalescence from tuberculosis had allowed him the leisure to assimilate the whole of Aquinas's *Summa* and key philosophical works by Maritain, Gabriel Marcel, and others. Flannery O'Connor liked Percy's first novel, *The Moviegoer,* "very much," so she said in 1962, and O'Connor and Percy knew each other slightly at this time; but their experiences of religion were very different, for while O'Connor was born and bred within the church, Percy always contemplated Catholicism in a more analytical manner, as one intellectual possibility among others.[38]

The Moviegoer (1961) is strongly influenced by the French tradition of existential alienation. Binx Bolling finds himself painfully adrift in "Gentilly," a suburb of New Orleans, where, like Camus's "outsider," Bolling sardonically remarks the insufficiency of all the paraphernalia of everyday life set up for his delectation. He is, he says, in "exile," oppressed by a sense that the world is "upside down" and that, in this falsely paradisiacal landscape of pristine air conditioners and sanitized deodorants, "what are generally considered to be the best times are for me the worst."[39] Finding that the "deep dumb convictions" (177) of his Catholic Uncle Jules appall him, Bolling takes his cue from the novel's Kierkegaardian epigraph and embarks instead upon what he terms a "vertical" search for the meaning of the universe (70). This is akin to the Puritan search for transcendence, a direct communication – or "vertical line," as Kierkegaard called it – between man and God, a path cleared of all intermediary obstructions such as ecclesiastical or social institutions.[40] Bolling's fascination with the cinema operates as an emblem of this transcendental aspiration, for the movies here connote a world of disembodied and denaturalized perfection. You can't touch a film star, he isn't there: in the cinema, as Percy's hero recognizes, the corporeal pressure of the flesh has been superseded by its flawless celluloid replication. Reluctantly, however, Bolling comes to appreciate the insufficiency of this perfectionist formula: "The only difficulty was that though the universe had been disposed of, I myself was left over" (70). As Percy himself

38 *The Habit of Being: The Letters of Flannery O'Connor,* p. 501.
39 Walker Percy, *The Moviegoer* (New York: Knopf, 1961), pp. 18, 10. Subsequent page references are given in parentheses in the text.
40 Lawson and Kramer, *Conversations with Walker Percy,* p. 123.

has pointed out, this is a direct echo of Kierkegaard's judgment on Hegel: "Hegel told everything about the world except one thing: what it is to be a man and to live and to die."[41] The moviegoer comes to realize those transcendent images up on the silver screen do not possess a human body, whereas he himself inexorably does.

Bolling's "vertical" search, then, is associated with German romantic subjectivism, with the neo-scholastics' notion of "angelism," and also with the Faustian ambitions of science to encapsulate the universe within a few pithy equations: Bolling at one point talks of his desire to "understand more and more specimens by fewer and fewer formulae" (82). As the novel proceeds, however, Bolling opts to put aside his "vertical" search for a "horizontal" one; in other words, he exchanges transcendence for immanence. Such an exchange is predicated upon what French Catholic existentialist philosopher Gabriel Marcel understood as the conceptual superiority of *es denkt in mir* to *cogito ergo sum:* abandoning the "pure subjectivism" of Cartesian thought, as Marcel called it, Binx Bolling elects finally to marry his girlfriend, Kate, and to take his place within the community.[42] Rather than attempting to control and direct life, he allows life to flow through him. Bolling now declares of a humdrum Louisiana salesman that "like many businessmen, he is a better metaphysician than the romantic" (216). In this belief, Bolling echoes the view of an earlier Catholic philosopher, G. K. Chesterton, who has one of his fictional personae assert: "Materialists are all right; they are at least near enough to heaven to accept the earth and not imagine they made it. The dreadful doubts are not the doubts of the materialist. The dreadful doubts, the deadly and damnable doubts, are the doubts of the idealist."[43] In this abandonment of his former univocal romanticism, Percy's moviegoer nevertheless continues to talk of "my dark pilgrimage on this earth" (228), and his marriage to Kate takes on the form of something like a Pascalian bet, a leap of hope and faith rather than true knowledge. Pascal has tended to be viewed askance by neo-scholastic philosophers because, despite his proficiency in mathematics and science, the Frenchman denied there could be any direct correlation between human and divine knowledge: faith, said Pascal, is "God perceived by the heart, not by the reason."[44] Yet it is this kind of agnosticism that Percy's wayfaring heroes often share. For Will Barrett in *The Second Coming* (1980), it is

41 Ibid., p. 11.
42 Gabriel Marcel, *Being and Having,* trans. Katherine Farrer (Westminster: Dacre Press, 1949), p. 27.
43 Hugh Kenner stresses the theological implications of this passage in *Paradox in Chesterton* (London: Sheed and Ward, 1948), p. 6.
44 Gabriel Daly, O.S.A., *Transcendence and Immanence: A Study in Catholic Modernism and Integralism* (Oxford: Oxford Univ. Press, 1980), p. 22.

only Pascal, "the rare sane unbeliever," who "could at least make a modicum of sense" (191).

As a trained medical doctor, a product of what he called "Columbia University agnosticism" and only a relatively late convert to Catholicism, Percy was very attuned to the cultural differences between Protestant romanticism and Catholic materialism.[45] Many of his novels, in fact, rotate around this dichotomy. *The Last Gentleman* (1966) ridicules the fake secular ideals of orgasm and psychoanalysis, disparages "the old itch for omniscience" or "perfect angelic knowledge," and finds Will Barrett eventually abandoning the quest to "engineer" his own superior life.[46] Instead, he acquiesces in the ordinary business of marrying a wife and living a life: "Henceforth," he says, "I shall be what I am no matter how potential I am" (214). Forsaking the transcendent, angst-ridden landscapes of southwestern deserts for the more homely charms of a suburban golf course, Barrett chooses to live within the limitations of a gentle lewdness with his new wife, Kitty. Lewdness also has a central part to play in *The Second Coming,* where we find that the widowed Barrett has now relapsed into the German romantic folly of *"wahnsinnige Sehnsucht"* (302), inappropriate longing, before being bailed out of his misery by a new sexual relationship with Alison. Moreover, the novel's title, *The Second Coming,* does not refer simply to the imagery of Christian resurrection that permeates this book. When Alison is bathing Will, so we are told, the scene "reminded her of some paintings of the body of Christ taken down from the crucifix" (236); yet this religious rebirth promptly becomes associated with Alison's own sexual rejuvenation as the narrative describes how "she came against him, willingly" (257). The final pages of the novel even more explicitly define the central characters' reawakening in sexual terms: "Come, believe me, it's the ultimate come, not the first come which we all grow up dreaming about and which is never what we hoped, is it, but . . . the second, last and ultimate come to end all comes" (337).

What we find in this text, then, is that religious and sexual significances are eventually equated. The consolations of sexuality reconcile human beings to their corporeal status sub specie aeternitatis and offer Barrett a means "to reenter the world" (262) after his forlorn search for a direct revelation of God. "The answer," says the chaplain, "lies under our noses, so to speak" (138). For Barrett, the answer to this mystery of being comes to lie under his nose in a literal – comically literal – sense, for when he adjourns to a cave under Sourwood Mountain vowing to

---

45 Lawson and Kramer, *Conversations with Walker Percy,* p. 313.
46 Walker Percy, *The Last Gentleman* (New York: Farrar, Straus and Giroux, 1966), p. 170. Subsequent page references are given in parentheses in the text.

remain there until God manifests himself, Barrett is rewarded only with a toothache, as if to imply that it is the human responsibility to worry about bodily incarnation rather than ultimate metaphysical designs. Many of Flannery O'Connor's characters – the Misfit, Hazel Motes, Tarwater – also seek a direct sign of God's presence, but, as in Percy, this turns out to involve a misplaced yearning for pure transcendence, an illicit desire to rise above the limitations of one's imperfect human condition. Suicide, that other means of self-induced transcendence, is also considered in *The Second Coming:* Will Barrett's father is said to have killed himself, just as Percy's own real-life father did, while in this novel Sutter Vaught also constantly contemplates the terminal act. But Will Barrett evades that unhappy climax by his eventual immersion in limited human gratifications and by his cagey Pascalian admission to the Catholic priest, Father Weatherbee, that "though I am an unbeliever, it does not follow that your belief, the belief of the church, is untrue, that in fact it may be true" (358).

Percy remarked frequently upon his great admiration for Gabriel Marcel's work, and in this conclusion to *The Second Coming* we can see the influence of Marcel's conception of "intrasubjectivity."[47] Intrasubjectivity, for Marcel, was the faculty of apprehending oneself in terms of interaction with others rather than as an isolated individual. The intrasubjective state of mind indicates a preference for concrete social relations rather than solipsism. Along these same lines, it is noticeable that four of Percy's six novels are narrated in the first person, just as Marcel's philosophical work *Being and Having* and Sartre's existentialist novel *Nausea* also take diary forms. In all of these cases, the writer is implicitly sharing with the reader his own ineradicably human sensibility and so admitting that he cannot transcend time, cannot aspire to that old spectatorial position of authorial omniscience prized by Victorian novelists. Instead, the narrator is necessarily involved within the world he writes about. The ontological limitations of human beings are one of Percy's favorite themes, and, like O'Connor, Percy cherishes the novel form because it is necessarily an art of incarnation, bringing into being flawed individual characters rather than any scientific types or abstract examples. "It is," said Percy, "the novelist's responsibility to be chary of categories and rather to focus upon the mystery, the paradox, the *openness* of an individual human existence."[48]

Percy also takes up from Marcel and the French existentialists their

---

47 Marcel, *Being and Having,* p. 105.
48 Walker Percy, *The Message in the Bottle: How Queer Man Is, How Queer Language Is, and What One Has to Do with the Other* (New York: Farrar, Straus and Giroux, 1975), p. 108.

juggling of doubt and belief. Indeed, Percy's fictional world, like O'Connor's, is not so theologically clear-cut as it might appear. "It is," noted Percy in 1981, "a classical dispute between Catholics and Protestants whether faith is a form of knowledge"; and with Percy being a late-flowering Catholic, his texts fluctuate equivocally between Kierkegaardian uncertainty and Thomistic resolution.[49] Percy's essay "The Message in the Bottle" actually features two contradictory epigraphs: one from Aquinas insisting "The act of faith consists essentially in knowledge," the other from Kierkegaard declaring "Faith is not a form of knowledge."[50] Kierkegaard's point here is that "the eternal" and "the historical" are such mutually distinct categories that it is absurd attempting conceptually to reconcile them; whereas for Aquinas, of course, the historical is analogically related to eternal being. Nevertheless, this dichotomy may not ultimately be as divisive as it seems, for just as the deconstructive theology of Rahner and Tracy can reilluminate dark areas in Flannery O'Connor's writings, so the critique of neo-scholasticism that emerged from within the turmoils of Catholic modernist philosophy may afford some insight into Percy's reexamination of the quandaries of faith.

Looking back to the eighteenth century, we find Kant originally working out the terms "transcendence" and "immanence" and coming to influence the development of a radical Christian doctrine of "vital immanence," whereby religion is said to derive from the need for God that exists within the human psyche. Kant's subjectivism was of course the bête noire of the neo-scholastics, who looked for more "objective" proofs of God's existence than the vagaries of individual human consciousness. But Kant's emphasis on subjective faith rather than objective reason was in line with the earlier Pascalian position, as we have seen, and in the early twentieth century it was taken further by modernist Catholic theologians like Maurice Blondel, who believed this idea of immanence – that "nothing can enter into a man which does not emerge from him" – was a development in philosophy that Catholic theology should seek to come to terms with rather than simply ignore. Blondel's model was that of a man journeying toward the absolute end of Christian revelation and endowed with an intrinsic need for the transcendent and supernatural. Another Catholic modernist, Lucien Laberthonnière, considered that Aquinas's rigid scholasticism tended to paralyze the older reliance upon intellect and human will to be found within the Augustinian tradition, so that Laberthonnière believed the human task was not slavishly to follow the "objective" teachings of theological dogma but to rediscover subjectively how the transcendent is immanently incarnated within hu-

49 Lawson and Kramer, *Conversations with Walker Percy*, p. 204.
50 Percy, *The Message in the Bottle*, p. 119.

man experience: "Faith is thus an interior and free response of the good will stimulated by grace. It is not the same as belief on the authority of another: it is an interior affirmation of the being of oneself, the being of God, and the being of others."[51]

All of these subversive new ideas were, of course, officially stamped on by Pius X in his 1907 encyclical letter *Pascendi dominici gregis,* which roundly condemned "the doctrine of the Modernists." But it is interesting to note how Laberthonnière's reiteration of this stress upon "the being of oneself" finds an echo in Percy. In his essay "The Mystery of Language," Percy avowed that knowledge cannot be gleaned through science but must rather be sought through a Heideggerian perspective whereby man is "that being in the world whose calling is to find a name for Being."[52] It is noticeable also how often Percy would quote Gerard Manley Hopkins, the Jesuit poet who guiltily censored his own artistic productions because they project a similar intimation of divine being existing as an immanent force within the natural world. Hopkins's poems, looking back to the ideas of the medieval mystic Duns Scotus, express a sense that experience of God might be a subjective and irrational phenomenon, rather than – as Hopkins's Jesuit order would much have preferred – one based upon the impersonal and "objective" tenets of Thomistic orthodoxy. Yet Percy was clearly in sympathy with Hopkins's subversion of Jesuit orthodoxy, for in his essay "The Loss of the Creature" Percy praised Hopkins's intuitive ability "to see the thing . . . a rock or a cloud or a field" rather than feeling any need to refer the object to theological experts for certification and classification. Equally important in this subjectivist context are the existentialist philosophers, with their emphasis on being rather than having. As Marcel put it, one does not have a body, one is that body: "I cannot quite treat myself as a term distinct from my body. . . . I cannot validly say 'I and my body.' "[53]

This focus upon the existential reality of incarnated being necessarily brings into play as well the variables of temporality and contingency. To the mortification once again of theological traditionalists, the Catholic modernist thinker Friedrich von Hügel scorned what he called "that mania for deceptive and very superficial clarities" all too typical, so he thought, of the neo-scholastics.[54] Von Hügel moved instead toward a rejection of essentialism and toward an account of the role of the aleatory in making the transcendent reality of God available to man. All of these developments in Catholic theology are wrestling with the same problem

---

51 Daly, *Transcendence and Immanence,* pp. 8, 38, 101.
52 Percy, *The Message in the Bottle,* p. 158.
53 Ibid., p. 56; Marcel, *Being and Having,* pp. 12, 14.
54 Daly, *Transcendence and Immanence,* p. 128.

that Percy confronts in his novels and essays: the "Absolute Paradox," as he said in "The Message in the Bottle," of how divine knowledge might be apprehended within historical time, the dilemma of man as an unhoused Kierkegaardian castaway who nevertheless aspires to a comprehension of eternal truth. Gabriel Daly has described Blondel as attempting to "create a Catholic Kantianism," to bridge the conceptual gap between subjective faith and objective reason, and this phrase "Catholic Kantianism" might usefully be applied to Percy's artistic project as well.[55]

Percy admitted that a "good deal of my energy as a novelist comes from *malice* – the desire to attack things in our culture," and these satirical tendencies are very evident in *Love in the Ruins* (1971), *Lancelot* (1977), and *The Thanatos Syndrome* (1987).[56] *Love in the Ruins* mocks Percy's familiar kind of targets, the false new Edens of secular America, the angelic idealism and abstraction of university graduate students. Also ridiculed is the hero's first wife, Doris, who becomes an Episcopalian enamored of a vague religiosity that she expresses by making clay pots, having ruined her mind with books of "Gnostic pride" and "esoteric doctrine."[57] Doris's newfound transcendentalism conceives of religion as pure spirit, whereas the "bad Catholic" narrator, Thomas More, looks to religion to save him from this disembodied sphere as he corporeally digests the body of Christ, permitting the Eucharist access to his own flesh. More's eating habits, however, are just as much frowned upon by his new spouse, Ellen, who harbors an "ancient Presbyterian mistrust of *things,* things getting mixed up in religion," and who deeply mistrusts "the Old Church's traffic in things, sacraments, articles, bread, wine, salt, oil, water, ashes" (400). When Ellen reappears in *The Thanatos Syndrome,* she still finds repulsive this Catholic predilection for eating the Eucharist; Ellen herself prefers to preserve the kind of belief in dualism, the absolute separation of spirit from matter, that Percy's narrators scorn. In *Love in the Ruins,* Thomas More heaps abuse on Descartes who "ripped body loose from mind and turned the very soul into a ghost that haunts its own house" (191), thereby redefining the human being dualistically as "mythical monster, half angel, half beast, but no man" (383). This, of course, is a standard piece of neo-scholastic doctrine, which could have come straight out of Maritain or Lynch. In his addiction to worldly sensuality, Thomas More may be a "bad Catholic" (384) – just as Percy often called himself a "bad Catholic" in interviews – but

55 Percy, *The Message in the Bottle,* p. 146; Daly, *Transcendence and Immanence,* p. 48.
56 Lewis and Kramer, *Conversations with Walker Percy,* p. 14.
57 Walker Percy, *Love in the Ruins: The Adventures of a Bad Catholic at a Time near the End of the World* (New York: Farrar, Straus and Giroux, 1971), p. 64. Subsequent page references are given in parentheses in the text.

such venial transgressions appear greatly preferable to the Faustian proclivities of all those angelic "isms" propagated by secular or puritan
America. God, recalls Thomas More, "did not warn his people against
dirty books. He warned them against high places" (64). In *The Last
Gentleman,* "lewdness" is described by Sutter as "a kind of sacrament
(devilish, if you like)" (281) because it can put people in touch with the
concrete circumstances of their human incarnation in a way that abstract
science cannot.

In a similar way, *Lancelot* applauds the "old tolerant Catholic world-
weariness" (131) of New Orleans, a city of "comfortable Catholic limbo"
(23) where the Creoles are neither damned nor saved, as the Puritans
would have preferred, but rather know "the secret of living ordinary
lives well" (24) – a feat, declares Lancelot, more difficult than solving
"the mystery of the universe" (94). Again, the heresies of dualism and
angelism are attacked here, though in this novel such dualism becomes
associated specifically with the North: the northerner, declares Lancelot,
is "at heart a pornographer . . . an abstract mind with a genital attached.
His soul is at Harvard. . . . His body lives on Forty-second Street" (219).
Likewise, in *The Thanatos Syndrome* the dastardly plot to include a heavy
sodium additive in the water supply so as to guard against mental and
physical diseases is said to arise out of the desire of northern federalists
– "a bunch of ham-fisted social engineers," says Van Dorn – to impose
their own ideals upon the South. Van Dorn compares such federalists to
those "guilt-ridden Puritan transcendentalist assholes who wanted to save
their souls by freeing the slaves and castrating the planters."[58] According
to the eccentric priest Father Smith, a leading figure in this novel, idealistic philanthropy and "tenderness" (361) are devils in disguise that can
ultimately lead to people being executed in the gas chamber, supposedly
for their own good. Father Smith loathes the "professor-philosophers"
and "educated Episcopal-type unbelievers," and he claims that "the only
people I got along with were bums, outcasts, pariahs, family skeletons,
and the dying" (243). As in O'Connor, a sense of alienation from federal
American ideals results in sympathy with those marginalized by the
formulas of secular society.

Throughout his novels, Percy's scathing comedy operates to deflate
the pretensions of this technological society. Percy exploits the genre of
comedy as a radically antiidealist form that skeptically defuses the pretensions of human institutions. As with Flannery O'Connor, however,
one of the unresolved contradictions in Percy's art may arise from an
uneasy conjunction between this skeptical, comically concrete emphasis

58 Walker Percy, *The Thanatos Syndrome* (New York: Farrar, Straus and Giroux, 1987),
   p. 217. Subsequent page references are given in parentheses in the text.

and the higher principles of Catholic faith. Percy said he revered Kier-kegaard's essay *The Difference between a Genius and an Apostle,* where Kierkegaard stated that a "genius" is the person who sees or embodies the world for other people, whereas an "apostle" is that secondary figure who takes it upon himself to conceptualize his findings and preach to others what he perceives as truth. A novelist "least of all," said Percy, should be an apostle; he should embody concrete truths, not seek "to edify anyone or tell them good news." It is of course clear enough that Percy's novels avoid overt didacticism; still, in these perpetual dialogues between "vertical" and "horizontal," between Protestantism and Ca-tholicism, between transcendence and immanence, there occasionally lurks a suggestion that Percy does not altogether avoid in the form of his own writing that "angelic" or apostolic tendency the themes of his books so much deplore.[59] Father Smith in *The Thanatos Syndrome* could almost have stepped out of the Manichaean world of Graham Greene: Smith's is a privileged, "correct" position – as in Greene, the priest's worldly failure authenticates his spiritual integrity – and this formalistic conflict of good and evil unwittingly replicates that bifurcation between spirit and matter so typical of the Jansenist philosophy implicit within Greene's work. Percy, like Greene, was a Catholic convert who never quite shook off his cultural Protestantism; he is, perhaps, the Orestes Brownson of the late twentieth-century Catholic novel, a writer whose very rationalization and interrogation of the principles of Catholicism set him apart from the masses who absorb religious influences in a more unconscious cultural fashion.

Nevertheless, it is this recognition of a crossed heritage, Kierkegaard confronting Aquinas, that makes for some of the most interesting ten-sions in Percy's work. A sense of existentialist insecurity and a search for the paradoxical hybrid of "Catholic Kantianism" pervade his texts, so that his questers – Binx Bolling, Will Barrett, Lancelot – find the end of their journey is not what they thought they came for: the purpose is beyond the end they figured and is altered in fulfillment. As with O'Con-nor, we find in Percy's fiction not only Catholic apologetics but also, as *The Last Gentleman* puts it, an intimation of "*Lücken* or gaps . . . like a book with blank pages" (12), a general ambience of absence that plagues the life of Will Barrett in this novel and is a response to the mysterious indeterminacy of the postmodern world.

This confrontation between Kierkegaardian angst and Catholic theology in Percy's novels is echoed in the literary paradoxes of another prominent postmodernist writer, Donald Barthelme. Despite being brought up Ro-

59 Lawson and Kramer, *Conversations with Walker Percy,* pp. 64, 113.

man Catholic and attending parochial schools, Barthelme clearly cannot be thought of as a religious writer in any orthodox sense. Indeed, to affiliate him with Flannery O'Connor and Walker Percy rather than his more obvious generic postmodernist companions, fabulators such as John Barth or Robert Coover, might seem to some an act of critical perversity. It is true that, unlike O'Connor and Percy, Barthelme had almost nothing to say about his childhood religion or its influence upon his subsequent work – apart from one jokey comment about his writing practices, in an interview with Lois Gordon, when the author mentioned how "Sunday seems to be my best day, probably because I'm a lapsed Catholic."[60] It is evident enough as well that Barthelme's texts do not subscribe, either explicitly or implicitly, to Catholicism as an accredited system of belief. Nevertheless, the philosophical and theological paradoxes that Barthelme's works find themselves compelled to negotiate demonstrate a fascinating example of the Catholic literary sensibility at work. Despite his avowed atheism, Barthelme in fact shares at least as many conceptual characteristics with the avowed believer Walker Percy as he does with Barth or Coover or Pynchon.

There is also a historical and biographical link here, in that Barthelme – another southerner, brought up in Houston – published Percy's philosophy and fiction during his spells as editor of the University of Houston's *Forum* and *Location*, thereby helping Percy on his way to general public recognition. Part of *The Moviegoer* was first published in *Location* – "with great joy," said Barthelme – and Percy always remained one of Barthelme's favorite novelists.[61] Furthermore, Barthelme's work, like Percy's, evokes a marked antipathy toward the ideologies of both Enlightenment rationalism and Germanic romanticism. Kant saw the development of a faculty of autonomous human reason as one of the defining characteristics of the Enlightenment: abandoning the superannuated old religious myths, humanity would emerge from a period of "self-incurred immaturity" that necessarily involved "the inability to use one's own understanding without the guidance of another."[62] This Kantian or "angelic" conception, though, is peremptorily opposed by Barthelme's preference for the ludic arena of play and paradox, his focus upon those irrational tendencies that lurk within the supposedly rational perimeters of daily life. Barthelme's one book written especially for

60 Lois Gordon, *Donald Barthelme* (Boston: Twayne, 1981), p. 18.
61 Joe David Bellamy, *The New Fiction: Interviews with Innovative American Writers* (Urbana: Univ. of Illinois Press, 1974), p. 47; Larry McCaffrey, *The Metafictional Muse: The Works of Robert Coover, Donald Barthelme, and William H. Gass* (Pittsburgh: Univ. of Pittsburgh Press, 1982), p. 119.
62 Quoted in Robert A. Ferguson, "'What Is Enlightenment?': Some American Answers," *American Literary History*, 1 (1989), 246.

children (*The Slightly Irregular Fire Engine*), as well as his reworking of such juvenile legends as Batman (in the 1964 story "The Joker's Greatest Triumph") and *Snow White* (1967), also work against Kantian principles and the politics of Enlightenment.

In itself, of course, this rebellion against institutionalized forms of reason is a phenomenon familiar enough from the culture of the 1960s. Yet for Barthelme, as for Percy, this critique operates more specifically against the purported self-indulgence of romantic egoism in its contemporary as well as its more established forms. In "Heliotrope," for instance, Barthelme parodies the "Open University of San Francisco," which specializes in courses such as "Happiness and Freedom" and "Outdoor Motivation": the barbed wit here is aimed at targets similar to those satirized in Walker Percy's *Lost in the Cosmos,* Percy's spoof of the genre of the self-help book, with all its synthetic advice for the "fulfillment" of the individual.[63] Along the same lines, Goethe's self-important humanism is mocked several times in Barthelme's stories: in "The New Music," Goethe is quoted as boasting to his biographer Eckermann of how he has "devoted [his] whole life to the people and their improvement"; in "City Life," Goethe has another cameo role to assert that "theory is gray, but the golden tree of life is green"; while in "Conversations with Goethe" Eckermann is subjected to several pages of windy and in fact nonsensical aphorisms from his master, with Goethe rambling on about how "Youth . . . is the silky apple butter on the good brown bread of possibility," and so on.[64]

It has become a commonplace of Barthelme criticism that he prefers fragments rather than linear narratives, collage rather than thematic sequence, irony rather than direct statement. His is a world of "epistemological skepticism," as Larry McCaffrey put it, where authority in all its forms – father, priests, psychoanalysts – has been overturned, with the result that the authority of the text itself is also necessarily thrown into disarray. "God was the omniscient author, but he died," Ronald Sukenick famously claimed in "The Death of the Novel": authors can no longer manipulate their characters in imitation of a divine will, since divine will has absconded, leaving the earthlings grappling with metaphysical and textual confusion.[65] These are familiar arguments, and in their own way they are true enough. But while Barthelme can be inter-

---

63 Donald Barthelme, *Guilty Pleasures* (New York: Farrar, Straus and Giroux, 1974), p. 99.
64 "The New Music," in *Great Days* (New York: Farrar, Straus and Giroux, 1979), p. 28; "City Life," in *City Life* (New York: Farrar, Straus and Giroux, 1970), p. 166; "Conversations with Goethe," in *Overnight to Many Distant Cities* (New York: Putnam's, 1983), p. 73.
65 McCaffrey, *The Metafictional Muse,* p. 110; Ronald Sukenick, "The Death of the Novel," in *The Death of the Novel and Other Stories* (New York: Dial Press, 1969), p. 41.

preted synchronically, in terms of the postmodernist culture of his time, he can also be interpreted diachronically, through the perspective of a Catholic cultural tradition of radical antihumanism going back through Percy, Flannery O'Connor, even as far as James T. Farrell. Barthelme's version of a fragmented "city life" is not altogether dissimilar to Farrell's: in both cases we find fictional "heroes" marginalized by a corporate and ritualistic culture that becomes the dominating presence within the text and frustrates the attempts of any individual to manipulate or even understand it. Goethe, one feels, would have had as hard a time in James T. Farrell's world as he is faced with in Barthelme's. The ego is sidelined, and some kind of "system," whose very inscrutability constitutes its intimidating power, seems to be in control. It is ironically apposite that the traditional complaints about Farrell and Dreiser – about how they lack romantic imagination and possess an un-American sense of passive fatalism that compels them to reproduce their environment as a fait accompli rather than striving to construct a new "world elsewhere" – recurs in the way Alfred Kazin sought to relegate Barthelme to the status of a minor "antinovelist": "The almighty state is always in view," said Kazin. "So Barthelme sentences us to the complicity with the system that he suffers from more than anyone. . . . He is under the terrible discipline that the system inflicts on those who are most fascinated with its relentlessness."[66] Interesting also is the way Kazin's polemic – "almighty state," "system," "terrible discipline" – contains a strange echo of the populist anti-Catholic rhetoric of Paul Blanshard and his followers, with their complaints about the relentless and dehumanizing systems enforced by Rome. It is not that Kazin is consciously anti-Catholic here, of course, merely that he omits to acknowledge how D. H. Lawrence's ideology of the novel as an emblem of the vital individual flame, a "bright book of life," is itself a culturally partial and not an impartial idea.

In this sense, Catholicism for Barthelme operates in the paradoxical condition of *The Dead Father:* "Dead, but still with us, still with us, but dead."[67] Just as the figures in this 1975 novel make their confessions to the Dead Father despite the old man's defunct state, so Barthelme's texts seek to negotiate some kind of accommodation with the religion their author apparently no longer believes in. Throughout his career, though, Barthelme made various statements about his work that do not altogether accord with the familiar image of him as simply a ludic and lexical prankster. He told an audience at New York University in 1982 that he

---

66 Alfred Kazin, *Bright Book of Life: American Novelists and Storytellers from Hemingway to Mailer* (Boston: Little, Brown and Co., 1973), p. 273.
67 Donald Barthelme, *The Dead Father* (New York: Farrar, Straus and Giroux, 1975), p. 3. Subsequent page references are given in parentheses in the text.

especially respected Mallarmé because the French poet "shakes words loose from their attachments and bestows new meanings upon them, meanings which point not toward the external world, but toward the Absolute, acts of poetic intuition."[68] This reechoed the aspiration toward something "Absolute" that he expressed in a 1976 symposium on fiction with Grace Paley, Walker Percy, and William Gass, where Barthelme's postulation of a transcendent signified made him appear more closely aligned with Percy's emphasis on final (religious) knowledge than with Gass's all-encompassing skepticism. "I would suggest," said Barthelme,

> that there is a realm of possible knowledge which can be reached by artists, which is not susceptible of mathematical verification but which is true. This is sometimes spoken of as the ineffable. If there is any word I detest in the language, this would be it, but the fact that it exists, the word ineffable, is suspicious in that it suggests that there might be something that is ineffable. And I believe that's the place artists are trying to get to, and I further believe that when they are successful, they reach it; my painter friend, for example, reaches an area somewhere probably between mathematics and religion, in which what may fairly be called truth exists.[69]

This interesting area "somewhere probably between mathematics and religion" need not signify any benign divinity, of course: one thinks of the dark Neoplatonism of Samuel Beckett, for whom the austere rationalism of Cartesian "truth" dwarfs the squalid contingencies of worldly existence without offering to redeem human life in any way. In February 1989, a few months before they both died, Barthelme acknowledged Beckett to be an oedipal "problem" for him because of the "enormous strength of his style, his tone."[70]

Nevertheless, the idea of this quest for something "ineffable" helps to elucidate what many critics of Barthelme's fiction have felt, that his work does not simply celebrate anarchy but strives to put it in another perspective. Tony Tanner associated this "not-at-homeness" and "yearning for an unknown somewhere else" with the American romantic quest for a world elsewhere, Huckleberry Finn once again sailing up the paradigmatic river to escape from the Widow Douglas.[71] Jerome Klinkowitz preferred to see here the kind of moral impetus associated with modernism's search for principles of order amid the futility of contemporary

68 Herbert Mitgang, "Barthelme Takes on Task of Almost Deciphering His Fiction," *New York Times*, 18 Feb. 1982, Sec. C, p. 15.

69 Donald Barthelme, William Gass, Grace Paley, Walker Percy, "A Symposium on Fiction," *Shenandoah*, 27, no. 2 (1976), 11.

70 Terry Ross, "The Joker Is Wild," *Willamette Week*, 16–22 Feb. 1989, p. 10.

71 Tony Tanner, *City of Words: American Fiction 1950–1970* (New York: Harper and Row, 1971), p. 404.

civilization. Klinkowitz compared Barthelme with George Orwell in his exposure of the "empty phrases" of consumer society, and he suggested that Barthelme is in fact a "counterrevolutionary, opposing the new language of technology and manipulation with pleas for old-fashioned interest and imagination."[72] Neither a residual romanticism nor a residual modernism seems quite to fit, however, and I think it can be argued that a residual, desacralized Catholicism plays at least as significant a role in Barthelme's epistemological landscape.

Images from Catholic liturgy and traditions pop up in all kinds of unexpected places within Barthelme's stories. In "Critique de la Vie Quotidienne," Wanda rebukes her husband with "a look upon her face corresponding to that which St. Catherine of Siena bent upon Pope Gregory whilst reproaching him for the luxury of Avignon." In "The Genius," a man inspecting a church "because the nave is said to be a particularly fine example of Burgundian Gothic" becomes deeply intimidated by the icy stare of a nun. In "Departures," a "friendly Franciscan" enters "in his brown robes" to enquire why the narrator entered "None" in the space for "Religion" on his hospital form. At the end of "The Rise of Capitalism," we find assorted saints come marching in to deliver their "same old message" about placing hope "in the Word of God."[73] All of these examples come from Barthelme's 1972 collection *Sadness,* and the sadness in question here betokens a world of loss, a world where metaphysical presence has been promised but then denied. The random quality of these images, the way they are scattered throughout the texts without being subordinated to any kind of pattern of logical exegesis, suggests how Barthelme's ghostly Catholicism is no philosophical system but a lurking irrational shadow, an intimation of absence that seems to undermine the positivistic premises of quotidian life. The illusory specter of a bankrupt world of spirit continues to compromise empirical perspectives. In "On the Steps of the Conservatory," from *Great Days* (1979), one student asks another: "When are you going to change yourself, change yourself into a loaf or a fish?" There is no response to the miraculous suggestion. "Christian imagery is taught at the Conservatory," so we are told, along with "Islamic imagery and the imagery of Public Safety"; yet this kind of bathetic and flattening explanation cannot altogether cancel the aura of suggestiveness that Barthelme's religious references bring forth.[74] In this sense, Barthelme's cultural Catholicism contributes to his general subversion of liberal pieties, for, while his texts

72 Jerome Klinkowitz, *Literary Disruptions: The Making of a Post-Contemporary American Fiction* (Urbana: Univ. of Illinois Press, 1975), pp. 66, 76.

73 Donald Barthelme, *Sadness* (New York: Farrar, Straus and Giroux, 1972), pp. 5, 32, 106, 148.

74 Barthelme, *Great Days,* p. 134.

offer no metaphysical formulas, this sense of jarring or displacement works against any movement toward closure from within the comfortable middle-class environment they describe.

In an early Barthelme story like the 1961 "Hiding Man," it is relatively easy to see how Catholicism functions in the familiar modernist or Joycean manner as a repressive force to be escaped from. Here the narrator, Burlingame, fondly recalls how he shocked the "athletic priest," Father Blau, not only by avoiding a "wholesome sport" like basketball but also by discoursing philosophically upon the sacrament of confession while actually engaged in that penitential act. During confession, Burlingame suggested to Father Blau with a touch of Stephen Dedalus–like insouciance that "certain aspects of the ritual compared unfavorably with the resurrection scene in *Bride of Frankenstein*."[75] Horror movies, in fact, have now become Burlingame's surrogate religion: he hides in dark cinemas as he once took refuge in dark churches, and he fights off the advances of Bane-Hipkiss, whose true identity seems to be that of a priest in search of the lapsed. The lurid sense of guilt that is a common feature of both Catholic apostasy and gothic art is prominent here, as is the notion – again, very Joycean – of a dissolution of stable character into multiple and inconclusive fragments, some religious, some secular. Psychological discontinuity of this sort characterizes many of Barthelme's fictions: Paul, the bedraggled Prince Charming of *Snow White,* shops for one authority system after another, eventually ending up as a monk in the Abbey of Thélème. In "A Picture History of the War," Kellerman feels a strange and unexpected need to undergo confession, though he secretly hopes the priest will act like a friendly customs officer and generously wave his sins aside.[76]

While nearly all of Barthelme's religious references tend to be comic, indeed hilarious, they depend for that comedy upon recognition of an incongruity between their worldly and putatively "spiritual" frames of reference. One of the clearest examples of such incongruity is the monk in "Lightning" who feels that deprivation of rock music is the big drawback to a monastic career; he avows it would not be so bad to "retire to one's cell at night to read St. Augustine" if one could simultaneously listen to Rod Stewart and the B–52's.[77] Barthelme, however, extends this incongruity beyond simple comedy to produce an implicit critique of the more rigid and literal aspects of Catholic theology. In "The New Music," for instance, the narrator wonders, "Could Christ have per-

75 Donald Barthelme, *Come Back, Dr. Caligari* (Boston: Little, Brown and Co., 1964), p. 31.
76 "A Picture History of the War," in *Unspeakable Practices, Unnatural Acts* (New York: Farrar, Straus and Giroux, 1968), p. 137.
77 *Overnight to Many Distant Cities*, p. 50.

formed the work of the Redemption had He come into the world in the shape of a pea?"[78] In *Paradise,* Simon similarly asks himself whether Christ had to "visit each and every planet" in the solar system that supports life and "go through the same routine, the Agony in the Garden, the Crucifixion, and so on."[79] The point is not that these are nonsensical questions but that they appear, on the contrary, both logical and pertinent, and are in fact just the kind of issue with which old-fashioned Scholastic theologians used to concern themselves. The early story "Florence Green Is 81" recalls the fourth-grade classroom at Our Lady of the Sorrows, where Sister Scholastica "knew how many angels could dance on the head of a pin."[80] Hence, by taking the literalist tendencies of Catholic theology to their logical conclusion, Barthelme reduces them to absurdity. "Is there bluegrass in heaven? Make enquiries," the narrator of "The New Music" tells himself.[81] Sister Scholastica would presumably know the answer.

As we have seen, Paul Tillich's "Protestant principle" insisted on an absolute divergence between heaven and earth, but Catholic thought has traditionally attempted to forge links between the city of God and the city of man through its system of saints, sacraments, litanies, dogma, and so on. It is precisely these moments of alleged "intercession" that Barthelme's theological humor focuses upon. In "Overnight to Many Distant Cities," the narrator has lunch in Barcelona with the Holy Ghost, who pronounces himself generally pleased with the way the world is going. In "Henrietta and Alexandra," Alexandra's fondness for collecting indulgences induces her to petition Rome to annul her marriage, a move that sucks her into the labyrinthine, self-justifying system of the Catholic legal bureaucracy. For Alexandra, though, this system connotes psychic security, the reassuring hand of the dead father; furthermore, she cherishes the vision that "she will live forever, live after she is dead at the right hand of God in His glory with His power and His angels and His whatnot." Though he calls this idea "immature," the narrator gloomily concedes "I cannot persuade her otherwise."[82] There is an equation to be made here between Barthelme's subversion of Catholic Scholastic theology and his subversion of the traditional realistic novel. Both forms envision the world in an excessively literal way, ignoring those inconsistencies and absurdities inherent within each system. Barthelme par-

---

78 *Great Days,* p. 30.
79 Donald Barthelme, *Paradise* (New York: Putnam's, 1986), p. 98. Subsequent page references are given in parentheses in the text.
80 *Come Back, Dr. Caligari,* p. 13.
81 *Great Days,* p. 27.
82 *Overnight to Many Distant Cities,* pp. 174, 87.

odies these systems by his technique of taking their premises to a ludi-
crous, though not illogical, conclusion.

Yet this parody does not constitute simply a didactic satire upon the
folly of religious belief. What we find instead is a comedy of metaphysical
displacement, where the fracture of worldly and otherworldly systems
leaves Barthelme's heroes, like those of Walker Percy, with a sense of
being alienated wayfarers, searching for something "ineffable" but intangible. This, indeed, is the "new principle" the angels look for after
the death of God (in the story "On Angels"); it is the same "new principle" for which the characters in Snow White seek.[83] The idea that what
these people have is "not enough" echoes around both these texts, though
of course the quest for epistemological meaning itself is spoofed, no less
than the literalist fallacies of the Dictionary of Angels and the Walt Disney
legends. Similarly, in the Beckett-like story "The Leap" two unnamed
individuals talk about the possibility of making a leap of faith but then
decide, all things considered, to put it off until another time. It is the
black comedy of hesitation and doubt, where belief seems impossible,
yet every secular affair reverberates with the tantalizing suggestion of
metaphysical significance. In "Daumier," Ignatius Loyola's Jesuits attempt to recapture a troupe of au pair girls, among whom is to be found
the punning figure of "Celeste." Daumier looks at Celeste and sees "that
the legs on her were as long and slim as his hope of Heaven."[84] The
puns here slide between terrestrial and extraterrestrial significance:
"slim," for instance, is a positive adjective in the context of Celeste's
legs, but a negative adjective in the context of Daumier's hope of heaven.
Still, in the language of mock-heroic punning made famous by Joyce –
one of Barthelme's acknowledged masters – this image cuts both ways
at once, elevating "Celeste" with intimations of spiritual glamor at the
same time as it drags religious spirit down into a world of earthly matter.

There is a similarly tantalizing oscillation between presence and absence
in those lists and catalogues that throng Barthelme's pages, in parody,
as Klinkowitz said, of the litanies and catechisms characteristic of Catholic
dogma. This debt is made explicit in the story "The Catechist," and also
in "The Indian Uprising" where "Miss R" says, "The only form of
discourse of which I approve . . . is the litany."[85] Barthelme's lists, like
the Vatican's, are always straining toward completeness and finitude;
but, because his texts simultaneously deny that possibility of closure, the
lists also come to evoke a "terror of failure, loss and disintegration," as

83 "On Angels," in City Life, p. 130; Snow White (New York: Atheneum, 1967), p. 181.
   Subsequent page references for Snow White are given in parentheses in the text.
84 Sadness, p. 171.
85 Klinkowitz, Literary Disruptions, p. 65; "The Indian Uprising," in Unspeakable Practices,
   Unnatural Acts, p. 8.

Régis Durand put it. The attempt to erect perfect closed systems in an ontologically imperfect world is less a sign of religious devotion than of obsessional neurosis: as Colin MacCabe said of George Eliot, the monumental heaping up of lists and objects and categories betrays a frantic attempt to erase those irredeemable absences and differences upon which any textual construction is based.[86]

Barthelme's work is more conspicuously self-referential than George Eliot's, of course, and it is precisely within witty, playful dialogues between plenitude and lack that Barthelme's literary and theological paradoxes locate themselves. Nevertheless, it is these fleeting glimpses of an ideal order that induce Barthelme's texts to reject Ronald Sukenick's model of an opaque, self-sufficient, and "purely aesthetic surface"; instead, Barthelme's fiction always finds itself disturbed by something intangible and unverifiable.[87] As "Over the Sea of Hesitation" (1972) puts it:

> Wittgenstein was I think wrong when he said that about that which we do not know, we should not speak. He closed by fiat a great amusement park, there. Nothing gives me more pleasure than speaking about that which I do not know. I am not sure whether my ideas about various matters are correct or incorrect, but speak about them I must.[88]

While minimalism and skepticism remain the dominant impulses within Barthelme's fiction, they cannot entirely annul the kind of speculative tendency outlined here. However problematic such a quest may be, Barthelme's narrators continue to search for some glimmer of "truth," that sense of the "ineffable" – as the author himself put it in the 1976 fiction symposium – which might manifest itself when more mundane matters have slid into deliquescence. Alan Wilde called this a philosophy of "assent," an existential drive to discover not some essential truth or a modernist realm of order and the "an-ironic," but rather Heidegger's category of *Dasein,* "the contingency of being-in-the-world." Instead of attempting to flee into a nostalgic realm of symbolic order or romantic escapism, contended Wilde, Barthelme seeks to work through the ironies and contingencies of city life to reveal, in a "sacramental" way, "the extraordinary... amidst the quotidian." Wilde's highly interesting argument draws upon Barthelme's relationship with Sartrean existentialism as well as Heideggerian phenomenology, and it analyzes how this notion

---

86 Maurice Couturier and Régis Durand, *Donald Barthelme* (London: Methuen, 1982), p. 29; Colin MacCabe, *James Joyce and the Revolution of the Word* (London: Macmillan, 1978), pp. 13–38.
87 Alan Wilde, "Barthelme Unfair to Kierkegaard: Some Thoughts on Modern and Postmodern Irony," *boundary 2,* 5 (1976), 66.
88 *Overnight to Many Distant Cities,* p. 100.

of "assent" becomes for Barthelme an area of risk and possibility. Wilde gave as an example "The Temptation of St. Anthony," where in Barthelme's rewriting of the legend the saint finds himself located in contemporary America and tempted by the more worldly charms of everyday life.[89]

This Heideggerian perspective has some validity, and in many ways Barthelme's work fulfills that familiar mock-heroic dualism whereby the secular is sanctified at the same time the sacred is secularized. It is important to stress, however, how Barthelme's is a specifically Catholic version of phenomenology that in fact bears many resemblances to the kind of "Catholic Kantianism" we saw in Walker Percy. As with Percy, Barthelme's existential idiom is framed by a Catholic eschatology. In the story "Margins," Carl asks Edward: "Have you read *The Mystery of Being*, by Gabriel Marcel? I really liked that one. I thought that one was fine."[90] It is an apposite remark, for Marcel's emphasis on the essentially circumscribed nature of bodily incarnation works its way subliminally into many of Barthelme's fictions. Crucially, this is a metaphysic of human limitation rather than human transcendence. Like Marcel, Barthelme prioritizes *es denkt in mir* over *cogito ergo sum*: his characters cannot rationally understand truth, but they can – perhaps – irrationally embody it. This emphasis on the ontological limitations of the human condition is brought into focus once again in the quotation from Pascal that Kitchen advances in "A Shower of Gold": "The natural misfortune of our mortal and feeble condition is so wretched that when we consider it closely, nothing can console us."[91] There are, in fact, many interesting links between Pascal and Barthelme. Both disdained the Scholastic attempt to turn Catholic philosophy into dogma and concrete fact; both suggested instead that the "ineffable" was a question of hints, guesses, and wagers; both placed emphasis upon the limitations of the human domain. In the same paragraph of the *Pensées* from which Kitchen's quotation about man's "feeble condition" derives, we find Pascal's famous assertion of how "the sole cause of man's unhappiness is that he does not know how to stay quietly in his room"; and this outlook is oddly mirrored in the geographically constricted world of Barthelme's stories, where, one feels, some of the characters may have taken Pascal's advice to heart.[92]

One such character is Simon, the architect in *Paradise*, who finds himself cooped up in his Manhattan apartment with three lingerie models. The point about this paradise is that it is a distinctively earthly, materialist

89 Wilde, "Barthelme Unfair to Kierkegaard," pp. 59–65.
90 *Come Back, Dr. Caligari*, p. 143.
91 Ibid., p. 177.
92 Pascal, *Pensées*, trans. A. J. Krailsheimer (Harmondsworth: Penguin, 1966), p. 67.

phenomenon, a "hog heaven" (50) dependent upon the bounties of money and sex. It is certainly not a divine resting place, nor is it the kind of terrestrial utopia Emerson or Thoreau would have favored; Simon keeps his money in a book entitled *On Adam's House in Paradise,* as if to emphasize how his version of bliss diverges sharply from that of the "American Adam" in its more traditional pastoral paradigms. This kind of millennial vision is parodied again in Barthelme's last novel, *The King* (1990), which spoofs Malory's style of quest romance; Barthelme's "Blue Knight" here views with distaste any allegorical restitution of Eden, feeling that "even if Paradise were regained it would have music by Milhaud and frescoes by the Italian Futurists."[93] So, as in Percy's novels, we see a movement in Barthelme toward immanence rather than transcendence: for their Catholic sensibility, common materialism can be philosophically more satisfactory than the self-deceptions of human heroism or the pretensions of romantic idealism. In *Paradise,* Simon meditates upon the history of his profession and shakes his head sadly over the folly of Le Corbusier's modernist ambitions, "the messianic-maniacal idea that architecture will make people better, civilize them" (69). This is an idea presaged in *Snow White,* where one of the dwarves ironically contemplates how "clean buildings fill your eyes with sunlight, and your heart with the idea that man is perfectible" (8).

It is true, then, that Simon's paradisiacal idyll is a vulgar concept – "unearned," as he himself recognizes (186) – but in its very lack of pretentiousness it parodies not only the millennial apocalypses of the American Dream but also the kind of self-help perfectionism derided by Percy in *Lost in the Cosmos.* In both Percy and Barthelme, the advent of divine grace may be problematical but the prospect of God emitting direct signs of special election or favor is altogether impossible, for man is inexorably bound up within a material sphere and it is there that he must work out his destiny. Will Barrett's failure to be rewarded with a manifestation of God in *The Second Coming* is echoed in Barthelme's story "At the End of the Mechanical Age," where God attends Thomas's wedding but chooses to hide his divine self behind a tree, ignoring the bridegroom's request to provide the gathering with the "barest hint" about his celestial nature. Nevertheless, the end of the story still finds "the glow of hope not yet extinguished" and "standby generators ensuring the flow of grace to all of God's creatures at the end of the mechanical age."[94] Though God may be shy of freely showing his ef-

93 Donald Barthelme, *The King* (New York: Burlingame–Harper and Row, 1990), p. 78.
94 Donald Barthelme, *Amateurs* (New York: Farrar, Straus and Giroux, 1976), pp. 182–3.

fulgence, the apparatus of grace may not have disappeared entirely from the material world.

Barthelme's characters, then, find themselves compelled to work through the postlapsarian condition, but the Heideggerian conception of their existential being as endowed with a "sacramental" presence is, perhaps, not so prevalent in these texts as Alan Wilde's argument would imply. Barthelme's fictions manifest a "not-at-homeness," as Tanner put it, partly because they are adrift in the uncertain gap between transcendence and immanence. Barthelme's heroes, like Percy's, know they must confine their activities to this world, but they also possess the Kierkegaardian wayfaring sensibility that tells them this world is not enough. Even Snow White is to be found reading the Catholic existentialist philosopher Teilhard de Chardin. In the story "See the Moon," Barthelme uses the figure of a Catholic cardinal to highlight this perception that earthly accident no longer necessarily incorporates spiritual essence: "If there is any value that has value, then it must lie outside the sphere of what happens and is the case, for all that happens and is the case is accidental." The narrator promptly concludes that Cardinal Y is "not serious," but he himself seems to take up the cardinal's point just a few paragraphs later when he concludes: "One can measure and measure and miss the most essential thing."[95] Precisely: if accident and essence are no longer consubstantial, then all catalogues and litanies are useless, for worldly instruments can never be used to measure what is "ineffable." It is the old debate between Aquinas and Pascal: Aquinas claimed God could be embodied in material ways, Pascal asserted the two realms were quite distinct. Barthelme, like Percy, adheres more closely to the Pascalian position, a position that lends to his characters (as Maurice Couturier said) the sense of being chance, accidental figures "in a world teeming with universals."[96] Essence remains tantalizingly beyond their grasp.

Thus the sense of displacement and generalized guilt experienced by Simon in *Paradise* and by many other Barthelme characters may be traced to a detachment from the world that is neither purely ironic and playful nor simply contemptuous, in satirical fashion, of material decadence. Attempts to moralize Barthelme (especially as either "for" or "against" contemporary culture) fail every time because his texts remain quite elusive to any didactic category imposed upon them. Yet this elusiveness can itself be seen as characteristic of a certain form of cultural Catholicism. Barthelme's predilection, like that of his Dead Father, for "having it both

95 *Unspeakable Practices, Unnatural Acts*, pp. 167–8.
96 Couturier and Durand, *Donald Barthelme*, p. 19.

POSTMODERNISM AND DISPLACEMENT

ways" (15) mirrors the position of many other cultural Catholics like Scott Fitzgerald, Frank O'Hara, Robert Altman, Andy Warhol – artists whose work is neither a satire nor a celebration of American society but is rather positioned in a parodic relation to it. Barthelme's rewriting of the popular legend of Snow White, for instance, is very similar in spirit to Altman's reworking of Popeye and other American myths, and both have similarities with Warhol's blank reflections of Marilyn Monroe or Mickey Mouse. Whether or not these artists "believed" in God, their Catholic inheritance still directed them toward apprehending the secular world as accidental, a temporary resting place on the road to "higher" things, so that in their work we tend to find both a focus upon this material world as the proper state for fallen man and also, paradoxically, a sly detachment from that world as being ontologically incomplete. Satire is inapplicable, because satire would imply the possibility of human perfection in this world, which is inconceivable. Pure celebration is inapplicable, because that would imply the secular world is autonomous and self-sufficient, which is equally inconceivable. Catholic fictions prefer to negotiate an ironic position where they are neither totally of the world nor totally out of it, and the double-edged form of parody is the most appropriate form within which to express this metaphysical paradox.

Parody and paradox are, of course, the most consistent features of Barthelme's fiction. *Snow White* contains direct parodies of Henry James, Matthew Arnold, and many other writers. Another excellent example of Barthelme's comic paradoxes is the story "Some of Us Had Been Threatening Our Friend Colby," where preparations for Colby's hanging are described in terminology normally associated with preparations for a wedding.[97] Some sort of paradoxical shift in levels is typical of many literary genres, of course, and parody is also a staple diet of many forms of postmodernist fiction, so we should be wary of claiming these as specifically "Catholic" idiosyncrasies. Yet the postmodernist sensibility of Barthelme, O'Hara, Altman, and Warhol seems to differ in kind from that of (say) Barth, Coover, or Pynchon, and one way to characterize the former group might be to suggest they practice an art of deflation rather than excess. Coover's texts, by contrast, fabricate fantastically intricate systems and delight in exposing their own radically fictional status; Barth's characters generally find themselves absurdly displaced into other species or historical eras; Pynchon creates labyrinthine, overdetermined worlds that appear beyond the compass of the human intelligence to fathom. Elaine Safer has, in fact, spoken interestingly of how Pynchon's texts comically redefine the drive of Puritan hermeneutics toward some order and meaning "behind" the visible world: Stencil in

97 *Amateurs*, pp. 29–34.

V seeks to unscramble a pattern of revelatory signs, but the elaborate
mazes of Pynchon's world deny him any such reassurance.[98] There are
various references in Pynchon's texts to his own Puritan ancestors, the
Pyncheons, shadowy figures who also appear in Hawthorne's *The House
of the Seven Gables;* and it may be that – like Hawthorne – Pynchon is
implicitly acknowledging some affiliation between this secular quest to
decipher secret systems and the Puritans' effort to decode the world
according to hierophantic messages laid down in the Bible.

The point here is that if Pynchon can be seen as obliquely connected
with a definably Puritan idiom, so Barthelme is connected with a definably Catholic idiom. Barthelme's characters do not seek to resolve the
world into a system of transcendent order; instead they render themselves
passive, flattening themselves before the demands of an external environment. This process is analogous to the way Warhol's subjects flatten
themselves passively before the camera; appropriately enough, Warhol's
Interview magazine is actually mentioned in Barthelme's *Paradise* (112).
The pattern is analogous as well to the way Altman's characters become
accidental components of some overarching and central myth, and to
the way Frank O'Hara's narrators submerge themselves within the world
of Manhattan: Charles Altieri perceptively noted that in their common
rejection of the "high Romantic doctrine of the form-creating imagination" Barthelme is Frank O'Hara's "counterpart in prose fiction."[99]
The "death of the subject" is a standard postmodernist theme, of course,
but subjects can die in many different ways, and the slide toward deflation
and passivity in Barthelme is dissimilar in tone to that sense of the
excessive and fabulous in Barth or Pynchon. Couturier, who compared
Barthelme's work to "the Andy Warhol style," mentioned how the
author's linguistic use of the predicate tends to erase an individualistic
subject – in circumlocutions such as "was expressed," "was serious" –
and he noted how this also adds to the general feel of passivity in Barthelme's work.[100] It is the same kind of passivity critics have talked about
in the context of Scott Fitzgerald, the sense of characters not being able
to achieve dominance over their worlds. Moreover, Barthelme's use of
lists and catalogs recalls all those ritualistic litanies that permeate Fitzgerald's fiction and, again, tend to displace the subject, turning him into
a component of the world rather than its master. "'Why do I make
lists?'" asks Amory Blaine in *This Side of Paradise.* "'Because you're a
medievalist,'" replies Monsignor Darcy. "'It's the passion for classifying

98 Elaine Safer, "American Novelists and Their Ethnic Traditions," MLA Convention,
San Francisco, 29 Dec. 1987.
99 Charles Altieri, *Enlarging the Temple: New Directions in American Poetry during the 1960s*
(Lewisburg: Bucknell Univ. Press, 1979), p. 117.
100 Couturier and Durand, *Donald Barthelme*, pp. 66, 19.

and finding a type. . . . It's the nucleus of Scholastic philosophy'" (114). In Barthelme, as in Fitzgerald, we discover a Catholic analogical mind-set that rejects isolation and individuality in favor of contiguity and similarity. Forfeiting their status as Cartesian subjects, the characters are embodied instead as ritualistic objects. As Hogo puts it in *Snow White:* "My main point is that you should bear in mind multiplicity, and forget about uniqueness" (75).

In finally considering how the modernist sensibility of Katherine Anne Porter and earlier novelists is modified by the postmodernist tendencies within O'Connor, Percy, and Barthelme, it is clear that the latter writers believe the landscape of contemporary America – abstract, romantic, relativist – is the one they must confront in their fiction. The old orders of Porter's Texas are now no more a viable option than the ethnic communities of Pietro Di Donato or James T. Farrell. That myth of plenitude has long since disappeared: "I have," said O'Connor in a 1963 letter, "never been greatly tied emotionally or sentimentally to my own Irish background."[101] Nor can the Deep South itself be the last bastion of social order, as it was, at least potentially, for Allen Tate. Robert H. Brinkmeyer has suggested that Percy draws upon the conservative traditions of the South as an antidote to the modernistic liberalism and alienation prevalent in the North; but, unlike Tate, Percy never seems to conceive of the South as a satisfactorily all-encompassing myth. It is true that Percy wrote from within the South, and his texts sometimes use this vantage point to make fun of the North. At other times, though, they make fun of the South as well, and it may be truer to suggest, as Richard Gray does, that Percy re-creates ironic, pastiche versions of the southern patriarchal homestead – Vaught Castle in *The Last Gentleman,* Belle Isle in *Lancelot* – as if to signify that in the computerized late twentieth century the landscape of New Orleans consists of a series of absences no less than those of Los Angeles or New York do.[102] For Percy, southern icons have become defamiliarized and alien rather than sources of regional strength.

Along with the supersession of modernist regionalism and ethnicity, we find a rejection of political idealism. Modernist Catholic literature is strewn with characters who flirt with the dogmatism of (usually Marxist) politics as a substitute for the dogmatism of their Catholic upbringing: one thinks of Farrell's Danny O'Neill and Bernard Carr, several figures

101 *The Habit of Being: The Letters of Flannery O'Connor,* p. 531.
102 Robert H. Brinkmeyer, Jr., *Three Catholic Writers of the Modern South* (Jackson: Univ. Press of Mississippi, 1985), pp. 119–72; Richard Gray, *Writing the South: Ideas of an American Region* (Cambridge: Cambridge Univ. Press, 1986), pp. 251–70.

in Dreiser and Eugene O'Neill. The whole idea became so familiar that George Orwell in *The Road to Wigan Pier* (1937) spent several pages analyzing "the analogies between Communism and Roman Catholicism," while in his 1941 paper "Literature and Totalitarianism," and elsewhere, Orwell routinely compared twentieth-century political totalitarianism to "medieval Europe," where "the Church dictated what you should believe."[103] We find this modernist intersection of church and state reproduced in Katherine Anne Porter's 1930 story "Flowering Judas," where the cradle-Catholic Laura finds herself mixed up with the socialism of Braggoni, whose political beliefs manifest themselves as a mirrored inversion of the structure of Catholicism: the Mexican Catholics hold a festival in honor of the Blessed Virgin on the same day the socialists celebrate their own martyrs, for instance. For the later modernists like James T. Farrell, socialism sometimes fulfills the role of a political utopia, an updated political version of that characteristic form of modernist idealism we see in such earlier guises as Marinetti's futurism or D. H. Lawrence's primitivism or Le Corbusier's pure white buildings. But O'Connor and Percy are not interested in political activity in any shape or form. Just as for O'Connor the "topical" was "poison," so Percy's *The Thanatos Syndrome* ridicules the standard American political debates between liberals and conservatives where "after two years no one had convinced anyone else" and "neither party listened to the other" (34).

Such political quietism is itself a form of implicit conservatism, of course, and it is no surprise that O'Connor was hostile to the idea of the Mass in English, nor that Percy's *Lancelot* lampoons the idea of priests as psychological counsellors: "Why can't you priests stick to being priests for a change?" (159). Still, on examining the arc of twentieth-century American novels, one feels as well that a more profound cultural change has taken place. In the shadow of Maritain and the increased influence of neo-scholastic philosophy, the whole notion of social idealism became for American Catholic writers in the post–1945 period not only redundant but also dangerously "angelic," a dream of human reason that might deflect attention away from the inherent limitations of human kind. This is, curiously enough, a return to that reluctance within nineteenth-century American Catholic enclaves to mingle religious devotion with material or worldly ambition. O'Connor and Percy both share a "Christian skepticism," as she called it, about the efficacy of any plans for social self-improvement; and this skepticism marks a major shift away from

103 George Orwell, *The Road to Wigan Pier* (New York: Harcourt, Brace and Co., 1958), p. 209; "Literature and Totalitarianism," in *The Collected Essays, Journalism and Letters of George Orwell,* ed. Sonia Orwell and Ian Angus (New York: Harcourt, Brace and World, 1968), II, 136.

that dogmatism, transformed from a religious into a political context, which is represented in modernist texts like "Flowering Judas."[104] Added to this fear of angelism, we find also in O'Connor, Percy, and Barthelme a typically postmodernist understanding of the arbitrary and discontinuous nature of any kind of system. Unlike the utopian modernists, postmodernists tend not to cherish idylls of an ultimate, clean, well-lighted place. The allure of final closure has vanished out of sight.

When thinking of how these American Catholic novelists engage with postmodernism, though, one of the most significant aspects is the way they critique the postmodernist fetish of "difference." Writing on "Metaphor as Mistake," Percy admitted the differences and "wrongness" necessarily involved in linguistically bridging two distinct objects, but he went on to claim: "This 'wrongness' of metaphor is seen to be not a vagary of poets but a special case of that mysterious 'error' which is the very condition of our knowing anything at all."[105] In other words, the linguistic analogies inherent in metaphor establish what the theologians would call a bond of being. Recognizing the ineluctable differences between objects, the Catholic philosopher nevertheless posits their vital resemblances as well. Percy returned to this theme in a discussion of Hopkins's "extraordinary sense of metaphor":

> You see him using words, metaphors, which are like and yet very different from what they signify . . . he would use the strangest metaphors to describe, for example, clouds: rafts of clouds, slivers of clouds, shafts of clouds. He would go out of his way to distance the metaphor. Sometimes he overdid it, but he was very much aware of what he was doing.[106]

According to Percy, Hopkins chooses to foreground the process by which metaphors and analogies are created. By emphasizing how his language is "like" but at the same time "very different from" his objects, Hopkins turns his texts into self-reflexive artifacts that deconstruct themselves, but deconstruct themselves to emphasize similarity rather than – as Derrida would have preferred – difference. Admitting difference, Hopkins at the same time refuses to essentialize it; the idea of similarity is equally important, even if within a worldly milieu such similarities can be fabricated only in a provisional fashion.

As we have seen, ontological similarity, expressed within the trope of materialized analogy, is one of the dominant characteristics of Catholic fictions. The recurring idea is of human beings bound together on a common enterprise, a common ship of fools. The litanies and catalogs

---

104 *The Habit of Being: The Letters of Flannery O'Connor*, p. 478.
105 Percy, *The Message in the Bottle*, p. 111.
106 Lawson and Kramer, *Conversations with Walker Percy*, p. 241.

in Barthelme's work represent an excellent example of this emphasis upon mirrored multiplicity rather than uniqueness. The names of some of the narrators in Walker Percy's books – Thomas More in *The Thanatos Syndrome* and *Love in the Ruins,* the hero of *Lancelot* whose name harks back to "that old nonexistent Catholic brawler and adulterer Lancelot du Lac" (116) – imply even more clearly how these Catholic writers envision processes of repetition and analogy to be at work throughout temporal history, so that human beings are seen as bound together in what Joyce's *Finnegans Wake* calls the "commodius vicus of recirculation."[107]

107 James Joyce, *Finnegans Wake,* 3rd ed. (London: Faber, 1964), p. 3.

16

The Beatific Vision:
J. P. Donleavy and
Jack Kerouac

As we have seen, Flannery O'Connor and Walker Percy maintain within their fiction a trace of "univocal" idealism. They tend at times to reveal religious patterns diagrammatically to the reader, even though in both cases their theories of art insist upon the redundant quality of didacticism and the necessity instead for a representation of concrete, fully incarnated manners and mystery. This tension between art and dogma is heightened by the fact that they are both very conscious of the status of their minority beliefs within American culture: adhering in theory to an art celebrating "the good of that which is made," both writers nevertheless preserve a certain defensiveness and resistance to the world around them, a resistance that impels their texts toward prescription rather than description. Yet if we take these aesthetic formulas of O'Connor and Percy to their logical conclusion, the "Catholic" novelist could be one who does not discuss the church at all, who represents life in a "sacramental" way without necessarily even being aware of how his or her view of the world has been produced. One might indeed argue that the notion of "Catholic" writing in the modern era has become too narrow and rigid precisely because of its associations with the explicitly Catholic fiction of O'Connor, Graham Greene, Evelyn Waugh, and others, although the attempt of David Tracy to reconcile postmodern theology with cultural pluralism would imply that "Catholic" authors might be found outside this kind of framework. J. P. Donleavy and Jack Kerouac, for example, are by no means Catholic writers in any orthodox sense, but both emerged out of a culture of Catholicism that has continued to influence the shape and direction of their work.

Flannery O'Connor herself wrote to Ted Spivey in 1959 that reading "the beat writers ... makes me think that there is a lot of ill-directed good in them. Certainly some revolt against our exaggerated materialism is long overdue. They seem to know a good many of the right things

394

to run away from, but to lack any necessary discipline."[1] O'Connor's typically neo-scholastic emphasis upon spiritual "discipline" brings to mind Max Weber's point in *The Sociology of Religion* about how Catholicism has traditionally tended to suppress idiosyncratic or romantic forms of mysticism, preferring to stress instead that clear-cut objectivity laid down in articles of faith. And yet, as Gabriel Daly said, an emphasis upon mysticism – which might be broadly defined as belief through experience of God, rather than through knowledge about him – became more prevalent in liberal Catholic circles during the twentieth century, and the term was used loosely by modernist theologians to imply a mode of thought antithetical to the remorseless logic of orthodox Thomism.[2] James Terence Fisher has written of how this form of Catholic romanticism, or "personalism" as he described it, became especially popular in mid-twentieth-century America: social rebels like Dorothy Day, Thomas Dooley, Thomas Merton, and Kerouac himself attempted to forge "a new Catholic identity in which the story of one's soul could be told as part of an American adventure." Fisher's point is that by emphasizing subjective experience of the world rather than its objective interpretation according to the tenets of preestablished dogma, writers like Kerouac "managed to move Catholic personalism close to the sources of classic American selfhood and self-expression." It is an "irony," said Fisher, that these rebellious beat writers were in fact reviving the kind of antinomian ideas fundamental to the American pastoral tradition.[3] In Kerouac's *The Town and the City* (1950), we find the narrator making fun of dour young Irish-Americans who are studying Aquinas at Boston College; similarly, in *On the Road* (1957) Sal Paradise accuses two "Jesuit boys" from an "Eastern college" of being encumbered with "a lot of ill-understood Aquinas," the implication being that Sal's own version of paradise comes closer to essential verities than this tired Scholastic dogma.[4] Kerouac once informed the priest in his Massachusetts hometown that Catholicism was too repressive because "Christ is joy, not damnation. That's why He cursed the fucking Pharisees"; and what we

---

1 Sally Fitzgerald, ed., *The Habit of Being: The Letters of Flannery O'Connor* (New York: Farrar, Straus and Giroux, 1979), p. 336.
2 Max Weber, *The Sociology of Religion,* trans. Ephraim Fischoff (London: Methuen, 1965), pp. 187–9; Gabriel Daly, O.S.A., *Transcendence and Immanence: A Study in Catholic Modernism and Integralism* (Oxford: Oxford Univ. Press, 1980), p. 228.
3 James Terence Fisher, *The Catholic Counterculture in America, 1933–1962* (Chapel Hill: Univ. of North Carolina Press, 1989), pp. 203–4, 199.
4 Jack Kerouac, *The Town and the City* (New York: Harcourt Brace Jovanovich, 1978), p. 184; *On the Road* (New York: Viking, 1957), p. 227. For both novels, subsequent page references are given in parentheses in the text.

see in the postwar Catholic "beat" writers is an attempt to incorporate within literature highly personalized forms of this beatific "joy."[5]

While Kerouac's subjective mysticism was partly fueled by a sense of dissatisfaction with what he conceived to be the desiccated nature of American Catholicism during the 1940s and 1950s, the rebellion in J. P. Donleavy's work is more broadly cultural. *The Ginger Man* (1955) enunciates an urgent desire to escape from Boston's Beacon Hill and the frigid materialism of Radcliffe girls, who harbor excessively rigid ideas of social status, into an environment not so "corrosive of the spirit," as Donleavy put it in his essay "An Expatriate Looks at America."[6] Because both Donleavy and Kerouac find their Catholic sensibility to be at odds with the dominant ethos of American culture, this leads them toward psychological flight and a desire to collapse within their texts all conventional social structures. Binx Bolling, in Percy's *The Moviegoer,* deems the beats to be "heartbreaking" (41) precisely because of their sense of loss and displacement, although this idiom of absence is not something Bolling himself is entirely immune from. This again reflects the central quandary of the Catholic writer within a generally non-Catholic culture, the same dilemma as Flannery O'Connor's texts find themselves riven by: charged with celebrating the immanent wonder of creation, the American Catholic writer finds the surrounding creation appears to be firmly resistant to any such metaphysical design.

This ironic disjunction between spirit and matter arises, of course, out of the especially tense situation of Catholicism within the United States. Albert Sonnenfeld has pointed out that while in the Catholic cultures of Spain and Italy religious literature tends to be "celebrative," with "its sign the adoration of the Virgin," in Protestant Germany and England – and, by extension, America – "the emblem of the Catholic writer is Holbein's picture of the still-suffering dead Christ."[7] The miseries endured by Graham Greene's characters, like those uneasy gaps and absences within Flannery O'Connor's texts, seem to betoken the differences that exist between a secular or Protestant environment as opposed to one imbued with Catholic "grace." Peter Hebblethwaite has similarly written of how French Catholic novelists like George Bernanos and François Mauriac tended to denounce the stolid materialism and literary (Balzacian) realism of bourgeois France in order to advance those aspects of Catholic faith that are "most paradoxical and craggy." Bernanos and Mauriac found themselves needing to subvert the anticlerical, rationalistic

5 Gerald Nicosia, *Memory Babe: A Critical Biography of Jack Kerouac* (New York: Grove Press, 1983), p. 86.
6 J. P. Donleavy, "An Expatriate Looks at America," *Atlantic Monthly,* Dec. 1976, p. 46.
7 Albert Sonnenfeld, "Twentieth Century Gothic: Reflections on the Catholic Novel," *Southern Review,* NS 1 (1965), 390.

temper of postrevolutionary France before they could open the eyes of
their audience to religious issues. Kerouac, with his French-Canadian
heritage, reconstitutes within his texts elements of this French style of
paradox and irony, cerebrally inverting the mundane materialistic world
so as to reveal what lies "at the boundary of that which escapes cohesion,"
to quote from Georges Bataille's theory of religion.[8]

Bernanos and Mauriac, then, conceived of their work as necessarily
oppositional to the genre of the novel. This interpretation of the novel
as a quintessentially humanist and therefore antimetaphysical literary
form was pursued by Bernard Bergonzi, who followed Ian Watt's familiar argument about how the development of the novel in the eighteenth century was intimately connected with the social and economic
growth of the bourgeoisie. This ensured, according to Bergonzi, that:

> The novelist whose Catholic beliefs were explicit in his work was work-
> ing against the grain of the novel form, with whatever advantages and
> disadvantages that could bring. The novel as it had developed since the
> eighteenth century was *bürgerlich,* this-worldly, realistic, empirical, phe-
> nomenological; unlike the romance, which it had partly replaced, it was
> not well adapted to miraculous or supernatural happenings. If religion
> appeared at all it was as a matter of social behavior or ethical conviction.
> The Catholic novelists occupied a world that was less solid and com-
> placently materialistic; it was partly transparent to other worlds, re-
> flecting the flames of Hell or, less frequently, the radiance of Heaven.[9]

Bergonzi's thesis is more obviously applicable to the English novel,
rotating as it does upon the axis of marriage and property, than to an
American tradition where more abstract forms of "romance" have lasted
longer. By their blithe disregard of the *"bürgerlich"* and their accessibility
to "miraculous or supernatural happenings," the texts of Kerouac and
Donleavy are in one sense reworking the old antinomian quests of American frontier romance – James Fenimore Cooper, Melville, Ralph Ellison
– albeit within a putatively metaphysical idiom. This is where the self-
centered "personalism" of Kerouac's version of religion dovetails neatly
with American romantic culture, as Fisher noted: it is no coincidence
that Kerouac's novels (and those of Donleavy) are nearly always narrated
in the first person, implying the same kind of individualistic search for
"salvation" that we find in the work of the most celebrated American
romancers.

This notion of Catholicism as an idiosyncratic personal style also sug-

8 Peter Hebblethwaite, "How Catholic Is the Catholic Novel?," *Times Literary Supplement,*
  27 July 1967, p. 678; Georges Bataille, *Theory of Religion,* trans. Robert Hurley (New
  York: Zone, 1989), p. 10.
9 Bernard Bergonzi, "A Conspicuous Absentee: The Decline and Fall of the Catholic
  Novel," *Encounter,* 55, nos. 2–3 (Aug.–Sept. 1980), 44.

gests why the religion suddenly became fashionable in the late 1950s and
early 1960s, when rebellion against old WASP norms was de rigueur for
intellectuals of all kinds. Norman O. Brown's *Life against Death* (1959)
– an account of "the psychoanalytical meaning of history" – postulated
an equation between money-grabbing Protestant capitalism and anal re-
tentiveness: "In the Protestant era," claimed Brown, "life becomes a
pure culture of the death instinct." For similar reasons, Norman Mailer's
list of "The Hip and the Square" in the same year assigned Catholicism
to the "hip" category and Protestantism to the "square."[10] Some of the
less ambitious beat writers have drawn upon the transiently modish
manner of this Catholic heritage to construct fairly simplistic parallels
between the terrestrial world and a "beatific" vision. Gregory Corso's
sentimental elegy, "For John Lennon," for instance, equates the assas-
sinated ex-Beatle with the martyred Christ, promising the songster a
quasi-divine "resurrection" when his acolytes will happily "wade in the
hosannahs of new water."[11]

Traces of this kind of radical chic persevere even in the more complex
projects of Kerouac and Donleavy. The tone of these authors is substantially different from that of earlier American Catholic novelists such
as Dreiser and Farrell, where the focus is much more upon communal
narratives and the meager rituals of alienated social groups. By foregrounding instead the role of the fashionable existential hero, Kerouac
and Donleavy appear to integrate their fiction within that "self-made
man" ethic more central to the American experience. This is a paradox
we have encountered before: in the language of American romanticism,
rebellious independence seems natural, while passive conformity seems
preternatural. Yet, ironically, the Catholic heroes of Kerouac and Donleavy never quite attain that freedom and independence characteristic of
American romance, nor indeed that sturdy self-reliance associated with
the more rotund heroes of the English empirical tradition. A novel whose
title derives from the name of its leading character usually negotiates
some kind of code of personal moral freedom, however much that freedom may find itself under pressure from the circumstances of society:
we might think of *David Copperfield,* or *The Adventures of Huckleberry
Finn,* or *The Adventures of Augie March.* It would be difficult, though, to
imagine *On the Road* appearing under the title "The Adventures of Sal
Paradise," because the character of Sal Paradise is never conceived of as
existing in the same self-defining, humanistically responsible way.

10 Norman O. Brown, *Life against Death: The Psychoanalytical Meaning of History* (Middletown: Wesleyan Univ. Press, 1959), p. 216; Norman Mailer, "The Hip and the
   Square," in *Advertisements for Myself* (New York: Putnam's, 1959), pp. 424–8.
11 Gregory Corso, *Herald of the Autochtonic Spirit* (New York: New Directions, 1981),
   p. 28.

It is true enough that Kerouac's works are close enough in spirit to the free world of American romance to draw sustenance from the energy of that genre: Alfred Corn, for instance, called Kerouac "a late avatar / Of Whitman" in his propensity to embark upon "Perpetual journeys."[12] But Kerouac's works are also far enough away in spirit from Whitmanian principles to cast a quizzical eye over such visionary interpretations of America. The apocalyptic quest that might radically rearrange the world into a nationalized version of the new millennium is, in Kerouac, disallowed; in *On the Road*, the nation cannot grow or change any more than Sal Paradise himself can. One subversive aspect of Kerouac's quests, in fact, is that they always seem to end up exactly where they began. The quest is undertaken, but then, in a disarming way, parodied. Similarly with that *"bürgerlich"* eradication of metaphysical designs Bergonzi claimed was integral to the novel: Kerouac and Donleavy appear to divest their world of anything spiritual in favor of the iconoclastic, earth-bound joys of the flesh, but both authors end up, paradoxically, letting the "miraculous" sneak in again through the back door. It is precisely this sense of an enigmatic, otherworldly dimension that operates mysteriously to displace these fictional characters toward the margins of their own lives. Characters like Sal Paradise become accidents, shadowy contingencies dependent for their incorporation upon some larger design. They are not, as in Dickens or Balzac, solid propertied figures, nor, as in Ralph Ellison or Saul Bellow, triumphantly self-validating humanistic essences. Instead, the personae of Kerouac and Donleavy become "partly transparent to other worlds" in the way Bergonzi said was characteristic of Catholic fiction. It is their very attenuated quality that seems to hint at these characters' otherworldly status.

J. P. Donleavy is not generally rated among the "beat" writers, though in fact he shares many of their themes and some of their vocabulary. "I've been beaten, beaten," complains O'Keefe to Sebastian Dangerfield in *The Ginger Man*.[13] As in Kerouac, this state of being "beaten" or defeated leads toward the possibility of a higher, "beatific" vision.

Donleavy was born into a Catholic family in Brooklyn in 1926. His father was an Irish immigrant, but Donleavy himself "ceased practising the religion at an early age" and questions of religious identity rarely surface overtly within his texts.[14] What is much more apparent, however, is an overall sense of social unease and psychological displacement. Don-

---

12 Alfred Corn, *Notes from a Child of Paradise* (New York: Viking Press, 1984), p. 80.
13 J. P. Donleavy, *The Ginger Man* (New York: Delacorte Press–Seymour Lawrence, 1965), p. 40. Subsequent page references are given in parentheses in the text.
14 I owe this information to a personal letter from Jacqueline Maguire, Secretary to J. P. Donleavy, 28 Sept. 1988.

leavy's own feeling that his lower-class Irish "cultural background isolated me in America" is replicated within the fictional lives of his heroes,
who are never able to find themselves quite at home within any given
setting. In a 1975 *Paris Review* interview, Donleavy talked of how his
Irish-American friend A. K. Donoghue perceived himself to be "ostra-
cized" at Harvard: Donoghue "couldn't join any of the good clubs," said
Donleavy, a comment evoking shades of Scott Fitzgerald's experiences
at Princeton.[15]

Throughout Donleavy's novels, we encounter various attempts to
overcome this kind of alienation. One such attempt involves migrating
to Ireland. During his American youth, Donleavy first set eyes on Ireland,
or its simulacrum, in John Ford's film *The Informer*. In a similar mental
projection (or fantasy) of "home," Donleavy's fictional heroes shuttle
from country to country in the forlorn attempt to recover an ancestral
ethnic plenitude. In the Dublin of *The Ginger Man*, exiled American
Sebastian Dangerfield feels nostalgic for fall and football in New England,
following a pattern set by Donleavy himself, who wrote of experiencing
longing for America in Ireland and for Ireland in America.[16] Donleavy's
novels are set in America (*A Singular Man*) and England (*Schultz*) as well
as in Ireland, and this internationality betokens a strange kind of interchangeability where alienation becomes conceptual as well as geographic.
The heroes are always looking for "home," but no place is home, and
eventually all places come to seem the same. As in Kerouac, the idea of
travel and exile ultimately implies a sense of ontological loss, the expulsion from paradise. "Till they re-establish paradise on earth," says
Kerouac's narrator in *Desolation Angels,* the beats will be "nothing but
bums."[17] The undermining of this fundamental notion of "home" reduces these wayfarers to bedraggled pilgrims on the stony paths of postlapsarian life.

It is obvious enough that Donleavy's novels represent Ireland as a
provisional structure, a state of mind. Yet the shadowy and insubstantial
nature of this environment can itself become an asset to the themes of
his fiction, concerned as Donleavy is to eradicate that rigidly conventional
mentality he associates with the United States. As an exile, the author
naturally feels a sense of psychological distance from the social and class
hierarchies of his adopted country; consequently, in his work more attention comes to be focused upon matters that are altogether asocial. *The
Ginger Man,* like Donleavy's other novels, thrives upon what John Rees

15 "The Art of Fiction LIII: J. P. Donleavy," *Paris Review*, no. 63 (Fall 1975), pp. 161–2.
16 *J. P. Donleavy's Ireland: In All Her Sins and in Some of Her Graces* (New York: Viking
Press, 1986), pp. 11, 185.
17 Jack Kerouac, *Desolation Angels* (New York: Coward-McCann, 1965), p. 112.

Moore called an "instinct for catastrophe," catastrophe that is always welcome because it breaks down the rigid dimensions of the everyday self and permits the text to become – in Bergonzi's phrase – "partly transparent to other worlds."[18] Poverty introduces a welcome atavism: to be "beat," as so many of Donleavy's characters are, destroys the Protestant shibboleths of "decency" and moral "fibre" Sebastian Dangerfield deems so antipathetic to his "Catholic blood" (167).

In place of this decency, Donleavy's texts substitute the beastly beatitudes of human sexuality. Sebastian Dangerfield implicitly spiritualizes the flesh by making love to his wife against the sound of a Gregorian chant wafting up from Saint Patrick's Cathedral. When his marriage flounders and Dangerfield takes up with the Puritan-minded "Miss Frost," the hero advises her not to worry too much about her sense of sin by quoting reassuringly from the teachings of Aquinas:

> I comforted her with readings from this Aquinas because he says it's good for you. And I said, tenderly earwards, heads on the pillow, that from manure, lilies grow. To know the real goodness one had to be bad and of sin. What good is it to God, dear Miss Frost, for a child to be born pure, to live purely and die purely. Where was the grace in that shallow, white sterility? You don't want that stuff. No. Get down in it, down. The greatest whiteness is touched with black. The righteous were a sneaky bunch anyway. (210)

This is the classic Catholic doctrine we have seen refracted in Frank O'Hara, Robert Altman, and other authors: evil is intricately interwoven with good, not – as in the Puritan doctrine – its antithesis. To claim that Aquinas believed extramarital sex to be "good for you" is, of course, an overstatement; still, the Angelic Doctor did hold that fornication, adultery, and seduction were all less serious sins than masturbation, since the former activities at least revealed a transgressor's involvement with the bounty of God's creation – nature being by definition good – while the latter vice implied only solipsism.[19] In the eyes of Aquinas, both fornicator and masturbator were sinning against the laws of society and the church, but only the masturbator was sinning also against the laws of nature.

For Sebastian Dangerfield, then, God is a comedian tolerant of human peccadilloes: Dangerfield envisions the deity "splitting his sides up there over this tender little scene" between Miss Frost and himself (256). Likewise, in Donleavy's short story "Meet My Maker" (1964), God appears

18 John Rees Moore, "J. P. Donleavy's Season of Discontent," *Critique,* 9, no. 2 (1966), 97.
19 Peter Gardella, *Innocent Ecstasy: How Christianity Gave America an Ethic of Sexual Pleasure* (New York: Oxford Univ. Press, 1985), p. 10.

as a pipe-smoking *homme moyen sensuel,* a figure kitted out in blue jeans, partial to well-cooked veal and fine vintages, and fond of alleviating his divine burden by working out in the gym. In Donleavy's fiction, access to this companionable maker tends to derive from a sense of detachment from the pomp and circumstance of worldly events. The rich business-man George Smith, hero of *A Singular Man* (1963), would prefer, he says, to secede from respectability and become "a great criminal." As in Kerouac, becoming an outcast from society seems good for the soul: "I haven't got much religion," claims George Smith at one point, "but I believe I'll just get down on my knees here for a moment."[20] In similar fashion, at the end of *The Destinies of Darcy Dancer, Gentleman* (1977) Darcy falls, "Knees sunk in the soft, moist grass. Praying to sexton's Stations of the Cross."[21] For Darcy Dancer, images of Christ and of his love Clarissa have become equated.

   The Onion Eaters (1971) again consecrates human sexuality, this time by punningly aligning it with worship of the Madonna. "Let the current of deep faith sweep you into the arms of our lady," the Catholic priest in this novel ambiguously advises Bligh.[22] Albert Sonnenfeld's suggestion that it is the crucified Christ who is the archetypal image for Catholic writers in Protestant cultures has some relevance to Donleavy: motifs of martyrdom appear throughout *The Ginger Man,* where the beaten/bea-tific Dangerfield dreams of himself "tacked up on a cross and looking down" at the "passive, mystifying sorrow" of Dublin (234). But images celebrating the Blessed Virgin, which Sonnenfeld adjudged more typical of Catholic writers in Catholic cultures, can also be seen here, though they are generally transferred from a divine to a secular significance. By moving beyond the theological aspects of Catholicism, Donleavy permits himself to reinvent his landscapes of nature within a broader Catholic cultural perspective.

   Sexuality in fact becomes so ubiquitous throughout Donleavy's texts that it achieves the status of an essentialism in itself. Donleavy replaces the lost plenitude of Christian heaven with the earthly plenitude of human congress, whose necessary shadow of mortality is also a constant presence in his work. This reinterpretation of spiritual ideas within a materialist idiom is another aspect of what Thomas LeClair has called Donleavy's

20 J. P. Donleavy, "Meet My Maker," in *Meet My Maker The Mad Molecule* (New York: Delacorte Press–Seymour Lawrence, 1964), pp. 157–9; *A Singular Man* (Boston: Little, Brown and Co., 1963), pp. 154, 294.

21 J. P. Donleavy, *The Destinies of Darcy Dancer, Gentleman* (New York: Delacorte Press–Seymour Lawrence, 1977), p. 401. Subsequent page references are given in parentheses in the text.

22 J. P. Donleavy, *The Onion Eaters* (New York: Delacorte Press–Seymour Lawrence, 1971), p. 282. Subsequent page references are given in parentheses in the text.

"ironic denial of religion and covert affirmation of it": *The Onion Eaters* talks of a "holy hell" (306); *Schultz* describes how the protagonists "screwed each other in every direction. Tongues up each other's asses. That's how deep love can get. Holy shit." From this angle, even excreta become sacramental. Especially in *Schultz*, the author's use of profanity veers away from being a mere throwaway use of language and suggests instead the covert sanctification of earthbound activities: "Holy jesus is it two fingers she's sticking in."[23] These blasphemous inversions, philosophical and linguistic, depend of course upon a preexistent religious structure: transgression has no rationale unless there is something to transgress against. The most thorough working out of these inversions occurs in *The Beastly Beatitudes of Balthazar B* (1969) where, as the title implies, heaven and hell are yoked by violence together, as Beefy, an expert in "combining lechery and religion," plans to take holy orders – "but not before I've had my fill of the diabolical."[24]

In Donleavy, then, burlesque becomes a moral imperative. Social order and individual human dignity are annihilated as material becomes spiritual, and vice versa: "Before the night's over we'll see bottoms up and tops down," declares Percival in *The Onion Eaters* (290). Because of these kinds of ironic reversal, the dominant movement of Donleavy's humor is bathos, the establishment of a conventional idea that is subsequently trumped by a subversive lower meaning. In *Darcy Dancer,* for instance, the narrator talks of how "love hits you a blinding flash between the eyes if you are a gentleman. And between the legs if you are not" (75). Given this carefully constructed form of antiidealism, it is hard to think of Donleavy as epitomizing what Ihab Hassan called "radical innocence," for nihilism in Donleavy never exists simply as pure, unobstructed nihilism. All Hassan said about the dangerous and violent edge to Donleavy's work is true, but this "crackling laughter" of absurdity does not imply a glad escape from social and religious hierarchies so much as a constant rebellion against them. Donleavy's heroes oscillate between the poles of conventionality and transgression, and within this rebellious framework the Oedipal parent of Catholicism continues to exercise a powerful signifying charge.[25] The laughter in Donleavy retains elements of religious

23 Thomas LeClair, "A Case of Death: The Fiction of J. P. Donleavy," *Contemporary Literature,* 12 (1971), 336; J. P. Donleavy, *Schultz* (New York: Delacorte Press–Seymour Lawrence, 1979), pp. 394, 243. For *Schultz,* subsequent page references are given in parentheses in the text.
24 J. P. Donleavy, *The Beastly Beatitudes of Balthazar B* (New York: Delacorte Press–Seymour Lawrence, 1968), pp. 224, 195. Subsequent page references are given in parentheses in the text.
25 Ihab Hassan, *Radical Innocence: Studies in the Contemporary American Novel* (Princeton: Princeton Univ. Press, 1961), p. 196.

celebration because it depends partly upon residual energies lodged within religious icons and ideas, icons and ideas the texts are explicitly denying. Thus the textual apotheosis of sexuality in Donleavy's work can be seen as a reworking of religious apotheosis. Though of course their works are not of equal artistic merit, it is a similar aesthetic and cultural pattern to the one we find in the works of James Joyce, a writer whom Donleavy openly reveres.[26]

The artistic status of Donleavy's work is, in fact, an interesting question. Conventional wisdom insists that after the zany iconoclasm of *The Ginger Man* his texts tended to repeat themselves and become increasingly predictable. Donleavy's reputation has hardly been boosted by his own admission that he is driven to write by "money, above all things. Fame goes, but money never does. It's got its own beauty."[27] Yet this subversion of liberal pieties about the integrity of the creative imagination may have its own validity in terms of Donleavy's work. His novels undercut social structures in order to allow access to a radical materialism, even atavism, which subsequently becomes sanctified. The idea is, as *Schultz* puts it, that one has "to accept people for what they are, dirty rats" (288), greedy for the dirt of money and sex. "Old Europe is so wise to people's frailties," asserts Schultz later on: "Guys exist to screw women and women exist to make them pay for it" (404). This is, in its more savage way, an updating of Henry James's theme about the endemic corruption within Europe as opposed to the abstract idealism prevalent within the United States. Like his fellow exile James, Donleavy prefers Europe, the Europe where "a fart might be called a fart," where (as in *The Onion Eaters*) the priest who hears confessions turns out to be a greedy gambler himself, where the Puritan zeal for human perfectibility is held of no account.[28]

This rejection of idealism has led some critics to claim Donleavy's works are bereft of intelligence. "If Donleavy's work were informed by intellectual concepts," complained Charles E. Masinton, "or were the occasions for him to develop ideas relative to important issues or problems, then they might have displayed greater variety or ingenuity."[29] But in fact these novels are informed by "intellectual concepts": the idea that abstract intellectual concepts are more or less worthless, the belief

---

26 *J. P. Donleavy's Ireland*, p. 221. Here Donleavy recounts how he moved with his family to Levington Park in County Westmeath, "a mellow stone mansion where James Joyce came as a young man and stayed to walk in its halls."

27 Donleavy, "The Art of Fiction LIII," p. 141.

28 *J. P. Donleavy's Ireland*, p. 20.

29 Charles E. Masinton, *J. P. Donleavy: The Style of His Sadness and Humor* (Bowling Green, Ohio: Bowling Green Univ. Popular Press, 1975), p. 4.

that lust, greed, and death comprise the sum of the human cycle. As *Darcy Dancer* puts it:

> Haven't I read all the great Irish thinkers and metaphysicians from Johannes Scottus Erigena at the court of Charles the Bald in France right down to the latest from Berkeley. And let me tell you, not one of them knew better than a cow does when she goes to shelter behind a hedge in a winter's gale. And none of them could give you a better definition of confidence than I'm giving you now. It's a pound sterling in your pocket. (341)

It is the familiar American insistence that "intellectual concepts" must be synonymous with some form of idealism that has resulted for so long in the fetishizing of individual liberty, with its concomitant ideologies of pastoralism and transcendentalism. Donleavy's work has more affinities with a brutal Hobbesian attitude, and in this he stands as a challenge to, and critique of, American literary and philosophical traditions. When Donleavy refused to consider cutting *The Ginger Man* to ease its path toward publication because he felt certain the book "held itself together on the basis of these scatological parts," the author knew exactly what he was doing.[30] Scatology, in the widest sense of that term, is Donleavy's essential milieu. From this angle, the author's assertion that he writes for money could be seen to reflect back upon the antiidealistic form of his work, for the production of these novels, as much as their thematic content, revolves around the desire for filthy lucre.

The accusations of antiintellectualism directed at Donleavy were echoed in various forms of hostility toward the beat writers in general. Writing in the *Partisan Review* in 1958, Norman Podhoretz gave it as his version of "the plain truth . . . that the primitivism of the Beat Generations serves first of all as a cover for an anti-intellectualism so bitter that it makes the ordinary American's hatred of eggheads seem positively benign." Kerouac came in for particular abuse from Podhoretz, who talked of the writer's "know-nothing populist sentiment," his "simple inability to express anything in words" and his intellectual pretensions, which were "only a form of newspeak."[31]

The word "newspeak," taken from Orwell's *1984,* is particularly revealing here. In Orwell's novel, newspeak is the sinister language of the mass media disseminated by Big Brother in order to control the thought processes of the population. In American intellectual circles during the 1950s, there was a similar fear of the media – especially, in this case,

30 Donleavy, "The Art of Fiction LIII," p. 128.
31 Norman Podhoretz, "The Know-Nothing Bohemians," *Partisan Review,* 25 (1958), 313, 307.

406 POSTMODERNISM AND DISPLACEMENT

television – becoming an agent for dehumanization and social control. In the late 1950s and early 1960s, Kerouac himself was very popular and effective on television talk shows: according to John Clellon Holmes, in fact, he came to be thought of primarily as a "show-biz guy."[32] This would certainly not have endeared Kerouac to the *Partisan Review* liberal establishment and other academics of the time for whom anything popular was by definition inferior. (We might remember the hostility toward Robert Frost in the 1950s from Yvor Winters and other critics on account of the widespread popularity of his poetry. Even defenders of Frost, such as Lionel Trilling, saw the mass appeal of his work as a potential liability rather than an asset.)[33]

As we have seen, however, Catholic art and thought have tended to be centered around what is familiar and communal rather than what is private and transcendental. This, as William Lynch perceived, has created a different kind of Catholic vocabulary: "Much of the public strength of Protestantism lies in its magnificent poetic defense of the unconditional transcendence of God, and its glowing picture of human nothingness, while Catholicism is often caught, as a result of its own logic, in a state of 'non-magnificence.'"[34] It is no coincidence that many of the ablest American theorists of mass media – Warhol, McLuhan, Ong – have been Catholic. The ubiquitous banality of popular culture, its mass appeal, is a quality the intellectual and spiritual disciplines of Protestantism and Judaism have often tended to resist. The purpose here is not triumphantly to vindicate Kerouac, but to suggest that Kerouac's attempt to bridge "high" and "low" culture was partly a product of his Catholic identity. From this perspective, Podhoretz's claim that "being for or against what the Beat Generation stands for . . . has to do . . . with being for or against intelligence itself" implies a rather too partial and culturally specific notion of what constitutes "intelligence."[35] There may be other models.

Other models, though, were not easy to come by within the homogenizing social climate of the 1950s. This was an era of comfort and consensus, intellectual as well as suburban and materialistic. (It is curious how the intellectuals' mode of liberal protest became as monolithic, in its way, as the very forms of mass culture they were protesting against.) It was the time when Catholic thinkers like Walter J. Ong were striving

---

32 Holmes made this assertion on the film *Kerouac,* dir. John Antonelli, Wonder Productions, 1984.

33 Yvor Winters, *The Function of Criticism: Problems and Exercises* (Denver: Alan Swallow, 1957), pp. 157–87; Lionel Trilling, "A Speech on Robert Frost: A Cultural Episode," *Partisan Review,* 26 (1959), 445–52.

34 William F. Lynch, S.J., *Christ and Apollo: The Dimensions of the Literary Imagination* (New York: Sheed and Ward, 1960), p. 16.

35 Podhoretz, "The Know-Nothing Bohemians," p. 318.

to reconcile the seemingly unassailable hegemony of American liberal optimism with a reinvigorated Catholic modernity; in *Frontiers in American Catholicism* (1957), Ong wrote of how the defensive ethnicity of Catholicism in the 1930s was becoming supplanted by keen participation in the rituals of Eisenhowerian consumerism. One side of Kerouac cooperates enthusiastically with this rejection of the narrower focus of ethnic identity: in many ways, Kerouac's texts are predicated upon a buoyant validation of all the new icons of 1950s materialism. Still, an uneasy note of estrangement can never quite be suppressed. If Scott Fitzgerald's Irish-Catholic heritage impairs a full commitment to the American Dream of the 1920s, Kerouac's French-Catholic heritage impairs full commitment to the American Dream of the 1950s. Kerouac's novels, like Fitzgerald's, negotiate that uneasy space between assimilation and alienation, between consensus and ethnicity; and, as with Fitzgerald, this double-edged perspective pushes Kerouac's novels toward the form of a gentle parody of institutionalized American romanticism.

Fellow beat writer Diane di Prima expressed the opinion that Kerouac should actually be thought of as an immigrant writer. This, surely, is to overstate the case; but even though ethnicity was such an unfashionable subject in the 1950s, it is noticeable that Kerouac did choose to describe his nationality as "Franco-American."[36] Brittany was the ancestral home of the Kerouacs, and French Canada the intermediate point on the way to Lowell, Massachusetts, where the writer was born and brought up. The old Yankee view of Catholic French Canada as "the North American Babylon," a perception prevalent during the French wars of the mid-eighteenth century, was by now generally in abeyance, of course; nevertheless, a residual suspicion of the traditionally close nature of French-Canadian family and ethnic ties still lingered in northern New England communities.[37] Canadians had immigrated to these communities in large numbers during the nineteenth century, with "Dénationaliser, c'est démoraliser" being the slogan of those who attempted to keep French loyalties alive. Yankees, meanwhile, thought back darkly to George Washington's famous farewell address warning against "the insidious wiles of foreign influence" and judged this attempt by French-Canadians to preserve their national identity to be socially undesirable. According to Kerouac's *Visions of Gerard* (1963), Lowell in 1925 was "a close knit truly French community such as you might not find any more (with the

---

36 Di Prima makes this suggestion on the film *The Beat Generation: An American Dream,* dir. Janet Forman, Renaissance Pictures, 1987; Jack Kerouac, *Lonesome Traveller* (New York: McGraw-Hill, 1960), p. iv. Subsequent page references appear in parentheses in the text.

37 Sacvan Bercovitch, *The American Jeremiad* (Madison: Univ. of Wisconsin Press, 1978), p. 115.

peculiar Medieval Gallic closed-in flavor) in modern long-eared France."[38] French, indeed, was the first language Kerouac heard at home; he could not speak English until he was five or six, and he was still talking "with a halting accent" ten years later.[39] Some sense of the English language as a strange, unfamiliar entity, acquired rather than inherited, can be traced throughout the prose of his novels. Like the Germanic Dreiser, for whom also English was a second language, Kerouac juggles words in a self-conscious fashion rather than according to the unstated norms of inherited custom. Also much like Dreiser is the way Kerouac's struggle with the articulation of speech is intimately tied to wider issues of cultural articulation, the struggle to find a voice that might speak for his marginalized community.

The imminent loss of this ethnic plenitude, however, is a theme that permeates Kerouac's fiction, just as it does Donleavy's. Kerouac's first novel, *The Town and the City* (1950), describes a transition from the ethnic security of a small town to the postmodern contingencies of life in a big city, with nostalgia for the lost comforts of family ritual being inextricably combined with nostalgia for the Catholic faith of childhood: "The mother had always taught the legend of the Catholic religion to those of her children who seemed most interested" (24). The name of the family in *The Town and the City* is the Martins, which was also the surname of Thérèse of Lisieux, the Breton saint beatified in 1923 to whom Kerouac – educated at parochial schools until the age of seven – was taught to pray. *Visions of Gerard* recollects this Catholic schooling as it narrates the story of Kerouac's brother's early death and his supposed transposition into the happy condition of a martyred "little saint" (136). *Maggie Cassidy* (1959) also associates memories of home with the pain of loss, in this case the loss of the hero's small-town Irish-Catholic sweetheart, and again this narrative introduces larger issues about the loss of innocence and the loss of community. *On the Road* (1957) is even more explicit on this theme of lost innocence: "The one thing that we yearn for in our living days, that makes us sigh and groan and undergo sweet nauseas of all kinds, is the remembrance of some lost bliss that was probably experienced in the womb and can only be reproduced (though we hate to admit it) in death" (124).

It would of course be easy enough to proffer psychoanalytical readings of this "lost bliss." The devotion to "Dean Moriarty" in *On the Road* might be seen as a search for a father figure, while the relapse into

---

38 Jack Kerouac, *Visions of Gerard* (New York: McGraw-Hill, 1976), p. 80. Subsequent page references appear in parentheses in the text.
39 According to Kerouac's "confession" in *The Subterraneans* (New York: Grove Press, 1958), p. 3. Subsequent page references appear in parentheses in the text.

maternal cohabitation with "Memère" at the end of *Desolation Angels* (1965) could be read as a regressive form of tranquillity, a dysfunctional attempt to escape from the symbolic order of society into the imaginary plenitude of original narcissism. We know, of course, that Kerouac did indeed end up in the 1960s living with his mother in Massachusetts and Florida. Still, *The Subterraneans* (1958) warily resists the whole idea of therapy on the grounds that "it's a big world and psychoanalysis is a small way to explain it" (71). While psychological maladjustment might be one interpretation of Kerouac's dilemmas, this maladjustment was also a condition – an integral condition, in fact – of the metaphysical displacement that underlies his work.

Vanity of Duluoz (1967) adumbrates this displacement when the narrator chastises secular "materialists" who, in "their clunkheaded ignorance of their own broken hearts," fail to perceive that the only human "sin" is "the sin of birth."[40] In this novel, Kerouac relates all earthly suffering to the necessary tragedy of terrestrial incarnation, the original expulsion from paradise, a sorrow brought to focus in the symbol of the cross with "its mysterious penetration into all this brutality" (276). Taking issue with Bertrand Russell, he says one should not attribute worldly troubles to the deficiencies of the government; instead, "metaphysical causes" (277) are deemed to be the root cause of all human anguish. According to James Terence Fisher, many Catholic political activists of the 1940s and 1950s followed in Dorothy Day's *Catholic Worker* tradition by perceiving self-denial and suffering to be their primary responsibilities, and something of these antitriumphalist, self-immolating tendencies linger in Kerouac's rhetoric of self-abnegation. French-Canadian Catholicism, like its Irish-American counterpart, was shaped partly by the doctrines of Jansenism, and we can see a trace of these austere influences in Kerouac's infatuation with Original Sin: "Sin is sin," declares the narrator in *Visions of Gerard,* "and there's no erasing it" (42).[41]

Nevertheless, the "mission" of Kerouac's writing – a word he himself used in the 1960 *Lonesome Traveller* (171) – was to redeem the suffering of this beaten world by revealing, or at least implying, the salvation of a beatific vision. Like Donleavy, Kerouac subverts social and material categories in order to allow access within his texts to the translucency of a religious aura. As in Donleavy also, this undermining of social convention involves a form of psychological collapse, the cracking open of the self so as not to be "completely safe," like the smug, self-absorbed

40 Jack Kerouac, *Vanity of Duluoz: An Adventurous Education, 1935–46* (New York: Coward-McCann, 1967), p. 276. Subsequent page references appear in parentheses in the text.
41 Fisher, *The Catholic Counterculture in America,* p. 69; for Canadian Jansenism, see Richard S. Sorrell, "The Catholicism of Jack Kerouac," *Studies in Religion,* 11 (1982), 197.

individual in a "Scandinavian ski sweater" depicted in *Visions of Cody* (1972).[42] In *Visions of Gerard,* we are told that collapse of the "ego-personality" (140) is a necessary precondition of the journey toward a "divine and perfect ecstasy" (147). *On the Road* similarly embraces a radical sense of self-dissolution: the narrator starts by recalling how this was "the one distinct time in my life, the strangest moment of all, when I didn't know who I was" (17), and he concludes by reckoning that in the course of his quest he "had lived a whole life and many others in the poor atomistic husk of my flesh" (302). This assumption of multiple personalities, the sense of being split between heaven and earth, becomes essential to Kerouac's visionary endeavors, which is why the label of "schizophrenic" may be reductive in this context, even if according to the formulas of psychoanalysis it is "true." (According to Gerald Nicosia, Kerouac fell at times into the delusion that he actually was God.)[43]

Kerouac's texts are bestrewn with images of crucifixes and suffering, suffering that looks forward to being redeemed in a better world. In *Visions of Gerard,* punishment from the nuns is acceptable because "it was all secondary, it was all for the bosom of the Grave Church, which we all know was Pure Gold, Pure Light" (40–1). In *The Town and the City,* Peter attends church on Good Friday to see "Jesus suffering and heroic, dark, dark Jesus and his cross"; then he returns on "the bell-golden Easter mornings of sun and flowers" to find "Jesus arisen triumphant, immortal, radiant and true." Peter feels this heroic pattern is one he and his brothers must imitate: "They had to be heroes or nothing" (121). Thus the personae of Kerouac's novels are, like Christ, socially disenfranchised martyrs who possess the heroic faculty of "divine" vision, although this vision usually becomes recast within earthly terms. It is the sacred quality of the here-and-now Kerouac is most often concerned with; as the saintly hero of *Visions of Gerard* tells his teacher, Sister Marie: "We're all in Heaven – but we don't know it" (68). This is the same pattern we saw in Donleavy's work, the paradoxical inversion of theology so as to sanctify the fallen human world. In *Doctor Sax* (1959), the narrator finds himself "suddenly realizing that the world was upside down and the bottom of the world was gold."[44] Here even the imagery of inversion recalls Donleavy's *The Onion Eaters,* which talks of "bottoms up and tops down" (290). Similar metaphors are found in *On the Road,* where Sal Paradise claims that "the bottom of the world is gold and the world is upside down" (254).

42 Jack Kerouac, *Visions of Cody* (New York: McGraw-Hill, 1972), p. 48. Subsequent page references appear in parentheses in the text.
43 Nicosia, *Memory Babe,* p. 49.
44 Jack Kerouac, *Doctor Sax: Faust Part Three* (New York: Grove Press, 1959), p. 196.

This reinvention of spiritual concepts in material terms is the essence of Kerouac's famous "beatific" vision, the product of a self-described "strange solitary crazy Catholic mystic."[45] In his essay "The Origins of the Beat Generation," Kerouac disparaged the equation of "beat" with juvenile delinquency and said "the vision of the word Beat as being to mean beatific" first came to him in a Catholic church in 1954.[46] In *On the Road*, Sal Paradise is, so he says, "mad to be saved" (8), and he embarks with Dean Moriarty on a pilgrimage to expand his soubriquet "Sal" into the full glory of salvation. (The character of Moriarty was based upon Neal Cassady, who, like Kerouac himself, was a former Catholic altar boy.)[47] Various potential promised lands – Denver, San Francisco, Mexico – are driven toward and then through. In Mexico, Sal is surprised to find the external landscape offering an objective correlative to his own psychological Catholicism; this perception becomes even more explicit in *Lonesome Traveller*, where the central character remarks on how "it amazed me to remember that we were all Catholics" (29). Such a shock of recognition implicitly reveals the sense of alienation that Kerouac's narrators experience at other times, a disjunction the texts strive heroically and at times hyperbolically to overcome. In *On the Road*, Dean is described as "a new kind of American saint" (39) who deciphers the world about him "like a monk peering into the manuscripts of the snow" (112). By reading correctly the book of the secular world, Kerouac's characters hope to locate that spiritual essence latent within the accidents of matter.

In this prophetic task, these heroes reembody the aspirations of the thirteenth-century Franciscans, friars who followed Saint Francis by rejecting the monastic enclosures of the Benedictines and opting instead for a career of poverty and perpetual travel. The Franciscans, said Lawrence Cunningham, saw themselves as "contemplatives on the move" whose faith would not be encumbered by materialistic hoarding.[48] Kerouac's novels reveal a similar radical asceticism. "Everything belongs to me because I am poor," claims the narrator in *Visions of Cody* (33). The hero of *Desolation Angels* categorically asserts that "I love St. Francis of Assisi as well as anybody in the world" (69) before going on to speculate about how Saint Francis would have coped with the intellectual climate of the 1960s.

According to Ann Charters, Kerouac remained a believing Catholic throughout his life, though his commitment to the faith did at times

45 See Kerouac's Introduction to *Lonesome Traveller*, p. vi.
46 Jack Kerouac, "The Origins of the Beat Generation," *Playboy*, June 1959, p. 42.
47 Sorrell, "The Catholicism of Jack Kerouac," p. 192.
48 Lawrence Cunningham, *The Catholic Heritage* (New York: Crossroad, 1983), p. 37.

waver.[49] Most obviously, he became attracted by the holistic formulas of Buddhism, cherishing the Zen *nada* or void in *Tristessa* (1960), coming to think Christ had been too political, longing instead for the transcendental quietism of Eastern religions. All of this is most apparent in *The Dharma Bums* (1958), where the empty tranquillity of northwestern mountains becomes an emblem of the grand passivity of Buddha: "Think of the patience, hundreds of thousands of years just sittin there bein perfectly silent."[50] In *Desolation Angels* we are told that "those who believe in a personal God who cares about good and bad are hallucinating themselves" (70), while in the same novel the narrator professes surprise that Cody, the product of an "Irish Jesuit school" (159), still insists upon believing "that all does really good-and-bad matter" (168). The narrator here also (rather uneasily) defends Buddhism against the Catholic philosophies of David D'Angeli, a fictional character based on Philip Lamantia. D'Angeli, however, assures narrator Jack that he has no reason to be concerned because Jack will remain a Catholic whether he likes it or not. "You've been baptized," says D'Angeli, "the mystery of the water has touched you" (187).

It is true the more worldly aspects of Catholicism often troubled Kerouac, though Regina Weinreich's claim that "the influence of Gary Snyder and the teachings of Buddha . . . assuaged the cruel disappointments of Kerouac's Catholicism" surely gets the balance wrong. Kerouac himself said later: "I'm a Catholic all along. I was really kidding Gary Snyder."[51] Though we should not necessarily take that last statement at face value, by the time of *Big Sur* (1962) we can see the image of the cross beginning to supersede the compulsions of Zen: "I lie there in cold sweat wondering what's come over me for years my Buddhist studies and pipesmoking assured meditations in emptiness and all of a sudden the Cross is manifested to me."[52] This would give support to Philip Whalen's contention that "when push came to shove" it was the "Catholic saints" Kerouac was "hung up on."[53]

Still, Kerouac's form of Catholicism was fairly close in spirit to Zen insofar as it was specifically Franciscan: nondogmatic, nonjudgmental,

49 Ann Charters, *Kerouac: A Biography* (San Francisco: Straight Arrow Books, 1973), p. 199.
50 Jack Kerouac, *The Dharma Bums* (New York: Viking Press, 1958), p. 67.
51 Regina Weinreich, *The Spontaneous Poetics of Jack Kerouac: A Study of the Fiction* (Carbondale: Southern Illinois Univ. Press, 1987), p. 127; Kerouac quoted in Sorrell, "The Catholicism of Jack Kerouac," p. 195.
52 Jack Kerouac, *Big Sur* (New York: Farrar, Straus and Cudahy, 1962), p. 205. Subsequent page references are given in parentheses in the text.
53 Barry Gifford and Lawrence Lee, *Jack's Book: An Oral Biography of Jack Kerouac* (New York: St. Martin's Press, 1978), p. 217.

and concerned with the grace of nature rather than the strictures of morality. In *On the Road,* Sal Paradise talks of how "a saint called Doctor Sax" will "destroy" a snake called "Satan" and how "it may also be disclosed that the snake is just a husk of doves" (171–2). As in Donleavy, Frank O'Hara, and other textual transformations of Catholicism, evil manifests itself as a subset of good rather than its polar opposite; grace extends into and redeems the world of fallen nature. Kerouac's poem "Heaven" dramatically rejects any form of ethical judgment and looks forward to "Universal Freeing Day," when the hero will find himself socializing on high with incumbents of the divine sphere such as his late brother Gerard, Giorgio de Chirico, and Jesus Christ. While the appearance of these particular revelers may be predictable enough, we also find here, less obviously, the good-humored figure of Adolf Hitler "stroking his mustache."[54] Aquinas's understanding of evil as a mere absence of good has elided, more radically, into Origen's heretical vision of an entirely empty hell, a vision John Berryman was also moved by. There was some debate within the church at the beginning of the thirteenth century over the wisdom of Pope Innocent III's decision to recognize the Franciscan order, an order that more conservative churchmen regarded as too morally passive as well as dangerously pantheistic, and any consideration of Kerouac's Catholicism raises exactly the same kind of issue.

True to the philosophy of his universalist heritage, Kerouac's perennial stylistic preoccupation is with similitude, those materialized analogies and resemblances that bind the United States into an ideal form of unity. As I noted earlier when discussing how Kerouac diverges from the Emersonian tradition of vatic prophecy, *On the Road* celebrates the fact that the floors of Greyhound bus stations are the same the continent over (35). It also cherishes the image of telephone poles linking together all America's different geographic areas: "I told Dean that the thing that bound us all together in this world was invisible, and to prove it pointed to long lines of telephone poles that curved off out of sight over the bend of a hundred miles of salt" (210). Emerson might have agreed with the first half of this sentence, but he would probably have been uneasy about Kerouac's attempt to make this spirit visibly incarnate within such dubious "sacramental" instruments as telephone poles. Perhaps Emerson would have been willing to look upon these telephone poles as symbols or conduits of a transcendent spirit; but Kerouac's own emphasis is on the writer as a priest celebrating what is present rather than a prophet intuiting what is absent. Accordingly, Kerouac sees his mission as to

54 Jack Kerouac, *Heaven and Other Poems* (Bolinas, Ca.: Grey Fox Press, 1977), pp. 23–30.

consecrate these terrestrial objects in and for themselves, relocating the earthly accident – "transubstantially," as it were – within an essential, unifying design. Such an effort to invest the contingent world with analogical, all-encompassing significance highlights that incongruity familiar to us from other American Catholic writers, whereby a minority culture within the United States is charged with an all-embracing, Catholic temper. Although Kerouac's culture emanates from one ideological source, he is forever attempting to aggrandize that idiom into a global truth: in universalist mood, he finds mystical meaning in the fact that "it's Friday night all over America" (in *Desolation Angels*, 102) or that in California "everybody looked like a broken-down movie extra" (in *On the Road*, 170). Surely not everybody, the protesting reader wants to say; yet Kerouac's catholic style is one that advocates synthesis rather than analysis, similitude rather than difference. "I knew like mad that everything I had ever known and would ever know was One," declares Sal Paradise ecstatically at one point in his travels (147). *Maggie Cassidy* is similarly celebrated for her "universal blood" – she is, the narrator is pleased to remark, a typical small-town girl – while *Visions of Gerard* ends up seeking to bridge the contingent historical circumstances of Lowell, Massachusetts, with an apotheosized vision of essential truth: "Sometime in the same night that's everywhere the same night now and forevermore amen" (147).[55]

The grammatical counterpart to this universalist similitude is the use of analogy and simile, the binding of disparate events into one syntactical unit. In *On the Road*, everything is related through reflective simile to everything else: "everybody sleeping like lambs" (165), Dean Moriarty looking "like God," Mexico "like . . . some gloriously riddled glittering treasure-box" (285), and so on. This idiom is predicated upon what Giles Gunn has called the "neo-Thomist assumption that the Christic imagination is essentially analogical and integrative."[56] It reflects also the analogical interactions posited by Kerouac's texts between material and "spiritual" reality: in Mexico, for instance, Sal Paradise finds the eyes of Indian girls to be "like the eyes of the Virgin Mother when she was with child" (298). The flowing form of Kerouac's writing, where each event merges into the next without clear or logical demarcation, is consistent with this language whereby everything is "inter-allied in one rich united universe of showery light," as *Maggie Cassidy* puts it (78).

Coming across a Catholic poet watching the "Mud Bowl" on tele-

55 Jack Kerouac, *Maggie Cassidy* (New York: McGraw-Hill, 1978), p. 20. Subsequent page references are given in parentheses in the text.
56 Giles Gunn, *The Interpretation of Otherness: Literature, Religion, and the American Imagination* (New York: Oxford Univ. Press, 1979), p. 34.

vision in *Desolation Angels,* the narrator makes a casual remark about how "Jesuits always seem to be interested in football" (279); and it could be that the image of a football match – where no event or play has any meaning in itself, every action being necessarily related to every other part of the game – comprises something like a secularized reflection of the neo-scholastic emphasis upon forms of analogy. Kerouac was himself a star football player in his high school and early college days, and for him, as for Jesuit intellectuals, the football field may have operated subliminally as an externalization of this analogical consciousness. Imagine, by contrast, the impossibility of Kerouac's fellow beat writer William Burroughs ever becoming enthused with football activities. Burroughs has said that his "basic fear" is that of "possession . . . the shame and fear of not being fully in control" of himself.[57] For Burroughs, who emerges from a gaunt, Puritan tradition of self-determination, the analogical interactions of football would be anathema. The Catholic Kerouac, on the other hand, is inspired precisely by a desire to lose his individuality, to transpose it analogically into the service of some higher system or purpose.

This difference between the self-preservation of Burroughs and the self-dissolution of Kerouac might be understood as the difference between repressive and polymorphous styles of literary invention. In *Anti-Oedipus,* Gilles Deleuze and Felix Guattari celebrated the kind of writing that transgresses "territorialities" so as "to scramble the codes, to cause flows to circulate"; consequently, they declared themselves opposed to rigid rationalizing structures that are forever erecting Freudian or other classifications to arrest and control such desire. Deleuze and Guattari specifically cited Kerouac as a writer whose work challenges the reductive categories of Oedipal explanations.[58] This may be true in Kerouac's case – and Donleavy as well prioritizes the flow of essential similitude over the narrow logic of human ratiocination. But it is important to recognize that Deleuze and Guattari's theory is itself not a culturally innocent phenomenon: as Terry Eagleton has said, the authors are surreptitious "metaphysicians" holding to a "covert essentialism" in the way they idealize the nature of this flow of desire, translating it into a dehistoricized and quasi-religious (French Catholic) construct.[59] By way of highlighting this kind of cultural context, another writer who ideologically hypostatizes

57 Victor Bockris, *With William Burroughs: A Report from the Bunker* (London: Hutchinson-Vermilion, 1982), p. 37.
58 Gilles Deleuze and Felix Guattari, *Anti-Oedipus: Capitalism and Schizophrenia,* trans. Robert Hurley, Mark Seem, and Helen R. Lane (New York: Viking Press, 1977), pp. 132–3.
59 Terry Eagleton, "Capitalism, Modernism and Postmodernism," in *Against the Grain: Essays 1975–1985* (London: Verso, 1986), p. 142.

an idea of analogical flow is the "Catholic" James Joyce, especially in *Finnegans Wake,* where mountains and rivers are forever metamorphosing themselves into human entities punningly bound together through time and space. *Finnegans Wake* is mentioned several times in Kerouac's texts: a reference to Joyce's Earwicker illuminates for the hero of *Lonesome Traveller* a cycle of days and nights in New York City (105), while in *Desolation Angels* Maggie Cassidy is nostalgically remembered for her proximity to Joyce's Anna Livia Plurabelle. Kerouac's hero broods here on how he "might have married her and been old Finnegan to her Irish lass Plurabelle" (29), exemplifying his homely theme by falling into a pastiche of Joyce's language: "I'd fall down ladders, brabac, and wash me river underwear" (30).

This concentration upon idealist essence has important ramifications for Kerouac's conceptions of truth and fiction. "I do believe," declares the narrator in *Vanity of Duluoz*, "that lying is a sin, unless it's an innocent lie based on lack of memory" (12). Kerouac's famous (or infamous) style of spontaneous creation upon long scrolls of paper might, therefore, be seen not so much as a radical form of poetics as an ascetic attempt to recapture the essence of final truth. This is made especially clear in *Desolation Angels,* where the author avows the moral imperative of narrative to be "innocent go-ahead confession, the discipline of making the mind the slave of the tongue with no chance to lie or re-elaborate (in keeping not only with the dictums of Dichtung Wahreit Goethe but those of the Catholic Church my childhood)" (229). Lying, in novel writing as in the confessional, is a "sin." Kerouac keeps rewriting his past not, like Nabokov, out of a tricksy desire to play with multiple angles of narrative perspective, but rather in the hope of attaining the final plenitude of confessional revelation. Accordingly, *Vanity of Duluoz,* one of Kerouac's last books, sets about rewriting the history already offered fictionally in *The Town and the City,* only this time stripping away Duluoz's artistic vanity, his guilty pleasure in fictional fabrication, so as to reflect (supposedly) the essence of God's good truth. As in Frank O'Hara, the human maker feels uneasy about attempting to usurp the creative abilities of his divine master; God's book, it is implied, is superior to any human version.

Such final truth was, as Kerouac realized, impossible to achieve through the world of human fiction, and not only because the libel laws required the names of actual people be changed. The title *Visions of Cody* punningly outlines not just the visions Cody himself enjoys, but also the narrator's visions of Cody from within his own memory. The narrator quotes from Proust's *Remembrance of Things Past,* invoking Proust's recognition of the necessary distortions and transformations wrought by memory, and in this sense *Visions of Cody* self-reflexively comments upon the text's own inability to portray what it calls "the actual impulse that everything is happening exactly as you see it" (307). In this light, Allen Ginsberg's account of *Visions of Cody* as "a single universe of perception with no mental manoeuvers or selfconscious manipulation of any reader's mind" is, I think, an example of the highly simplistic criticism with which Kerouac's work has been dogged.[60] The point is not that the book succeeds in abolishing fictional distance, but that it attempts to do so. In *Visions of Cody*, this textual chasing of one's own tail involves incorporating transcripts of taped conversations into the body of the narrative. Malcolm Cowley's comment on how Kerouac was reluctant to admit to artistic revision even though he actually did "a good deal" suggests rather more than simply an attempt to guard a public image of bohemian insouciance; it implies also a deep unwillingness on Kerouac's part to admit to an awareness of the postlapsarian and ironic status of his texts.[61] It hurt the author to concede they were simply fictions, aesthetic recreations, lies.

This emphasis upon original speech rather than its fictional reduplication ties in with Kerouac's essay "The Origins of Joy in Poetry," in which he defined poetry in "its origin, in the bardic child" as "truly ORAL." Relieved of the burden of secondary "abstractions or explanations," these "new pure poets confess forth for the sheer joy of confession."[62] Kerouac's prioritizing of speech over writing bears a striking resemblance to the literary theories of his fellow Catholic, Jesuit critic Walter Ong, who in *The Presence of the Word* (1967) and other books has argued for the idea of oral speech as betokening an essential "presence" and "participation" qualitatively different from the solipsism introduced by the written alphabet. The alphabet, according to Ong, brought forth a fragmented world where "a kind of pretense, a remoteness from actuality, becomes institutionalized."[63] Venerating communities such as Cork, Ireland, where he alleged this "primary orality" might still be found, Ong asserted that "primary orality fosters personality structures that in certain ways are more communal and externalized, and less introspective than those common among literates. Oral communication unites people in groups. Writing and reading are solitary activities that throw the psyche back on itself." Print, Ong went on, similarly encourages "a sense of closure, a sense that what is found in a text has been finalized," whereas oral culture thrives upon the use of memory to su-

60 Allen Ginsberg, Introd., *Visions of Cody*, p. xx.
61 Gifford and Lee, *Jack's Book*, p. 206.
62 Jack Kerouac, "The Origins of Joy in Poetry," in *Scattered Poems* (San Francisco: City Lights Books, 1971), p. v.
63 Walter J. Ong, *The Presence of the Word: Some Prolegomena for Cultural and Religious History* (New Haven: Yale Univ. Press, 1967), pp. 101, 137.

perimpose layer upon layer of consciousness in a more random, open, and therefore "in a profound sense more natural" fashion.[64]

My purpose here is not to vindicate Ong's theories, of course. In a 1968 essay, Frank Kermode expressed doubt about Ong's categorical distinction between the glad naïveté of orality as opposed to the hapless fragmentations of modernist literacy, concluding sardonically that "we seem to have been a long time in the wilderness out of which Father Ong now seeks to show us the way."[65] The point is simply that the equivalences between Kerouac's ideas and those of Ong highlight the ways in which both were shaped by an implicit ideology of Catholicism. At the end of *The Presence of the Word*, Ong tried to deny his own Catholic partiality by asserting that "faith or no, we must all deal with the same data." But this "data" – about how the "mystery of sound" is inextricably entwined with "understanding and unity" – is itself manifestly produced by Ong's concern for the incarnation of divine presence within a typographical world which has, so he claimed, brought about a "displacement of mimesis by irony."[66] Kerouac's attempt to eradicate ironic fictional distance is of a similar order. Indeed, one might see Kerouac's exploitation of new electronic media – the tape recorder in *Visions of Cody*, the frequent television appearances, the tendency to call long lost friends out of the blue on the telephone – as an effort to reembody the "participatory mystique" of an oral world that exists prior to the disruptive interventions of print. For Ong, the electronic media constituted a "secondary orality," as he put it, somewhere between the primal presence of the spoken word and the fatal absence of print. An updated version of this electronic simultaneity can be found in Hugh Kenner's tribute to the participatory mystique of computer programs, whose sophisticated modems link the user with "a vast assortment of other people" on the same system.[67] The Catholic sensibility of Kenner – who wrote his first book on G. K. Chesterton – reveres this new global village whose inhabitants can be invisibly linked together without recourse to the fragmentation and distance of letter writing.

For all his bohemian iconoclasm, then, Kerouac preserved in many ways a traditionalist sensibility. His Catholic essentialism led him in the direction of a fundamental social conformity. One aspect of this con-

64 Walter J. Ong, *Orality and Literacy: The Technologizing of the Word* (London: Methuen, 1982), pp. 69, 132, 40.
65 Frank Kermode, "Father Ong," in *Modern Essays* (London: Collins-Fontana, 1971), p. 107.
66 Ong, *The Presence of the Word*, p. 324; Walter J. Ong, *Interfaces of the Word: Studies in the Evolution of Consciousness and Culture* (Ithaca: Cornell Univ. Press, 1977), p. 287.
67 Ong, *Orality and Literacy*, p. 136; Hugh Kenner, "Out My Computer Window," *Harper's*, Nov. 1989, p. 76.

formity was a continual sense of guilt about having failed to fulfill the materialistic aspirations of his immigrant parents. Another was his attitude toward gender: his texts retain a conservative – even stereotyped – view of gender roles, seeing men as priestly travelers and women as corporeally rooted in the earth's womb: "A man may spend the night tracing the course of the stars above the earth," says *The Town and the City*, "but the woman never has to worry her head about the course of the stars above the earth, because she lives in the earth and the earth is her home" (69). In the traditional Catholic fashion, spiritual quests in Kerouac's novels are the prerogative of male characters. In *On the Road*, Dean advises Sal to make a woman "mind your soul" (186), while *Visions of Cody* recapitulates this fear of "men enslaved to cunts" (116) by expressing incredulity at the way Joyce managed to create his artistic monuments with all those women in his family hemming him in (156). At the same time, of course, there is an intense desire to return home to domestic security, to relapse into *On the Road*'s primordial fantasy of "comfortable little homes . . . with buttermilk and beans" (161) as an antidote to all this wearisome priestly striving. "I couldn't meet a girl without saying to myself, what kind of wife would she make?" broods Sal Paradise (116). Women are seen not as equals of the men but as Madonnas, agents of final grace and redemption.

It is such grace and redemption that proves to be the ultimate goal of Kerouac's quests. In their end is their beginning: all knowledge, finally, comes from home, and the final destiny of the traveler is to circle back to where he started from. This idea is anticipated in *The Town and the City*, where Peter Martin, returning from New York to his home town in New Hampshire, "realized now with strong conviction that nothing which could be taught him in the university could ever touch the wild joy in his heart, the plain powerful knowledge of things, the boyish glee and wonder he felt now as the train bore him back to the weather and veritable landscape of his soul" (147). The "landscape of his soul" has proved too strong a force for the secular university to modify. Similarly, in *Desolation Angels* the narrator ridicules the tiresome materialistic emphasis of classes at Columbia University and instead plays truant to contemplate his own vision of "the Golden Eternity" (37). This pattern can be seen as rooted within the Catholic upbringing of Kerouac's characters: the religious education inculcated in youth brings about a rejection of all subsequent agnostic thought and the relocation of foundational value within primary childhood landscapes. In *Big Sur*, the narrator finally turns with relief to "go back home across autumn America and it'll all be like it was in the beginning – simple golden eternity blessing all – Nothing ever happened" (216). At the end of *Vanity of Duluoz*, Jack proclaims that "no 'generation' is 'new.' There's 'nothing new under the sun.' 'All is vanity'" (279). Even the elaborate pattern of inverted commas here testifies to a narrative desire to escape individuation by taking refuge within the primal comfort of old maxims. All that is left to Jack is the old Roman liturgy, *Hic calix,* to drink from the chalice of redemption "and be sure there's wine in it" (280).

William Burroughs, talking of how "it's generally construed that Jack underwent some sort of a change and became more conservative" in later life, pointed out that in fact "he was always conservative" and that these central "ideas never changed."[68] In a political sense, Kerouac's Catholic conservatism induced him to support American involvement in Vietnam and William Buckley's *National Review,* as well as leading him toward a general detestation of atheistic communism. *Big Sur* remarks upon the narrator's fear of "this secret poisoning society," which he reads as "a big anti-Catholic scheme... Communists destroying everybody" (203). According to Peter Orlovsky, Kerouac even vowed that he would get up in a tree and start "shooting the Communists if it came to that, if he had to."[69] Naturally enough, Kerouac's pioneerlike conception of America as being ideally "as free as that wild wind, out there," as *Desolation Angels* puts it (19), would make him antagonistic to bureaucratic regulation of any kind: in this narrative, the American Forest Service's "effort to restrict the use of the forest to people" (44) promptly becomes equated with a "totalitarian beastliness" (18). But more than this, Kerouac's implicit devotion to the golden values of his youth – football, baseball, patriotism, religion – ensured his hostility to any secular philosophy that might try to dislodge these fundamental "truths." Kerouac's metaphysical fatalism, his doctrine that there is nothing new under the sun and that the linear quest ultimately circles back toward the redemptive power of the chalice, becomes conflated in *Desolation Angels* (and elsewhere) with a social and political fatalism whereby conceptions of gender are reified and "nasty intellectuals and Communists and existentialists" (69) are pummeled into submission by the "ecstasy of the golden eternity" (28).

The dematerializing impulse of Kerouac's writing, therefore, produces concrete political consequences. Kerouac's spiritual concerns do not occupy simply a marginal status within his work; on the contrary, the Catholic spirit of his fiction strives to eradicate terrestrial difference. Just as linguistic difference is subsumed by simile and analogy, just as geographic locality and difference is abolished by the texts' homogenizing universalism, so any materialist philosophies that might disrupt the sanctified circle of this spiritual pilgrimage are met with vehement abuse.

---

68 Gifford and Lee, *Jack's Book,* p. 303.
69 Ibid., p. 264.

The necessary failure of the linear quest, the fact that at the end of the journey to the "Promised Land" of San Francisco in *On the Road* there is nowhere to go but home again, is anticipated in that text by the frequent image of a Ferris wheel revolving, as if to signify how the earthly journey cannot move forward forever but must eventually recapitulate and recycle itself.

This is why *On the Road* has such an odd relationship with the existentially oriented literature of the 1950s. On the one hand, its theme of flight and freedom echoes the journey pursued by any number of other American fictional heroes of this time: Bellow's Augie March, Ellison's Invisible Man, and so on. On the other hand, the existential ideal of individualistic autonomy is undermined by the circular direction of Kerouac's enterprise. The paradox here is similar to that which Jean-Paul Sartre wrestled with in his 1952 book on Jean Genet, in which Sartre attempted to untangle the freedom of becoming from the determinism of being in Genet's work. Sartre's book, brilliant as it is, is an example of a cultural Protestant attempting to reinvent a cultural Catholic in his own image. Holding that the idea of essential "being is . . . a subtle and radical perversion of freedom," Sartre acknowledged that Genet's psychology had been shaped by the Catholic systems of his childhood; nevertheless, claimed Sartre, in a bold act of existential freedom Genet had subsequently chosen to be what crime made of him, so that "the victim of misfortune carries out, proudly and rebelliously, the superb project of being self-caused."[70] Sartre described Genet as the product of "two incompatible world systems: substance and will, soul and consciousness, magic and freedom"; but he went on to assert that Genet had eventually succeeded in redefining Catholic substance as Protestant will, reinventing fatalism as existentialism. This, incidentally, was not a conclusion Genet himself concurred with.[71] Still, Sartre's perception of the presence in Genet of "two incompatible world systems" might with equal aptness be applied to Kerouac's texts. Kerouac is another "Catholic" writer who balances off the contradictory impulses of existential "becoming" and essential "being," though in his case it is clearer that "the ragged and ecstatic joy of pure being," as *On the Road* puts it (195), is ultimately triumphant.

Genet himself is mentioned several times in Kerouac's novels, and we know from the *Paris Review* interview that Sartre's *Saint Genet* was a book Kerouac read. (It is a mistake to think of Kerouac as a literary naïf:

---

70 Jean-Paul Sartre, *Saint Genet: Author and Martyr,* trans. Bernard Frechtman (New York: George Braziller, 1963), pp. 19–69.
71 Sartre, *Saint Genet,* p. 61; Hubert Fichte, "Jean Genet: An Interview," trans. Patrick McCarthy, *New Review,* no. 37 (Apr. 1977), p. 20.

he was extremely well informed, though he generally tended to suppress his learning in favor of a more bohemian image.) Tony Tanner, writing of John Barth, assumed that the ability freely to remake one's environment and avoid "getting trapped in fixed patterns" is "a very recognizable American dream," and if this is the case then Kerouac is not an orthodox American writer, for his novels are finally meditations upon a welcome loss of individual freedom.[72]

This is to come back to the strange, parodic relationship Kerouac enjoys with the romantic traditions of American literature. At the beginning of On the Road, Sal Paradise reads books about the old pioneers (12), apparently girding himself up to reembody the millennial westering myths. Later on, the book describes Dean Moriarty as "that mad Ahab at the wheel" (234), as if to connote a self-consciously intertextual relationship with the American questers of old. The concern in The Dharma Bums and elsewhere to forge an interpenetration between man and nature through the framework of mystical Eastern religions creates another link with Emerson, Thoreau, and those other transcendentalists who were interested in Oriental philosophy. Yet for all of these familiar literary associations, there remains something slippery about Kerouac. He does not seem quite to fit within this famous American heritage, and one explanation may be that throughout his work we have an intimation – slight, but persistent – of the texts' concern with ulterior Catholic motives. Kerouac seems to play at being a Dharma bum; he does not quite believe in any of it. In the end, the image of the crucifix will be too strong. We might recall the old stereotype of the "ingenious Jesuit" and the ways in which Jesuits would often disguise themselves by conforming to the manners of the country they were seeking to infiltrate, for it is something of this sinister ambivalence that lingers in Kerouac's work. Kerouac himself in fact told (a shocked) Gary Snyder that he was a "lay Jesuit," while the narrator in Vanity of Duluoz portrays himself as "one of the world's secret Jesuits, everything I do is based on some kind of proselytization" (48). Similarly, in his 1967 Paris Review interview, Kerouac acknowledged that he always used to pray before writing, claiming that in the final analysis all he wanted to write about was "Jesus."[73]

This constitutes the same "subtle and radical perversion of freedom" that Sartre talked about in relation to Genet, though here the perverted "freedom" constitutes a swerving away from America's Enlightenment, romantic and secular ideals. Ginsberg, for all his anarchic howling, ac-

72 Tony Tanner, City of Words: American Fiction 1950–1970 (New York: Harper and Row, 1971), pp. 258, 233.

73 Gifford and Lee, Jack's Book, p. 294; "Jack Kerouac," in Writers at Work: The Paris Review Interviews, ed. George Plimpton, 4th ser. (New York: Viking Press, 1976), pp. 382, 379.

tually fits much more comfortably into a line of humanistic self-assertion and protest going back through Whitman. In walking this tense tightrope between conformity and alienation, freedom and perversion, Kerouac's work echoes that uneasily parodic ambivalence of many American Catholic texts: Dreiser, Farrell, and Fitzgerald were all writers who acquiesced in the rules of American society without ever finding themselves entirely at home there. Kerouac told the *Paris Review* that the United States had given his immigrant family "a good break," which was why he was now patriotically "pro-American," but *On the Road* does not quite fulfill the philosophical logic of this brave New World.[74] After his joust with the brilliant wonders of the American landscape, the hero hurries back to his cosy home and his mother, a pattern that repeats itself several times in this and other Kerouac novels. One cannot imagine Melville's Ishmael being so compliant.

The works of both Kerouac and Donleavy, then, can be seen as less concerned with challenging social and political structures than with collapsing the linear boundaries and material concerns of fiction so as to allow their texts access to "divine" grace. For Kerouac, even though he never formally returned to the church, this grace seems to present itself as a genuinely divine phenomenon; in the lapsed Catholic Donleavy it manifests itself more ironically as a spiritualization of human sexuality; but in both writers the metaphors are shaped by a figurative metaphysical source. Sartre said in Genet the reader finds "a kind of passive and contemplative state of mind," the idea that "one must be open to Being as the mystic is open to his God," and it is just this same kind of openness in Donleavy and in (the French Catholic) Kerouac that resists the rationalistic closed systems of the "realistic" novel.[75]

This faculty of being "transparent to other worlds" is not, of course, an unproblematical issue for the postmodernist "Catholic" writer. Deprived of any clear-cut analogies between earth and heaven such as old-style neo-scholastic theologians (or novelists) would have favored, Donleavy and Kerouac find themselves negotiating those enigmatic gaps and absences of contemporary epistemology. These beat novelists work toward a beatific universalism, not in the (impossible) expectation of being able fully to incorporate any such vision within their texts, but so as to reveal the very inadequacy of fictional narratives as a medium for the incarnation of "grace." In a reworking of martyrology, novelistic failure becomes, at least potentially, spiritual triumph. Sartre, dedicated to psychological and political amelioration on a more earthly plane, observed disapprovingly that Genet "wills the impossible in order to be

74 *Paris Review Interviews,* 4th ser., p. 393.
75 Sartre, *Saint Genet,* p. 63.

sure of being unable to achieve it and in order to derive from the tragic grandeur of this defeat the assurance that there is something other than the possible."[76] Similarly, in Kerouac and Donleavy the characters' sense of rootlessness and displacement connotes not just the human exile from paradise but also a failure of language permanently to coincide with the ideal visions that these beatific fictions can only imply.

76 Sartre, *Saint Genet*, p. 191.

Part VI

Legalism and the Fictions of Society

17

Social Politics:
J. F. Powers, John O'Hara,
Mary McCarthy

In the period following the Second World War, American Catholicism came to be part of that social consensus that was characteristic of the Eisenhower years. In 1960, Daniel Bell declared the era of the 1950s had witnessed "the end of ideology," the exhaustion of Marxism and other dogmatic social theories in favor of a new flexible secular humanism based upon a skeptical refusal to accept any given abstract system as conclusive. Bell's rather too sunny prognosis was that ethnic and class differentials within the United States were being sutured within an enlightened language of universal detachment. According to Bell, this detachment was itself part of that matrix of postwar philosophical "alienation" that, he said, "is not nihilism but a positive role" insofar as it "guards one against being submerged in any cause."[1]

One difficulty here is that Bell's hypostatization of alienation as ideologically neutral ignores the ideological basis of alienation itself, an intense quandary for the conformist temper of Kerouac, as we have seen, and a similar source of ambiguity in Mary McCarthy's writing. Nor is it true to suggest the old ethnic ideologies and antagonisms had altogether evaporated by this time. Kerouac was in some ways always nostalgic for his French-Canadian ghetto, while Paul Blanshard's *American Freedom and Catholic Power* – which was already in its sixth printing by August 1949, having been first published only five months earlier – raised the old specter of a Vatican takeover and called for the registration of American Catholic higher officials under the Foreign Agents Registration Law. Nevertheless, the dominant mood at this time was, as Bell implied, synthesis and homogeneity, the integration of Protestant, Catholic, and Jew into what religious sociologist Will Herberg approvingly termed a communal "Interfaith," the "highest expression of religious coexistence

---

1 Daniel Bell, *The End of Ideology: On the Exhaustion of Political Ideas in the Fifties* (Glencoe, Ill.: Free Press, 1960), p. 16.

427

and co-operation within the American understanding of religion." Eisenhower himself, with a blithe prioritizing of form over content, announced in 1952 that "our government makes no sense unless it is founded in a deeply felt religious faith, and I don't care what it is."[2] Consequently, the work of J. F. Powers and Mary McCarthy shows the separatist ethos of Catholicism becoming less apparent than it had been in the literature of the early twentieth century. On the contrary, Powers, McCarthy, and John O'Hara concern themselves more with the arrival of a Catholic sensibility within the central arenas of American social and political life.

This increasing embourgeoisment and invisibility of Catholicism was assisted by various factors, the most obvious of which was the increasing economic prosperity of Catholic groups, especially the Irish Americans. Various sociological studies have suggested that by the early 1960s Catholics were actually beginning to surpass Protestants in terms of income and social status.[3] Another incentive toward "Americanization" came from liberal Jesuit theologians such as John Courtney Murray, Gustave Weigel, and Walter J. Ong, all of whom strove to reconcile the tenets of Catholicism with loyalty to the secular ideals of materialistic, middle-class America. In his 1957 book *Frontiers in American Catholicism,* Ong proclaimed that the church was finally on its way to recovering from the "blow to American Catholic self-confidence" brought about by Leo XIII's 1899 apostolic letter *Testem benevolentiae,* in which the pontiff had denounced the heretical errors of modern American liberalism. American Catholics were now sloughing off their "minority complex," suggested Ong. Rather than feeling the old "cosmic nostalgia" for a medieval age of faith, they were recognizing the need to face the challenges of new technology "in the historical spirit." Ong here was anticipating by a few years the direction of the Second Vatican Council, which stressed Catholicism's function as a religion of incarnation and emphasized the theological significance of "inculturation," the adaptation of the Word of God to fit the patterns of any given culture. For Ong, the essence of Catholic faith was to be reincarnated amid the mass culture of American business, advertising, and television, a transition that should not be so impossibly incongruous as some people might imagine: "The charges urged against Catholicism in the United States," he said, "– superficiality,

2 Will Herberg, *Protestant-Catholic-Jew: An Essay in American Religious Sociology,* 2nd ed. (New York: Anchor-Doubleday, 1960), p. 259; Eisenhower quoted in Will Herberg, "Religion and Culture in Present-Day America," in *America as a Mass Society: Changing Community and Identity,* ed. Philip Olson (New York: Macmillan–Free Press of Glencoe, 1963), p. 380.

3 See, for example, Norman D. Glenn and Ruth Hyland, "Religious Prejudice and Worldly Success," *American Sociological Review,* 32 (1967), 84–5.

mechanization, routine – are exactly the charges which are leveled against mass culture itself, and which are, we are beginning to see, themselves rather superficial charges."[4]

Ong's association between the popularizing instincts of Catholic institutions and the broadly based appeal of American mass culture is an interesting one. We have already seen the *Partisan Review* circle's disdain for Kerouac's engagement with the popular culture of the 1950s, and there could perhaps be just a trace of covert anti-Catholicism in their critical contumely. It is one of the most curious and ironic developments in American Catholicism that it began to embrace the communal icons of this era more enthusiastically than did the literary and political establishment: whereas anti-Catholicism in the 1850s was fueled by a fear of the barbarian tendencies of impoverished immigrants, anti-Catholicism in the 1950s was engendered by a suspicion that Catholics were becoming just too conformist, too patriotic, so conformist and patriotic in fact that they were undermining the "natural" American temper of sturdy self-reliance. The response to Senator Joseph McCarthy is one example of this phenomenon: cherished by blue-collar workers and by what Daniel Bell called "the rising middle-class strata of the various ethnic groups" for his anti-Communist purges, McCarthy was frequently abhorred by intellectuals as a demagogue whose very zeal for conformity threatened to subvert the constitutional freedom of the American spirit.[5]

The stories and novels of J. F. Powers reflect and refract the moves toward theological inculturation and social conformity that framed American Catholic thought in the postwar period. Powers's texts posit comfortable styles of assimilation and materialism for their Catholic personnel, although in the end they work to disrupt any form of complacency that may have arisen from this process of homogenization. In Powers's first novel, *Morte D'Urban* (1962), the midwestern Catholic priest Father Urban initially takes the kind of delight in American corporate life of which Walter J. Ong would have been proud. Noting with approval that *Time* magazine had declared the Catholic church second only to Standard Oil in efficiency among large corporations, Urban works to reincarnate the essence of spiritual truths amid the accidents of baseball and business life. Just as Ong hoped for "a real Christian *mystique*" of technology and industry, so Urban befriends the rich Chicago businessman Billy Cosgrove and extracts gifts from Cosgrove for various Catholic organizations.[6] Father Urban is operating here on the principle

4 Walter J. Ong, S.J., *Frontiers in American Catholicism: Essays on Ideology and Culture* (New York: Macmillan, 1957), pp. 125, 4, 102, 10.
5 Bell, *The End of Ideology*, p. 101.
6 Ong, *Frontiers in American Catholicism*, p. 121.

that "merchants" should be "paying homage in the way best suited to them and their real talents," just as the prayer of the mute tumbler took the form of a display of acrobatics before the altar of Mary.[7]

In the same way, Ong's call for a Christian mystique "of such things as sports and lunch clubs" is mirrored by Urban's Saturday morning cartoon shows for the children – he resists every stuffy clerical effort to drop "short subjects of a religious nature" into these programs (164) – and by his chummy devotion to football and golf.[8] Indeed, the sporting metaphors of *Morte D'Urban* – Urban "now went to bat for himself" (115), "I'd go down the line for you" (238), and so on – assist in this process of "Americanizing" the text, of recasting its otherworldly goals within the colloquial idiom of the American vernacular. The idea of Father Louis leaving the Jesuits after a theological dispute and joining "the Clementines on the first bounce, as a divorced man takes up with the first floosie he meets" (198) is another example of this predilection for domesticating strange and apparently exotic ideas by a skillful deployment of the familiar tongues of this world; it is, of course, not too far removed from the old Jesuit tricks of disguise and infiltration that Blanshard and the Protestant fundamentalists so much feared. Father Urban also sees an important role for television in the future dissemination of an American Catholic spirit, and here his views echo those of Fulton Sheen, national director of the Society for the Propagation of the Faith and a regular television performer during the 1950s. Sheen, another ebullient proponent of mass culture, opined that the American Catholic church was in urgent need of a saint who knew what it was to eat hot dogs and drink Coca-Cola in a public park.[9]

Powers himself implicitly sympathized with this sanctification of mundane life when he remarked in a letter of 1951 that "all stories today should take place in modern supermarkets; the modern square, battlefield and manger."[10] We have already seen how Walker Percy's futuristic *Love in the Ruins* lampoons the schismatic "American Catholic Church whose new Rome is Cicero, Illinois" (5), and which is concerned above all with "property rights" (6). Still, Percy's satire notwithstanding, the business of establishing the church as a communal and socially visible institution has always played an important role within the structures of Catholicism. The significance attached in *Morte D'Urban* to erecting a new house of God in the parish of Saint Monica's epitomizes this desire

7 J. F. Powers, *Morte D'Urban* (Garden City: Doubleday, 1962), p. 96. Subsequent page references are given in parentheses in the text.
8 Ong, *Frontiers in American Catholicism*, p. 122.
9 Lawrence Cunningham, *The Catholic Heritage* (New York: Crossroad, 1983), p. 212.
10 Quoted in George Scouffas, "J. F. Powers: On the Vitality of Disorder," *Critique*, 2, no. 2 (Fall 1958), 51.

for material foundations, which (for instance) Quakers, with their idea of faith as a highly privatized and spiritualized affair, have never shared. In Catholic terms, then, the worldliness of Father Urban is not necessarily immoral. Urban remarks upon his admiration for Lanfranc, that eleventh-century English archbishop of Canterbury who operated politically with "great finesse" to outmaneuver William the Conqueror; Urban notes with approval how Lanfranc was one of "those who had remained on the scene and got on with the job" rather than seeking out the "martyr's crown" (286). Urban's own political and social networks are constructed with similar aims in mind: the guiding idea is, as he puts it, that one should take "good care to conquer the profane world before tackling the other one" (188). This is not simply cynicism because, according to traditional Catholic thought, the road to salvation consists of a communal pilgrimage along worldly paths. The *ecclesia* is inevitably a corporate and heterogeneous enterprise.

In the end, though, Father Urban's problem is that he becomes just too worldly, worldly at the expense of his spiritual duties. Having failed to be chastened by the experience of exile to a remote monastery in Minnesota, it is only after he is struck on the head by a golf ball and disabled that he begins to see the light. The analogy with Saul's conversion on the road to Damascus is made explicit. Urban gradually distances himself from the rowdy extravagances of Billy Cosgrove, renounces his dreams of television stardom, and moves toward saving his soul by becoming a devoted leader of the monastic order. This is the kind of narrative reversal we find several times in Powers's work, where the stern, impersonal dictates of Christian theology usurp that more comfortable sense of a humanly sympathetic happy ending the reader may have been expecting. Another example of this is the short story "Prince of Darkness" (1946), in which the forlorn and shabby figure of Father Burner, the last member of his seminary class still without his own parish, engages the reader's sense of pity as he becomes increasingly bitter year after year waiting for his ship to come in. Nevertheless, contrary to our (sentimental) expectations, at the end of the story the archbishop continues to deny Burner the fulfillment of his humble dream.

Powers's worldly clergymen have often been compared to those of Balzac and Trollope – "Trollope Romanized," was Robert Daniel's description of Powers's work.[11] The crucial difference, however, is that in Powers comic human foibles are never allowed to usurp the injunctions of "divine truth." Father Burner may be pathetically endearing, as are many of Trollope's clerics; but he is also – more importantly – a sinner, a priest who has abused his office in various ways and whose association

---

11 Robert Daniel, "No Place to Go," *Sewanee Review*, 56 (1948), 527.

with imagery of black and burning testifies to his close affiliation with a more famous prince of darkness. Burner is a devotee of Farrell's *Studs Lonigan* – "the best thing since the Bible," in his opinion – but that old-fashioned attachment to underdog ethnic fighting spirit is now seen as a kind of self-indulgence on the priest's part.[12] The eccentricities of human psychology are not what primarily concern Powers: he is, as he said in a 1948 essay, interested not in "morals" or in "trying to edify" but in "theology" and "grace." As John P. Sisk has written, American literature is accustomed to confronting the issue of "evil" in violent and apocalyptic terms, but the unusual thing about "Prince of Darkness" is that evil emerges in this story as a "small and unexciting thing," a form of banality and self-centeredness.[13] As we discover more about Father Burner, we come to recognize the aptness of the archbishop's remark that the old classic villains are now "extinct" (273) and that the devil today is the more insidious and ordinary "devil in us" (274).

This is not to say that Father Burner is allegorically condemned, as he might have been in Bunyan or Hawthorne. "The decision will not be rendered in this ring," said Powers in a 1964 interview: it is the function of the novelist to describe human affairs, not to usurp the divine pre-rogative of final judgment.[14] But what we do get from Burner, Urban, and the other Powers characters is a sense of the ontological limitations of the human condition: the recognition that no "natural perfection" is possible, as Powers himself said in 1948, echoing a phrase of Jacques Maritain. This, of course, sets Powers apart from New World nostrums of social progress and limitless possibility. "Too many Americans think they will live forever," remarked Powers in 1964, "I do not go for that." In 1987, he similarly disparaged "growth" as "one of those would-be positive *now* words I always give a minus to."[15]

Powers's narrative style of bathos and understatement exemplifies this language of essential limitation. His second novel, *Wheat That Springeth Green* (1988), starts off with a scene in which future priest Joe Hackett performs a remarkable series of sexual exploits, all of which are however described in the most understated fashion, as though sex (like money) should be seen as nothing more or less than a fact of incarnated life. It

12 J. F. Powers, *Prince of Darkness, and Other Stories* (Garden City: Doubleday, 1947), p. 244. Subsequent page references are given in parentheses in the text.
13 J. F. Powers, "Art, the Moon Prince," *Commonweal*, 48 (1948), 104; John P. Sisk, "The Complex Moral Vision of J. F. Powers," *Critique*, 2, no. 2 (Fall 1958), 37.
14 J. F. Powers, "The Catholic and Creativity," *American Benedictine Review*, 15 (1964), 64.
15 Powers, "Art, the Moon Prince," p. 105; "The Catholic and Creativity," p. 76; "On Reading about My Faith and Fiction in a Secular Age," *U. S. Catholic Historian*, 6 (1987), 141.

is this disillusioning, deromanticizing tone that perseveres throughout the book. At first, Joe finds collecting money from parishioners to be demeaning and much prefers questing in the safely interiorized world of the spirit. As the narrative proceeds, though, Joe becomes more clear-eyed about the earthly conditions of money, sex, and society; he abandons his desire for sainthood and chooses instead to acquiesce in terrestrial limitation, coming to recognize that "life's not a cookout by Brueghel the Elder." As Father Day advises him, the sin of "despair" is "really presumption," predicated upon the fallacy of "expecting too much" and the impossible dream of attempting to "change the world."[16] Again, this rejection of heightened romanticism distances Powers from those millennial strains of American literature and culture predicated upon the confident quest for an earthly paradise. As Sisk remarked, Powers preserves a strict detachment from "the literature of innocence," with its "pastoral yearning for the clear vision and spontaneous virtue of childhood."[17]

In Powers's eyes, the complexity of social and ecclesiastical politics constitutes an ontological as well as a literal reality, for it comes to represent another aspect of this denial of transcendental idealism. Aquinas described man as by nature "a social and political animal," arguing that "even in the state of innocence" human beings would have lived in society and been governed by laws laid down for the common welfare; in the same way, Powers sees politics, the interactions of human beings within a given community, as constituting a truer image of man's worldly status than the escapism of pastoral genres. As Alfred Kazin noted, it is not the representation of subjective psychology that interests Powers but the representation of an objective world, which also becomes a world where humans are themselves objectified.[18] This impersonal mode of deflation and irony ensures that Catholic triumphalism is no more welcome in Powers's texts than Puritan apocalypse: in the story "One of Them," Simpson, a convert to Catholicism, persists in exuding a heroic and triumphalist air that the rest of his seminary colleagues have shrugged off. Although the exotic dogfights between sin and grace in the novels of a Catholic convert like Graham Greene may be more agreeably spicy for most readers – including Catholics – that kind of melodrama is not the context within which Powers chooses to situate his own literary or religious battles.

Rather than allegorizing or proselytizing overtly, Powers's work

16 J. F. Powers, *Wheat That Springeth Green* (New York: Knopf, 1988), pp. 199, 106.
17 Sisk, "The Complex Moral Vision of J. F. Powers," p. 39.
18 Mary T. Clark, ed., *An Aquinas Reader* (Garden City: Doubleday–Image, 1972), p. 367; Alfred Kazin, "Gravity and Grace," *New Republic,* 30 Apr. 1956, p. 19.

comes to imply an otherworldly level through techniques of indirection and covert displacement. As we have seen, the materialized form of analogy can be read as a characteristically Catholic literary figure, linking together accident and essence or visible and latent worlds, as in Joyce's *Ulysses*. This idiom is clearly prevalent in *Morte D'Urban:* Urban himself is intertwined with Malory's Lancelot, the knight who renounced worldly interests for spiritual devotions, while Sally Hopwood is associated with the temptress Guinevere. Powers signals these and other analogies to the reader not only through the title of his novel but also through the fact that one of these monks in Minnesota is preparing "a scholarly children's edition of *Le Morte d'Arthur,* by Sir Thomas Malory" (256). Critics such as John Hagopian and Marie Henault have chased down these motifs further, pointing out how some of Powers's metaphors derive from medieval sources: Father Urban "enters the lists," endures an "ordeal by combat," and so on.[19] All of this is significant; but equally significant is the way this metaphorical stratum is hinted at rather than clearly revealed. When we read a Powers text, we gradually begin to get some intimation that we are witnessing events from a limited point of view and that there may be something beyond the surface that is not yet exposed to our full sight. The imperfection of the narrative perspective comes to connote how the reader is necessarily seeing the textual world through a glass darkly, just as Urban himself is the victim of a distorted perspective throughout most of *Morte D'Urban.* Similarly with Father Burner in "Prince of Darkness": we experience a kind of double take in reading, as the imagery of darkness and hell slowly convinces us this is not just another comically errant clergyman. In this way, we find our reception of the text jolted from a literal to a theological level.

We witness these subtle shifts in perspective again in "Death of a Favorite" (1950) and "Defection of a Favorite" (1951), stories narrated by Fritz, the rectory cat. Fritz's sardonic comments upon ecclesiastical power struggles not only work as a parody of church politics but also imply that these local disputes between liberal and conservative clergymen matter very little in the larger scheme of things. To hear human affairs narrated by a cat is like looking at earthly objects through the wrong end of a telescope: it radically diminishes our scale of worldly significance. The story "Look How the Fish Live" (1957) similarly creates analogical mirrors between human beings and "insects, birds, and animals of all kinds," working toward the conclusion that, as Mr. Hahn

---

19 John Hagopian, "Irony and Involution in J. F. Powers' *Morte D'Urban*," *Contemporary Literature,* 9 (1968), 163–6; Marie J. Henault, "The Saving of Father Urban," *America,* 2 Mar. 1963, pp. 290–2.

puts it here, "A man had to accept his God-given limitations."[20] Flannery O'Connor, Evelyn Waugh, and some of Powers's other astute readers have taken violent exception to the rectory cat, seeing it as an altogether too cute excrescence; but in fact this reflective interaction between humans and animals, like the interaction in these texts between the mundane and the mythic, skillfully hints at the deflationary antihumanism and sense of metaphysical displacement that permeate Powers's fiction.[21]

This antihumanism also diminishes the possibility of large-scale psychological development for Powers's characters. The reader is urged all the time specifically to look at how the fish live, to apprehend those "truths" already lodged within the world. This is one reason for the seemingly inconsequential and casual narrative direction of his novels. Some critics have suggested that Powers is more naturally skilled in the short story, which may be true, but it is important also to bear in mind the author's philosophical aversion to constructing chains of linear cause and effect that would lead events in the direction of radical change. For Powers, all has been determined in advance, and the business of narrative should be gradual revelation of preexistent truth rather than the quest for new knowledge. Again, this traduces the more familiar American genre of the novel as romance and exploration. Powers said in 1960 that he doubted if he was quite descriptive enough for a novelist, but he defended himself against the charge of rarefied impersonality by confiding to the interviewer that he did not "believe in" such "intangible things as atmosphere, place or country." Rather, he said, he holds with a de-localized, universalist notion of the "reality of art," which "has an existence whether you experience it or not."[22]

This is a bold stance for an American novelist, not only because it rejects the whole tradition of homage to the natural environment based upon the exclusivist "atmosphere" of a pastoral world elsewhere, but also because it implicitly critiques the idea of "American" literature being fundamentally different from the literature of Europe or other countries. F. O. Matthiessen's version of American Studies, like the pilgrim fathers' conception of their newfound land, was founded on a vision of the essential difference between the United States and the corrupt Old World; but for Powers, in his characteristically Catholic way, art, like life, is essentially the same wherever you are. This is not to say, of course, that a sense of place becomes irrelevant in Powers, but that it becomes in-

20 J. F. Powers, Look How the Fish Live (New York: Knopf, 1975), pp. 18, 19.
21 Sally Fitzgerald, ed., The Habit of Being: The Letters of Flannery O'Connor (New York: Farrar, Straus and Giroux, 1979), p. 159; Evelyn Waugh, "Scenes of Clerical Life," Commonweal, 63 (1956), 667–8.
22 Donald McDonald, "Interview with J. F. Powers," The Critic, 19, no. 2 (Oct.–Nov. 1960), 21, 88.

cidental and accidental. It matters little in the end whether the characters
are in Lutheran Minnesota, or – as in the story "Tinkers" – searching
(hopelessly) for family roots in Ireland. Nobody can ever feel themselves
quite at home, since exile from the world of spirit to the world of
corporeal substance is represented in Powers as being the crux of man's
earthly condition.

It is this paradoxical conjunction between essence and accident that
underlies Powers's view of "the human situation as essentially comic,"
as he put it.[23] In the story "Lions, Harts, Leaping Does," from *Prince of
Darkness,* the Christian "cross" is said to epitomize "everywhere the sign
of contradiction, and always" (66). This contradiction is, as Naomi Lebowitz has written, the "dialectical tension involving secularism and
divinity" that leads toward the crucial ironies within Powers's fiction.[24]
It is one of the curious aspects of Powers criticism that some of the
clearest responses have emerged from those who have not shared the
author's religious vision: F. W. Dupee, for instance, wrote an excellent
article in the 1963 *Partisan Review,* discussing how Powers's work shows
the American Catholic church beset by contradictions between this world
and the next, whereas too many Catholic critics have preferred to categorize Powers not as an ironist but as a satirist. For Gene Kellogg, for
instance, Powers makes "the American unspiritual priest" the subject
of "savage satire": Father Urban is said by Kellogg to be an instance of
"spiritual bankruptcy," signifying the "flatly earthbound" sensibility of
a church ripe for the broadside of another papal encyclical along the lines
of *Testem benevolentiae.*[25] The Jesuit critic Harold C. Gardiner similarly
proffered his opinion that Powers was a superficial smart aleck who had
failed to elucidate the genuine "deep and Christ-like friendships among
priests." Bill Oliver, in the *U.S. Catholic Historian,* was another who
insisted upon how Powers "satirizes an age in which even self-professed
Christians have become immersed in secular concerns and have, as a
consequence, grown oblivious to God."[26]

Now it is true, of course, that the *contemptus mundi* theme forms one
important strand in Powers's work. It is true also that in Catholic criticism of Powers's fiction we see the old "Americanization" controversies

23 Powers, "The Catholic and Creativity," p. 65.
24 Naomi Lebowitz, "The Stories of J. F. Powers: The Sign of the Contradiction," *Kenyon
    Review,* 20 (1958), 494.
25 F. W. Dupee, "In the Powers Country," *Partisan Review,* 30 (1963), 113–16; Gene
    Kellogg, *The Vital Tradition: The Catholic Novel in a Period of Convergence* (Chicago:
    Loyola Univ. Press, 1970), pp. 160, 168, 227, 178.
26 Gardiner quoted in Stanley Poss, "J. F. Powers: The Gin of Irony," *Twentieth Century
    Literature,* 14 (1968), 67; Bill Oliver, "Faith and Fiction in a Secular Age," *U.S. Catholic
    Historian,* 6 (1987), 119.

come round again: should the Church assimilate and Americanize itself, as Walter J. Ong and others advocated, or should it preserve its spiritual integrity by scrupulously alienating itself from the decadent agendas of American materialism, as Gene Kellogg would doubtless have preferred? This is a complex social and theological issue, to which there is no easy answer; yet it is the very lack of an easy answer that Powers's texts are negotiating. His work ironically surveys the contradictions between spirit and matter rather than simply relapsing into that easier satirical mode of denigrating all secular interests. In the Catholic insistence that Powers must be a satirist, we may have a sense of those implicated within his humor trying to distance themselves from the charges of excessive worldliness: Powers must be a satirist, so the argument runs, because no Catholic priest ought to be more concerned with building churches than with praying inside them. In an abstract sense this may be true, but in Powers it is rarely a choice between one or the other. In the comic earthly condition, the soul must be joined to a body, the church must have money, the human spirit must be enmeshed in social politics. The process of incarnation leads inexorably to contradiction and ironic incongruity. Consequently there is a lack of certainty and closure in Powers's texts that most Catholic critics, too keen to pick out satirical moralizing, have been oblivious to.

This is not to deny that, as Barclay W. Bates argued, Powers is a writer in the tradition of Catholic orthodoxy. But, as Bates himself noted, this tradition characteristically involves not an individualistic, angst-ridden search for God – that quandary typically faced by the heroes of John Updike or Philip Roth – but rather a quietist patience, a willingness to wait for God to reveal himself in his own good time. We can trace such differences in American culture back to the seventeenth century, where, said Perry Miller, hundreds of Puritan Reformers wrote in what they called "just refutation of that Popish Doctrine, that thinke it impossible for a man to know that he is in an estate of grace."[27] Whereas the Puritans individually sought an assurance of salvation, Catholics denied that any such certainty could exist this side of the grave. This acquiescence in that necessarily limited knowledge available to the human spirit is the position assumed by Powers's hero at the end of *Morte D'Urban*; the style of Catholicism opts to downplay personal mysticism, preferring to let God make the first move. In a 1988 interview with the *New York Times*, Powers even expressed doubts about the divinity's existence: "There are people who believe nothing I've said about there

27 Barclay W. Bates, "Flares of Special Grace: The Orthodoxy of J. F. Powers," *Midwest Quarterly*, 11 (1969), 105; Perry Miller, *The New England Mind: The Seventeenth Century* (New York: Macmillan, 1939), p. 50.

being a God and a next world. Maybe they're right. Sometimes I bet the other way. I believe the difference between the two is slight."[28] These are the areas of unknowability and contradiction that Powers's texts uncover, and to explain them away as narrow corrective tracts does a disservice to the complexity of his fiction.

What it is manifestly untrue to say, however, is that the materialism of Powers's fiction betokens a lack of interest in religious affairs. Granville Hicks alleged there to be "no large issues" in *Morte D'Urban;* William Gass found religious feeling "conspicuously absent" in the novel; Saul Bellow declared "there is curiously little talk of souls in this book about a priest," adding that "spiritually, its quality is very thin." Bellow went on to complain of how Father Urban does not seem "furious at . . . abuses of the soul and eager to show what's positive and powerful in his faith. The lack of such power makes faith itself shadowy, more like obscure tenacity than spiritual conviction. In this sense Mr. Powers's book is disappointing."[29] Here again, though, we can recognize an unconscious ideological impulse putting itself forward as objective criticism, for that arduous "spiritual" quest common to traditional Puritan and Jewish cultures forms a less essential part of the Catholic sensibility. Bellow has always loathed being pigeonholed as a "Jewish" novelist, and of course his work cannot be reduced to such a narrow ethnic category; nevertheless, residual cultural assumptions from a Judaic heritage inevitably continue to inform the viewpoints of his writing.

In American literature of the 1950s, then, we find the confluence of quite different religious traditions. Powers was writing in the legalistic mode of Aquinas, choosing to prioritize the community over the individual and to regard external constraints as altogether necessary within human society: "It is by law," insisted Aquinas, "that man is directed to proper actions in relation to his final end."[30] It was, though, Bellow's alternative kind of "spiritual conviction" that became institutionalized in artistic and intellectual circles during the 1950s: Powers's conception of the church as an inherently social establishment carried less weight than the protest-ant notion of society as a necessary evil, an obstruction to the higher visionary impulses of the "soul." Whereas for Aquinas the perfect community was the city, the place of law and regulation, for

---

28 Mervyn Rothstein, "Though Fascinated by Priesthood, Catholic Author Didn't Join," *New York Times,* 15 Sept. 1988, p. 18.
29 Granville Hicks, "The Foibles of Good Men," *Saturday Review,* 15 Sept. 1962, p. 21; William Gass, "Bingo Game at the Foot of the Cross," *Nation,* 29 Sept. 1962, p. 183; Saul Bellow, "Some Notes on Recent American Fiction," *Encounter,* 21, no. 5 (Nov. 1963), 25.
30 *Aquinas Reader,* ed. Clark, p. 386.

American romantic questers the city was more often seen as constituting a threat to the autonomy of an individual spirit. Hence the American romance has traditionally preferred to secede from civilization and locate itself within the wide open spaces of the river, the ocean, the forest, the frontier. In the works of mid-twentieth-century romancers such as Bellow, Ralph Ellison, and Philip Roth, this visionary quest came to be defined in largely secular rather than metaphysical terms, the protagonists being concerned with the fulfillment of a human self in this world rather than the next. Nevertheless, that underlying premise of an individualistic journey remained the same.

In American intellectual discourse of this postwar era, the term "religious" worked silently to exclude the organizing conceptual principles of Catholicism. R. P. Blackmur's 1961 essay "Religious Poetry in the United States," for instance, postulated a relationship between the privileged self and some ideal "other," unproblematically defined by Blackmur as "the numinous force; the force within the self, other than the self, greater than the self, which, as one cultivates it, moves one beyond the self."[31] Again, the demand is that the individual mind turn back upon itself, probing for what is "numinous" within the psyche rather than what might be "sacramental" within the external world; it is a classic American form of self-expression, with roots in the introverted musings of seventeenth-century Puritan journals. Giles Gunn similarly suggested it is this dialectic between self and self-transcendence that constitutes "the essential paradigm of the American experience": hence the title of Gunn's 1979 book, *The Interpretation of Otherness: Literature, Religion, and the American Imagination.*[32] Yet all of this seems another unwarranted cultural assumption, insofar as such a view of "otherness" could be read as an extrapolation from Karl Barth's specifically Protestant notion of God as an alien and unknowable force, radically disjunct from human affairs. Whereas Catholicism stresses analogical interaction between God and man, Barth's form of Protestantism emphasizes instead this chasm or "otherness," a chasm that might be bridged only by the uncertain leap of human faith. It is not difficult to appreciate the consistency between the desire of Barth to project faith onto an unknowable God and the confidence of American prophetic writers, from John Winthrop through to Alice Walker, in some form of millennial triumph, an unknown but better future: anything rather than circumscription by the here-and-now.

It was a secularized version of this "otherness" that came to dominate

---

31 R. P. Blackmur, "Religious Poetry in the United States," in *Religious Perspectives in American Culture,* ed. James W. Smith and A. Leland Jamison (Princeton: Princeton Univ. Press, 1961), p. 286.

32 Giles Gunn, *The Interpretation of Otherness: Literature, Religion, and the American Imagination* (New York: Oxford Univ. Press, 1979), p. 201.

the intellectual climate of the 1950s, as alienation and nonconformity became a standard intellectual response to mindless consumerism and political tranquillity. As we have seen, expansions in the mass media were generally viewed askance by the academic classes, for whom the image of Bing Crosby dressed up as a Hollywood priest – "a Santa Claus of the adult Catholic imagination," according to Arnold J. Sparr – seemed to represent everything about the church that was apparently anachronistic and centered around a desire for infantile security.[33] In the period after the Second World War, the role of "intellectual" became almost synonymous with the positions of existentialism or alienation outlined most famously by Sartre, Theodor Adorno, and other theoreticians of the Frankfurt School. The austere late modernist geometries of Kafka and Beckett, as valorized by this Frankfurt School, seemed irreparably divorced from the sentimental pieties regurgitated by Hollywood and television: in *The Oasis* (1949), Mary McCarthy records without comment, as if taking for granted, Will Taub's "alienation as an intellectual from the mass-culture of the drugstore and the radio serial."[34] This separation of Catholics and intellectuals into two divergent camps was helped along by the antiintellectual postures of Senator Joe McCarthy, himself a graduate of the Catholic Marquette University, whose campaign against what he called the "networks of professors and teachers who are getting their orders from Moscow" was endorsed, at least to some extent, by Fulton Sheen, Cardinal Spellman, and other key figures in the American Catholic hierarchy.[35] Support for the anti-Communist movement from William Buckley's *National Review* added to the general impression that American Catholicism in the 1950s was moving out of its oppositional ghettoes and beginning to associate itself, in the most conventional kind of way, with the forces of middle-class, lace-curtain reaction.

It is at just this point that self-consciousness starts to emerge in American Catholic academic circles about the lack of a reputable indigenous intellectual tradition. John Tracy Ellis's 1955 essay "The American Catholic and the Intellectual Life" sparked widespread debate about the reasons for this supposed lack of intellectual ambition. Monsignor Ellis attributed the blame partly to economic reasons – the confinement of immigrant Catholics to impoverished communities, where the acquisition of culture was naturally of secondary importance – and partly to the inculcated

33 Arnold J. Sparr, "From Self-Congratulation to Self-Criticism: Main Currents in American Catholic Fiction, 1900–1960," *U.S. Catholic Historian*, 6 (1987), 233.

34 Mary McCarthy, *The Oasis* (New York: Random House, 1949), p. 100. Subsequent page references are given in parentheses in the text.

35 Robert Von Hallberg, *American Poetry and Culture, 1945–1980* (Cambridge, Mass.: Harvard Univ. Press, 1985), p. 119.

Catholic habit of personal humility and deference to authority. Ellis quoted from Thomas à Kempis's *Imitation of Christ:* "What doth it avail thee to discourse profoundly of the Trinity, if thou be void of humility, and consequently displeasing to the Trinity?"[36] In his subsequent treatise *American Catholicism,* Ellis cited the words of American prelate Archbishop Vagnozzi, who was echoing these medieval sentiments as late as 1961. Noting with disapprobation that Catholic intellectuals have conceived themselves to be "underestimated," Vagnozzi continued:

> The question is whether we are confronted with true and genuine intellectuals, who are inspired by a sincere love of truth, humbly disposed to submit to God's Revelation and the authority of the Church, or whether we are confronted with intellectuals who believe, first of all, in the absolute supremacy and unlimited freedom of human reason, a reason which has shown itself so often fallacious and subject to error.[37]

Interviewed in 1988, Ellis again lamented the fact that, "unlike our Jewish fellow citizens," American Catholics have tended to be "only superficially interested in intellectual pursuits, while they are deeply engrossed in material concerns."[38]

Ellis's thesis has been enormously influential, though other possible explanations have been advanced for the kind of defensive conformity he outlined. Gustave Weigel, S.J., and Andrew Greeley suggested that as Irish-American families could never quite forget how long and difficult had been the path toward social respectability, they tended to urge their children not to take any risks with social status; as a result, members of these communities usually avoided potentially insecure areas like the arts and academia, opting instead for business, medicine, and the law. Stephen Steinberg, writing from a more hardheaded sociological perspective, reckoned this "myth" of inherent Catholic antiintellectualism to be simply a delusion, a fictive rationalization arising out of American Catholics' traditionally low position on the social and economic scale.[39] Steinberg's analysis brings to mind the conceptual limitations of sociological posi-

---

36 John Tracy Ellis, "The American Catholic and the Intellectual Life," in *The Catholic Church, U.S.A.,* ed. Louis J. Putz, C.S.C. (Chicago: Fides Publishers, 1956), p. 345.

37 John Tracy Ellis, *American Catholicism,* 2nd ed. (Chicago: Univ. of Chicago Press, 1969), p. 220.

38 Dolores Liptak and Timothy Walch, "American Catholics and the Intellectual Life: An Interview with Monsignor John Tracy Ellis," *U. S. Catholic Historian,* 4 (1985), 192–4.

39 Gustave Weigel, S.J., "An Introduction to American Catholicism," in *The Catholic Church, U.S.A.,* ed. Putz, p. 9; Andrew M. Greeley, *That Most Distressful Nation: The Taming of the American Irish* (Chicago: Quadrangle, 1972), pp. 189–90; Stephen Steinberg, *The Ethnic Myth: Race, Ethnicity, and Class in America* (New York: Atheneum, 1981), p. 144.

tivism, a topic we discussed earlier; still, on the whole it seems likely that it was a combination of economic and psychological factors that helped to push American Catholicism toward cultural conformity in the postwar years.

It is surely a mistake, though, for Ellis to accept without question an equation between conformity and antiintellectualism. It is as if Ellis and his allies had internalized and unconsciously reproduced the critical arguments of the Frankfurt School without being aware of Frankfurt's narrow ideological base. This reaction was understandable enough in the light of the intellectual mood of the 1950s, but it led many Catholic thinkers into erratic interpretations of their own culture. "To be an intellectual," declared Catholic scholar Thomas F. O'Dea in 1958, "means to be engaged in a quest."[40] But this is a gross oversimplification: as we have seen, the "quest" in Kerouac and Powers, if it exists, is ironic and parodic, turning full circle to end up precisely where it began. It is this typical 1950s assumption that intellectualism must always coincide with nonconformity that needs rigorous interrogation: the search for the "numinous force" of "otherness" may be appropriate for Bellow and Updike, but it is by no means the only procedure available. This is not, of course, to denigrate these excellent novelists, merely to point out that the cultural assumptions implicit within their texts comprise relative, not absolute, truths.

By contrast, Donald Phelps wrote in 1969 that "the comedy of manners is *the* literary métier of American Catholicism." Phelps aligned J. F. Powers with writers such as John O'Hara and Mary McCarthy, all of whom manifest "a total seriousness about the world" in which their stories take place.[41] For Catholic novelists, the corporate *ecclesia* necessarily embodies familiar social landscapes as well as Christian principles, whereas in the tradition of Bellow and Updike this abject material world tends to oppress the putative freedom of the spirit. Such prioritizing of spiritual autonomy is one reason for Bellow's attempt to resist classification as a "Jewish" novelist: he aspires to fly free of the shackles of ethnic heritage so as to achieve an abstract, idealized humanism. This was a theme much in vogue in the 1950s: we see it replicated in James Baldwin's desire to transcend his blackness and, indeed, in J. F. Powers's own admission that he much disliked the term "Catholic literature" – though Powers also admitted he supposed it was, in the end, a "meaningful" term.[42] In all of these cases, there is resistance to the idea of ethnic

---

40 Thomas F. O'Dea, *American Catholic Dilemma: An Inquiry into the Intellectual Life* (New York: Sheed and Ward, 1958), p. 112.
41 Donald Phelps, "Reasonable, Holy and Living," *Minnesota Review*, 9 (1969), 57, 61.
42 Powers, "The Catholic and Creativity," p. 64.

and religious difference and a desire instead to approach a universally valid, transcendent "truth." Bearing in mind the supposedly oppositional status of intellectuals at this time, it is ironic that such a process represents another version of Eisenhowerian homogenization, the abolition of local peculiarities in the interests of philosophical unity. We may be reminded of Althusser's work on "interpellation," where supposedly free subjects are in fact invented by their social and historical context, being "subjects [only] by and for their subjection": Eisenhower's intellectuals were under the subjection of the very forces they thought they were reacting against.[43]

Other aspects of this universalizing mode can be recognized in the literary criticism of the 1950s. It is apparent in the ambition of New Criticism to depoliticize and dehistoricize texts so as to unlock their essential "spirit," an entity supposed to fly freely across the boundaries of historical change. We see it also in the popularity of "myth" criticism, especially Northrop Frye's Anatomy of Criticism (1957), which sought to diminish the merely material, corporeal part of a text by subsuming its essential spirit under the banners of timeless archetypes. It is a sardonic paradox that all these attempts to depoliticize and universalize literary texts should have been so dependent upon the historical and material circumstances of one particular time. But it is also true that the culture of the 1950s did no more than reinvigorate a transcendental strain that, in one form or another, has enjoyed enormous prestige within American cultural history, so much so that many literary critics have taken it to be the one and only American language. We find a later version of this dualistic "otherness" in Harold Bloom's notions of transcendent misprision, whereby the texts of master spirits like Wordsworth, Nietzsche, Yeats, and Stevens uproot themselves from their banal material conditions of production and begin to converse intertextually with each other. How, for instance, would a "Catholic" poet like Frank O'Hara fit into Bloom's charmed circle? Frank O'Hara's concern with the quidditas of material objects, his stress upon the immanent rather than transcendent world, would seem impertinently to disrupt Bloom's rarefied air of spirit.

In the same way, John O'Hara, whose novels also prefer solid immanence to disembodied transcendence, has come to be associated with "antiintellectualism" both by critics in the Bloom mold and also by those who followed Ellis's line that to be an intellectual was necessarily to be a questing radical. A radical in political terms John O'Hara certainly was not, as his crusty support for Barry Goldwater and bad-tempered News-

43 Louis Althusser, "Ideology and Ideological State Apparatuses (Notes towards an Investigation)," in Lenin and Philosophy and Other Essays, trans. Ben Brewster (London: New Left Books, 1971), p. 169.

day column in the 1960s indicated. One aspect of this devotion to the status quo is O'Hara's insistence upon the ineradicable, indeed reified, nature of ethnic difference and racial loyalty. "Fantastically overspecialized in the social signs," according to Alfred Kazin, O'Hara chronicles the rigid rules of "polite" society and the external badges of social affiliation or (equally importantly) disaffiliation.[44] In *Appointment in Samarra* (1935), the socially naive Julian English omits to "consider the Catholic point of view" before insulting Harry Reilly, kingpin of the Irish community in Gibbsville, Pennsylvania. English subsequently finds the Catholics in this town protectively "stick together," thus pushing him toward social ostracism and, eventually, suicide. Conversely, in *Ourselves to Know* (1960) Jerry MacMahon discovers that he will not be allowed to become president of the local bank because of "strong anti-Catholic feeling in the Valley."[45]

There are in O'Hara innumerable instances of this kind of religious heritage creating insurmountable barriers between people. It is the very reverse of that universalizing spirit prevalent in postwar America, which may be one reason O'Hara has been generally so much scorned in American literary circles. O'Hara is deemed to have, as Matthew J. Bruccoli argued, no "ennobling view of humanity."[46] Sheldon Norman Grebstein complained of how the writer was foolish enough to acquiesce in a "fundamental acceptance of society as given," with the consequence that he professes no interest in "ultimates, the quest for fundamental verities"; accordingly, said Grebstein, O'Hara's work sadly lacks "all metaphysical, religious, and spiritual dimension." At times, Grebstein's complaint against the supposed superficiality of O'Hara's texts lurches into comic melodrama: "One gets nowhere . . . the sense of crisis, the apocalyptic vision, the moral agony, the assault upon sanity, the excruciating inquiry into the basic conditions of human existence." Joseph Browne's conclusion was more laconic: O'Hara's "eyes and ears aren't connected to a brain."[47]

Confronted with literary analysis of this order, it is no wonder that O'Hara's letters and essays reveal a testy suspicion of the whole enterprise

---

44 Alfred Kazin, *Bright Book of Life: American Novelists and Storytellers from Hemingway to Mailer* (Boston: Little, Brown and Co., 1973), p. 106.
45 John O'Hara, *Appointment in Samarra* (New York: Modern Library–Random House, 1953), pp. 106, 119; *Ourselves to Know* (New York: Random House, 1960), p. 310.
46 Matthew J. Bruccoli, *The O'Hara Concern: A Biography of John O'Hara* (New York: Random House, 1975), p. 344.
47 Sheldon Norman Grebstein, *John O'Hara* (New York: Twayne, 1966), pp. 144, 146, 111; Joseph Browne, "John O'Hara and Tom McHale: How Green Is Their Valley?," in *Irish-American Fiction: Essays in Criticism,* ed. Daniel J. Casey and Robert E. Rhodes (New York: AMS Press, 1979), p. 129.

of criticism. His basic defense was simply that while his books continued to sell well, the critics could go and paddle their own canoes. On a more conceptual level, though, it may be that O'Hara has been underrated by American critics for the same kind of reasons Scott Fitzgerald was out of fashion for so long. Like Fitzgerald, O'Hara focuses upon the external circumstances of society, whereas American critics have traditionally preferred the development of an internalized spirit: O'Hara's characters have "no inner resources," complained Norman Podhoretz.[48] Concomitantly, O'Hara is profoundly uninterested in ethics per se because, like Fitzgerald (and Powers), O'Hara sees character as largely a passive product of cultural circumstances rather than an autonomous entity capable of exercising existential free will and therefore independent moral judgment. The Jesuit theologian Gustave Weigel once wrote of how "there is an energetic passivity in American Catholics, but they are weak in initiative," and it is exactly this sense of "energetic passivity" that we find in O'Hara's characterizations.[49] Another reason for the mutual hostility between O'Hara and his critics is that this whole business of rigid social classification is anathema to a society whose central myths revolve around democracy, classlessness, and freedom of spirit. It is a central irony that so many of O'Hara's stories of religious intolerance should be set in his native Pennsylvania, a state founded upon the Quaker principle of religious freedom, but a locale that turns out in O'Hara's texts to be a hotbed of intolerance. O'Hara, like Powers, offers a radical critique of American pastoral idealism by implying that the same kind of religious prejudices and class hostilities are to be found everywhere, in the New World of the United States as well as the Old World of Europe. It is not that American critics consciously disapprove of O'Hara on ideological grounds, of course, nor indeed that O'Hara consciously writes from the cultural perspective of Catholicism (a devout churchgoer as a boy, he abandoned practicing the faith in his late teens). It is simply that because the latent assumptions in O'Hara's novels are quite different from those most critics have come to expect, many of them cannot fathom where the author's angle on the world could possibly derive from.

This is, one suspects, the same kind of bewilderment experienced by liberal intellectuals when confronted by the strictures of Senator McCarthy. In traditional Catholic theology, a person's allegiance to the church is measured by adherence to external laws and objects – participation in the sacraments, for example – with the idiosyncrasies of per-

---

48 Norman Podhoretz, "Gibbsville and New Leeds: The America of John O'Hara and Mary McCarthy," *Commentary*, 21 (1956), 270.
49 Weigel, "An Introduction to American Catholicism," p. 19.

sonal faith being of decidedly secondary importance. In similar fashion, McCarthy's anticommunism was predicated upon a lack of interest in – indeed, contempt for – the vagaries of individual conscience; instead, McCarthy insisted upon the need for firm commitment to visible communal loyalties. This sensibility derives from the same ideological family as O'Hara's prioritizing of social signs over psychological depth: the group, the organization, is more significant than the individual. Alfred Kazin called O'Hara's work "energetically superficial in the fashion of . . . metropolitan journalism" and thus an example of "the rejection or corruption of all conscious values"; but this is unfair because O'Hara rejected "values" not out of a personal disdain for them but because, in a philosophical sense, he – like Joe McCarthy – conceived subjective human values to be less important than the objective law.[50] In McCarthy, this law was anticommunism; in O'Hara, it is the iron law through which class and ethnicity determine social behavior. In both cases, though, the pressure is toward forms of conformity that usurp the private consciousness, and it is precisely that sense of conformity critics like Kazin have reacted against.

"The people were right, the talk was right, the clothes, the cars" were real, said O'Hara in his obituary notice for Scott Fitzgerald. Like Fitzgerald, O'Hara cherished this visible materialism, "the patent solidity of society" as Malcolm Bradbury put it. (Interestingly, the English critic Bradbury saw O'Hara's novels as forming "an essential chronicle of Thirties America": an example, perhaps, of the advantages of reading O'Hara from a different, un-American cultural perspective.)[51] If searching for substantiation of his grumble about the excessive materialism of American Catholics, John Tracy Ellis would find rich pickings in O'Hara: this kind of materialism surfaces not only in the behavior of fictional characters – such as Thornton McBride in *BUtterfield 8* (1935), a man fresh "out of a high-priced Catholic prep school, Yale, and Fordham Law School" who "was with his father in the law firm and cared about nothing except the law and golf" – but also in the author's dogged insistence upon himself as a professional writer more concerned with money than moral idealism.[52] As with J. P. Donleavy, money for John O'Hara became an image of the ubiquitous bathos of the human condition, the way no high aesthetic or spiritual ideas can ever gainsay the need to grub around in the mucky material world. Categorically rejecting

50 Alfred Kazin, *On Native Grounds: An Interpretation of Modern American Prose Literature* (New York: Harcourt, Brace and World, 1942), pp. 389–90, 387.
51 John O'Hara, "In Memory of Scott Fitzgerald," *New Republic*, 3 Mar. 1941, p. 311; Malcolm Bradbury, *The Modern American Novel* (Oxford: Oxford Univ. Press, 1983), p. 108.
52 John O'Hara, *BUtterfield 8* (New York: Harcourt, Brace and Co., 1935), p. 19.

the romantic image of the writer as seer, O'Hara perceived himself more in a medievalist mode, as an impersonal technician content humbly to imitate the preexistent world.

Given this lack of any larger ethical idealism, it follows that the political intrigues in O'Hara's texts should revolve upon an axis of pure self-interest. As Lee Sigelman put it, for these characters "political activity is . . . motivated not by conviction but by their desire to feather their own nest."[53] More than this, though, the political machine in novels like *Ten North Frederick* (1956) becomes an emblem of that acknowledgment of ontological human limitation we saw in Powers. In *Ten North Frederick*, the Episcopalian idealist Joe Chapin, who cherishes dreams of becoming president, is brought low by the jesuitical machinations of local Irish politician Mike Slattery, whom Chapin unwisely chose to ignore. One of Slattery's strengths is that he is remorselessly undeceived about the less noble elements in human character, his own included. Slattery's understanding is described as "in part . . . traceable to frequent examinations of conscience before visiting the confessional"; whereas Chapin falls foul of that abiding temptation of the Puritan temperament, a hypocritical lack of honesty about one's own motives.[54] Chapin is also compromised by his exceeding reluctance to reduce himself to a cog caught up within Slattery's political machine; he is, in the end, a romantic subjectivist who refuses demeaningly to objectify himself in the required manner. In this way, as Sigelman said, the limitations placed upon human behavior by such political frameworks come to imply that "more encompassing machine . . . society itself," which is "based on scrupulous adherence to carefully-defined rules and roles." A kindred emphasis upon impersonality is also, appropriately enough, the law of O'Hara's fictional style: as John Updike said, "it is hard to think of another significant twentieth-century fiction writer who was less of an egoist – less of an autobiographical self-celebrator."[55]

As in Powers, this social matrix in O'Hara becomes an ontological necessity that annuls the idealistic visions of American romanticism. Purity in O'Hara's world is quite impossible: there is no question of a "world elsewhere," for all are inextricably embroiled in human corruption. No man is "exempt from sin any more than he can avoid a trip to the toilet," the nuns in Jack Kerouac's parochial school used to tell him; it is that perception of the inevitability of "sin," translated into its secularized form of social and political corruption, which permeates

---

53 Lee Sigelman, "Politics and the Social Order in the Work of John O'Hara," *Journal of American Studies*, 20 (1986), 244.
54 John O'Hara, *Ten North Frederick* (New York: Random House, 1955), p. 209.
55 Sigelman, "Politics and the Social Order," p. 254; John Updike, "The Doctor's Son," in *Hugging the Shore: Essays and Criticism* (New York: Knopf, 1983), p. 181.

O'Hara's world.[56] His focus upon latent antagonisms and subtle badges
of ethnic difference becomes all the more truculent precisely because this
was a time when such differences were becoming less and less visible
and also less in tune with the consensual temper of the nation. In *BUtterfield 8,* we are told "the Farleys were Roman Catholic, although when
they were married . . . you would not have been able to guess from their
dossiers in the newspapers" (18): the recognition of a Catholic heritage
has now become a kind of secret signal flashed from one party to another.
In the same novel, Jimmy Malloy's girlfriend notes his resemblance to
Jimmy Cagney, whereupon Malloy himself concludes, albeit a touch
reluctantly: "I am a Mick. I wear Brooks clothes and I don't eat salad
with a spoon and I probably could play five-goal polo in two years, but
I am a Mick. . . . There are not two kinds of Irishmen. There's only one
kind" (67). This is reminiscent of Scott Fitzgerald's obsession with his
marks of ethnic inferiority, although Jimmy Malloy seems to cherish his
social outsiderhood much more explicitly than any Fitzgerald character
does. When he reappears in *Sermons and Soda Water* (1960), Malloy is still
caressing the idea of himself as a "heretic" and agreeing with his girlfriend, Julie Moore, that he will never be anything other than "a non-
practising member of the [Catholic] faithful."[57] Joseph Browne saw in
O'Hara a latent inferiority complex and an urgent desire to eradicate his
own Irish heritage, but it is at least as plausible to argue that O'Hara
cultivated ethnic and religious difference because it justified his fatalistic
view of human society, the way no person is finally able to transcend
his or her social background.

One also suspects – though this is less tangible – that in the very
belligerence of O'Hara's concentration upon surfaces there lurks a sense
of the absence of any "spiritual" dimension and a nostalgia for the loss
of his childhood faith. Because of their very multiplicity of detail,
O'Hara's texts sometimes seem to veer strangely out of conventional
aesthetic proportions, like a surrealist landscape where familiar objects
have become oddly and inexplicably magnified. It is this magnification
of minutiae that implicitly draws attention to the vacancies they are
covering up. In *Hope of Heaven* (1939), Malloy tells Peggy Kennedy that
only poor people believe when you die your soul goes up in the sky; the
"educated," he says, "believe that heaven is a state, a sort of metaphysical
state."[58] But the conversation tails off laconically. In O'Hara, there is no
"sort of metaphysical state," nor any hope of heaven.

*   *   *

56 Jack Kerouac, *Visions of Gerard* (New York: McGraw-Hill, 1976), p. 42.
57 John O'Hara, *Sermons and Soda Water* (New York: Random House, 1960), III, 55.
58 John O'Hara, *Hope of Heaven,* in *Here's O'Hara: Three Novels and Twenty Short Stories*
    (New York: Duell, Sloan and Pearce, 1946), p. 376.

Writing in 1957, Mary McCarthy described her religious upbringing as no more than a "memory," something belonging to the distant past. *Memories of a Catholic Girlhood* ostensibly regards religion as a childish phenomenon, to be dismissed when the protagonist achieves maturity. Catholicism is also associated by the author with the historical past, with glamorous warriors of old like Charlemagne and Bonnie Prince Charlie, as idolized by her Catholic convent school teachers. In the narrative of her own life, she describes herself as encountering a more primitive form of ethnic Catholicism locked fatalistically within its ghetto; McCarthy's grandmother would apparently pray assiduously for the "extermination of Protestantism."[59] McCarthy's sardonic intellectualism distances her from all this, however. She herself abandoned the practice of religion in adolescence and later greatly perturbed Flannery O'Connor at a dinner party by suggesting the Holy Ghost was no more than a symbol, albeit "a pretty good one."[60] McCarthy generally associated Catholicism with the repression of free thought: by her own account, she was forbidden by her primitive Catholic guardians to read anything except a "*Lives of the Saints,* full of graphic accounts of every manner of martyrdom," while her first parochial school offered not books but "readers that had stories in them." Accordingly, McCarthy credited her origination as an intellectual to liberation from this Catholic milieu by her Protestant grandfather and the consequent "opening up of libraries to me." "I was born as a mind during 1925, my bodily birth having taken place in 1912," she announces in *How I Grew* (1987).[61] This dualism of mind and body is itself symptomatic of that cerebral alienation enjoyed by intellectuals during the postwar period, when the emphasis was upon existential rebellion, autonomous will, an escape from the "body" of any determining social context. One thinks of Sartre's *Les Mots* (1964), where Sartre similarly proclaims a loathing of his childhood and all that remained of it. Like McCarthy, Sartre sought dualistically to cancel the material burden of his past so as to be born again as pure mind, will, and intellect.

The novelist Mary Gordon said in a 1988 interview that it was only her "father's Jewishness" that gave her "a kind of license to speak," the courage to write and express herself despite the "interdicting" and "silencing environment" of her Irish-Catholic childhood.[62] There is something of this crossed ethnic heritage in McCarthy as well. Her Protestant

---

59 Mary McCarthy, *Memories of a Catholic Girlhood* (New York: Harcourt Brace Jovanovich, 1957), p. 34.
60 *The Habit of Being: The Letters of Flannery O'Connor,* p. 125.
61 Mary McCarthy, *How I Grew* (San Diego: Harcourt Brace Jovanovich, 1987), pp. 3, 23, 1.
62 M. Deiter Keyishian, "Radical Damage: An Interview with Mary Gordon," *Literary Review,* 32, no. 1 (Fall 1988), 81.

maternal grandfather was complemented by her Jewish maternal grandmother, inciting McCarthy to describe herself as "a quarter Jewish" and
so even further removed in spirit from the coercions of Catholicism.[63]
Indeed, in good existentialist fashion, a sense of desiring not to belong
anywhere is something that comes across strongly in her writings. If her
parents had lived, McCarthy muses, she would probably have become
a "wholesome" Catholic married to an Irish lawyer; if she had gone to
a private high school in California, as at one point she wished, she might
well have become a standard West Coast type; whereas the marginalized
world of Puget Sound allowed her to preserve a spiky independence.[64]
Moreover, McCarthy attempts to validate this independence through the
form of autobiography, which is in itself an existentialist enterprise, an
attempt to invent and control the self.

One of the revealing aspects about McCarthy's texts, though, is that
in the end existentialism is found to lack authority. Alfred Kazin wrote
of how there is "always one theme" in her books, "none of these awful
people is going to catch *me*. The heroine is always distinctly right, and
gives herself all possible marks for taste, integrity and indomitability."[65]
But this is not entirely just: for while it is true that McCarthy's acerbic
style seems to betoken a contempt for those alien to herself, we should
also see how a series of displacements is operating throughout Mc-
Carthy's writing so that the narrator or heroine is never as much in
control of events as she would like to be. The "Protestant" side of
McCarthy, emphasizing existential freedom, must always confront those
aspects of her "Catholic" heritage that have become lodged in the unconscious interstices of her texts and work to compromise individual
independence by engendering patterns of psychological and cultural
fatalism.

This collapse into divided or multiple selves is played out in *Memories
of a Catholic Girlhood*. Hedged around by prefaces, footnotes, and retractions, *Memories* is, as Martha Lifson said, "an almost frantic" and
"unrelenting" attempt to "grasp" the "hidden" meanings of childhood,
together with an implicit recognition that this "center secret" must remain "hidden . . . unknown and unknowable." So far from the journey
toward an "integrated self" which Rosalie Hewitt found here, the identity
of McCarthy and her narrative alter ego becomes more and more problematical: did events happen just this way, she wonders, is memory
playing tricks, am I distorting the past in the interests of aesthetic self-

63 Mary McCarthy, "Artists in Uniform," in *On the Contrary: Articles of Belief, 1946–1961*
     (New York: Farrar, Straus and Cudahy, 1961), p. 61.
64 McCarthy, *Memories of a Catholic Girlhood*, p. 16; *How I Grew*, p. 29.
65 Kazin, *Bright Book of Life*, p. 188.

gratification?[66] The expression of these doubts serves paradoxically to heighten our conviction of the author's conscientiousness and veracity, as Derrida said in his discussion of Rousseau's autobiographical *Confessions;* nevertheless, as with Rousseau, McCarthy's interweaving of irony and memory eventually convinces the reader that any aspiration toward the self-authenticating presence of true identity must be a chimera. *Memories* appears to invite us to look through its writing to the original state of McCarthy's childhood, but in the end this ambition is denied, for the reader necessarily becomes arrested at the level of the writing itself. McCarthy's writing is simply (brilliant) writing. As Lifson said, the autobiographical work reflects back upon itself, retaining knowledge within its closed circle; we come to realize the text cannot grant us access to primary truth.

Yet this introduces into McCarthy's *Memories* an agreeable Derridean *aporia,* the paradox of a revelatory blind spot. The narrator aspires to slough off Catholicism, which she associates with an un-American dwelling on the legacy of the past, a lack of interest in secular morality, and also a self-indulgent delight in aesthetics as "prior to and beyond utility ('Consider the lilies of the field; they toil not, neither do they spin')." This latter "idea of sheer wastefulness," says McCarthy's persona, "is always shocking to non-Catholics": for Max Weber's Lutherans and Calvinists, we will recall, aesthetic luxury involved moral decadence while assiduous toil implied moral virtue.[67] So far from being rejected, however, all of these Catholic cultural traits the narrator affects to scorn surreptitiously manifest themselves in the aesthetic form of McCarthy's text: the conscious authorial "mind" is again compromised by the unconscious textual "body." *Memories of a Catholic Girlhood* denies access to the original content of McCarthy's childhood but allows this Catholicism to renew itself, albeit in a transformed status, by its displacement into a residual cultural determinant in terms of artistic form and style if not in content. Timothy Dow Adams has gone so far as to suggest the style of *Memories* constitutes a deliberate parody of the Catholic sacrament of confession, a memoir in which McCarthy chooses to boast about her "sins" of pride, deceit, and so on rather than humbly expressing contrition for them. Perhaps this is so; still, the very fact of turning her transgressions into a public event necessarily preserves an element of the

66 Martha F. Lifson, "Allegory of the Secret: Mary McCarthy," *Biography,* 4 (1981), 253, 263; Rosalie Hewitt, "A 'Home Address for the Self': Mary McCarthy's Autobiographical Journey," *Journal of Narrative Technique,* 12 (1982), 102. On the self-consciously fictive elements in McCarthy's *Memories,* see also Paul John Eakin, *Fictions in Autobiography: Studies in the Art of Self-Invention* (Princeton: Princeton Univ. Press, 1985), pp. 3–55.
67 McCarthy, *Memories of a Catholic Girlhood,* p. 26.

original penitential impulse: as Adams noted, "she is simultaneously trying to confess and to undercut the act of confession."[68] What we encounter here, in fact, is a Buñuelesque double bind where the aesthetic act of blasphemy is inextricably intertwined with the moral object it is blaspheming against.

Furthermore, the narrator's assumption of an identity predicated upon lying and equivocation also interpellates her within a mode of cultural Catholicism, for, as Newman famously remarked in *Apologia pro Vita Sua:* "If there is one thing more than another which prejudices Englishmen against the Catholic Church, it is the doctrine of great authorities on the subject of equivocation. For myself," Newman went on, in a stab at self-exculpation, "I can fancy myself thinking it was allowable in extreme cases for me to lie, but never to equivocate."[69] Yet the title of the last chapter of McCarthy's *Memories,* "Ask Me No Questions," implies a Catholic teaching technically called "mental reservation," which entitles the faithful to employ equivocation and ambiguity so as to withhold facts from any interrogator they believe has no moral right to know the whole truth. Throughout *Memories,* the narrator represents her young alter ego practicing this kind of duplicity as a way of life: she lies to the nuns about her preparations for First Communion, she lies to her grandparents about visiting Yellowstone Park, she lies to her college principal about staying out with a boy. In all of these instances, the deceit involves not so much a sense of personal immorality as a "jesuitical" understanding of how to conform externally to accepted social standards; recalling her interview with the college principal, for instance, she tells us: "I was going to equivocate, not for selfish reasons but in the interests of the community, like a grown-up, responsible person."[70] For the Catholic-trained mind of the young McCarthy, the lie has become merely a venial failing, almost an accepted manner of social behavior. But of course the secular, humanist side of McCarthy could never willingly accept such obfuscations; indeed, these early negotiations with duplicity may have been one reason McCarthy was so assertive in her later career on the subject of truth. She came to associate the practice of deception with repressive and authoritarian regimes of various kinds, whereas her own existentialist integrity required her to be "monotheistic," as she put it in *How I Grew,* where truth was concerned: "It has been an article of faith with me, going back to college days, that there is a truth and that it is

68 Timothy Dow Adams, *Telling Lies in Modern American Autobiography* (Chapel Hill: Univ. of North Carolina Press, 1990), p. 88.

69 John Henry Newman, *Apologia pro Vita Sua,* ed. A. Dwight Culler (Boston: Houghton Mifflin, 1956), p. 328.

70 McCarthy, *Memories of a Catholic Girlhood,* p. 162.

knowable."[71] Such zeal for demystification may help to explain her attempt to revise and correct *Memories of a Catholic Girlhood* in this later autobiography. *How I Grew* seems motivated by an existentialist drive to undercut every layer of deceptive artifice, to scrutinize the object of enquiry in its purest and most unadorned state.

Yet McCarthy's work ironically dramatizes the impossibility of any pure form of demystification, for it characteristically establishes a textual dialectic where the secular freedom to which her personae aspire is opposed by those psychological determinants and aspects of religious conditioning to which her narratives are bound. In many of McCarthy's early short stories, for instance, we find the fictional heroine indulging in various retrospective reveries as she seeks to come to terms with aspects of her past that threaten the freedom of a newly independent self. In "The Man in the Brooks Brothers Shirt," from *The Company She Keeps* (1942), the heroine is thrown into moral confusion by her rejection of the Catholic "Church's filing system," as she calls it, and she masochistically welcomes the feelings of "guilt and shame" a chance sexual encounter produces.[72] She even rejoices in the physical discomfort this episode brings about, seeing herself as like a "mendicant saint" (117) engaged in "mortification of the flesh" (114). Sexuality in McCarthy's fiction tends to involve a renegotiation of the protagonists' pasts rather than simply a celebration of their existence in the present moment, and so, as Doris Grumbach remarked, lovemaking is often viewed here as an absurd rather than a romantic phenomenon. Barbara McKenzie went so far as to claim McCarthy "has set the cause of the heterosexual novel in America back twenty years" by her refusal "to celebrate 'romantic' love" – a bizarre ideological insistence on McKenzie's part that romantic humanism should be the sine qua non of American fiction.[73]

The character of Margaret, an "Irish offspring" (265), is the thread linking all of the stories in this first collection. "The Genial Host" again hints at the heroine's temperamental masochism by chronicling her attachment to history's beautiful losers – "the South, the Dauphin, Bonnie Prince Charlie" (155). Another story, "Portrait of the Intellectual as a Yale Man," contrasts Margaret's temperament with the "puritan conscience" (192) of Jim Bennett, who, "like all good Yale men . . . feared systems as his great-grandfather had feared the devil, the saloon, and the pope" (172). Systematization, or the interpellation of individuals within structures of corporate or philosophical belief, is anathema to the fierce

---

71 McCarthy, *How I Grew*, p. 199.
72 Mary McCarthy, *The Company She Keeps* (New York: Harcourt, Brace and World, 1942), pp. 101, 100. Subsequent page references are given in parentheses in the text.
73 Doris Grumbach, *The Company She Kept* (New York: Coward-McCann, 1967), p. 138; Barbara McKenzie, *Mary McCarthy* (New York: Twayne, 1966), p. 177.

nonconformity of Jim's dissenting mind. For the Catholic consciousness of Margaret, however, nonconformity does not come so easily, and in "Ghostly Father, I Confess," the last story in this collection, the heroine finds her rationally motivated dissent summarily turned on its head. Terrified by God as a child, Margaret nevertheless feels a compulsion to replace the Christian deity with some substitute god or authority figure. She confesses to a psychoanalyst as once she confessed to a priest, finding relief in repeating to him the traumas of her past: "It happened again and again, and always there was this sense of recognition, this feeling that she was only repeating combinations of words she had memorized long ago" (293). Meg's Catholicism is a subject that intimidates both her and the psychoanalyst "for it suggested to them that the universe is mechanical, utterly predictable, frozen," a conception said to be "in its own way . . . quite as terrible as the notion that the universe is chaotic" (262). It is this internalization of Catholicism, its transposition into a form of psychological fatalism, that undermines the heroine's autonomy and confidence in her integral self.

This subversion of existentialism becomes, in McCarthy's longer novels, a subversion of liberalism and utopianism, abstractions that are similarly predicated upon the possibility of a perfection of the will. In *The Oasis* (1949) and *The Groves of Academe* (1952), collective idealism eventually becomes fragmented in much the same way as did the psychological idealism of McCarthy's earlier heroines. The high-minded community in *The Oasis* collapses when Will Taub's "analogical intellect" (165) comes to realize there is no essential difference between intellectuals and society at large. Taub tells Katy Norell with "the sonority of a black benediction" that she is "just like everybody else" (177), thereby annulling the possibility of some kind of exclusive spiritual election, which is implied in the novel's epigraph, taken from Rousseau's *Confessions*. A Rousseauesque belief in the sanctity of a romanticized version of the self and in the validity of disaffiliation from assumptions of the common herd is echoed in the idealistic visions of Howard Furness, chairman of Jocelyn College's English department in *The Groves of Academe*. Ensconced in Jocelyn's rural milieu, Furness disparages the old "medieval standard of scholarship as an end in itself," choosing to privilege instead the college's "progressive methodology . . . with its emphasis on faith and individual salvation," which Furness understands as "a Protestant return to the Old Testament."[74] Yet the naïveté of this liberal belief in the essential goodness of mankind is exposed when Henry Mulcahy, an Irish-American Joyce scholar, comes to feel himself victimized by the

74 Mary McCarthy, *The Groves of Academe* (New York: Harcourt, Brace and World, 1952), pp. 127, 296. Subsequent page references are given in parentheses in the text.

college authorities and starts pulling all kinds of political strings to undo its higher administration. As in John O'Hara's *Ten North Frederick,* political cunning – or "infernal jesuitry," as Henry Mulcahy calls it (154) – deflates the claims of ethical idealism. In *The Groves of Academe,* such idealism is represented as limited and provincial, too much locked inside the thin wish fulfillment fantasies of American pastoral. Henry Mulcahy, on the other hand, was formed by "Jesuit training . . . in an older mold and his Joyce studies confirmed him in the habit of universalization"; *Finnegans Wake* is for Henry "one book which shall be all books, the Book of Life" (210). As with Will Taub in *The Oasis,* Mulcahy's awareness of analogical similitude opens his eyes to the idealistic self-deceptions of the Jocelyn College faculty, for Mulcahy, like Taub – and like Joyce, and indeed like John O'Hara – recognizes that all mankind is in the same corrupt boat. This perception would appear to render the separatist pretensions of moral utopianism null and void. Still, this kind of universalism, like the pastoral idealism it competes with, is itself a limited and relative ideology: Mulcahy attempts to punish his rivals by erecting his transformed Catholicism into an omnicompetent idiom, but his own persecution complex, along with his narcissistic view of himself as a martyr and outsider in the heroic tradition of Jesus Christ and James Joyce, clearly identifies the particular cultural tradition from which his style of thought emanates.

McCarthy said in a 1961 interview that she thought religion offers to Americans "very often the only history and philosophy they ever get" and that "a reference to it somehow opens up that historical vista."[75] Certainly it is true that McCarthy's texts are especially alert to the differences between Protestant and Catholic modes of history and philosophy. *A Charmed Life* (1955) features a long discussion among the inhabitants of a New England community about why Corneille might be more of a "Catholic" dramatist and Racine more of a Jansenist or "Protestant."[76] The Jesuit-educated Miles Murphy, who for "a hardboiled unbeliever . . . had a strange admiration for the rules and observances of the church" (37), holds that the "imperial" Corneille is more concerned with a typically Catholic form of "world-domination" (182), whereas the more psychologically oriented Racine contents himself, like Luther, with focusing upon an individual person's "beast within" (183). One unusual aspect of Miles's philosophical systematizations, though, is that they are based upon apparent inconsistencies: "Like all the outstand-

75 *Writers at Work: The Paris Review Interviews,* 2nd ser., ed. George Plimpton (New York: Viking, 1963), p. 306.
76 Mary McCarthy, *A Charmed Life* (New York: Harcourt, Brace and Co., 1955), pp. 180–9. Subsequent page references are given in parentheses in the text.

ing people Warren had ever known, Miles was inconsistent" (37). In trying to yoke together heterogeneous ideas and perceptions, Miles's universalism must necessarily find itself confronted by the charge of illogicality and irrationality on a worldly level. His is not a logical but an analogical intellect, discovering points of resemblance even in the midst of rational difference – a very neo-scholastic inclination, as we have seen. At the end of *A Charmed Life,* the enigmatic vicomte offers Warren an explanation for this kind of inconsistency:

> "Do you really believe in a life after death?" "Naturally," said the vicomte, with an air of astonishment. "I am a Catholic." "But how do you reconcile that –?" "Reconcile, reconcile," pronounced the vicomte, impatiently. "That is all I hear from you atheists and Protestants. 'Paul, how do you reconcile . . . ?' I do not need to reconcile; I leave that to God." (303)

Marx, we may recall, defined God as the illusory sun that man revolved around as long as he was too ignorant to recognize how his world actually revolves around himself. Although she was no self-evidently "religious" writer, the texts of McCarthy leave gaps and ambiguities that implicitly deny Marx's kind of rationalistic positivism. McCarthy's vicomte may not be certain of what he believes, but, rather like J. F. Powers, he does not reckon the decision will be rendered in this ring. The claims of human logic are less significant than the paradoxes of divine disbelief.

Rather than successfully projecting a heroic, synthesizing ego upon the inchoate contradictions of the material world, McCarthy's work dramatizes the lack of continuity between subjective and objective reality. The subjectivity of her central characters becomes ironized and decentered. In McCarthy's 1972 narrative *Hanoi,* as Gordon O. Taylor has pointed out, her account of political events in Asia implicitly contrasts the geometric conic sections on a blackboard, sections that proclaim the "binding universal" of a "disinterested world of pure forms," with the erratic muddle of the Vietnam war itself.[77] *The Group* (1963) and *Birds of America* (1971) likewise signal the demise of this kind of romantic, Emersonian doctrine wherein the soul and oversoul might be mutually interpenetrating. In *The Group,* a clique of Vassar girls finds itself obliged to travel the grooved rails of social change in 1930s America. As in Fitzgerald and John O'Hara, McCarthy's characters are not so much idiosyncratic individuals as passive products of their time and circumstances: Kay Petersen fears her husband Harald might be "repeating his father's pattern" by "*needing* to fail"; Mrs. Renfrew feels that in her daughter Dottie's dubious marital choice it is "as if some dreadful pattern

77 Gordon O. Taylor, *Studies in Modern American Autobiography* (London: Macmillan, 1983), p. 93.

were being repeated."[78] *The Group* is a novel predicated upon various patterns of this kind where people are denied free will and portrayed instead as the victims of history. It is also, and concomitantly, a novel of corporate identity, of the ways in which no one individual can successfully secede from the cultural patterns of his or her time. The complaint of the *New Statesman* was that the girls are "as hard to tell apart as Disney dwarfs" so that the novel "celebrates everything that drags down the human spirit and boxes it in"; yet this could be seen from another ideological angle as one of the novel's great successes, for McCarthy is concerned not with the independence of the "spirit" but with the interdependence of destinies.[79] "The interdependence of spiritual destinies, the plan of salvation; for me, that is the sublime and unique feature of Catholicism," wrote Gabriel Marcel; Marcel was concerned not with autonomy but with "heteronomy," the "intersubjective nexus" where the fate of one individual is inextricably bound up with a communal destiny.[80] Translated from a spiritual to a material context, this is exactly what we find in *The Group*. Here, of course, it is secular rather than spiritual destinies that are at stake, but the sense of these lives as a communal enterprise rests upon a characteristically Catholic viewpoint. Max Weber made the same kind of point in *The Sociology of Religion* when he said the rituals of Catholicism enjoin passive membership rather than any deliberate act of conscious will.[81] McCarthy's characters are objects implicated within the rituals of their time whether they like it or not.

Birds of America again transposes the status of its characters from subjective consciousness to reified object by uprooting its scene from New England to Europe, where Peter Levi, former admirer of Thoreau and the solitary pleasures of transcendentalism, comes reluctantly to realize how "being abroad makes you conscious of the whole imitative side of human behavior."[82] At the end of this novel, Levi imitates the route of medieval pilgrims by undertaking an expedition to Rome, where, in the Sistine Chapel, he thinks in exasperation of how "there has to be *something* left to explore. To give you the illusion that you're blazing a trail, al-

---

78 Mary McCarthy, *The Group* (New York: Harcourt, Brace and World, 1963), pp. 92–3, 179.
79 Quoted in Grumbach, *The Company She Kept*, p. 194.
80 Gabriel Marcel, *Being and Having*, trans. Katherine Farrer (Westminster: Dacre Press, 1949), pp. 21, 167; Erwin W. Straus and Michael A. Machado, "Gabriel Marcel's Notion of Incarnate Being," in *The Philosophy of Gabriel Marcel*, ed. Paul Arthur Schlipp and Lewis Edwin Hahn (La Salle, Ill.: Open Court, 1984), p. 126.
81 Max Weber, *The Sociology of Religion*, trans. Ephraim Fischoff (London: Methuen, 1965), p. 187.
82 Mary McCarthy, *Birds of America* (New York: Harcourt Brace Jovanovich, 1971), p. 138. Subsequent page references are given in parentheses in the text.

though you know that thousands of others have been there before you"
(296). According to the terms of this text, however, there is nothing
new under the sun; the Emersonian notion of an "original relation to
the universe" seems peremptorily invalidated. The French Revolution
reckoned it was making everything new, says Peter, but its dream of
reason failed because conscious rationality can never drain dry those
deeper, murky well pools of the historical and psychological unconscious:
"They would have had to abolish all past literature and art, including
the *lumières*. Grinning Voltaire *and* the Holy Virgin" (146).

In the same way, Kant's quest for the definition of a "universal moral
faculty" is shown at the end of this novel to be, if not a romantic illusion,
then at least part of the limited ideology of romanticism. Coming across
a dilapidated *clocharde* in Paris, Peter Levi articulates to himself the
thought that: "If it was not the *clocharde*'s choice that she had got into
this grisly state, then there was no freedom of the will, and if it *was* her
choice, of which tonight he felt convinced, then the will's objects were
not the same for everybody" (333). The last words of the novel take up
this collapse of the Kantian imperative by proclaiming that "Nature is
dead" (344). In other words, the notion of some form of moral idealism
that might be sanctioned by "nature" – the dream of Thoreau, as well
as Kant – is overturned. The experience of Europe undermines Peter
Levi's transcendental visions and convinces him of how the relation of
subjective self to objective world is problematic and contingent. To talk
of a "natural" interpenetration between man and his local environment
becomes meaningless. McCarthy wrote in 1963 of how she thought "the
national novel, like the national state, was dying, and that a new kind
of novel, based on statelessness was beginning to be written," and it is
evident that *Birds of America* locates itself very much within this internationalist line.[83] Once again we can notice a kinship with J. F. Powers,
who has asserted that he does not believe in "atmosphere, place or country." In New England, Peter Levi can imagine he enjoys an "original
relation to the universe"; in Rome, he realizes such ideas are impossible.
What seems local and unique is in fact merely a small fraction and imitation of the grand universal.

Cannibals and Missionaries (1979) is another thesis-novel pitting the
cultural values of Catholicism against those of Protestantism. Here an
airplane hijack in the Netherlands offers the practicing Catholic Senator
James Carey a leisurely opportunity to review his political career. The
Achilles heel of Carey – a character based, as the author admitted, upon

---

83 Mary McCarthy, "Burroughs' *Naked Lunch,*" in *The Writing on the Wall and Other
    Literary Essays* (New York: Harcourt, Brace and World, 1970), p. 42.

Eugene McCarthy – appears to be that he will not "'throw himself into' whatever he was doing"; there is "always a playful element," a detachment from moral concerns, some hint of otherworldliness.[84] This maverick touch has led newspapers to dub Carey a "spoiled priest" (102) with a secret desire to renounce the world and gain the martyr's crown. As if to demonstrate how this is a wider cultural phenomenon rather than just an idiosyncratic quirk of Carey's temperament, McCarthy's novel makes its Dutch politician Van Vliet de Jonge another lapsed Catholic who suffers from problems similar to those experienced by Carey. The ingenious de Jonge would like to show the Iranian hijackers how best to extricate themselves from the difficulties they have created for all concerned, but he fears his political career in Holland would fall into disrepair if he were seen "to appear as privy counselor to a ruthless gang of terrorists" (135). Like Carey, de Jonge is too playful and not ethically "serious" enough to be trusted in the role of national politician. Both men are keen on aesthetic puzzles, and both have insufficient patience with that fundamentalist sense of morality seemingly required of state leaders. Carey and de Jonge see too many sides of a question rather than that reassuringly dualistic conflict between good and evil as institutionalized by the ethos of Puritanism.

McCarthy shared with Carey and de Jonge this sense of outsiderhood, of being "the Catholic among Protestants," as Doris Grumbach described her.[85] A perennial note of disengagement from common cultural assumptions can be detected in McCarthy's critical writing as well; she remarked upon her admiration and sympathy for J. F. Powers, for instance, whom she characterized as another "marginal figure, a minority, in the contemporary republic of letters."[86] In *The Stones of Florence* (1959), we can sense how she identifies her own mixed heritage with that of this Italian city, where one finds the "Protestant" spirit of plainness, sobriety, and humanism entering into dialogue with that sensuality and "snaky dissimulation" more common within Italian Catholic culture. Florence, with its "iconoclastic, image-breaking nature," was in the late Middle Ages heretically breaking away from traditional dogmas of medieval thought in just the same way as the author herself strove to assert her own project of individuation upon the circumstances of a tyrannical

---

84 Mary McCarthy, *Cannibals and Missionaries* (New York: Harcourt Brace Jovanovich, 1979), p. 105. Subsequent page references are given in parentheses in the text. For Eugene McCarthy, see Carol Gelderman, *Mary McCarthy: A Life* (New York: St. Martin's Press, 1988), p. 324.

85 Grumbach, *The Company She Kept*, p. 215.

86 Mary McCarthy, "On F. W. Dupee," in *Occasional Prose* (San Diego: Harcourt Brace Jovanovich, 1985), p. 250.

Catholic upbringing.[87] The city of Venice, though, is for McCarthy manifestly a Catholic wonder. In *Venice Observed* (1956), she describes how this "painted deception" and "gold idol with clay feet" has aroused the wrath of Anglo-Saxon rationalists like Edward Gibbon (who expressed his "disgust" with the place), Puritan-minded iconoclasts like D. H. Lawrence (who scorned the "abhorrent green, slippery city"), and fervent romantics such as Jean-Jacques Rousseau. "It was not a 'warm' city," McCarthy notes. "That warm soul, Jean-Jacques Rousseau, found himself impotent on the two occasions when Venetian prostitutes tried to initiate him." Rather than Rousseau, McCarthy nominates Casanova as a person with "the true Venetian temperament: cool, ebullient, and licentious."[88]

McCarthy's own literary style is often accused of a similarly "cool" quality. As Carol Gelderman has noted, "cold," "heartless," "clever," "cerebral" are all epithets commonly applied to McCarthy's writing.[89] However, it is interesting to note that these epithets correspond to just the same kind of charges traditionally leveled by the "Rousseau" type against the "Casanova" type, and indeed by Protestant fundamentalists against the Jesuits. There is certainly a jesuitical element in McCarthy's style, just as there was in Casanova's; but it is also important to remember that, as someone who characterized her political opinion as "dissident," she evades any clear adherence to one party or the other.[90] When writing about Watergate, she reestablishes her hostility to Catholicism by attributing John Mitchell's "steady dosage of lies" to his training by Jesuits at Fordham Law School. McCarthy observes here also that the *Washington Post*'s role in the Watergate affair could be seen as reviving the old spirit of the Reformation, where the written word stood as a corrective to the totalitarian impulses of government and mass media: "Printer's ink and domestic liberty have an old association," she remarks.[91] We are back with the young McCarthy receiving her first library card through the good offices of her Protestant grandfather so as to get her away from all those parochial school storybooks. Writing *Vietnam* in 1968, McCarthy similarly protests against the brainless images produced by American television programs, which she sees reproduced on Vietnamese screens:

87 Mary McCarthy, *The Stones of Florence* (New York: Harcourt Brace Jovanovich, 1963), pp. 32, 112, 74.

88 Mary McCarthy, *Venice Observed* (New York: Harcourt Brace Jovanovich, 1963), pp. 3, 144.

89 Gelderman, *Mary McCarthy*, p. xi.

90 *Paris Review Interviews*, 2nd ser., p. 300.

91 Mary McCarthy, *The Mask of State: Watergate Portraits* (New York: Harcourt Brace Jovanovich, 1974), pp. 54, 5.

"Maybe TV, too, is catholic," she remarks, "and the words do not matter."[92]

It is, though, within the formal design of her writing that McCarthy's residual Catholicism operates at its most intangible but also at its most profound. We have seen the temperamental passivity of many of her fictional personae: the "impotence" of "good intentions against instinct and impulse," as Norman Podhoretz recognized in McCarthy's themes, the "failure of Reason as a substitute for Grace, and the illusion of free will," the specter of "a high-minded adult under the tyranny of a five-year-old brat."[93] But this psychological regression also becomes conflated with an interpretation of social and historical stasis: *The Group*, declared McCarthy, is a novel about "the loss of faith in progress." The author attributed her characters' failure to grow and change to a predicament of cultural stagnation that she claimed was prevalent within American society. Quoting Henri Bergson's theory of how comic characters have a kind of immortality – "Like Mr. and Mrs. Micawber: they all have to go on forever and be invulnerable" – McCarthy elaborated her theory of how the girls in *The Group* were "essentially comic figures, and it's awfully hard to make anything happen to them."[94] Yet this inability to change is only another version of – perhaps even an extrapolation from – the psychological passivity that dogs so many of McCarthy's heroines. McCarthy attempted to explain the "comic" qualities of her characters in terms of secular historical and philosophical causes when it is equally likely this phenomenon may have a religious determinant.

McCarthy's fictional characters are "comic" because they are almost totally objectified, dragooned into line by the conceptual systems of her novels. For Kant, the one great moral failing was to regard people merely as means rather than as ends in themselves; but, as we saw in *Birds of America*, Kant's romanticism finds itself trumped in these texts by McCarthy's universalism, and the author has no more qualms than the Jesuits of old about manipulating her people as a means toward her own intellectual designs. Subjective freedom is summarily disallowed as McCarthy turns her characters into comic objects, a process wrought through the acerbic quality of her textual style as much as by her schematic moral designs. This is one reason for Barbara McKenzie's allegation that McCarthy's characters lack "spiritual qualities," a criticism all too reminiscent of the complaints against John O'Hara.[95] For the Catholic sensibilities of McCarthy and O'Hara, freedom of the "spirit" is rarely

92 Mary McCarthy, *The Seventeenth Degree: How It Went, Vietnam, Hanoi, Medina, Sons of the Morning* (New York: Harcourt Brace Jovanovich, 1974), p. 68.
93 Podhoretz, "Gibbsville and New Leeds," pp. 272–3.
94 *Paris Review Interviews*, 2nd ser., pp. 288, 308–9.
95 McKenzie, *Mary McCarthy*, p. 78.

an issue. Ironically, it is one of the most recognizable aspects of American "Catholic" writers that they squeeze "spirit" out of their texts because of a belief that the immanent material world, not its transcendent or metaphysical counterpart, is the arena within which mankind can best fulfill its appointed task of bodily incarnation.

This also helps to explain why McCarthy was always so antipathetic to the Jamesian tradition of the American novel, with its tendencies toward idealized disembodiment. Henry James set himself, said Mc-Carthy, "a resolve, very American, to scrape his sacred texts clean of the material factor."[96] Absenting his own authorial voice from the novels, James grants his characters license to wander around in a world seemingly evacuated of religious, philosophical, and political disturbance; he occasionally even grants them license to divorce themselves from their bodies, as we see in the ghostly antics of Ralph Touchett in *The Portrait of a Lady*. McCarthy, by contrast, concentrates upon the grossly corporeal: in her 1960 essay "The Fact in Fiction," she defended her view that the novelist should "believe again in the reality, the factuality, of the world"; while in her 1980 lectures, *Ideas and the Novel,* she praised the nineteenth-century European novel for managing to constitute itself as a forum where the open interplay of ideas could exist among the representations of "human flesh and blood."[97]

This apology for ideas in fiction is rather different from an admiration for the kind of allegory and symbolism Hawthorne and James favored. In her 1954 essay, "Settling the Colonel's Hash," McCarthy distinguished what she called "natural symbolism," with its "centripetal intention" of trying to discover what an object actually is, from the less praiseworthy "literary symbolism," which "is centrifugal and flees from the object, the event, into the incorporeal distance, where concepts are taken for substance and floating ideas and archetypes assume a hieratic authority." The latter takes us into the realm of myth and symbol, where, said McCarthy, "qualitative differences vanish, and there is only a single, monotonous story." (This, of course, is the universe of Northrop Frye, with his disembodied archetypes.) McCarthy, however, preferred the kind of analogical method where symbolism heightens rather than dematerializes the "real" object. An example of this, she claimed, is to be found in Joyce's representation of Leopold Bloom in *Ulysses* where "the point is transubstantiation: Bloom and Ulysses are transfused into each other and neither reality is diminished. Both realities are locked together,

96 Mary McCarthy, *Ideas and the Novel* (New York: Harcourt Brace Jovanovich, 1980), p. 6.
97 McCarthy, *On the Contrary,* p. 270; *Ideas and the Novel,* p. 113.

like the protons and neutrons of an atom."[98] The word "transubstantiation" is revealing. As we have seen, this style of materialized analogy is
characteristic of many "Catholic" writers, from Joyce to Scott Fitzgerald
through to Powers in *Morte D'Urban*.

It is not difficult to see how McCarthy's interest in the materialistic
impulse of the nineteenth-century European novel takes her in a direction
quite different to that pursued by Richard Chase in *The American Novel
and Its Tradition;* Chase chose to endorse just the kind of abstract pastoral
romances that McCarthy's term "literary symbolism" was concerned to
denigrate. McCarthy's work can be aligned more with the tradition of
Dreiser, Farrell, and Fitzgerald: her texts are stuffed with the "real"
objects of society rather than rarefied into attenuated allegories of an
American frontier world. It is odd, though, that McCarthy never seems
to have recognized how her literary preferences derived, at least partly,
from her particular religious heritage. Despite what she describes in *How
I Grew* as her "amused interest in theology," she does not align Henry
James with a culturally relative form of displaced Puritanism and James
Joyce with a culturally relative form of displaced Catholicism.[99] Instead
she claims, more straightforwardly, that Henry James was wrong and
James Joyce was right. From a more detached and analytical point of
view, that kind of value judgment seems unimportant, if not actually
nonsensical. Nevertheless, it is significant that Powers, O'Hara, and
McCarthy all prefer to focus upon the comic politics of society rather
than any solitary quest for spiritual salvation. It is important also to
recognize how the literary criticism that faults these texts for lacking the
quintessential "American" energy of romanticism – and there is a lot of
such criticism to be found – is analysis that fails to acknowledge its own
(latent) ideological agenda. "The comic element," said McCarthy, "is
the incorrigible element in every human being," not excluding "what is
comic in you and me."[100] It is the purpose of McCarthy's texts, like
those of Powers and O'Hara, to reveal how the comedy of social politics
can be read as an ontological reality as well as a literary genre.

98 McCarthy, *On the Contrary*, pp. 232–5.
99 McCarthy, *How I Grew*, p. 26.
100 McCarthy, "Characters in Fiction," in *On the Contrary*, p. 289.

18

Criminal Politics:
Edwin O'Connor,
George V. Higgins,
William Kennedy, Mario Puzo,
Francis Ford Coppola

In the representation of legislative politics within American Catholic fictions, we see a magnified version of those dilemmas that the idea of social politics creates within the national consciousness. In John O'Hara, the tentacles of society objectify and interpellate its inhabitants so that none, finally, can evade the prison-house of social rank and status. In a similar kind of way, within the worlds of Edwin O'Connor and William Kennedy none can avoid becoming implicated within local or national politics. For Catholic writers, political organizations, like social institutions, appear to be not only psychologically supportive but also ontologically inevitable. Yet, as Irving Howe noted in 1957, there is an old tradition whereby this machinery of politics does not seem "natural" in the United States: "The uniqueness of our history, the freshness of our land, the plenitude of our resources – all these have made possible, and rendered plausible, a style of political improvisation and intellectual free-wheeling."[1] It was precisely this emphasis upon "freewheeling" that led William James to declare Americans should "work to keep our precious birthright of individualism, and freedom from ... institutions" since "*every* great institution is perforce a means of corruption." Thus we find a long-standing uneasiness within the United States about overdetermined, politicized interpretations of society because in such detailed and intricate accounts of how the body politic constitutes itself we may detect a potential threat to what Frank Lentricchia has called "the principal myth of American myths – that of autonomous selfhood itself."[2]

If the political novel challenges the pastoral vision of "a world elsewhere," the novel of criminal activity similarly subverts the font of

1 Irving Howe, *Politics and the Novel* (New York: Horizon, 1957), p. 159.
2 Richard Hofstadter, *Anti-Intellectualism in American Life* (London: Cape, 1964), p. 39; Frank Lentricchia, "Lyric in the Culture of Capitalism," *American Literary History*, 1 (1979), 84.

idealism upon which such pastoral romanticism is founded. William Kennedy and George V. Higgins do not just write "crime novels"; they write novels that imply that everyone is a potential criminal, that man is ineluctably a fallen animal, that the empire of crime – like the empire of society and the empire of politics – can lock all creation within its clutches. These writers pay little heed to the old antitheses between good and evil, purity and impurity; indeed, they depict the boundary between legality and illegality in political operations as very thin, if not actually invisible. In Edwin O'Connor's *The Last Hurrah* (1956), Nathaniel Gardiner broods on how Mayor Frank Skeffington's "entire career seemed to have been devoted to the contravention of the law," while Skeffington himself counts it as one of his prime accomplishments that he has managed to stay out of jail.[3]

In socioeconomic terms, one reason for this close proximity of legitimate to illegitimate lifestyles is that crime used to be seen as a ladder of social mobility for impoverished immigrants. Daniel Bell wrote of how the illicit activities of marginalized ethnic groups might be understood as "a Coney Island mirror, caricaturing the morals and manners of society," since the "gangster elements" were simply "'getting ahead,' just as Horatio Alger had urged."[4] It is also true that the more notorious urban political machines, such as that portrayed in *The Last Hurrah*, flourished on the promise of providing ethnic loyalists with a more stable social and economic status through its customary trading of jobs for votes. "It was only when we gained a measure of political control," says Skeffington in *The Last Hurrah*, "that our people" – by which he means the Boston Irish – "were able to come up for a little fresh air" (220).

When considering the dubious probity of characters like Skeffington, it is relevant to recall that a suspicion of – or sometimes even an open disdain for – the idea of "law" has energized many American romantic heroes, from James Fenimore Cooper's Natty Bumpo through to the maverick policemen portrayed on the cinema screen by Clint Eastwood. What Natty Bumpo and Eastwood's Dirty Harry have in common is a contempt for the bureaucracies of legalism because such forces obstruct the heroes' own vision of a higher, "natural" law. Such outlaw idealism is, though, radically different in kind from Skeffington's venial transgressions. By evading all the bothersome procedures of the San Francisco district attorney's office, Dirty Harry can establish a (supposedly) nobler justice by heroically eliminating society's impure elements. His distinc-

---

3 Edwin O'Connor, *The Last Hurrah* (Boston: Little, Brown and Co., 1956), pp. 409, 108. Subsequent page references are given in parentheses in the text.
4 Daniel Bell, *The End of Ideology: On the Exhaustion of Political Ideas in the Fifties* (Glencoe, Ill.: Free Press, 1960), p. 116.

tion between the trivial restrictions of society and the higher laws of
nature works as a revised version of the Puritan nonconformist conscience, where ecclesiastical institutions were deemed to be merely an
obstruction between individual man and his God. As Catherine L. Albanese has written, in that tradition of dissent running from the New
England colonists through the Quaker conception of "Inner Light," there
was "always the possibility that disobedience to human law was the
greatest of the virtues."[5] In Catholic ideology, by contrast, no such
division between lower and higher laws can be valid. The social law or
mediating institution may of course be arbitrary and should not be taken
as a guarantee of final truth: it is an implicit recognition of this arbitrariness that licenses much of the chicanery and double-dealing in Edwin
O'Connor, for example. Yet though the law may be ironized and trans-
gressed against, it can never be confidently inverted, since any claim to
secular idealism or "natural" justice must itself be a doomed enterprise.
The law may be fundamentally inadequate, but it still operates as a
necessary bulwark against what Catholic thought conceives to be the less
reliable impulses of the individual human spirit. Writing of the Catholic
mind-set, William F. Lynch, S.J., talked of how this "imagination" often
"composes reality with irony and with ironic images" on account of its
assumption that all worldly and ethical positions must be relative rather
than absolute. Catholic faith, said Lynch, recognizes the inevitable gap
or disjunction between spiritual aspiration and worldly "reality," and it
flourishes by emphasizing this difference. Since no form of secular idealism or "prophetic authenticity" can be definitive or self-sufficient, every
abstract idea must be subject to the intrusions of an irony that "knows
how to de-absolutize things."[6]

Lynch's notion of irony can usefully illuminate some of the ideas
associated with Catholic conceptions of the politician. Whereas President
Eisenhower, according to Gore Vidal, entertained an "open disdain of
politics" and a "conviction that 'politician' was a dirty word," John F.
Kennedy tended to regard politics as an "honorable" profession and was
a "master" of the game.[7] For Eisenhower, essential values were to be
found in an abstract, idealized realm beyond the tawdry machinations
of politics – as Lynch put it, "The pure ought has no faith in anything
but the pure idea" – whereas in Vidal's understanding, at least, Kennedy
saw unfettered human idealism as a contradiction in terms. In the Catholic

5 Catherine L. Albanese, *America: Religions and Religion* (Belmont, Ca.: Wadsworth, 1981),
   p. 273.
6 William F. Lynch, S. J., *Images of Faith: An Exploration of the Ironic Imagination* (Notre
   Dame: Univ. of Notre Dame Press, 1973), pp. 83, 81, 102.
7 Gore Vidal, "President Kennedy," in *Homage to Daniel Shays: Collected Essays, 1952–
   1972* (New York: Random House, 1972), p. 93.

"analogical imagination," to use another of Lynch's phrases, angelic philanthropists and gangsters with dirty faces are mirror images of each other, bound together by theological analogy and separated only by the random chances of worldly fortune.[8] Conversant as he was with this idiom, Kennedy rarely elided the pragmatic and secular art of politics into a higher wisdom of moral perfection. Back in 1963, William V. Shannon wrote about how that millennial vision, handed down from Protestant and evangelical theologians to latter-day liberal idealists, seemed scarcely to impinge upon Kennedy's sensibility:

> More than he may realize... Kennedy has an approach to the funda-
> mentals of politics identical with Catholic teaching. Politics, the Church
> holds, is the search for justice. But since the kingdom of God is not of
> this world, heavenly perfection is not to be expected in politics....
> Perfection in politics, it has been said, is a Protestant vision.... An
> outlook and habits of mind that were real and natural for most liberals
> were unreal and unnatural for Kennedy.[9]

In Edwin O'Connor's novel *All in the Family* (1966) – a novel clearly influenced by the context of the Kennedys although equally clearly not a roman à clef – Phil Kinsella becomes increasingly disillusioned at the propensity of his brother Charles, a newly elected state governor, to compromise with the corrupt machinery of local government rather than attempt to purify it. Phil complains that Charles is becoming too interested in "politics itself: every high-minded, low-minded, statesmanlike ward-heeling second of it – he's crazy about it. He's found his natural habitat... that's why he keeps to all the rules of the game."[10]

In its extreme form, politics glides over any kind of moral purpose and turns into exactly this kind of "game," a sport with self-enclosed rules of its own. "Politics," said the Boston Catholic novelist George V. Higgins, "is a variable-sum game, just like the sports from which it draws so many of its metaphors."[11] William Kennedy's novel centered on Albany politics, *Billy Phelan's Greatest Game* (1978), is an example of how in the "Catholic" vernacular politics has a tendency to become an end in itself: for Phelan, his frequent games of pool and poker are simply another version of the games he plays with the Democratic party's urban machine. The novel's epigraph, from Johan Huizinga's *Homo Ludens* –

8 Lynch, *Images of Faith*, p. 106; William F. Lynch, *Christ and Apollo: The Dimensions of the Literary Imagination* (New York: Sheed and Ward, 1960), p. 133.
9 William V. Shannon, *The American Irish* (New York: Macmillan, 1963), pp. 402–3, 405.
10 Edwin O'Connor, *All in the Family* (Boston: Little, Brown and Co., 1966), p. 344. Subsequent page references are given in parentheses in the text.
11 George V. Higgins, *Style versus Substance: Boston, Kevin White, and the Politics of Illusion* (New York: Macmillan, 1984), p. 137.

"The great archetypal activities of human society are all permeated with play from the start" – attempts to universalize this phenomenon, but in William Kennedy's novels it should be seen as more particularly related to an ideology of transformed Catholicism. We discover here none of that weighty concern with affairs of state such as Anthony Trollope's novels discuss. In Trollope, political positions are usually identified explicitly with moral beliefs, whereas political operations in Kennedy's novels approximate more to a spirit of self-referential play.

We saw earlier how Jack Kerouac, himself an enthusiastic football player, remarked on how many Jesuit scholars were enamored of this all-American game. Moreover, Jay P. Dolan, in his work *The American Catholic Experience,* quoted a prefect of religion at Notre Dame as making extravagant claims for the larger significance of the football metaphor after Notre Dame had won the national championship in 1924:

> The world is beginning to realize the source of Notre Dame's brand of sportsmanship. The teamwork of a Notre Dame eleven is not inspired by the philosophy of Nietzsche, it has none of the earmarks of Schopenhauer or Kant... it is a red-blooded play of men full of hope, full of charity, of men who learn at the foot of the altar what it means to love one another, of men who believe that clean play can be offered as a prayer in honor of the Queen of Heaven.[12]

This harangue is interesting from a cultural point of view not only in its contempt for the philosophers of German romanticism but also in its emphasis upon what Gabriel Marcel called "heteronomy" rather than autonomy: the players on a football team are all dependent upon each other, just as in Catholic doctrine the quest for salvation is a communal, interdependent effort.[13] Equally significant is the way the prefect prioritized "play" as a self-fulfilling category in itself. In Catholic culture, the idea of "play" takes on ontological overtones because in the absence of conclusive moral authority or humanist idealism the spirit of play becomes a quintessential image of all human activity sub specie aeternitatis. Notre Dame's football players cannot actually achieve anything other than an arbitrary goal, just as a "goal" in football has no significance unless demarcated as such. Goalposts in themselves embody no profound moral purpose; nevertheless, in Catholic eyes, the process of the communal spirit of play that such goalposts bring about comes to constitute an image of salvation, so that the vacancy of the game's end result itself becomes unimportant. In the same way, the Catholic imagination rarely

12 Jay P. Dolan, *The American Catholic Experience: A History from Colonial Times to the Present* (Garden City: Doubleday, 1985), p. 391.
13 Gabriel Marcel, *Being and Having,* trans. Katherine Farrer (Westminster: Dacre Press, 1949), p. 167.

deludes itself that politics can ever finally accomplish any worldly goal, but it either recognizes these provisional and half-achieved goals as useful ends in themselves, or, like William Kennedy's Billy Phelan, it turns the very game of politics into an image of communal destiny. In this sense, the institutions of politics become a reflection of the Catholic church itself, where membership in the privileged *ecclesia* is a more certain route to (divine or human) preferment than the eccentricities of personal charisma or merit.

What we see in many "Catholic" novels, then, is a convergence of various impersonal systems that become analogical mirrors of each other as well as partial reflections of the legalistic structure of the Catholic church. In Edwin O'Connor's 1951 novel *The Oracle,* this system becomes that of the radio networks, as expertly manipulated by former sports journalist Christopher Usher. Usher's background in sports earns him barbed compliments from his father-in-law, who remarks with bitter sarcasm on how the fact that Usher "is of limited intelligence is not a drawback; to the contrary, it is a decided asset. He brings to every problem in statecraft the uncomplicated instincts of the sports reporter. All the world is a playing field."[14] Unlike the cantankerous Dr. Wrenn, however, Usher perceives this relinquishment of individual consciousness to be an unmitigated advantage. In Usher's eyes, the great boon of the sports system is that – as in the political system, the broadcasting system, and the theological system of the Catholic church – all possibility of self-determination becomes nullified; appropriately enough, Usher actually joins the Catholic church at one point during the novel. Usher's successful evasion of meritocracy here brings to mind a point made in 1967 by Gore Vidal, who said one of the most troubling aspects for Americans about the political machine established by the Kennedys' "Holy Family" was how it threatened the traditional self-reliant "belief that by working hard and being good one will deserve (and if fortunate, receive) promotion." In the Kennedy clan, as in the Catholic church, it was the fact of belonging rather than the merit of the individual soul that was the crucial distinction. In *The Sociology of Religion,* Max Weber defined this phenomenon as the Catholic notion of "institutional grace": salvation was to be obtained not so much by personal distinction as by membership in a corporate body vested with the control of divine favor.[15]

Transferred into a lower-class ethnic context, we can see this outlook already at work in the 1870s, when John Kelly assumed control of New

14 Edwin O'Connor, *The Oracle* (Boston: Little, Brown and Co., 1951), p. 21. Subsequent page references are given in parentheses in the text.
15 Vidal, "The Holy Family," in *Homage to Daniel Shays: Collected Essays,* p. 252; Max Weber, *The Sociology of Religion,* trans. Ephraim Fischoff (London: Methuen, 1965), p. 187.

York's Tammany Hall and, as Lawrence J. McCaffrey said, "consolidated a loosely structured feudal system into a centralized monarchy, very much in the image of his beloved Catholic church."[16] Appropriately enough, O'Connor's *The Last Hurrah* describes the Irish as "supplicants" for the favor of Mayor Skeffington (11). Daniel Moynihan attributed the tenacity of this Irish political system in eastern cities to its deep roots in "the social system of an Irish village," and it is true that the more legalistic aspects of Catholicism have become, especially in America, closely associated with Irish ethnic traditions.[17] Yet I would argue neither ethnicity nor sociology is in itself a sufficient explanation of why these patterns of elaborate systematization have preserved such a firm hold upon the American Catholic consciousness, and it is necessary also to be aware of the displaced theological context at work here.

In Weber's definition of institutional or "sacramental" grace, the burden of achieving salvation is, to a considerable extent, removed from any one individual person's shoulders. He or she is, said Weber, spared from "the necessity of developing an individual planned pattern of life based on ethical foundations. The sinner knows that he may always receive absolution by engaging in some occasional religious practice or by performing some religious rite." From this perspective, vice and virtue are not mutually exclusive opposites but should rather be seen as different aspects of the same cycle of sin and redemption. This is another angle on Aquinas's teaching that evil is not in essence evil but merely corrupt "through the goodness it lacks," although of course it is just this cast of mind that has caused unfriendly commentators to see in the Catholic sensibility not only duplicity but outright immorality.[18] Whereas Puritan cultures tend to believe that idealism and corruption, the soul and the body, are dualistically divided, Catholicism by contrast accepts corruption as a necessary fact of incarnated human life. For Bernie Morgan, Speaker of the Massachusetts House in George V. Higgins's novel *A Choice of Enemies* (1984), John F. Kennedy's friendships with Marilyn Monroe and the Mafia highlighted how the President was not only an enlightened liberal but also a Massachusetts crook, one of that "bunch of low-down dirty animals" who populate political life in Boston.[19] Like

---

16 Lawrence J. McCaffrey, *The Irish Diaspora in America* (Bloomington: Indiana Univ. Press, 1976), p. 140.
17 Nathan Glazer and Daniel Patrick Moynihan, *Beyond the Melting Pot: The Negroes, Puerto Ricans, Jews, Italians, and Irish of New York City* (Cambridge, Mass.: M.I.T. Press and Harvard Univ. Press, 1963), p. 226.
18 Weber, *The Sociology of Religion*, p. 188; Mary T. Clark, ed., *An Aquinas Reader* (Garden City: Doubleday–Image, 1972), p. 54.
19 George V. Higgins, *A Choice of Enemies* (New York: Knopf, 1984), p. 274.

the heroes of Higgins's own fictions, Kennedy is seen to have disaffiliated himself from unambiguous concepts of good and evil.

Coming back to the arguments of William F. Lynch, we can see how this is a classic case of Catholic irony at work: "the unexpected coexistence, to the point of identity, of certain contraries."[20] Just as transubstantiation ironically conjoins the disparate categories of spirit and matter, so, in the Catholic politician's secularized version of the church, good and evil, idealism and corruption, interpenetrate each other. It is not a question of one or the other, not a question of attempting to uncover and root out some dark evil that "really" resides at the heart of good, as in traditional Calvinist hermeneutics. Nor should these Catholic politicians necessarily be written off as amoral relativists – though that is a familiar enough American position, going back through Mark Twain's attacks on European statesmen in *The Innocents Abroad* and seen again in the perspective of more recent critics such as Joseph Blotner, who disparaged the politicians of *The Last Hurrah* as cynics for whom "a word such as 'evil' has little meaning."[21] Blotner ignored the fact that Skeffington sometimes employs his arts of duplicity to do unequivocal good, as when he tells the impoverished Gert that her late friend Kate had bequeathed money to her, thereby skillfully concealing his own part in the financial arrangements. But, more substantially, Blotner assumes, in the Enlightenment and Kantian manner, that integrity and corruption are mutually exclusive conceptions, that the ends can never justify the means.

Within American culture, the implications of this dualistic cast of mind – New World/Old World, idealism/corruption, soul/body – are very extensive. The various financial scandals associated with the papacy have never posed any serious internal threat to the authority of the Vatican – evil being in the Catholic experience merely a falling away from good – but the existence of bugging devices in a rival political party's headquarters proved to be an insuperable difficulty for a president in a country that has institutionally prided itself on a rhetorical idealism (of one kind or another) and has consequently needed to expel the taint of immorality from its purview. Although emanating from within an American idiom, Catholic irony has often functioned as a threat to the integrity of this rhetorical idealism. Like the heroes of Jack Kerouac, Catholic politicians in the novels of Edwin O'Connor and William Kennedy seem to carry with them an inherent elusiveness, a duplicity in that word's original sense of being doubled up, caught between two different worlds. This

---

20 Lynch, *Images of Faith*, p. 84.
21 Joseph Blotner, *The Modern American Political Novel, 1900–1960* (Austin: Univ. of Texas Press, 1966), p. 61.

duplicity may have derived originally from theological sources – the analogical interchange between heaven and earth – but in a more worldly context it comes to connote the ironic interplay between ends and means. Such duplicity finds what may be its natural home – or "objective correlative," as T. S. Eliot would have said – in these texts of crime and politics, whose distinguishing characteristic is duplicity, deception, the double identity.

Parallels between political and religious organizations are quite explicit in the novels of Edwin O'Connor, whose overt theme is the decline of Irish ethnic traditions in Boston – though this city is never named openly. In *The Last Hurrah,* Mayor Skeffington's old-fashioned party machine finds itself usurped by the slick media images and "unlooked-for plasticity" (282) of Kevin McCluskey's campaign, while in *The Edge of Sadness* (1961) Father Hugh Kennedy elegiacally witnesses the decline of the parish system. Religious parishes are represented as akin to political wards: once centers of community life, they now seem to be in irredeemable decline. Replacing these old local interests is the new global village of technology and the media, the universalized electronic community toward which radio commentator Christopher Usher aspires in *The Oracle* with his talks on "One World and Your World" (88). This global village is also the framework for *All in the Family,* where Irish-Americans nostalgic about their ancestral land need no longer dream sentimentally about Edenic green fields, being provided instead with frequent opportunities to board airplanes and match their fantasies with empirical reality.

Some critics have queried O'Connor's portrayal of the Irish emergence from ethnic ghettoes into acculturated affluence on the grounds that his novels lack sociological accuracy. His depiction of the demise of the Irish urban political machine was premature, protested Lawrence J. McCaffrey, pointing to the powerful networks subsequently established by Mayor Richard Daley in Chicago. In the same vein, Steven Erie has argued that the explanation for decline put forward by Jack Mangan in *The Last Hurrah* – how Roosevelt's New Deal destroyed the power of the old-time bosses by taking "the handouts out of the local hands" (374) – is of dubious historical accuracy.[22] But one cannot invalidate O'Connor's fiction on the grounds of social misrepresentation any more than one would veto Dickens's *Little Dorrit* by saying the Circumlocution Office is not a fair and accurate portrayal of the English civil service. It

22 McCaffrey, *The Irish Diaspora,* p. 161; Steven P. Erie, *Rainbow's End: Irish-Americans and the Dilemmas of Urban Machine Politics, 1840–1985* (Berkeley: Univ. of California Press, 1988), p. 223.

is true that O'Connor's texts have generally tended to be judged for their sociological verisimilitude, not least because they seem to embody the last hurrah of the conventional realist novel at a time when Barth and Pynchon were starting to get lost in their labyrinthine funhouses. Actually, though, O'Connor's "realism" is itself a tricksy illusion, a skillful *mise-en-abîme* created by a technique of presenting and then undermining fictional stereotypes so as to give the reader a (spurious) sense of greater authenticity, as in *The Edge of Sadness:*

> This ludicrous Disney-parson, provoking these electric responses: all right. Or rather, *not* all right, but at least expected. Any priest in any movie is almost by definition a parody. Which in a way is understandable enough. I don't think many people know very much about priests ... the ordinary simple matter of how priests live from day to day, how they fill in their idle hours – and those who do know aren't necessarily in Hollywood.[23]

O'Connor's deflationary style is clearly designed to give the reader a sense of heightened "realism." Yet this realism is implicit and psychological, not explicit and sociological, for what these texts discuss is not so much the "death of Irishness," as David Dillon suggested, but ways in which "Irishness" and Catholicism become redefined as interior, almost invisible but still powerful states of mind.[24] Although O'Connor himself continued to be a practicing Catholic throughout his life, his novels are not centered exclusively around manifestations of Catholicism as a literal system of belief; they also, more surreptitiously, chronicle the psychology of those who share Catholicism's cultural assumptions without sharing its theological premises.

In *The Last Hurrah*, for instance, Frank Skeffington lacks all sense of civic duty and brazenly regards politics as an end in itself. He is the Catholic political game player par excellence, a figure deemed "genuinely subversive" by a critic such as Anthony West, who found it abhorrent that Skeffington should perceive "mean vices" and "virtues" as altogether interchangeable. Writing in the *New Yorker*, West declared himself more in favor of "traditional New England Puritan ethics," a preference that makes visible the otherwise unacknowledged (and probably unconscious) ethnocentricity framing his critical notice.[25] Nevertheless, in *All in the Family*, a novel set in the same city as *The Last Hurrah*, duplicitous Charles Kinsella declares himself sympathetic to Skeffington's ingenious inter-

23 Edwin O'Connor, *The Edge of Sadness* (Boston: Little, Brown and Co., 1961), p. 105. Subsequent page references are given in parentheses in the text.
24 David Dillon, "Priests and Politicians: The Fiction of Edwin O'Connor," *Critique*, 16, no. 2 (1974), 108.
25 Anthony West, "When in Rome...," *New Yorker*, 11 Feb. 1956, pp. 123–4.

mingling of crime and politics. Skeffington, says Charles, "wasn't a crook at all. Or not much of one. By the standards of his time, that is: remember that those were the days of 'honest graft'" (181). Like Skeffington, Charles treats politics as an end in itself and abides by the rules of the game, cheerfully transforming his private identity into a double-edged public image to suit his political motives. Charles admits that he rakes in the Catholic vote because the Catholics know he is one of them, while also raking in the non-Catholic vote "because the others don't think I'm a very good one" (187). *All in the Family* altogether disproves Dillon's "death of Irishness" thesis by its insistence that subconscious traces of ethnic and religious loyalties linger long after one might have expected the brave new world of secular rationalism to have washed them away. Charles says he has listened to academics talking about how "the old antagonisms and prejudices are melting away in the face of a growing tolerance," but he declares this to be, in his experience, quite untrue: "The more you know them, and the closer you get to bedrock, the more you find that they still think and feel – and vote – precisely as their fathers and grandfathers did, and for pretty much the same reason. Or lack of reason" (367). This "lack of reason" is a pervasive theme in the novel: Charles's Irish-American wife, Marie, a "fashionable, sophisticated, extremely contemporary woman," is described as having "a stubborn, almost a peasant's, belief in her intuition" about what sex her baby will be (293).

Charles Kinsella's political duplicity is another expression of this residual Catholic sensibility, for the double-sided nature he presents to the world is itself a transformed version of Catholic doctrine, predicated upon an ironic imagination that, as William Lynch said, oscillates ambiguously between this world and the next. At any given time, nobody can quite tell which persona Charles is assuming, which level his language is functioning on; he displays a political elusiveness that might be understood as a worldly replication of theological irony. In a strictly religious sense, the Kinsellas may be only "token Catholics," as David Dillon argued; but it is Charles who takes up Catholic cultural conceptions of mankind's essential limitations and of the inextricable weaving together of good and evil, while his brother Phil would prefer an idealistic "moral crusade" (363) to clean up the city's institutionalized corruption.[26] Charles insists that politicians have to work with "living, breathing men" (364) – "whether you believe it or not," he says, "you have to work within the limitations they place upon you" (367) – and he is firmly of the opinion that utopian dreams are impracticable, that the kingdom of God is not of this world. One of the strengths of this novel, though, is that

26 Dillon, "Priests and Politicians," p. 118.

it does not heavily weight the argument on one side or the other: Charles's emphasis on human limitations is an idea we can trace back through J. F. Powers and other Catholic writers, while Phil's radical idealism would have qualified him for a place among the New England transcendentalists on Brook Farm. *All in the Family* is an excellent novel because it reveals how ethnic and religious determinants intersect in oblique and unpredictable ways with the political complexities of the contemporary world.

Compared with *All in the Family*, *The Last Hurrah* seems somewhat sentimental and parochial. Still, one aspect of the latter book, which is highlighted in John Ford's 1958 film version of the novel and given more prominence in O'Connor's later work, is the idea of vaudeville. Frank Skeffington is perturbed by the fact that his ne'er-do-well son, Francis, Jr., appears an "unkind mockery" of himself (17); Frank feels threatened by this materialization of analogical similitude whereby his individuality is grinningly compromised and reflected back to him. Skeffington has the same sensation when confronted with his rival, Charlie Hennessey: "Looking at Charlie in full flight was for Skeffington a little like looking into a mirror in a fun house" (204). This process of internal reflection can be seen as a correlative to the Catholic principle of visible analogy, through which disparate entities are drawn together within one universal bond of being. This is another example of an apparently neutral theme being intimately connected with a religious determinant, because the concomitant compromising of individual autonomy clears the way for that subversion of free will and undermining of human idealism that is a theme throughout O'Connor's texts. We see this same principle of burlesque at work in *All in the Family*, where Phil Kinsella vows never to appear with Charles on the same political platform because they "look too much alike. Or we remind people of each other, which comes to the same thing. Charles alone is fine; Charles with me is vaudeville. Comedy stuff" (203). Yet, despite Phil's strictures, this idea of comic similitude becomes in O'Connor some kind of structural principle and ontological necessity. In another small example of how human dignity here is mercilessly burlesqued by the crazy-mirror hall of analogy, Jean Kinsella casually mentions an "Italian cardinal who's always being embarrassed because he has a brother who's a midget" (248).

Just as in John Ford's films, these burlesque tendencies become associated with a recognition of the boundaries of human endeavor. At the beginning of his political career, Charles Kinsella complains of how "this gang of shanty clowns has been playing the city like a slot machine for years" (121), but by the end of the book he is taking a more relaxed and acquiescent attitude toward such turpitude, believing the city will always have "that extra little dimension of clownishness, of shabby corruption" (366). Again, the deflation of idealism is filtered through a "metaphysical" perspective. Charles may be a political realist, but as a cultural Catholic he is also tolerant toward what he conceives as the more venial weaknesses of the human spirit. The high-minded Phil Kinsella, on the other hand, strikes an appropriate match with a woman described by her in-laws as "la-di-da"; Phil's wife is too reminiscent for their tastes of "Episcopal bishops" (162). O'Connor remarked in a 1956 interview that Irish-American fiction had tended to be "depressed" and "sullen stuff," without sufficient humor; within his own texts, though, this humor functions not merely as entertainment but also as an aesthetic and philosophical principle designed to mock pretentiousness through imagery of internal analogy so as to bring the characters down to an immanent, earthly level.[27] This idea of burlesque becomes especially foregrounded in O'Connor's short 1964 novel I Was Dancing, where an aging Irish vaudeville star, Daniel Considine, runs up against his son, Tom, who is reluctant to take Daniel into his house in the time-honored Boston Irish manner. The anxiety experienced here by Tom Considine relates not so much to a dislike of his father's personality as to a fear of psychological displacement, an apprehension that he and his father will be diminished to parodic reflections of each other. In this sense, Tom and his wife fear their internal autonomy and independence might become compromised.

In The Edge of Sadness, however, similar intimations of displacement are eventually welcomed as a religious duty by the novel's central character, Father Kennedy. Marginalized by his age and alcoholism to a rundown parish on the outskirts of town, Kennedy finally refuses an invitation to return to the more prosperous and sociable St. Raymond's parish, where he used to work. For Kennedy, spiritual education involves coming to terms with this sense of ontological irony: "If you're a priest," he concludes, "to speak of belonging in this way makes no sense at all" (427). The "edge of sadness" in the novel remains necessarily amorphous, because it connotes what Kennedy conceives as a necessary absence of plenitude within the earthly condition, the fact that no kind of human idealism can ever quite be fulfilled. "Some element of happiness was missing," Kennedy muses to himself of one of his relatives. "The edge of sadness was visible; it was clear that she hadn't found . . . what?" (407). The point is that O'Connor is not simply an anthropologist charting the decline of parochial or ethnic systems of administration; he is also describing the inevitable moods of melancholy experienced by those who imagine themselves, consciously or not, to be voyagers en route from this world to the next. O'Connor's elegiac strain in The Edge of Sadness thus has a theological as well as a sociological rationale. The novel's shifts

27 Lewis Nichols, "Talk with Mr. O'Connor," New York Times Book Review, 5 Feb. 1956, p. 19.

in conceptual and geographical perspective – notably to the Arizona desert, where Kennedy's "steady strides forward" seem to be like "the steps of an ant up the side of a mountain" (142) – testify to this demarcated and imperfect human condition where, says the narrator, "as we are, we can see, but only to the corner; we cannot begin to see the whole design" (129).

The Edge of Sadness is in many ways a text of classic Christian paradox and martyrology: worldly defeat becomes a spiritual triumph. Edmund Wilson, who was a great admirer of O'Connor's, preferred this novel to *The Last Hurrah,* and certainly *The Edge of Sadness* has more depth and complexity than the earlier book – although it is true, as Roger Dooley noted, that the general mediocrity in O'Connor's portrayal of female characters is highlighted here.[28] *All in the Family,* however, seems to me O'Connor's best work: the scope is wider, the psychological tensions analyzed more subtly, the overall tone more cognizant of cultural incongruities and differences. John Kenneth Galbraith called O'Connor "a writer of first rate importance" and one of the few American authors to master the art of the political novel, and it may be that O'Connor has been undervalued (in academic circles, at least) since his early death in 1968 precisely because this Catholic ideology of theological irony and criminal politics is inimical to that more established "world elsewhere" American idiom.[29] In the 1960s, this romanticism reworked itself into the transformed pastoral of (utopian or dystopian) science fiction, or the new frontier spirit of the experimental novel, as manifested for example in John Barth's ceaseless forays onto lexical playfields and his "very American disinclination to accept any shapes as fixed and final," as Tony Tanner put it.[30] It is the old American irony of conventional protest come round again: nothing is more familiar in American culture than Ezra Pound's injunction to "make it new," nothing more predictable than "pioneering" fiction, nothing less conventional than conventionality. This may help to explain why the (socially and aesthetically) conventional surfaces of O'Connor's texts have met with so much critical scorn. Leslie Fiedler, for instance, complained that the political world in O'Connor appears "empty" and "meaningless" because his work is too mundane and obvious, lacking "complex inwardness" and "the authority of ter-

---

28 Edmund Wilson, "'Baldini': A Memoir and a Collaboration," in *The Best and the Last of Edwin O'Connor,* ed. Arthur Schlesinger, Jr. (Boston: Little, Brown and Co., 1970), p. 346; Roger Dooley, "The Womanless World of Edwin O'Connor," *Saturday Review,* 21 Mar. 1964, pp. 34–6.
29 Galbraith made this statement in a letter to Hugh Rank. See Hugh Rank, *Edwin O'Connor* (New York: Twayne, 1974), p. 86.
30 Tony Tanner, *City of Words: American Fiction 1950–1970* (New York: Harper and Row, 1971), p. 231.

ror."[31] The "authority of terror" may be all very well, and, as Fiedler said, many classic American authors have dealt with this area expertly. But simply to equate authenticity with terror is nothing more than a rhetorical strategy, an unwarranted aggrandizement of self-induced alienation and withdrawal from society into an all-encompassing artistic and intellectual norm.

One heir of Edwin O'Connor is George V. Higgins, another Catholic writer whose novels rotate upon the axis of politics and crime in the city of Boston. Though Higgins's work is less overtly directed toward religion than O'Connor's, a social framework of parochial schools, convents, and Catholic charities forms the backcloth to Higgins's fiction. For Higgins, as for O'Connor, politics and crime are closely interlinked, making up self-defining and self-perpetuating systems. Nevertheless, Higgins said in a 1987 interview that he much disliked the label "crime writer": "It infuriates me. I've never written a crime novel. Crime novels are novels about crime. I write novels about characters and what happens in their lives."[32] Higgins's point is that crime cannot be circumscribed within the safe confines of a detective novel; it is, on the contrary, a ubiquitous phenomenon compromising us all. At the end of *The Friends of Eddie Coyle* (1971), lawyer Foster Clark meditates upon the perpetual cycle of crime and punishment, the fact that wrongdoing seems to be ineradicable: "Is there any end to this shit? Does anything ever change in this racket?"[33] The answer, of course, is that no great good utopian place is available. Like O'Connor, Higgins conceives the kingdom of God to be not of this world.

But if sin is inevitable, it is also, for Higgins, a relativistic rather than essentialist construction. In *Eddie Coyle,* policemen and villains appear more or less interchangeable. Even the priests are corrupt: "I bet," says gunrunner Jackie Brown, "if I was to go down to the Shrine there and go to confession I'd get three Hail Marys and the priest'd ask me confidentially if I could get him something light he could carry under his coat" (8). Again, evil is not the Manichaean opposite of good, but a temporary lapse to be assuaged with a swift penance: in *Impostors* (1985), one of the murderers confides to a friend his belief that "there is forgiveness, if you ask for it," adding drolly "I hope I am right, you know,

31 Leslie Fiedler, "Some Footnotes on the Fiction of '56," *The Reporter,* 13 Dec. 1956, pp. 45–6.
32 Melvyn Bragg, "George V. Higgins," *The South Bank Show,* London Weekend Television, 5 Apr. 1987.
33 George V. Higgins, *The Friends of Eddie Coyle* (New York: Knopf, 1972), p. 183. Subsequent page references are given in parentheses in the text.

because I'm going to have to ask."[34] Similarly, for the "engaging rogue" Harry Mapes in *Penance for Jerry Kennedy* (1985), prison is seen not as a deep social shame but simply "a hazard of his occupation, which is burglary."[35] To some extent, this representation of policemen and criminals as on opposite sides of the same game can be related to the circumstances of an ethnic heritage: in Higgins, the Irish-American law enforcers realize – subconsciously, perhaps – that what they have in common with Irish-American law breakers is just as significant as the differences between them. Nevertheless, a barely suppressed theological context is also relevant here: policemen, lawyers, judges, and priests are but the mirror images of thieves, swindlers, and murderers. Higgins's legal machine, like Edwin O'Connor's political machine, catches up everyone within its toils, so that whether you are on the right or the wrong side of the line seems to be a matter of luck rather than individual merit. "In my estimation," said Higgins in 1987 – defending himself against the supposed "immorality" of his stories – "a man who has options in his life about whether to be dishonest or corrupt and who takes the paths of wickedness is more responsible for what the consequences of his behavior are than someone who had no choice."[36] Yet in Higgins's fiction, nobody does seem to have any choice. Pressurized by the brutal material demands of urban life, Jerry Kennedy would – as his friend Peter Cooper says – "defend Adolf Hitler if he came in with the cash" (89). The Catholic principle of analogical similitude is exaggerated here so that nearly all distinctions between good and evil become erased. It is not, of course, that Higgins is writing from an official "Catholic" point of view; but his work transforms and distorts this culture of Catholicism to produce fictional angles and ideologies that would not otherwise have materialized.

These savage cycles of greed, money, and self-preservation in Higgins's texts not only form an implicit critique of the liberal hegemonies institutionalized in Massachusetts academic and political life, but also involve the reader in an uneasy complicity with the activities represented. As Glenn V. Most wrote of Elmore Leonard, these postmodernist novels of crime and punishment hold up a looking glass to the reader's moral complacency and reflect back to us "splitting images of ourselves. . . . What reason do we have to believe that our own capacity for evil will be, not exacerbated, but purged by these novels?"[37] Higgins, like Leon-

34 George V. Higgins, *Impostors* (New York: Henry Holt, 1985), p. 208.
35 George V. Higgins, *Penance for Jerry Kennedy* (New York: Knopf, 1985), p. 7. Subsequent page references are given in parentheses in the text.
36 "George V. Higgins," *The South Bank Show*.
37 Glenn V. Most, "Elmore Leonard: Splitting Images," in *The Sleuth and the Scholar:*

ard, abolishes any reassuring distance between the reader and the various illicit activities described. No longer can the reader experience a comfortably detached ethical superiority: "It is," said Higgins in his description of the criminality of Richard Nixon, "what abashes all of us . . . Original Sin."[38] Far from being confined to W. H. Auden's "guilty vicarage," where the old-fashioned detective novel could engender a cosy catharsis by siphoning off an amorphous sense of evil through its restitution of social order, Higgins's novels deal with a world where sin can never be closed down. Auden welcomed the fact that by solving mysteries Sherlock Holmes could shrive communal guilt and so indulge our "fantasy of being restored to the Garden of Eden"; but in Higgins no such final solutions are possible, for – as in *Eddie Coyle* – the cycles of corruption will continue to revolve indefinitely.[39]

There are, then, several pressures that help to account for the lack of closure in Higgins's fiction. One is the context of postmodernism, whose labyrinthine style has produced what Stefano Tani has called the "anti-detective" novels of Thomas Pynchon, Jorge Luis Borges, and Umberto Eco, where, instead of "the detective as central and ordering character," we find "the decentering and chaotic admission of mystery, of nonsolution."[40] Another context is that of the American frontier novel, the James Fenimore Cooper paradigm, where upright pioneers were shadowed by Indians rather more closely than they might have liked and where white law tends to be represented as a provisional rather than immutable concept. This frontier tradition modulates into the hard-boiled genre of Raymond Chandler, whom Auden specifically excluded from his guilty vicarage on the grounds that Chandler's "powerful but extremely depressing books" deal with evil in a less tangible, more all-pervasive sense.[41] However, in a 1972 essay "The Private Detective as Illegal Hero," Higgins took exception to this Chandleresque idea of the "Private Eye" or "Western Hero" reacting to the chaos of the urban mean streets by establishing a vigilante order of his own. Paying special attention to Don Siegel's 1971 film *Dirty Harry*, where Clint Eastwood eventually throws away his police badge in exasperation at the bureaucratic restrictions placed upon his actions by the legal machinery of the

Origins, Evolution, and Current Trends in Detective Fiction (New York: Greenwood Press, 1988), p. 109.

38 George V. Higgins, *The Friends of Richard Nixon* (Boston: Little, Brown and Co., 1975), p. 277.

39 W. H. Auden, "The Guilty Vicarage," in *The Dyer's Hand and Other Essays* (London: Faber, 1975), p. 158.

40 Stefano Tani, *The Doomed Detective: The Contribution of the Detective Novel to Postmodern American and Italian Fiction* (Carbondale: Southern Illinois Univ. Press, 1984), p. 40.

41 Auden, "The Guilty Vicarage," p. 151.

justice system, Higgins noted that "Dirty Harry hates evil. . . . But Dirty Harry is a jerk." Like a crazed fundamentalist preacher, Eastwood's Harry Callahan takes it upon himself to root out (what he sees as) evil, indulging in several bouts of psychopathic violence in order to further this "moral" purpose. Dirty Harry feeds into American fantasies about the power of individual freedom, with its traditional dislike of cumbersome legal procedures and "the rules of Due Process"; but, said Higgins, Harry Callahan's anarchic romanticism embodies greater dangers of its own.[42]

Higgins's position here is that while the processes of law may be imperfect, they are greatly preferable to granting unfettered license to the "wild purist," that individualistic hero who, said William Ruehlman, "is entitled to mete out justice because he is *already* pure."[43] This mythological purity of the cowboy or private eye is a powerful idea in American popular culture, but it is a self-willed and self-defined purity that Higgins, as a Catholic legalist, instinctively dislikes. Higgins's theology of imperfection disallows the antinomian impulses of American romanticism and consequently rejects the possibility of individual purity. It is this philosophical skepticism that provides another crucial context for the lack of narrative closure: as Higgins writes out of a Catholic sense of corruption as unending and inevitable, his texts preclude the appearance of any kind of idealistic Dirty Harry who might take it upon himself to clean the world up. According to Walker Percy, G. K. Chesterton, and other Catholic writers, the really dangerous people are not the petty villains but the human perfectionists. Auden in "The Guilty Vicarage" cannily noted that the detective story in its traditional form "has flourished most in predominantly Protestant countries," for the dream of reconstituting Eden has never made a great impression upon Catholic sensibilities.[44]

This lack of trust in human perfectibility reworks itself in Higgins's nonfiction as a radical critique of liberal idealism. *The Friends of Richard Nixon* (1975) chronicles Higgins's astonishment at what he alleges to be public hypocrisy over Watergate. Higgins's line is that while Nixon was certainly a criminal, so was (and is) everybody else, including those who assailed the president. "The tension between what we know about viciousness, and what we would prefer to believe about human nature, is constant," says Higgins, and from this perspective Nixon becomes a scapegoat upon which the public projects its own fear of being inextric-

42 George V. Higgins, "The Private Detective as Illegal Hero," *Esquire*, Dec. 1972, pp. 350–1.
43 William Ruehlman, *Saint with a Gun: The Unlawful American Private Eye* (New York: New York Univ. Press, 1974), pp. 145, 129.
44 Auden, "The Guilty Vicarage," p. 151.

ably caught up within a world of "Original Sin."[45] "Fantasy" is one of Higgins's favorite words in this book, and Higgins relates Nixon's predicament to the continual disjunction within United States culture between idealistic vision and hard, objective fact. In the courtroom, for instance, Higgins finds that judges are reticent about handing out more lenient sentences to those who admit their crimes because the idealism of the system insists there should be no additional penalty imposed for exertion of the constitutional right to a trial. The judges are obliged to suppress their scruples, however, "because the idealism doesn't take into account the fact that the system erected upon it would break down in short order if everyone insisted upon that privilege . . . our system of law enforcement is so determinedly idealistic in formal terms that it is gravely inefficient in practice." The author goes on to relate this high-mindedness to the erroneously abstract notions of the Founding Fathers, whose theoretical spirit induced them to invent America as: "a government of laws, not of men – when in fact we are a nation, like every other, which is governed by men who either obey the law in its governance, or do not. And we are wedded to it. It's unrealistic, naive, impractical, and it contravenes every aspect of human experience that we know about."[46]

Higgins distances himself here from all suggestions of the manifest destiny or pastoral originality of the United States by asserting that America is only "a nation, like every other." In a 1987 interview, Higgins again registered his disapproval of this Enlightenment idea, implicit in the American Constitution, "that mankind is infinitely perfectible," either by nature or by government.[47] Higgins's Catholic theology of imperfection deconstructs the traditional view of American literature and culture as a city on a hill, a brave new world of natural freedom; on the contrary, Higgins – like Powers, John O'Hara, and other Catholic authors – believes that the social and psychological tensions within American life are essentially the same as those anywhere else. In the late nineteenth century, the predominant fear of anti-Catholic groups revolved around how the papists were planning to requisition the United States as part of their global empire, and though writers like O'Hara, O'Connor, and Higgins have no plans to send in the troops, we can see that this threat of globalism now poses itself in a more intangible, cultural manner. Higgins divests America of its philosophical uniqueness and instead conscripts "nature's nation" into a universal church of self-interest and corruption.

For Higgins, then, politics and the law become images of those on-

45 Higgins, *The Friends of Richard Nixon,* pp. 103, 277.
46 Ibid., pp. 32, 103, 278.
47 "George V. Higgins," *The South Bank Show.*

tological restrictions circumscribing the human spirit. In *The Judgment of Deke Hunter* (1976), the policeman talks of life as resembling a team game: "Everything," says Hunter, "almost everything you're ever gonna do in this life, is going to be that you got one job to do and there's another guy next to you that's got the next job to do."[48] In this sense, the political and legal games in Higgins's texts, which marginalize individual heroes and foreground instead the complex processes of jurisdiction, highlight a Catholic notion of communal and interdependent human destiny. This is the same tendency toward systematization of various kinds that we saw in Edwin O'Connor. In party political terms, Higgins's rejection of liberal idealism places him firmly in the right-wing, Republican camp: in *Style Versus Substance,* his 1984 nonfiction account of Boston politics, Higgins rails against Harvard, "modern academic liberalism," child psychology, and notions of "abstract social justice" with all the ferocity of a hard-nosed Boston cop. In his eyes, all this misplaced idealism can be traced back, once again, to the baleful influence of the Puritans, with their clear-cut division between the forces of light and the forces of darkness: "The Puritans are all dead now, but the Commonwealth they founded to this day venerates their example by the practice of a secular form of their infuriating code and calls it *liberalism*."[49] Such radical skepticism finds its way into Higgins's novels as well. In *A Choice of Enemies,* veteran Massachusetts politician Bernie Morgan inveighs against "professors from the universities" who went to "one of them prep places" and consequently think the government is run along the lines of Plato's *Republic;* while in *Impostors,* Connie Gates nepotistically obtains a job for which she is ill-qualified and says to herself: "Welcome to the real world, kiddo" (108).[50] The author seems to take delight in how the pretensions of the high-minded are trumped by the exigencies of the low-minded.

It should be emphasized that Higgins's burlesque of social idealism is often very funny. Indeed, the pleasure of his writing derives primarily from this style of comic sadism rather than from the pertinency of any of the philosophical views espoused in these texts. Like Sade, Higgins reduces human character to an externalized, objectified entity – a machine of sexual and financial desires – and uses this representation as a basis for exploding the institutionalized hypocrisies upon which social custom is based. Governor Tierney's high-mindedness in *A Choice of Enemies* is peremptorily overturned by Frank Costello's sardonic observation that

48 George V. Higgins, *The Judgment of Deke Hunter* (Boston: Little, Brown and Co., 1976), p. 100. Subsequent page references are given in parentheses in the text.
49 Higgins, *Style versus Substance,* pp. 121, 123–4.
50 Higgins, *A Choice of Enemies,* pp. 274–5. Subsequent page references are given in parentheses in the text.

Tierney "can rattle off that social justice shit like he was Bing Crosby rolling into 'White Christmas,'" though "he hasn't got the foggiest idea of how on earth to do it" (44). In *Penance for Jerry Kennedy*, the lawyer Kennedy wearily notes how Judge Luther Dawes's postures of moral authority derive basically from a love of entertaining his audience and creating stagey monologues for the television evening news. Dawes, a "patrician Yankee" (8) whose Christian name "Luther" is also significant, attempts to aggrandize and objectify his ethical authority; but, as in Sade, this authority is exposed as a self-interested phenomenon, pleasing only himself.

Such skepticism reinforces Higgins's textual analogies between judges and criminals, lawyers and villains. In the eyes of "God," Luther Dawes is as bad as Harry Mapes; it is only through the arbitrary and provisional system of human justice that Dawes sits on the bench while Mapes stands convicted. Life is not a question of good and evil but of winners and losers, of the luck needed to come out on top. *Penance* features frequent references to the Boston Red Sox, and, as in O'Connor, the idea of the game takes on in Higgins a metaphysical significance. To be happy is not to be good, but to be a winner, to be rich. It is true there are occasional rumblings of class or underdog discontent, as in *Deke Hunter* when Shanley says petty thieves get fifteen years in prison for stealing a hundred dollars with a gun while more sociable types get "an apology from the Judge" for stealing a million dollars without one (255). Nevertheless, the legal system, even though arbitrary, is presented as a regrettable, imperfect necessity. There is none of the Sadeian revolutionary fervor in Higgins; the social alternative, in his mind, is not the fall of the Bastille but the monomania of Dirty Harry. Given the limitations of the human project, the best Jerry Kennedy can muster is not to confuse worldly fortune with ultimate ethical value. While frequently reminding "God about the necessity of luck" in *Kennedy for the Defense* (1980), the lawyer nevertheless acknowledges that he doesn't "like people who were lucky and decided it was talent."[51] This, of course, is a clear-cut inversion of Calvinist ideology, where earthly success was taken to be a sure sign of divine favor.

This assiduous materialism in Higgins's novels is another version of the Catholic concern for immanence rather than transcendence; still, it cannot quite conceal a lurking sense of loss throughout his work. "Miracles don't happen anymore," says Kennedy's wife Mack in *Penance* (35), a sentiment echoed later in the same novel by Lou Schwartz: "Miracles

51 George V. Higgins, *Kennedy for the Defense* (New York: Knopf, 1980), pp. 41, 87. Subsequent page references are given in parentheses in the text.

I don't expect. I'm not a Catholic" (158). Yet, in both cases, the implication is that these characters would rather welcome some agent of divine grace to bail them out of the squalid merry-go-round of corporeal greed they see around them. In keeping with this tone of loss and disillusionment, one of the noticeable things about Higgins's work is that his dramatic climaxes actually work as understated anticlimaxes. In *Kennedy for the Defense,* for example, Jerry and his wife celebrate a major legal victory by taking their daughter to a "ski sale at the South Shore Plaza" (225). In *Impostors,* Mark Baldwin reacts to his ex-lover's suicide by assuming a detached and dismissive tone: "the only sensible thing to do," he says, "is cut your losses" and not worry about the past (350). These texts present a determinedly secular quality, a brutal concentration upon the ordinary, a rejection of hyperbolic emotion, qualities that in fact reverse the reader's expectations of what would normally happen in scenes like these. Subjective ecstasies of grief or delight are suppressed in favor of concentration upon the external processes of the worldly machine, where nothing seems to come as a surprise. It is as if Higgins's characters know their human selves are not substantial enough, in a traditional humanist sense, for individual emotions to contain a great deal of significance.

Yet Jerry Kennedy describes his father as a devout Catholic, a Knight of Columbus, and he claims that he himself left the church only out of displeasure at its stand on birth control. In *Penance,* Kennedy seems to feel that some form of religious contrition might bring to his world that sense of cohesion it so evidently lacks. At the end of this novel, Kennedy's wife Mack suggests that the idea of God wanting them to make peace with him "would explain a lot of things that I don't understand" (321), while the lawyer himself is advised by his Irish friend Mike Curran to seek out a priest and receive the sacrament of penance. Just as Jerry Kennedy searches for the divine father he has lost, so the inchoate nature of Higgins's postmodernist fiction may be covertly searching for some kind of authority that might lend it a sense of textual order and coherence. Despite the hardheaded surfaces of Higgins's narratives, there lurks here an uncertain, residual element of Catholic "grace" against which his savage materialism is played off in dialogical rebellion, a rebellion that – as in Bakhtin's model of dialogics – does not foreclose the possibility of continued interaction between sacramental and demystified spheres. Although reacting against the ghost of Catholicism, Higgins's fiction ironically works that specter into the subtext of its secular world.

"I believe what I was taught in my childhood religious classes," said Higgins in his 1987 interview with Melvyn Bragg: "I do not think we were put upon this earth to be happy. The best that we can possibly do is to be content and sometimes amused."[52] If we were pursuing John Tracy Ellis's line about the "anti-intellectualism" of American Catholic writers and thinkers, then Higgins might figure prominently in that category; the materialism and social conservatism within his texts evidently preclude that association between the idea of an "intellectual" and the business of being "engaged in a quest," such as Thomas F. O'Dea and other prominent Catholics of the 1950s talked about.[53] Higgins's novels are hardly quests, and yet their apparent antiintellectualism is based not upon bovine stupidity, but upon – whether we happen to agree with these ideas or not – a logical series of philosophical and quasi-theological propositions about man's place in the world. Thus Higgins interrogates this banal dualism of intellectual against antiintellectual, just as he rejects the Puritans' dualism of good against evil. As he wrote in *Style and Substance,* it "is the vicious aspect of the public orthodoxy which requires candidates to profess moral, ethical, and intellectual perfection; it implies that the alternative is utter degradation."[54] For Higgins, by contrast, nothing is ever pure white or pure black. Like Edwin O'Connor, Higgins evades this dualistic mentality by showing how his criminals and politicians are analogical reflections of each other, two halves of the same package. Yet even while mocking and deconstructing the American system of government, Higgins's heroes choose to stay inside its boundaries; like O'Connor's Charles Kinsella, or indeed like Fitzgerald's Gatsby, Jerry Kennedy opts to play the game according to the rules. This produces in Higgins's texts that ironic bifurcation so characteristic of American Catholic fiction, whereby the protagonists are inside and outside the system at one and the same time.

The works of William Kennedy again focus upon one particular community, though in this case the *ecclesia* is not Boston but Albany, New York. Whereas Catholicism in Higgins carries an enigmatic psychological power that threatens his characters' doggedly materialistic interests, Catholicism in Kennedy has expired as a literal system of belief but has been reborn, in postmodernist fashion, as a self-subverting cultural fiction. Kennedy has talked of how he has a "feeling for Catholicism" not as religious practice but "as ritual, as spiritual history, as metaphor."[55] Consequently, images from liturgical sources recur frequently in Kennedy's texts. Take an example from his 1969 novel, *The Ink Truck:*

52 "George V. Higgins," *The South Bank Show.*
53 Thomas F. O'Dea, *American Catholic Dilemma: An Inquiry into the Intellectual Life* (New York: Sheed and Ward, 1958), p. 112.
54 Higgins, *Style versus Substance,* pp. 21–2.
55 Tony Gould, "In the Underworld: An Interview with William Kennedy," BBC Radio 3, 21 Sept. 1986.

"When Bailey first stepped aboard the ancient trolley, clad in the formless robes of his hopeless faith (not a conventional faith, of course; religion was his ho-ho; but he enjoyed the hair-shirt quality of the robe's inner lining, enjoyed its itch, its tickle)."[56] Whereas Steinbeck's *In Dubious Battle* draws upon images of martyrdom in an effort realistically to represent the anguish of a California fruit pickers' strike, in this journalists' strike of *The Ink Truck* torture and martyrdom are conditions that can be requisitioned only with a knowing irony. Kennedy reinvents Albany's Catholic landscape as a mythic construction, a self-conscious fable, like the cinematic projections of John Ford's Ireland or Martin Scorsese's Little Italy.

This ambiguity does not, of course, annul the fictional significance of Kennedy's Catholic culture. Announcing quizzically in 1986 that "I am not Irish but I am," Kennedy went on to claim: "There's a particular quality of appreciation of that heritage as you grow older; you realize that you may like German music but you're not German, you *are* Irish."[57] One sign of this celebration of his Irish (Catholic) rather than German (Protestant) heritage manifests itself in *The Ink Truck,* when Bailey's girlfriend, Irma, symbolically kicks a pile of books by idealist philosophers off the library truck while she and Bailey are making love. Plato, Spinoza, Descartes, Schopenhauer, Sartre, and "Emerson, the transcendentalist" – all inkmongers of dualism and sublimation – are brought low by the immanent immediacy of human passion (198). Spinoza makes a return appearance in *Billy Phelan's Greatest Game,* but in an equally deflationary context, as he, Plutarch, Schubert, and Cardinal Wolsey are counted by Martin Phelan as the great "nipple fetishists of history."[58] Again, we witness the collapse of high-minded idealism: in *Ironweed* (1983), Francis Phelan's "most familiar notion" is "the desire not to aspire," the rejection of what he sees as Protestant shibboleths like individualism and the natural self in favor of acquiescence in laws laid down by God or fate.[59] Kennedy said in 1983 that one of the reasons his creative energies have become so intertwined with the historical city of Albany is that Albany's "political machine" used to produce a "kind of controlled environment" where "the individual became a totally subordinate figure whose freedom was very much in question." In this light, we can see how in Kennedy's texts the political world of Albany becomes

56 William Kennedy, *The Ink Truck* (New York: Viking, 1984), p. 211. Subsequent page references are given in the text.

57 Gould, "In the Underworld."

58 William Kennedy, *Billy Phelan's Greatest Game* (New York: Viking, 1978), p. 189. Subsequent page references are given in the text.

59 William Kennedy, *Ironweed* (New York: Viking, 1983), p. 75. Subsequent page references are given in the text.

a metaphor for a characteristically Catholic withdrawal from subjectivity. Kennedy works instead with an "experience of human limitation" that Flannery O'Connor postulated as "the basic experience of everyone."[60]

Within this Irish ethnic world of Albany, all abstract notions of "justice" become interrogated and relativized. Kennedy's characters, like those of Higgins, place little trust in American ideals founded upon the principles of the eighteenth-century Enlightenment. In Albany, said Kennedy, "What was immoral was to be out of office, and out of a job."[61] In his nonfictional account, O Albany! (1983), he tells of a police captain being upbraided by his wife for refusing the profits of corruption: "'Who are you,' she howled, 'not to take a bribe?'"[62] Money and corruption appear as the great levelers, concrete embodiments of that impulse toward burlesque that subverts the pretensions of human pomp and dignity. In Albany, everybody is on the same level, part of the merry-go-round of an urban political machine where gambling and corruption have become institutionalized as a way of life. In a 1986 interview, Kennedy talked of the kindred moralities of the politician and the gangster, both "very pragmatic," and he went on to assert more specifically that the mindsets of Dan O'Connell – longtime boss of the Albany Democrats – and of notorious Albany criminal Jack "Legs" Diamond were just about interchangeable.[63] For these ruffians, as for Edwin O'Connor's Frank Skeffington, the concept of secular idealism was well-nigh meaningless.

Here again we see at work the Catholic principle of materialized analogy and similitude. We find in Kennedy's texts the eradication from both politics and crime of any overarching ethical significance and the reconstitution of these systems as mirror images of each other, systems organized purely along worldly and self-referential lines, like a sport or game. Besides the affiliation between politics and sport in Billy Phelan's Greatest Game, we also learn in Legs (1975) that Jack Diamond is an aficionado of bowling and miniature golf, pastimes that are represented as parallels to his professional criminal activities. Diamond, we are told, was "one of the truly new American Irishmen of his day; Horatio Alger out of Finn McCool and Jesse James, shaping the dream that you could

60 Larry McCaffrey and Sinda Gregory, eds., Alive and Writing: Interviews with Some American Authors of the 1980s (Urbana: Univ. of Illinois Press, 1987), p. 158; Flannery O'Connor, "The Teaching of Literature," in Mystery and Manners: Occasional Prose, ed. Sally and Robert Fitzgerald (New York: Farrar, Straus and Giroux, 1969), p. 131.
61 Gould, "In the Underworld."
62 William Kennedy, O Albany! (New York: Viking, 1983), p. 300. Subsequent page references are given in parentheses in the text.
63 Gould, "In the Underworld."

grow up in America and shoot your way to glory and riches."[64] Like the Great Gatsby, Diamond imitates Alger's rise to success; but again it is a parodic imitation, for Diamond participates playfully in the American rags-to-riches myth, celebrating his accumulation of wealth but refusing to invest this triumph with the moral legacy demanded by Alger's Protestant idiom. For Calvinists, material wealth was a sign of God's favor; for Alger, a sign of moral virtue; but for Legs Diamond, it is a sign merely of brilliant technique and his superb manipulation of the political and criminal underworld in Albany. The narrator in *Legs* talks of Diamond as a student of the gangster genre, including *Gatsby,* and in fact he goes on to chronicle a meeting between Diamond and Scott Fitzgerald on board a transatlantic liner in 1926. (Kennedy said later this reference was an intertextual acknowledgment of the way he was using *Gatsby* as "a conscious model" when writing *Legs.*)[65] The shipboard encounter is a highly appropriate one, for Gatsby and Diamond both work out their careers as ambivalent parodies of the American Dream, a situation symbolically reinforced here by the narrative account of Diamond's involvement with Joe Delaney's "Parody Club," a saloon opened in Albany in 1894 (261). As is customary in Kennedy's texts, the historical landscape becomes "magically" metamorphosed into a metaphorical one.

At the time of his trial, Legs Diamond is described by a sympathetic nun as "one of the most devout Catholic children she has ever known" (283); indeed, Diamond still carries a rosary even when executing his nefarious deeds later in life. While evading the police by taking a trip to Germany, the gangster is saluted by a German playwright, Weissberg, for his success in embodying the Nietzschean ideal of moving beyond good and evil to exist in a world of pure will. Weissberg's adulation is, however, rewarded merely by a bullet in the foot from Diamond's gun, for Kennedy's hero has no interest in Weissberg's romantic formula. On the contrary, he cherishes the dark energy of transgression, loves ideas of "furtiveness" and "wickedness" (68), actively courts the evil that would assure him of self-immolation and death. "Jack failed thoroughly as a hypocrite," the narrator tells us. "He was a liar, of course, a perjurer, all of that, but he was also a venal man of integrity, for he never ceased to renew his vulnerability to punishment, death, and damnation" (118). As in Genet, villainy becomes a paradoxical image of sanctity, for a villain cognizant of his own corruption can never fall into the sin of complacent human pride. Simple morality belongs to a world of self-

---

64 William Kennedy, *Legs* (New York: Coward, McCann and Geoghegan, 1975), p. 13. Subsequent page references are given in parentheses in the text.
65 McCaffrey and Gregory, *Alive and Writing,* p. 167.

important secular idealism Diamond has no truck with. Marcus Gorman, Diamond's attorney, who is the narrative voice of this novel, talks of how he is "bored by people who keep returning life to a moral plane, as if we were reducible, now, to some Biblical concept or its opposite." Gorman wants to "get off the moral gold standard," as he puts it (285), and he perceives in Diamond a glorious demonic power that seems to render social ethics redundant; Diamond's *élan vital* appears closer in spirit to some satanic energy that might become magically transubstantiated and redeemed by an act of divine grace. In the same way, Diamond's wife Alice stays loyal to her errant husband because the idea of "evil" does not harass her with any threatening finality. Alice is not especially bothered by her husband's worldly transgressions because she has been brought up to respect "grace and transubstantiation as the only way to get to heaven" (179).

It is this search for transubstantiation and grace, conceived as a far more powerful force than mere human "good," that propels Kennedy's fiction. In its secularized aesthetic form, this transubstantiation becomes the magic power of art to transform and mythologize the world, as in Kennedy's own "magic realism." Kennedy himself said that a "central" theme of *Legs* is the "idea of how myth is created," a "sense of the gangster as myth"; yet *Legs* openly flaunts the differences between the "real" and the mythic Diamond, as if to acknowledge that the text is meditating upon the limits of its own capacities to transubstantiate mundane circumstances into these magic realist forms.[66] "All backward in the mirror image," comments Marcus Gorman. "Nobody would ever know which image was the real Jack" (292). Kennedy thus creates a *mode rétro* designed to blend past and present, literal and metaphorical, into a resplendent image of Albany as "a magical place where the past becomes visible if one is willing to track the multiple incarnations of the city's soul," as *O Albany!* puts it (7). However, by simultaneously foregrounding the human processes of writing and memory – the newspapers in *The Ink Truck* and *Quinn's Book* (1988), Gorman's reminiscences in *Legs* – Kennedy is also nudging the reader into recognition of how this language of literary transubstantiation may itself be no more than an imagined equivalence, a cultural fiction. If, as *O Albany!* says, the task of writing is "to peer into the heart of this always-shifting past, to be there . . . when it turns so magically, so inevitably, from then into now" (7), then it does not become difficult to see a parallel between the author's style of writing and Legs Diamond's attempts to transport himself from the mundane moral limits of this world into the glamorous grace of the next. In both cases, though, the magical projection is held in suspension.

66 Ibid., pp. 164, 162.

Kennedy's Catholic culture fabricates a dream of redemptive simultaneity and plenitude that the more skeptical, writerly aspects of his texts keep in check.

Yet if the yearning for transubstantiation in Kennedy's novels is never quite fulfilled, the more secular materials of Catholicism nevertheless engender those ironic incongruities whose "way of comedy" is symptomatic of this religious heritage.[67] In *Billy Phelan's Greatest Game*, history and tradition still pursue their course, even if theology does not. Of Martin Phelan, we learn that "despite his infidel ways, the remnants of tattered faith still had power over his mind" (172); while Martin's son Billy seconds Legs Diamond's rejection of the Nietzschean *uebermensch* in his avowal that "suckers must be stomped for their love of ignorance, for expecting too much from life" (93). Within this community, romantic self-aggrandizement seems to be the one unpardonable sin. In *Ironweed*, the characters are once again circumscribed by their (social and religious) past, and Francis Phelan's remorse for the manslaughter of his son is attended by a plethora of metaphors betokening sins of omission, guilt, and confession. The novel moves toward a fiction of salvation as Francis's "empty soul" (87) is baptized anew in the family bathroom, where the "sacred" faucets and "holy" drainpipe convince him it is "as if some angel of beatific lucidity were hovering outside the bathroom window" (172). As if, but only as if: the various scholarly articles pointing out Dantesque and other mythological echoes in this Pulitzer Prize–winning novel generally fail to observe that Kennedy's text is playing with these analogies in an ambiguous, flirtatious, postmodernist way.[68] Nevertheless, such hints of the magical and the mythical do convey an impression that Francis Phelan's pilgrimage, like that of Joyce's Leopold Bloom, is a journey undertaken many times before. Just as the Homeric paradigm works as a metaphor for the way Bloom is sanctified through the process of forfeiting his romantic freedom, so within Kennedy's texts the mythical status of Albany operates as a psychological state of mind, an expressionistic interpretation of how these characters are invented and controlled by the patterns of their local cultural heritage.

The epigraph to *Quinn's Book*, from Camus, reworks this sense of entrapment in its suggestion that "a man's work is nothing but this slow trek to rediscover, through the detours of art, those two or three great and simple images in whose presence his heart first opened." *Quinn's Book* pursues the implications of this statement by probing Daniel

67 Lynch, *Christ and Apollo*, p. 94.
68 See, for instance, Edward C. Reilly, "Dante's *Purgatorio* and Kennedy's *Ironweed*: Journeys to Redemption," *Notes on Contemporary Literature*, 17, no. 3 (1987), 5–8; Peter P. Clarke, "Classical Myth in William Kennedy's *Ironweed*," *Critique*, 27, no. 3 (1986), 167–76.

Quinn's struggle "with the power the past seemed to have over him: power to imprison him in dead agonies and divine riddles."[69] Part of the freedom Quinn seeks is a freedom of expression in art and love away "from dead language, from the repetitions of conventions" (265). Quinn is aided in his endeavors by Will Caraday, editor of the *Albany Chronicle,* who loans Quinn his copy of Montaigne and offers appropriately Montaignesque advice about the need to "move toward the verification of freedom, and avoid gratuitous absolutes" (135). Yet of course Montaigne, the quintessential skeptic, himself emerged out of a tradition of Catholic philosophy: in Montaigne, transcendental idealism and abstraction is disparaged at the expense of an ironic acknowledgment of how the contingencies of worldly existence limit the potential of human endeavor. It may in fact be one of the characteristics of Catholicism's status as an oppositional culture within the United States that it foregrounds this skepticism and irony as a means "to de-absolutize things," in Lynch's phrase.[70] Just as Montaigne's skepticism preserved a salutary distance from disembodied forms of philosophical idealism, so American Catholic writers, aware of their own differential status, look warily upon any gesture toward abstract or Neoplatonic modes of absolutism. Kennedy once remarked that Samuel Beckett's works, for instance, should not be seen as "universal" accounts of the human condition since they emerged from particular forms of (Protestant) cultural experience in Dublin and Paris.[71] Kennedy's own fiction participates in exactly this kind of relativizing process by the way it self-reflexively draws attention to its manipulation of idiosyncratically Catholic narratives from within Albany.

Just as the Catholic icons of Kennedy's Albany function on a postmodernist and self-consciously metaphorical level, so Francis Ford Coppola's *Godfather* films can be seen as a highly charged myth of the Catholic experience in America. Though the saga originated in a 1969 novel by Mario Puzo, it receives its most luminous incarnation in Coppola's three films, released in 1972, 1974 and 1990. Writing in 1979, James Monaco claimed the first two parts of *The Godfather* taken together represent "the most significant American film since *Citizen Kane*."[72]

Puzo's earlier novel about Italian immigrants, *The Fortunate Pilgrim* (1965), locates itself within a more recognizable pattern of social realism that looks back to the grinding world of Pietro di Donato. The familiar

69 William Kennedy, *Quinn's Book* (New York: Viking, 1988), p. 288. Subsequent page references are given in parentheses in the text.
70 Lynch, *Images of Faith,* p. 102.
71 Gould, "In the Underworld."
72 James Monaco, *American Film Now* (New York: Plume–New American Library, 1979), p. 345.

dichotomies in *The Fortunate Pilgrim* revolve around the innocence of Italy set against the corruption of America: America connotes for the immigrants a "blasphemous dream," an ideal of wealth and power that involves leaving behind that European "homeland" and so tearing "a vital root from their minds."[73] The anxieties of these fortunate pilgrims arise mainly from questions of money; indeed, an intense concern for money is looked upon here as a sign of maturity. Thus Gino Angeluzzi is disparaged because his "childish dreams did not include thoughts of money. He dreamed of bravery on a battlefield, of greatness on a baseball diamond. He dreamed of his own uniqueness" (137). But Gino must learn to grow up and sell out, as Puzo said later in relation to his own writing career, for such romantic idealism will never buy the house on Long Island that the Angeluzzi family covets as a totem of their cultural assimilation and social success.

Gino's mother especially distrusts all "high ambition, high aims" (150) because of the excessive material risks they involve. In particular, she is hostile toward the immaterial frivolity of the printed word: "They who read books," she declares, "will let their families starve" (221). In his essay "The Italians, American Style," Puzo wrote that an Italian parent used to view her child's library card with the same horror "today's middle-class mother" would feel about her "son's taste for drugs," and so it is not surprising that Mrs. Angeluzzi is most perturbed by the idea of her daughter Octavia marrying the book-reading Jewish boy, Norman Bergeron.[74] Given this disinclination for abstraction, Puzo's pilgrims prefer to devote their energies to more concrete and corporeal activities, notably those involving pleasures of the flesh and of money. The Angeluzzi family quickly realizes that American "justice" can be incorporated within this latter category, being a concrete rather than an abstract or impersonal phenomenon. When Larry sees a handshake between racketeering chief Mr. di Lucca and an American detective, "the whole majesty of law . . . crumbled before his eyes" (211), as Larry comes to realize the pertinence of the old Sicilian proverb "If you seek justice, put a gift in the scale" (221). Mr. di Lucca himself is eloquent upon how American law is a relativistic category, a system inappropriate for those immured in New York tenements to follow: "Poor people cannot live by all the laws. There would not be one alive. Only the *padroni* would be left" (212).

So here again we find the ironic juxtaposition of intense desire for

73 Mario Puzo, *The Fortunate Pilgrim* (New York: Atheneum, 1965), pp. 299, 115. Subsequent page references are given in parentheses in the text.
74 Mario Puzo, *The Godfather Papers and Other Confessions* (Greenwich, Conn.: Fawcett Crest, 1973), p. 188.

material success coupled with lack of faith in the moral principles of society. Like Gatsby, these Italian immigrants desire to play the game according to the rules of big business because that is the only path to the fulfillment of their grossly materialistic dreams, the cherished mansion on Long Island. Yet a powerful residue of ethnic and religious spirit ensures these pilgrims cannot buy into the (Protestant) ethical values associated with the institutions of capitalism and so, as with Gatsby, their dogged fight to the top takes on the air of a parody of the American Dream. *The Godfather* mythologizes this duplicity whereby American Catholic communities are, as *Gatsby* puts it, "within and without, simultaneously enchanted and repelled" by American culture (36). Robert K. Johnson complained that Coppola's films are "only partially realistic" and that Gay Talese's *Honor Thy Father,* a nonfictional account of the decline of the Mafia, is "by far, the more convincing"; yet Puzo was more concerned about what he called the "mythic" qualities of his central character, while in a 1975 interview Coppola also talked about the self-consciously "mythic aspects of the Godfather" as being those areas where the films most obviously depart from empirical fact.[75] Whereas Puzo's novel emphasizes plot and fast action, Coppola's films emphasize lavish, operatic ritual. Suspense plays a lesser part in the cinematic versions, especially in *The Godfather Part II,* where the scene fluctuates between past and present generations of the Corleone family, as if to emphasize the inevitability of their criminal empire's decline and fall. The fact that the iconography of *The Godfather* has passed into public legend testifies to Coppola's success in transubstantiating a mediocre gangster story into the high realm of myth, a transformation that in itself resembles the Catholic process of sacramentally investing mundane reality with a form of magical grace.

The hyperbolic and operatic elements in the films – the decapitated horses, the ritual slaughters, and so on – do in fact add to the effectiveness of the cinematic experience by covertly opening up for the audience windows of self-reflexivity. We know, and the picturesque excesses of the films continually remind us, that Marlon Brando is actually Marlon Brando, not Don Vito Corleone. This institutionalized unreality, the perpetual sliding between different levels of plot and ritual, lends to Coppola's films a radical instability that appropriately reflects the duplicitous, tensile quality of myth: Coppola's myth, like many others, is always implicitly admitting that it is not really true. Whereas Puzo's more naturalistic novel encourages the reader's suspension of disbelief,

75 Robert K. Johnson, *Francis Ford Coppola* (Boston: Twayne, 1977), pp. 109, 112; Puzo, *Godfather Papers,* p. 41; "*Playboy* Interview: Francis Ford Coppola," *Playboy,* July 1975, p. 60.

Coppola's Don Corleone no more invites the viewer to worry about the people he has murdered than Mozart's Don Giovanni invites us to worry about the women he has deflowered. This is not to say either Don can be dismissed simply as a fantasy figure; like Don Giovanni, Don Corleone is genuinely disturbing because he is a nexus where we see the convergence of various sinister cultural, historical, and psychological forces. As in the Mozart opera, the charismatic allure of transgression throws back a dark and troubling shadow over the apparatus of "respectable" society. The point is, however, that this shadow cannot be pinned down or understood too literally. Just as it would have been futile to attempt to vitiate the power of Mozart's work by saying most seventeenth-century Spanish noblemen were not in fact philanderers, so all the "smear" complaints about the stereotyping of Italian-Americans that emerged when Coppola's films were released, all the barrages of statistics proving most Italian-Americans were not in fact criminals, seem more than a touch pedantic. Coppola's *Godfather* films do not concern themselves with sociological accuracy. Instead, they take the old *Scarface* myth of Italian criminals as deracinated and ultimately doomed victims of American society and redeem that myth by inverting it, by transposing these marginalized elements into well-organized and successful American businessmen.

The mass appeal of *The Godfather* has been much debated. Daniel Bell has suggested that Americans find it reassuring to believe in the popular demonology of a Mafia because by turning the inchoate idea of crime into an abstraction – like "Wall Street" or "Big Business" – the unstated assumption is that this world of evil can be circumscribed and finally controlled.[76] Richard Gambino, however, saw the "key to the Mafia mania" as a projection of widespread yearning within the anomic landscape of contemporary America for older family values of "belonging," "loyalty" and "security."[77] John Paul Russo has similarly written of the dialectic between "plenitude" and "absence" in these films, "plenitude" connoting Italian family roots, "absence" the world of dehumanized American big business into which Michael Corleone (Al Pacino) has moved by the time of *Godfather II*.[78] Fredric Jameson gave this sociopolitical argument another twist by seeing an implicit anticapitalist ideology in the way the "Utopian longing" for collectivity epitomized by

76 Gordon Hawkins, "God and the Mafia," *The Public Interest*, no. 14 (Winter 1969), p. 32.
77 Richard Gambino, *Blood of My Blood: The Dilemma of the Italian-Americans* (Garden City: Doubleday, 1974), pp. 322, 282.
78 John Paul Russo, "The Hidden Godfather: Plenitude and Absence in Francis Ford Coppola's *Godfather I and II*," in *Support and Struggle: Italians and Italian Americans in a Contemporary Perspective*, ed. Joseph L. Tropea, James E. Miller, and Cheryl Beattie-Repetti (Staten Island: American Italian Historical Association, 1986), p. 256.

Vito Corleone's close-knit immigrant family gradually gives way to the alienating (and structurally homologous) forces of crime and big business. This dichotomy between the innocence (of Italy) and the experience (of America) is certainly a pattern that dominates *The Fortunate Pilgrim*, but, as Thomas J. Ferraro has argued, *The Godfather* problematizes that simplified binary opposition because here the ethnic organization and the capitalist world operate simultaneously. The idea of business does not corrupt the family; the family is already corrupt. In fact, the power of the Corleones' organization in the business world is directly related to the strength of these family ties.[79]

As if to highlight parallels between ethnic and capitalist dynasties, the heads of the five Mafia families meet after the murder of Sonny Corleone in the boardroom of a bank where a portrait of archetypal American financier Alexander Hamilton hangs on the wall. These Mafia directors sign an agreement that is, as Rose Basile Green said, "like the Constitution of the United States, respecting fully the internal authority of each member in his state or city."[80] In keeping with the American Catholic spirit of parody, both novel and films repeatedly insist upon the fact that this Mafia activity is only a mirror of how more orthodox power structures operate within the United States. When Michael's wife, Kay, expresses reservations about the affairs of his family, he tells her how many American presidents had fathers and grandfathers "who were lucky they didn't get hanged" and insists, with barely a trace of irony, that his father is an American businessman like any other.[81] Coppola reinforced these analogies between business, politics, and crime by remarking in an interview that *The Godfather* is essentially "a film about power. It could have been the Kennedys."[82] The frequently expressed desire of both Vito and Michael Corleone for eventual social legitimacy exemplifies again this close proximity between legal and illegal organizations, a proximity that subverts the image of the American Constitution as God-given and "natural": give the family organization a few years, Michael implies, and it might seem as naturally and heroically American as the old outlaws of the Wild West seem today. In Michael's eyes, American rhetoric about freedom of opportunity is inevitably ideologically slanted; Michael feels that his father, a "man of extraordinary force and character," had no

---

79 Thomas J. Ferraro, "Blood in the Marketplace: The Business of Family in the *Godfather* Narratives," in *The Invention of Ethnicity,* ed. Werner Sollors (New York: Oxford Univ. Press, 1989), pp. 178, 185–207.

80 Rose Basile Green, *The Italian-American Novel: A Document of the Interaction of Two Cultures* (Rutherford: Fairleigh Dickinson Univ. Press, 1974), p. 360.

81 Mario Puzo, *The Godfather* (New York: Putnam's, 1969), p. 364. Subsequent page references are given in parentheses in the text.

82 "*Playboy* Interview: Francis Ford Coppola," p. 60.

choice but to refuse "to live by rules set up by others, rules which condemn him to a defeated life" (365). Still, the ultimate aim of both men is not to overturn those rules but rather to manipulate them for their own advantage: the Corleones aspire not to becoming an oppositional faction but toward insinuating themselves, in jesuitical fashion, into the mainstream of capitalist society. In *Godfather II,* Michael says one thing he learnt from "Pop" is "to try to think as people around you think," a chameleonic mode of behavior that leads Michael ostentatiously to make a large philanthropic benefaction to a university in his adopted state, Nevada. Coppola's characters know that no final freedom from legalistic restrictions is possible, that all rules are ultimately unfair, that no pastoral utopias are viable; they do not try romantically to change the rules, but to make these rules more malleable so the law comes to work for them rather than against them. They conceive the law in corporeal, fleshly terms rather than as an abstract principle: not some attenuated ideal, but a human body to be fed, a machine to be oiled.

In these films, then, ethnic identity is fluid and unstable. The simple binary opposition of Old World and New becomes no longer tenable, for the Corleones are a complex mixture of different cultural heritages. The Mafia functions not so much as a direct image of America, as Jameson suggested, but as a double-edged parody of America, an organization structured along the same lines but fatally shadowed by its sense of being sundered from the main currents of American life. When in *Godfather II* young Vito Corleone (Robert De Niro) returns to Sicily to take revenge on the man who killed his father, he brings as a gift to his family a small replica of the Statue of Liberty; yet although Don Vito clearly models himself along the lines of an Ellis Island success story, he can never quite shake off the fetters of outsiderhood. This is why it is appropriate that in *Godfather II* the Corleone family should decamp to Nevada. For them – as for the politicians and gangsters in O'Connor, Higgins, and William Kennedy – society has become an enlarged game, a roulette wheel of skill and luck where investment of moral energies is irrelevant and the only imperative is to win. If the larger society is a flawed, arbitrary, and illogical structure – despite the misconception of itself as an Enlightenment ideal – then the gaming tables of Las Vegas shadow the ideology of capitalism in the same kind of way as does the Mafia itself, rendering naked capitalism's covert imperatives of greed and good fortune. Puzo's 1977 nonfiction account of life *Inside Las Vegas* takes delight in pointing out how the sailing of the Mayflower was financed by a lottery in England, how Harvard and Yale were built with funds raised by gaming, and so on: even the most elevated Puritan institutions are said not to be above "the premise that good things can come out of a little crookery." The concept of luck erases worldly logic through its egalitarian subver-

sion of the work ethic and any notion of personal meritocracy. Luck
scatters its favors randomly, like a benevolent god bestowing random
tokens of grace. As Puzo puts it: "No matter what our character, no
matter what our behavior, no matter if we are ugly, unkind, murderers,
saints, guilty sinners, foolish, or wise, *we can get lucky*."[83]

Puzo's belief in how Puritan idealism becomes inextricably entangled
with the crooked ways of gambling focuses attention upon how the
Catholic cultural system works its way through the *Godfather* saga. Good
and evil, honor and corruption become mutually sustaining rather than
irreconcilable contraries. We are confronted once again by Weber's notion
of "institutional grace," the grace that – as Flannery O'Connor noted in
a 1960 letter – can work through the medium of what is imperfect or
even hypocritical: participation in the communal sacraments paradoxically reverses worldly evil and brings the sinner absolution.[84] Parallels
between the Mafia "Godfather" and Catholic figures of divine authority
hardly need insisting upon: Puzo talks of how Vito Corleone listens to
Amerigo Bonasera "like a priest in the confessional" (30), Neri's father-
in-law petitions for the "intercession" of the Corleone family (422), the
opening titles of *The Godfather* reveal a dark figure pulling puppet strings
arranged in the shape of a cross, the opening of *Godfather II* features a
supplicant kissing Michael Corleone's hand as if he were kissing the hand
of the pope, and so on. Furthermore, Gordon Hawkins has written of
how the organization of the Mafia, with its elaborate hierarchical system
of *capi dei capi, consigliori,* lieutenants and other officials, bears more than
a passing resemblance to the Catholic system of heavenly governance,
where the Lord of Hosts is pictured as presiding over archangels, angels,
and cherubim.[85] By extension – though Hawkins does not push this
analogy – the Mafia parallel could extend to the Catholic scheme of
worldly governance, arranged as it is in mediating chains of cardinals,
archbishops, bishops, and so on. "God gives being by certain intermediate causes," said Aquinas in the *Summa:* "God created all things immediately, but in the creation itself He established an order among things,
so that some depend on others by which they are preserved in being,
though He remains the principal cause of their preservation."[86] Aquinas
here might have been talking directly about *The Godfather:* the celestial
bonds of being, those structures of materialized analogy, which for Aqui-

83 Mario Puzo, *Inside Las Vegas* (New York: Grosset and Dunlap, 1977), pp. 30, 244.
84 Sally Fitzgerald, ed., *The Habit of Being: The Letters of Flannery O'Connor* (New York:
    Farrar, Straus and Giroux, 1979), p. 389.
85 Hawkins, "God and the Mafia," p. 30.
86 *Summa Theologiae,* I, q. 104, art. 2. Quoted in H. Richard Niebuhr, *The Kingdom of
    God in America* (Chicago: Willett, Clark and Co., 1937), p. 200.

nas link heaven and earth, are terrestrially replicated in the bonds that hold the Mafia organization together.

Such structures of reduplication are made quite explicit in *Godfather III*, where Michael Corleone's attempts to make his family business "legitimate" lead him to donate a mammoth sum to the Vatican Bank in return for Vatican support of the Corleone company in a crucial takeover bid. Here the structures of the Mafia and of the Catholic church appear to mirror each other almost exactly: the Vatican, says the archbishop in charge of its financial operations, is like any other company in the world, and he hard-headedly promises the "whole past history" of the Corleone family "will be washed away" if Michael will only reciprocate by producing the $600 million necessary to "absolve" the Vatican Bank's debt. Yet the Vatican is also represented here as just like any other company in terms of its corporate intrigues, double-dealings, and murderous jealousies. "A pack of Borgias," Michael calls the Vatican cartel at one point; he feels that his quest for social legitimation is being compromised by the mires of treachery and corruption he can never seem to escape: "Just when I thought I was out," complains Michael, "they pull me back in." The larger question here revolves around whether any (ethical or social) purity is actually possible: Michael tells his sister he had hoped to rise in society and become more respectable, but "the higher I go, the crookeder it gets." Eventually, Michael finds himself forced to consult one of his veteran Sicilian cronies in order to find out if there might be anyone "friendly" to their cause inside the Vatican: "Politics and crime, they're the same thing," Michael sighs disconsolately as he pushes the wily old *mafioso* away in his wheelchair.

In this way, the Mafia works not only as a parody of American business corporations but also as a "grotesque parody," as Robert Viscusi said, of the Catholic mythos.[87] In *The Godfather*, big business, crime, and theology are represented as cognate, with each system ironizing and destabilizing the others. Hence the audience never quite knows at which level the text is functioning, just as the friends and acquaintances of Michael Corleone can never quite pin him down as an outright villain. If these films were simply indictments of American capitalism or exposés of organized crime, they would be far less complex and interesting; the strength of Coppola's work is to dramatize the interaction of opposites where sacred and profane are yoked together in a trembling instability of the balance. The films' tone oscillates between the suave and the savage. Soft-spoken Marlon Brando euphemistically makes people offers

87 Robert Viscusi, "Professions and Faiths: Critical Choices in the Italian American Novel," in *Italian Americans in the Professions*, ed. Remigio U. Pane (New York: American Italian Historical Association, 1983), p. 51.

they can't refuse, Senator Geary (G. D. Spradlin) is blackmailed with the utmost politesse after having been found with a dead girl in Fredo's brothel: "It will be as if she never existed," Tom Hagen (Robert Duvall) assures him, "All that's left is our friendship." Whereas the dominant mode of Puzo's novel is sensationalism, the dominant mode of Coppola's films is irony: for Coppola, words imply more than they appear to mean at first blush. Indeed, the films often delight in demonstrating an ironic incongruity between the understatements of the mafiosi and the gruesome visual consequences of those words as represented on the screen.

One of the clearest manifestations of this structural irony occurs at the end of the first film, where Michael, standing in church as godfather to his sister's child, ritualistically proclaims that he renounces Satan and all his works even while his henchmen are participating in a parallel ritual of mass slaughter. Coppola intercuts the murders with the church service in what Robert Phillip Kolker called an Eisenstein-like montage, "a complex of opposing shots that affect us by the way they play off each other."[88] There are many other ironic juxtapositions in these films, of course: the rural landscape of Sicily set against the urban jungle of New York City, the public spectacle of the wedding of Connie Corleone (Talia Shire) set against the darkened study where Brando's Don Corleone receives petitions for his favor, and so on. But the point about all these apparent dichotomies is that they are unmasked and shown to be different aspects of the same phenomenon. Sicily is not a place of pastoral calm, but equally as bloody as New York. The family is not a utopian escape from business, as Gambino suggested, but rather the source of its strength. Coppola's ironic mode of art pulls apparently competing discourses into the same unified thread, so that we can see how the church sacrament in which Michael Corleone participates does indeed have the power to redeem the sins he is committing: it is not simply a macabre or farcical contrast. This, of course, actually heightens the gruesome nature of the murders, for the audience is not allowed to channel its sense of outrage onto some clearly guilty party. Just as Michael duplicitously evades the police and (later) the Senate committees of inquiry, so he seems to slide out of responsibility for his own impious actions by taking refuge in the Catholic sacraments, impersonal phenomena that – to the chagrin of post-Reformation humanists – are understood to have a "magical power" (Pietro di Donato's phrase) enabling them to work under all circumstances.[89] In Godfather III, Michael actually makes his confes-

88 Robert Phillip Kolker, A Cinema of Loneliness: Penn, Kubrick, Coppola, Scorsese, Altman (New York: Oxford Univ. Press, 1980), p. 176.
89 Dorothée von Huene-Greenberg, "A MELUS Interview: Pietro Di Donato," MELUS, 14, nos. 3–4 (1987), 42.

sion to Cardinal Lamberto (Raf Vallone), who pronounces Michael's catalogue of misdeeds to be "terrible" and then proceeds unhesitatingly to absolve him.

Richard Gambino has written of how Italian culture, strongly influenced by pagan and Muhammadan customs, places greater emphasis upon the power of evil than does traditional Catholic neo-scholastic philosophy, and it is true that in *The Godfather* the force of evil pressurizes the rituals of Catholicism far more than in films by (say) Robert Altman, where any threat of evil is swiftly diminished to a mere human foible and incorporated into the great catholic world of good.[90] Nevertheless, both Puzo and Coppola represent evil as being in some way, even if ambiguously and stressfully, intertwined with redemptive grace. For all the carnage and corruption in *The Godfather*, we never infer any shift in moral perspective that would make the work consonant with the kind of neoorthodox Protestantism outlined by theologians like Reinhold Niebuhr, where man is understood to be an essentially sinful entity whose only hope for redemption rests in the quite undeserved love of God. Whereas Niebuhr postulated divine redemption beyond history, *The Godfather* magically sloughs off its burden of evil to describe the possibility of "grace" within history. Puzo's text talks of "a pattern [Michael Corleone] was to see often, the Don helping those in misfortune whose misfortune he had partly created. Not perhaps out of cunning or planning but because of his variety of interests or perhaps because of the nature of the universe, the interlinking of good and evil, natural of itself" (392). Again, this theological interaction of opposites betokens a similar secular interaction. Just as George V. Higgins's lawyers and criminals are represented as analogical mirrors of each other, separated only by the arbitrary boundaries of society, so in *The Godfather* Mafia chiefs, Vatican bankers, and national politicians become incorporated into one circle where good and evil are interlinked and interchangeable. In *Godfather II*, Michael Corleone is a corrupt man who also does good, while Senator Geary is a man doing good who is also corrupt. This self-perpetuating cycle implies, of course, a radically antihumanist outlook, one that denies any possibility of freedom for the altruistic soul or the ameliorating liberal imagination.

Coppola's style of cinematic irony, balancing these levels of crime, politics, and theology off against each other, is a brilliant correlative to the themes of duplicity his films enunciate. Al Pacino's Michael Corleone is a formidable liar, one of the best in the history of the cinema; at times his poker-faced facade almost convinces the cinema audience, even when it knows he is telling outright black lies. Michael's duplicity, our sense

90 Gambino, *Blood of My Blood*, pp. 194–207.

of him facing two different ways at once, is a (blasphemous) counterpart to that philosophical irony endemic to the Catholic tradition, where, as Lynch has said, matter is always attending its putative transubstantiation into spirit. John R. May has written well about Coppola's ability to entertain the ironic "coexistence of contraries" in his pictures, and in *The Godfather* all the contraries inherent within the duplicitous narrative carry larger reverberations extending into the duplicitous, doubled-up realm of Catholic theology.[91]

By demonstrating how the boss of a criminal empire is also a good father, by both celebrating "the family" and also exposing the Mafia myth as a mystification of commercial ruthlessness, by showing how corruption is inherent within all American institutions of government, Coppola is effectively deconstructing the various power bases his film treats. He is, as Kolker said, "the great sleight-of-hand artist in American film of the seventies – and the great subversive," an ironist whose texts resist becoming locked into any fixed ideological position.[92] Puzo's narrative is finally too sentimental about the Mafia: Michael's wife, Kay, converts to Catholicism at the end of the novel, for instance. But Coppola's films reject that sense of neat closure and instead show unresolved tensions within the family saga, as Italian ethnicity confronts the ever more intransigent world of American secular experience. In Coppola's films, Kay (Diane Keaton) and Michael are unable to transcend their cultural and religious differences, despite the personal affection they express for each other. In *Godfather III*, especially, Kay is represented as a Protestant outsider who is totally unable to comprehend, far less admire, the culture of duplicity within which her husband is enmeshed. The beginning of the film finds Michael being invested with the papal insignia of Saint Sebastian the Martyr as a reward for his services to the church; Michael then returns the favor by presenting the archbishop with a check for $100 million, supposedly for the "poor of Sicily." For Michael, all of this is just another day's work keeping the wheels of business spinning; yet Kay, more at home with the WASP emphasis on individual integrity, says she finds this investiture a "shameful" ceremony, another occasion where Michael is simply being "disguised" by his church. Later on, she tells him scornfully he is "still a liar." In Sicily, toward the end of the film, Michael assumes a penitential posture and asks Kay to "forgive" him, to which she replies dismissively: "Like God, huh?" Kay, accustomed to a moral idiom of self-reliance, simply fails to understand what Michael perceives as the enormous significance of this ritualistic act of

91 Lynch, *Images of Faith,* p. 83; John R. May, "Francis Coppola," in *Religion in Film,* ed. John R. May and Michael Bird (Knoxville: Univ. of Tennessee Press, 1982), p. 164.
92 Kolker, *A Cinema of Loneliness,* p. 193.

contrition. The failure of communication here is shown as genuinely tragic, the more so because of their enduring affection for each other, and because Michael himself is always torn psychologically between loyalty to Sicilian values and a desire to integrate himself within the kind of secular American society Kay epitomizes.

This double-edged idiom of irony to which Kay is so impervious is also apparent, though in a less compelling way, in other films made by Coppola. Determined ever since childhood to be "rich and famous," Coppola responds to questions about whether or not he has "sold out" to the Hollywood system by talking of how "people like myself... decide that it's necessary to work within a system" in order to be able eventually to change it.[93] It is the classic Gatsby answer: play the game according to somebody else's rules, beat them on their own terms, but preserve a sense of detachment. (Coppola in fact wrote the script for Jack Clayton's 1974 film *The Great Gatsby*.) This transposition of society's rules into a series of artificial codes to be played with and skillfully manipulated is seen most clearly in Coppola's 1982 film *One from the Heart*. Set on the Fourth of July in Las Vegas, this musical love story gleefully exposes all the American myths of romance and patriotism as cultural rather than natural productions. Such foregrounding of fictionality is highlighted by the fact that the movie was "filmed entirely on the stages of Zoetrope Studios" (as it proudly announces at the end) with the artificial props and lighting creating a strange, defamiliarizing effect where the film seems to be a close approximation of "reality" without ever quite erasing its dark glass of illusion. We are never allowed to forget that what we are seeing is not the Taj Mahal, but a plastic replica of the Taj Mahal. Although there are no conspicuously religious elements in *One from the Heart,* the film embodies Coppola's Catholic heritage in several ways: through the manner in which it flirtatiously and self-consciously investigates how humdrum reality might become transubstantiated into glittering myth; through its subversion of everything that is supposedly "natural" about American culture, so that the values of Independence Day become scrambled into arbitrary signs on a Las Vegas gaming table. One of the key scenes in this film centers on a daredevil tightrope-walking act undertaken by the Natassia Kinski character, whose performance embodies the ironic conceptual tightrope walking throughout Coppola's cinema, where to de-absolutize myths is not to satirize them but to engage in a style of gentle parody where the text can place itself inside and outside American traditions simultaneously.

93 Monaco, *American Film Now*, p. 339; "*Playboy* Interview: Francis Ford Coppola," p. 65.

19

Conclusion:
Aesthetic Universalism and
Catholic Skepticism

Raymond Williams once remarked how appropriate it was that the literary "canon" should be a phrase with a prominent religious connotation:
the "canon" of accepted texts, of religious orthodoxy.[1] Consequently,
it is not surprising that in recent times we can see challenges to the
"canon" of American literature and to the more traditional doctrines of
Catholicism working in parallel. Especially in the United States, there
has been much discussion at every level of the religious institution about
ways in which various strands of "liberal" and "conservative" thought
diverge. Many factions within the American church have been pressuring
Rome for more relaxed attitudes toward the rights of women, homosexuals, and other marginalized groups, just as the most illuminating of
recent texts emerging from within American Catholic culture have taken
an interrogative stance toward canonical assumptions.

There is surely nothing very unexpected about this continuing tension
between Roman dogma and American liberalism. As we have seen, these
supposedly deviant qualities of American subjectivism and modernity
have been an issue in the church since the days of Orestes Brownson.
Also in a direct line from Brownson, though, is that strategy of universalization through which American Catholic writers have tried to reconcile the various contradictions that have arisen not only within the
ecclesia itself but also out of the rebarbative relationship between this
church and its surrounding environment. These kinds of incongruity
have always been part of the necessary experience of American Catholics.
Whereas the European faithful could at least fantasize about the lost
harmony of the Middle Ages, American Catholics have been forced to
recognize the inescapable disjunctions between their spiritual faith and
their secular circumstances.

---

1 Raymond Williams, "Cultural Studies, Media Studies, Political Education," University
  of London Institute of Education, 18 Jan. 1986.

One result of this, ironically, has been to make American Catholicism more universalist in tendency, more willing to embrace conflicts and differences as part of some grand synoptic design. Just as Brownson liked to stress a compatibility between the universalist inclination of the American republic and the synthesizing tendencies of the Church of Rome, so contemporary American Catholic thinkers such as Jay P. Dolan have contended the church is of a "radically pluralistic nature" with "no one, Catholic way to pray, but a variety of ways for Catholics to pray."[2] Avery Dulles, S.J., in a 1989 lecture at Fordham University, again described how New World Catholics have historically "shunned the sectarian stances of American Protestantism" so that the differing philosophies of traditionalism, neoconservatism, liberalism, and "prophetic radicalism" could be subsumed within a mutually sustaining and mutually corrective relationship inside the church. "None of the four strategies is simply wrong," claimed Dulles: "The realities of American Catholicism and of American culture are complex and multi-faceted." Invoking the Joycean phrase "here comes everybody" to justify his universalist stance, Dulles maintained the church needs to preserve its "broad popular appeal" and not become too sidetracked into narrow channels of "sectarian militancy," whether of the left or the right.[3]

This multifaceted perspective is predicated upon the valorization of analogical "similarities-in-difference," a universalist understanding, which Catholic theologians take care to distinguish from any "deadening uniformity beloved by a univocal mind."[4] Such a position has been more tenable within the church since the early 1960s, when the Second Vatican Council sanctioned the idea of "inculturation," the recognition of how the church should become "incarnate" in many different types of culture. These Vatican II reforms were especially compatible with the American experience, where, as I have suggested, an acknowledgment of diversity and heterogeneity had long been an inevitable fact of life anyway. Still, the assumption that all philosophical positions are relative – that everything should be welcomed as possible and nothing accepted as final – must itself be problematic within an American culture built around an idealization of the soul and positive individual choices. Jonathan Edwards, one feels, would not have taken kindly to any suggestion that his interpretation of the world was simply one creative possibility among

---

2 Jay P. Dolan, *The American Catholic Experience: A History from Colonial Times to the Present* (Garden City: Doubleday, 1985), p. 433.

3 Avery Dulles, S.J., "Catholicism and American Culture: The Uneasy Dialogue," *America*, 27 Jan. 1990, pp. 54–9.

4 David Tracy, *The Analogical Imagination: Christian Theology and the Culture of Pluralism* (New York: Crossroad, 1981), p. 412.

many others. Avery Dulles's subtle defense of the principle of "accommodation" as a pragmatic missionary strategy could thus be seen from a Protestant perspective as yet another example of jesuitical guile, a refusal to stake out firm beliefs, a preference for facing many different ways all at once.[5]

In this way, the universalist temper of American Catholicism has gone hand in hand with a destabilizing tone of all-embracing skepticism. This skepticism has often involved a refusal to grant to any worldly position the approval of a final imprimatur. There is an elusiveness in American Catholic modes of discourse that is, for various reasons, less common within the imaginative styles of European Catholicism. Hence, in an American context at least, the notion that a Catholic cast of mind must infallibly be associated with dogmatism in one form or another is simply a popular misconception. Such a misconception is stereotypically reproduced in novels like Lionel Trilling's *The Middle of the Journey* (1947), where Communist party renegade Maxim Gifford converts to Catholicism, supposedly swapping one totalizing theory for another; and also in Gore Vidal's *Washington, D.C.* (1967), where at the end of the narrative Peter Sanford is surprised to find how Billy Thorne "was not yet a convert to Catholicism," described here as "the usual last harbor for disillusioned absolutists of the left.'"[6] It is true, of course, that the modernist drive toward architectonic systems in the earlier part of the twentieth century produced a situation where several writers traded Catholicism for communism, at least temporarily: one thinks of Dreiser, Farrell, O'Neill, and others. But in this respect the modernist era was exceptional, and of course other non-Catholic writers of that time – Pound, Yeats, Eliot – were also tempted by absolutist formulas. More recently, though, writers from a Catholic culture have tended to be particularly wary of idealism of all kinds. Writing in 1962 to Alfred Corn, after the young poet had expressed some disillusionment with his Catholic beliefs, Flannery O'Connor advised him: "Where you have absolute solutions . . . you have no need of faith. Faith is what you have in the absence of knowledge. . . . You can't fit the Almighty into your intellectual categories. . . . What kept me a sceptic in college was precisely my Christian faith. It always said: don't bite on this, get a wider picture, continue to read."[7] In one way, O'Connor is reworking an old Chestertonian paradox whereby the problem with atheism is not that you

5 Dulles, "Catholicism and American Culture," p. 59.
6 Gore Vidal, *Washington D.C.* (Boston: Little, Brown and Co., 1967), p. 375.
7 Sally Fitzgerald, ed., *The Habit of Being: The Letters of Flannery O'Connor* (New York: Farrar, Straus and Giroux, 1979), p. 477.

believe in nothing but that you believe in anything. Still, O'Connor gives this line a peculiarly American twist in her clear distinction between "absolute solutions" on the one hand and "faith" on the other.

This kind of Catholic skepticism is much more typical of Montaigne and the Reformation thinkers than it is of Aquinas and the medieval Scholastics. It highlights the way American Catholic fictions have been influenced more by a tradition of Renaissance relativism than by medieval absolutism – not actually a surprising circumstance, bearing in mind how America itself grew up from the Renaissance premises of skepticism, exploration, and discovery. In his 1965 analysis *Character and the Novel*, W. J. Harvey offered a familiar interpretation of the novel as a "distinct art form of liberalism" whose presentation of multiple characters and values ensures a generic "tolerance" that is inherently unable to convey the "monolithic creed" of a religious perspective.[8] But, as O'Connor emphasized in her letter to Corn, within the American Catholic idiom skepticism is the antithesis of dogmatism, not the antithesis of belief. "Assertion and dogmatism are positive signs of stupidity," remarked Montaigne back in the sixteenth century: "The best minds are those that are most various and most supple."[9] It is not a large step from Montaigne's fideistic promulgation of what is "most various" to Frank O'Hara's celebration of an artistic "Grace / to be born / and live as variously as possible" (256). This illumination of heterogeneity subverts all rigid linear conceptions of rationality and hierarchy; instead, the variety of "Grace" is positioned as a challenge to the institutions of human reason.

Again, this was a widely recognized philosophical stance in the Catholic Reformation, a position most famously articulated by Erasmus when he wrote in the praise of folly. Describing himself as a "false theologian," Erasmus ridiculed the pretensions of medieval Scholasticism to epistemological closure. In place of such anachronistic formalism, Erasmus gave priority to his perception of the irrational and the ridiculous as central ordering principles within human life: "Only I, Folly, embrace all men without distinction in my provident goodness... what else is the life of man but a kind of play in which men in various costumes perform until the director motions them off the stage. The director often orders the same actor to appear in different costumes."[10] Erasmus's rec-

---

8 W. J. Harvey, *Character and the Novel* (Ithaca: Cornell Univ. Press, 1965), p. 24.

9 Michel de Montaigne, *Essays,* trans. J. M. Cohen (Harmondsworth: Penguin, 1958), pp. 357, 251. For an elaboration of this point, see Richard H. Popkin, *The History of Scepticism from Erasmus to Spinoza* (Berkeley: Univ. of California Press, 1979), pp. xix–xxi.

10 Erasmus, *The Praise of Folly,* in *The Essential Erasmus,* trans. John P. Dolan (New York: Mentor-New American Library, 1964), pp. 167, 135, 119.

ognition of the arbitrary and interchangeable nature of social roles signifies a kind of ontological burlesque where all man-made systems of
authority are lampooned. It implies the tendency to erase worldly distinctions – or at least to regard them as temporary and provisional – that
Tocqueville noted as one of the defining characteristics of American
Catholic culture in the early nineteenth century. This is also the style of
ontological burlesque that we find in the films of John Ford or Robert
Altman, where comedy becomes a moral imperative designed to deflate
pomposity and hold all social categories in a state of suspension without
undermining them entirely. Because of this, comedy tends to be a more
common literary mode among Catholic authors than tragedy: "You have
to have very great moral authority to end a novel tragically," remarked
David Lodge.[11] Most "Catholic" authors, like Lodge himself, prefer to
relinquish that overarching authority to a power larger than any individual creative self, whether this power be God (for Flannery O'Connor),
or the secular world of Manhattan (for Frank O'Hara), or the rituals of
communal society (for Robert Altman).

Yet if that tragic "power of blackness" so cherished by Melville and
Poe is an unfamiliar subject within American Catholic fictions, that does
not necessarily mean this Catholic tradition is antiintellectual; more accurately, it might be described as antitranscendental. In his essay "On
Experience," Montaigne depicted himself as a "very earthy person" who
was keen to acquiesce in the given circumstances of this world. Montaigne gave it as his view that "supercelestial" thoughts too often go
together with bestial or "subterrestrial" conduct: "Transcendental hu-
mors frighten me," he said, "like lofty and inaccessible heights."[12] There
is a similar thematic critique of transcendentalism in the novels of Walker
Percy, J. F. Powers, Donald Barthelme, and other American Catholic
writers. Like Montaigne, they prefer to concentrate upon the limitations
of the human condition rather than aspire toward the celestial peaks of
Kantian or Emersonian romanticism. In the American Catholic imagination, tragedy is supplanted by burlesque comedy, just as difference is
supplanted by the universalist principles of similitude and materialized
analogy. This does not, of course, make such universalist designs universally valid; it simply suggests how the intellectual assumptions of one
particular cultural tradition are not necessarily compatible with the intellectual assumptions of another. Stanley Cavell, for instance, is an excellent critic who has frequently drawn upon Emerson and Thoreau to
elucidate what Cavell takes to be the truth of individualism and individual

11 Lodge quoted in Eden Ross Lipson, "Liberated by Thatcher," *New York Times Book
Review*, 23 July 1989, p. 20.
12 Montaigne, *Essays*, pp. 394, 405.

difference, the Kantian imperative of treating every human being as essentially "other." But the difficulty comes when, in a secularization of Kantian transcendence, Cavell tries to aggrandize that romantic idiom into a philosophical truth. For Fitzgerald and Kerouac and Mary McCarthy, all of whom emerge from an alternative cultural context and who secularize instead the Catholic doctrine of analogy, those processes that link one person to another seem to be far more significant, both aesthetically and ontologically, than Cavell's cherished categories of otherness and difference.[13]

Nevertheless, this predilection for universalism we see in Catholic fictions – a heightened form of analogy, where the whole world comes to resemble itself – should be critically redefined in material and ideological terms as a relative phenomenon. Marshall McLuhan's "delirious tribal optimism," as Jean Baudrillard put it, is one of the most obvious examples of this ironic phenomenon, for McLuhan's universalist aspirations emerge fairly clearly from one particular cultural source.[14] McLuhan, a fervent Catholic convert, conceived the new medium for the Holy Spirit to be television, an apparatus capable of fostering a global village of cosmic simultaneity and interconnectedness, thus ushering in a kind of universal harmony not witnessed since the Age of Faith. Like Walter J. Ong, to whose ideas his visions bear marked similarities, McLuhan despised the closed systems of narrow reason and logical consistency. McLuhan believed such linear modes of thought to have been fatally encouraged by the growth of the printed word, with all the opportunities for aberrant individualism (and study of the Bible) that this typological revolution had brought about. In other American Catholic fictions, impulses toward global villages are, happily, not so overt as this. Nevertheless, in the efforts of Altman or McCarthy or Fitzgerald to synchronize and ritualize historical events as an epitome of their times, we can glimpse the same kind of (partial) universalist sensibility at work.

In keeping with this double movement of universalism and skepticism, one recurrent pattern we see appearing throughout these texts is a move to synchronize and essentialize an ideal of "America," only to subvert it. The American flags and football in James T. Farrell, the tributes to Columbus and the "green breast of the new world" in *The Great Gatsby*, the Independence Day celebrations in Coppola's *One from the Heart* – all

13 See, for instance, Stanley Cavell, *Pursuits of Happiness: The Hollywood Comedy of Remarriage* (Cambridge, Mass.: Harvard Univ. Press, 1981), pp. 8–16, 73–80. For a discussion of Cavell and Kant, see Gerald L. Bruns, "The New Philosophy," in *Columbia Literary History of the United States*, ed. Emory Elliott (New York: Columbia Univ. Press, 1988), pp. 1057–9.

14 Jean Baudrillard, *For a Critique of the Political Economy of the Sign*, trans. Charles Levin (St. Louis: Telos Press, 1981), p. 172.

these suggest a desire to pin down an idealized "essence" of the United States. These universalizing motifs betoken a desire to become incorporated into those festivals and value systems that signify full membership in the American community; they are strategies to reconcile all disparities within the grand design of nationalistic iconography. Yet, as we have seen, very often the duplicitous Catholic spirit can never quite become assimilated into this dominant ideology, so that these texts hover uneasily between conformity to the system and rebellion against it. In this dualistic movement, American Catholic fictions operate on the margins of social legitimacy, maintaining a parodic distance from national icons without ever threatening altogether to satirize them. To take one offbeat example of this, Alan Rauch has written of the bizarre irony whereby during the 1984 presidential campaign Ronald Reagan tried to commandeer Bruce Springsteen's song "Born in the U.S.A." as a patriotic "message of hope," despite the fact that Springsteen's lyrics sardonically address the issue of alienation among Vietnam veterans. Springsteen diplomatically opted "to dissociate myself from the president's kind words," as he phrased it; yet the irony is an instructive one, for Springsteen, from an Italian-Catholic family, projects an ambience of patriotic zeal even when the substance of his songs is pulling in quite another direction.[15] This double-edged, parodic temper is characteristic of a particular cultural inheritance: the old pressure on Catholics in Britain and America "to integrate and conform, while privately preserving the faith" (as Terry Eagleton, himself a lapsed Catholic, put it) has led to the development of latent and at times even secretive elements within fictional texts.

In discussing the transformation of Catholics into secular intellectuals, Eagleton noted how they are usually "wary of individualism and the inner light," tending instead to grasp values and ideas "in institutional terms, as questions of common religious practice rather than private conscience."[16] For Hawthorne and Henry James, no less than for Warhol and McLuhan, the displacement of inner light into external iconography was a way of bridging the world of private conscience with a more communal, popular culture. In Italy, Hawthorne and James saw – with much ambivalence – how the pictorial and sculptural representations of an Old World culture brought the illiterate masses to prayer; more enthusiastically, Umberto Eco, in his essay "The Return of the Middle Ages," described an equation between the force of these medieval ca-

15 Alan Rauch, "Bruce Springsteen and the Dramatic Monologue," American Studies, 29, no. 1 (Spring 1988), pp. 29, 39.
16 Terry Eagleton, "The Silences of David Lodge," New Left Review, no. 172 (Nov.–Dec. 1988), p. 96.

thedrals and the iconographic dimensions of Hollywood.[17] In both a religious and a secular sense, Catholicism has always been concerned just as much with the culture of the masses as with the culture of a privileged "elect." According to Anthony Burgess, one of the characteristics of Catholic culture is precisely this kind of universalist momentum that tries to bring together "high" and "low" art, the sophisticated and the popular.[18] Defensive definitions of what might constitute polite "taste" are quite alien to this way of thinking. In Maureen Howard's *Not a Word about Nightingales* (1960), genteel New England heroine Rosemary Sedgeley cannot fathom how the Italians can be "surrounded by such marvellous churches" and yet "choose to live with these moulded plaster saints – I mean especially when one is from a good family."[19] But for Howard's Italian characters, what is exquisite and what is tawdry, what is high and what is low, revolve upon the same universalist axis. For these Italians, the narrow-minded aesthetic judgments of a "good" American family are altogether irrelevant.

Because of this universalist heritage and the propensity of American Catholicism to adapt itself to many different types of environment, there is not necessarily an irredeemable fissure between unfamiliar ethnic or feminist perspectives and the "canonical" imperatives of established tradition. Potential contradictions can be sutured and reconciled within the expansive framework of the institution's dominant ideology. Louise Erdrich, for instance, is a writer of German Catholic and Chippewa Indian extraction who has said she is "not a practicing Catholic now," although she claims still to be attached to Catholic "ritual" that "is full of symbols, mysteries, and the unsaid."[20] In Erdrich's novels, Catholicism appears as a form of magic realism, a prerogative of the human myth-making imagination, another facet of that mysterious anthropomorphic energy her texts recognize in Indian religious ceremonies. In *The Beet Queen* (1986), Mary Adare collapses upon a frozen pond where she may – or may not – miraculously witness the face of the crucified Christ. Erdrich's fiction creates a world, not unlike Toni Morrison's, of enigmatic intuitions, irrational mythopoeic desires, and ambiguous visions. It is clearly outside the narrower canons of (religious or literary) orthodoxy, yet in

---

17 Umberto Eco, *Travels in Hyperreality*, trans. William Weaver (San Diego: Harcourt Brace Jovanovich, 1986), p. 83.

18 Burgess made this assertion in a television interview with Russell Davies, *Saturday Review*, BBC2, 21 Feb. 1987.

19 Maureen Howard, *Not a Word about Nightingales* (New York: Atheneum, 1962), p. 74. This novel was first published in the U.K. in 1960.

20 Jan George, "Interview with Louise Erdrich," *North Dakota Quarterly*, 53, no. 2 (Spring 1985), 245.

their American Catholic universalist way these texts also work toward some kind of reconciliation between the Catholic imagination and native American culture.

In the late twentieth century, the relationship between the Catholic church and American women is one of the most frequent areas of theological tension and artistic interrogation. We find a scrutinizing of gender roles in Elizabeth Cullinan's 1970 novel *House of Gold*, where a contradiction develops between the role of motherhood sanctioned by the church and the desire of younger women for some measure of existential freedom. The domestic divinity at the center of *House of Gold* is one Mrs. Devlin, an eighty-three-year-old matriarch dying of cancer. Mrs. Devlin consoles herself for this imminent demise by meditating upon how four of her nine children devoted themselves to the religious life, some of them even achieving the status of martyrdom by dying young: "Surely," ruminates Mrs. Devlin, "there was something marvelous in store for a mother who had sacrificed so much."[21] As her sardonic daughter-in-law Claire remarks, Mrs. Devlin conceives the heaven of her eternal reward to be rather like a simple elevation to the top floor of her own house, an extension of the comfortable life she has hitherto enjoyed. Mrs. Devlin turns her material world into a series of superstitious fetishes, making primitive concrete equations between hearth and heaven; she is a great aficionado of television game shows and family comedies, so it is highly appropriate that her son, Father Phil, should actually deploy the television set as an altar when he comes to say mass in the family house at Easter. Cullinan's text, however, moves to ironize Mrs. Devlin's repressive and possessive environment, so that at the end of the novel her children exchange the closed world of family security for the brave new world of "risk, continual risk."[22] In some ways, this narrative replays the kind of antagonism between family "duty" and individual fulfillment we saw in James T. Farrell's novels of the 1930s. More than Farrell, however, Cullinan emphasizes the difficulties faced by young women as they strive guiltily to resist that stereotypical deification of motherhood sanctioned by the old-style Catholic church, with all the negative psychological consequences that role implies.

The claustrophobia of Catholic family life, with its perennial hostility toward forms of secularization and change, appears again in Maureen Howard's autobiography *Facts of Life* (1978), where the narrator recounts her father's support for Joseph McCarthy and his McCarthyite contempt

---

21 Elizabeth Cullinan, *House of Gold* (Boston: Houghton Mifflin, 1970), p. 3.
22 Ibid., p. 293.

for "educated" people in every shape and form.[23] Texts that turn upon this axis of memory and rebellion, where rebellion can never quite erase the memory of childhood conditioning, are heirs to what we might call the Mary McCarthy tradition of Catholic existentialism. One of the most visible heirs to this tradition is the novelist Mary Gordon. It is true Gordon's writing foregrounds the dilemmas of gender more than McCarthy does; but, like McCarthy, Gordon uneasily juggles the paradoxical oscillation between autonomous free will and religious conditioning. In fact, Gordon's heroines often turn to McCarthy novels in an effort to gear themselves up for their existential conflict: Isabel Moore in *Final Payments* (1978) is a reader of McCarthy, while Felicitas Taylor in *The Company of Women* (1980) is also to be found in her student days reading McCarthy's *Vietnam*, even though she had been

> warned against Mary McCarthy for years. Ever since *The Group*, nuns had shaken their heads and breathed her name as a warning to the better students. "What good do all those brains do her? Four husbands and writing filth," they said. It was a comfort to have that book with her; she felt accompanied by a daring older sister whom defiance had made glamorous.[24]

As in McCarthy's early fiction, Gordon's heroines desire to liberate themselves, to escape from the repressive circumstances of the church, but they also find the church acts as a kind of paternal superego from which they are ultimately unable or unwilling to free themselves. Isabel Moore discovers herself to be a devotee of "discipline" and "penance" despite the anger she feels at herself "for making the equation, my father's equation, the Church's equation, between suffering and value."[25] Gordon's heroines fluctuate uncertainly between secular freedom and spiritual devotion; as David Lodge noted, we find here a subconscious (and sometimes neurotic) "nostalgia for, as well as nausea at . . . the power structure of the authoritarian, paternalistic" church of more traditional days.[26]

Similar kinds of contradiction can be recognized in a public lecture Gordon gave in 1987 subtitled "A Writer's Reflections on a Religious Past." Here Gordon abhorred the way the Catholic church has been ruled by "celibate males," who, she said, have a "fear of the body"; she also denounced the "closed world" of the religious "orthodox," claiming such timid acquiescence in authority to be the reason American Catholics

---

23 Maureen Howard, *Facts of Life* (Boston: Little, Brown and Co., 1978), p. 25.
24 Mary Gordon, *The Company of Women* (New York: Random House, 1980), pp. 92–3.
25 Mary Gordon, *Final Payments* (New York: Random House, 1978), pp. 96, 134.
26 David Lodge, "The Arms of the Church," *Times Literary Supplement*, 1 Sept. 1978, p. 965.

"are scandalously underrepresented in the arts."[27] Gordon buttressed her complaint against misogynistic priests by further deploring "the twin dangers of the religious life," dangers categorized by her as "dualism and abstraction." "Abstractionism" she defined as "the error that results from refusing to admit that one has a body and is an inhabitant of the physical world. Dualism, its first cousin," she went on, "admits that there is a physical world but calls it evil and commands that it be shunned."[28] Yet Gordon's harangue does not, as she seemed to believe, constitute a fundamental critique of Catholic theology; at most, her attack could be said to indict the particular Jansenist tendencies of the Irish-American church she grew up in. It is in fact a consummate irony that her assertion of the "sinful" nature of dualism and abstraction might have come directly from a neo-scholastic treatise attacking Kant and Descartes. Gordon argued here against the Catholic church while apparently not fully realizing how precisely her philosophical priorities have been shaped by its cultural spirit. She has, so she said, "never been drawn to any kind of systematic theology, except as a curiosity, though as soon as I say this I want to qualify it, because what makes me even more nervous than the word 'spiritual' are the words 'evangelical,' or 'charismatic.' The religious impulse unmediated by reason terrifies me." Yet, as Max Weber remarked long ago, this scorn for the "evangelical" impulse, the "charismatic" individual, is itself a rigorously traditionalist Catholic position.[29] While claiming she has "never been drawn" to "systematic theology," Gordon succeeds in representing exactly the kind of viewpoint such Catholic theology would have promoted.

To be fair, Gordon's novels are not altogether unaware of their formal ironies, the way their assiduous displacement of romantic subjectivism surreptitiously endorses the Catholicism these texts are apparently rejecting. In *The Company of Women,* Father Cyprian points out to the heroine that "the love of nature for its own sake" is "a particularly American error," since it relies upon the caprices of intuitive response rather than the supposedly objective data of the catechism.[30] Although her religious views waver, the heroine in this novel conforms to her early training by always preserving a wary distance from the religiosity of nature worship, just as in her lecture Gordon recommended a wide berth be given to evangelical preachers: in both cases, the fervid emotional

27 Mary Gordon, "Getting Here from There: A Writer's Reflections on a Religious Past," in *Spiritual Quests: The Art and Craft of Religious Writing,* ed. William Zinsser (Boston: Houghton Mifflin, 1988), pp. 29, 45.
28 Ibid., p. 27.
29 Ibid., pp. 28–9; Max Weber, *The Sociology of Religion,* trans. Ephraim Fischoff (London: Methuen, 1965), p. 187.
30 Gordon, *The Company of Women,* p. 36

response is deemed to be self-indulgent and self-deluding. Concomitant with this skepticism is a strong sense of Protestantism as being "very limited in either a historical or a geographical context," as the author put it. Gordon talked of how she conceived the exclusivist predilections of romantic pastoralism to be hardly more than a form of institutionalized narcissism; whereas Catholicism, so she claimed, offers that "genuine humility which tells you that you are *not* the center of the universe." Like Mary McCarthy, Gordon draws upon a Catholic sensibility in an attempt to subvert the narrower understanding of "America," thus allowing access within her fiction to "a world wider than the vision allowed by the lens of one's own birth."[31] Yet such universalist pretensions themselves can never be conclusively universalist; no less than the sectarian nature of the American Protestantism she criticizes, Gordon's Catholicism is itself a culturally specific ideology.

Another aspect of this argument between gender identities approved by traditional Catholic teaching and the unshackled impulses of the United States revolves around attitudes toward homosexuality. This is not a new problem, of course: Frank O'Hara was exploring such a dilemma back in the 1950s. Still, we can see a marked difference of emphasis between the approaches of O'Hara and those of a younger poet such as Alfred Corn. While O'Hara perceived an immutable antithesis between the church and his sexuality, so that he felt himself obliged to scorn Catholicism in order to achieve personal fulfillment, Corn proposes a conceptual reconciliation between his homosexuality and the older institutions of church and state. In *Notes from a Child of Paradise* (1984), the narrator of this long poem recounts – among other things – his journey away from heterosexuality to homosexuality. This shift does not, however, alienate the protagonist from his former wife, who equates the narrator's newfound sexuality with women's new freedom from overly rigid social constructions of gender:

> A narrow channeling of desire was part
> And parcel of the "same patriarchal control
> That tries to keep women powerless and fearful."

The countering stress on fluidity, diversity, and innovation that this poem introduces as a response to such "control" invokes a mood characteristic of American romanticism.[32] Corn's poem acknowledges itself within this romantic mode by its frequent references to Emersonian transcenden-

---

31 Peter Occhiogrosso, *Once a Catholic: Prominent Catholics and Ex-Catholics Discuss the Influence of the Church on their Lives and Works* (Boston: Houghton Mifflin, 1987), pp. 77–8; Gordon, "Getting Here from There," p. 33.

32 Alfred Corn, *Notes from a Child of Paradise* (New York: Viking Press, 1984), p. 97. Subsequent page references appear in parentheses in the text.

talism as well as its narrative review of Lewis and Clark's epic expeditions of discovery. This tone of innovation and exploration is played off against the older paradigms of authority in Catholic Europe.

Not to abandon the landscapes of Catholicism entirely, however, Corn also draws upon analogies with Dante's *Divine Comedy* so as to promote his conception of art as a "feminizing" influence that might wean the church away from its excessive dependence on repressive patriarchal authority. Corn imagines a church reinvented in his own androgynous, postmodernist image:

> Sapientia, Caritas, Claritas –
> A host of feminine nouns, ancillary
> To the patriarchal Apostolic Church
> Moved to the place of honor.
>
> (68)

The burden of this poem is that such Dantean harmony is hard to come by: inevitably, concedes the narrator, "the imperfect was our paradise" (48). In this sense, the poem is about people "who met eternal things halfway," as it suggests in its first section (10): we find not paradise but notes from paradise, a locale where some intimation of provisionality and failure necessarily invades the gardens of eternal delight. In Paris, the narrator almost finds himself lighting a votive candle in Notre Dame Cathedral, but he then backs off, concluding "no, / Not quite" (20). In Rome, the Eternal City itself becomes subjected to metaphysical ambiguity:

> Bellissima Roma laminata:
> Among so many Eternal buried,
> Which City will the latest pilgrims seek?
>
> (18)

The oxymoronic construction of "Eternal buried" hints at how these "Eternal" dignitaries may, in fact, not be immortal at all, but simply "buried" within the temporal rubble of Rome.

This is the kind of double-edged paradox Corn plays with all the way through his long poem. In Italy, the modern city's "dim arcades" (16) are verbally and thematically intertwined with arcadia, just as "Dante's tomb in San Francesco" (91) is intertwined with the artificial paradise of San Francisco in the 1960s, a scene described elsewhere in the poem. In every case, though, the linguistic and conceptual difference appears as significant as the resemblance; unlike Dante, Corn constructs a world of analogies that never quite manage to fit together. This structural ambivalence not only suggests the lapse of Scholastic philosophy into contemporary American dialects of diversity but also evokes the internal sexual ambivalence of the narrator as he attempts to locate his identity within landscapes where he, like the analogical arrangement of his poem, never seems quite to fit. In Corn's poem, then, contradiction and suture are held in balance. The unorthodox nature of the narrator's sexuality cannot be comfortably reconciled with Catholicism; nor, though, does this sexual identity choose to define itself through a sharp antagonism to religious culture. Instead, the poem toys with the possibility of construing church authority within a new kind of skeptical, humanist, American idiom.

Within the culture of contemporary Catholicism, other pressures for change have arisen from issues of racial difference. The ethnic diversity of American Catholicism is an old story; although since the 1840s it is the Irish influence that has been strongest within the American church, it is surely an oversimplification for Mary Gordon to maintain that because of this Irish "controlling interest . . . we are all Irish Catholics in America, whatever our ethnicity."[33] As if to undermine any such hegemonic picture, Harold J. Abramson has succinctly analyzed many of the sociological differences among these various Catholic groups: the bilingual and bicultural consciousness of French-Canadians, the clannish midwestern temper of German-American Catholicism, the anticlerical impulses of American Italians. As these Italians were accustomed to associate the church with a reactionary political order back in Italy, they tended to regard Catholicism as an admirable influence upon the feminine realm of hearth and home but as a peripheral or even malevolent force when it came to the more serious, masculine business of making a living.[34] That kind of bifurcation may help to elucidate the division between the sanctity of the home and the profanity of the Mafia world that we saw in Coppola's *Godfather* films, just as a bilingual consciousness – the sense of being always a foreigner – materially affects the novels of Jack Kerouac. There are other important ethnic differences among American Catholic authors: Santayana and Katherine Anne Porter were negotiating with a Spanish heritage, Hitchcock with an English, while in Robert Altman's focus upon communal rituals we find a trace of German Catholicism's enthusiasm for ceremonial feasts and festivals.

Perhaps the most significant ethnic boundary within American Catholicism, however, marks the difference between black culture and white. Black American Catholic writers share some themes with white authors but tend to filter them through a distinctly more oppositional cultural perspective. Claude McKay, for instance, was a black writer

33 Occhiogrosso, *Once a Catholic*, p. 75.
34 Harold J. Abramson, *Ethnic Diversity in Catholic America* (New York: John Wiley, 1973), p. 137.

who was also a Catholic convert. Through his role in the Harlem Renaissance, McKay was part of the rebellion against Puritanism that was all the rage in the years following the First World War: the contempt for "the gray, gaunt Protestant church" that we find in McKay's first novel *Home to Harlem* (1928) is worthy of H. L. Mencken or Waldo Frank at their most vituperative. "The Ancient Respectability was getting ready to flee," declares the book's narrator, more perhaps in hope than anticipation. As if to slough off these tired repressions, McKay's narrator chooses to celebrate instead the "groups of loud-laughing-and-acting black swains and their sweethearts [who] had started in using the block for their afternoon promenade."[35]

McKay, born in Jamaica in 1899, did not convert to Catholicism until 1944. Even in this early novel, though, we see him associating black culture with motifs drawn from Catholic sources: he talks of the "grand blue benediction" of the Harlem sky, for instance.[36] These images make up an oppositional pressure designed to critique the stranglehold of white Protestant culture in the United States; McKay wrote elsewhere of how he saw Protestantism as a "source of evil," a power ensnared by its focus upon arrogant individualism, social exclusivity, and the worship of Mammon. In his essay "How Black Sees Green and Red," McKay preferred to think of himself as affiliated with what he took to be the more generous spirit of Irish Catholicism: "I suffer with the Irish," he said, "I think I understand the Irish. My belonging to a subject race entitles me to some understanding of them."[37] McKay entertained a similar kind of empathy for Spanish Catholicism, which emerges in his interpretation as an intuitive, folksy phenomenon, a welcome antidote to the brutal materialism of the United States. Waldo Frank's *Virgin Spain* (1926) embraces a similar kind of thesis; in fact, this rather sentimentalized version of the natural probity of the "soil" was much in vogue in American modernist circles around this time. Typically modernist, too, was McKay's search for some idealistic, all-encompassing mythic system that might act as a redemptive panacea upon the alienation of the modern world. Like Dreiser and Farrell, McKay flirted with communism for a while, and McKay's friend Max Eastman was appalled when Catholicism began to supplant communism in the black writer's mind toward the end of the 1930s.

A still more radical revision of Catholic faith is proposed in the writings of Leon Forrest, a Southern black novelist who aligns himself with "the eloquence of the Oral Tradition" in black culture. The presiding motif

35 Claude McKay, *Home to Harlem* (Chatham, N.J.: Chatham Bookseller, 1973), p. 301.
36 Ibid., p. 279.
37 James R. Giles, *Claude McKay* (Boston: Twayne, 1976), pp. 39, 37.

in Forrest's work is transformation. One of Forrest's nonfiction pieces celebrates his aunt, "a magical seamstress, a lady who was always transforming life," and the author implicitly associates her kind of folk art with the power of Christ to transform the world through the Eucharist.[38] He also links this metamorphic energy with his own fiction, which desires radically to transform the mundane world and embark upon a quest for spiritual wholeness. In *Two Wings to Veil My Face* (1983), the narrator scorns contemporary materialism with the kind of venom that would have alarmed all those Catholic writers who have advocated a more serpentine assimilation of the faithful into central currents of American life. Looking back on her life, ninety-one-year-old Sweetie Reed inveighs against: "the kind of thinking we are doomed to right here and now – thinking that the spirit of God is manifested in every seed of commercial folly flung broadcast, as the very trajectory of our seedy spiritual wasteland – wilderness: in the silver bullet upon the silver screen; in a Lincoln, in a Caddy . . . in an Electrolux."[39] This oppositional impetus should not be read simply in terms of secular politics or hostility toward American capitalism. In his 1988 autobiographical essay, Forrest asserted that "all great literature is at its backbone was and is and ever shall be, world without end, amen, about man's spiritual agony and ascendancy." Accordingly, he distanced himself from some of his literary friends of the 1960s, who, said Forrest, were attempting to "save the world . . . in a moment of some patched-up ideological miracle."[40]

Two Wings to Veil My Face, then, turns upon a series of metaphysical paradoxes where the "riddled soul" (18) of pain is transfigured into redemption, where earth is transfigured into heaven, where a human figure can take on "the holy glory of an angel's spirit" (256). The impulse is always to rent the earthly "veil of grief" and enter a state of blissful "revelation" (205). In this light, Forrest's novel can be seen as more Manichaean in tendency than most Catholic fiction, more concerned with a harsh dualistic antithesis between matter and spirit. The hero, Nathaniel Witherspoon, is, so we are told, "obsessed with . . . the need to have something spiritual going with a girl" (82); accordingly, when he finds the lower promptings of sexual desire become an obstruction to this elevated ideal, the tortured Witherspoon "howled at his body," a body "wrapped in flaming chains on that burning river to Hell" (150). The tongues of revivalist preaching are a hovering presence here, spiced with a touch of the southern gothic flavoring.

38 "Leon Forrest," in *Contemporary Authors: Autobiography Series,* ed. Mark Zadronzy, VII (Detroit: Gale, 1988), 23, 21.
39 Leon Forrest, *Two Wings to Veil My Face* (New York: Random House, 1983), p. 187. Subsequent page references are given in parentheses in the text.
40 *Contemporary Authors,* ed. Zadrozny, p. 34.

It is true that in this book Forrest is reconstituting a vision of Eden that is an old ideal in American literature. For Forrest's narrator, though, this utopian promise involves a vision of the next world – the aspiration to "ascend into the highest tree of God's invention" (174) – as well as a more earthly program of liberation for the black race, those "yoked-down people, who have been in the storm too long" (180). In this double sense, the sounding of God's trumpet signifies not only the storming of heaven's gates, but also a triumphant political liberation, the alleviation of material suffering. The narrator's rhetoric reaches its crescendo in the last few pages of the novel: "Oh, you may bury me in the east, bury me in the west, but I heard the trumpet radiant as the resonant bells of the morning; oh Kyrie eleison, oh Christie eleison" (294). Pouring scorn on Master Rollins Reed's belief that if any "darkies" were to go to heaven they would find themselves "in a different part or room, sealed off" from whites (123), Forrest's novel advocates the kind of liberation theology that holds there to be a necessary affinity between spiritual and political freedom.

The radical nature of this liberation theology, which originally emerged from among Hispanic Catholic workers, is another of those areas of potential contradiction within the church that Vatican authorities have not yet sutured to everyone's satisfaction. In literary terms, though, it is curious how in such a radical text the impulse toward baptism, the renewal of innocence and the regaining of paradise, should make Forrest's work more like a traditional American narrative than almost any other Catholic work of this modern era. Forrest is drawing upon standard American typologies of exodus and liberation, typologies that go back through the slave narratives to myths of the pilgrim fathers: indeed, the blacks are described by Forrest's text at one point as "like new world pilgrims and a long ways from home" (199). Anthony Burgess once remarked on how Catholic thought has always tended to be wary of utopias of all kinds, and doubtless some of the tensions between black Catholic communities and the institutional church in America have arisen from these communities' departure from familiar Catholic metaphors. Nevertheless, processes of change, in religious metaphors as well as in religious practices, are inevitable. If, as Karl Rahner has suggested, the era of "Eurocentrism" in the Catholic church is coming to an end, it is only to be expected that American Catholic literature should increasingly reflect the cultures and implicit values of groups that have previously found themselves to be the victims of an institutional absence.[41]

41 Anthony Burgess, *Little Wilson and Big God* (New York: Weidenfeld and Nicolson, 1986), pp. 148–9; Avery Dulles, S.J., *The Catholicity of the Church* (Oxford: Clarendon Press, 1985), p. 174.

Another important contemporary novelist, Robert Stone, writes out of sympathy for Hispanic Catholicism, a marginalized force that once again is coming to play an increasingly significant part in church affairs. Stone shares with some South American writers a language of "magic realism," where mundane circumstances appear to be shot through with some strange and irrational, perhaps spiritual, power. For Stone, a self-confessed lapsed Catholic, these icons tantalizingly promise some higher meaning, although in the end they seem to remain stranded within the banality of nonsignification. In *A Hall of Mirrors* (1967), New Orleans disc jockey Rheinhardt gazes at a crucifix where the "iron Christ stared down in wide-eyed rusty death from the gibbet of a green, oxided cross."[42] Rheinhardt desperately wants to believe in the magical power of this image. He remembers the lunchtime rosaries at his Catholic school; he toasts the Eucharist; he even perceives himself as a surrogate Christ figure in his role as disembodied spirit of the airwaves: "I got hired by WUSA which is the voice of Almighty God in this part of the forest," he says, "I get to call the faithful to prayer" (134). Nevertheless, throughout all of Stone's work there is something that does not quite connect. In *Dog Soldiers* (1974), Vietnam veteran Converse goes into a Catholic church in San Francisco, sits before a plaster image of St. Anthony of Padua and thinks about lighting a candle; but he cannot quite bring himself to do it because, as he later tells Danskin, "I don't believe in it anymore."[43] Thus in Stone's novels we are left with only vulgarized versions of transfiguration. The Hollywood actors in *Children of Light* (1986) inhabit a world of masks where the cinema offers a cheap form of magic realism: to speak the truth, says one actress, is possible, "but very Protestant."[44] The landscapes of churches and bell towers in Southern California and Mexico, where this novel is set, offer hints and echoes of transubstantiation, only to find themselves deprived of full sacramental splendor.

South America attracts Stone because its Catholic culture brings out the most pointed disjunctions between religious aspiration and material squalor. By subverting materialistic self-sufficiency, such disjunctions also allow for the possibility of some kind of intersection between the mundane and the otherworldly. For Stone – as for Flannery O'Connor, for example – the complacent bourgeois landscapes of North America choke the spirit: Stone claimed in a 1987 interview that "logical positivism has really been exhausted . . . and that optimistic, materialist, relatively

42 Robert Stone, *A Hall of Mirrors* (Boston: Houghton Mifflin, 1967), p. 196. Subsequent page references are given in parentheses in the text.
43 Robert Stone, *Dog Soldiers* (Boston: Houghton Mifflin, 1974), p. 160. Subsequent page references are given in parentheses in the text.
44 Robert Stone, *Children of Light* (New York: Knopf, 1986), p. 213.

comfortable world is breaking apart."[45] As a global generalization, this might seem absurd; yet the statement is certainly true in relation to Stone's own novels, where the "breaking apart" and dissolution of character become moral imperatives, keys to the accession of "grace." In *A Hall of Mirrors,* state's attorney Calvin Minnow – his Christian name, of course, is significant – gives a lecture on how poverty and sloth are "inextricably linked" (355). The attorney hopes to arouse the righteous ire of solid citizens against no-good "Jew communist beatniks" (361), but Stone's work goes on to contradict Calvin by implying it is the suffering outcast who is (spiritually) rich. In *A Hall of Mirrors,* Farley has "a mask of suffering intelligence" (68), which is the guarantee of how he is "basically of a religious nature" (71). In *Dog Soldiers,* it is war-torn Cambodia that provides Converse with images of suffering and martyrdom: "A man was nailed Christlike to a tree beside the road, a shrine" (185). The violence in *Dog Soldiers* seems perversely to be welcomed, because, as Frank W. Shelton has said, it corresponds to Stone's imagined "world in which brutality and illegality are the norm and not the exception." Stone once informed the *Washington Post* that "the myth of original sin is onto something," and certainly any mood of liberal optimism is quite alien to Stone's fields of textual activity.[46]

For Stone, then, Catholicism induces psychologically what he called "a perverse, masochistic element."[47] A hero such as Rheinhardt cherishes this style of martyrdom, drunkenly reciting Gerard Manley Hopkins's *Wreck of the Deutschland* as a way of indicating his triumph over the more banal concerns of the secular world. In *A Flag for Sunrise* (1981), an American army officer is quoted as remarking on how "the compulsion to lose was universal and only a handful of people could overcome it"; but for Stone's heroes – as for other Catholic literary martyrs like Jake La Motta and Dick Diver – the earthly defeat mysteriously betokens some kind of higher victory, even if heaven itself is a locale of doubtful status.[48] The plot of *A Flag for Sunrise* revolves around American government agents battling with Catholic missionaries for political influence in the South American countries of "Tecan" and "Compostela," but the optimistic Marxist liberation theology espoused by Father Goday and Sister Justin cannot withstand the compulsions toward violence and failure that seem to be inherent within this sinister landscape. The "only meaning in all of things," suggests Father Egan, is "that little radiant

45 Occhiogrosso, *Once a Catholic,* p. 50.
46 Frank W. Shelton, "Robert Stone's *Dog Soldiers*: Vietnam Comes Home to America," *Critique,* 24 (1983), 81; Occhiogrosso, *Once a Catholic,* p. 39.
47 Occhiogrosso, *Once a Catholic,* p. 47.
48 Robert Stone, *A Flag for Sunrise* (New York: Knopf, 1981), p. 244. Subsequent page references are given in parentheses in the text.

thing" (319), the "Jewel" that "is in the Lotus" (332). Egan believes there is some barely tangible but nevertheless persistent strain of spirituality that can transcend the corruption and mortality of the lotus. Like Dieter in *Dog Soldiers* who believes the "good stuff" occurs only in a redemptive "flash" (273), Father Egan holds that "a gleam in the muck" (369) is the only hint of spirituality available on man's terrestrial plane.

To be sure, this pattern of self-immolation and hankering after something "higher" constitutes one of the clichés of Catholic culture, at least in the eyes of outside observers. We see similar obsessions in the plays of Tennessee Williams, for example: craving for alcohol, tortured homosexuality, yearning for the luxury of crucifixion as a sign of superiority to the demands of a crass material world. Some of Williams's *maudits* characters are represented as Catholics – failed priest Lawrence Shannon in *The Night of the Iguana* (1961), for instance – although Williams himself was brought up within a strictly Protestant community and did not convert to Catholicism until 1969. Williams's theater analyzes, often very powerfully, the theme of repression; yet it is difficult not to feel all this imagery of Orpheus descending and Christ rising is essentially fake, a self-consciously fictive metaphor for that terrifying energy of sexuality, along with all its necessary social disguises, that makes up Williams's central subject. Just as Williams manipulated his "plastic" theater to draw attention to the fictionality of his performances and to imply how this visible drama can but hint at the invisible forces for which it so evidently yearns, so Williams exploited the cultural significance of Saint Sebastian and other religious icons as a displacement of, and as a mask for, more secular concerns.

Catholic critic Garry Wills took exception to Williams's appropriation of Catholic imagery for his own idiosyncratic purposes, comparing it to the fascination for Rome among exotic aesthetes like Aubrey Beardsley and Ronald Firbank, for whom the "bawdy glamor" of gold chalices offered a frivolous "avenue for escape."[49] Wills's judgment is a touch prudish, in that many more sober writers – Charles Eliot Norton, Henry James, Henry Adams – have also been interested in the metaphorical rather than literal connotations of Catholic culture. Nevertheless, there does seem to be a crucial difference between Williams, for whom Catholicism is an aesthetic or metaphorical phenomenon, and Stone, for whom the aesthetic surface gives rise to a desperate quest for metaphysical value. In *A Flag for Sunrise*, Father Egan is described as like "some heterodox doctor of the Renaissance, a man condemned by his times but sustained by faith in God and the Spirit among men" (3). The word

---

49 Garry Wills, *Bare Ruined Choirs: Doubt, Prophecy, and Radical Religion* (Garden City, N.Y.: Doubleday, 1972), p. 96.

"heterodox" is especially interesting, for it is Egan's intimation of religious faith as a slippery, inconclusive category that permeates all of Stone's work. As the author acknowledged in one interview: "there is a certain aspect of Catholicism that, to me, is its most appealing and attractive tradition, and that is the tradition of Catholic skepticism which I associate with people like Montaigne and Erasmus and Pascal. I think that's a very intellectually wholesome tradition, and I can still identify with that to some degree."[50] As Stone suggested, Montaigne, Erasmus, and Pascal all posited a fundamental breach between reason and faith. While staying within the broad compass of the Catholic church, these Renaissance thinkers disparaged the notion that God might be comprehended within a framework of human logic. Accordingly, they came to reject all the dogmatic rules and systems of medieval Scholasticism. Stone's view of divinity as "nonrational," a "kind of dynamic absence that is a constant challenge," squares precisely with Montaigne's maxim on how "it is folly to measure truth and error by our own capacity."[51] Montaigne found himself placed on the papal Index in 1676, and of course Stone's Catholic sensibility is anything but orthodox in a theological sense, but both men were attempting subtly to construct bridges between faith and skepticism in an epistemologically uncertain era.

Looking back over the range of Catholic writers, it seems possible that this Renaissance tradition of "Catholic skepticism," as Robert Stone put it, might be a more useful summation of the American experience than those models of systematic theology going back through Aquinas and the medieval reworking of Aristotle. In many twentieth-century European Catholic writers – Evelyn Waugh, George Bernanos – there is a sense of exile and nostalgia for the lost enchanted garden, a garden associated with the social order and ecclesiastical authority of an Age of Faith.[52] But this medieval ideal has never existed anyway in the United States. Jack Kerouac and Frank O'Hara find no compulsion to revisit Brideshead; instead, they search for elements of the irrational or "spiritual" within the debris of contemporary civilization. In this, their project bears distinct resemblances to that of Montaigne and Pascal, who glimpsed the possibilities of faith not within the archaic structures of feudalism but amid those lacunae and absences lurking within the brave new world of humanist reason.

Consistent with this refusal of arcadian nostalgia is the fact that the

50 Occhiogrosso, Once a Catholic, p. 43.
51 Ibid., pp. 43, 49; Montaigne, Essays, p. 86.
52 Conor Cruise O'Brien, Maria Cross: Imaginative Patterns in a Group of Modern Catholic Writers (1954; rpt. London: Burns and Oates, 1963), pp. 213–15.

American Catholic church, with its large number of immigrants, has in modern times been largely an urban phenomenon. In Europe, we often find an urban secularism threatening to invade the pieties of rural faith, as in Bernanos's *Diary of a Country Priest,* for example; in the United States, however, this process usually works the other way around, with urban Catholicism positioned as the sinister force threatening to subvert the pastoral calm of the pilgrim fathers' newfound land. By a similar topsy-turvy process, in medieval Europe the Catholic faith was intimately bound up with institutional structures of law and state government, but in the United States this Catholic impulse has generally stood in opposition to the Enlightenment rhetoric of the Constitution. The humanist optimism that summarily declared an inalienable right to "life, liberty and the pursuit of happiness" could never make much impact upon a Catholic frame of mind, which, as Anthony Burgess remarked, tends to be more Augustinian than Pelagian, more convinced of the ubiquity of Original Sin than of human perfectibility.[53]

Consequently, one of the contributions of Catholicism within American culture may be to problematize the idea of what is considered "natural." Thoreau's god of nature is a very different thing from the Catholic conception of *lex naturalis,* the natural law that, according to Jacques Maritain, is "the normality of functioning of the human being" in the "essential inclinations of human nature."[54] For the Catholic, natural law is participation in the eternal law, which insists that man is a social being who must work out his life and salvation through interaction with others. Those communities and rituals that are so prevalent in American Catholic fictions testify to the way these artists tend to focus upon people in groups rather than as individuals. It is not, of course, that Thoreau's view of nature is right or wrong; it is simply that the countercultural discourse of Catholic fictions implies how this "nature" is always an ideologically determined entity. For Thoreau, it is natural for a person to be alone, but for Mary McCarthy it is natural for a person to be in a group.

Through a similar kind of distinction, as we have seen, utopian and millennial thought has not played a prominent role within the American Catholic literary tradition. Emerson and Whitman prophetically envisioned a better world to come; Berryman and Frank O'Hara did not. Cotton Mather hoped for and expected the world to end in 1697; Santayana made no such predictions. By refusing to participate in the Protestant quest for "purity," and by generally refusing to equate subjective

53 Burgess, *Little Wilson and Big God,* p. 148.
54 Will Herberg, ed., *Four Existentialist Theologians: A Reader from the Works of Jacques Maritain, Nicolas Berdyaev, Martin Buber, and Paul Tillich* (Garden City: Doubleday-Anchor, 1958), p. 81.

desire with the objective world, Catholic writers have resisted that temptation to resolve their external environment into dualistic polarities of good and evil, a process that leads inexorably toward the imagination of apocalypse. Catholic writers more often see the world as a "provisional combination of the pure and impure" and therefore as not susceptible of being radically overhauled by the romantic designs of a willful, transcendental ego.[55]

The range of American authors who have felt compelled to negotiate with Catholicism is a wide one, though we must recognize the subject of "Catholicism" itself is less a fixed structure of beliefs than a product of complex, evasive, and shifting discourses. If nothing else, consideration of this wide spectrum of writers should dispense with the unhappy stereotype of Catholic fiction as being enmeshed in dark cycles of guilt and perversion. That old humanist adage of Catholicism failing to present "a healthy, broad-minded approach to either sex or religion," as Francis Kunkel put it, is illegitimate: Kunkel regretted that Catholic literature has become generally associated in the mind of secular readers with neurosis and obsession, but his altogether too narrow selection of "Catholic" authors – Waugh, Greene, Claudel, Tennessee Williams – works simply to shore up that kind of archaic reification.[56] Yet it is one of the commonplaces of poststructuralist practice that essentialist categories should become historicized and revealed as "collective fictions that are continually reinvented," in Werner Sollors's phrase, and the culture of Catholicism needs to be interpreted in this provisional, interrogative light as well.[57] The whole subject is much more complex and amorphous than Kunkel's narrow field of vision would imply.

To risk one structural generalization, though, I would suggest the deepest divisions in "religious" sensibility among these writers can be traced not to different ethnic characteristics, nor to any distinction between apostates and "true" believers, but rather to a difference between those born and raised as Catholics and those who later converted to the faith. The latter group – Orestes Brownson, Allen Tate, Robert Lowell, Walker Percy – tend to experience Catholicism in a much more self-consciously theoretical way, as a cerebral rather than subliminal phenomenon. Anthony Burgess wrote in his autobiography that "the converted Catholics of modern literature seem to be concerned with a different faith from the one I was nurtured in," adding how the "naively

55 Jean Guitton, *The Church and the Gospel,* trans. Emma Craufurd (Chicago: Henry Regnery, 1961), p. 225.
56 Francis L. Kunkel, *Passion and the Passion: Sex and Religion in Modern Literature* (Philadelphia: Westminster Press, 1975), pp. 167–8.
57 Werner Sollors, "Introduction: The Invention of Ethnicity," in *The Invention of Ethnicity,* ed. Sollors (New York: Oxford Univ. Press, 1989), p. xi.

romantic, pedantically scrupulous" novels of Evelyn Waugh seem to "falsify the faith by over-dramatising it." Lapsed Catholic poet Craig Raine has also talked about how the religious angst that permeates the novels of Graham Greene, another convert, is altogether foreign to his own experience.[58] One would wish to avoid Burgess's presumption that a convert's faith is more "false" than his own preoccupations, of course; still, it would be true to say there is a distinct difference of emphasis in their approaches.

For all these assumptions of philosophical relativism, it should be clear that in aesthetic terms cultural pluralism is not sufficient as an end in itself. Tired liberal conceptions of a "multicultural" literary landscape can induce a slack self-indulgence, the inference that no works can be assessed for their intrinsic literary merit because they are simply "genuine" expressions of divergent cultures. But this notion, as Sollors has argued, has two deleterious consequences: first, the prioritizing of a mystique of insiderhood, the idea that only "authentic" ethnics can "really" understand their own native culture; and second, the presupposition that the power of ethnic, religious, and other cultural boundaries is permanent and unchanging.[59] In fact, of course, there is no such thing as a homogeneous American Catholic literature, any more than there is a homogeneous Italian-American literature. The quest for "roots" is always a doomed enterprise; ethnic characteristics overlap between different groups, and they further relinquish whatever distinguishing marks they "originally" enjoyed by the inevitable process of interaction with a new, polysemous American culture. In just the same way, Catholic authors interact with their environment, negotiate with the forces of difference, so that we find the dense, complex, and inchoate nature of an insistently other world emerging within their fictional texts. It is the bad American Catholic novelist – Cardinal Spellman (Flannery O'Connor's bête noire) or whoever – who refuses this process of interaction and prefers to write from within the hermetically sealed world of true faith. Analysis of how religious culture works through literature does not preclude aesthetic values; indeed, it is vitally dependent upon them. Just as Nabokov tells us a great deal about the Russian-American immigrant experience through the very sophistication and intensity of his novels, so Scott Fitzgerald reveals more about Irish Catholicism in the

58 Burgess, *Little Wilson and Big God,* p. 8; Raine made this remark in a television interview with Richard Hoggart, *Writers on Writing,* ITV South, 14 Mar. 1986.

59 Werner Sollors, *Beyond Ethnicity: Consent and Descent in American Culture* (New York: Oxford Univ. Press, 1986), p. 30; Werner Sollors, "On a Critique of Pure Pluralism," in *Reconstructing American Literary History,* ed. Sacvan Bercovitch (Cambridge, Mass.: Harvard Univ. Press, 1986), pp. 250–79.

United States precisely because of those ambiguities, hesitancies, and lacunae the reader can locate within his multifaceted fictions.

Having said this, it would seem reasonable to suggest that certain excellent writers have been undervalued because the (explicit or implicit) ideologies of their texts do not accord with what are conceived, often unconsciously, to be American literary values. As we have noted, it is this kind of unexamined assumption that has led to Robert Lowell's later poems being generally judged superior to his early ones. It is this assumption also that may have contributed to the continued underestimation of Dreiser, Kerouac, Mary McCarthy, John O'Hara, J. F. Powers, Edwin O'Connor. The Emerson–Frost–Stevens triad is a familiar combination in American literary history; Santayana–Tate–Frank O'Hara less so. This is not, of course, to promulgate the idea of "religious" art in any theological sense at all. The great French composer Olivier Messiaen, a devout Catholic, has sometimes complained of how his work is praised by those who altogether ignore its religious significance; still, secular musicologists within French culture will at least recognize the significance of the religious framework Messiaen is working with, even if they do not themselves adhere to these Catholic principles. One wonders how Messiaen's music would have been critically received if he had been working in the United States, where the Catholic cultural matrix is much more suppressed and inscrutable.

One obvious ramification of this alternative American "Catholic" tradition is to reveal the "Protestant" cultural tradition as a relative phenomenon. In his 1937 work, *The Kingdom of God in America,* H. Richard Niebuhr argued that the United States could be seen as the embodiment of the Protestant gospel, just as Augustine's city of God was materially embodied in the Catholic Middle Ages. Thirty years later, Howard Mumford Jones was still asserting that "our literary tradition has been overwhelmingly Protestant and individualistic."[60] Today, however, the challenge to this once-accepted "canon" is an old story. America, as Sacvan Bercovitch has argued, should be seen as neither utopia nor dystopia but as "a certain political system" with its own "social limits" that can be located and relocated at specific junctures within history. The themes and patterns of American literature are not so exclusively different from those elsewhere in the world; as Bercovitch remarked, Emerson's work must be read in the larger context of Kant and Carlyle as well as in the light of Emerson's affinity with Thoreau and Hawthorne.[61] "Cath-

60 H. Richard Niebuhr, *The Kingdom of God in America* (Chicago: Willett, Clark and Co., 1937), p. 164; Howard Mumford Jones, *Belief and Disbelief in American Literature* (Chicago: Univ. of Chicago Press, 1967), p. 144.
61 Sacvan Bercovitch, "The Problem of Ideology in American Literary History," *Critical Inquiry,* 12 (1986), 645–6.

olic" literature is well placed to help break down these artificial national boundaries because, as Anthony Burgess said, its spirit of a universal church engenders a certain contempt for small patriotisms. This universalism compels a recognition that human nature in America may have more essential similarities than differences with human nature in other places.[62] Just as in Hawthorne and Twain the reification of Catholicism as an oppositional force gradually becomes compromised by an acknowledgment of equivalences between Old World and New, so the characters in John O'Hara's novels, for instance, are accidentally but not essentially different from those in the novels of Anthony Trollope or C. P. Snow. The antiheroic, often mean-minded temper of O'Hara's social climbers was supposed to debar them from the grand and "genuine" American spirit of manifest destiny, the heroism of "man in the open air," in the phrase F. O. Matthiessen took from Whitman. While "manifest destiny" itself might seem an impossibly anachronistic notion, we have seen how the moralistic assumptions stemming from this understanding of America as the great good place have lingered with remarkable obstinacy in twentieth-century literary criticism.

In his foreword to Allan Bloom's *The Closing of the American Mind,* Saul Bellow recalled his own immigrant childhood in Chicago and adduced his subsequent literary career as a rebuke to those who would attempt to replace classical learning with mere celebration of ethnic difference. "I did not intend to be wholly dependent on history and culture," said Bellow: "Full dependency must mean that I was done for."[63] Without arguing with this, surely the crucial words here are "wholly" and "full." To say Bellow's works contain residual traces of Jewish immigrant culture is not at all to claim they can be "wholly" reduced to that category, any more than it would be appropriate to relate Frank O'Hara's poetry to a "full dependency" upon his Catholic background. In themselves, ethnic and religious differences do not constitute art; but no art can altogether avoid the material influence of such differences. Good art reworks these differences in a dense and interesting way; bad art does not.

One critical strategy that might be useful here is what Jean-François Lyotard has called "sveltesse," an agility enabling readers ironically to detach themselves from the impositions of all grand conceptual systems. In Lyotard's treatise *The Postmodern Condition,* the teleological status of religion and other "metanarratives" is dismantled and supplanted by more "discontinuous" modes of knowledge, modes characterized by

---

62 Burgess, *Little Wilson and Big God,* p. 148.
63 Saul Bellow, Foreword, *The Closing of the American Mind,* by Allan Bloom (New York: Simon and Schuster, 1987), p. 13.

"incomplete information" and "pragmatic paradoxes."[64] Art is well placed to produce such strategies of evasion, because good art contains a superfluity of meaning that renders it not wholly dependent upon any given scheme or conceptualization. One of the many paradoxes involved in elucidating a tradition of American Catholic fictions is to recognize how the best texts incorporate, but then move beyond to reflect upon, the premises of Catholicism. Indeed, we can see a cycle of deconstruction at work here. The culture of Catholicism deconstructs the more celebrated American ideologies (Protestant pastoral, and so on) to reveal them as provisional systems; Catholic arts and fictions in turn deconstruct the theological and philosophical bases of Catholicism, to reveal art's own irrepressible superfluity of signification; but the critical impulse of deconstruction in turn illuminates the fictional status of all these aesthetic creations, reconstituting them as inventions of the human imagination at particular times and places within history.

Nor should this paradoxical cycle of fiction spinning be seen simply as a negative or nihilist phenomenon. Toward the end of his life, Jean Genet was asked how such a "nonreligious" person as himself could possibly claim there was "nothing happier or more joyful" than Monteverdi's *Vespers of the Blessed Virgin*.[65] Genet replied: "I read the *Iliad* twenty years ago, it's very very beautiful. Does that mean I believe in the religion of Zeus?"

64 Jean-François Lyotard, *The Postmodern Condition: A Report on Knowledge*, trans. Geoff Bennington, Brian Massumi, and Regis Durand (Minneapolis: Univ. of Minnesota Press, 1984), p. 60. For Lyotard and "sveltesse," see Ihab Hassan, "Fictions of Power: A Note on Ideological Discourse in the Humanities," *American Literary History*, 1 (1989), 141.
65 Hubert Fichte, "Jean Genet: An Interview," trans. Patrick McCarthy, *New Review*, no. 37 (Apr. 1977), p. 10.

Index

Fate, 243; "The Imaginary Jew,"
245; *Love and Fame*, 233, 243, 244,
247; "New Year's Eve," 234;
"Nones," 245; "Not to Live," 234;
Recovery, 244, 245, 246; "The
Search," 246; "Sext," 245; "The
Song of the Demented Priest,"
234; "A Usual Prayer," 243
Bersani, Leo, 92, 135
Blackmur, R. P., 193, 216, 231, 242,
439
Blanshard, Paul, 378, 427, 430
Blondel, Maurice, 371, 373
Bloom, Allan, 530
Bloom, Harold, 19, 117, 121, 356,
443
Boelhower, William, 162, 301–2, 303
Bradbury, Malcolm, 121, 446
Bradstreet, Anne, 35
Brando, Marlon, 343, 494, 499–500
Brassai, Georges, 293
Brecht, Bertolt, 279
Brooks, Van Wyck, 59, 70, 113, 114
Brown, Norman O., 398
Brownson, Orestes, 25, 53, 56–60,
62–74, 75, 76, 125, 204, 206, 225,
230, 316–17, 375, 505, 506, 527;
The American Republic, 68–9;
"Catholic Secular Literature," 70;
Charles Elwood, 70–1; *The Convert*,
59, 63, 66; "Extra Ecclesiam Nulla
Salus," 72; "Harmony of Faith and
Reason," 63; "Nature and Grace,"
63; *New Views of Christianity,
Society, and the Church*, 64, 69;
"Philosophy and Catholicity," 62,
72; "Public and Parochial Schools,"
65; "Religious Novels," 70; "Rome
or Reason," 72; "Slavery and the
Church," 63; *The Spirit Rapper*, 71
Bruccoli, Matthew J., 172, 444
Buckley, William F., 420, 440
Buddhism, 192, 412–13
Buñuel, Luis, 6, 193, 283, 315, 452
Bunyan, John, 432
Burgess, Anthony, 172, 512, 521,
526, 527–8, 530
Burlesque, 282, 298, 333, 403, 475–6,

483, 488, 509; in Altman, 315, 317,
322; in Ford, 306, 307–8, 322
Burrell, David, 28n, 365–6
Burroughs, William S., 415, 420

Cagney, James, 296, 297, 298, 336,
448
Calvin, John, 37, 38, 39, 64, 80, 81,
82, 85, 97, 114, 115, 225, 451; and
aesthetics, 274, 276, 337; and
capitalism, 11–12, 139, 180, 484,
489; and dualism, 106–7; and evil,
135–6; and Melville, 82, 134
Camus, Albert, 254, 367, 491
Capra, Frank, 297–8
Carroll, John, Bishop, 39–40, 44
Cartesianism, *see* Descartes, René
Cartier-Bresson, Henri, 289
Casanova, Giacomo, 460
Cather, Willa, 40, 128
Catholic League for Social Justice,
141
Catholic Worker Movement, 141
Catholicity, *see* Universalism
Cavell, Stanley, 509–10
Chabrol, Claude, 326, 328, 329, 330,
335
Chandler, Raymond, 480
Chardin, Teilhard de, 387
Chase, Richard, 135–8, 139, 144, 168,
176, 463
Chesterton, G.K., 14–15, 23, 193,
207, 306–7, 308, 316, 368, 418,
481, 507–8
Chopin, Kate, 111, 127–9, 130, 135,
139
Ciardi, John, 264
Claudel, Paul, 125, 245, 527
Coleridge, Samuel Taylor, 258
Cooper, James Fenimore, 45, 76, 77,
84, 274, 397, 465, 480
Coover, Robert, 376, 388
Coppola, Francis Ford, 504; *The
Godfather*, 492, 494–503, 518; *One
From the Heart*, 503, 510–11
Corn, Alfred, 399, 507, 508, 516–18
Corneille, Pierre, 23, 455
Corso, Gregory, 398
Cotton, John, 27

Continued from the front of the book